THE NIV
APPLICATION
COMMENTARY

From biblical text . . . to contemporary life

PETER ENNS

ZondervanPublishingHouse
Grand Rapids, Michigan

A Division of HarperCollinsPublishers

The NIV Application Commentary: Exodus
Copyright © 2000 by Peter Enns

Requests for information should be addressed to:

ZondervanPublishingHouse
Grand Rapids, Michigan 49530

Library of Congress Cataloging-in-Publication Data

Enns, Peter, 1961–.
    Exodus / Peter Enns.
        p. cm.—(NIV application commentary)
        Includes bibliographical references and indexes.
        ISBN: 0–310–20607–3
        1. Bible. O.T. Exodus—Commentaries. I. Title. II. Series.
BS 1245.3 .E55 2000
222'.1277—dc21
                                                 99–53001
                                                    CIP

This edition printed on acid-free paper.

Printed in the United States of America

00 01 02 03 04 05 06 /❖ DC/ 10 9 8 7 6 5 4 3 2

To the memory

of

Raymond B. Dillard, Ph.D.

(1944–1993)

For we do not preach ourselves, but Jesus Christ as Lord. (2 Corinthians 4:5)

Contents

The NIV Application Commentary Series

When complete, the NIV Application Commentary
will include the following volumes:

Old Testament Volumes

Genesis, John H. Walton
Exodus, Peter Enns
Leviticus/Numbers, Roy Gane
Deuteronomy, Daniel I. Block
Joshua, Robert Hubbard
Judges/Ruth, K. Lawson Younger
1-2 Samuel, Bill T. Arnold
1-2 Kings, Michael S. Moore
1-2 Chronicles, Andrew E. Hill
Ezra/Nehemiah, Douglas J. Green
Esther, Karen H. Jobes
Job, Dennis R. Magary
Psalms Volume 1, Gerald H. Wilson
Psalms Volume 2, Gerald H. Wilson
Proverbs, Paul Koptak
Ecclesiastes/Song of Songs, Iain Provan
Isaiah, John N. Oswalt
Jeremiah/Lamentations, J. Andrew Dearman
Ezekiel, Iain M. Duguid
Daniel, Tremper Longman III
Hosea/Amos/Micah, Gary V. Smith
Jonah/Nahum/Habakkuk/Zephaniah
    David M. Howard Jr.
Joel/Obadiah/Malachi, David W. Baker
Haggai/Zechariah, Mark J. Boda

New Testament Volumes

Matthew, Michael J. Wilkins
Mark, David E. Garland
Luke, Darrell L. Bock
John, Gary M. Burge
Acts, Ajith Fernando
Romans, Douglas J. Moo
1 Corinthians, Craig Blomberg
2 Corinthians, Scott Hafemann
Galatians, Scot McKnight
Ephesians, Klyne Snodgrass
Philippians, Frank Thielman
Colossians/Philemon, David E. Garland
1-2 Thessalonians, Michael W. Holmes
1-2 Timothy/Titus, Walter L. Liefeld
Hebrews, George H. Guthrie
James, David P. Nystrom
1 Peter, Scot McKnight
2 Peter/Jude, Douglas J. Moo
Letters of John, Gary M. Burge
Revelation, Craig S. Keener

To see which titles are available,
visit our web site at http://www.zondervan.com

NIV Application Commentary
Series Introduction

THE NIV APPLICATION COMMENTARY SERIES is unique. Most commentaries help us make the journey from our world back to the world of the Bible. They enable us to cross the barriers of time, culture, language, and geography that separate us from the biblical world. Yet they only offer a one-way ticket to the past and assume that we can somehow make the return journey on our own. Once they have explained the *original meaning* of a book or passage, these commentaries give us little or no help in exploring its *contemporary significance*. The information they offer is valuable, but the job is only half done.

Recently, a few commentaries have included some contemporary application as *one* of their goals. Yet that application is often sketchy or moralistic, and some volumes sound more like printed sermons than commentaries.

The primary goal of the NIV Application Commentary Series is to help you with the difficult but vital task of bringing an ancient message into a modern context. The series not only focuses on application as a finished product but also helps you think through the *process* of moving from the original meaning of a passage to its contemporary significance. These are commentaries, not popular expositions. They are works of reference, not devotional literature.

The format of the series is designed to achieve the goals of the series. Each passage is treated in three sections: *Original Meaning, Bridging Contexts,* and *Contemporary Significance.*

THIS SECTION HELPS you understand the meaning of the biblical text in its original context. All of the elements of traditional exegesis—in concise form—are discussed here. These include the historical, literary, and cultural context of the passage. The authors discuss matters related to grammar and syntax and the meaning of biblical words.[1] They also seek to explore the main ideas of the passage and how the biblical author develops those ideas.

---

1. Please note that in general, when the authors discuss words in the original biblical languages, the series uses a general rather than a scholarly method of transliteration.

After reading this section, you will understand the problems, questions, and concerns of the *original audience* and how the biblical author addressed those issues. This understanding is foundational to any legitimate application of the text today.

THIS SECTION BUILDS a bridge between the world of the Bible and the world of today, between the original context and the contemporary context, by focusing on both the timely and timeless aspects of the text.

God's Word is *timely*. The authors of Scripture spoke to specific situations, problems, and questions. The author of Joshua encouraged the faith of his original readers by narrating the destruction of Jericho, a seemingly impregnable city, at the hands of an angry warrior God (Josh. 6). Paul warned the Galatians about the consequences of circumcision and the dangers of trying to be justified by law (Gal. 5:2–5). The author of Hebrews tried to convince his readers that Christ is superior to Moses, the Aaronic priests, and the Old Testament sacrifices. John urged his readers to "test the spirits" of those who taught a form of incipient Gnosticism (1 John 4:1–6). In each of these cases, the timely nature of Scripture enables us to hear God's Word in situations that were *concrete* rather than abstract.

Yet the timely nature of Scripture also creates problems. Our situations, difficulties, and questions are not always directly related to those faced by the people in the Bible. Therefore, God's word to them does not always seem relevant to us. For example, when was the last time someone urged you to be circumcised, claiming that it was a necessary part of justification? How many people today care whether Christ is superior to the Aaronic priests? And how can a "test" designed to expose incipient Gnosticism be of any value in a modern culture?

Fortunately, Scripture is not only timely but *timeless*. Just as God spoke to the original audience, so he still speaks to us through the pages of Scripture. Because we share a common humanity with the people of the Bible, we discover a *universal dimension* in the problems they faced and the solutions God gave them. The timeless nature of Scripture enables it to speak with power in every time and in every culture.

Those who fail to recognize that Scripture is both timely and timeless run into a host of problems. For example, those who are intimidated by timely books such as Hebrews, Galatians, or Deuteronomy might avoid reading them because they seem meaningless today. At the other extreme, those who are convinced of the timeless nature of Scripture, but who fail to discern its timely element, may "wax eloquent" about the Melchizedekian priest-hood to a sleeping congregation, or worse still, try to apply the holy wars of the Old Testament in a physical way to God's enemies today.

The purpose of this section, therefore, is to help you discern what is timeless in the timely pages of the Bible—and what is not. For example, how do the holy wars of the Old Testament relate to the spiritual warfare of the New? If Paul's primary concern is not circumcision (as he tells us in Gal. 5:6), what *is* he concerned about? If discussions about the Aaronic priesthood or Melchizedek seem irrelevant today, what is of abiding value in these pas-sages? If people try to "test the spirits" today with a test designed for a spe-cific first-century heresy, what other biblical test might be more appropriate?

Yet this section does not merely uncover that which is timeless in a passage but also helps you to see *how* it is uncovered. The authors of the commentaries seek to take what is implicit in the text and make it explicit, to take a process that normally is intuitive and explain it in a logical, orderly fashion. How do we know that circumcision is not Paul's primary concern? What clues in the text or its context help us realize that Paul's real concern is at a deeper level?

Of course, those passages in which the historical distance between us and the original readers is greatest require a longer treatment. Conversely, those passages in which the historical distance is smaller or seemingly nonex-istent require less attention.

One final clarification. Because this section prepares the way for dis-cussing the contemporary significance of the passage, there is not always a sharp distinction or a clear break between this section and the one that fol-lows. Yet when both sections are read together, you should have a strong sense of moving from the world of the Bible to the world of today.

THIS SECTION ALLOWS the biblical message to speak with as much power today as it did when it was first written. How can you apply what you learned about Jerusalem, Ephesus, or Corinth to our present-day needs in Chicago, Los Angeles, or London? How can you take a message originally spoken in Greek, Hebrew, and Aramaic and com-municate it clearly in our own language? How can you take the eternal truths originally spoken in a different time and culture and apply them to the sim-ilar-yet-different needs of our culture?

In order to achieve these goals, this section gives you help in several key areas.

(1) It helps you identify contemporary situations, problems, or questions that are truly comparable to those faced by the original audience. Because

contemporary situations are seldom identical to those faced by the original audience, you must seek situations that are analogous if your applications are to be relevant.

(2) This section explores a variety of contexts in which the passage might be applied today. You will look at personal applications, but you will also be encouraged to think beyond private concerns to the society and culture at large.

(3) This section will alert you to any problems or difficulties you might encounter in seeking to apply the passage. And if there are several legitimate ways to apply a passage (areas in which Christians disagree), the author will bring these to your attention and help you think through the issues involved.

In seeking to achieve these goals, the contributors to this series attempt to avoid two extremes. They avoid making such specific applications that the commentary might quickly become dated. They also avoid discussing the significance of the passage in such a general way that it fails to engage contemporary life and culture.

Above all, contributors to this series have made a diligent effort not to sound moralistic or preachy. The NIV Application Commentary Series does not seek to provide ready-made sermon materials but rather tools, ideas, and insights that will help you communicate God's Word with power. If we help you to achieve that goal, then we have fulfilled the purpose for this series.

The Editors

General Editor's Preface

EXODUS MAKES GREAT THEATER.

- An exciting plot: a dramatic escape by thousands of people from an abusive despot
- Special effects: an escape accompanied by miracles galore
- Great actors: Moses, a charismatic leader, negotiating the release of God's people

It is a gripping story.

It is a story made even more gripping because its underlying theme—leaving an unacceptable situation in search of a better one—is one to which we can all relate. Indeed, one might say that life itself is precisely such a journey. We undertake countless journeys, large and small, in search of life abundant.

These countless, private exoduses are anything but certain as to their outcome. When we first undertake them and as we undergo them, we do not know if we will succeed. Sometimes we know the destination, but often we don't. Sometimes we know the route, but often we are reduced to aimless wandering. We exit from a known evil in search of an unknown good.

Is it any wonder that under such nebulous circumstances, we frequently wonder about the meaning of our exoduses? How can we possibly understand why evil befell us in the first place (the Job question)? How can we hope for guidance in the deserts of our journeys (the psalmist's question)? How in the world will we know when we have arrived at the correct destination (the _____ question)? In the midst of these massive uncertainties, don't we need an anchor, a hermeneutical certainty to orient us?

In this excellent commentary on the book of Exodus, Peter Enns says, "Yes, we need such an anchor, and yes, we have such an anchor. The anchor is Jesus Christ—the story of Jesus Christ contained in the New Testament." But since the story of Jesus Christ occurred hundreds of years after the Exodus, the meaning we seek in the Exodus and in our exoduses has special features.

(1) Life is dynamic. We are meant to move. Or, more accurately perhaps, we are not meant to stay rooted in our sufferings. It is okay to try to escape persecution, to seek better conditions elsewhere. God is not a sadist, gleefully pulling wings off insects or angels or people. We are meant to fly to seek God's will and God's blessings. It is true that we will likely experience some sufferings and persecution for our faith. But God does not require either that

we seek suffering or that we passively endure it if and when it comes. The Exodus is not a once-for-all historical oddity but part of the Christian lifestyle.

(2) Our exodus is uncertain—at least in the details. We move not knowing everything about the reasons, the journey, or the destination. The details of Moses' exodus only become clear in light of the life of Jesus Christ hundreds of years later. The details of our exoduses may only become clear in the future, in the events of the move itself or even later. If we wait until we know all the details we will probably never go. True exodus requires faith.

(3) Because of our faith we can be sure there is meaning in our moving even when it is not entirely clear to us. Part of that meaning is a confidence that our lives are of a single piece. Often our reluctance is rooted in an exodus's strangeness. It doesn't seem to fit the trajectory of our life. But that is often part of what we cannot see—how it does fit. Exodus leads to more life, not less; more exodus means more meaning.

The most important events of Moses' exodus occurred on the journey. The discovery of God's will at every step of the way was provided on a need-to-know basis. Moses never reached the Promised Land, but his trip was still a success—for him and for his people.

Exodus is more than a gripping story. It is the nature of our life together in Christ.

Terry C. Muck

Author's Preface

MY ACADEMIC ASSOCIATION with the book of Exodus began during my years of doctoral study. My dissertation topic was the apocryphal book Wisdom of Solomon, and I explored the ways in which this ancient author interpreted the Exodus for his specific setting.

Although I have taken great care never once to mention my dissertation in this commentary (quite an accomplishment for a professional academic),[1] the issues I began addressing there have come into play as I worked through my thoughts on Exodus here. For one thing, the dissertation forced me to read through Exodus in Hebrew seemingly countless times, a discipline that helped me gain a stronger familiarity with its unique contours. Also, studying the manner in which the author of the Wisdom of Solomon interpreted Exodus helped me to become even more self-conscious about the task of interpreting Exodus specifically and the Old Testament in general.

In view of this, I think it appropriate to thank my professors—particularly my dissertation advisor, Dr. James L. Kugel. His teaching, along with that of my other professors, not only helped bring some clarity to what Exodus is about, but also affected the types of questions I bring into the interpretive task.

I also wish to acknowledge my teachers at Westminster Theological Seminary, many of whom are now my colleagues. Their influence continues to be profound. I consider it a gift and privilege to be associated with them. Also, I deeply appreciate the editing work of my research assistant, Erick Allen. Amid a busy teaching and study schedule, he found time to proofread the manuscript twice and to prepare the indexes. His careful attention to detail caught many mistakes and problems that would otherwise have gone unnoticed. His theological instincts also helped me look at several issues from different angles.

Finally, I wish to thank my extremely patient wife and usually patient children, who, for the past three years or so, have seen a little less of me than they would have liked. They mean more to me than the writing of books.

Yes, Elizabeth, Daddy is done now.

---

1. At the risk of contradicting myself, I will mention here once—and only once— my dissertation: *Exodus Retold: Ancient Exegesis of the Departure From Egypt in Wis 10:15–21 and 19:1–9* (Harvard Semitic Monographs 57; Atlanta: Scholars, 1997).

Abbreviations

AB	Anchor Bible
ABD	*Anchor Bible Dictionary*
AO	*Aula orientalis*
ASOR	American Schools of Oriental Research
ASORDS	American Schools of Oriental Research Dissertation Series
AUSS	*Andrews University Seminary Studies*
BA	*Biblical Archaeologist*
BAR	*Biblical Archaeology Review*
BASOR	*Bulletin of the American Schools of Oriental Research*
BBR	*Bulletin for Biblical Research*
BDB	F. Brown, S. R. Driver, and C. A. Briggs, *The New Brown-Driver-Briggs-Gesenius Hebrew-English Lexicon*
Bib	*Biblica*
BibOr	*Biblica et orientalia*
BSac	*Bibliotheca Sacra*
BZAW	Beihefte zur Zeitschrift für die alttestamentliche Wissenschaft
CBQ	*Catholic Biblical Quarterly*
ExpTim	*Expository Times*
GKC	W. Gesenius, E. Kautzsch, and A. E. Cowley, *Gesenius' Hebrew Grammar*
HAR	*Hebrew Annual Review*
HTR	*Harvard Theological Review*
HUCA	*Hebrew Union College Annual*
IBHS	B. K. Waltke and M. O'Connor, *An Introduction to Biblical Hebrew Syntax*
ICC	International Critical Commentary
JBL	*Journal of Biblical Literature*
JBLMS	Journal of Biblical Literature Monograph Series
JETS	*Journal of the Evangelical Theological Society*
JNES	*Journal of Near Eastern Studies*
JNSL	*Journal of Northwest Semitic Languages*

JPS	Jewish Publication Society
JSOT	*Journal for the Study of the Old Testament*
JSOTSup	Journal for the Study of the Old Testament Supplement Series
JTS	*Journal of Theological Studies*
LCC	Library of Christian Classics
LXX	Septuagint
MT	Masoretic Text
NIV	New International Version
OBT	Overtures to Biblical Theology
OTL	Old Testament Library
PTR	*Princeton Theological Review*
ResQ	*Restoration Quarterly*
SBLDS	Society of Biblical Literature Dissertation Series
SBT	Studies in Biblical Theology
SHR	Study in the History of Religions
TZ	*Theologische Zeitschrift*
USQR	*Union Seminary Quarterly Review*
VT	*Vetus Testamentum*
VTSup	Vetus Testamentum Supplements
WBC	Word Biblical Commentary
WTJ	*Westminster Theological Journal*
ZAW	*Zeitschrift für die alttestamentliche Wissenschaft*

Introduction

WRITING A COMMENTARY on a book of the Old Testament, particularly in a series geared toward application, is not a straightforward enterprise. It is hard to imagine anyone working on a commentary such as this who would not feel pressed to work out deliberately an approach to Old Testament interpretation that leads to application.

Toward that end, the question that has been my constant companion over the past three years or so since I began this commentary has been a simple one to ask, but exceedingly difficult to answer: How should a Christian interpret the Old Testament? Answers to this question will vary among Christians, and I certainly respect the diverse thinking among those who confess the name of Christ. Indeed, even in the process of writing this commentary there have been some extremely fruitful discussions among several of the authors and editors regarding the best way to answer this question. Input from a variety of sources greatly enriches the insights that any one person would have if left to himself or herself, and so I have benefited from this interaction.

The approach taken in this commentary is one that, like the question it answers, seems straightforward at first but is in fact difficult to address: A Christian should interpret the Old Testament from the point of view of Christ as the final word in the story of redemption. That final word is displayed for all the world to see in the cross, the empty tomb, and the existence of the church by God's Spirit.

Such an approach to Old Testament interpretation is not a personal idiosyncrasy. Although the specific comments on Exodus that follow are certainly my own (unless cited otherwise, of course), reading the Old Testament in light of the person and work of Christ is one with a long and honored history—going back to the New Testament authors themselves. Moreover, several of the commentaries in this series share a similar perspective.

Hence, in view of this overarching principle, it seems wise at the outset to offer some words of explanation for how I handle the three categories that form the structure of every commentary in this series: Original Meaning, Bridging Contexts, and Contemporary Significance.

What Is "Original Meaning"?

WHAT IS IMPLIED by "original meaning" is the meaning as it was intended by the writer to be understood by his audience. In one sense, such a quest is a welcome corrective to many unfortunate trends in modern biblical interpretation (and literature in general) that are prone to flights of fancy and absurdity. Most will quickly acknowledge the benefits of having our interpretations "anchored" somehow in what the writer himself wanted to say. No effective communication can occur when an author's intention is simply brushed aside.

The Question of Authorship

THE PROBLEM, HOWEVER, is that arriving at a text's original meaning is not a simple task. For one thing, a good number of biblical books are essentially anonymous, so the quest for uncovering an *author's* intention takes on a dimension of difficulty. Exodus seems to fit into this category.

As is well known, the authorship of Exodus (and the Pentateuch) has been a disputed point, not only over the past three hundred years of Old Testament scholarship, but earlier as well. A number of theories to account for the present state of the Pentateuch have without doubt overreached the biblical evidence. In my view, the well-known Documentary Hypothesis, popularized by the German scholar Julius Wellhausen in the latter half of the nineteenth century, is certainly guilty of this. Recent dissatisfaction with this theory among scholars of various stripes is a welcome countertrend.[1] The criticisms of this hypothesis offered by conservative scholars over the past 150 years (e.g., W. H. Green, U. Cassuto, O. T. Allis, E. J. Young) have largely been vindicated. The thoughtful exegetical works of these and other scholars, therefore, deserve renewed and careful attention, not simply by conservative scholars but by the academic community as a whole.

It is equally clear, however, that data in the Pentateuch and the book of Exodus complicate the matter of identifying an author with any certainty. In a manner of speaking, it is the Pentateuch itself that raises the question of authorship. For instance, nowhere in the Pentateuch is Moses described as the writer of the whole work. To be sure, he is said to write—the first instance being the episode with the Amalekites (see Ex. 17:14). Elsewhere in the Pentateuch where Moses is said to write, the reference is to the law (24:4; 34:1, 27, 28; Deut. 31:9, 24), the only exception being Deuteronomy 31:19, 22, which tells us that Moses wrote down the words of a song (Deut. 32:1–43). The Pentateuch has no more to say on the subject. To say more is to go beyond the pentateuchal evidence.

---

1. Two prominent examples of this countertrend are R. Rendtorff, *The Problem of the Process of the Transmission of the Pentateuch,* trans. J. J. Scullion (JSOTSup 89; Sheffield: Sheffield Academic, 1990), and R. N. Whybray, *The Making of the Pentateuch: A Methodological Study* (JSOT-Sup 53; Sheffield: Sheffield Academic, 1989). For helpful overviews of the history of the debate see R. N. Whybray, *Introduction to the Pentateuch* (Grand Rapids: Eerdmans, 1995), 12–28, and G. Wenham, "Pentateuchal Studies Today," *Themelios* 22/1 (1996): 3–13.

Furthermore, it seems difficult to maintain that Moses wrote the account of his own death (Deut. 34) or that he referred to himself as "more humble than anyone else on the face of the earth" (Num. 12:3).[2] Few would dispute this. However, despite the glaring inadequacies of the Documentary Hypothesis, strongly dismissing this theory does not in and of itself settle the question of authorship. An attitude of reverential open-mindedness seems most consistent with the evidence.

A similar situation involves the identification of the original audience. The precise identity of the audiences of biblical books is often difficult to determine. To be sure, some general observations can be made with a fair degree of certainty. For example, many, if not most, books may safely be labeled "postexilic," or "monarchic," or "premonarchic," and so forth. These designations are helpful for interpretation and in many cases virtually certain (no one would label Ezra or Nehemiah "preexilic").[3] But such designations do not actually identify the original *audience* but the general *time period* in which that audience might have lived.

The result of this relative lack of firm evidence, however, is not interpretive chaos. To acknowledge that the author and the audience cannot be precisely identified is not to say that we can freely mold the text to any shape we desire. Even though we do not have access to the mind of an author, we most certainly have the words he has produced, and it is to these *words* that we are bound. Our starting point for interpreting the text, therefore, is not a private notion of what an author intended. It is the other way around: A correct handling of the words on the page—the only "objective" data we have—allows us in due time to offer some suggestions as to what the author's intention might have been. In other words, understanding an author's intention comes at the end of the interpretive process, not the beginning.

One important factor to keep in mind in interpreting the Bible is that the question of biblical authorship is more than simply identifying the *person* who did the writing. All Christians who confess some notion of inspiration believe that the Bible is "authored" by God in some sense. Theories of how inspiration works vary, though we cannot get into a discussion on that issue here. The point to be made is that simply the question of authorship

---

2. These are two of a number of "standard" difficulties with Mosaic authorship raised by the Pentateuch itself. It should be made clear, however, that these non-Mosaic elements have no bearing whatsoever on whether Moses is responsible for some writing. In fact, the passages listed in the previous paragraph demonstrate that Moses did write. I might also add that many of these standard difficulties have been routinely pointed out by conservative scholars, so I am offering nothing new here.

3. On the other hand, determining the dates of many psalms is still uncertain, since historical markers in the psalms are for the most part conspicuously absent.

of any biblical book—precisely because it is God's Word—*must* go beyond merely the question of human authorship, his historical setting, and the setting of his audience. Scripture ultimately reaches beyond its own time and place, for it is a book that ultimately comes from God. The fact that all Scripture has not only a human author but a divine author is vital to any investigation of a text's meaning.

These authors, the human and the divine, do not compete with each other, nor do they contradict each other. But to say that the divine author inspires the human author does not mean that a human author at any one time knows fully the grand scheme of God's revelation. The divine author is perfectly cognizant of the "big picture" at every moment. The human author is not privy to the same total grasp of the sweep of history. In other words, the intention of the divine author, the Holy Spirit, is ultimate. I often wonder what advantage there is in limiting meaning to what the human author intended. If there is anything we *do* know about Scripture, it is "God-breathed" (2 Tim. 3:16). This is something Scripture itself makes plain. The Bible is God's book, and it seems wise to allow this fact to enter into the equation. I have often mused that the reason why the Bible itself is so relatively mute and even ambiguous on the question of human authorship is to remind us of who the ultimate author is.

Of course, to speak of God's intention is not to say that we can get into God's head and see what he intended! But just as a human author's intention can only be discerned by working backward from his final product (the words he has produced), so, too, can God's intention be discerned. And the final literary product that God has produced is the Bible as a whole. To speak of God's intention, therefore, is not to look at the bits and pieces of Scripture to ask what his intention was here or there. Rather, it is to take a step *back* from the details and look at the sweep of Scripture as a whole.

This is where the gospel comes into play. To look at God's intention is ultimately to look to the *end of the story and work backward*. We know how the story winds up; not every detail, but the bold contours of the story are clear—we are living in the still, fresh blast of light from the empty tomb. Like the mystery buff who sneaks a peek at the final chapter, we know the conclusion, and that knowledge forms the proper setting within which Christian interpretation of the Old Testament takes place.

If I can put this another way, for a Christian it seems that the "meaning" of an Old Testament text cannot simply be equated with what was intended by its human author and what it meant to its original audience. It means more. Ultimately, the question turns to the connection between the meaning of a text in its original setting and the effect the resurrection of Christ has on our understanding of that meaning. (We are getting a bit ahead of ourselves here, so we will come back to this below.)

None of this is to imply that discerning the meaning of the text, once you know the conclusion, is an easy thing to do and that every Christian will agree. People have been engaging in biblical interpretation in some sense for well over three thousand years, and the end is nowhere in sight. There have been points of agreement and disagreement throughout this great span of time. Even reasonably like-minded Christians who live in a similar social setting and in the same time period will both agree and disagree over certain matters. This is because the quest for meaning in the Bible is an arduous, ongoing process, which no one can claim to have mastered. Quite to the contrary, we are mastered by it.

This is to say that biblical interpretation is a spiritual matter, taken up by spiritual people, whose object is ultimately the deeper understanding of who God is and what he has done (1 Cor. 2:14–16). When we interpret Scripture, we are involved in a spiritual exercise. It is therefore not simply a matter of applying some "neutral" tools and methods to the text. It is both an adventure and a journey. Hence, to say a text means such and such may not always be the end of the matter but actually the beginning. All of us engaged in biblical interpretation, whether professionally or privately, enter into a long and honored stream of faithful people of God who have done likewise. Knowing that we are surrounded by this "great cloud of witnesses," it is best to keep an open mind, which is what I have tried to do in this commentary. Toward that end, I will not hesitate to offer explanations when I feel it is justified. Neither will I hesitate to confess ignorance where needed.

The Question of History

THERE IS AN IMPORTANT MATTER related to original meaning that should be touched on briefly here, especially since it comes up so frequently in discussions over Exodus. This is the perennial, thorny question of historicity. The historical veracity of the Old Testament has been rigorously attacked in modern biblical scholarship, and this fact has no doubt contributed toward the conservative tendency to spend much effort in defending the Bible as a reliable historical document. Such defense is often needed and has paid off important dividends, especially in recent years.[4] The point to be raised here,

---

4. A well-known example in recent years is the discovery of an inscription in Tel Dan that makes reference to the "House of David," thus lending extrabiblical support for the historicity of David's reign. The discovery and interpretation of this inscription has sparked a great deal of controversy. See A. Biran, "'David' Found at Dan," *BAR* 20 (March-April 1994): 26–39; W. Schiedewind, "Tel Dan Stela: New Light on Aramaic and Jehu's Revolt," *BASOR* 302 (1996): 75–90. With respect to the historicity of Exodus specifically I suggest the recent study by J. K. Hoffmeier, *Israel in Egypt: The Evidence for the Authenticity of the Exodus Tradition* (New York: Oxford Univ. Press, 1997).

however, is the relevance of history for ascertaining original meaning. The matter will come up now and then in the commentary itself, so it is appropriate to outline the issue here.

It is often simply stated that if what the Bible says happened did *not* happen, then the truth claims of the Bible are rendered suspect and we have little reason to trust it. Defense of the Bible's historicity is, of course, important, but it is not the *goal of biblical interpretation*. To use an obviously relevant example, you have not *understood* the book of Exodus when you have successfully defended the historicity of the event of the Exodus. There is more to interpreting the book than demonstrating that this or that happened.

The Old Testament is not a journalistic, dispassionate, objective account of events. Its purpose is not just to tell us "what happened" so that we can "look objectively at the data" and arrive at the proper conclusions. The Old Testament is *theological* history. It has been written to teach lessons. The primary lesson I would argue is to teach us what God is like and what it means for his people to live with that knowledge.

If I can put it another way, the Bible is an *argument* to God's people that God is worthy of our worship. It is not designed merely to set out "objective data." It is a deeply spiritual book that has deeply personal implications. It is not a book to be held at a distance, but a book that the interpreter is required to enter into, because it is God's book and we are his people. That the Bible has such a purpose should rightly affect the types of questions we bring to that reading, which in turn affects our interpretation of the text. We must be careful to expect from the Bible only those things it is prepared to yield. And it is not a science textbook or owner's manual. It is a book about God and his creation. It is about who he is, who we are, and how the former determines the standing of the latter.

To push this one slight step further, to say that the Bible is theological history, history with a driving theological purpose, is not to concede that it is somehow "less objective" than what we might see in history textbooks or newspapers. The fact of the matter is that there is no objective history in the commonly understood sense of the word. There is no account of events that is free from one's bias, one's perspective. All one has to do is watch the major news networks report on the same "objective" event, or read high school American history textbooks written in the wake of the Second World War, or read differing evaluations of the Civil War from northern or southern observers. What reporters choose to include in their accounts, how they report it, and the conclusions they draw differ from station to station and between books of different eras. Who we are *always* determines what we see and how we interpret it.

In this sense, what the Bible gives us is the *divine* perspective on events, that is, what God wants us to see and understand. I am not suggesting that

God's perspective is in any way faulty or merely one among many. Rather, simply put—what the Bible contains is what God wants to present. This is why I hesitate in this commentary to introduce prolonged discussions on historicity. It is not because history is unimportant. *These things really happened!* But what we have is the text in front of us, which is a gift from God. It is the text that is the focus of our attention, not what might lie behind it. To be sure, the Bible has a referential subject matter, but when the topic turns to *biblical interpretation*, there is no "behind it." The "it" is the object of study. Some concrete examples will be explored in the commentary.

One final matter concerning history is the fact that a good many historical issues remain hopelessly unresolved. In what century the Exodus took place will remain a point of debate for some time, even among evangelicals. We still do not know who the pharaoh of the Exodus was. Curiously enough, we are not told (see Ex. 1:8). To this day we do not know what route the Israelites took, what specific body of water they crossed,[5] or where Mount Sinai is. These events form the very basic historical contours of Exodus and yet they continue to elude us. Can proper interpretation of the book proceed only after these basic questions are answered? No. In fact, the church has been deriving spiritual benefit from Exodus for a long time without such firm knowledge.

The Text in Front of Us

WHAT, THEN, ARE WE to make of original meaning? It is, as mentioned above, located in the text. I realize, as does anyone familiar with the debate, that this does not settle every matter. My focus, nevertheless, will be on the *words in front of me*—ultimately the Hebrew text—and how those words form impressions in my mind as to how an ancient Israelite audience might have understood those words.

This means that the goal of the Original Meaning sections will be to draw out the *theology* of the text. We must remember that the original purpose of Exodus was theological, to teach God's people about himself and their relationship to him. It was not to have its readers enter into discussions of who the pharaoh was or some other piece of historical trivia. Exodus was written as a theological treatise, and hence any original meaning we might discern from the text will have to proceed firmly from that basis. Such an approach does not claim a basis in an objective point of departure outside of the text. It claims rather to immerse itself in the text and to come up with some informed and defensible (but not necessarily final) answers that will hopefully contribute to the church's understanding of Exodus.

---

5. On the lack of the precise identification of the location of the Red Sea, see Hoffmeier, *Israel in Egypt*, 215.

Since the theology of Exodus is communicated through the words on the page, my efforts to disclose the theological message of the book will require / me to pay attention to things like wordplays, unusual turns of phrases, repetitions of themes, and so forth, in the Original Meaning section, not the Bridging Contexts section. In other words, it is precisely because original meaning is theological and textually bound that we must discuss already in the first section the principles involved in making certain interpretive decisions. The Bridging Contexts section will be reserved for designing a different kind of bridge for bringing meaning into our contemporary setting.

What Does It Mean to "Bridge the Contexts"?

I MENTIONED ABOVE that the following question has been my constant companion in writing this commentary: "How should a Christian interpret the Old Testament?" This is not the same as asking, "How should *I as a Christian* interpret the Old Testament for my life?" We have not yet arrived at the "I" question. That comes next. The question we are asking here is still much more basic. It is a topic where opinions among Christians differ sharply. Let me say again that I am aware of these differences and that I greatly respect other approaches. No interpreter is omniscient.

Nevertheless, I have become firmly convinced that Christian interpretation of the Old Testament has its own flavor, so to speak. It looks different, or at least should look different, from what others do. This has been the case throughout the history of the church, and indeed it should be. Is there nothing about Christian interpretation that makes it look different from, say, Jewish exegesis or secular exegesis? Yes. We believe that God has raised Jesus from the dead. We know the end of the story, and now we can—must—go back and read Israel's story in light of that great culminating event. In doing so, Israel's story becomes ours. This is why Christian interpretation is not a neutral undertaking, but one that, like every other area of our lives, rests in the reality of the gospel.[6]

To put it another way, a Christian reads the Old Testament armed with the knowledge that Christ actually did rise from the dead, and that that fact affects the interpretive process. The resurrection of Christ is the absolute center of our existence. It is the event that has shaped us as a people of God. It was not just a trick that God pulled off at the last minute to prove how powerful he is. It was a new beginning for all the world and for all God's people. This highest of all

---

6. A seminary professor of mine, the late Raymond Dillard, would evaluate student sermons on the Old Testament by asking, "Could this sermon have been preached in a synagogue?" The answer had better be "no"! His point was that there should be something distinct about Christian preaching of the Old Testament.

realities makes a difference in everything we do and think. It should also make a difference in how we approach Old Testament interpretation.

The Old Testament is not an ancient text with which *we* have to struggle somehow to find creative ways to bring its timeless principles into our world. God has already "interpreted" the Old Testament by raising Christ from the dead. In doing so, God has put the period and exclamation point on Israel's story. This is something that the New Testament writers go to great lengths to demonstrate. Israel's story must now be understood in light of the coming of Christ and of his death and resurrection. The fact that these things have happened, by God's design and purpose, is what drove the New Testament writers *back* to the Old Testament in an effort to understand the *entire* Old Testament—not just an isolated prophecy here and there—from this new, fresh point of view.

Let me illustrate. Have you ever read the New Testament where it quotes an Old Testament passage, and then gone back and looked at the Old Testament context only to find, perhaps with a slight sense of awkwardness and embarrassment, that it doesn't really "fit"? (As a professor, I get this question a lot.) This could be demonstrated dozens of times within the pages of the New Testament, and several will come up in the course of the commentary. One example is worth bringing up here in order to illustrate the point.

In 2 Corinthians 6:2 Paul cites Isaiah 49:8: "In the time of my favor I heard you, and in the day of salvation I helped you." Paul then goes on to declare, "I tell you, now is the time of God's favor, now is the day of salvation." What does Paul mean here? A look at the context of Isaiah 49:8 makes it plain that Isaiah's words speak to the situation of the Babylonian captivity, that is, the period of Judah's exile in Babylon in the sixth century B.C. Isaiah's prophecy certainly seems to concern Israel's eventual release from Babylon and their return home beginning in 539–538 B.C. Isaiah is not prophesying about the coming of Christ. There is really no indication *in Isaiah* that suggests he is referring to Christ. Paul, however, does not allow the fact that Isaiah's words do *not* speak of Christ to prevent *him* from doing so.

Paul quotes Isaiah and then says, "I tell you, *now* is the time of God's favor, *now* is the day of salvation." The salvation that Isaiah spoke of several centuries earlier is happening *now*. What is this "now"? Paul clarifies this in the closing verse of chapter 5: "God made him who had no sin to be sin for us, so that in him we might become the righteousness of God" (2 Cor. 5:21). The apostle is not contradicting Isaiah. Rather, he is building on his words. He is saying that the salvation of which Isaiah spoke was merely a *prelude* to the fullness of God's salvation as seen in the cross and the empty tomb. The "now" that Isaiah referred to (Israel's release from Babylon) was real and true, but foreshadowed the final *Now* with the coming of Christ.

There is nothing in Isaiah 49:8 that an "objective" reading would lead one to think of Christ! You can only see Christ there if you are standing at the end of the story, as Paul was and as we still are today. In other words, Paul, knowing that Jesus is the final answer to Israel's story, *goes back* to the Old Testament, rereads Israel's story, and then says, "Oh, now I get it." He claims Israel's story and puts it at the feet of King Jesus, saying as it were, "Now we know the whole story, now we know what God was ultimately saying through Isaiah."

This is just one example, but it demonstrates an interpretive principle repeated throughout the New Testament. What we call the Old Testament[7] is rightly understood fully only in light of the resurrection of Christ. This is because the resurrection of Christ is the ultimate fulfillment of everything the Old Testament—God's book, Holy Scripture—pointed toward in the first place. My contention is that proper Christian interpretation of the Old Testament cannot and must not proceed without taking seriously into account the interpretive stance of the apostles themselves. The New Testament itself drives us in this direction.

This, then, is how the contexts between the Old Testament and our contemporary setting will be bridged in this commentary—not by seeking timeless moral principles in the Old Testament and then seeking to apply them to our lives, but rather by asking ourselves what the Old Testament tells us about the nature of God (i.e., how he acts, what he expects of his people) and then seeing how these things can be understood in light of the gospel. It is reading *back into* the Old Testament the final word that God has stamped onto the pages of history—the death and resurrection of his Son. This event is the "answer" to Israel's story, and God, by his grace, has given us, Jews and Gentiles, the privilege of participating in the final chapter of that story.

This great fact should indeed enter our interpretive activity of the Old Testament. Let me say, however, that a commitment to this approach does not in any way imply that the matter of interpretation is easy! To interpret the Old Testament is to interact with it with an intimacy that characterizes the high view of Scripture that Christians confess. It is in the pages of Scripture that we get to know God better. Such personal interaction implies struggling and wrestling with the text. What God has done in Christ is the proper subject of a lifetime of discovery, where each of us experiences both highs and lows.

What God has done in Christ, in other words, is the proper *context* within which we interpret the Old Testament. But this does not mean that Jesus is

---

7. Jesus and the apostles typically referred to this as "the Scriptures." It seems to me that sometimes the term "Old Testament" puts up barriers for contemporary interpretation that would have been wholly foreign to what the New Testament itself not only presents but assumes.

a magic key that quickly unlocks the door to every corner. Knowing the end of the story does not mean that Old Testament interpretation is a superficial process! We are, after all, dealing with the Word of God. Its author is deep and even mysterious.

It is with this thought in mind that I proceed to bridge the contexts of then and now. How I see the gospel fulfilling the book of Exodus is the result of my own wrestling with the text, but I do not presume to have the final word on the matter. The *gospel* is the final word, not *my understanding* of how the gospel is the final word! Our thinking will always develop as we continue to live with Scripture and ponder the nature of the gospel.

To anticipate perhaps another objection, reading the Old Testament from the point of view of the resurrection does not mean, as it is commonly misunderstood, that we must find Jesus in every verse. The "Christocentric" interpretation I am advocating is not mechanical. There are places in the Old Testament, of course, where the gospel is more transparent than others. Isaiah, for example, has sometimes been called in the history of Christianity "the fifth Gospel." But not everything has such an obvious Christological dimension as, say, Isaiah 52:13–53:12 (even here the precise nature of this Christological dimension is up for discussion).

The fact that Christ has been raised from the dead and that we are raised with him to a new life should affect our reading of the Old Testament. At times that means seeing clearly how the Old Testament prepares the way for the gospel. At other times, however, there is no one-to-one correspondence between the Old Testament and Christ, and in such instances the matter should not be pushed.

Let me use the example of the tabernacle in Exodus to illustrate. As we will see later on, the fact that the glory of God is seen in Christ and that the New Testament refers to Christ both as the tabernacle and the temple (see John 1–2) is clearly intended to challenge Christians to see Christ as somehow fulfilling the role that the tabernacle (and later the temple) had in the Old Testament. Briefly stated, the tabernacle is the premier symbol of God's continued presence with his people, a role assumed by Christ at his first coming.

But recognizing this explicit theological connection between Christ and the tabernacle does not mean that we have to find Christological significance in every detail in the tabernacle. For example, I have no interest in "finding Jesus" in the goat hair curtains or the acacia wood crossbars. A Christological reading is not like a hermeneutical "Where's Waldo." Rather, to read the tabernacle section of Exodus Christologically means to see how the *theological significance of the whole* can be seen from the point of view of the gospel. Again, it is the *theology* of Exodus that is our focus for deriving original meaning. Likewise, it is that same theology that encourages us to expand our interpretive horizons to appreciate how Christ's coming helps us to see these Old Testament realities in a different, fuller light. As we will see clearly in the case of the tabernacle, the New Testament itself drives us toward that end.

In light of this, there are a number of times in the commentary where I do not provide a separate Original Meaning, Bridging Contexts, and Contemporary Significance section for each section of Exodus. A rigid adherence to this threefold scheme would run into some significant problems in treating, for example, the plagues. Each plague does not have to be *individually* bridged to our contemporary setting. It would be tedious indeed to bridge the plague of flies narrative separately from the plague of gnats. Moreover, it would be rather ridiculous to try to argue that each plague offers its own application to the contemporary setting (can you apply the plague of gnats any differently than the plague of flies!?). Hence, the nature of the book of Exodus at times lends itself to drawing theological implications from larger blocks of text. I have tried to be as sensitive as I can to where this approach is appropriate. At each of these sections I have offered an explanation for why I think it is so.

The Question of "Contemporary Significance"

THE QUESTION OF APPLICATION follows directly from bridging the contexts. That is, we understand the significance of the Old Testament for us by first understanding what the Old Testament has to say about God and how the gospel expresses this in final form. We typically approach the question of application with two assumptions. (1) Application means bringing the Old Testament into our lives. It has to be understood in such a way that it "speaks to us where we are." (2) Application is something demonstrable and concrete. Specifically, it pushes us to *do* something; that is, it has to be "practical." Both of these assumptions are at the same time right and wrong.

(1) As for the first assumption, it is certainly true that the Old Testament, as God's Word, must enter our lives in some way. It is not an artifact from a bygone era, a book of law and wrath that can be dismissed now that Jesus is here. The Old Testament has always spoken powerfully to the church throughout its two-thousand-year history, and we are right to expect it to do the same in our day. The problem with this assumption, however, is that it does not account easily for the fact that much of the Old Testament is *narrative*.

Narrative portions of the Old Testament are notoriously difficult to apply. One need only go to Christian bookstores and see copies of the "New Testament and Psalms." The reason why the book of Psalms is included is because it is perceived as having more immediate relevance for our lives today (although I think that the interpretive issues surrounding the Psalms are difficult in their own right). Still, just once I'd like to see "New Testament and 2 Kings," "New Testament and Judges," or even "New Testament and Genesis." The reason why Psalms (and I might add Proverbs) are apparently so much easier to bring into our lives is that they are not as bound to a particular place and time. Exodus, however, is; it is a *story* about something that *happened*, and therefore it is not as apparent how that story should be applied.

But the problem may not be with Exodus. It is not nearly as stubborn a book when we learn to ask the right questions of it. When we think of application, we tend to think of *ourselves* as the immovable point and the Old Testament as something that has to be *brought into* our lives. We think that it has to speak to *our* circumstances without always considering whether it is our particular circumstances that the Bible is designed to speak to.

There is another way of thinking about application. The book of Exodus is not waiting there for *us* to bring *it* into *our* world. Rather, it is standing there defining what our world should look like and then inviting us to enter that world. That may sound a bit esoteric, so allow me to explain. Who we are and what we are experiencing should not always be the starting point for thinking about how the Old Testament relates to us. To give a specific example, the story of Exodus is not designed to tell us what God will do to those people who oppress us today, say, if you as a Christian are facing hostile opposition from unbelievers. True, oppressed people may be able to identify with certain aspects of the book and thus connect with it differently from nonoppressed people. The story of Exodus, however, is designed to tell us what *God is like*, how he thinks of his people, the lengths to which he will go to deliver them, and the proper response of God's people to this great deed. Applying the book of Exodus begins with understanding what the story is supposed to do and then seeing how we, as God's people, fit into that story.

And the way we today fit into that story is, first and foremost, by understanding that the Exodus story is ultimately not a self-contained unit whose boundaries must not be crossed. The story of Exodus does not actually end until we come to the cross and the empty tomb—or even beyond, not until the Second Coming. In other words, seeing how *we as Christians* fit into the story must be seen in light of how *Christ completes* the story. We do not draw a straight line from something in Exodus to our lives. We take a part of the story, we see how it fits into the whole story, which comes to a conclusion in Christ, and *then* we begin to see more fully how this story affects how we look at ourselves and our God. Hence, application follows upon bridging the contexts.

(2) Related to this is the second assumption: The ultimate goal of application may not always be to tell us how we should act. It may also be to change how we *think*, how we look at the world around us, and how we understand what it means to be a child of God. "Application" may mean that

we grow in our understanding of how great God is and how full of love he is. Proper application may be no more than coming to the truly heartfelt conclusion that our God is indeed great. Application is worship.

Maybe it is the society in which we live, but we are always asking, "What's the payoff?" If one's understanding of a biblical text does not translate into concrete action, something demonstrable and "practical," then it is not thought to be something worthwhile for God's people. I understand and sympathize with the motives behind this sentiment. It is all too common for our Bible study to become merely an arid intellectual or academic exercise. This is wrong. What I am saying, however, is that "practical" application need not always translate into something we do. Rather, what may be in order is to change how we define "practical."

Let me put it this way. The goal of Old Testament application may not be to "love your wife more" or to "be kinder to your husband." We may not get this directly from the Old Testament. Rather it may be, "Now that I have come to understand this story better, I see that I have become selfish and shortsighted. I have forgotten how great God is, how wonderful he is. But now I see Jesus more clearly, and therefore myself more clearly." And as a result of gaining (or relearning) this practical insight, the Christian goes out and has a renewed motivation for doing such things as loving a spouse.

This commentary attempts to explain Exodus in light of Christ's coming. In doing so, I have tried to listen as carefully as I can first to what the story would have communicated to ancient Israelite readers of the book. The theology of the book pushes me outward to consider how that theology fits into the whole story, a story that culminates in the person and work of Christ. It is knowing how the story ends up that forms the proper context within which we who are "in Christ" (to use Paul's words) apply those words to ourselves.

In working toward this goal, I do not hesitate to say I have much to learn. This commentary is an attempt to work out the implications of what a Christian interpretation of Exodus looks like in principle. Nothing would make me happier than to be completely outdone by others in this task, if it would lead to greater understanding of who the God of Exodus is and what it means to be bound to him through the death and resurrection of his Son.

Outline

EXODUS IS A LONG BOOK. One danger in outlining a book of this length is that one can get lost in the minutia. Outlines of any sort sometimes obfuscate the highlights with endless sub-points and sub-sub-points. How much more the case with a book as busy as Exodus!

In an effort to avoid such trouble, the following is an attempt to present the contents of Exodus in ways that will hopefully bring to the foreground the essential divisions and forward movement of the book. An outline is not an end in itself but a means to an end, which is to understand what the book as a whole is communicating.

Nor is there any one outline that by itself catches the essence of the book. Exodus may be depicted in several outlines, each of which serves to help the reader grasp the book on various levels. Several outlines of varying detail are given below, and the reader is invited to make use of the one that proves most helpful.

In its simplest outline, Exodus may be divided into two parts that highlight the Israelites' departure from Egypt and their stay at the foot of Mount Sinai:

    I. Departure From Egypt (chs. 1–15)
    II. Journey to and Arrival at Mount Sinai (chs. 16–40).

A subdivision of Part II can easily be justified, since two basic activities are recounted in chapters 16–40: the giving of the law and the building of the tabernacle:

    I. Departure From Egypt (chs. 1–15)
    II. Mount Sinai: Law (chs. 16–24)
    III. Mount Sinai: Tabernacle (chs. 25–40).

This three-point outline gives the broad contours of Exodus, but a bit more detail will perhaps provide a more useful presentation of the book's contents.

    I. Departure From Egypt (chs. 1–15)
      A. Prelude (chs. 1–6)
      B. Plagues (chs. 7–12)
      C. Departure (chs. 13–15)
    II. Mount Sinai: Law (chs. 16–24)
      A. Journey to Sinai (chs. 16–18)
      B. Ten Commandments (chs. 19–20)

Although imperfect and far from complete, this outline is a reliable guide to the main divisions and flow of Exodus. As such, it is perhaps a good, basic outline to memorize. A more detailed outline (and one that I trust does not suffer from too much detail!) follows below. The rough chapter divisions given above are helpful for the purpose of memorization. Below, however, chapter and verse divisions are given more precisely.

It should also be observed that this more detailed outline is a compromise of sorts. It is not an "ideal" outline. Rather, the way in which I have finally outlined the book reflects the needs of this commentary series. The most obvious tinkering with the structure of Exodus can be seen with respect to chapters 25–40. Specifically, the golden calf episode (chs. 32–34) is treated after the entire tabernacle section, not at the midway point as the book of Exodus actually presents it. Also the tabernacle section (chs. 25–31 and 35–40) is collapsed, with parallel passages treated together. This is to avoid tedious repetition in the commentary. A fuller explanation for this and other organizational matters is given at the appropriate junctures in the commentary itself.

Annotated Bibliography

THIS IS BY NO MEANS an exhaustive list of works cited in this commentary. Rather, these are the books and commentaries I have found most useful in developing my own thinking on Exodus, and they are all highly recommended for one reason or another.

Cassuto, Umberto. *A Commentary on the Book of Exodus*. Jerusalem: Magnes, 1967. A standard conservative treatment of Exodus. Based on the Hebrew text but still profitable for general consultation.

Childs, Brevard. *The Book of Exodus*. OTL. Philadelphia: Westminster, 1974. Original attempt to discuss Exodus not simply as an ancient book but as Scripture. Comes to fairly standard critical conclusions on a number of matters, but Childs is to be commended for bringing into his discussion the history of interpretation and the theological significance of the canonical form of Exodus for the church.

Durham, John I. *Exodus*. WBC 3. Waco, Tex.: Word, 1987. Becoming a standard commentary on Exodus. Some will find Durham's interaction with source criticism disruptive, as it tends to add little to his conclusions. Many fine exegetical insights.

— Fretheim, Terence E. *Exodus*. Interpretation. Louisville: John Knox, 1991. Wonderful commentary full of rich and creative theological insights. Definitely to be consulted for sermon preparation and other types of popular expositions.

Gowan, Donald E. *Theology in Exodus: Biblical Theology in the Form of a Commentary*. Louisville: Westminster/John Knox, 1994. Thoughtful interaction with the theology of Exodus. Treats not only Exodus itself but Exodus within its canonical context, as well as from the point of view of the history of Jewish and Christian thought. Gowan deals with large blocks of material, which aids the reader in coming away with the broad scope of the biblical book.

— Houtman, Cornelis. *Exodus*. 3 vols. Trans. by J. Rebel and S. Woudstra. Kampen: Kok, 1993–1999. Probably the most well-rounded and balanced commentary on Exodus available. To date, volume 3 has not yet been translated into English. Houtman is judicious while being creative in his insights. His comments range from detailed philological and syntactical points to discussions on the history of interpretation and theological significance. This work is a mine of valuable information.

Janzen, J. Gerald. *Exodus*. Westminster Bible Companion. Louisville: West-minster/John Knox, 1997. As with other contributors in this series, Janzen's insights are geared toward a basic theological grasp of the book. This purpose is well met.

Plastaras, James. *The God of Exodus: The Theology of the Exodus Narratives*. Mil-waukee: Bruce, 1966. Explores the theology of Exodus and how that theology is reflected elsewhere in Scripture, particularly in the New Testament. As with Durham's commentary, it is not always clear how his discussions of critical issues affect the broader goals of the book. Nev-ertheless, it is a sensitive and helpful treatment.

— Sarna, Nahum M. *Exodus*. JPS. Philadelphia: JPS, 1991. Perhaps the most careful and penetrating shorter one-volume commentary on Exodus available in any language. Sarna's knowledge of rabbinic writings allows him to direct the reader to elements of the text that Christian readers might otherwise pass over too quickly. Along with Houtman and Fretheim, Sarna's commentary is a "must."

_____. *Exploring Exodus: The Heritage of Biblical Israel*. New York: Schocken, 1986. A more detailed discussion of some major themes and issues of Exodus than are treated in his commentary. A valuable "second step" for many issues raised in his commentary.

Exodus 1:1–22

THESE ARE THE names of the sons of Israel who went to Egypt with Jacob, each with his family: ²Reuben, Simeon, Levi and Judah; ³Issachar, Zebulun and Benjamin; ⁴Dan and Naphtali; Gad and Asher. ⁵The descendants of Jacob numbered seventy in all; Joseph was already in Egypt.

⁶Now Joseph and all his brothers and all that generation died, ⁷but the Israelites were fruitful and multiplied greatly and became exceedingly numerous, so that the land was filled with them.

⁸Then a new king, who did not know about Joseph, came to power in Egypt. ⁹"Look," he said to his people, "the Israelites have become much too numerous for us. ¹⁰Come, we must deal shrewdly with them or they will become even more numerous and, if war breaks out, will join our enemies, fight against us and leave the country."

¹¹So they put slave masters over them to oppress them with forced labor, and they built Pithom and Rameses as store cities for Pharaoh. ¹²But the more they were oppressed, the more they multiplied and spread; so the Egyptians came to dread the Israelites ¹³and worked them ruthlessly. ¹⁴They made their lives bitter with hard labor in brick and mortar and with all kinds of work in the fields; in all their hard labor the Egyptians used them ruthlessly.

¹⁵The king of Egypt said to the Hebrew midwives, whose names were Shiphrah and Puah, ¹⁶"When you help the Hebrew women in childbirth and observe them on the delivery stool, if it is a boy, kill him; but if it is a girl, let her live." ¹⁷The midwives, however, feared God and did not do what the king of Egypt had told them to do; they let the boys live. ¹⁸Then the king of Egypt summoned the midwives and asked them, "Why have you done this? Why have you let the boys live?"

¹⁹The midwives answered Pharaoh, "Hebrew women are not like Egyptian women; they are vigorous and give birth before the midwives arrive."

²⁰So God was kind to the midwives and the people increased and became even more numerous. ²¹And because the midwives feared God, he gave them families of their own.

²²Then Pharaoh gave this order to all his people: "Every boy that is born you must throw into the Nile, but let every girl live."

 ONE CAN BEGIN to understand Exodus by thinking of it more as a chapter of a book (the Pentateuch) than a book in its own right. Exodus is not meant to be read in isolation from the surrounding material in the Pentateuch. Rather, it describes one stage of Israel's story that began with creation in Genesis 1 and ends with the Israelites poised at the borders of the land of Canaan at the end of Deuteronomy.

In Exodus 1, a number of elements draw the reader back to Genesis, thus driving us to read Exodus in light of what has come before. The connection to Genesis (esp. creation and the patriarchs) will prove to be an important theme in Exodus, so it is worth our while to see how this theme is initiated here.

The first such element is the first word of the book. Although not reflected in the NIV, the Hebrew text shows that 1:1 does not begin simply with the words "These are the names. . . ." Rather, it begins with the harmless word "and" (the Hebrew letter *waw*). This is not academic hair-splitting or forcing meaning from the text. Although the presence of "and" at the beginning of the book may seem odd,[1] it functions here to join Exodus to what has come before. This book continues the story begun in Genesis: God chose a people for himself and brought them down into Egypt.[2] Their presence there is an outworking of his presence with the patriarchs. It is no by-product of chance. This insight will soon prove to be most valuable for the Israelites.

Second, the first six words of 1:1 are an exact repetition of Genesis 46:8. The words are the same, but the contexts of the two passages are different. The context of Genesis 46 is the imminent move of the Israelites into Egypt. Joseph had just revealed his identity to his brothers. They report back to Jacob, who then sets out to see his long lost son once more before he dies. An appropriate translation for Genesis 46:8 is: "Now these are the names of sons of Israel who were traveling [better English: who journeyed] to Egypt."

---

1. "And" also begins the books of Leviticus and Numbers, although there it is attached to verbs, which is somewhat less unexpected. Deuteronomy begins with "These," but a few ancient manuscripts include "and." See comments by C. Houtman, *Exodus*, 1:226–27.

2. The commentaries are in routine agreement over this. See, e.g., U. Cassuto, *Commentary on Exodus*, 7, and J. I. Durham, *Exodus*, 3–5. James S. Ackerman argues that Ex. 1:1–14 as a whole acts as a bridge linking the patriarchal narratives and the Exodus ("The Literary Context of the Moses Birth Story [Exodus 1–2]," *Literary Interpretations of Biblical Narratives*, ed. K. Gros. Louis, J. Ackerman, and T. S. Warshaw [Nashville: Abingdon, 1974], 74–119).

And after this opening statement, as we also see in the opening paragraph of Exodus 1, Genesis 46:8–27 provides a genealogy of those who made the trek.

The perspective of Exodus 1:1, however, in contrast to Genesis 46:8, is that of looking *back* from an Egyptian setting to the *past* event of the Israelites' move from Canaan to Egypt under Jacob. But in an effort to reproduce Genesis 46:8, Exodus 1:1 also uses the participle. This grammatical construction is striking. One would expect the standard past-tense narrative formula that is used throughout Hebrew narrative: *waw* ("and") followed by the imperfect verbal form.[3] The repetition of Genesis 46:8 in Exodus 1:1, including "and" and followed by the genealogies, indicates a clear connection between them. Exodus is to be read as a continuation of the past; it is one part of a larger story.[4]

A third element in Exodus 1 serves to remind its readers of Genesis. The language of 1:7 is creation language, calling to mind the language found in Genesis 1:28 and 9:1: The Israelites became "fruitful and multiplied greatly and became exceedingly numerous."[5] The Hebrew of Exodus 1:7 is even more explicit than the NIV: "The Israelites became fruitful and swarmed; they increased in number and became exceedingly strong" ("swarm," also used in Gen. 1:21 and 8:17, is another description of what God's *created* beings do).

The Israelites' increasing number in Egypt was a sign of God's presence and blessing. They, like their forefathers, were fulfilling the creation mandate. The presence of such creation language in Exodus 1 is another indication that this book is to be read in the context of Genesis.[6] The Exodus (deliverance) and Genesis (creation) connection will become more explicit later in the book with the plagues and the crossing of the sea. To anticipate those discussions: God will deliver the Israelites from bondage by unleashing the forces of creation against the Egyptians.

The new pharaoh who came into power (1:8) apparently did not "know" Joseph, which may mean that he was either wholly ignorant of his own

---

3. Verb tense in Hebrew is determined by context as much as by form. Hence, in Exodus 1:1, the participle is certainly to be translated as past (*IBHS*, 623; GKC, §116.d). Nevertheless, the use of the participle in 1:1 is no doubt an echo of Gen. 46:8.

4. In this regard, see also J. Plastaras, *The God of Exodus*, 8–11; T. E. Fretheim, *Exodus*, 24–26.

5. See also the similarity in wording between Ex. 1:7 and Gen. 47:27: "Now the Israelites settled in Egypt in the region of Goshen. They acquired property there and *were fruitful and increased greatly in number*." For a fuller discussion, see Houtman, *Exodus*, 1:230–34. The Exodus/Noah connection (Gen. 9:1) is made more explicit in Ex. 2:3 (see below): Moses, like Noah, is placed in an "ark" (Heb. *tebah*). This Hebrew word occurs only in Ex. 2 and Gen. 6–9. Apparently, the Exodus is meant to be understood in light of several past events.

6. J. Ackerman speaks of "repeated allusions in Exodus 1–2 to the primeval stories in Genesis 1–11" ("Literary Context," 74). See also his discussion of Ex. 1:1–7 (ibid., 75–79).

---

nation's history, or (more likely) that he simply chose to act in ignorance of Joseph's wise counsel and how the Egyptians had benefited from it (Gen. 41). Verse 8 is also a striking example of a characteristic not only of Exodus in general but of many portions of biblical narrative: The writer does not provide a full, detailed account of what he is reporting.

Two immediate questions come to mind with respect to verse 8. (1) Who is this pharaoh? (2) How much time has passed since the demise of Joseph's generation? The biblical writer, however, is not interested in giving these details. Why not? This is anyone's guess. It may be that in providing too many concrete historical details he runs the danger of limiting the timelessness of the message of Exodus[7] (although then one must explain why the biblical writer does choose to be specific elsewhere, e.g., the names of the store cities in v. 11). Another reason may be that some of these "incidental" details[8] are simply not worth mentioning since they do not add to his purpose, a purpose that is evidently more theological than journalistic. Exodus is the story of *God's* deliverance of his people.

Although this latter view is likely the case, another possibility should be given due consideration. It may be that some of the details are not mentioned because they do not need to be. We must not think that the original audience was encountering this or any other biblical story *for the first time* in writing.[9] Although the omission of names and chronological markers may present a problem for modern interpreters, this difficulty should not be projected on ancient readers. An adequate explanation may be no more involved than appealing to the familiarity of the ancient audience with the story that we see only in its inscripturated form. It is likely that by the time the narrative received its "official" (i.e., biblical) written form, the story had already been in wide circulation for considerable time. The biblical form then presents a story that for modern readers appears fresh, but for an ancient audience was the very stuff of their cultural and spiritual fabric.[10]

---

7. This is similar to B. Childs's view that Pharaoh and the midwives represent ideal types, i.e., figures that represent patterns of conduct rather than specific individuals (*Book of Exodus*, 13).

8. No one, however, should refer to these gaps in the narrative as "incidental" when speaking to biblical archaeologists or historians! It is precisely the terseness of passages such as these that has led to considerable debate over the identity of the pharaoh of the Exodus, the Israelites' precise location during their stay in Egypt, etc.

9. C. Isbell advocates reading Exodus "as if for the first time" ("Exodus 1–2 in the Context of Exodus 1–14: Story Lines and Key Words," in *Art and Meaning: Rhetoric in Biblical Literature*, ed. D. J. A. Clines, D. M. Gunn, and A. J. Hauser [JSOTSup 19; Sheffield: JSOT, 1982], 38). This is all well and good and is profitable advice for who those want to encounter the text afresh. Still, it appears to be more of a modern convention than ancient.

10. J. Goldingay discusses "The Role of Ambiguity and Openness in Stories" in *Models for Interpretation of Scripture* (Grand Rapids: Eerdmans, 1995), 39–41.

Although some of the details of the story are lacking, what is clear is that this new pharaoh is not at all happy with what he sees. What troubles him is the increasing number of Israelites (v. 9).[11] To put it another way, Pharaoh is opposed to their fulfillment of the creation mandate to be fruitful and increase (cf. Pharaoh's words in v. 9 with vv. 6–7). In this respect, Pharaoh represents not only a force hostile to God's people by enslaving them (vv. 11–14), but a force hostile to God himself, who wills that his people multiply.

We see, then, already at this early stage of the book, what will become much more pronounced later on: the real antagonists in the book of Exodus. This is not a battle of Israel versus Pharaoh, or even of Moses versus Pharaoh, but of *God* versus Pharaoh. The Egyptian king, as we will see in the following chapters, is presented as an anti-God figure; he repeatedly places himself in direct opposition to God's redemptive plan, and this behavior is already anticipated here. Pharaoh's ultimate sin is not simply making slaves of God's people. This is merely his solution to get at a much more basic problem: The Israelites are becoming too numerous, and as such present a possible military threat to Egypt (v. 10).[12]

The very oppression of the Egyptians in wanting to reduce the number of Israelites is antithetical to the created order. *This* is the sin of Egyptian slavery, which anticipates a point to be elaborated in subsequent chapters: Since the increase of the Israelites in Egypt is a fulfillment of the creation command, it is fitting to speak of the Israelites' deliverance from Egypt in creation language and to punish the Egyptians by means of a series of creation reversals (the plagues and the crossing of the Red Sea).[13]

Enslavement is one of three solutions by which Pharaoh attempts to keep the Israelites' numbers to a manageable mass: enough for forced labor, but not enough to encourage rebellion.[14] This proves futile as oppression merely

---

11. Moreover, most commentators agree that "Israelites" in v. 7 (Hebrew "sons of Israel") should be understood as an expression of national identity (e.g., Childs, *Book of Exodus*, 2). This is to be contrasted to the use of the same phrase in v. 1 where a patriarchal, familial meaning is intended. The point is that Israel's stay in Egypt was a formative event in its move from family to nation status. The Israelites were now a *people* with whom Pharaoh had to reckon.

12. Ackerman correctly compares Pharaoh's machinations in v. 10 to those of the inhabitants of Babel in Gen. 11:3–4 ("Come, let us . . . lest they . . ."). A comparison of the Hebrew of Ex. 1:10 and Gen. 11:3–4 shows clear similarities in wording. This is further support that Exodus should be read in light of Genesis.

13. Fretheim speaks of Pharaoh as "a symbol for the anticreation forces of death" (*Exodus*, 27).

14. Many commentators consider it contradictory that Pharaoh would want to reduce the numbers of his labor force. Killing one's own slaves makes little economic sense. J. Nohrnberg attributes Pharaoh's strategy to "the politics of terror" (*Like Unto Moses: The Constituting of an Interruption* [Bloomington: Indiana Univ. Press, 1995], 243).

results in further increase, and, as if to drive this point home, verse 12 repeats the "increase" language of verse 7. Pharaoh is no match for the Creator-God. Verse 12 hints at the eventual outcome of this battle.

The second solution is to command the midwives[15] to kill all Israelite male children at birth (since only males posed any military threat). This, too, proves futile and even results in blessing for the midwives. Ironically, they are blessed by the very thing Pharaoh enlisted their help to prevent: population increase.[16]

The final solution is the murder of all male infants (v. 22) by throwing them into the Nile. Thus, what for the Egyptians is a life-giving force is intended as an instrument of death for the Israelites. The significance of this act, both for Egypt's future destruction and Israel's deliverance, cannot be overstated. Water will play a central role in bringing this struggle to a close.

In keeping with his taciturn prose, the writer does not tell us anything that transpires after the giving of this insidious decree. His only concern is to move the narrative to Moses and *his* escape. It is evident, however, that either many other male infants escaped as well or (more likely) that the decree was eventually rescinded, since Moses was not the only male of his generation to survive! The existence of male offspring is assumed throughout Exodus 1– 14 (e.g., 3:22). Nevertheless, the text does not give us information regarding the sweeping ramifications of this decree. All we are told is that one special child escaped Pharaoh's evil intention.[17]

---

15. Here is another curiosity in the opening chapter of Exodus that raises some basic questions. Why are the midwives mentioned by name? Are they so integral to the story? Also, were there only two Hebrew midwives to supervise the entire population? Or perhaps were these only two of many midwives, the two whose particularly brave adherence to the Lord ensured their continued remembrance (cf. Matt. 26:13)? The text simply does not provide us with adequate information to answer these questions. Cassuto suggests that the mention of their names is an indication of the "poetic" nature of the narrative, although he does not explain this further (*Commentary on Exodus*, 12–14).

16. There is some ambiguity in the text whether this refers to the midwives bearing their own children, or to their becoming "tribal" mothers (i.e., matriarchal heads) of families (cf. Houtman, *Exodus*, 1:259–60).

17. Furthermore (cf. above) great reduction in male population would undermine Pharaoh's efforts to assemble a suitably sized male workforce to build his cities (J. Cohen, *The Origins and Evolution of the Moses Nativity Story* [SHR 58; Leiden: Brill, 1993], 5, n. 2). It is a popular point of view among ancient Jewish interpreters to assume that Pharaoh rescinded the edict after he had been told by his court astrologers that the promised redeemer (Moses) had already been born (e.g., *Jubilees* 47:3). This, of course, is not a point of fact in the biblical text. Rather, it is an explanation developed to fill this narrative gap.

Bridging Contexts

CONTINUITY WITH THE PAST. The first chapter of Exodus is the beginning of the story of Israel's deliverance from her enemy, Egypt. Yet it is more than this. Already at this early stage we see the author's concern that his readers understand that story of deliverance fully and properly. From the very first word he demonstrates his intention to put the Israelites' stay in Egypt in its true historical perspective. Israel, through a variety of circumstances, finds herself in a foreign and hostile place. However the people might choose to view that present circumstance, the author reminds them that the full story is one that stretches back to their ancient ancestors and even to the very beginning of the world itself. It is only in seeing their situation from the broad, divine point of view that the readers can hope to gain a full understanding of their lot in life. It is this divine point of view that transcends the millennia and finds a ready audience today.

God's people are never alone. They belong to him who rules creation and history. The story of the Israelites' captivity in and eventual escape from Egypt does not hurry to chapter 14 and the crossing of the Red Sea. Rather it lingers, not only in the present captivity but in the past—the past of ancient ancestors and even creation itself. The writer is somewhat emphatic to show the Israelites that "who you are now" must be understood in connection with "who came before you and who they were." What the Israelites could come to expect from God in their present situation is directly related to how he dealt with the Israelites in the past.

A need to emphasize the present community's connection with the past is not unique to Exodus 1. In fact, it is a common theme throughout the Old Testament. (1) One prominent example is the book of Isaiah, particularly several passages beginning in chapter 40. The setting is the imminent release of the Israelites from their captivity in Babylon, not unlike the imminent release at the beginning of Exodus. Isaiah again and again pushes his readers to view their situation not merely in terms of their present circumstances, but in terms of the past. Specifically, he points back to two formative events: the creation of the world and the "creation" of Israel in the Exodus. For example, in 45:18, Yahweh speaks of the certainty of future deliverance by reminding the captives of who it was who created the universe:

> For this is what the LORD says—
> he who created the heavens,
>   he is God;
> he who fashioned and made the earth,
>   he founded it;

> he did not create it to be empty,
>> but formed it to be inhabited. . . .

God has not "spoken in secret" (Isa. 45:19). Rather, what he has done in the past is plain to all. He has demonstrated by his *past* actions that he is fully capable of bringing about Israel's deliverance from Babylon *now*. So, "turn to me and be saved, all you ends of the earth; for I am God, and there is no other" (v. 22). Isaiah's message is: "Do you want some assurance of how God will bring you out of captivity? Just look back to creation, that is proof enough. The Creator will save you." In other words, the God of creation is the God of salvation. This is a theme, as we will see, that finds expression throughout Exodus.

Elsewhere, Isaiah links the impending deliverance of God's people from Babylon to the past deliverance from Egypt. For example, in Isaiah 43:16–17 he offers the following assurance for their deliverance:

> This is what the LORD says—
>> he who made a way through the sea,
>> a path through the mighty waters,
> who drew out the chariots and horses,
>> the army and reinforcements together,
> and they lay there, never to rise again,
>> extinguished, snuffed out like a wick. . . .

The certainty of Israel's deliverance *now* is based on God's *past* actions. In this second example from Isaiah, the past action is the Exodus.[18] God's message in the opening chapter of Exodus is similar: "If you want to know what will happen to you, my special people, you must remember who I am and what I have done in the past. I do not change, and my care for my people does not change."

(2) Another example to illustrate the importance the Old Testament places on continuity with the past occurs in those portions of Scripture that we are quick to pass over: genealogies. Although these genealogies sometimes appear disruptive to the flow of the book, they serve a theological purpose. They give the people periodic reminders of where they came from. Genealogies connect the present with the past. Perhaps nowhere is this more obvious than the opening chapters of 1 Chronicles. This is not the stuff of which mighty sermons are made. Here we have nine solid chapters of (yawn) names. Yet these chapters are not a spiritual exercise designed to test our patience. Rather, they make a precise theological point.

---

18. On this point, see also P. Enns, "Creation and Re-creation: Psalm 95 and Its Interpretation in Hebrews 3:1–4:13," *WTJ* 55 (1993): 255–80, esp. 258–64.

The two books of Chronicles present Israel's history from the perspective of the postexilic world. The writer wants to demonstrate that even though times have changed (the land is ravaged, the people have taken up residency with pagans, and the temple lies in ruins), God is the *same* and remains with his people. This is why the genealogy stretches back not simply to David or Moses, or even Abraham, but to the beginning—to Adam. The present is not divorced from the past. The present, however chaotic it might seem, must be seen in light of the past.[19]

When seen in terms of the broader Old Testament theme of continuity with the past, the manner in which the writer describes the Israelites' situation in Exodus 1 seems well at home. It is merely one of many Old Testament examples that force readers to view their present in terms of their past, because God is the same, yesterday, today, and forever. Viewing the present in terms of the past not only provides security now but gives assurance of what will be. We learn from the past, from what we have seen and heard, that the future outcome is certain.

The New Testament shows the church's connection with the past in several ways. (1) For one thing, the New Testament is not without its genealogies. We see in Matthew 1:1–17 a three-tiered genealogy tracing Jesus' lineage from Abraham to David, from David to Babylonian exile, and from the exile to his birth.[20] The Gospel writer begins his account of the Christ by placing him in the context of the past: "Who is Jesus? Review God's dealings in the past and see." Luke also includes a genealogy, but his extends back to Adam. This serves not only to provide a more universal appeal (cf. previous footnote) but to show that the story of Jesus is one that must be viewed, biblically speaking, from the most comprehensive context: from Adam onward.

What clearly distinguishes the Matthean and Lukan genealogies from their Old Testament predecessors, however, is not where they begin but where they end. *Jesus* is the goal of the New Testament genealogies and not

---

19. Further information on the theology of the genealogies in Chronicles can be found in H. G. M. Williamson, *1 and 2 Chronicles* (Grand Rapids: Eerdmans, 1982), 38–92, esp. 38–40 (pp. 2 and 38 are reversed in this volume), and R. Braun, *1 Chronicles* (WBC 14; Waco, Tex.: Word, 1986), 3–5.

20. The purpose of the structure of Matthew's genealogy is a debated point (see D. A. Hagner, *Matthew 1–13* [WBC 33A; Dallas, Tex.: Word, 1993], 5–9). The genealogy as a whole, however, should be viewed in light of what is generally recognized as a characteristic of Matthew's Gospel: It is directed (albeit not exclusively) to a Jewish-Christian audience (ibid., lxiv). Furthermore, the genealogy's focus on Abraham, David, and Jesus serves to present Jesus as "King of the Jews," as Matt. 2:2 makes explicit (R. H. Gundry, *Matthew: A Commentary on His Handbook for a Mixed Church Under Persecution* [2d ed.; Grand Rapids: Eerdmans, 1994], 14).

Israel, as we see in 1 Chronicles. The Gospel writers show the continuity that *Jesus* has with the past (i.e., the entire Old Testament), and it is precisely here that we begin to see how this applies to Christ's church. Having Jesus as the goal of these genealogies is not to say that God's people are now left out of the picture. Rather, what is distinct in the New Testament is that now the people of God have their identity in Christ. They "participate" in the past, as it were, insofar as they participate "in Christ" (to use Paul's repeated phrase).

The church's continuity with the *past* is defined by her *present* relationship with the crucified and risen Christ. This is the proper starting point for today's Christians to understand their own continuity with the past. The question of who we are can only be answered in terms of who God is, specifically, in terms of what he has done *in Christ* and of our relationship to Christ. The Christian connects with the past by virtue of his or her union with Christ (Rom. 5:12—6:14), in whom the past itself is fulfilled.

Linking Adam and Christ in the same genealogy also serves to place Christ in the broadest of all contexts, creation itself. Twice Paul presents Jesus as a "new Adam" (Rom. 5:12—21; 1 Cor. 15:20—28). Jesus is like Adam in that both are representatives of a larger group. The continuity between the two, however, is not absolute, since both heads represent different groups of people. Through Christ life is given to his people, but through Adam's disobedience comes condemnation. Despite this discontinuity, the force of presenting Jesus as a new Adam should not be lost. The second Adam does what the first did not do: He is obedient to God and thereby brings life to his people.

(2) Aside from the Adam/Christ typology, other passages illustrate the connection between Jesus and creation. Note, for example, John 1:1—18. It is difficult to escape the conclusion that John's "in the beginning" (1:1) is anything other than an explicit attempt to tie together the person and work of Christ and creation. In fact, he even goes a step further: John does not tie Christ to the point of creation, but beyond it.[21] For John, Jesus was not created—he simply "was"; he is the Creator himself (cf. 1:2—3). And one of the great marvels of this Gospel is that Jesus the Creator is also Jesus the Savior.

The twin concepts of salvation and creation, which we have already glimpsed in Exodus 1, are brought together in the New Testament in the person of Christ. The New Testament further brings these two concepts together by describing the salvation of believers as an act of creation (a point that will also be seen in Exodus). Most notable, perhaps, is 2 Corinthians 5:17: "Therefore, if anyone is in Christ, he is a new creation; the old has gone, the new

---

21. See, e.g., R. E. Brown, *The Gospel According to John (i–xii)* (AB 29; Garden City, N.Y.: Doubleday, 1966), 4.

has come!" Being in Christ (salvation) means being a "new creation." By virtue of the church's relationship to Christ the Creator, the Christian's salvation is a new beginning. The church's link with the past extends to creation, since its very identity is found in its relationship with the Creator himself.

(3) The continuity the church has with the past—that is, the fact that its present identity is defined in terms of the past—can be seen in the New Testament in a number of other ways. Three brief examples will illustrate the point: Romans 4, Hebrews 11, and 1 Corinthians 10. In all three passages, the biblical writer bases a point of teaching for the church in the present on the experiences of Israel in the past.

For example, do you want to understand the nature of faith? Observe Abraham's example (Rom. 4). Paul's choice of Abraham is not arbitrary. He is the one from whom all Israelites descended, and his faith is portrayed as not simply a moralistic model for the church to follow, but as a summary of the true form of Israelite spirituality. Faith in Christ *now* means participating in the *Israelite* ideal of faith. Hebrews 11 makes the point even more explicitly. Not only is Abraham held up as a model of faith (vv. 8–19), but the Old Testament saints parade across the page one by one: Abel, Enoch, Noah, Abraham, Isaac, Jacob, Joseph, Moses, Rahab, and many more; yet even then, the writer acknowledges that he is only skimming the surface (v. 32).[22]

By having faith in Christ, Christian, you are doing what God's people in the past have always done. And if a warning is in order, Paul recounts Israel's desert rebellion in 1 Corinthians 10. The events that transpired back then "were written down as warnings for us, on whom the fulfillment of the ages has come" (10:11). The continuity between the Israel of the past and the church of the present is a basic assumption that the New Testament writers make in applying the Old Testament to the life of the Christian.

We could multiply examples such as these many times over, since the church's present is described throughout the New Testament by referring to the past. This is because the Christian era is understood as a fulfillment, and therefore a continuation, of Israel's story. Note the manner and extent to which the New Testament writers cite the Old Testament. The New Testament message as a whole—that is, the person and work of Christ and God's people in relation to Christ—is connected to the past. Thus, Christians today must understand their connection with the past not simply by looking back to the New Testament, but by rounding off the picture through a look to the Old Testament as well, which is where the New Testament writers themselves locate the roots of the church's identity.

---

22. It is worth noting that the catalog of Old Testament saints in Heb. 11 begins with creation (v. 3). This is similar to Isaiah's appeal to creation mentioned above.

Although chronologically in the past, the New Testament era is nevertheless part of today's Christian's "theological" present, insofar as all Christians through all time have been living in the age inaugurated by Christ's coming. Yet, the church today must understand itself more fully by looking backward through the millennia to the very dawn of the universe itself, "for he chose us in him before the creation of the world" (Eph. 1:4).

The Lord rules despite appearances. Another theological message of Exodus 1 is seen in the way God is presented—or better, not presented. Scholars have noted the theological significance of God's apparent absence in this chapter, extending to the end of chapter 2.[23] The sense of God's absence in our daily affairs is a common theme in the Psalms, Prophets, and wisdom literature,[24] and is also a topic in the New Testament, although there the emphasis on the "triumph of the resurrection" receives more attention.[25]

There is no doubt that God is *presented* in Exodus 1 as one who is not actively engaged in overseeing the unfolding circumstances in which the Israelites find themselves. Joseph and his brothers are not said to have been brought down to Egypt *by God;* they just seem to go on their own. The new king's plans to remove the Israelite threat are not brought on *by God's* hardening the king's heart, as we often see in the plague narrative that follows. Rather, it is his own doing. Moreover, the Israelites' success at thwarting all three of Pharaoh's hideous attempts is nowhere attributed *to God.* In fact the midwives, although motivated by their fear of God (1:17), seem to obviate Pharaoh's wrath by their own cunning: They cook up a story about the rugged Israelite mothers who give birth before they can get to them.[26]

This extends to chapter 2: Even Moses' deliverance from Pharaoh's final decree is due to his mother's and sister's ingenuity, not a mighty act of God. In reading this opening chapter of Exodus, we should take care not to jump too quickly ahead to where God takes on a more active role. For now at least, we must allow chapter 1 to speak, and we must hear what it has to say.

As Gowan suggests, the *portrayal* of God as "absent" in chapter 1 comes into clearer focus in light of the immediate, directive role he takes beginning

---

23. This notion has most recently been discussed by D. A. Gowan, *Theology in Exodus,* 1–24. B. Childs makes the observation that the "absence" of God in ch. 2 is one of several indicators that the story of Moses' birth may have been a product of wisdom circles ("The Birth of Moses," *JBL* 84 [1965]: 118–22). God is mentioned in Ex. 1:17, 20–21, though not as an active player, but as someone behind the scenes.

24. Gowan, *Theology in Exodus,* 7–12.

25. Ibid., 16.

26. It is difficult to reconcile the midwives' pious *refusal* to obey Pharaoh in v. 17 with their *excuse* in v. 19 that the safe birth of the Israelite children was simply a result of the mothers' vigor. Why did they not simply declare openly their obedience to God rather than to Pharaoh?

in 2:23–25 and throughout the remainder of Exodus—"the author's explicit and powerful statement ... that now something different is about to happen."[27] It is Yahweh who delivers the Israelites, who fights for them, who cripples the Egyptian army, and who renders Pharaoh impotent. The "absence" of God in chapter 1 is sorely felt by the Hebrew slaves, and it is important for understanding the thrust of the first two chapters of Exodus that we allow this tension to remain. The appearance of God in 2:23–25 must be seen in light of the Israelites' perception of his absence in chapter 1. "How could God allow this terrible turn of events to take place? Why has the God of our fathers, the God who promised his abiding faithfulness to us and our ancestors, allowed us to become slaves? Look at this young upstart pharaoh, flexing his muscles. Why doesn't God just snap his fingers and make him go away? Why has God forgotten us?"

The answer, of course—as is made plain beginning at 2:23–25—is that God *is* with his people even though it does not appear to be so. An old pharaoh dies, a friend of the Israelites. Generations pass, and another pharaoh comes into power, but this one has no love for the growing Israelites. God, however, is with them, regardless of the turn of political events—whether for good or for bad. It is *he* who directs their paths, who brings blessing in times of peace, and who, as, and when he sees fit, brings deliverance in times of trouble.

To put it another way, Yahweh is the Lord of history. This is a fact. He is not any less the Lord of history in times of trouble, nor do good times suggest a mere temporary spasm of control over events. He is steady and sure, and the Israelites are to see their prolonged enslavement in light of God's character rather than to make conclusions about God's presence or absence on the basis of their circumstances.

The specific sociopolitical setting of Exodus 1 is common to the Old Testament. If there is any topic that consistently finds expression throughout the various Old Testament genres, it is the struggles that God's people face against foreign enemies and oppressors. For example, in the Pentateuch, apart from the Exodus, we see Abraham's rescue of Lot from Kedorlaomer and his alliance (Gen. 14), the perennial struggles with Edom/Esau inaugurated in Genesis 27, war with the Amalekites (Ex. 17), the defeat of Sihon of Heshbon and Og of Bashan (Num. 21; Deut. 2–3), and recurring contention with the Moabites (Num. 25).

Moreover, the conquest of the land in Joshua and Judges is a truly international struggle. The period of the monarchy is dotted with tense undercurrents and open conflict with the Egyptians, Assyrians, and

---

27. Gowan, *Theology in Exodus,* 2.

Babylonians—the latter two eventually bringing the northern and southern kingdoms respectively into captivity in a foreign land. How Israel ought and ought not to view their relationship to the nations is a regular topic in the prophetic literature. Many of the psalms also reflect on the struggles that the righteous Israelite (e.g., David) has with his enemies, often foreign.

The Old Testament, in other words, is not reticent about Israel's politics. The drama of the Israelites' place in the world is told against the backdrop of the political machinations of their neighbors. It is sometimes the case that God intervenes quickly to bring an imminent end to the conflict, such as the defeat of the Amalekites in Exodus 17 and the defeat of Sihon and Og. Other times, more patience is required of God's people, as in the case of the release from Babylon after (roughly) a fifty-year captivity, or four hundred years as we see in Exodus. At still other times, the ultimate resolution of conflict takes on an apocalyptic, otherworldly flavor (e.g., Zech. 14). The point, however, is that Israel's political fate is never left to the caprice of international events. Rather, God is in control and he will, sooner or later, bring all of history to its proper conclusion.

The NT presents God's lordship over history in terms of the person and work of Christ:

> For by him all things were created: things in heaven and on earth, visible and invisible, whether thrones or powers or rulers or authorities; all things were created by him and for him. (Col. 1:16)

> All authority in heaven and on earth has been given to me. (Matt. 28:18)

> Therefore God exalted him to the highest place
> and gave him the name that is above every name,
> that at the name of Jesus every knee should bow,
> in heaven and on earth and under the earth,
> and every tongue confess that Jesus Christ is Lord,
> to the glory of God the Father. (Phil. 2:9–10)

Jesus reigns supreme and all powers are subject to him. Revelation speaks of the struggles that the saints of God endure at the hands of God's enemies. Yet the present circumstances of the believer do not tell the whole picture. With every painful "How long, Sovereign Lord?" (Rev. 6:10), the saints are given a glimpse of the true state of affairs. "Wait a little longer," they are told (v. 11). Soon the rider on the white horse will be revealed and with him the new heaven and new earth, when God "will wipe every tear from their eyes. There will be no more death or mourning or crying or pain, for the old order of things has passed away" (21:4). The Lord Jesus is the Lord of history. He is ever true and faithful. He does not change. Despite appearances, the outcome is assured in Christ.[28]

YOU ARE OF CHRIST, and Christ is of God (1 Cor. 3:23). Who am I? Where did I come from? Where do I fit in? Where is my niche in life?

Nearly everyone asks questions such as these at one time or another. Despite outward appearances, few people are content to stroll through life without even an ounce of introspective energy, focused solely on the present (at least I know no one like that). Rather, even a glance at the history of human thought displays a universal desire to explain who we are, where we came from, and what we are doing here. Although answers to these questions have always been and continue to be diverse, the motive that impels us to ask such questions in some form is common to all and is, to use the expression, "what separates us from the animals." Human beings, from the dawn of recorded history, have pondered how they, in their particular point in time, "fit" with those who have gone before and those who will come after.

In recent generations, for example, such questions have been asked on the grand scale: evolution or creation? Are human beings the product of a natural development of species specialization and diversification, or is our existence the clearest imprint of God's creative stamp? And how then does our understanding of where we came from influence how we define our present and future? Likewise, but on a more narrow scale, are issues of ethnicity. Who are my people? With which of the diverse peoples of this earth do I invest my identity? And what bearing does this have on how I see myself?

On a still narrower level are questions of individual identity. Our identities are largely derived from our parents. Were they immigrants? of high social standing? powerful? well educated? How do our parents' experiences affect who we are now and how we see ourselves? Families have rituals and traditions that give them identity over against other families with other rituals and traditions. What holidays do you celebrate, and how do you celebrate them? Do you have a traditional yearly vacation spot? Do the children follow in their parents' vocational footsteps? On any scale, we see ourselves as connected to our past, and we see that past as an integral element in how we see ourselves in the present.

---

28. God's presence with his people on the world stage touches on the pervasive "divine warrior" theme in Scripture; see T. Longman III and D. G. Reid, *God Is a Warrior* (Grand Rapids: Zondervan, 1995). This is a recurring theme in Exodus.

One's spiritual identity is no different. Christians are connected to the past because their spiritual identity is in Christ, the Lord of history and the Creator of the universe. Christians are so intimately identified with God in Christ that they are considered Christ's brothers (and sisters) (Heb. 2:5–18), and therefore children of God (1 John 3:1) and co-heirs with Christ in glory (Rom. 8:17). The church is Christ's bride (Rev. 19:7; 21:2, 9; 22:17), and, as with human marriages, the two become one (Eph. 5:31). The church is the body of Christ (1 Cor. 12:27). Christians are united with Christ (Rom. 6:5). "Who am I?" the Christian asks. "Where do I come from? How do I 'fit'?" The answer: You are in Christ. Your past is noble, your present secure, and your future certain. You are in Christ and he does not change.

It is part of the Christian proclamation that one's identity can only be properly understood in terms of one's relationship to God in Christ. Rebels though we are, all human beings are created by God and therefore are already "tied" to him in some sense (however distorted that tie may be through sin). Hence, as John Calvin argued, one comes to a better self-understanding as one comes to know God: "It is certain that man never achieves a clear knowledge of himself unless he has first looked upon God's face, and then descends from contemplating him to scrutinize himself."[29] One's self-understanding is, by the very fact that we are God's creatures, bound up with one's relationship to the Creator.

There is no quick fix to the problems people face in the world today. Believers and unbelievers alike share many of the same afflictions and difficulties. Nevertheless, for the believer there is a tie that binds us, in Christ, to the Creator. All of God's fullness dwells in Christ (Col. 1:19), yet Christ is not ashamed to call us his brothers and sisters (Heb. 2:11). We are intimate with God through Christ, and we view all our present circumstances, whether joyful, mundane, or horrific, in light of this reality. We are of Christ and Christ is of God.

When God Isn't There. "Why does God let this happen? Doesn't he see what's happening? I thought being a Christian meant always feeling God's presence." God's people through all time have struggled with his apparent disinterest in their personal affairs.

This is by no means a modern dilemma. "Where are you, God?" is the refrain of Job and forms the substance of many of the psalms. Wondering where God is and what he is doing is not a mark of spiritual immaturity or distrust in God. Rather, it represents the honest yearnings of God's people living in this world, who long to feel his presence in their affairs.

---

29. J. Calvin, *Institutes of the Christian Religion*, ed. J. T. McNeill; trans. F. L. Battles (LCC 20; Philadelphia: Westminster, 1960), 37.

The biblical approach to this dilemma, however, is one worthy of profound contemplation. Many psalms, for example, question God's apparent absence, but they do so from the ultimate point of view of what the writer *knows* to be the case. His present struggles and periods of doubt are endured in the context of his broader understanding of who God is. Psalm 73 is one example. Note verse 1:

> Surely God is good to Israel,
>   to those who are pure in heart.

The psalmist *knows* how things work. He understands the means by which God operates. Yet things are not the way he knows they are supposed to be. Note verse 2:

> But as for me, my feet had almost slipped;
>   I had nearly lost my foothold.

What is the psalmist's specific problem? He sees around him, contrary to what he knows ought to be the case, the prosperity of the arrogant and the suffering of the righteous. How can this be? Where is God? What he sees around him is in such blatant tension with how God is supposed to be running things that the psalmist is beside himself with anguish and inner turmoil.

What can he do? He certainly cannot begin telling others that God is not true to his promises. This would be too much for others to bear. Note Psalm 73:15: "If I had said, 'I will speak thus,' I would have betrayed your children." But neither can he keep it all inside—this is too much to bear as well: "When I tried to understand all this, it was oppressive to me" (v. 16). So what can he do? To whom can he explain his dilemma? He goes directly to the Lord; that is, all of this is oppressive "till I entered the sanctuary of God" (v. 17). Even when he doubts God's presence, the psalmist turns to God for solace. Why? Because in a sense in which we only too often do not understand, God *is* there. Doubts of his presence will come—this is our lot in life. Nevertheless, how we perceive the matter does not determine its reality. God *is* present, he *does* care. Hence, our sense of his absence must be met head-on, as the psalmist does. We are honest with him, and the result is a deeper, more trusting, and thus more intimate relationship with him.

Such an approach to God's apparent absence has many applications. All believers go through periods of spiritual dryness where they struggle with feelings of God's absence. Many of us have felt the unexpected and senseless loss of someone dear to us, or experienced problems in our family or with our savings account. These things do not happen because of lack of faith (as many are saying today). Would anyone level such a charge against the psalmists? The lesson, rather, is that neither our present circumstances nor our perceptions of God's absence determine reality. We cry out to the Lord honestly, and he hears us.

> The Israelites groaned in their slavery and cried out, and their cry for help because of their slavery went up to God. God heard their groaning and he remembered his covenant with Abraham, with Isaac and with Jacob. So God looked on the Israelites and was concerned about them. (Ex. 2:23–25)

In addition to such a personal vein, applying biblical understanding to God's apparent absence is also relevant for political affairs, just as it was for the ancient Israelites. The church (for better or for worse) has had quite a track record of drawing together the religious and political spheres. Some would say that the Christian faith began a downward spiral of corruption with the "conversion" of Emperor Constantine at the Battle of the Milvian Bridge in A.D. 312. The general failure of the Crusades (A.D. 1095–1291) is frequently mentioned as a textbook example of what happens when the church freely employs the power of the state. This is not to say, of course, that church and state should have no mutual influence. Nevertheless, in election years in particular, it seems that there are many in the church today who do not see the behind-the-scenes God of the Exodus.

For some, the very fate of the country depends on whether the right people are elected into office. The spiritual character of our country (if there even is such a thing) seems to be determined more by the character of the "new pharaoh" we elect rather than by the character of the ever-present God by whose command rulers rise and fall. All this is not to say that political involvement by Christians ought to be discouraged, nor is it to say that all earthly rulers are of equal merit. Rather, the reality of God's presence in the lives of Americans, Germans, Mexicans, Koreans, and whomever, does not depend on politics. Even if God's people today, like the Israelites of Exodus 1, were to suffer inhumane treatment at the hands of the government, the big picture should not be lost. It is maintaining this big picture that is a mark of the mature Christian life. We doubt and we struggle, but we trust God. Things are not the way they ought to be, but we rest in God's promises. We have faith.

Exodus 2:1–10

NOW A MAN of the house of Levi married a Levite woman, ²and she became pregnant and gave birth to a son. When she saw that he was a fine child, she hid him for three months. ³But when she could hide him no longer, she got a papyrus basket for him and coated it with tar and pitch. Then she placed the child in it and put it among the reeds along the bank of the Nile. ⁴His sister stood at a distance to see what would happen to him.

⁵Then Pharaoh's daughter went down to the Nile to bathe, and her attendants were walking along the river bank. She saw the basket among the reeds and sent her slave girl to get it. ⁶She opened it and saw the baby. He was crying, and she felt sorry for him. "This is one of the Hebrew babies," she said.

⁷Then his sister asked Pharaoh's daughter, "Shall I go and get one of the Hebrew women to nurse the baby for you?"

⁸"Yes, go," she answered. And the girl went and got the baby's mother. ⁹Pharaoh's daughter said to her, "Take this baby and nurse him for me, and I will pay you." So the woman took the baby and nursed him. ¹⁰When the child grew older, she took him to Pharaoh's daughter and he became her son. She named him Moses, saying, "I drew him out of the water."

Original Meaning

THE DESPAIR AND apparent hopelessness of chapter 1 are "interrupted" by the report that a child is born to a Levite household. Just what relevance this child's birth has to the oppression of his countrymen is not indicated at this point. All we are told is that he is born, hidden, abandoned, found by Pharaoh's daughter, and adopted, as it were, as her own son. This Levite has become an Egyptian; for what purpose remains to be seen.

These ten verses must be seen against the backdrop of chapter 1. The menace and vile poison of Pharaoh's attempt at genocide yields to the story of the birth of an innocent child. This story is also the story of one more frustration of Pharaoh's plan. His previous two attempts have been neutralized. The readers are now poised to see how—or perhaps if—this last plan is to be thwarted; and it is. One child, one very special child, is spared.

As we have already glimpsed in chapter 1, the author is not concerned to provide many of the details one might expect. Although the names of this child's parents are mentioned in 6:20 (Amram and Jochebed), in 2:1 it seems sufficient simply to tell us of their lineage: They are of the "house of Levi."[1] Specifying the child's tribal lineage, which appears of greater importance than giving other details, such as his parents' names, likely indicates the author's concern to promote the child's priestly pedigree, the importance of which will be seen later in the book as well as the rest of the Pentateuch. Suffice it to say now that Moses will later play the ultimate priestly role by being the one through whom God's law is given to the people. Further genealogical ambiguities involve the child's older sister, who simply appears on the scene suddenly (v. 4), as does Aaron later (4:14). Their stories are ancillary to that of the child who proves so central to the unfolding story. Our attention is driven to the birth of this child.[2]

The manner in which the writer of Exodus presents Moses' birth has often been compared to the ubiquitous "child exposure" motif in ancient Near Eastern literature. Anyone familiar with Old Testament scholarship knows only too well how the discoveries of ancient Near Eastern texts over the past hundred years have presented challenges to one's understanding of the uniqueness and historicity of certain biblical narratives. Well known, perhaps, are the Babylonian version of creation and the ubiquity of flood stories found throughout the world.[3] The presence of these extrabiblical parallels have led to a virtual scholarly consensus that the ancient Near Eastern texts and their biblical counterparts are on the same plane, so to speak; they are "stories," which imply to these scholars the

---

1. As Cassuto puts it, the narrative's main focus is not "details of secondary import," such as "genealogical particulars" (*Commentary on Exodus*, 17).

2. S. R. Driver is certainly correct in pointing out that the mention of "taking" (*laqaḥ*) a wife (v. 1), followed immediately by the announcement of the child's conception, *implies* that Moses was their first child (*The Book of Exodus in the Revised Version* [Cambridge: Cambridge Univ. Press, 1929], 8). Since reference to the child's older sister in v. 4 clearly indicates the opposite, some have reasoned that Miriam and Aaron were children of Amram by a previous marriage. There is, however, no mention of this elsewhere in the Old Testament. Cassuto explains the difficulty by suggesting that this child was merely the first born *after* Pharaoh's decree (*Commentary on Exodus*, 18). Although this is a possible explanation, it is certainly in order, with the writer's selectivity evinced repeatedly in the previous passage, that the manner in which the child's conception is mentioned expresses nothing more than the writer's desire to draw the reader's attention to the birth of Moses.

3. The standard commentaries typically draw attention to this issue: J. Skinner, *A Critical and Exegetical Commentary on Genesis* (ICC; Edinburgh: T. & T. Clark, 1956), 41–50; 174–81; G. J. Wenham, *Genesis 1–15* (WBC 1; Waco, Tex.: Word, 1987), xlvi-l; C. Westermann, *Genesis 1–11: A Commentary*, trans. J. J. Scullion (Minneapolis: Augsburg, 1984), 399–406. See also A. Heidel, *The Babylonian Genesis: The Story of Creation* (Chicago: Univ. of Chicago Press, 1963).

questionable historical value not only of the ancient Near Eastern material but the Bible as well.

No one can doubt that Moses' birth bears similarities to other stories of the ancient Near East. Scholars have thus argued that Exodus 2:1–10 represents a legendary pattern, a motif, of an "exposed infant." Even a glance at the Sargon legend lends support to this conclusion.[4] Donald Redford has provided an exhaustive treatment of the topic, finding no less than thirty-two examples of this motif throughout ancient Near Eastern literature.[5] It would seem a *tour de force* to attempt to understand the historicity of Moses' birth (and by implication the historicity of Moses himself) in isolation from what on the surface appears to be clear: The story of Moses' birth participates in some way in this popular motif.

Yet it would be impulsive to conclude that Moses' birth is entirely, or even essentially, legendary simply because it is presented in such a manner that has so many literary parallels. Although we cannot settle the complex issue of the relationship between "history" and "literature" here in the space of several sentences, a comment or two is in order. For one thing, we should keep in mind what is often forgotten when the discussion turns to the question of historicity for any Old Testament narrative: *All* biblical narrative has a story-like quality.[6]

Making this observation is not to say that the Old Testament is without basis in history. This is decidedly not the case.[7] What we do have is a

---

4. Sargon was a king of ancient Akkad (2300 B.C.) whose mother, as the story goes, put him at birth in a reed basket treated with bitumen and placed him on a river. He was found by a drawer of water, who raised him as his son. Sargon grew up to be a mighty king (see J. B. Pritchard, ed., *Ancient Near Eastern Texts Relating to the Old Testament*, 3d ed. [Princeton: Princeton Univ. Press, 1969], 119). Virtually no commentary on Exodus fails to draw a connection between this legend and Ex. 2:1–10. See N. Sarna, *Exodus*, 267–68; B. Lewis, *The Sargon Birth Legend: A Study of the Akkadian Text and the Tale of the Hero Who Was Exposed at Birth* (ASORDS 4; Cambridge, Mass.: ASOR, 1984); T. Longman III, *Fictional Akkadian Autobiography: A Generic and Comparative Study* (Winona Lake, Ind.: Eisenbrauns, 1991), 53–60.

5. "The Literary Motif of the Exposed Child," *Numen* 14 (1967): 209–28. Redford's conclusions can certainly be challenged on a case-by-case basis, but the general thrust of the data remains.

6. For two recent evangelical treatments of this broader issue see, R. L. Pratt Jr., *He Gave Us Stories: The Bible Student's Guide to Interpreting Old Testament Narratives* (Brentwood, Tenn.: Wolgemuth & Hyatt, 1990), and V. P. Long, *The Art of Biblical History* (Foundations of Contemporary Interpretation 5; Grand Rapids: Zondervan, 1994).

7. See also J. Plastaras's discussion on "folkloric" elements in Moses' birth story (*The God of Exodus*, 43–44). Concerning the historicity of the abandonment motif in the ancient Near East, particularly with respect to the Sargon legend, T. Longman III argues: "While certainly a folklore theme, the practice of placing a child in the river may have been a widely practiced form of abandonment, similar to the more modern practice of leaving a child on the doorstep of a house" (*Fictional Akkadian Autobiography*, 56). See also Hoffmeier, *Israel in Egypt*, 136–38.

presentation of history that is firmly at home in the *literary conventions* of the ancient world. We must take great care not to allow our modern conventions of what constitutes "history" or "story" to color our understanding of biblical texts. It is not just with these obvious examples (creation, Flood, Moses' birth) that we see biblical writers following literary conventions of their day; the Old Testament *as a whole* is a literary production of the ancient world. The story of the birth of Moses is not unique in the ancient Near Eastern world. Rather, it is stories such as this that bring us face-to-face with what is in fact characteristic of the Old Testament as a whole.

To put the matter in a more positive way, would it not be too much to expect a biblical narrative to take on a literary quality that is *unique* to its historical setting? In fact, if I may touch on the subject here, one might argue that it is the very nature of a revealed, inspired text that it takes on the feel of its historical circumstances. God does not merely speak—he speaks to someone, somewhere, at sometime. In the Old Testament, he is speaking (originally) to ancient Israelites. And when God speaks to someone, he speaks *their* language. When stated this way, the presence of an ancient Near Eastern literary motif that parallels 2:1—10 should not be seen as a threat to a high view of Scripture. One might even state that it is the very nature of what we mean by "inspiration" that the *divine* word takes on a *human* form.

This in no way diminishes the truth of the Word. Rather, the eternal Word becomes "incarnate"; it enters into the very lives of God's people. Christ himself is *the* Word of God incarnate (John 1:1—14). In becoming a human being—in identifying with us, in becoming like us—Christ is no less the Creator and Ruler over all (Col. 1:15—20). Let me suggest here that not only Moses' birth narrative, but much of the Old Testament ought to be understood in terms of this same "incarnational analogy."[8] This approach has

---

8. The incarnational analogy is an approach to understanding Scripture that has a long and honored history. Strong undercurrents are evident, for example, in Reformed theology, e.g., the writings of Calvin (his theory of "accommodation" and the "lisping" of God), the Old Princeton School (J. A. Alexander, W. H. Green, B. B. Warfield), as well as the Dutch Reformed tradition (H. Bavinck, G. C. Berkouwer). Some examples of explicit treatments of the incarnational model are the following: J. P. Smyth, *How God Inspired the Bible: Thoughts for the Present Disquiet* (New York: James Pott, 1892), esp. 119–35; J. Hannah, *The Relation Between the Divine and Human Elements in Holy Scripture* (London: John Murray, 1863); K. B. Trembath, *Evangelical Theories of Biblical Inspiration: A Review and Proposal* (New York: Oxford Univ. Press, 1987). Two essays (with responses) in *The Proceedings of the Conference on Biblical Inerrancy 1987* (Nashville: Broadman, 1987) are dedicated to this issue: J. I. Packer, "Inerrancy and the Divinity and the Humanity of the Bible," 135–51, and K. Kantzer, "Inerrancy and the Humanity and Divinity of the Bible," 153–73. Two Catholic treatments include B. Vawter, *Biblical Inspiration* (Philadelphia: Westminster, 1972), 95–113, and L. Alonso Schökel, *The Inspired Word: Scripture in the Light of Language and Literature* (London: Burns & Oates, 1967), esp. 49–53. One recent investigation of the Chris-

the advantage of neither explaining away nor ignoring what seems clearly to be the case here, that Exodus 2:1–10 has many close affinities with the popular ancient Near Eastern motif of the exposed child.[9]

When Moses' mother looked at the child after his birth, she saw that he was "fine" or "good" (*tob*, 2:2). Just what is meant by this comment is hardly clear and has exercised commentators since before the time of Christ. The LXX uses *asteios* (handsome) for the Hebrew *tob*, a Greek word also found in Acts 7:20 and Hebrews 11:23, influenced no doubt by the LXX. This does not solve the problem, however, of what the comment means. Why did the writer feel it necessary to include such an apparently incidental comment in this otherwise terse narrative? Are we really to conclude that Moses' mother simply saw how good-looking he was? It was, after all, that observation that influenced her to hide the child. Are we to presume that the child's mother would not have hid him had he been ugly? What mother would *not* think her newborn son to be handsome?[10] Also, why would physical beauty warrant his salvation rather than some other trait? Early rabbis thought, for example, that *tob* indicated that Moses was circumcised at birth. Hence, he was truly special, and this was a justifiable motive for his mother's actions.[11]

A more fruitful line of inquiry is to understand *tob* in terms of creation language, something we have already seen in chapter 1. Sarna, for example, argues that the phrase *ki tob* (NIV: "that he was a fine child") in 2:2 is an echo of the refrain in Genesis 1, where God pronounces "good" what he has created.[12] The birth of Moses, in keeping with the re-creation theme in chapter

---

tological analogy in Karl Barth's thinking is F. M. Hasel, "The Christological Analogy of Scripture in Karl Barth," *TZ* 50 (1994): 41–49. See also P. Enns, "The 'Moveable Well' in 1 Cor 10:4: An Extra-Biblical Tradition in an Apostolic Text," *BBR* 6 (1996): 23–38.

9. On the other hand, Ex. 2:1–10 is not simply a reproduction of the motif without its own flavor. B. Childs, for example, has argued that the ancient Near Eastern motif has been modified in Exodus by wisdom influences, which may be seen by the presence of various wisdom themes in these verses, e.g., God's absence, a positive attitude toward foreigners, the piety of the midwives ("The Birth of Moses," *JBL* 84 [1965]: 109–22; see also Childs, *Book of Exodus*, 13).

10. I disagree with Cassuto and others, who feel that the child's physical beauty would have made the mother *especially* distraught at the potential loss of a child such as this (*Commentary on Exodus*, 19; see also Childs, *Book of Exodus*, 18). Likewise, Calvin argues at some length that the parents showed an excusable timidity in abandoning Moses in the first place, particularly since God had made Moses so handsome so as to indicate to the parents that the child was someone worth holding on to (*Commentaries on the Four Last Books of Moses Arranged in the Form of a Harmony*, trans. C. W. Bingham [Grand Rapids: Baker, 1979], 40–42).

11. For other attempts by ancient interpreters to explain *tob*, see Houtman, *Exodus*, 1:273–74, and Sarna, *Exodus*, 9.

12. Sarna, *Exodus*, 9. E.g., after God created the light in Gen. 1:3, v. 4 says, "God saw the light, *ki tob*," i.e., "that it was good."

1, is not merely about the birth of one man, but represents the birth of a people. The savior of God's people is born, and through him they will receive a new beginning. Their slavery will end and their savior will bring them safely into their rest, the Promised Land.[13]

The boy is set in an "ark" (*tebah*) and set afloat on the Nile (v. 3). Like *ki tob*, *tebah* provides a clear connection to Genesis. In all of the Old Testament, this Hebrew word is found only here and in the Flood story (Gen. 6:14–9:18). The theological connection between these two events is self-evident.[14] (1) Both Noah and Moses are specifically selected to forego a tragic, watery fate; (2) both are placed on an "ark" treated with bitumen and are carried to safety on the very body of water that brings destruction to others; and (3) both are the vehicles through whom God "creates" a new people for his own purposes. Furthermore, Moses' safe passage through the waters of the Nile not only looks backward to the Flood story, but forward to the passage through the sea in Exodus 14 for all of God's people.

Ironically, this child, once doomed to death by Pharaoh's decree, will become the very instrument of Pharaoh's destruction and the means through which *all* Israel escapes not merely Pharaoh's decree, but Egypt itself. The child once abandoned in the reeds (*suph*) along the shore of the Nile (v. 3) will later lead his people in triumph through the Reed Sea (*yam suph*, cf. 13:18). Moses' redemption as an infant will be replayed later with respect to Israel at the very infancy of her existence as a nation. We see, then, already in the first two chapters of Exodus, an interweaving of creation and redemption themes that extend from Genesis through Exodus.

Big sister (presumably Miriam, not mentioned by name until 15:20) watches her little brother float along and sees the vessel retrieved by the handmaidens of Pharaoh's daughter, who, like her father (1:8), is left anony-

---

13. We are also told that the boy's mother hid him for three months. The motive seems clear enough: to protect the boy from Pharaoh's harsh decree in 1:22. Note Heb. 11:23, that hiding Moses was an act of faith on the part of Moses' parents. The reasons for the three-month period are not made explicit, nor are the means that they chose to hide him or the reasons why the day came when they were no longer able to do so. See Houtman, *Exodus*, 1:274, for ancient exegesis of the significance of "three months." Some, including Cassuto, suggest that the infant's crying became too loud by this time (*Commentary on Exodus*, 18), although anyone acquainted with a newborn's shrill, nighttime serenade might find Cassuto's explanation wanting.

14. See, for example, Cassuto, *Commentary on Exodus*, 18–19; Sarna, *Exodus*, 9.

mous (2:4–5). To what was certainly Moses' sister's relief, Pharaoh's daughter has pity on the child rather than helping her father carry out his plan. The sister seizes the moment and offers, somewhat matter-of-factly, that it might be of benefit to all concerned if the child were nursed—at least for the time being—by someone else, say, a Hebrew woman she just happens to know (vv. 7–8). Pharaoh's daughter agrees to this arrangement and even pays the nurse for her efforts (v. 9).

After an unspecified length of time,[15] the boy is returned to Pharaoh's daughter, whom she then claims as her own and names *Mošeh*, Moses (v. 10). Some have remarked that the manner in which Moses came to be a son of Pharaoh's daughter "is almost the identical pattern found in a series of bilingual Sumerian-Akkadian legal texts known as *ana ittišu*."[16] To what extent this pattern is reproduced in 2:1–10 is a matter of debate.[17] What is clear in any case is that Moses did become her son.[18]

What has received considerably more scholarly attention is the etymology of Moses' name. We should first observe that it is Pharaoh's daughter who gives the boy his name. Not only does she name him, but she also offers the rationale for the name itself: "I *drew* him out of the water" (v. 10). The verb "to draw" is the Hebrew *mašah*, and from one of its forms we get the name Moses.[19] On the surface, this seems to settle the matter of the origin of Moses' name, yet one ought not overlook the fact that such an etymology would require a daughter of an Egyptian pharaoh to speak Hebrew. Even allowing for this (unlikely) possibility,[20] one would have to wonder why she would give this child, the object of her father's wrath, a Hebrew name that would likely reveal his true identity.

Most scholars are quick to point out that the name Moses is ultimately of Egyptian derivation, not Hebrew. The name is based on the Egyptian verb *ms(w)*, meaning "to bear, give birth to." "Moses," then, is probably a shortened form of an originally longer name—something analogous, for

---

15. Driver mentions that the length of time is likely three to four years, at which point the child would have been weaned and returned to Pharaoh's daughter (*Book of Exodus*, 11). Houtman suggests a span of two to three years (*Exodus*, 1:288).

16. Childs, "The Birth of Moses," 111.

17. Childs considers 2:1–10 to be "a free adaptation of this traditional material within a narrative setting" (ibid.). He feels that there is enough evidence "to make highly plausible a common Near Eastern tradition which is reflected in Exod 2" (112).

18. The Hebrew idiom is the verb *hayah* plus the preposition *lamed*. This idiom is often to be translated as "to become" (e.g., Ex. 4:3 and 9:24).

19. The English "Moses" derives more directly from the Greek *Mōüsēs*.

20. Calvin's arguments to the contrary are unconvincing. He cites Ps. 81:5 and Gen. 42:23 as possible support for Pharaoh's daughter being able to speak Hebrew (*Four Last Books of Moses*, 45–46).

example, to the famous Egyptian name "Thutmose," meaning either "Thoth [a god] is born" or "Born of the god Thoth."[21]

What, then, is to be made of the Hebrew etymology in 2:10? Likely this is either an etymology worked out by the biblical writer himself or a traditional, popular etymology that the people held to, which the writer simply records here.[22] Some scholars add that the biblical writer could not have known Egyptian, for if he had, he certainly would have supplied the "proper" genealogy.[23] Such a view, however, goes beyond the evidence. It is not stretching the point to suggest that the writer could have known Egyptian and still recorded the popular etymology. Whether his readers would have shared that knowledge of Egyptian, however, is another matter. In this respect, the popular etymology serves the writer's purposes better. We see something similar in how Paul cites the Old Testament. Rather than cite the Hebrew, he uses the LXX for his Greek-speaking audience even though he is an educated Jew, well versed in Hebrew, and there are at times significant textual differences between the Hebrew and Greek texts.

We may take a moment here to draw some implications from the etymology of Moses' name. First, although there seems to be some tension between the Hebrew etymology in 2:10 and the ultimate Egyptian derivation of the name, at the very least the Egyptian derivation lends strong support to the historicity of Moses. The name "Moses" would have been firmly at home in ancient Egypt.[24] Moreover, the popular etymology has decided theological significance. Not only has the boy been "drawn out" of the water, but it is under his leadership (God's role, of course, notwithstanding!) that all Israel will later be brought through the water of the sea.

It is missing the theological point to ask simply whether the Hebrew or Egyptian etymology is "true," as if a choice must be made between them. The nature of biblical narrative shows us time and time again that there is a truth that transcends simple issues of historicity. The Hebrew etymology is most definitely *true*. Moses' name meant for the Israelites (and therefore for God, whose Spirit inspired the writers) that he was drawn out of water and would

---

21. See the discussions by J. P. Hyatt, *Commentary on Exodus* (London: Oliphints, 1971), 65; Sarna, *Exodus*, 9; G. Widengren, "What Do We Know About Moses?" *Proclamation and Presence: Old Testament Essays in Honour of Gwynne Henton Davies*, ed. J. I. Durham and J. R. Porter (Macon, Ga.: Mercer Univ. Press, 1983), 28. The complex matter of Egyptian derivation is dealt with thoroughly by J. G. Griffiths, "The Egyptian Derivation of the Name Moses," *JNES* 12 (1952): 225–31.

22. I prefer the second explanation (see Cassuto, *Commentary on Exodus*, 20).

23. E.g., Childs, *Book of Exodus*, 12.

24. Hoffmeier makes a point of this (*Israel in Egypt*, 140–42). See also J. G. Griffiths, "Egyptian Derivation," 231.

draw them out of water. Such an etymology was more "true" and spoke more clearly and pointedly to the ancient Israelites than a distant, isolated appeal to a piece of Egyptian linguistic trivia.

A CHILD IS BORN. We have seen how Moses' birth continues the creation theme of Exodus 1. The boy is *ṭob*, and he is set on an "ark" so that he might be delivered from a watery death. This represents not simply the birth and deliverance of one man, but is symbolic of the birth and deliverance of an entire nation. Israel as a nation is "born," so to speak, at the Exodus. A mass of upstart slaves crosses the sea and emerges as a nation. This theme of deliverance as a new beginning, a new creation, will be seen again in subsequent chapters.

Moses' birth story is just one example of a common Old Testament theme. At various crucial junctures the birth of a child is instrumental to God's plan of delivering his people from some dire situation. This theme typically entails a miraculous birth—or at least, as in the case of Moses, a birth that is "against the odds" (think of Pharaoh's decree). This theme culminates many centuries later in a manger in Bethlehem.

One such example is the birth of Isaac. God promised Abraham[25] that he would become a "great nation" (Gen. 12:2) and that his descendants would multiply greatly and receive God's "reward," which was the Promised Land (e.g., 15:5, 7). But Abraham and Sarah do not seem able to have children. How, then, will there be any descendants to live in this new land? Perhaps out of frustration or impatience (see 15:1–3), Sarah insists that Abraham sleep with her maidservant, Hagar (16:1–3). Since Hagar is Sarah's property, all Hagar's offspring are legally Sarah's offspring, and hence the promise may be realized through Hagar.[26] In this way, God's promise to Abraham in 15:4, that he will have a son "from your own body," would be fulfilled.

But Sarah's plan apparently does not work out. She herself attempts to thwart the plan when she becomes jealous of Hagar and drives her and her newborn son, Ishmael, into the desert (Gen. 16:4–6). Now all seems lost—until God appears to Abraham (ch. 17). In his time, when other efforts have failed,

---

25. The patriarch is not called Abraham until Gen. 17:5, where his name is changed from Abram. Likewise, Sarah is known as Sarai before 17:15. Nevertheless, for sake of simplicity, the names Abraham and Sarah will be used here regardless of what portion of Genesis we are in.

26. Sarah's strategy represents a fairly well-attested ancient Near Eastern practice. C. Westermann provides both primary and secondary sources (*Genesis 12–36: A Commentary*, trans. J. J. Scullion [Minneapolis: Augsburg, 1985], 239).

God announces that he will establish his covenant with Abraham, which will result in many descendants (v. 2). First in order are name changes, from Abram to Abraham and from Sarai to Sarah—a new beginning of sorts for the couple God has chosen to bear his covenant promise. God promises Abraham offspring and land and stipulates that he and all his male descendants (including any slave or foreigner in their midst) are to be circumcised as a sign of this covenant; otherwise, they are to be "cut off" from God's people (vv. 9–14).

The main obstacle to all this is that both Abraham and Sarah are past the age when bearing children usually occurs; he is ninety-nine (or one hundred; cf. vv. 1 and 17) and she is ninety (v. 17). Abraham's reaction is understandable: He laughs (v. 17). God responds that by this time next year Sarah will give birth to a son and his name will be "Isaac," which in Hebrew means "he laughs," perhaps a constant reminder of the miracle, the "against all odds" nature, of the boy's birth. Isaac is the physical evidence of God's faithfulness to Abraham. It is through this son that God's far-reaching covenant with Abraham's descendants will be realized: "I will establish my covenant with him [Isaac] as an everlasting covenant for his descendants after him" (v. 19). Isaac is God's unexpected surprise, the one through whom redemption will come for God's people. When such a thing seems beyond any reasonable expectation, Sarah conceives, but only by God's direct intervention.

Another example of this theme is the birth of Samson (Judg. 13). Manoah's wife is sterile and childless, yet God intends to give them a son (vv. 2–3). As with other birth stories, the importance of this event lies beyond the obvious joy experienced by the parents. The child born to them is no ordinary child, but a mighty deliverer, who, although far from an exemplary moral model (e.g., his desire for a foreign wife in ch. 14 and his weakness for Delilah in ch. 16), becomes Israel's leader to oppose the Philistines. His twenty-year reign (15:20; 16:31) is hardly a standard for others to emulate, but his famous death deals a crippling blow to Israel's enemies.

The book of Ruth as a whole is concerned with the tragedy of one woman's childlessness and her subsequent, unexpected deliverance from that state. Ruth, her sister-in-law (Orpah), and her mother-in-law (Naomi) all lose their husbands (Ruth 1:3–5). The great tragedy in this is that Naomi, an Israelite woman, is now both childless and without the means of bearing other children. All she has left is two daughters-in-law, and foreigners at that (from Moab!).[27] All is not lost, however. Naomi has a relative in Bethlehem named Boaz. Ruth goes to work in his fields in the hopes of providing food

---

27. Pertinent here is the command in Deuteronomy to exclude any Ammonite or Moabite from entering the assembly of the Lord—even to the tenth generation (Deut. 23:3). Naomi's grief truly must have been great.

for herself and her aging mother-in-law. Boaz is taken by Ruth's faithfulness and commitment to Naomi and pronounces a blessing on her (2:11–12).

Naomi, in a manner of speaking, plays the matchmaker.[28] She has Ruth dress up and go to Boaz at night to impress on him his obligation as a near relative to marry Ruth (ch. 3).[29] They do eventually marry and have a son, Obed (4:13–17). Deliverance through this child is on two levels. (1) This male heir remedies not only Ruth's childlessness but Naomi's as well (see esp. 4:14). (2) This child becomes the grandfather of David, the king of Israel (4:17). In other words, once again this birth is the means by which God has chosen to bring deliverance to his people and ensure his presence with them.

A fourth example of this theme is the story of Hannah and the birth of Samuel (1 Sam. 1:1–2:11). Hannah too is childless and suffers much indignation at the hands of her husband's other wife, Peninnah (1:4–6). The heartbroken woman goes to Shiloh to fast, weep, and above all pray. God hears her prayers and announces through Eli, the priest at Shiloh, that she will be granted her request. She conceives and bears a son whom she calls Samuel, meaning "heard of God" (1:17–20). Hannah gives her son back to the Lord to serve as priest at Shiloh. The significance of Samuel lies in his transitionary role as both the last of the judges of Israel, who were leaders of God's people before the inauguration of the monarchy, and the first prophet to anoint a king and to chasten Israel's kings under God's direction.

Samuel's birth is not just an isolated, shortsighted response to one woman's desire to have children. God's purpose is more far-reaching. Samuel is to be the priest-leader through whom the Lord will bring about the kingdom of Israel, which although ruled by human kings is ultimately God's kingdom, a lesson the Israelites learn only too late.[30]

Each of these birth stories has its own distinctive flavor and purpose, with its own particular literary and historical context. Nevertheless, one should not overemphasize the distinctives features at the expense of those elements that serve to bring these stories together under a general theological theme. In seeing how the parts of Scripture work together we begin to discern biblical

---

28. As with the midwives in Ex. 1 and Moses' mother and sister in Ex. 2, we see a degree of ingenuity being displayed by Naomi. God is once again behind the scenes of the narrative, but he directs the actions, as Ruth 4:13–15 clearly implies.

29. Boaz is called a "kinsman-redeemer" (e.g., 2:20; 3:9, 12). The legal obligation for a close relative to take care of his departed brother's widow is set out in Deut. 25:5–10 (see also Lev. 25:25–28, 47–49).

30. We could note also the birth of Jeremiah alluded to in Jer. 1:4–10 and the birth of Isaiah's son in Isa. 7:14. On this latter one, the birth of the child was a concrete testimony to God's presence with his people, as the name Immanuel itself indicates.

"patterns of behavior," which lead us to recognize better the God with whom Scripture as a whole is ultimately concerned.

For Christians, this Old Testament pattern of birth and deliverance comes to its fullest and most moving theological expression in the birth of Christ. There are a number of parallels, both in individual details and theological themes, between the story of Christ's birth and the Old Testament stories. As with the birth of Samuel, the child is given a special name, in this case by an angel. Mary is to name the boy Jesus (Luke 1:31; cf. Matt. 1:21), a name that is itself the bearer of a theological message.[31] Isaac, Samson, and Samuel were all born to mothers who, if things had been left to the normal course of physical events, would have remained childless. So too with Jesus, we have a mother who is a virgin (Matt. 1:23; Luke 1:34–35). In all these cases it takes God's direct intervention to work contrary to normal child-bearing procedure.[32]

Several important theological themes serve not only to draw a parallel between Jesus and the Old Testament stories but also to highlight the distinctiveness of Christ's coming. (1) Both Moses and Jesus undergo periods of humiliation followed by exaltation. Moses was born in humble surroundings, abandoned in a basket, and placed on the Nile. Although he came to live in Pharaoh's house, his temporary rise to power and prestige comes to an abrupt end when he flees Pharaoh's wrath (Ex. 2:15).

Later, however, his true exaltation, his exaltation in God's eyes, begins. Yahweh meets him on Mount Horeb, at which time he receives a commission to lead the Israelites out of Egypt. In time, he not only brings God's people through the sea, but receives the Torah on that very same mountain (chs. 19–24). He receives instructions to build the tabernacle with all its ceremonial furnishings and trappings (chs. 25–40). It is Moses alone who is permitted to see God's glory (33:12–23) and who brings the Israelites safely through a forty-year desert march to the borders of the Promised Land, though because of one tragic error is himself not permitted to enter (Num.

---

31. The Greek for Jesus, *Iesous*, is the same name for the Hebrew Joshua (*yehošuaᶜ*). Joshua in turn is derived from the Hebrew verb *yašaᶜ*, to save, deliver. The name Joshua means "the LORD saves."

32. Note too that in Matt. 2:13–18 we see how Jesus' birth incites strong reaction from Herod, the ruler at that time. The parallel to Pharaoh's decree in Ex. 1:22 is self-evident. Both Jesus and Moses endure the forces of a powerful political machine and emerge triumphant. The parallels between Jesus and Moses extend beyond their birth stories. Heb. 3:1–4:13 and the Gospel of John expound on many direct parallels between the two, some of which will be discussed later. On Hebrews and John, see M. R. D'Angelo, *Moses in the Letter to the Hebrews* (SBLDS 42; Missoula: Scholars, 1979), and T. F. Glasson, *Moses in the Fourth Gospel* (SBT; London: SCM, 1963).

20:1–13). Finally, he alone of all of the Old Testament saints is worthy of this posthumous description (Deut. 34:10–12):

> Since then, no prophet has risen in Israel like Moses, whom the LORD knew face to face, who did all those miraculous signs and wonders the LORD sent him to do in Egypt—to Pharaoh and to all his officials and to his whole land. For no one has ever shown the mighty power or performed the awesome deeds that Moses did in the sight of all Israel.

Jesus, too, suffers humiliation, but on a far grander scale and on different levels. Although God himself, he "made himself nothing, taking the very nature of a servant, being made in human likeness" (Phil. 2:7). He not only subjects himself to the humiliation of the limitations of our flesh, but he is born in the most humble of circumstances. Rather than the comfort and privacy of even a simple room, Mary has to settle for a stable and the company of beasts. Jesus lives among his people, yet is not accorded the respect and reverence due him: "He came to that which was his own, but his own did not receive him" (John 1:11). In time he enters into conflicts with those who oppose him, particularly teachers of Scripture, who, denying the very Christ of Scripture, have him who is free from all sin and wrongdoing condemned to a sickening and humiliating death.

But this humiliation is only temporary. He rises from the grave, having defeated the power of death, the greatest enemy, and ascends on high to sit at the right hand of the Father. Jesus is the church's Moses (cf. Heb. 3:1–6). His triumphant exaltation leads his people not from Pharaoh's slavery to a new land, but from the slavery of sin and death to "a better country—a heavenly one" (Heb. 11:16). Christ has risen from the dead, and so his people rise with him to the newness of the Christian life, where their sin is behind them and glory before them (Rom. 6:4).

(2) Like Isaac, Jesus' birth represents the vehicle through which God fulfills his covenant promises to his people. Their births are not isolated miracles but have a larger purpose; they are primarily for the benefit of others. Isaac was born so that God could establish an "everlasting covenant" with his people (Gen. 17:19). He in time fathered Jacob, whose twelve sons and their offspring became the nation of Israel, the countless numbers God had promised to Abraham in Genesis 15:1–6. Christ's birth signified the beginning of the "new covenant," which did not replace the old as much as extend its scope to include not merely national Israelites, but those who are spiritual children of Abraham (Luke 3:8; John 8:31–47).

(3) Moreover, like Obed, Christ's birth has redemptive significance. Obed's birth brings deliverance for a barren Naomi and ensures that she will not die childless. The point, of course, is not simply that Naomi can have a

child through Ruth, but that the line of her husband, Elimelech, can be perpetuated. In this sense, Obed's act of redemption has both immediate and distant significance. In a similar vein, Jesus' birth ensures a continual (eternal) line of spiritual heirs.[33]

(4) A final theological theme links with how Christ's earthly and heavenly ministry is described as that of priest (Heb. 8–10). Samuel was dedicated to the service of God at Shiloh and grew to fulfill that task. Jesus' death on the cross is truly the ultimate priestly sacrifice. As the author of Hebrews tells us, he now has a permanent priesthood, by which "he is able to save completely those who come to God through him, because he always lives to intercede for them" (7:24–25).

We could explore other themes, and those themes that have been mentioned could be peeled further back to reveal many layers of meaning. But it suffices here to say that the birth of Christ is one that signals the fulfillment of many of God's promises in the Old Testament: "For no matter how many promises God has made, they are 'Yes' in Christ. And so through him the 'Amen'" (2 Cor. 1:20). Birth and deliverance form a common Old Testament theme, and each instance has its own particular flavor and significance. In Christ these many strands are brought together, for in Christ the Father's plan of deliverance sees its fullest expression.

Unexpected help. Another theme in Exodus 2:1–10 is the surprising and unexpected nature that God's deliverance sometimes takes. This is in part related to the theme of God's absence mentioned in connection with Exodus 1: God may seem to be distant from his people, but all along he is working behind the scenes to bring about an unexpected climax. This theme also overlaps with the birth of Moses and others of the Lord's deliverers in the Old Testament. Their births are either miraculous or against the odds, and therefore "unexpected."

Since there is some overlap between this theme and the others discussed above, I will not belabor the point here. But one element that works itself out in 2:1–10 needs comment. We should not lose sight of the fact that it is Pharaoh's decree to kill the firstborn male infants that drove Moses' parents to take their chances by placing the infant in a basket and setting him afloat on a river. The thought of employing such a strategy on a three-month-old is enough to numb any parent. How ironic that the very plan to rescue the infant from Pharaoh's decree, to take him as far from Pharaoh's influence as possible, actually results in his being raised in Pharaoh's house.

---

33. There is another sense in which Jesus is our kinsman-redeemer. He parallels not only Obed, but Boaz, who is called "kinsman-redeemer" in Ruth. As Naomi through Ruth sought deliverance from a close relative, Jesus is our close relative. He was made our brother, as the author of Hebrews puts it (Heb. 2:11, 17), in order to redeem his people from the helplessness of sin.

To put it another way, Pharaoh first brings death, then life to Moses. As we see often in Scripture, the Lord shows his strength by meeting his people precisely in the depths of their despair and working *those* very circumstances for ultimate good. Pharaoh wishes to counter God's plan by casting infants *into* the Nile. God saves Moses by casting him *onto* the Nile and bringing him to Pharaoh's front door. Truly the power of God is at work in this boy's life.

The story of Joseph readily comes to mind as another illustration of this point. By his brothers' treachery he becomes a slave in Egypt to Potiphar, the captain of Pharaoh's guard (Gen. 37:36). While a slave, he has his famous encounter with Potiphar's wife (ch. 39). He is falsely accused and lands promptly in jail. The slave has sunk lower; he is now a prisoner. But "the LORD was with him" (Gen. 39:21), and eventually Joseph finds himself with the prestigious position of interpreting Pharaoh's dreams. The climax of the story is not so much the bettering of Joseph's condition but that of his entire family. Egypt meant death for Joseph—he could just as well have simply rotted in jail. It also meant death for his father, Jacob, who mourned for his lost son (37:34–35).

But as it turns out, Joseph's stay in Egypt becomes the very vehicle through which God provides for his people. Joseph's brothers come down to find food during the famine. What they get is more than simply food; they receive a whole new beginning, for not only does their stay in Egypt provide for them as a family, Egypt is also the bitter cup that Israel has to drink before God makes her a nation in her own right. For both Joseph and the Israelites centuries later, Egypt first poses both a threat to their existence but later turns out to be the means by which God showers blessings on his people.

In this respect, Moses' infancy, his "death and rebirth" on the Nile, is itself a microcosm of the people's plight as a whole. As their leader, he experiences what the Israelites will experience later on. This identification of Moses' and the people's plight is similar to how Paul describes the effects of Christ's death and resurrection. By virtue of Christ's work, the church has been *united* to him (Rom. 6:5; Phil. 2:1). One way this union works itself out is in the believer's journey from death to life, from being an enemy of God to being reconciled to him by the blood of Christ. Becoming a Christian means in a real (but imperfect) sense going through what Christ went through. In Romans 6:1–6, Paul teaches us that being a Christian means dying and being raised from the dead. Note verse 4:

> We were therefore buried with him through baptism into death in order that, just as Christ was raised from the dead through the glory of the Father, we too may live a new life.

Paul is not simply speaking here of future realities but of the present experience of those who are in Christ. Being a Christian means experiencing now in a proleptic but real way the resurrection from the dead. Since we have been raised from the dead, Paul can also add that God has *"seated* us with him in the heavenly realms in Christ Jesus" (Eph. 2:6; cf. Col. 3:1). Not only this, but we are co-heirs with Christ (Rom. 8:17), to whom God has given all power and authority.

We see, then, that it is precisely in Christ's death that he brings life to his people. As with Joseph and Moses, the Father turns the tables on his enemies. Death itself has been defeated, and out of death comes life, not only for Christ but for all those who believe: "And having disarmed the powers and authorities, he made a public spectacle of them, triumphing over them by the cross" (Col. 2:15).

"IN ALL THINGS God works for . . . good" (Rom. 8:28). Anyone who has been a Christian for more than five minutes knows full well that being a Christian does not in any way guarantee immunity from daily trials and challenges that beset the rest of humanity. The mark of a Christian life is not in what happens to us. I know too many people, both those inside God's kingdom and those standing outside the gates, who think that being a Christian means that bad things won't happen to you. In fact, I remember once in high school sharing the gospel with a friend who said, "I can't become a Christian. Do you expect me to believe that God is going to keep me from getting cancer?" Such an expectation is a standard that not only the New Testament saints, but Christ himself could not emulate.

Being a Christian does not mean that everyday circumstances that affect us all are somehow suspended by the Lord. Our focus in living the Christian life is not on the outside pressing in but on the inner strength of those who have been called by God to participate in his kingdom and how that inner strength determines how a person perceives one's circumstances.

We should be reminded here of Romans 8:28: "And we know that in *all* things God works for the good of those who love him, who have been called according to his purpose." Paul does not say that nothing bad will happen to Christians. Rather, he writes that *whatever* does happen will somehow, eventually, work out for good. This may call for temporary suffering on the part of the believer, or at the very least the exercise of Christian patience, for we know that *all* will work for the good. We may see this good now or later, though we may never see it in this lifetime; but that does not nullify God's promise of his care for his people and his directing their paths. This is not an encouraging pat on the back that Paul gives us here, nor is it a naive, Pollyanna view of life. It is nothing less than the benefits of Christ's death and resurrection bestowed on his brothers and sisters, on those who are in Christ and who therefore participate in what Christ has done.

Too frequently passages such as Romans 8:28 are thought to mean that God works *against* our everyday trials to bring some good out of it. Although it is true that God can and does at times deliver his people *from* such circumstances, most Christians would agree that it is more common for the Lord to work *through* our circumstances; indeed, he puts us *in* certain difficult situations precisely because he plans to work some good in our lives. And that "good" is not a temporary shot in the arm but nothing less than God's conforming us ever more to the image of his Son. The point, then, is that God works not so much *despite* our circumstances as in them, through them, with them.

Look back now at Exodus 2:1–10. God did not oversee Moses' birth despite Pharaoh's edict to kill all newborn males. It was not as if the Lord "reacted" to the decree and thought, "What am I going to do now?" Rather, it is precisely by means of this decree that God brings deliverance to his people. God is in full control both of Moses' birth and of the external circumstances that threaten to undo it. God does not remove Moses from the situation, nor does he strike down Pharaoh who dares to oppose him, both of which he certainly could have done. Instead, God places Moses in the same Nile that Pharaoh intends for the boy's harm, brings the boy right to Pharaoh's doorstep, and has him raised in Pharaoh's house. Why? To defeat the enemy decisively at his own game, at the very heart of his strength. Now the savior of Israel can grow up safe and secure, free not only from Pharaoh's wrath but from the debilitating effects of slavery. It is also from his "Egyptian" vantage point that Moses can see more clearly the cruelty with which the Egyptians are treating the Israelites (Ex. 2:11–12).

We should think of the resurrection of Christ in the same way. Christ worked salvation for his people not despite his death but precisely in his death. It is because he died and rose again that those who believe in him are also raised to a new life. To put it another way, Christ triumphed *over* death because he first *endured* death. He defeated death because he participated in it. He suffered the ultimate ignominy to bring the greatest glory to himself and therefore to those whom he calls his brothers and sisters. This is why Scripture encourages the Christian to look on his or her circumstances, however horrible they may be, not stoically but joyously, with anticipation, because the heavenly Father is sure to have some great blessing waiting on the other side. This is why Paul can say in Romans 5:2–5:

And we rejoice in the hope of the glory of God. Not only so, but we also rejoice in our sufferings, because we know that suffering produces perseverance; perseverance, character; and character, hope. And hope does not disappoint us, because God has poured out his love into our hearts by the Holy Spirit, whom he has given us.

Paul is not encouraging his readers to ignore their circumstances and rejoice anyway, to keep a stiff upper lip. Rather, we are to rejoice *because* we suffer, for we know that the end product is hope that "does not disappoint." James expresses the same view in James 1:2—4:

Consider it pure joy, my brothers, whenever you face trials of many kinds, because you know that the testing of your faith develops perseverance. Perseverance must finish its work so that you may be mature and complete, not lacking anything.

Perhaps we begin to see in these passages the "good" that Paul refers to in Romans 8:28. The ultimate reason for enduring harsh circumstances is to promote Christian maturity (cf. James 2:4). What is always on the Christian's horizon is the hope that God has confirmed by virtue of Christ's death and resurrection. This same resurrection power that raised Christ from the dead is also at work in the lives of those who are called according to God's purpose in Christ. In the same way that God's resurrection power brought Christ victory *through* death, so too does this resurrection power bring us through all our trials and challenges, and, like Christ, ultimately through the greatest challenge, death itself.

Most Christians can readily give testimony to God's faithfulness in their lives. The individual circumstances are as varied as the testimonies. Some reading this have no doubt their own story to tell of real, deep pain felt right now. It is a great comfort to know that the Lord is so mighty that he actually uses these circumstances for our good—what a mystery this is! He does not always "do battle" with them and defeat them. As Moses' birth and Christ's resurrection show, he sometimes actually converts those same debilitating circumstances into some benefit for his saints.

In one sense, it is easy to talk this way in a commentary or from a pulpit, but no one is suggesting that this is a simple solution to make all of life run without a hitch. We should not forget that involved in this process may be a period of intense suffering, longing, questioning, and doubt. Nevertheless, God has shown himself faithful in the past and will complete a good work in his people. "Who shall separate us from the love of Christ?" Paul asks (Rom. 8:35). Any trouble or danger? "No, *in* all these things we are more than conquerors through him who loved us" (v. 37).

"I am going to do something in your days that you would not believe" (Hab. 1:5). This is how the Lord begins his answer to Habakkuk's first complaint. Habakkuk is concerned about rampant injustice in Judah, and God responds by telling him that help is on the way—albeit from an unlikely source. To punish the unlawful people of Judah, the Lord is "raising up the Babylonians, that ruthless and impetuous people" (v. 6) to exact punishment. For Habakkuk, this is not only an unexpected move on the Lord's part, but disconcerting as well. How can God possibly call upon a pagan, unclean, godless nation to punish his own people?

Habakkuk's complaint surely represents the sentiments of any Israelite who worshiped a holy God. Yet we see in Scripture time and time again how God works through anyone he pleases. We see it in the Lord's choice of Cyrus, the Persian king, at whose hands the Babylonians were defeated. The Lord even calls him "my shepherd" (Isa. 44:28) and "[my] anointed" (45:1). The Lord will work as he pleases by whatever means he chooses, in accordance with his good pleasure.

The Lord God is Lord over all his creation and over everyone who lives on his earth. He, in some mysterious way that rarely makes perfect sense to us, directs the steps of everyone who treads his earth and breathes his air. And he is not at all hesitant about bringing any part of that creation to bear on his dealings with his people. With Habakkuk and Isaiah we see this playing out on a grand scale: God will direct the national superpowers of the day to serve his purpose. In the case of Moses' birth, the situation is somewhat different. Although in one sense the focus of God's activity is to deliver Moses from the threat of another superpower, Egypt, the narrative itself focuses on the compassion of Pharaoh's daughter.

Before I left seminary to begin doctoral work in Old Testament in a large secular university, I was given some advice by one of my professors: "Unbelievers are some of the nicest people you'll ever meet." This is not to say, of course, that believers are not cordial (although sometimes you have to wonder!). His point was that living in that intense academic environment can quickly make it difficult to foster the "us versus them" mentality: "I am an evangelical, and they are not." One of the biggest spiritual challenges I had to face was not by those who were antagonistic to the gospel (or anything religious), but by those unbelievers whom I got to know, with whom I spent considerable time, and with whom I sweated over exams. I enjoyed their company and derived much personal benefit from knowing them. They continue to be some of my best friends and hold for me some of my most prized memories of graduate school years.

This, of course, is a challenge. I did not meet the enemy to be conquered. Rather, I got to know some people and left thinking how thankful I was to the Lord for the chance to be a part of their lives and for them to be a part of my life. As a result, through much struggle, my faith in Christ has grown precisely because it is not as parochial as it once was. I would like to think that God put me in that situation, not simply to get a Ph.D., but to change me, and he used unbelievers with good hearts (humanly speaking—I am not forgetting Paul's words in Rom. 3!) to bring this about. The Lord also used me to bear witness to them about his goodness, but that is another story.

Did Moses grow up hating his new mother because she was not an Israelite? Did he think, "OK, I'll live in her house, but she's Egyptian. As soon as I'm able, I'm getting out of here to join my own people"? Or is it more likely that he came to rely on her, look up to her, depend on her—love her? Once again, Exodus does not provide us with the psychological details of Moses' relationship to Pharaoh's daughter. Nevertheless, what is clear is that God could have chosen any way to deliver his people, yet he chose to work through a non-Israelite, an Egyptian, an enemy. One cannot help but conjecture what effect this close association with Pharaoh's house had on Israel's redeemer. One can say, however, that this was not a random act of God but a purposeful one.

What is our proper posture toward an unbeliever? There is more than one biblical model. The model of "opposition" is certainly well known and has ample biblical precedent. This model, however, is not deserving of universal application. We share with others the love of Christ, who was a friend to sinners. In doing so, we bring the good news to them in many different ways, which is something that God's people are called to do. But do not be surprised if in the process the Lord uses these same people to change you. Our neighbors, coworkers, and relatives are not so much projects to be won, notches on our salvation belt, but people who are created in God's image and whose lives are in God's hands. They, too, may be his instruments for purposes we cannot fathom. It is his will to employ many facets of his creation for his sake and for his glory.

Exodus 2:11–25

ONE DAY, AFTER Moses had grown up, he went out to where his own people were and watched them at their hard labor. He saw an Egyptian beating a Hebrew, one of his own people. ¹²Glancing this way and that and seeing no one, he killed the Egyptian and hid him in the sand. ¹³The next day he went out and saw two Hebrews fighting. He asked the one in the wrong, "Why are you hitting your fellow Hebrew?"

¹⁴The man said, "Who made you ruler and judge over us? Are you thinking of killing me as you killed the Egyptian?" Then Moses was afraid and thought, "What I did must have become known."

¹⁵When Pharaoh heard of this, he tried to kill Moses, but Moses fled from Pharaoh and went to live in Midian, where he sat down by a well. ¹⁶Now a priest of Midian had seven daughters, and they came to draw water and fill the troughs to water their father's flock. ¹⁷Some shepherds came along and drove them away, but Moses got up and came to their rescue and watered their flock.

¹⁸When the girls returned to Reuel their father, he asked them, "Why have you returned so early today?"

¹⁹They answered, "An Egyptian rescued us from the shepherds. He even drew water for us and watered the flock."

²⁰"And where is he?" he asked his daughters. "Why did you leave him? Invite him to have something to eat."

²¹Moses agreed to stay with the man, who gave his daughter Zipporah to Moses in marriage. ²²Zipporah gave birth to a son, and Moses named him Gershom, saying, "I have become an alien in a foreign land."

²³During that long period, the king of Egypt died. The Israelites groaned in their slavery and cried out, and their cry for help because of their slavery went up to God. ²⁴God heard their groaning and he remembered his covenant with Abraham, with Isaac and with Jacob. ²⁵So God looked on the Israelites and was concerned about them.

Original Meaning

THE BIBLICAL NARRATIVE moves quickly from the story of Moses' birth to a series of pivotal events that bring him to his initial meeting with Yahweh on Mount Horeb in 3:1ff. (the name "Sinai" is not used until 16:1). In the space of these few verses, Israel's deliverer goes from privileged status in Pharaoh's house, to fugitive, to virtual exile in a foreign land.

By the time we reach 2:11, Moses has apparently grown to be a man, as the following narrative makes clear. Just how much time elapses between verses 10 and 11 is not specified by the text, although Stephen speaks of Moses as being forty years old at the time (Acts 7:23; see also *Exodus Rabbah* 1.27). The number forty may have been deduced in antiquity by the fact that Moses was eighty years old when he confronted Pharaoh (Ex. 7:7) and 120 years old when he died (Deut. 34:7); it seems that main epochs of his life were divided into thirds. In any event, we know nothing of Moses' life during these intervening years (Charlton Heston's portrayal in Cecil B. DeMille's *The Ten Commandments* notwithstanding!).

Moses goes out to be with his people (lit., "his brothers"; 2:11). It is not clear whether he at this point has already consciously identified himself with his true countrymen. Nowhere in this passage do we see Moses consider himself an Israelite. (In v. 19 Jethro's daughters assume Moses is Egyptian, likely by his dress, but this tells us nothing of his self-identity.) The fact that he goes out to observe the suffering of his countrymen certainly suggests a strong degree of compassion[1] but not necessarily blood-kinship. We are left to conjecture whether the distinction between Moses' identification with "his brothers" and the "Egyptians" with whom he contends is in Moses' mind or the author's. This is ultimately an unanswerable question.

Another way of posing the problem is to ask whether it is more likely for a Hebrew child, who was secretly delivered from Pharaoh's wrath but who nevertheless grew up in Pharaoh's household, to have grown up conscious of his true heritage, or whether that heritage would have been kept from him for his own safety. If Moses is unaware of his Israelite birth, he would have seen himself as a compassionate Egyptian whose conscience is finally stricken to the point where action is demanded. It is the opinion of the vast majority of commentators,[2] not to mention the New Testament (Heb. 11:24–25), that Moses is aware at least by this time of his true pedigree.

---

1. The Hebrew phrase *wayyarʾ bᵉsiblotam* (NIV: "[he] watched them at their hard labor") suggests more emotional investment on Moses' part than mere "observance" (see Durham, *Exodus*, 19; Driver, *Book of Exodus*, 13), although we should perhaps not put too much stress on this.

2. See, for example, Childs, *Book of Exodus*, 30; Sarna, *Exodus*, 11. See also *Exodus Rabbah* 1.32.

One may also conjecture that Moses' fear of being caught and Pharaoh's wrath against him (Ex. 2:12–15) suggest that both he and Pharaoh are operating under the assumption that Moses is an Israelite. After all, we may presume that an Egyptian prince would have been within his rights to kill whomever he wished without fearing the pharaoh's reprisal. On the other hand, Moses may have feared that his Israelite identity is now discernible, since killing an Egyptian slave driver would show where his true sympathies lie. But all this is conjecture.

Whatever may have been in Moses' mind, however, it seems clear from the context of this passage that the writer wishes to place Moses' Israelite heritage in the foreground. We see already in verse 11 two subtle hints of his subsequent role as deliverer of his people. (1) He is said to "go out" to his people (Heb. vb. *yaṣaʾ*). Both this verb and *ʿalah* ("go up") will become refrains throughout Exodus and other books of the Old Testament to describe how God brought the Israelites out of Egypt. Here Moses makes a first step: He "goes out" of Egypt himself.[3]

(2) The Egyptian's "beating" the Hebrew slave evokes a strong action on Moses' part. The Hebrew root is *nakah*, which appears again in 5:14 with respect to the Israelite foremen who are beaten by the Egyptian slave drivers for not meeting their quota of bricks. Moses' response to the beating of the Hebrew slave foreshadows the unjust treatment of the Israelites by Pharaoh's Egyptian slave drivers in 5:14 and their subsequent deliverance. Hence, in light of the context of these verses, Moses' action here (see also *nakah* in v. 12) should not be interpreted as an act of vengeance or rash zeal but as a proleptic execution of divine justice against Egypt.[4]

To be sure, one is left wondering about some of the circumstances surrounding Moses' act. Why does he hide the body? Is it out of fear?[5] But why would the future deliverer be frightened about doing the right thing? Perhaps he has not yet grown into his position. Or, as some suggest, perhaps he does not really mean to kill the Egyptian, only teach him a lesson.[6] There is no need, however, to defend Moses against the charge of premeditated murder. Since he is acting, albeit imperfectly, as God's instrument of justice, it is more than fitting that Moses would exact the same type of punishment here as

---

3. See also Plastaras, *The God of Exodus*, 45.

4. See also 12:12–13, where God "strikes" (*nakah*) the firstborn of Egypt. The tenth plague is the final prelude to the Exodus.

5. This is B. Jacob's opinion (*The Second Book of the Bible: Exodus*, trans. W. Jacob [Hoboken, N.J.: Ktav, 1992], 38).

6. See Durham, *Exodus*, 19. The fact that Moses looked "this way and that" (v. 12), however, seems to indicate that he knows quite well what he is about to do. Jacob, however, adduces Isa. 59:15–16 as proof to the contrary (*Exodus*, 37–38).

Yahweh will later do in the intentional killing of the firstborn in Exodus 12 or the drowning of the Egyptian army in Exodus 14. In any event, however conscious Moses is of his own background and despite the questions that may arise in our minds concerning some of the particulars, it is clear that Moses is incensed enough at what he sees to kill the Egyptian, thus severing his ties with the Egyptian aristocracy.

In verse 13, Moses intercedes in another conflict, but now between two Israelites. Although the narrator relates that the two men are "fighting" (*naṣab*), Moses asks the perpetrator, "Why are you hitting [*nakah*] your fellow Hebrew?" The implication is that the Hebrew's treatment of his countryman is for Moses no different from that of the Egyptian in verse 11, where the same root *nakah* is used (or any different from the slaver drivers' treatment of the Israelite foremen in 5:14). It is bad enough for God's people to be oppressed by the Egyptians, but has it gone this far that Israelites mistreat each other?

This incident serves to introduce two interconnected themes that recur throughout the Pentateuch: Israel's rebellion and the rejection of Moses. When asked by Moses why he is hitting his countryman, the Hebrew man replies in effect, "Who are you? Who do you think you are? Who gave you the right to tell me or anyone else here what to do?" Although it would be too much to expect of this Hebrew slave to recognize Israel's future deliverer in his presence,[7] from a literary and theological point of view his reaction is striking. Moses' role as redeemer at its very beginning is already met with his own people's questioning his authority. One could expect such behavior from the Egyptians (e.g., 5:1–5 and Pharaoh's hardness of heart regarding the plagues), but certainly not from those whom he has been sent to deliver.

Israelite rebellion and rejection of Moses' leadership is a frequent occurrence in Exodus and throughout the Pentateuch. In the burning bush narrative (3:1–4:17), even Moses himself doubts God's choice for the deliverer of Israel, thus in essence rejecting his own leadership. After Moses confronts Pharaoh for the first time, the Israelites are left to make bricks without straw (5:1–19), which admittedly does not inspire much confidence among the people in Moses' leadership (5:20–21), even after God assures Moses of his calling (5:22–6:12, esp. 6:9–12). After the Lord displays his power in the ten plagues, it seems that the Israelites have finally caught on. Still, with their backs against the sea and with the approaching Egyptian army in sight, they complain again: (14:11–12)

> Was it because there were no graves in Egypt that you brought us to the desert to die? What have you done to us by bringing us out of

---

7. This is especially true, since Moses is not officially commissioned until he meets Yahweh on Mount Horeb in chs. 3–4.

Egypt? Didn't we say to you in Egypt, "Leave us alone; let us serve the Egyptians"? It would have been better for us to serve the Egyptians than to die in the desert!

How soon they forget! Yahweh responds by opening a path in the sea for the Israelites (and a watery grave for the Egyptian soldiers). The Israelites sing a song of praise in 15:1–21, but by the time we get to 15:24, they are complaining again, this time because they have no water; God gives them water. In chapter 16, they complain because they have no food, and God gives them bread from heaven (manna) and quail. In 17:1–7 they complain again about the lack of water; the Lord responds by providing water from a rock.[8]

In chapters 19–31, Moses is on Mount Sinai receiving the commandments from God (the Ten Commandments, the Book of the Covenant, and matters concerning the tabernacle). While he is away, the Israelites rebel by making an idol out of gold (ch. 32). In Numbers 12:1–16 both Miriam and Aaron, Moses' siblings, oppose his leadership and receive swift rebuke. Immediately after exploring the new land, the people rebel by refusing to enter it out of fear of the Nephilim (13:1–33). In the next chapter, the entire Israelite community rebels (except Joshua and Caleb), in words reminiscent of Exodus 14:12, even threatening to elect a new leader and go back to Egypt (Num. 14:1–4). Korah, Dathan, and Abiram rebel in Numbers 16 and are swallowed up by the ground (16:31–32), while their 250 followers are consumed by fire from the Lord (v. 35).

In fact, in an unexpected twist, things get so bad by Numbers 20 that Moses himself rebels. He strikes the rock with his staff rather than speaking to it as he was commanded. Thus, he is denied entrance into the land of Canaan. Later on the Israelites rebel by allowing themselves to be seduced by Moabite women (Num. 25). Opposition to God and his chosen deliverer is a common theme in the Pentateuch, and we see strong hints of this already at the beginning of Moses' adult life, even before his official role has been announced.

In refusing to acknowledge Moses' right to interfere in his affairs, the Hebrew slave reminds Moses of his crime the day before: "Are you thinking of killing me as you killed the Egyptian?" Despite his attempt to cover up his act by hiding the body in the sand, it is clear that the deed "must have become known" (v. 14). Pharaoh apparently gets wind of it as well and seeks to kill Moses, which prompts him to flee to Midian (v. 15).

---

8. The Israelites rebel in virtually the same way in Num. 20:1–13. These two parallel rebellious acts occur near the beginning and end of the forty-year desert period. By framing the entire desert experience, these episodes present the picture of those forty years as a time of constant rebellion.

In one sense, Pharaoh's response to Moses' act seems extreme: Would the king really want to kill his son for behaving in such a way without some other precipitating motive? Perhaps something else is going on behind the scenes, something that, once again, the narrative itself does not bring to the surface. Was it against the law for a prince to kill one of his subjects? Or might there be another reason for Pharaoh's reaction? We have already seen, with his planned genocide in chapter 1, that he is prone to irrational outbursts. Could this simply be further evidence of Pharaoh's capriciousness? Perhaps, as mentioned above, his strong reaction may be evidence that he is well aware of Moses' Hebrew birth, or that Moses' act of murder actually betrays his true national allegiance.

For whatever reason Pharaoh reacted the way he did, his determination to kill Moses drives Moses away to Midian.[9] His choice of haven is significant in three respects. (1) Midian becomes a prominent entity in successive biblical narratives. Moses eventually marries a Midianite woman and has children by her (2:21–22; 18:2–4). He also receives helpful advice from his father-in-law about how best to settle disputes among the Israelites (18:13–27). Later on the Midianites become a cause of stumbling for the Israelites (Num. 25) and are eventually defeated by Gideon (Judg. 6–8).

(2) Midian serves to tie Moses to the patriarchs, something we have seen as a central concern of the writer of Exodus in chapter 1. Not only was Midian one of Abraham's sons by Keturah (Gen. 25:1–6), but it was the Midianite traders who brought Joseph down into Egypt (37:25–36). Note, then, the parallel: The Midianites brought the patriarch Joseph to exile in Egypt; Moses winds up with the Midianites after his exile from Egypt. Also, like Joseph, Moses spends his early years in Egypt in good graces, only to be considered an enemy later on; yet in the end, both emerge triumphant over hostile Egyptian opposition. Similarities also occur between Moses and Jacob.[10] Both flee from threat of physical harm to a foreign country; both meet their wives by a well; and both return home with their future wives to meet her father.

(3) Perhaps most significant, Moses' departure from Egypt into the Sinai desert foreshadows the Exodus itself. As we have seen above and will see below, Moses' activity in chapter 2 anticipates a number of elements of the Exodus in general.[11] Here, he foreshadows Israel's departure from Egypt. Fur-

---

9. Midian is a term that describes more an ethnic or political entity than a location, although archaeological research has safely demonstrated Midianite presence near the Gulf of Aqaba in the Sinai Peninsula. See G. E. Mendenhall, "Midian," *ABD*, 4:815–18.

10. See M. D. Dunnam, *Exodus* (Communicator's Commentary Series; Waco, Tex.: Word, 1987), 50.

11. T. Fretheim is especially helpful in highlighting this feature in the narrative. In fact, the subtitle for 2:11–22 of his commentary is "Moses As Embodiment of the Future" (*Exodus*, 41–46).

thermore, Moses' intervention in the conflicts in verses 11–14 foreshadows God's future deliverance of the Israelites.

Moses arrives in Midian and sits down by a well. This scene serves two immediate purposes: (1) It describes Moses' initial contact with the Midianites and his marriage to Zipporah; (2) it provides yet another example of Moses' actions as anticipating subsequent elements in Exodus. Regarding Moses' marriage, anyone familiar with the patriarchal narratives will be reminded of Genesis 24 and 29, where Isaac and Jacob, respectively, meet their wives.[12] The clear difference between these narratives is that Isaac and Jacob marry descendants of Abraham, while Moses marries a foreign woman.[13] The theological significance of this foreign marriage seems to highlight Israel's rejection of her deliverer (v. 14). Moses finds acceptance only apart from his own people, first by being raised in an Egyptian household and now by starting his own household on foreign soil with a foreign wife. Once again, Moses' circumstances anticipate Israel's forty-year "exile" in the desert.

Particularly striking is what Moses does at the well to gain Reuel's admiration. His action here anticipates his character as future redeemer and leader of his people. Some shepherds come and drive away the flock that Reuel's daughters are trying to water. Moses' role as shepherd of the sheep, reiterated in 3:1, foreshadows his shepherd-like role as leader of the Israelites out of Egypt and through the desert.[14] He is their guide and protector. Not only does Moses care for the daughters' sheep but he "rescues" the daughters

---

12. *Exodus Rabbah* 1.32 states: "He [Moses] adopted the practice of his ancestors. Three met their marriage partners at the well—Isaac, Jacob, and Moses." Another parallel often mentioned is the Egyptian story of Sinuhe, which exhibits noticeable similarities to Moses' sojourn in Midian (Houtman, *Exodus*, 1:318; Pritchard, *Ancient Near Eastern Texts*, 18–22). In this respect, the comments in the previous section regarding the Sargon legend and Moses' birth are relevant.

13. There is some discrepancy between 2:16–22, where the clear implication is that Zipporah is a Midianite, and Num. 12:1–2, where she is called a Cushite. Another discrepancy is the name of Zipporah's father. His name is Reuel in Ex. 2:18, but in 3:1 and 18:2ff. his name is Jethro (see also Jeter in 4:18, although the NIV translators prefer the variant reading Jethro). Not surprisingly, theories abound, but two names for one person should not pose a significant difficulty. In any event, a precise explanation is lacking. For various attempts at solving this issue, see Driver, *Book of Exodus*, 15; G. W. Coats, "Moses in Midian," *JBL* 92 (1973): 3–10; W. F. Albright, "Jethro, Hobab and Reuel in Early Hebrew Tradition" *CBQ* 25 (1963): 1–11. Sarna suggests that Jethro is not a name but a title: "his excellency" (*Exodus*, 12).

14. See, e.g., Ps. 77:20. Speaking of the Exodus we read, "You [God] led your people like a flock by the hand of Moses and Aaron." See also Num. 27:15–17, where Moses is to "shepherd" the people into Canaan, but because of his disobedience in 20:1–13, that task is given to Joshua.

themselves.[15] In fact, he not only drives the shepherds away but goes so far as to water the Reuel's daughters' sheep, something that they feel is worthy of special mention.[16] Moses' attempt to help his fellow Israelite in need in verses 13–14 is met with resistance, but the Midianites greet him with open arms.

So this stranger is accepted into Reuel's family. Moses marries one of his daughters and has a child by her. Every indication is that he has found a new home and has every intention of settling down. He is a man in exile from his home country and from the people of his birth. Moses is an alien, as are his Israelite countrymen in Egypt; he is finally experiencing their plight. He names his son appropriately, Gershom, which stems either from the two Hebrew words *ger* and *šam* ("an alien there") or from the verb *garaš* ("to drive out").[17] His son's name is a constant reminder of his banishment.

In verses 23–25 the writer returns for a moment to Egypt to remind us of the big scene ("meanwhile, back at the ranch," so to speak). The pharaoh who has sought to kill Moses is dead, but the Israelites are still being oppressed by their slave drivers. Moses may have settled down, but the situation in Egypt is anything but settled. The Israelites "groan" and "cry out." It is here that the God of Israel enters the scene explicitly. Their cry goes up to him, and he hears it. The behind-the-scenes God of chapters 1–2 is not absent.

Why does God respond to their cry? The answer to this question is crucial for understanding this book, and we will keep returning to it below. God responds because he remembers "his covenant with Abraham, with Isaac and with Jacob" (2:24). Once again, we see how the Israelites' present circumstances must be seen from the broad, divine perspective. In saving them, God displays his faithfulness to his earlier promise. The Israelites' deliverance is certain, for what is at stake is nothing less than God's character.

Throughout this section we have seen how Moses' acts of deliverance foreshadow subsequent events in Exodus. But now for the first time the iden-

---

15. The feminine plural suffix *an* on the verb *wayyoši'an* ("he delivered them"; NIV, "he came to their rescue") either stands for the flock (a collective noun) or for the daughters. The latter is likely, esp. in light of v. 19, where the daughters (not the sheep) are said to have been delivered (*nasal*) from the shepherds.

16. The Hebrew verbal construction in v. 19 is emphatic, *daloh dalah*, which can be translated, "Why, he even drew water!"

17. The etymology is a debated point. If the former is in the mind of the author, we have another example of a theologically rather than linguistically motivated etymology, as we have already seen with the name Moses in 2:10 (see comments on 2:10). I do not concur with Durham's judgment that this popular etymology is "incorrect" (*Exodus*, 23); it is *theological*. Furthermore, although worth considering, I also disagree with Durham's judgment that the foreign land Moses refers to in v. 22 is Egypt, i.e., Moses has finally found his home in Midian. Rather, the point of this pericope seems to accent Moses' displacement away from his country and people (see also Houtman, *Exodus*, 1:317).

tity of Israel's true redeemer is introduced. It is God who sees the Israelites' plight. The use of the verb *ra'ah* in verse 25 and in verse 11 is interesting. Moses "sees" the oppression of the Hebrew slave at the hands of the Egyptian in verse 11. Here the God of Moses sees it as well. And he knows; so rest assured, God is in complete control. With these concluding verses the stage is set. The next scene of the drama of Israel's redemption is about to unfold. How, then, will God aid his covenant people?

 CHARACTERISTICS OF ISRAEL'S REDEEMER. In the relatively brief span of fifteen verses, we see a number of elements that together introduce the complex portrait of Moses as the redeemer of Israel. He is Israel's protector (vv. 11, 17) and shepherd (vv. 17–19). He is an outcast (vv. 15, 22) and despised by his own people (v. 14). A number of these elements are found in varying degrees elsewhere in Scripture.

We have already noted the similarities between Joseph and Moses and how this serves to join Exodus with the patriarchal narratives. Rejection by one's own brothers (literally for Joseph) and eventual triumph over their circumstances (Joseph by becoming a leader under Pharaoh, Moses in the opposite fashion by the destruction of the Egyptian army at the Red Sea), in addition to the obvious connection to Egypt they share, are significant points of comparison.

Moses as protector of his oppressed people is played out more fully later in his lifetime, particularly at the Red Sea, where the Israelites see the oncoming Egyptian army. It should be noted that Pharaoh decides to pursue the Israelites not to destroy them but to enslave them again (14:5–7, although 15:9 seems to offer a different perspective). The victory at the sea, which is ultimately a military victory at the hands of Yahweh as divine warrior (14:30–31), protects the Israelites from renewed oppression. This same theme is revisited in Joshua's leadership after Moses' death, but now the twist is that Israel, by God's command, has become the aggressor: Joshua leads the Israelites in a systematic military conquest of Canaan. The cycle of judges in the book of Judges likewise exhibits the protective role of Israel's warrior. Israel is oppressed by outsiders and subjected to their rule. After varying periods of time God raises up military leaders to bring Israel out from domination of these hostile peoples.

The cycle in Judges also clearly reminds us of the theme of the rejection of God's redemptive work seen in Exodus. The Israelites in those days did not reject their earthly leaders, but their recurring retreat back to sin after the death of these judges was nothing less than a rejection of God, who had repeatedly delivered them from their enemies. It is worth noting here in the early chapters of Exodus the community's rejection not only of Moses' leadership, but also their subsequent rejection of God's leadership (lack of faith at the sea, manna and quail, need for water). The rejection of Israel's leader is essentially rejection of Israel's God.

David also embodies many of the themes introduced in Exodus. He is Israel's protector. When defeat at the hands of the Philistines seems imminent, the young David exhibits uncanny savvy and courage by sinking a stone into Goliath's forehead (1 Sam. 17). Not unlike Moses in Exodus 2, David's victory over Goliath serves to presage his leadership as king over all Israel. David's other military exploits also manifest this theme (e.g., his protection of Keilah against the Philistines in 1 Sam. 23:1–6).

The theme of protector overlaps in certain respects with that of shepherd. David, as ruler over Israel, is the shepherd of his people (2 Sam. 5:2; 7:7). As shepherd, his role is to guide and protect his sheep.[18] But David is also rejected by his people. He first has to dodge Saul's attempts to kill him (1 Sam. 18–19; 23:7–29). Although David is anointed by Samuel, Saul does not recognize that divine call. David's woes do not end with Saul's death (1 Sam. 31), for wars between the two houses persist for a time (2 Sam. 2–4). His sin with Bathsheba (ch. 11) begins a cycle of discord that leads to further rejection of his leadership, even by members of his own family; for a time he becomes an outcast, just as Moses had once been (chs. 13–20).

Eventually, the rejection of God's appointed leaders leads to a division of the kingdom of Israel into the northern and southern kingdoms. During Solomon's lifetime, Jeroboam, one of his officials, rebels against him (1 Kings 11:26–40), which sows the seeds of full-blown rebellion after Solomon's death. Israel (the northern kingdom) rebels against Solomon's rightful heir, Rehoboam, and declares Jeroboam their king (12:1–24). Two nations are born, and both eventually meet a similar fate: exile.

In addition to judges and kings, prophets are also leaders of the people; many of these same themes are found in the prophetic books. Apart from the ubiquitous mention of Israel's rejection of the Lord against which so much of the prophetic literature is directed, the lives of certain prophets embody these themes. Jeremiah, for example, is the object of repeated scorn by the very people he is directed to help. The men of Anathoth, Jeremiah's hometown, plot to kill him (Jer. 11:18–23). The priest Pashhur has him beaten for

---

18. Cyrus, king of Persia, is called "my shepherd" in Isa. 44:28 (see also Hos. 12:12–13). Sheep is a common way of describing the Israelites (see Ps. 23:1; 74:1; 95:7; 100:3; Isa. 53:6; Jer. 50:6; Ezek. 34:11; Zech. 13:7). Often in these contexts, it is God himself who is the shepherd rather than an earthly king.

prophesying Jerusalem's destruction (20:1–6). Unlike Moses, however, his fortunes do not change with the passing of power from one king to the next (cf. Ex. 2:23; 4:19); thanks only to the thoughtful words of some elders, Jeremiah escapes another attempt on his life after Jehoiakim assumes the throne (ch. 26).

Later, Zedekiah has Jeremiah put in prison and then into a cistern (Jer. 37–38); he is released only after his predictions of Jerusalem's capture by the Babylonians come true (chs. 39–40). And like Joseph and the baby Moses, Jeremiah lived in Egypt for part of his life (41:16–44:30). Some of these same themes recur in the lives of other prophets (e.g., Ezek. 34 [shepherds]; Amos 7:10–17 [rejection]; Zech. 11:4–17 [shepherds]).

There are many ways, both implicit and explicit, in which Christ's redemptive work is presented in the Old Testament imagery just discussed. In the previous section we saw the theological connection between Christ's birth and that of Moses. A connection between Moses the redeemer in Exodus 2 and Christ is also apparent. (1) Christ protects his church, though now the sphere of conflict is primarily in the spiritual realm. The church certainly suffers persecution from earthly sources, but the powers ultimately behind this persecution are demonic. It is Satan who wishes to destroy the church of Christ, and it is Christ who, by virtue of his death, resurrection, and present intercession, protects the church from this foe.

Satan is a devouring lion on the prowl against the sheep (1 Peter 5:8). Therefore, our defenses are not primarily directed toward "flesh and blood, but against the rulers, against the authorities, against the powers of this dark world and against the spiritual forces of evil in the heavenly realms" (Eph. 6:12). For this reason, Paul warns us, we must put on God's full armor to resist this struggle and remain faithful to the end (vv. 13–18). This armor is impenetrable since it is a gift of the risen Christ, who has already defeated these powers of the dark world.

(2) Like Moses and David, Christ is also the shepherd of his flock; he was born for this very purpose (Matt. 2:6; cf. Mic. 5:2). He is the good shepherd, who lays down his own life for the sheep (John 10:11); he is the great shepherd, whom the God of peace brought back to life (Heb. 13:20). He does not lead his people astray but leads them through peril and danger until they are safely in their fold (Luke 12:32; 1 Peter 2:25; 5:4).

(3) Like Moses and David, Christ was rejected by his own. Stephen makes the explicit connection between Moses' rejection by his people and that of Christ (Acts 7:39, 51–53). But Christ was not a fledgling redeemer, difficult to recognize as Moses may have been. He was God's Son, sent from the Father. One would expect the possibility of rejection to be remote. Yet, "he was in the world, and though the world was made through him, the world

did not recognize him. He came to that which was his own, but his own did not receive him" (John 1:10–11). Christ's life was permeated with rejection. It began at his birth (Herod's plot in Matt. 2:1–18) and continued throughout his ministry (constant opposition by the religious leaders of his day). His final rejection came in his betrayal and crucifixion.

One element of Moses' rejection helps to bring this theme into sharper focus with respect to both Christ and the church. As we have noted, Moses' circumstances in the opening chapters of Exodus presage his subsequent role as redeemer as well as Israel's future redemption. Moses, in other words, foreshadows both the redeemer and the redeemed. He first experienced Israel's rejection and became an outcast and alien before he himself became worthy to be her redeemer. Christ, too, became like us before he could deliver us (Heb. 2:17). But he did not simply descend from the comfort and prestige of an Egyptian palace, but from heaven itself, becoming not only a man but a despised man—for our sake. As Moses became Israel's savior by truly embodying her suffering, Christ from highest heaven took onto his own body the sin of humanity. He is the Savior through suffering.

This angle helps us to appreciate how Christ's rejection relates to us. There are many ways in which Christ fulfills the Old Testament. There is, for example, the well-known triad of prophet, priest, and king, each of which is ultimately realized fully in Christ. But there are other ways as well, reflected in his person and work. Christ not only fulfills the ideals of certain individuals (e.g., David) and offices (e.g., priest), but of Israel as a whole. Christ is the embodiment of Israel's experience. This is what lies behind Matthew's unexpected (at least for us) citation of Hosea 11:1 (cf. Matt. 2:15): "Out of Egypt I called my son." The context of Hosea 11 clearly shows that Hosea is speaking not of Christ's but of Israel's coming out of Egypt during the Exodus. Matthew, however, interprets Hosea 11:1 as referring to Jesus as a child coming out of Egypt after Herod's death.

The precise nature of Matthew's use of Hosea 11:1 has been debated, particularly by evangelicals concerned about Matthew's somewhat startling lack of concern for the original context of Hosea's statement. Nevertheless, the more basic theological point should not be lost: Matthew sees Israel's Exodus experience as fulfilled in the person of Christ. Since, therefore, Christ serves as a focal point for Israel's experience, it is important for the church today, which is the body of Christ, to consider its application of the Old Testament message to itself in Christological terms. How we apply Exodus 2:11–25 to our situation is, therefore, a Christocentric exercise. We see our daily Christian walk in light of the condescension and victory of Christ, who, like Moses, was scorned in order that he might redeem. The significance of 2:11–25 for today is bound to the character of Israel's redeemer.

"CLOTHE YOURSELVES WITH HUMILITY" (**1 Peter
5:5**): **Characteristics of the redeemed.** A theme
that Exodus 2:11–25 shares with chapter 1 is that
of the suffering of Israel while in captivity. Suf-
fering will remain a recurring theme in Exodus until the departure from Egypt
in chapter 14. Hence, there is a certain degree of theological overlap among
the opening chapters of Exodus, a fact that speaks not of the writer's lack of
imagination but of the central importance of this theme, among others, to
the portrait he is painting.

What distinguishes Exodus 2 from chapter 1, however, is the identification of Moses with the suffering of his people. No longer a lofty bystander,
observing the people's plight from the security of his privileged status, he now
comes down to experience firsthand what it means to be scorned by Egypt.
He does not play the role of a slave temporarily—to see if he likes it. Rather,
by attempting to interfere with Egyptian policy, he pays the price for his zeal:
He assumes their lowly position.

Christ showed even greater humility, and it is a New Testament refrain that
we must look to Christ as our example. Jesus exemplifies the ideal of humiliation seen in 2:11–15, and his standard sets the goal for Christian life and conduct, for those who have been called out of darkness and into his light.

A prominent Christian speaker once remarked to me how he was often
introduced before a message or lecture he was invited to give as someone who
was a "humble" man—which in his case is true to a striking degree. This always
bothered him: Why did this particular trait need *special* mention? I have thought
over the years about what he said, and it seems to me that he has a point.
Humility should not be a Christian virtue that is worthy of special mention,
as if some Christians possess this trait while others do not. Rather, humility is
at the center of the character of one who knows Christ and is known by him.
It is not a word that describes a "super-Christian," but a quality that is supposed to be a distinguishing characteristic of all Christians. To be sure, Christians at different stages of spiritual growth will exhibit this quality in varying
degrees; in fact, no one mirrors perfectly the standard set by Christ. Nevertheless, humility is a basic ingredient of those who have learned to hate their
sin and to be thankful to the Lord for his incomparable mercy.

Still, humility is a trait that many of us find hard to come by, which may
be one reason why some feel it necessary to make special mention of it when
they find it. Lack of humility comes in many shapes and sizes, but most of
us, I imagine, do not encounter the issue on such a grand scale as Moses.
Instead, our daily battles to be conformed to the image of Christ are far more
subtle and therefore much harder to recognize. We are pastors and scholars

who live in the spotlight, but who serve a Christ who hid himself from the crowds. We are students who revel in a quest and thirst for knowledge, but who serve a Christ of lowly birth and little education. We are homeowners who take great pride in the appearance of our homes, but who serve a Christ who had no place to lay his head.

Humility is selflessness, and this is not a quality taught or cherished by our world. As C. S. Lewis reminds us, humility is not thinking less about ourselves, but thinking about ourselves less. It is not looking back after a day of struggles and remarking at how humble we were today. It is being in such a state (albeit imperfect) of conformity to Christ that the question does not even enter our heads. This is the type of humility that we are all called to exhibit but few achieve.

Humility is a central quality that defines the Christian. It is part of who we are as re-created in Christ's image, but it still requires perseverance and discipline to achieve. There are times, however, when humility is not something we choose, but is thrust upon us. It is not a question of practicing humility, but of being humiliated. Although Moses humbled himself, so to speak, by intercepting the Egyptian's blows, his resulting exile was in effect imposed on him by Pharaoh's desire to have him killed. Moses chose to help his Hebrew brother; he never intended to flee his home as a result. Christ not only humbled himself by taking on flesh and blood, but he suffered humiliation throughout his lifetime, especially on the cross, but also whenever he was scorned or rejected by the people of his day.

Christians often find themselves in a state of enforced humility simply by virtue of their Christian witness. We who are Christ's ambassadors (2 Cor. 5:20) can expect nothing less than that which our Lord himself endured (John 15:20). We all know how difficult it can sometimes be simply to live the Christian life outside of the safe confines of a Sunday service. At work, play, or school, we are bound to pay some sort of price for living consistent Christian lives—and many of us have our own stories to tell. When we, like Moses, take a stand by bringing the gospel of Christ to bear on *all* of our lives, the world, which did not recognize the Savior when he came, is bound to react in a manner consistent with its unregenerate character.

The Lord is not absent in this process. In fact, humiliation is one of the means by which the Lord builds Christian character. Moses' exile is what prepared him to shepherd Israel out of Egypt. His flight from Egypt to Midian was the beginning of a lengthy spiritual journey. It came to a climax on Mount Horeb (ch. 3), where Yahweh announces that he is going to use Moses for a mighty purpose. We can even say that it is the Lord's hand that drives Moses out of his comfort zone and into the desert. Would Moses have been adequately prepared for his ministry had he remained adorned in royal splendor? I think not. Rather, he is humbled by the Lord precisely so that he may be made into an instrument of deliverance.

A close college friend of mine was a talented baseball pitcher. During his senior year, he was actively scouted by a number of teams. It had been his dream since early childhood to play in the major leagues. He finished his college career in May and had already been invited to a number of tryouts later that month. One week after his college career ended, he injured his elbow— an injury that swiftly ended any hope of fulfilling his dream. He went to the tryouts anyway, but his performance was clearly below the necessary standard. Ever since he was a boy, he had thought of little else than baseball. And for over two years after his mishap, he struggled with the Lord: "Why did this happen? I could have made it. Why didn't you give me a chance to show what I can do?" He struggled with his faith and the purpose of his life. He was undone.

But the Lord was merciful. This man's struggles did not last forever. He was crushed, but his grief instigated his own long spiritual journey. I would love to say that the Lord healed his arm and that he became the next Nolan Ryan, but he didn't. I would at least like to be able to say that the Lord took my friend from a life of baseball and made him into the next Billy Graham, but this didn't happen either. He is just a regular guy with a wife and children. He has a regular job and a home in the suburbs. But the Lord drove him into his desert for a purpose too. He has learned many valuable lessons of faith. He is closer to the Lord than he was before. His faith is active and vibrant. How true it is that the Lord will drive us out of our comfort zones in order that we may learn the painful lesson that only he is our comfort.

By being forced to rely on his grace more fully, we are being prepared for service to him (cf. 2 Cor. 12:7–10). In making this spiritual journey, we are not only living out Moses' experience but Christ's as well. Is this not what the writer of Hebrews had in mind? "Although he was a son, he learned obedience from what he suffered" (Heb. 5:8). We cannot say that Christ "learned" in the same sense as we do. Nevertheless, there is a tie that binds us to Christ, our brother. We, too, learn obedience from what we suffer. The Lord drives us into our desert to conform us to the likeness of his son: "And we, who with unveiled faces all reflect the Lord's glory, are being transformed into his likeness with ever-increasing glory, which comes from the Lord, who is the Spirit" (2 Cor. 3:18).

The Moses of Exodus 2:11–25 must precede the Moses of Exodus 14. The Christ born of lowly circumstances, who was despised and rejected by men, who died with great shame, must precede the Christ of the resurrection. We, too, must be broken before we can be built up again, for his sake.

Exodus 3:1–4:17

NOW MOSES WAS tending the flock of Jethro his father-in-law, the priest of Midian, and he led the flock to the far side of the desert and came to Horeb, the mountain of God. ²There the angel of the LORD appeared to him in flames of fire from within a bush. Moses saw that though the bush was on fire it did not burn up. ³So Moses thought, "I will go over and see this strange sight—why the bush does not burn up."

⁴When the LORD saw that he had gone over to look, God called to him from within the bush, "Moses! Moses!"

And Moses said, "Here I am."

⁵"Do not come any closer," God said. "Take off your sandals, for the place where you are standing is holy ground." ⁶Then he said, "I am the God of your father, the God of Abraham, the God of Isaac and the God of Jacob." At this, Moses hid his face, because he was afraid to look at God.

⁷The LORD said, "I have indeed seen the misery of my people in Egypt. I have heard them crying out because of their slave drivers, and I am concerned about their suffering. ⁸So I have come down to rescue them from the hand of the Egyptians and to bring them up out of that land into a good and spacious land, a land flowing with milk and honey—the home of the Canaanites, Hittites, Amorites, Perizzites, Hivites and Jebusites. ⁹And now the cry of the Israelites has reached me, and I have seen the way the Egyptians are oppressing them. ¹⁰So now, go. I am sending you to Pharaoh to bring my people the Israelites out of Egypt."

¹¹But Moses said to God, "Who am I, that I should go to Pharaoh and bring the Israelites out of Egypt?"

¹²And God said, "I will be with you. And this will be the sign to you that it is I who have sent you: When you have brought the people out of Egypt, you will worship God on this mountain."

¹³Moses said to God, "Suppose I go to the Israelites and say to them, 'The God of your fathers has sent me to you,' and they ask me, 'What is his name?' Then what shall I tell them?"

¹⁴God said to Moses, "I AM WHO I AM. This is what you are to say to the Israelites: 'I AM has sent me to you.'"

¹⁵God also said to Moses, "Say to the Israelites, 'The LORD, the God of your fathers—the God of Abraham, the God of Isaac and the God of Jacob—has sent me to you.' This is my name <u>forever</u>, the name by which I am to be remembered from generation to generation.

¹⁶"Go, assemble the elders of Israel and say to them, 'The LORD, the God of your fathers—the God of Abraham, Isaac and Jacob—appeared to me and said: I have watched over you and have seen what has been done to you in Egypt. ¹⁷And I have promised to bring you up out of your misery in Egypt into the land of the Canaanites, Hittites, Amorites, Perizzites, Hivites and Jebusites—a land flowing with milk and honey.'

¹⁸"The elders of Israel will listen to you. Then you and the elders are to go to the king of Egypt and say to him, 'The LORD, the God of the Hebrews, has met with us. Let us take a three-day journey into the desert to offer sacrifices to the LORD our God.' ¹⁹But I know that the king of Egypt will not let you go unless a mighty hand compels him. ²⁰So I will stretch out my hand and strike the Egyptians with all the wonders that I will perform among them. After that, he will let you go.

²¹"And I will make the Egyptians favorably disposed toward this people, so that when you leave you will not go empty-handed. ²²Every woman is to ask her neighbor and any woman living in her house for articles of silver and gold and for clothing, which you will put on your sons and daughters. And so you will <u>plunder the Egyptians</u>." — *to make the golden calf?* — *to build the tabernacle?*

⁴:¹Moses answered, "What if they do not believe me or listen to me and say, 'The LORD did not appear to you'?"

²Then the LORD said to him, "What is that in your hand?"

A staff," he replied.

³The LORD said, "Throw it on the ground."

Moses threw it on the ground and it became a snake, and he ran from it. ⁴Then the LORD said to him, "Reach out your hand and take it by the tail." So Moses reached out and took hold of the snake and it turned back into a staff in his hand. ⁵"This," said the LORD, "is so that they may believe that the LORD, the God of their fathers—the God of Abraham, the God of Isaac and the God of Jacob—has appeared to you."

⁶Then the LORD said, "Put your hand inside your cloak." So Moses put his hand into his cloak, and when he took it out, it was leprous, like snow.

⁷"Now put it back into your cloak," he said. So Moses put his hand back into his cloak, and when he took it out, it was restored, like the rest of his flesh.

⁸Then the LORD said, "If they do not believe you or pay attention to the first miraculous sign, they may believe the second. ⁹But if they do not believe these two signs or listen to you, take some water from the Nile and pour it on the dry ground. The water you take from the river will become blood on the ground."

¹⁰Moses said to the LORD, "O Lord, I have never been eloquent, neither in the past nor since you have spoken to your servant. I am slow of speech and tongue."

¹¹The LORD said to him, "Who gave man his mouth? Who makes him deaf or mute? Who gives him sight or makes him blind? Is it not I, the LORD? ¹²Now go; I will help you speak and will teach you what to say."

¹³But Moses said, "O Lord, please send someone else to do it."

¹⁴Then the LORD's anger burned against Moses and he said, "What about your brother, Aaron the Levite? I know he can speak well. He is already on his way to meet you, and his heart will be glad when he sees you. ¹⁵You shall speak to him and put words in his mouth; I will help both of you speak and will teach you what to do. ¹⁶He will speak to the people for you, and it will be as if he were your mouth and as if you were God to him. ¹⁷But take this staff in your hand so you can perform miraculous signs with it."

BEFORE BEGINNING OUR DISCUSSION of this section, we should say a word or two about its length. Exodus 3:1–4:17 cannot be further subdivided without affecting its theological message. As mentioned in the introduction, this is not the only section of Exodus that will have to be dealt with in this fashion. The plagues, the Book of the Covenant, and the tabernacle sections likewise form theologically coherent passages.

The Burning Bush (3:1–10)

THE ABRUPT ANNUNCIATION in 2:23–25 of God's presence with his people sets the stage for what is commonly referred to as the "call of Moses." Yahweh is indeed with his people, and he is about to show precisely how his presence will be manifest to them. Our introduction to Moses in this phase of his life finds him pasturing the flock of his father-in-law, Jethro.[1] He leads the sheep to the "far side of the desert," which piques one's curiosity: Why? Is there a lack of suitable grazing pasture available near his home? What possible benefit would a shepherd derive from herding his flock a significant distance through the desert? Is it possible that Moses drives his sheep to a certain location because he himself is being driven by a higher force?

Of course, it is no accident that Moses winds up at "Horeb,[2] the mountain of God." As he was driven from his home to Midian in 2:11–25, Israel's deliverer is driven further into the desert; he is to be prepared there for the task ahead. Even his vocation serves to shape his character. Shepherding was a common occupation in the ancient Near East, so it is no surprise to find Moses occupied with such work. From a theological point of view, however, the significance of such an occupation cannot be missed: He who will soon become the shepherd of God's people undergoes training in Midian.[3]

Moses arrives near the mountain and sees an astonishing sight: a bush that burns without being consumed. The narrator tells us at the outset the significance of this sight: "The angel of the LORD appeared[4] to him" (3:2). Moses

---

1. There is some discrepancy between 3:1 and 2:18, where Moses' father-in-law's name is Reuel (see comments on 2:18). In my view, the two names do not suggest two traditions or sources brought together by a redactor, a conclusion reached by a number of commentators. It seems to me that it is best not to ferret out any meaning in these alternative names, but to treat them simply as two names for the same person (e.g., George Ruth, better known as Babe Ruth), or perhaps Jethro as a priestly title. An unequivocal solution is not forthcoming.

2. Horeb and Sinai, somewhat like Jethro and Reuel, seem to be alternate names for the same site, although some commentators suggest that Horeb may be "a slightly wider term than 'Sinai,' " designating the region rather than simply the mountain (Driver, *Book of Exodus*, 19; see also Sarna, *Exodus*, 14). On the centuries-old debate on the possible locations of the mountain, see Houtman, *Exodus*, 1:116–20; R. L. Cate, *Exodus* (Layman's Bible Book Commentary; Nashville: Broadman, 1979), 28–29. The word "Sinai" is not used in Exodus until 16:1.

3. See comments above on 2:16–17. See also Ps. 77:20 and Num. 27:15–17. Ancient reflection on this theological theme may be found in *Ex. Rab.* 2.2–3. An excerpt from this passage reads as follows: "Our Rabbis said that when Moses our teacher, peace be upon him, was tending the flock of Jethro in the wilderness, a little kid escaped from him. He ran after it until it reached a shady place. When it reached the shady place, there appeared to view a pool of water and the kid stopped to drink. When Moses approached it, he said: 'I did not know that you ran away because of thirst; you must be weary.' So he placed the kid on his shoulder and walked away. Thereupon God said: 'Because thou hast mercy in leading the flock of a mortal, thou wilt assuredly tend my flock Israel'" (*Midrash Rabbah: Exodus*, trans. S. M. Lehrman [London/New York: Soncino, 1983], 49).

4. "Appeared" is the Niphal (passive) of the verb *ra'ah*, "to see." This root serves to connect the announcement in 2:25 that God "saw" the Israelites and the various repetitions of this verb in 3:2, 4, 7 (emphatic: "I have indeed seen"), 9, 16; 4:1, 5, 14. Houtman, however, does not consider the use of this root to be of any significance (*Exodus*, 1:335).

is not yet aware of this, but he is about to come face-to-face with the God of his ancestors. The precise identity of the angel of the Lord has always been a matter of debate. The Hebrew can also be translated "messenger of the LORD," which is precisely the role this angel plays. Throughout the Old Testament, this mysterious figure is closely identified, if not equated, with Yahweh himself. We see this already in verse 4: "The LORD saw. . . ." Obviously, there is a close identity between these two.

Nevertheless, it is best not to think of the two figures as simply equated. We should see this in the context of the ancient Near East, where messengers normally spoke for the sender. We see this phenomenon throughout the prophetic writings of the Old Testament. When the prophets brought God's message to Israel, they typically spoke for God in the first person; e.g., "The LORD said, 'I am bringing a nation against you,'" rather than, "The LORD said that he is bringing a nation against you." Simply equating the angel of the Lord with Yahweh tends to obliterate the clear fact that they are presented as two distinct figures in the Old Testament.[5]

These two, then, are to be identified in some sense, yet they are distinct from each other. This close relationship has led many to suggest that the angel of the Lord is an Old Testament manifestation of the incarnate Christ. This notion is worth considering. It is, if anything, certainly true from a theological point of view. The notion of the close relationship in the Old Testament between the messenger/angel of the Lord and Yahweh himself is something that is fully manifested in the person of Christ, who is both one with the Father yet distinct from him as the second person of the Trinity. This not to say, however, that the angel of the Lord *is* a preincarnate manifestation of Christ. Rather, the angel of the Lord foreshadows Christ in the same way that Moses, the priesthood, or the sacrificial system do (see Heb. 3:1—6; 8:1—10:18). In the final analysis, the angel of the Lord remains a mysterious but prominent figure in the context of God's self-revelation to his people, and his role is ultimately fulfilled in Christ.

Another common element that regularly accompanies God's self-revelation is fire, seen here in the bush. Fire is a frequent sign of God's presence in Exodus (13:21; 19:18; 24:17; cf. Gen. 15:17; Ezek. 1:27; 8:2). Various explanations have been suggested for why this is the case. Philo, for example, offers an allegorical explanation, that the fire's inability to consume the bush symbolizes the Egyptians' inability to destroy Israel.[6] Such an explanation

---

5. Other Old Testament passages that speak of the angel of the Lord are: Gen. 16:7, 9, 11; 22:15; 31:11, 13; Num. 22:22–35; Judg. 2:1–5; 6:11–23; Zech. 3:1–6; 12:8.

6. Philo wrote extensively on Moses in a work called *De vita Mosis* (*On the Life of Moses*; see Loeb Classical Library, *Philo*, vol. 6. See p. 311 in that volume for Philo's explanation of the fire.

might find some support in the fiery furnace episode in Daniel 3:1–30 and Isaiah 43:2 ("when you walk through the fire, you will not be burned; the flames will not set you ablaze"). In the context of Exodus, however, a more suitable explanation presents itself. The fact that the bush is not consumed demonstrates that the fire's natural property is temporarily suspended. Fire normally burns wood, but here God holds it in abeyance.

This episode, then, presages the upheaval of the natural phenomena in the plagues and the crossing of the Red Sea. Bushes do not remain unscorched when on fire, but neither do rivers turn to blood. Frogs, flies, and locusts do not normally invade a nation. Gnats are not formed from dust. Hail and darkness do not fall on command. The firstborn of a nation do not die all in one night. Seas do not form walls of water. Moses would have been wise to learn a lesson from this burning bush. The God who is calling him is the God over creation. The natural phenomena do his bidding; all are under his control. In light of this fact, made clear in the burning bush, Moses' excuses in 4:1–17 to be exonerated from his responsibility are almost comical.

The burning bush and its significance remain a curiosity for us as it did for Moses. We would like to go over and take a closer look, much as Moses did (3:3), but we cannot. We should respect the mystery that neither we nor the writer himself can fully explain. What is known, however, is that Moses draws near to the bush and is met by God. We come, then, to that point in the narrative that informed readers (as the Israelites certainly were) have been anticipating since the opening verses of the book. Moses—the Hebrew turned Egyptian, turned exile, turned shepherd—has an audience with Yahweh. Now God's plan of deliverance begins in earnest.

God initiates the encounter by calling "Moses! Moses!" (3:4). This repetition of one's name is a common feature in the Old Testament when God speaks to someone (cf. Abraham in Gen. 22:11; Jacob in 46:2; Samuel in 1 Sam. 3:10). Moses' response ("Here I am") is somewhat abrupt.[7] Does he know who is speaking to him? Is this his first encounter with Yahweh, the God of Israel? Is he expecting some sort of divine encounter as he makes his way to see the bush? We have here another all-too-typical gap in the narrative. It would be nice to know the degree to which Moses knew about Israel's God before this time. Access to such information would also help us understand the alleged "revelation" of the divine name Yahweh in 3:14–15 (see below).

---

7. "Here I am" seems like an inappropriate response, almost flippant, in light of the magnitude of the encounter. This phrase is a translation of the Hebrew *hinneni*, which can also be translated (albeit inadequately), "It is I" or "Behold, it is I." No translation captures the essence of the original. Perhaps it would be best simply to think of it as a "yes" response. Plastaras suggests, "Here I am! At your service!" (*The God of Exodus*, 64).

Yahweh sets the tone immediately: Moses must know first and foremost that he is in the presence of a holy God. In 3:5, God gives him two commands, both of which are justified on the basis that Moses is on holy ground. "Do not come any closer. . . .[8] Take off your sandals." It is worth noting that Moses is *not* told to stop advancing *until* he removes his sandals, for a command to come closer is never given. The site is so holy that Moses has no right to be there: "Stay where you are—not another step."

Why then must he remove his sandals? This is a sign of reverence common in the ancient Near East, a practice that continues to this day.[9] Joshua is commanded to do the same in Joshua 5:15. There the "commander of LORD's army " (another messenger reminiscent of "the angel of the LORD") appears to Joshua just before the fall of Jericho. As in Exodus 3, through a divine encounter a leader is commissioned to do battle with those forces that oppose God's people.

Yahweh announces himself to Moses as the "God of your father, the God of Abraham, the God of Isaac and the God of Jacob" (3:6). Whereas God's first words to Moses are an announcement of his holiness, his second words are a reminder of the past; we revisit here the theme of the previous chapters—"continuity with the past." God makes known to Moses who he is: the God of Moses' father Amram[10] and the God of their ancient ancestors. Yahweh is the God of the present and the past. Here God is either informing Moses of what he has forgotten during his long exile from his people or is being told for the first time who God is. The former is more likely, since the reference to the patriarchs implies that Moses is aware, at least to a certain extent, of his Israelite heritage.

The emphasis of 3:6 is not on the message spoken, but on this voice in the bush identifying himself as that God. The first person pronoun (*ʾanoki*) makes the Hebrew phrase emphatic: "*I* am the God of your father . . ." (see also 3:12). In other words, "I am the one you have heard about [albeit vaguely]; I am the God of your ancestors, I am the God of your very own father." Moses responds appropriately by hiding his face, too afraid to look on him whom he had earlier casually gone over to look at. What begins as a curiosity in verse 3 turns into a source of fear and reverence. Moses is getting a crash course in holy etiquette. He is to be the redeemer of Israel.

Yahweh continues speaking in 3:7; he gets closer to the point of why he has called this audience with Moses, the shepherd. The Lord has seen, has

---

8. The Hebrew is more abrupt than the English implies: "Do not come near here."

9. See Houtman, *Exodus*, 1:351–53; Durham, *Exodus*, 31; see also Sarna, *Exodus*, 15.

10. The Hebrew of v. 6 is singular, "God of your [i.e., Moses'] father" rather than "God of your fathers." Some ancient versions (see also Acts 7:32, which follows LXX) have "God of your fathers," which make the following phrase "the God of Abraham . . ." appositional, i.e., further defining "God of your fathers."

heard, and knows what his people have been enduring under Egyptian oppression. The language of this verse unmistakably echoes that of 2:24—25.[11] Yahweh is well aware of what the situation is and he will soon do something about it. Israel is "my people." He has a special interest in their safety. He is, after all, the God of Abraham, Isaac, and Jacob. His relationship with them has a long history. He has heard their cry and tells Moses that he has "come down to rescue them." To "come down" is typical biblical language to describe what God does when he intervenes in human affairs (e.g., Gen. 11:5, 7; 18:21). He will "bring them up" from one land and into another, from the land of Egypt, which meant captivity and slavery, and into "a land flowing with milk and honey."

Both of these phrases in quotation marks are common refrains to those familiar with the content not only of Exodus but of the Pentateuch as a whole. The verb "to bring up" (a form of which has already appeared in 1:10; see comment there) is the typical expression used to describe Israel's deliverance from Egypt.[12] The description given of the Promised Land is also a familiar one (Ex. 3:17; 13:5; 33:3; Lev. 20:24; Num. 13:27; 14:8; 16:14; Deut. 6:3; 8:7—9; 11:9ff.).[13] The list of the nations that occupy that land also provides a connection to passages throughout the Pentateuch and the conquest narratives.[14] This verse serves as a focal point that brings together God's impending redemptive act and a broad sweep of biblical imagery.

In 3:9—10 God makes the announcement: The Israelites' cry has reached high to heaven,[15] and this is what Yahweh tells Moses: "So now, go. I am sending you to Pharaoh." God's plan is revealed. The outcast is chosen to bring God's special people out of Egypt. This announcement, however, seems somewhat at odds with verse 8, which clearly implies that God is the one who will be doing the delivering. Of course, no contradiction exists. Moses is the *means* by which God will work his own redemptive strength. There is, in

---

11. See Houtman, *Exodus*, 1:354; Cassuto, *Commentary on Exodus*, 33; Fretheim, *Exodus*, 59—61.

12. The verb is ʿalah. Another commonly used verb is yaṣaʾ, "to go out."

13. Houtman (*Exodus*, 1:357) suggests that the reference to milk and honey is mythological language referring to divine sustenance, which evokes images of paradise. Fretheim seems to be in line with this view, for he sees a connection here between paradise and the "new creation" theme (*Exodus*, 58—59). In this respect, the allusion to paradise is another example of deliverance spoken of in creation language, a theme encountered already in chapter 1 (see comments), and to which we will return repeatedly. Entrance into Canaan is, in a manner of speaking, a return to the garden.

14. A similar list of nations occurs in Gen. 15:19—21; Ex. 13:5; 23:23, 28; 33:2; 34:11; Deut. 7:1; 20:17; Josh. 3:10; 9:1; 11:3; 12:8; 24:11, although the number of nations varies considerably.

15. The allusion to the Sodom episode (Gen. 18:21) seems clear, thus providing another connection to Genesis.

---

fact, a recurring ambiguity throughout Exodus concerning who is doing the delivering: God or Moses? But this ambiguity is intentional and is expressed as early as 4:16, where Moses "becomes like God" (pers. trans.)[16] to Aaron. Moses and Yahweh's roles are sometimes difficult to distinguish.

Thus far, Yahweh has done all the talking. The announcement has been made. As soon as the chosen messenger relays God's word to the Israelites, they will be begin to feel the sought-after relief from their misery. But how will this messenger react? Will he be a willing participant in God's mighty act?

Moses Doubts Himself: "Who Am I?" (3:11–12)

ONE MIGHT THINK that Moses would skip with joy all the way from Mount Horeb to Egypt with the good news. The promise of redemption from Egyptian cruelty was foretold as far back as Abraham's day (Gen. 15:13–14). Now Yahweh is finally going to do something about it, and Moses is privileged to bear the news. But in a fashion more like a pouting child than a warrior singled out by his commander for an honorable task, Moses begins to question God's wisdom—not once, not twice, but no less than <u>five times.</u>

Moses' first question is actually quite reasonable: "Who am I?" This can be read not so much as a declaration of Moses' own lack of self-confidence as his refusing to usurp God's glory. After all, God says in verse 8 that *he* will deliver them, as he had promised Jacob in Genesis 46:3–4:

> "I am God, the God of your father," he said. "Do not be afraid to go down to Egypt, for I will make you into a great nation there. I will go down to Egypt with you and *I will surely bring you back again.* And Joseph's own hand will close your eyes." (italics added)

Is it not the divine prerogative to save? This should not be a human being's responsibility. Perhaps Moses' question is actually a show of true humility. He is not God, and hence *he* cannot bring the Israelites out of Egypt.

Moses seems to be making a legitimate point. Verses 6–9 give the clear impression that *Yahweh* is about to do a mighty deed (see v. 6 and the emphatic verbal construction in verse 7: "I have indeed seen . . . my people"; "I have heard"; "I am concerned"). One expects Yahweh to say in verse 10: "I will go to Pharaoh and give my people decisive victory." Unexpectedly, however, this verse throws it all in Moses' lap. This is what Moses objects to, and we can perhaps sympathize with him.

Moses repeats the pronoun in his response to God in verse 11: "Who am I [*'anoki*]?" In other words, who is the "I" that is going to be doing the sav-

---

16. The word "like" is not in the Hebrew of 4:16 but is implied. The point is that Moses is being infused with divine strength for the task at hand. See further comments below.

ing, Moses or Yahweh? God's response to Moses' question in verse 12 settles the matter: "I will be with you." Here we have a clear play on words with the "I AM" phrase in verse 14 ("I will be" and "I am" are the same word in Hebrew). The "I AM" is with Moses. Moses' assertion that *he* cannot do this task is correct but entirely beside the point. He is not doing the saving. Moses says, "I cannot do this." Yahweh responds, "You're not, I am."

In addition, God offers Moses a sign that he will be with him. This is a common theme in Exodus.[17] The question, however, is the precise identity of the sign in 3:12. The NIV offers one possible interpretation: that the Israelites will worship God on Mount Horeb after they have come out of Egypt. The problem with this interpretation, however, is that this sign will not be validated until after the Exodus, which does not help Moses at this particular moment, since the sign is for Moses' benefit.[18] Others suggest that the sign might be the bush itself.[19] It is perhaps Moses' dissatisfaction with this sign that prompts him to query God further.

Moses Doubts His Reception: "What Is Your Name?" (3:13–22)

MOSES IS NOT only conscious of his own lack of qualifications, he is also concerned about how his lack of qualifications will be perceived by the very Israelites he is being sent to deliver. The central issue surrounding this passage is the disclosure of the divine name to Moses. These verses (esp. vv. 14–15) have attracted much scholarly activity, documented as far back as intertestamental Judaism, and the discussion has lost little momentum.

Moses projects onto the Israelites themselves his own doubts about the task set before him. Again, to a certain extent this makes perfect sense. All the Israelites know of Moses, if they know anything at all, is that he was brought up as an Egyptian, committed murder, and is a wanted man. What credentials does he carry? If the first sign was meant to convince Moses, the second is meant to convince the Israelites. Whereas the first objection Moses brings is, "I don't think I can do this," the second objection is, "No one else will think I can do this, either."

To buttress his argument, Moses anticipates a question he expects to hear from the Israelites: "What is God's name?" This raises a number of

---

17. See 4:8, 9, 17, 28, 30; 7:3, 5; 8:16–19; 10:1; 12:13; 13:9, 16; 31:13, 17.

18. Durham, however, suggests a rationale for this delayed sign: The reason the gathering of the Israelites at Mount Horeb is mentioned as the sign is that the Israelites *then* will experience what Moses is experiencing *now*, i.e., theophany (*Exodus*, 33). Such an explanation, although still dissatisfying in light of Moses' self-doubt, fits nicely into the theme discussed in the previous section, i.e., Moses' experiences foreshadow those of the Israelites. ✓

19. For solutions and discussions on this issue, see Childs, *Book of Exodus*, 56–60; Sarna, *Exodus*, 17; Houtman, *Exodus*, 1:364–65.

questions. (1) Does Moses anticipate this question because the Israelites do not know the name of their God? In other words, would the Israelites be saying that they have heard of him but they just have no idea what his name is? (2) Or have the Israelites forgotten the name of their God because of their prolonged stay in a foreign land? (3) Or is this question designed to test Moses' knowledge? In other words, "We know God's name, Moses, but let's see if you know it too."[20] (4) Perhaps Moses is asking for his own benefit, so that he, too, can know the name of him who has sent him and thus gain more credibility in their eyes. Although Moses' question is valid from his point of view, he still seems to be fixated on his role in God's plan more than on what God will do through him. We see once again the repetition of the pronoun *ʾanoki*: "Suppose *I* go to the Israelites" (v. 13). Moses has still not learned that it is by the Lord's might that this great deed will be accomplished.

In 3:14, God appears to give a direct response to Moses' request. The central issues before us are: (1) What exactly is the name that God gives? (2) Is this a new name not known before, or is it the reiteration of a known (though perhaps forgotten) name?

God answers Moses by saying "I AM WHO I AM." These three Hebrew words (*ʾehyeh ʾašer ʾehyeh*) are among the most discussed of any in the Old Testament. The clause is made up of the first person singular imperfect of the verb *hayah* ("to be") plus the relative pronoun *ʾašer* plus the verb repeated. One question that has always vexed commentators is how this clause should be translated. Options include "I am who I am," "I will be who I will be," "I create what I create."[21] But more important than simply translating the words is that matter of what the words convey. Houtman suggests "What does it matter who I am?"[22] This is a promising solution. It does not seem that "I AM WHO I AM" is the name itself, but a preparatory

---

20. On this third option, see Houtman, *Exodus*, 1:366. This may also reflect the "rejection of the leader" theme seen in chapter 2, which becomes more pronounced in later chapters.

21. In addition to the commentaries (see esp. Childs, *Book of Exodus*, 60–70), the following articles are helpful in laying out the various issues involved: D. N. Freedman, "The Name of the God of Moses," *JBL* 79 (1960): 151–56; R. Abba, "The Divine Name Yahweh," *JBL* 80 (1961): 320–28; E. C. B. MacLaurin, "YHWH: The Origin of the Tetragrammaton," *VT* 12 (1962): 439–63; B. Albrektson, "On the Syntax of אהיה אשר אהיה in Exodus 3:14," in *Words and Meanings: Essays Presented to David Winton Thomas*, ed. P. R. Ackroyd and B. Lindars (Cambridge: Cambridge Univ. Press, 1968), 15–28; D. J. McCarthy, "Exod. 3:14: History, Philology and Theology," *CBQ* 40 (1978): 311–22; C. D. Isbell, "The Divine Name אהיה As a Symbol of Presence in Israelite Tradition," *HAR* 2 (1978): 101–18; G. S. Ogden, "Idem per Idem: Its Use and Meaning," *JSOT* 53 (1992): 107–20. See also Plastaras, *The God of Exodus*, 86–100; Gowan, *Theology in Exodus*, 80–85.

22. *Exodus*, 1:367; see also 1:94–100.

comment before the name is given. The name itself seems to be announced in the following clause in v. 14: "This is what you are to say to the Israelites, 'I AM has sent me to you.'"

In this sense, "I AM WHO I AM" can be understood (and this is the solution I prefer) as a near refusal to dignify Moses' question with an answer: "I AM WHO I AM; they know very well who I am. What a question!" What follows is the announcement of the name Moses is to give to the Israelites: "I AM" (*?ehyeh*).[23] The play on the verb "to be" may also suggest God's unswerving existence with his people from the patriarchal period onward. This is supported fairly clearly by the pun with verse 12: "I will be (*?ehyeh*) with you." At least one of the reasons for using this name is to highlight God's continued existence with his people. What follows in verse 15 is further elaboration on God's name: "The LORD [Yahweh], the God of your fathers—the God of Abraham, the God of Isaac and the God of Jacob." Both "Yahweh" (*yhwh*) and "I AM" (*?ehyeh*) are apparently derived from the same root "to be" (*hyh*).

With this in mind, we return to the two questions asked above: Which of these is actually God's name, and is it a revelation of a name hitherto unknown? Regarding the first question, "I AM WHO I AM" is not God's name but a preparatory comment that introduces the following announcement. The divine name, instead, seems to be "I AM": "This is what you are to say to the Israelites: 'I AM has sent me to you'" (v. 14). What follows in verse 15 is not the divine name itself but an elaboration of verse 14.[24] "Say to the Israelites, 'The LORD, the God of your fathers—the God of Abraham, the God of Isaac and the God of Jacob—has sent me to you.'"

The second question is equally important and is connected to the first: Is there any new information imparted to Moses here? To be more specific, is there anything here that is revealed for the first time, or is it simply a reiteration of a name that has been known? As is well known, 3:14—15 has been a crucial passage adduced in support for the widely accepted Documentary Hypothesis. It is far beyond the scope of these few pages to interact in any great depth with this hypothesis, but a word or two is in order.

---

23. See C. D. Isbell, "The Divine Name," 102–5 along with some of the sources cited in his bibliography.

24. For a thoughtful presentation of the opposite view, see R. W. L. Moberly, *The Old Testament of the Old Testament: Patriarchal Narratives and Mosaic Yahwism* (Minneapolis: Fortress, 1992), 13–26. Moberly essentially argues that 3:14 *introduces* the revelation of the divine name in v. 15 rather than being the answer to Moses' question, which, in my opinion, is *elaborated* in v. 15. Although I disagree, Moberly's insights are quite perceptive (although not as firm as he seems to suggest) and should prove helpful to readers who may not be convinced by the analysis I have offered here.

Exodus 3:14—15 has typically been understood by source critics as a product of the E (Elohist)[25] source. According to this hypothesis, the name of Yahweh is revealed here for the first time. But one asks, then, what of the recurring uses of "Yahweh" throughout Genesis? How can God's name "Yahweh" be revealed here for the first time if it has been used regularly previously? The answer given is that the previous uses of Yahweh in the Pentateuch are from a different source, the J source.[26]

It should be noted, however, that if Exodus 3:14—15 does not refer to the *revelation* of God's name but merely to the reiteration of a known name, it would require some rethinking on the part of those who hold to some form of the Documentary Hypothesis. But the argument I have outlined above pushes us in another direction. If the "name" that God gives Moses to bring to the Israelites is "I AM" and not "Yahweh," then discussions over whether Yahweh's name is new or not are misdirected. In the scheme I have presented, the name Yahweh is not the focus of attention here; this name is not presented as anything novel. The answer to Moses' question, "What is your name," is answered in verse 14, not verse 15. Moreover, the fact that the God of Israel is nowhere else in the Old Testament called "I AM" (with the possible, though unlikely, exception of Hos. 1:9) suggests that "I AM" was never intended as a serious answer to Moses' query.

---

25. This is the E in the well-known JEDP of the Documentary Hypothesis. It stands for the Elohist source, since, it is argued, Elohim is the name of God used by this writer throughout Genesis and up to Ex. 3:14—15, where "Yahweh" is supposedly revealed for the first time. E is thought to stem from roughly the eighth century B.C. The Documentary Hypothesis reached its clearest and most forceful expression in the work of Julius Wellhausen in the second half of the nineteenth century, although the antecedents of Wellhausen's theory reach back at least to the time of the philosopher Spinoza in the middle third of the seventeenth century. Discussions of the history of this scholarly debate can be found in most commentaries on this verse and will not be repeated here. B. Childs does a particularly good job of highlighting the important issues (*Book of Exodus*, 112—14). See also R. E. Friedman's popular (although somewhat overconfident and at times even self-congratulatory) presentation of one dominant understanding of the Documentary Hypothesis, *Who Wrote the Bible?* (New York: Harper and Row, 1989). Recently, two helpful and concise overviews of the history of Pentateuchal studies have appeared: G. Wenham, "Pentateuchal Studies Today," *Themelios* 22 (1996): 3—13; D. L. Peterson, "The Formation of the Pentateuch," *Old Testament Interpretation: Past, Present, and Future*, ed. J. L. Mays et al. (Nashville: Abingdon, 1995), 31—45. In recent years, however, this scholarly "consensus" is being questioned more and more. There have always been diverse opinions on the authorship of the Pentateuch, and this is more so the case today than ever. A thorough consensus does not exist. See R. N. Whybray, *Introduction to the Pentateuch* (Grand Rapids: Eerdmans, 1995), 12—28, and G. Wenham, "Pentateuchal Studies Today," *Themelios* 22 (1996): 3—13.

26. "J" is the first letter in the German spelling of Yahweh, a reminder of the pervasive influence German scholarship has had on modern notions of Pentateuchal authorship.

Nevertheless, if we concede for a moment the possibility that "Yahweh" is the name that Moses is told to give to the people, there still remain several factors that militate against understanding "Yahweh" as a new, hitherto unknown appellation.[27]

(1) A new name would not have helped Moses if the problem he is facing is a lack of credibility on the part of the Israelites.[28] Moses needs to establish his authority. Bringing to the Israelites a new name would only bear weight if Moses' authority were already established. That establishing Moses' authority is a central concern here is supported by verse 16. Moses is to gather the elders together first in an effort to legitimize his mission in their eyes. Of course, the name may be new to Moses, but this speaks only to his lack of knowledge and not to the question whether "Yahweh" was an unknown name before this encounter.

(2) The clause *"This* is my name forever, the name by which I am to be remembered from generation to generation" in the latter half of verse 15 refers most naturally not simply to the tetragrammaton toward the beginning of the verse but to the entire preceding phrase: "Yahweh, the God of your fathers—the God of Abraham, the God of Isaac and the God of Jacob." I do not think anyone maintains that God's association with the patriarchs is first revealed now to Moses. If "God of your fathers," and so forth, is not revealed here for the first time, then neither is "Yahweh." Furthermore, subsequent references in this narrative to how Moses is to present God's name to the Israelites (3:16; 4:5) show that the crucial element in Yahweh's self-description in 3:15 is precisely this connection to the patriarchs, not the tetragrammaton.

(3) The use of "Yahweh" in 3:2, 4, 7 clearly indicates that it is not a term introduced here in 3:14–15 for the first time. Of course, by source-critical standards as noted above, this is a weak argument, since these verses can simply be assigned to the J source (which a redactor has brought together and allowed the tension to stand). Yet source critics are left to explain why this tension was allowed to remain and if the flow of the narrative before us lends itself to another, perhaps more straightforward explanation.[29] If there

---

27. I should also make clear that my reason for adopting this solution is not a broader desire to debunk the Documentary Hypothesis. Although I have found this hypothesis to be wholly inadequate for explaining the Pentateuch, my views on the proper interpretation of 3:14–15 are not fueled by any such negative concerns. I am attempting to argue as best as I can from the data the narrative provides.

28. See similarly Sarna, *Exodus*, 18.

29. Too often, appeal is made to a theory of a "mindless redactor," who evidently is not bothered by such tensions as the presence of the name Yahweh in the immediate context of vv. 14–15, where that name is supposedly introduced for the first time. In my view, it has never been adequately explained why, according to source criticism, *authors* are assumed to be consistent in their use of names for God and other terms, but redactors are perfectly happy to bring these sources together in seemingly contradictory ways.

is variation between "God" (²*lohim*) and "LORD" (*yhwh*) both before and after 3:14—15, then at least from a literary point of view, the narrative cannot be read as a new revelation of God's name.[30] This factor should not simply be ignored.

(4) Moreover, the mention of the patriarchs in verse 6 precludes reading verse 15 as a new name, since (cf. [2], above) the reference to the patriarchs should be included as part of the announcement.

(5) The phrase "forever" (*l*ᶜ*olam*) in verse 15 likely refers to perpetuity through all time, that is, backwards and forwards (see the similar use of "forever" in 15:18). In other words, Yahweh has always been God's name. This is further supported by Yahweh's specific answer to Moses in verse 15. In verse 13, Moses intends to tell the Israelites that "the God of your fathers" had appeared to him. The response that Yahweh gives in verse 15 can be understood as a correction of Moses' truncated designation. Moses says that he will refer to God simply as "the God of your fathers." God, however, insists that he spell it out fully, as if to say, "No, Moses. Tell them that I am Yahweh, the God of their fathers, the God of Abraham. . . ."[31] The force of verse 15 rests on the assumption that Yahweh is not a new name. Its proper understanding is: "I am Yahweh, the God of the patriarchs. This has always been my name."

(6) If "Yahweh" is the new name revealed here for the first time, and if this is the vital piece of information the Israelites need to verify Moses' status, why is it not mentioned in Moses' initial meeting with the Israelites in 4:29—31?[32] Why does this momentous event, the revelation of the divine name, recede into oblivion?

It seems, then, that the purpose of 3:14—15 is not to introduce a new name, but to underscore the precise identity of the God who is now addressing Moses. In fact, the force of this divine encounter is considerably lessened if Moses were hearing God's name for the first time. Moses is not receiving a new bit of information. Rather, God is leaving no doubt in Moses' mind who it is that is speaking with him. God is saying to him: "I am Yahweh, the 'I AM,' the God of the patriarchs. The one you have heard about is the one speaking with you now."

But if this is not the revelation of a new name, what does the question Moses asks in verse 13 mean: "What is your name?" I suggest what seems to be the straightforward implication of the question: The name is not known (or perhaps has been forgotten) by Moses. Nothing here implies that the

---

30. See E. J. Young, "The Call of Moses," *WTJ* 29 (1966—67): 117—35 and 30 (1967—68): 1—23 (see esp. Young's comments in 29:129).

31. See Houtman, *Exodus*, 1:368.

32. See also Jacob, *Exodus*, 65—71.

Israelites in general are ignorant of it. Again, they would have to know the name if Moses' appeal to it is to have any force in legitimizing his message.[33]

Moses is to bring his message to the elders of Israel (3:16) and must tell them that God will bring them up (again, the Heb. verb ʿalah) out of Egypt and into the Promised Land (3:17, similar to 3:8). In a somewhat unexpected development, after the elders listen to Moses they are *all* to go to Pharaoh and demand release (3:18). As noted above, there is some ambiguity concerning who is the one bringing the Israelites out of Egypt, Moses or God. Here, everyone gets into the act.

What is of more immediate concern is the nature of the request that Moses and the elders are to make: "Let us take a three-day journey into the desert to offer sacrifices to the LORD our God." How are we to understand this? The tension, of course, is that verses 8, 10, and 17 leave no impression whatsoever that a three-day journey is all that God has in mind. Calling for a three-day journey seems to imply that after three days the Israelites will return to Egypt. How might this be understood?

One possible explanation is that this is another "cunning" response, similar to that given by the midwives in 1:19. Although they have no intention of returning after three days, the request serves to show Pharaoh for what he really is: an oppressive ruler who won't even let the Israelites fulfill their responsibilities to their God.[34] But most commentators suggest that "three-day journey" simply indicates a lengthy journey of some sort, that is, the amount of time needed to get to where they need to go for their celebration without necessarily implying a return trip.[35] One can hardly think that Moses is to go into Pharaoh's presence and communicate to him anything other than God's full demand: release of the slaves. Moses' words, according to this explanation, are not a display of cunning, but a bold command to let the people go.

Another element that may raise an eyebrow is the elders' declaration that "the God of the Hebrews has met with *us*." On the surface, this appears to be pure fantasy. The point, however, is that this is an implicit statement of the reception of Moses' authority. They accept Moses' testimony as their own. This is another hint of a theme we have seen previously: Moses'

---

33. Another solution offered is that Moses is not asking for God to reveal the name, but for God to explain the significance of the name (Young, "Call of Moses," 19 and n. 42). This is worth considering seriously, but seems a bit too subtle in the context of the narrative.

34. See Driver, *Book of Exodus*, 25; Houtman, *Exodus*, 1:375–77. Houtman underscores the point that Moses is to introduce Yahweh to Pharaoh as a national God ("the God of the *Hebrews*"). In accordance with ancient Near Eastern customs, Pharaoh should have respected the Israelites' request and let them leave to perform their required religious duties. Fretheim refers to Moses' request as an "initial negotiating stance" (*Exodus*, 66).

35. Sarna, *Exodus*, 19; G. A. F. Knight, *Theology As Narration: A Commentary on the Book of Exodus* (Grand Rapids: Eerdmans, 1976), 26.

experiences are representative of the group as a whole. The theophany Moses witnesses is on behalf of the entire community. The community's vicarious experience of the initial theophany here foreshadows their own experience later on at the mountain (19:1–20:21).

Yahweh continues his speech to Moses by predicting that Pharaoh will not listen to reasoned persuasion, even if the demands are couched in as nonthreatening a manner as possible (3:19). Only a "mighty hand" will compel him. This phrase foreshadows the entire plague narrative and deliverance through the sea, where Yahweh displays his power with a "mighty hand and an outstretched arm" (e.g., Deut. 4:34; 5:15). Yahweh will "stretch out" (*ša-lah*) his hand against Pharaoh by a series of "wonders" (plagues), and, in a delightful pun, Pharaoh will succumb and release (*šalah*) the slaves: Pharaoh "sends" the Israelites away in response to God's "sending" the plagues.[36]

Not only will Pharaoh send them away, but the Egyptians will have such pity for the slaves that they will not allow the Israelites to go away empty-handed (3:21–22). The women are to ask for silver, gold, and clothing for their children, a theme repeated in 11:2–3 and 12:35–36. Why is this important? Perhaps they are being prepared for the long desert march to Mount Horeb, although one wonders whether food and water might not serve them better in the desert than silver and gold. It has been argued since the intertestamental period[37] that this is payment to the Israelites from their Egyptian captors for years of slavery. Part of the motive for such a interpretation is to alleviate the possible moral difficulty of God's people "plundering" (v. 22) the Egyptians, since this would seem somewhat spiteful for a holy nation.

Yet this moral difficulty is hardly surprising in light of some of the things the Israelites are justified in doing later on (e.g., total destruction of Ai and Jericho). "Plundering" implies a degree of hostility, but this is no rare commodity in Israelite history, nor can one say that the Egyptians did not deserve it. Why only women were to do the plundering may suggest the decisive triumph of Israel over Egypt: The women, the weaker members of the population, are to carry out the deed after God has made the Egyptians favorably disposed toward them.[38]

Moses Doubts His Reception: Three Signs Are Given (4:1–9)

THE ANSWERS GOD gives to Moses' first two questions are apparently not enough to convince him (4:1). The reader may begin to get suspicious at this point: Is Moses relaying legitimate concerns, or is he just trying to extricate

---

36. Cassuto, *Commentary on Exodus*, 43.

37. For example, *Jubilees* 48:18; Philo's *De vita Mosis* 1.140–42; Ezekiel the Tragedian's *Exagoge* 162–66. See also Houtman, *Exodus*, 1:382–86; Cassuto, *Commentary on Exodus*, 44.

38. Houtman, *Exodus*, 1:386.

himself from his responsibility? For whatever reason, Moses feels that simply dropping God's name will not be enough to convince the Israelites. Simply showing that he knows the name of the God of Israel is no proof that he is God's deliverer, since God's name is widely known. Moses needs to bring them more proof.

As noted above, can one really blame Moses in light of previous experience in 2:14? The obvious point should not be missed: Moses is concerned not with whether *Pharaoh* will recognize his authority, but whether *Israel* will. (The people's reaction as early as ch. 5, and intermittently throughout the Pentateuch, bears out Moses' concern.) God answers Moses' objection by providing him with three signs that he is to perform before the Israelites.

(1) The first sign is turning Moses' shepherd staff into a snake (4:2–5). Naturally Moses, being a shepherd, would have a staff in his hand. God uses the ordinary to do the extraordinary. In a manner of speaking, this first sign has much in common with the ten plagues that follow. The plagues are ordinary phenomena that God uses to do extraordinary things. There is nothing unusual about gnats, flies, frogs, and so forth. Had he wished, God could have conjured up hideous beasts and other supernatural phenomena to terrify the Egyptians into immediate submission.[39] Here too in 4:2–5, God could have performed some mind-boggling trick (make the sun stand still, an earthquake, a violent storm) to remove any doubt from Moses' mind that God is with him. Instead he asks, "What is that in your hand? A staff? Let me show you a little of who I am by doing something unexpected with it."

The staff turns into a snake. Why a snake? Likely because the snake represents a sign of Egyptian royal authority (think of a pharaoh's cobra-like headdress worn as a symbol of his authority).[40] Moses reacts to the snake by fleeing, which is to be expected. His reaction also serves to adumbrate the Egyptians' response to God's activity later in this book (9:20; 14:25, 27), where they, too, are said to flee.

Moses is then told to grab the snake by the tail, a dangerous move that demonstrates further God's dominion over creation for his purposes.[41] God's turning Moses' staff into a snake and Moses' grabbing the snake to turn it back into a staff symbolize the spiritual and political authority that God will impose through Moses on Egypt. The purpose of the sign is to demonstrate to the Israelites that Yahweh, the God of the patriarchs, has appeared to

---

39. See the apocryphal book the Wisd. Sol. 11:15–20.

40. Sarna writes, "The snake, the uraeus, represented the patron cobra-goddess of Lower Egypt" (*Exodus*, 20). Others suggest that turning the staff into a snake symbolizes God's power over the magic of snake-charming (Houtman, *Exodus*, 1:391).

41. Sarna (*Exodus*, 20) and Knight (*Theology As Narration*, 28–29) consider this a sign of Moses' faith in God.

Moses (4:5). This should be read in light of 3:15—that God wishes to establish in Moses' mind and in the minds of the Israelites that he is the God of the fathers. The God whom they have heard about is now revealed to them.

(2) The second sign is the skin disease that God first inflicts on Moses and then cures (4:6–7). It is not clear what kind of skin disease is referred to, but it almost certainly is not "leprosy" as we think of it today.[42] The significance of this second sign seems to be authority over disease and sickness, and as such may anticipate the infliction of pain in some of the plagues (e.g., boils). It may also prefigure Israel's experience: God will take an unclean nation and make it clean.[43] In this sense, Moses' experiences again represent those of the group.

(3) The first two signs are clearly intended to demonstrate to the Israelites that Moses is God's chosen deliverer. This is why they are given to Moses in the first place. Although none of the signs are explicitly said to be demonstrated before the Israelites, 4:29–31 clearly implies as much. The third sign (4:8–9), like the first one, is repeated before the Egyptians. The "staff to snake" sign is Moses' first demonstration to Pharaoh of God's power. For the most part Pharaoh remains unimpressed (7:10–13).

The third sign, changing water to blood, however, is different. For one thing, it is not actually performed before Moses here as the other two are. Moreover, this is an actual preview of the first plague (7:14–24). In fact, 4:8–9 seems careful to avoid calling this a "sign" (*ʾot*), as were the other two. Blood is a symbol of life and death, in this case life for the Egyptian slaves and death for their Egyptian captors. If the first two signs are not enough to convince the Israelites, the third "sign," which represents the onset of the plagues, will certainly do the trick. Turning water into blood symbolizes God's power over the elements, similar to the burning bush. It also symbolizes the power of Israel's God over the power of the Egyptian gods and the Egyptian nation, whose life force was the Nile.[44]

Moses Doubts His Reception: "I Am Ineloquent" (4:10–12)

MOSES' FOURTH OBJECTION focuses on another reason why he might not be received by his countrymen. He insists he is not an eloquent speaker; surely, anyone called to confront the king of Egypt and motivate his own people to follow must have powers of verbal persuasion. The precise nature of Moses' problem is difficult to identify. The Hebrew literally says, "I am not a man of

---

42. Houtman, *Exodus*, 1:395–96. A similar event happens to Miriam in Num. 12:10 and Gehazi in 2 Kings 5:27—both times as a sign of God's punishment.

43. Ibid., 1:399.

44. This aspect of the narrative will be brought out more fully below regarding the plagues.

words ... I am heavy [dull] of mouth and heavy [dull] of tongue" (4:10). But what exactly is the problem? Stuttering is one possibility, which is how the LXX seems to take it, but this is not explicit in the Hebrew.[45] Could it be that Moses had lost his command of Egyptian (the likely language with which he would have to confront Pharaoh) because of his years in exile? Or perhaps he has spent far too much time with the shepherding "blue-collar" set to have the diplomacy skills needed to engage a world leader in conversation.

Whatever the problem, legitimate or illegitimate, it is not enough to deflect God from his path of action. The significance of God's answer in 4:11–12 is that God is in control not only of the elements and of the Egyptian government (cf. the previous signs), but he is also in control over the messenger. The Lord directs the mouth, ears, and eyes (v. 11). Moses' "speech problem" is hardly a challenge.

We see here again the battle over which "I" should be the focus of attention. At the end of 4:10 Moses says, "I [ʾanoki] am slow of speech and tongue." Yahweh responds:

> Who gave man his mouth? Who makes him deaf or mute? Who gives him sight or makes him blind? Is it not I [ʾanoki], the LORD? Now go; I [ʾanoki] will help you speak and will teach you what to say.[46]

This play on words is hardly noticeable in the English. Moses feels his "I" is inadequate for the task; Yahweh responds by saying that it is his "I" that is to be reckoned with. Verse 12 is particularly striking. The clause "I will help you speak" literally translates, "I will be [ʾanoki ʾehyeh] with your mouth." The crowning rebuttal to Moses' complaint is an unmistakable allusion to the earlier conflict between the "I" of Moses and that of Yahweh (see esp. 3:14–15). Moses has nothing to argue about; "I AM" is with his mouth.

" *I* "

This exchange between Moses and Yahweh gets at the heart of Moses' repeated attempts to extricate himself from God's call. Moses seems to resist God's call because he assumes that he is playing the central role in the deliverance of the Israelites, whom God calls "*my* people" (3:7). What Moses does not yet understand is that God cares more about Israel's deliverance than he does, and God is fully capable of directing the means to bring this about. It is God who will bring his people out of Egypt. He will display his might precisely by working through weak and ordinary means. Moses has not yet learned that salvation is of the Lord.

---

45. It is possible, however, that some speech impediment is implied by v. 11. See Fretheim, *Exodus*, 71.

46. See also Deut. 18:18, which uses similar wording and seems to set up Moses as a paradigm for all future prophetic activity, those through whom God will speak.

Moses Refuses God's Call (4:13–17)

BY NOW MOSES should have learned this lesson, particularly in light of the reiteration of the "I AM" speech in God's last rebuttal to Moses. God could not have made it any clearer to Moses that his objections are inconsequential. Moses sees this and, left with no further "reasonable" argument against God's call, blurts out one final attempt to convince God of the error of his plan: "O Lord, please send someone else to do it" (4:13). The Hebrew of this verse is not entirely clear, but a striking thing is the manner in which Moses addresses God. Apparently, the stinging reminder in 4:12, that "I AM" is with him, shames Moses into using a "lesser" name for God than Yahweh, namely, *ʾadonay* ("Lord" in the NIV rather than "LORD").

No matter what, signs or no signs, whether or not God promises to be with him, Moses does not want to go. He is still viewing his call in light of his circumstances. But the point that Moses has yet to learn is that *his* circumstances are not the proper light in which to view his call. His earlier objections have been legitimate, and God met these objections head on, one by one. This last objection, however, is not based on some legitimate circumstance; Moses just doesn't want to do it. This is not a complaint God can address. Moses is not giving him a point that can be debated. He is simply putting his foot down and saying "no." Hence, the Lord becomes angry with him for the first time (4:14).

Yahweh not only becomes angry, but he also seems to give in to Moses' stubbornness. God is prepared to cripple the power of Egypt through Moses, but Moses is not to be the deliverer, as if the success of the mission rests on his shoulders. He is to occupy a more exalted position: God's "right-hand man." But he doesn't want the position. So now God finally gives in: "Aaron, your brother, is coming to meet you. Tell him what I have told you, and I will be *with your mouth and with his mouth*" [lit. trans.]. The wording of 4:15 is similar to that of verse 12: God will be *with* them and *teach* them. From Moses' point of view, he is now sharing the burden with someone else, but he is actually sharing the glory.

Verses 15–16 suggest that Moses' final refusal is closely related to his previous objection. Apparently, what still concerns Moses is his speech difficulty. To remedy this, God assigns Aaron to Moses to be "[his] mouth" (v. 16). Aaron's introduction here is somewhat startling. The text mentions that he is from the tribe of Levi. Certainly Moses does not need to hear this, as if he is not sure which Aaron the Lord is speaking about. After all, Moses is Aaron's brother, and so Moses is a Levite as well. Clearly this information is written more for the reader's benefit than Moses'. Reference to Aaron here as a Levite signals to the alert reader that Aaron's levitical pedigree will become important later on in his role as the leader of Israel's priesthood.

And we see Aaron's priestly role suggested here in the context of this passage: Aaron will speak for Moses. Moses is the mediator of the message, but Aaron is the one who will relay that message as he receives it from Moses, who will be, as it were, "God to him."

Moses and Aaron will now become a team, but not a team of equal partners. Aaron will be Moses' mouth, but Moses will be Aaron's God (4:16). This striking phrase suggests not only Moses' authority over Aaron, but also the close identification between God and his messenger. Moses is still God's chosen instrument; Aaron is only a concession.

The prominence of Moses' role over that of Aaron's is played out most clearly in the following chapters in that Aaron's role in the deliverance is minimal, particularly as the narrative progresses toward chapter 14. In fact, Moses has a number of extended dialogues with Pharaoh in the course of the plagues. What happened to Aaron as Moses' mouthpiece? Why does Moses do so much talking later on when here God goes out of his way to make a special provision for Moses so that he will not have to talk? One can only conjecture, but the surface implication underscores the importance of Moses' role as God's instrument of deliverance.

The dialogue between Moses and God ends somewhat abruptly: "Don't forget your staff, Moses." One could envision a number of alternative endings to this dramatic encounter. We could see Moses groveling on his knees begging the Lord for patience and mercy for his continued stubbornness. Or perhaps God could round off the discussion by reiterating the promise to deliver the Israelites. The reminder to take the staff seems somewhat anticlimactic.

But perhaps Moses needs some reminding. He is about to leave behind forever the world of shepherding. What will he need a staff for? But the staff is to become a conspicuous player in the plague narratives. The shepherd's staff will humble the world power at the time. The raised staff will cause the water of the sea to part and allow Moses to shepherd his people through to the other side and on to Mount Horeb. God will use this symbol of lowliness and unimportance to bring about the central salvific act of the Old Testament. "Don't forget your staff, Moses."

Bridging Contexts

THE RELUCTANT LEADER. The narrative of Moses' call revisits a number of themes that have been introduced in the preceding chapters. We see, for example, the rejection of Moses' leadership, which is what fuels Moses' concerns about his own ability to carry out God's call. To push this a step further, Moses' self-doubt in this passage is an extension of the rejection theme and reminds us of how pervasive resistance against

Moses' leadership was. The recurring reference to the patriarchs as well as the creation overtones of the three signs remind us of another theme: "continuity with the past," which was so central to Exodus 1.

The main theme addressed in this passage, however, is God's call to Moses and Moses' reluctance to answer that call. His reluctance seems to be a cross between true humility, an appreciation for the difficulties that will confront him in his role, and simple stubbornness. The complexity of his response presents an ambiguous picture of the redeemer. One would expect Israel's deliverer to have more resolve and less hesitation. Nevertheless, such a human presentation of Moses is one that even God's people today can readily understand.

We can gain a fuller understanding of Moses' call if we place 3:1—4:17 in the context of Scripture as a whole. Frequently in the Old Testament God "calls" someone, thereby setting him aside for a particular purpose. These "call narratives," as they are titled,[47] bear varying degrees of similarity to our passage. The most pertinent call narratives include Joshua (Josh. 1), Gideon (Judg. 6), Samuel (1 Sam. 3), Isaiah (Isa. 6 and 40), Jeremiah (Jer. 1), and Ezekiel (Ezek. 1).

The broader canonical context of these other narratives provides the proper theological framework for viewing not only Moses' call but the others as well. We will look briefly at the characteristics of each of these narratives and then make general conclusions. It should be pointed out that no attempt will be made to force any of these call narratives into a single pattern, thus blurring the distinctive elements of each. In fact, those elements that are not in common are as significant as the areas of overlap.

Joshua's call is the logical place to start, since he is Moses' successor. After the death of Moses, the Lord commissions Joshua to lead the Israelites into the Promised Land. He is to finish the job that God began through Moses. Hence, God's presence with Joshua is as vital for his mission as it was for Moses. The Lord tells Joshua, "As I was with Moses, so I will be with you; I will never leave you nor forsake you" (Josh. 1:5; cf. Deut. 31:23). God promises his presence with Joshua as Israel's new leader sets out to perform the task assigned to him by the Lord. There is no Mount Horeb experience or back and forth dialogue between Joshua and the Lord, but the promise of God's presence to Joshua for fulfilling Moses' aborted assignment[48] indicates some similarity between Joshua's call and that of Moses.

---

47. For a technical discussion, see N. Habel, "The Form and Significance of the Call Narratives," *ZAW* 77 (1965): 297–323. See also Plastaras, *The God of Exodus*, 77–82.

48. Moses would have been the one to complete the mission and lead the people into the Promised Land had he remained faithful to the Lord (Num. 20:12).

Gideon's call presents more striking parallels to Moses' call. As with Moses, the angel of the Lord appears to Gideon in close proximity to a tree (Judg. 6:11). This supernatural encounter in a mundane setting (he is busy thresh- ing his father's wheat) closely resembles God's call to Moses (who is shep- herding Jethro's sheep). As with Moses, the angel announces to Gideon, "The LORD is with you" (v. 12; cf. Ex. 3:12). Gideon, like Moses, although much more briefly, questions God's actions (Judg. 6:13). He even objects to God's plan to use him as an instrument to defeat the Midianites (v. 15). God responds to Gideon's complaint by reassuring him of his continued pres- ence: "Am I not sending you?" (v. 14); "I will be with you" (v. 16).[49]

Gideon is apparently not fully convinced of God's reassurance, so he, like Moses, asks for a sign (Judg. 6:17). The sign consists of fire (cf. Ex. 3:2, a typical characteristic of theophany) consuming the meat and bread Gideon has offered to him (Judg. 6:21). Being finally convinced that it is indeed the Lord who is speaking with him, Gideon becomes frightened at being in God's presence (v. 23; cf. Ex. 3:6). As we will see below, one of Moses' early encounters with the Israelites he is sent to deliver does not go smoothly; they are actually hostile toward him. Hostility is also the Israelites' initial reaction toward Gideon (Judg. 6:30).[50]

Samuel's call is similar to Moses' in a number of ways. We have the direct address "Samuel," twice explicitly (1 Sam. 3:6, 10) and twice implied (3:4, 8). As in Exodus 3:4, at the climactic moment, the name is repeated twice in 1 Samuel 3:10, "Samuel! Samuel!" Also, in 1 Samuel 3:4, 5, 6, and 8, Samuel responds to God's call with *hinneni/hin⁽e⁾ni* ("Here I am"), as does Moses in Exo- dus 3:4. Like Moses and Gideon, God calls Samuel to announce to him some plan that he is about to carry out (1 Sam. 3:11–14). Two noticeable differ- ences are Samuel's lack of any explicit objection to being part of God's plan (although he is afraid to tell Eli of the vision, v. 15), and Eli's submission to the message that God gives Samuel (vv. 17–18), different from the Israelites' hostility toward Moses.

Isaiah's call (Isa. 6:1–13) begins with the prophet in God's awesome pres- ence (vv. 1–3). Like Moses, Isaiah feels the weight of being in the presence of the holy God, and it is too much for him to bear: "Woe to me! . . . I am ruined!" (v. 5; cf. Ex. 3:6). Isaiah's recognition of his own sin is also a form of objection. Since he is sinful, he realizes he has no place being in God's

---

49. "I will be with you" in Judg. 6:16 is the same Hebrew clause as in Ex. 3:12.

50. The question of the literary relationship between the call narratives of Moses and Gideon (was there a genre of call narratives that dictated the form both narratives took? is one narrative dependent upon the other?) will not detain us here. In their theological, canonical context, what is important is reading each call narrative in light of the others.

presence. Yet the divine response is to make it so Isaiah can remain before the Lord (vv. 6–7):

> Then one of the seraphs flew to me with a live coal in his hand, which he had taken with tongs from the altar. With it he touched my mouth and said, "See, this has touched your lips; your guilt is taken away and your sin atoned for."

This is somewhat similar to the "I will be with you" response that Moses gets. The deficiencies of the one receiving the call do not determine God's actions. He will see to it that his chosen vessel is adequately prepared.[51] Furthermore, Isaiah is called to perform a certain task (Isa. 6:8–9). He responds in the familiar manner, "Here am I" (*hineni*). The distinctive feature we find in Isaiah's call, however, is that he is not sent to deliver his people, but rather to announce God's word of judgment against his people (vv. 9–13).

Jeremiah too is confronted by God (Jer. 1:4–19) and told that he has been set apart from the womb as a prophet to the nations (v. 5). In response, Jeremiah offers a complaint of his own reminiscent of Moses: "Ah, Sovereign LORD ... I do not know how to speak; I am only a child" (v. 6); precisely what Jeremiah means is not clear. But as with Moses, God responds by declaring his presence with Jeremiah: "Do not be afraid of them, for I am with you" (v. 8).[52] God demonstrates to Jeremiah more concretely his presence with him. The "sign," so to speak, that God gives is like what we have seen with Isaiah: God reaches out, touches the prophet's mouth, and says, "Now, I have put my words in your mouth" (v. 9). The connection to Moses' complaint of his speech problem and God's response, "Now go; I will help you speak and will teach you what to say" (Ex. 4:12; lit., "I will be with your mouth") should not escape our notice.[53]

Ezekiel's call includes an extended description of the divine confrontation (Ezek. 1: the windstorm, the four living creatures, and the wheel). The

---

51. Mention here should also be made of Solomon's humility in 1 Kings 3, where he asks for wisdom to rule Israel. This is not a call narrative in any proper sense, but the humility that accompanies Solomon's request for wisdom (vv. 7–8) is a mark of several of the call narratives. That humility is the proper response to God's plan for him. God rewards Solomon by giving him not only wisdom, but wealth and honor as well. Had Moses responded too quickly to God's call on his life, his suitableness for the task may have been rendered suspect.

52. The Hebrew is somewhat different here from the other instances of this clause (see also Jer. 1:19).

53. In this context, it is also at least worth glancing at Isa. 40, which has certain characteristics of a call narrative. There the prophet is also confronted by God and told to give a message of judgment, but this time to the nations, specifically Babylon. Jeremiah, too, is called as a prophet to the nations (Jer. 1:5).

description of this confrontation concludes in 1:28, where the prophet reacts in a way that reminds one of Moses at the mountain: The prophet falls face-down in fear and reverence (cf. Ex. 3:6). God then calls Ezekiel to special service; like Isaiah before him, he is to speak God's word of judgment to rebellious Israel (Ezek. 2:3). Unlike other call narratives, Ezekiel offers no complaint. In fact, he plays a rather passive role throughout his initial meeting with God. Yet, like Moses and Jeremiah, Ezekiel is given divine empowerment to help him speak. In his case, he is made to eat a scroll on which are written "words of lament and mourning and woe" (2:10). Being God's messenger to the people requires being enabled to speak God's words.[54]

Although each of the call narratives has its own character and integrity, there are several elements common to most or all of them. Highlighting these elements will help us to have a better grasp of the coherence of these narratives in general. (1) God initiates the contact. These are, after all, *call* narratives. Moses is on no quest to find God. He and the other chosen servants were simply minding their own business (Jeremiah was in the womb!) when God called them away from what they were doing and put them on a new and unexpected path.

(2) Some of these narratives seem to go out of their way to mention the mundane or ordinary vocation the leaders were engaged in at the time of their ✓ calling. A primary factor in God's choice was not the individual's résumé or experience. Rather, he calls people out of ordinary circumstances for extraordinary tasks.

(3) The recipients of God's call are often jolted by the thought of what ✓ God intends for them. Hence, they respond in humility or disbelief. A feeling of inadequacy and even reluctance is a perfectly normal reaction. In fact, complying too quickly with God's call would suggest one's true inadequacy for the task set before him. Thus, we see repeated questioning, denial, pleading, requests for signs, and in Jonah's case, fleeing to the opposite end of the world. This period of doubt and questioning should be viewed generally in a positive light. God does not chide any of his leaders for taking him to task. None are punished or upbraided for not acquiescing immediately to God's call. Rather, in a certain sense, it is this struggle with their call that begins to *good reflections* prepare them for the task ahead.

Moses' questions, which are really challenges to God, serve to draw out more concretely the nature of God's continued presence with Moses and

---

54. We could also mention here the calls of Amos and Jonah. Like Moses' call, Amos's comes unexpectedly as he is doing his work, and like Moses, he has no desire to be a mouthpiece for God (Amos 7:14–15). The book of Jonah does not include a call, but it does indicate Jonah's reluctance: He flees to Tarshish. But God triumphs through him all the same.

the manner in which his power will be displayed to Egypt. God answers each of Moses' questions patiently. He does not become angry with Moses until his fifth challenge. Moses' concerns seem legitimate (at least in his mind), but the Lord is patient with that, and those concerns provide a vehicle for God to reveal himself.

Even after God's patient assurances of his presence with Moses for the task ahead, Moses simply puts his foot down and says "no." This is why the Lord became angry with him. It is not because he dared confront the Lord or because the Lord has patience with four questions but five is one too many. Moses' error is in refusing to trust God's answers.[55]

√ (4) The lesson these leaders learn is that "salvation comes from the LORD" (Jonah 2:9). However legitimate their concerns may be, they are in the final analysis irrelevant. God is greater than their inadequacies, lack of experience, or talent. In fact, he surprises the ill-prepared and calls them out of unlikely settings precisely to leave no doubt that it is his power and might that is at work. "I will be with you" is a refrain, either explicit or implicit, that dominates these call narratives. Salvation is in God's hands; he will work his might through whomever he chooses.

There is much in these call narratives that believers today can relate to. God meets us where we are. Our initial response is awe, but as time goes on we begin to question the Lord and wonder whether he has made a mistake. (Actually, this line of thinking puts us comfortably in the world of the Psalms.) So we struggle back and forth with the Lord, and as a result we grow, slowly but surely, to have a better grasp of the role God has called us to in his kingdom.

Although such a scenario speaks to us directly—and further reflection would prove more profitable—we should perhaps exercise some patience first. Before we begin serious reflection on the application of the call narratives to our lives, it behooves us as Christians, who serve a Christ of whom all of Scripture speaks, to bring to the foreground the Christological dimension of these call narratives. The significance of the call of Moses and other Old Testament characters is not diminished but accented when we allow the person and work of Christ to mediate that significance to us.

Although there is no specific, localized "call narrative" in the Gospels, many of the elements of the Old Testament call narratives present themselves in the life of Christ. First, Christ is "sent" by the Father to perform a

---

55. The extreme example of this is Jonah. Jonah doesn't even confront God directly with what he perceives to be a great injustice: the evangelization and eventual conversion of the pagan Ninevites. The Lord is angry with Jonah because the reluctant prophet simply refuses the order and attempts to run away. As a result, God gives him time to think it over while sitting in the belly of a fish for three days.

specific task, a refrain noted especially in John's Gospel (John 5:36). Although we cannot speak of the "divine initiative" of the Father in the same way that we can with the call of Moses and the others, it is still the Father who initiates Christ's mission. Of course, this touches on the great mystery of the inter-Trinitarian relationship between the Father and the Son, and these matters will not be resolved here. Still the Son, in his role as the incarnate Christ, speaks as one who was given a message by the Father to bring to the world.

On a different level, the setting apart of Christ's role as the mediator of God's word is given concrete expression at his baptism (Matt. 3:13–17; Mark 1:9–11; Luke 3:21–22). Christ's baptism by John serves to give open testimony to the Father's sanction of his ministry: "You are my Son, whom I love; with you I am well pleased" (Mark 1:11). It is at this point that Jesus' public ministry, his proclamation of God's word, begins. Moreover, the purpose for which the Father sent the Son was to deliver God's people, an element common to the Old Testament call narratives. Of course, here the nature of that deliverance takes on a new meaning: not from political oppression or social injustice but to cross "over from death to life" (John 5:24).

Like Moses, Jesus' earthly circumstances hardly lead one to expect the gravity of his assigned mission. He was, to all appearances, of ordinary birth and upbringing, a carpenter's son from Galilee. He was not invested with any prestige, at least in the way that we normally reckon such things. This is not to say that Jesus was surprised by the role he was to play in God's redemptive plan; he was not "minding his own business," as were Moses and others. Still, it is striking that Christ, too, was leading an "ordinary" life before his extraordinary mission began.

The similarities between Christ's "call" and those in the Old Testament break down, at least a bit, when we consider Christ's response to the task for which the Father sent him. There were certainly periods of intense struggle, as we see in the Garden of Gethsemane ("Take this cup from me") and on the cross ("My God, my God, why have you forsaken me?"). What we do not see, however, is the degree of obstinate objection, feelings of inadequacy, or stubborn reluctance that we find exhibited by the Old Testament characters. The reason for this is straightforward: The Son and the Father are one. There is a unanimity of purpose between them. The Son does not need a sign from the Father to ensure his continued presence.

The Father and the Son are so in harmony that knowing the one means knowing the other (John 5:16–18; 8:19; 10:30). There is no "distance" between the two as there was in the Old Testament. In Christ, the Father has the perfect messenger to proclaim his word. He needs no special pep talk to fulfill the task. He needs no special assurance that "I will be with you," because the Father and the Son are already one and their wills cohere perfectly (6:38–40). Christ's role as messenger completes to perfection the trajectory begun in the Old Testament.

THE CALL OF GOD on our lives. In contrast to the degree to which Christ fulfills the role for which the Father had sent him, the Old Testament characters, however nobly they perform their respective tasks, are found lacking. It is for Christians, then, who are in Christ, to understand the call narratives in general and Exodus 3:1–4:17 in particular in the broader context of redemptive history as a whole. When we turn to applying these narratives to our lives, we ask ourselves, "What does it mean for a Christian to be 'called' by God?"

This question can be addressed on two different levels: (1) God calls us as sinners into his kingdom; (2) having done so, God calls each of us to some kingdom service. In other words, God's call concerns salvation and vocation. Exodus 3:1–4:17 and the other call narratives, as understood in their Christological dimension, speak to Christians today.

(1) Let us first look at how God calls us into his kingdom in the context of the call narratives. A central theme of these narratives is that God initiates the call. This is true also of our entrance into God's kingdom. Speaking of a "call" to describe our salvation is not intended to create divisions between Calvinists and other Christians; most Christians can readily agree that we do not initiate our relationship to the Lord but that the Spirit must be at work in us. True, this notion of election is a mark of Calvinism, but my purpose for raising it here is not to engender debate. Rather, it is to highlight what every Christian believes, that we are unholy people who, by some great wonder, now have a relationship with a holy God. As Paul writes in 2 Corinthians 4:6, "For God, who said, 'Let light shine out of darkness,' made his light shine in our hearts to give us the light of the knowledge of the glory of God in the face of Christ."

However one may want to understand the election theme in the New Testament, the idea that God shines *his* light into our dark hearts is something that rings true in all our ears. Whatever the dynamic may be between God's call and our response (this is perhaps the proper locus for the election debate), it is difficult to maintain scripturally that we "initiate" our own salvation. Rather, we are called into God's kingdom.

There are ready parallels between Moses' call and ours. Many Christians, particularly those who have come to a saving knowledge of the Lord in their adolescent and adult years, have testimonies that bear similarity to Moses' call.

For example, we might think of the unexpected nature of our conversion:[56] an invitation to an evangelistic meeting or a "chance" encounter with an old friend who first spoke with you about the Lord. Theologically speaking, many of us were minding our own business, so to speak, when God shined his light in our hearts, when the Lord took us from our mundane lives and placed us on a new, extraordinary path that we never really expected to take. Many Christians have had a Mount Horeb experience of sorts, not because they saw a burning bush or a miraculous sign, but because they were changed. Yet, from a Christological point of view, we can say that our call to Christ was accompanied by even greater signs than Moses' call or anyone else's. We who are living at the "end of the age" have the Spirit of Christ himself dwelling in us, and we see things that even the Old Testament prophets and angels longed to look at (1 Peter 1:10–12).

Like Moses, the direction our lost lives were taking was eternally altered by God. Also like Moses, our call may have been accompanied by a certain degree of resistance. Speaking for myself, my focused resistance lasted a couple of years after my initial conversion (and struggles still linger today). As Moses did not trust the Lord's repeated promise to be with him, the ever-present grace and love of God is a lesson that many of us need to keep learning day after day.

Sometimes the numbing reality of God's unconditional love inspires true humility in us. Other times, we carefully count the cost of our conversion and debate with the Lord that we are not sufficiently endowed to receive this great gift. Still other times, we may shift the focus far too much on our own abilities and qualities, and we stubbornly resist the sustaining grace of the Lord that he offers every day. There are patterns in our own behavior that are similar to Moses' reactions to the Lord's call on Mount Horeb. And, like Moses, the Lord patiently teaches his church that it is his presence with us, in the brilliant light of Christ's resurrection, that counts. It is precisely in our inability that his light shines brightest in our hearts.

We must remember that we are not simply called by God to enter his kingdom, but we are called "in Christ." The inexorable union between the Father and the Son is also at work in those who are called to be co-heirs with Christ, his brothers and sisters. Our call into his kingdom must be seen against the backdrop of Christ's first fulfilling God's call to him: to become a human being and reconcile fallen humanity to the Father. When God calls us now into his kingdom, he does not do so apart from what he has accomplished in Christ but precisely by virtue of what he has done. Our call to

---

56. One thinks here of C. S. Lewis's famous account of his own conversion, *Surprised by Joy: The Shape of My Early Life* (New York: Harcourt Brace Jovanovich, 1955).

salvation, therefore, should not be seen immediately in the context of the Old Testament call narratives, but the message of the call narratives should first be mediated to us through the "call" of Christ. What begins to develop, then, is a stronger sense of God's unfailing presence with those whom he has called.

Although doubts and struggles will certainly arise in conjunction with God's call, it is the very Spirit of Christ that the Father imparts to us in that call. God's promise to be with Moses is fulfilled in us to a degree that neither Moses nor any of the Old Testament saints ever envisioned. God is not *with* us, but *in* us—and we are *in* Christ. This intimacy is greater than what Moses experienced, plagues and miracles notwithstanding. This powerful presence of God in our lives does not preclude doubt and struggle. Rather, it serves as the proper theological setting in which to view our struggle. Brothers and sisters of the risen Christ are in a privileged situation.

(2) Another level at which we can apply the call narratives concerns our call to kingdom service. The Lord does not simply call us to save us. He also calls us to be active servants in his kingdom, to be the salt of the earth to bring every thought captive under the universal rule of the risen Christ. We are all called in order to be sent out on a mission. We are ambassadors of King Jesus, and each of us has a task to perform. Of course, God does not call each of us to the same task. Some may traverse the globe, others may go no further than their own neighborhoods or families. Some may earn the respect and admiration of thousands, most others may remain anonymous. But each of us is called to serve in some way.

God's call to kingdom service, like that of Moses, is the Lord's doing. There truly is a sense of "calling" that Christians feel, even though we may belittle that notion from time to time. Sensing the Lord's call is not just something that seminarians feel, but eventually everyone who serves the Lord. Fifteen years ago, if anyone had told me that I would one day be teaching Hebrew in a seminary and writing a commentary, I would have suggested that they begin wearing a hat when in direct sunlight. Old friends I haven't seen for years cannot be fooled. They know that something extraordinary must have happened for me to be doing what I am doing.

We can all reflect on how different our lives would have been had the Lord not called us to where we are now. Most of can attest to how the Lord has put ministry opportunities in our paths. You move into a new neighborhood and you "happen" to meet some people who are young Christians or perhaps close to entering the kingdom. And there you are, called to minister to them. Perhaps someone new was hired at work who is particularly open to the gospel because of a personal problem. When we stop to think about it, we, like Moses, are being called continually to serve in a variety of capacities. We may not be called to be a great deliverer, sent to lead an entire people from bondage—Christ has done that already. But the Lord uses us where we are to do his work, and he makes sure the opportunities are there.

Of course, the analogy between Moses' call and ours does not stop there. With each opportunity we accept, there are others where we resist, doubt, struggle, and even rebel. Most likely, we have all at one time or another felt embarrassed about witnessing to strangers, or, even worse, to friends, family members, classmates, or coworkers. Pastors in particular often feel weighed down by the responsibilities of their calling, perhaps to the point where they doubt the calling itself. Such doubt, as in Moses' case, may arise from an appreciation for the great responsibilities they bear and a recognition of their own inability to fulfill their obligations.

Such periods of discomfort are often nothing less than the honest struggling of God's people, and it is precisely through such a process that the Lord strengthens us for the task ahead and causes us to grow to meet greater challenges. Like children, we are not expected immediately to comprehend our situation and distinguish the long-term results from the present, apparently dire, circumstances. So we plunge ahead, somewhat reluctantly, into the task the Lord has set before us. We begin that conversation with a neighbor about spiritual matters. We bear witness to what the Lord has done in our lives.

In doing so, we truly learn that the Lord is "with our mouths," just as he was with Moses' mouth. When the Lord calls us to a task, he is faithful to see us through it, despite our feelings. Moses began to learn from his back-and-forth with the Lord that his perception of the situation should not dictate his actions. How successfully we fulfill the Lord's call on our lives does not depend on our ability to act, but on the sovereign Lord who is with us and acts through us. It is *his* work; we are his instruments. If he chooses to use us, the clay has no right to argue with the potter. Again, none of this is to minimize the dimension of honest doubt and struggling that Christians feel in varying degrees and at varying times in their lives. But it is precisely at those times that we would profit most from remembering that *he* is amply fitted for carrying out the task in which he has graciously allowed us to participate. The Spirit of Christ in us is the continual reminder that God is truly present with us.

No task undertaken alone. A brief mention of two related matters of application in Exodus 3:1–4:17 will conclude our discussion. The task Moses was given to confront Pharaoh was not to be undertaken alone. Rather, he *and the elders* were to go to Pharaoh and demand the release of the Israelite slaves (3:18). Likewise, God provided Aaron to Moses as a helper to carry out God's plan. Although this addition was more of a concession to Moses' lack of faith than anything else, both Aaron's role and that of the elders underscore the role of the group in carrying out God's purpose. Moses is not to be a lone ranger deliverer, but he is to work for the group by working with the group. He must first gain the group's confidence before he can carry out his task (3:16—17). This helps us make sense of the fact that Moses does not seem to doubt so much his ability to confront Pharaoh as his reception by his own people.

Likewise, we should not assume that our own calling is necessarily a private matter. How often have we heard someone claim to have had a private vision that the Lord wants him or her to do such and such, and, come what may, nothing will get in that person's way. We must remember that the church is a corporate body. We are all members of that body. God's call on our lives must be checked or confirmed by the whole. For example, if someone feels called to be a pastor, we do not just take that person's word for it. Every denomination that I know of has some sort of process, whether formal (seminary, ordination exams) or less formal (a perception of the candidate's spiritual maturity and ability to lead people), whereby that call is scrutinized. Bypassing that process can have disastrous effects.

Likewise, if one feels called to teach Sunday school or serve as a deacon, it is the church's responsibility to play a role in the particulars of how that individual carries out his or her task. Even in terms of some other ministry (neighborhood evangelism, helping the poor) the individual ought to call on the resources of the body of Christ rather than proceed in isolation.

Being confronted by God's holiness. A second area of application, one that can easily be lost in the shuffle, is that being called by God means being confronted by his holiness. This was the first lesson Moses learned as God was preparing him for the task ahead (3:5). God's "otherness," his purity, his holiness, is not something we readily bring into our reflection on our calling. Yet Moses is startled; he approaches the burning bush, curious to find out what is happening. But the Lord does not allow it to remain there. "Stop, Moses. Come no further. I am not a matter of curiosity. I am holy."

It is the same holy God that confronts us today. Perhaps we do not fully appreciate how incredible it is that a holy God calls *us* into his service. But we should recapture the biblical model of true reverence and piety when in God's presence. Speaking for myself, I am not nearly enough in awe of God's presence with me throughout the day and throughout those times when I am particularly struggling with who I am as a Christian. Here we arrive at the heart of the matter. God is holy. As we reflect on *him* rather than ourselves, we approach our calling with a peace that passes all understanding. The holy God calls us into his kingdom and even allows us to participate in his kingdom work. In the end, the only proper response is worship.

Exodus 4:18–31

THEN MOSES WENT back to Jethro his father-in-law and said to him, "Let me go back to my own people in Egypt to see if any of them are still alive."
Jethro said, "Go, and I wish you well."

¹⁹Now the LORD had said to Moses in Midian, "Go back to Egypt, for all the men who wanted to kill you are dead." ²⁰So Moses took his wife and sons, put them on a donkey and started back to Egypt. And he took the staff of God in his hand.

²¹The LORD said to Moses, "When you return to Egypt, see that you perform before Pharaoh all the wonders I have given you the power to do. But I will harden his heart so that he will not let the people go. ²²Then say to Pharaoh, 'This is what the LORD says: Israel is my firstborn son, ²³and I told you, "Let my son go, so he may worship me." But you refused to let him go; so I will kill your firstborn son.'"

²⁴At a lodging place on the way, the LORD met Moses and was about to kill him. ²⁵But Zipporah took a flint knife, cut off her son's foreskin and touched Moses' feet with it. "Surely you are a bridegroom of blood to me," she said. ²⁶So the LORD let him alone. (At that time she said "bridegroom of blood," referring to circumcision.)

²⁷The LORD said to Aaron, "Go into the desert to meet Moses." So he met Moses at the mountain of God and kissed him. ²⁸Then Moses told Aaron everything the LORD had sent him to say, and also about all the miraculous signs he had commanded him to perform.

²⁹Moses and Aaron brought together all the elders of the Israelites, ³⁰and Aaron told them everything the LORD had said to Moses. He also performed the signs before the people, ³¹and they believed. And when they heard that the LORD was concerned about them and had seen their misery, they bowed down and worshiped.

Original Meaning

THIS PASSAGE TAKES US from Moses' departure from Midian to his arrival in Egypt, where he and Aaron meet with the Israelites. Moses obeys the call he had resisted so stubbornly in the previous verses. The narrative may be divided into three parts: (1) Moses' departure (vv. 18–23), (2) the mysterious incident that happened along the way (vv. 24–26), and (3) Moses' meeting with Aaron and the demonstration of God's might before the Israelites (vv. 27–31). This passage is fraught with interpretive challenges that have perplexed interpreters for centuries.

Moses' Departure (4:18–23)

SOMETIME AFTER MOSES left the Lord's presence on Mount Horeb (most likely immediately thereafter), he asks his father-in-law, Jethro,[1] for permission to leave. In doing so, he is probably simply showing respect to one who showed him hospitality when he sorely needed it (2:20) and who gave him his daughter in marriage. What is curious, however, is the precise nature of the request he makes. Had he simply said, "Let me go back to my own people in Egypt," there would be no problem. One could conclude that, for whatever reason, Moses is simply choosing not to go into any great detail about why he wants to leave.

But Moses does provide a motive for leaving his father-in-law's family: "to see if any of them [his countrymen] are still alive." The problem, of course, is that this is not why God has told Moses to go back to Egypt in 3:1–4:17. He is to go back in order to bring the Israelites out of Egypt, not merely to see how they are doing. Moses' statement to Jethro is similar to what we have seen in 3:18, where Moses is commanded by God to tell Pharaoh that the Israelites are to go on a three-day trip into the desert, when in fact God intends nothing of the sort (see comments on 3:18). What is the big secret? What is keeping Moses from laying it all out on the table?

Perhaps 4:18 can be understood in the context of Moses' self-doubt in the preceding section. We must remember that Moses did not leave his initial √ encounter with the Lord brimming with self-confidence. All we know is that he is reprimanded for his last of five challenges to God and that he leaves Mount Horeb with staff in hand (4:13–17). Sometimes our English Bibles can be misleading. Ancient texts had no chapter or verse divisions or section

---

1. The name in Hebrew here is *Jeter*, which is likely a variant spelling of Jethro. Many ancient translations of the Hebrew changed Jeter to Jethro, no doubt to make it conform to 3:1. Cassuto suggests that "Jethro" reflects an earlier Hebrew spelling of the name (*Commentary on Exodus*, 52).

headings.[2] We should not drive an artificial wedge between verses 17 and 18, as if verse 18 is starting something new. Although we cannot be dogmatic here, reading difficult statements such as this in their immediate contexts is a fruitful place to begin reflection.

In this case, Moses may be somewhat embarrassed at the thought of what Jethro's incredulous reaction might be if he claims to have had a conversation with God in a burning bush, telling him that he is to humble the powers of Egypt. Perhaps blurting this out would cause more problems than it is worth.[3] Some things are better left unsaid. Perhaps this, too, is why Moses cannot simply ask Jethro to leave without giving him some excuse. If he simply asks to leave without giving a reason, Jethro will undoubtedly ask why, which will oblige Moses to produce some excuse on the spot and may make Jethro suspicious. However morally questionable this might be for us, in the final analysis it probably serves to expedite Moses' mission. Our intention should not be to sanitize Moses' statement to Jethro, and the rationale offered here is not aimed in that direction. But neither can we simply brush it aside. We must try to explain statements such as this by assuming that it serves some meaningful purpose here.

Another approach to this problem is theological rather than psychological. Houtman points out that 4:18 is similar to 2:11 in that both passages refer to Moses going out to see his countrymen.[4] As discussed above, 2:11 foreshadows the Exodus: Moses goes out to see the mistreatment of his people and attempts to deliver them. In 4:18, Moses intends to go back to Egypt to see how his countrymen are doing; this is a further development of 2:11.

The main difference here, however, is that Moses is now going with God. He has met the Lord on Mount Horeb and has been commissioned for the great task. What Moses meant to do in 2:11 in a narrow, myopic sense, God now begins to unfold. Whereas Moses had earlier left Egypt (symbolically) to see his countrymen's plight, Moses now returns to Egypt, back to his countrymen, to do something about it. But this time he will not react as brashly as he did earlier. Now he is going with God. Moses' statement that he wants to go see his countrymen is, on the surface of things at least, at best a partial truth. In the context of the Exodus narrative as a whole, however, it serves a subtle yet powerful theological purpose. Verse 18 begins to escort the reader further into the narrative flow of events that will climax in Israel's release from captivity.

---

2. Chapter and verse divisions were introduced in the medieval period.
3. Jethro later comes to support and even aid Moses in his role as deliverer (18:1–27).
4. *Exodus*, 1:419.

Verse 19 also raises some questions. (1) Why does the Lord give Moses the command to leave Midian *after* he has apparently already resolved to do so in verse 18? Doesn't verse 19 logically precede verse 18? (2) Verse 19 seems to imply that since Pharaoh and the others who wanted to kill him are now dead, it is now *safe* for Moses to return. Why would the Creator of heaven and earth, who is about to dismantle the forces of Egypt, have to wait until the previous Pharaoh is dead before he moves in with a display of his might?

(1) Again, we are confronted with questions that offer no easy answers. We should not, of course, overestimate the importance of some of these issues, but neither should we ignore the tension that problems such as these create. We should also be aware that we are not the first to see incongruities in the narrative, for careful readers of the Bible have been thinking and writing about these things for a long time. Thus, it would be a bit foolish to think that we can arrive at definitive solutions in the pages of this or any other commentary. As we engage the biblical text, we are doing nothing less than entering into the interpretive process that has gripped Christians (and in the case of the Old Testament, Jews as well) for centuries.

What we can do, however, is engage the text on an intimate level and try to understand the purpose of this verse in this context. Our concern should not always be to "solve the problem" but to allow what *we* think is a "problem" to shape our understanding of the text as a whole. One approach to understanding the position of verse 19 after verse 18 is reflected in the NIV: "Now the LORD *had said* to Moses." Unlike English, the Hebrew language has no pluperfect tense. Typically, the verb here would simply be translated "said" rather than "had said." But the pluperfect is an acceptable translation, provided the context allows it, which is certainly what we see here. By saying "had said," the NIV is actually *interpreting* verse 19 as being chronologically prior to verse 18. When understood in this way, the *contextual* order of verses 18 and 19 should not be equated with the *chronological* order.[5]

(2) The other issue is the apparent necessity of Pharaoh and his leaders to die first before the Lord sends Moses back. But, like verse 18, sensitivity to the theological thrust of this verse sheds light on the subject. Note how verse 19 echoes the deliverance from Egypt of the following chapters. When Moses left Egypt, he was a wanted man: Pharaoh and presumably his officials (hence the plural "all the men" in v. 19) were seeking to kill him. But now those who intended him harm are themselves dead. Later in the book, the Egyptians who seek to harm the Israelites meet their own demise in the Red Sea. In this sense, verse 19 is not saying, "OK, Moses, it's safe for you to come back." This would make very little sense in the context of God's measured, con-

---

5. See also Jacob, *Exodus*, 101.

trolled, sovereign display of power throughout the book. Rather, it is an announcement to Moses that the first installment of the Exodus has commenced. Those who enslaved the Israelites are dead—the process has begun. ✓

The interpretive challenges in verse 20 concern Moses' family and where they lived while the deliverance was going on. First of all, Moses is said to leave with his wife and *sons*, but 2:22 has mentioned only the birth of Gershom. His other son, Eliezer, is not mentioned until 18:4. Of course, as we have seen elsewhere in the book, Exodus and biblical narratives in general tend to be somewhat laconic. Original readers likely would not have been troubled by the abrupt mention of more than one son when only Gershom's birth had been mentioned. The original readers knew who Moses was, who his wife was, and that he had two sons. The likely reason why only Gershom's name was mentioned in chapter 2 is because the etymology of his name served the writer's theological purpose in that context: He wished to highlight Moses' sojourning in a foreign land (see 2:22). What is more curious is not the mention of "sons" here in light of 2:22, but the mention of only one son just below in that most vexing of passages, 4:24–26, to which we will turn in a moment.

A more pressing matter is the destination of Moses' wife and sons. In one sense, the sentence gives the clear impression that Moses puts his family on a donkey in order that they may accompany him to Egypt. The problem here is that Moses' family is nowhere mentioned explicitly as arriving in Egypt with Moses. In fact, they are never heard from again until 18:2–7, which describes Moses' *reunion* with his family after the departure from Egypt. Exodus 18:2 is explicit in telling us that Moses had previously sent his family away to live with Jethro, presumably to keep his loved ones out of harm's way. The only way to reconcile this explicit state of affairs with 4:20 is either to assume that Moses took his family with him to Egypt but sent them away later, or that 4:20 describes Moses leaving them behind.

The former option assumes something that is not expressed in the text, whereas the latter option, apart from itself not being explicit in 4:20, actually seems to disrupt the sense of the verse. Moreover, *leaving* his family in Midian is not the same as *sending them away*, as we read in 18:2. Readers who know nothing of 18:2–7 would take 4:20 to mean that Moses goes back to Egypt with his family. Critical commentators typically argue, partly on the basis of inconsistencies such as this, that the book of Exodus preserves variant, originally separate traditions of Moses and his family that cannot be reconciled. Although a straightforward solution to this matter is not obvious, the ambiguities of 4:20 do not, in my opinion, lend themselves to such an approach. Terseness seems to be a stock characteristic of Old Testament narratives. The fact that something may not make sense to us does not mean that it made no sense to the original readers. Where Moses' family went in 4:20 or how they might have gotten to Midian is not something the narrative is pleased to disclose.[6]

What we are told at the end of verse 20, however, is that Moses is dutiful in bringing his staff with him. The writer brings the narrative back to its focus: Moses is going to Egypt to deliver the Israelites by God's mighty deeds. God gives Moses one last charge: He is to perform the signs before Pharaoh (v. 21). This is the first mention in Exodus that Moses is to perform the signs before *Pharaoh*. Up to this point, we are led to expect that the signs are for the purpose of convincing the Israelites of Moses' commission. True, in 3:19 it is hinted that God will perform wonders before the Egyptians, but 4:21 implies that the wonders in question are those performed in 4:1–9, and these wonders are clearly directed at Israelite unbelief.

So, is this a new announcement, that now the wonders are to be performed before Pharaoh? Perhaps this is a new twist, an introduction of the identity of Moses' true adversary. Although Israelite disbelief is a theme that appears throughout the Pentateuch, the clear conflict in the subsequent chapters of Exodus involves Egyptian opposition more than Israelite. What we have in verse 21, as we have seen in verses 18–20, is another indication that the true conflict is about to begin. Moses' focus is now redirected toward the ultimate enemy.[7]

Verse 21 also introduces an inherent theme in Exodus that raises serious questions about God's justice and the freedom of the human will. Moses is to perform the signs before Pharaoh, but God will actually keep Pharaoh from heeding the signs—he will harden Pharaoh's heart (i.e., make him stubborn). There is little one can do to make this verse say something different. It seems that God is not playing fairly. This is not the place to rehearse the centuries-old debate between free will and predestination. Our focus is more narrow—the immediate context and the book of Exodus as a whole. What is clear is that, for whatever reason, God will prevent Pharaoh from acting in such a way as to save his own neck and the neck of his kingdom.

We should understand verse 21 as another hint of the deliverance from Egypt. Here, God is revealing to Moses the mysteries of his plan of attack. As this passage progresses, we are allowed to peer further and further into the plan that God has for dealing with Israel's enemy. In 3:19, all we are told is that God is *aware* that Pharaoh will react stubbornly. In fact, 3:19 seems to contradict 4:21. In 3:19, God says that he *knows* Pharaoh will resist "*unless a*

---

6. I lean toward the opinion that Moses left his family in Midian in 4:20, but I cannot give convincing reasons.

7. Houtman plausibly suggests that v. 21 is evidence of an unrecorded exchange between the Lord and Moses (*Exodus*, 1:428–29). I prefer to read v. 21 as having more an explicit theological purpose in the narrative rather than being an example of terseness, but the reader is invited to assess the arguments of both options.

mighty hand compels him." In other words, according to 3:19, it will not be until God displays his power that Pharaoh will relent. But in 4:21, God will make Pharaoh resist those very mighty acts that in 3:19 are supposed to break Pharaoh's will. The point is clear: In 3:19, Pharaoh's resistance seems to be his own doing; in 4:21, it is the will of God. This is the real tension of the narrative. It is not simply that God will harden Pharaoh's heart, but that the cause of Pharaoh's hardness is said to come from two sources.

Allowing us here to peer into the inner workings of God's plan serves to introduce the back-and-forth of God's role in the hardening of Pharaoh's heart that will surface repeatedly in the subsequent chapters. I understand 4:21 not to contradict 3:19, but to take 3:19 to another level, one that is ultimately unfathomable by our standards. The verbal connection between 3:19 and 4:21 is lost in the NIV. In 3:19, a "mighty hand" is needed to compel Pharaoh to acquiesce. In 4:21, God will "harden" Pharaoh's heart. Both "mighty" and "harden" are formed from the Hebrew root *ḥzq*. This overlap is striking. On the one hand, in 3:19 it is God's *ḥzq* that will serve to convince Pharaoh to release the Israelites; this is what finally happens after the death of the firstborn. But in 4:21 it is God's *ḥzq* that will *prevent* Pharaoh from heeding Moses' demand to release the Israelites. This is essentially what happens throughout the first nine plagues. Pharaoh is God's plaything. God will do as he wishes to the king. God will not only act mightily and sovereignly in delivering Israel, he will also dictate Pharaoh's response.

The obvious point of all this should not be lost: The deliverance of Israel from Egypt is entirely God's doing and under his complete control. The impending Exodus is a play in which God is author, producer, director, and principal actor. The purpose of 4:21, then, is not to introduce some abstract philosophical notion of God's sovereignty. Rather, it is further confirmation of what we have seen earlier in chapter 4, that God is with Moses and with Israel. Now we begin to see just how pervasive his presence truly is. The words of comfort we read in 2:23–25 take on a new dimension. God's apparent absence in chapter 1 and the announcement in 2:23–25 of his impending activity gives way to a greater revelation of what God's role is in the deliverance of his beloved people. Not only is Israel's fate in God's hands but Egypt's as well.

Verses 22–23 conclude the Lord's final talk to Moses before beginning his mission. Here, the Lord tells Moses what he is to say to Pharaoh—the first fulfillment of God's promise to be "with Moses' mouth" (4:12, see comments).[8]

---

8. Apparently, Moses is to speak to Pharaoh the words of vv. 22–23 just before the commencement of the tenth plague. Hence, v. 23 might better be translated, "I *have been saying* to you, 'Let my people go so that they might serve me,' but you *have kept refusing* to let them, so I am *about* to kill your firstborn son."

These verses are important in the context of the deliverance story that concludes in chapter 15. Israel is not simply one nation among others; rather, Israel is God's firstborn son. This nation of slaves and outcasts is special to God, and God wants Moses to make sure that Pharaoh knows it. Israel has a privileged status among the nations.[9] As God's son, Israel has an obligation to serve him and him alone: "Let my son go, *so he may worship me.*" God's demand for Israel's release is not simply for Israel to be free *from* service to Egypt, but for Israel *to* serve the Lord.

The reason for Israel's release goes beyond vague notions of "freedom from oppression." Rather, God's son is now to enter into a close father-son relationship with God. Since Israel is God's firstborn son, the appropriate punishment against Egypt for harming Israel is for God to harm Egypt's firstborn son. Verse 23 is an explicit allusion to the tenth plague, where God kills Egypt's firstborn sons, which is what finally persuades Pharaoh to release the Israelites. These verses, then, recount the Exodus by bringing us to the very end of Israelite captivity: the death of the firstborn and departure from Egypt. Verses 18–23 as a whole are a climax to the preceding chapters and serve as a bridge connecting these chapters to the powerful deeds that follow.

The Circumcision of Moses' Son (4:24–26)

THE FLOW OF verses 18–23 seems to be rudely interrupted by verses 24–26. Anyone familiar with the legion of interpretive challenges that surround this next passage and the oppressive amount of scholarly activity it has generated will be relieved to know that they will not be treated here in as much detail as they might otherwise deserve. Why? (1) There is little anyone can say about this brief passage that has not already been treated (too) thoroughly elsewhere.[10] (2) After the dust clears and the debate subsides, few definitive conclusions can be drawn.

---

9. Houtman's words are worth citing: "In the dispute about the question to whom Israel belongs and who is her legitimate ruler, Pharaoh or YHWH, YHWH at last will show that he has intimate emotional ties with Israel. Pharaoh had better know that to YHWH Israel is not just his own people, they are also dear to him, and therefore he will go to bat for them all the way. Pharaoh is going to be hit (4:23) at his most sensitive spot, the spot where he has touched YHWH himself, viz. in the love for the firstborn" (*Exodus*, 1:430).

10. A sampling of the scholarly literature includes the following: H. Kosmala, "The 'Bloody Husband,'" *VT* 12 (1962): 14–28; J. Morgenstern, "The 'Bloody Husband' (?) (Exod. 4:24–26) Once Again," *HUCA* 34 (1963): 35–70; W. Dumbrell, "Exodus 4:24–26: A Textual Re-examination," *HTR* 65 (1972): 285–90; L. Kaplan, "'And the Lord Sought to Kill Him' (Exod 4:24): Yet Once Again," *HAR* 5 (1981): 65–74; C. Houtman, "Exodus 4:24–26 and Its Interpretation," *JNSL* 11 (1983): 81–105; B. P. Robinson, "Zipporah to the Rescue: A Contextual Study of Exodus IV 24–6," *VT* 36 (1986): 447–61; W. H. Propp, "That

Some of the difficulties of this passage are obscured by the translation of the NIV. The following translation attempts to preserve the ambiguity of the Hebrew and thus helps us better to appreciate the problems:

> Now, at the lodging place along the way, the Lord met him and sought to kill him. So Zipporah took a flint knife, cut off the foreskin of her son, and touched his "feet."[11] She said, "You are a bridegroom of blood to me." So he let him alone. (At that time she said "bridegroom of blood," referring to circumcision.)

There are a number of ambiguities that beset this passage in the Hebrew that no English translation can adequately capture, but even this translation (other translations are possible) points out several ambiguities that cry out for explanation. Who is it that the Lord wants to kill? Assuming it is Moses, why would the Lord want to kill him after he just gave him the command to go? Why is Zipporah able to appreciate the gravity of the situation and, more important, know exactly how to alleviate it? If the object of God's anger is Moses, why does Zipporah circumcise her son? Which son was it (more than one is mentioned in v. 20)? Whose "feet" does she touch with the foreskin? Who let whom alone? And what does "bridegroom of blood" mean?[12]

Again, answering each of these questions (there are more) will not detain us. Nevertheless, we are obliged to make some sense of this section, since it is here for a purpose. Without wading through the interpretive muck and mire, let me suggest that these verses presage the importance of circumcision in 12:43–49.[13] We are able to make several fairly safe assumptions: (1) The object of God's wrath is Moses; no one really disputes this, and it makes the most sense in the context. (2) God is probably angry with Moses because his son (or perhaps both he and his son) is not circumcised. In any event, circumcision has something to do with it. (3) Zipporah's[14] circumcision of her son appeases God's wrath and causes him to relent.

We have seen above how verses 18–23 introduce us to how God's plan of deliverance will be worked out in the following chapters; they are a

---

Bloody Bridegroom (Exodus IV 24–6)," *VT* 43 (1993): 495–518; R. B. Allen, "The 'Bloody Bridegroom' in Exodus 4:24–26," *BSac* 153 (1996): 259–69. For additional bibliography, see Durham, *Exodus*, 51–52; Houtman, *Exodus*, 1:432–33.

11. "Feet" is likely a euphemism for genitals (Plastaras, *The God of Exodus*, 103; Sarna, *Exodus*, 26 and n. 38).

12. For brief synopsis of the various views of this passage, see Durham, *Exodus*, 57; Jacob, *Exodus*, 106–10; Childs, *Book of Exodus*, 95–101.

13. Sarna discusses this approach in his commentary (*Exodus*, 25; see also Childs, *Book of Exodus*, 104).

14. It is worth pointing out that, once again, a woman comes to the rescue to deliver Moses (cf. chs. 1–2).

foreshadowing of the events to come. If we look at verses 24–26 in the same way, we can begin (and only begin!) to make some sense of them. Verses 18–23 tell us what God is going to do to Egypt in the subsequent chapters; verses 24–26 tell us something about God and Israel. The importance of circumcision (and Passover) in 12:43–49 can be seen in how it is so stressed on the eve of the Exodus. Of all the things that the Israelites need to hear before their departure, why is so much time spent pointing out the necessity of circumcision, a rite that won't even become relevant until well after their departure?

What we see in 4:24–26 is the zeal with which the Lord guards this most important rite. We must remember that circumcision as a sign of God's covenant was commanded of the patriarch Abraham (Gen. 17:1–27). Throughout the opening chapters of Exodus we have noted the importance God attaches to the patriarchs, particularly in connection with God's name (Ex. 3:15–16; 4:5). It is in his connection to the patriarchs that God is to be known, and it is for the sake of the patriarchs that God will deliver Israel (2:24). Yet this connection to the patriarchs also imposes a covenant obligation on Moses and the Israelites. They have been delivered by the God of Abraham, Isaac, and Jacob. They are, therefore, to observe the command given to them: Circumcise your male children.

In the same way, then, that verses 18–23 presage Egypt's consequences for not obeying the Lord, verses 24–26 presage Israel's consequences for not obeying the command to circumcise. This is apparently such a serious concern that the Lord is willing to kill Moses, whom he had just taken so much time to convince of his role in God's plan. Moses can argue, pout, whine, and hold his breath about going to Egypt and God will deal patiently with him— but circumcision is another matter. Failure to circumcise meets with swift punishment. The story of God's attack "at a lodging place" symbolizes Israel's and Moses' subsequent rebellions and God's just anger, followed by propitiation. Were there less ambiguity in this passage, or if explicit reference to this passage had been made elsewhere in Exodus, more definitive statements could be made. But as it stands, the best we can do is take some of the clues and trace the trajectory of this passage within the context of the Exodus narrative.

Moses, Aaron, and the Israelites (4:27–31)

THE MENTION OF Aaron in 4:27 recalls 4:14–17. In fact, verse 27 might be better translated, "Now the Lord *had* (previously) said to Aaron, 'Go into the desert to meet Moses,'" referring to some previous conversation God had with Aaron implied in 4:14–17.[15] In verses 27–31, God's words to Moses on

---

15. Jacob, *Exodus*, 110.

Mount Horeb are realized: Moses meets with Aaron as promised (4:14). The fact that Aaron and Moses meet on the "mountain of God" is significant. As God had earlier commissioned Moses on Mount Horeb, Moses is now inaugurating Aaron.[16] Moses proceeds to relay to Aaron what God has told him and the signs he has been given to perform. Moses, thus, becomes "God" for Aaron (4:16) in bringing God's message to him.

After Aaron's initial debriefing, they both go to meet with the elders of Israel (see 3:16–18). In this meeting, Aaron, not Moses, is the one who relays the message to the people, thus fulfilling God's earlier promise that Aaron will speak for Moses (4:16). In speaking on Moses' behalf and performing the wonders,[17] this initial contact with the people gives us a glimpse of what is ahead in Exodus. Throughout the next ten chapters, Aaron and Moses will confront Pharaoh with both word and deed in an effort to get him to release the Israelites.

The good news for Moses is that the people seem to accept him enthusiastically, thus allaying his fear of rejection (v. 31). Aaron performs the signs before them and they believe. As noted earlier, what convinces the people of Moses' divine call are the signs he performs, not the fact that he knows God's name. Throughout this passage, there is, somewhat curiously, no mention of the fact that God has "revealed" his name to Moses in 3:13–15. This bit of information is not necessary to convince the Israelites because they are well aware of who their God is. Moreover, the matter-of-fact reference to Yahweh (NIV, "LORD") in verse 31 implies that the name is familiar to them. No explanation of this allegedly new name is needed.

In any event, the people seem to be on board now, although, as we will see later, this is merely a lull in the rejection theme. They are moved to worship at seeing how the Lord is "concerned" with them (the same word used in 3:16). Worship is the appropriate response to God's love for them. It is also the ultimate reason for which he is bringing them out of Egypt (v. 23).

Exodus 4:18–31 is an important passage in the flow of the narrative. Here we see the final preparation for Moses' task. Elements of both previous chapters and subsequent events are drawn together for the purpose of preparing the reader for the narrative that follows. Moses has returned to Egypt and the Israelites are beginning to realize that God's promised deliverance will be

---

16. Houtman, *Exodus*, 1:450.

17. Since Moses originally seems to have requested these signs in anticipation of Israelite incredulity (4:1), the fact that the wonders are performed before the people seems to imply that they *need* to be performed, i.e., that these elders offer some resistance to Moses' message. See also Houtman, *Exodus*, 1:453.

realized in their lifetime. The stage is set for the confrontation between Moses and Pharaoh.

Bridging Contexts

"THIS IS MY SON, whom I love" (Matt. 3:17). That God refers to Israel as his "firstborn son" in 4:22 is no throw-away line or mere expression of sentimentality. Rather, it gets at the heart of the special relationship that God has with his people. This statement is a powerful summary of how close God truly is to his people; the Exodus is the expression of the father's love for his son. Sonship language is not restricted to 4:22. Elsewhere in the Old Testament sonship language is used generally in two ways: to describe Israel's relationship to God (as we see in 4:22) and to describe the relationship between God and Israel's king. The theological thrusts of both these images ultimately converge on the love of God for his firstborn Son, Christ, and the love he has for Christ's church.

Israel is God's son, not only according to 4:22 but also according to such passages as Jeremiah 3:19; 31:9 and Hosea 11:1. These passages remind us that being God's son means not only enjoying a privileged relationship with God but also living up to the responsibilities that this relationship entails. These passages remind us that being a son is a high calling. In the context of the book of Exodus as a whole, we know that Israel the son is not always faithful to the Father. Israel's periodic rebellions are especially grievous to God precisely because of the intimacy between them as expressed in 4:22.

As all parents know, children can give parents both inexpressible joy and grievous suffering and heartache. Jeremiah is a prophet called by God to deal head-on with Israel's rebelliousness, which eventually brought the punishment of the Exile on them. God called Israel as his own, but they continued to go their own way. The Lord says (Jer. 3:19):

> How gladly would I treat you like sons
>   and give you a desirable land,
>   the most beautiful inheritance of any nation.
> I thought you would call "Father"
>   and not turn away from me following me.

God's feelings of both anger and heartbreak are evident. A son should not treat his father with such contempt, particularly this Father who had shown so dramatically time and time again how much he loves his son.[18] When a

---

18. The unrequited love God has for Israel is also expressed in terms of the husband/wife metaphor (e.g., Isa. 50:1–2; Hos. 1–3, where Israel is an adulterous wife).

son is unfaithful, he is punished. In the case of Jeremiah it is the exile to Babylon. Yet the punishment is not permanent; there is a restoration of the relationship between Father and son. The period of captivity ends and Israel returns to her home.

> They will come with weeping;
>> they will pray as I bring them back.
> I will lead them beside streams of water
>> on a level path where they will not stumble,
> because I am Israel's father,
>> and Ephraim is my firstborn son. (Jer. 31:9)

God restores Israel to himself because Israel is his firstborn son. As most of us can attest, the family relationship brings out in us intense emotions, both love and anger, even hate. We become angry and punish our children, but not long afterward they are sitting in our laps while we wipe away the last lingering tears. Israel's relationship to God is similar. His wrath is severe when Israel rebels, but his faithfulness and fatherly love rise as sure as the sun.

God's faithfulness to his son Israel is also expressed in Hosea 11:1–11, a passage particularly important since it is cited in Matthew 2:15. Hosea recounts how God delivered his son Israel from Egyptian slavery: "When Israel was a child, I loved him, and out of Egypt I called my son" (Hos. 11:1; the sonship language seems to recall Ex. 4:22). Part of Hosea's point is to highlight Israel's rebellion despite God's deliverance from Egypt (Hos. 11:2– 7). Verses 5–7 even suggest that Israel will return to Egypt because of their disobedience. But here, too, as we have seen in Jeremiah, punishment is not the final word between father and son. There is always restoration. The Lord resolves that he cannot leave his children alone: "How can I give you up, Ephraim? How can I hand you over, Israel?" (v. 8). God will not leave them but will lead them back to their homes (v. 11). Though they are sinful, he will forgive them and bring them home.

The link between Israel as God's son and Christ as God's Son seems obvious, but the connection between them is more than merely lexical, as a reading of Matthew 2:15 brings out.[19] The point here is that Matthew identifies Israel with Christ—both are God's son. This is the motive behind the somewhat unexpected (by our exegetical standards, at any rate) appeal to Hosea 11:1 as being fulfilled in Jesus' coming out of Egypt after the death of Herod. Christ is the Son of God; better, he is the true Son of God. What applied to

---

19. See also Matt. 17:5; Rom. 8:29; Col. 1:15, 18; Heb. 1:5; 5:5. The relationship between Hos. 11:1–11 and Matt. 2:15 has already been mentioned in the Bridging Contexts section of Ex. 2:11–25.

Israel the son only proleptically is *fulfilled* (this is Matthew's word) in the life of Christ, *the* Son. Christ is the ultimate embodiment of the true intimacy between the Father and his people. Christ is the new Israel.

Moreover, we should not lose sight of the context of Hosea 11. Israel is God's son, but because of utter rebellion, Israel is threatened with exile. Yet God cannot punish the Israelites for long; he brings them back and restores them (v. 11). Israel is sinful, but the Father forgives his son. Christ, however, is truly God's Son. His intimacy with the Father far exceeds that of Old Testament Israel because his will is perfectly in harmony with the Father's. Unlike Israel, Christ is without sin. Yet he is the one who will one day bear the full brunt of God's anger. Historical Israel is sinful but forgiven. Christ, the new Israel, is without sin but receives no mercy. He is the object of God's wrath. By drawing the analogy between Christ and Israel, Matthew is also drawing out the great distinction between the two. Christ fulfills the ideal of a wholly perfect, obedient son: "This is my Son, whom I love; with him I am well pleased" (Matt. 3:17).

The church, made up of both Jews and Gentiles, is now heir to God's promises to Israel. But the church appropriates these promises only in light of the work of Christ. We are God's son, the new Israel, *only* because Christ is God's Son first. The church is God's son by virtue of its relationship to Christ, the true Son. That relationship is repeatedly described by Paul as "in Christ." As mentioned throughout this commentary, Christians are united with Christ (Rom. 6:5). With respect to the Old Testament, this means that Christians should read passages such as Exodus 4:22 in light of the person and work of Christ, who first fulfilled this passage. Old Testament sonship language should be applied to the church Christologically.

Another way of putting this is to say that Christ is the representative of his people. A similar representative role is played by Old Testament kings with respect to their people. Israel is God's son, but so is the king. The classic passage here is Psalm 2. This psalm describes the anointing and installation of an Israelite king. In verse 7 the Lord says, "You are my Son; today I have become your Father."[20] The king is God's son (or better, he "becomes" God's son at his installation). It should be no surprise that this psalm is cited several times in the New Testament to refer to Christ (Acts 4:25–26; 13:33; Heb. 1:5; 5:5; Rev. 2:27; 19:15). Although the king of Israel is God's son, that title finds its ultimate expression in the true Son of God and King of his people. This is not to say that the author of Psalm 2 knew that his words would apply fully to Christ. Rather, in light of Christ's coming the New Testament authors could begin reading the Old Testament as a book that spoke ulti-

union with Christ

---

20. Similar language is also found in Ps. 89:26–29.

mately of the risen Lord. Christ fulfills both the Israelite and kingly ideal of sonship. He is the true King; he is fully obedient to the Father.

Such an understanding of the church's position as son serves as the proper basis for viewing ourselves as God's people. We, too, are God's "son." We enjoy that special relationship with him as did the ancient Israelites. But however intimate that relationship may have been between God and Israel, it is more intense between God and the church because the church is intimately united to the true Son. Christ is not simply the Father's firstborn son, he is "the firstborn among many brothers" (Rom. 8:29; cf. Col. 1:15, 18). Christ came so that those who believe in him can share in that sonship, be a part of God's family. We are, to use John's language, "born again" or "born from above."[21] Our new birth puts us in God's family, which has significant implications for how we view our Christian lives (cf. below).

The potter and the clay. By any standard, the way in which Pharaoh is treated in 4:21 is startling. In the final analysis, all of us, regardless of theological persuasion, are left to ponder the seeming injustice, or at least the profound mystery, of God's hardening Pharaoh's heart. It could be suggested that such hardening must be "balanced" with 3:19, where the hardening of Pharaoh's heart is his own doing. Yet this does not alleviate the problem. Frankly, it would be easier to make sense of God's justice if he controlled Pharaoh's reaction throughout as he does in 4:22 and not just once in a while. But what we see is Egypt's king as a toy on a string that God can pick up and manipulate now and then as he pleases.

The role that God takes in directing human affairs is an issue that comes up from time to time in Scripture. The tension created in our minds between God's sovereignty and human freedom is a tension that not only we but biblical authors themselves struggle with. It is not the place here to engage the debate between predestination and free will or to provide a list of proof texts to defend any particular position. The Esau and Jacob narrative, where God chooses to love Jacob but hate Esau, is familiar enough.[22] We also have the famous "potter/clay" passages in Isaiah 29 and 45 and Jeremiah 18. These passages offer an added dimension to the discussion. Whereas Exodus 4 and the Esau narrative refer to God's directing the actions of non-Israelites (although this is not technically true of Esau), Isaiah and Jeremiah speak of

---

21. John 3:3. The Greek word *anothen* can mean either "again" or "above." The ambiguity may well be intentional: to be born again means that you have received the birth that comes from God, who is above.

22. The story of Jacob and Esau is found in Gen. 27–33. The famous statement, "Yet I have loved Jacob, but Esau I have hated" is found in Mal. 1:2–3. Echoes of this can be seen in the Cain and Abel story, where God chooses to accept Abel's offering but not Cain's (no explicit reason is given, but see Heb. 11:4 and 1 John 3:12).

God's directing Israel's fortunes as a potter shapes clay. The issue is brought closer to home.

In Roman's 9, Paul deals with the matter of God's sovereign choice and brings into his discussion the passages mentioned above, including Pharaoh's hard heart (he cites Ex. 9:16). As Christian readers of the Old Testament, we must direct our attention to Paul's words if we hope to understand how God's sovereignty plays out in our lives. We will not attempt to unravel the mysteries of this chapter in Romans that have for centuries inspired both awe toward God and contempt for Paul. Still, the heart of Paul's argument is expressed in Romans 9:19–21, where he addresses, with his usual pointedness and energy, the central problem:

> One of you will say to me: "Then why does God still blame us? For who resists his will?" But who are you, O man, to talk back to God? "Shall what is formed say to him who formed it, 'Why did you make me like this?'" Does not the potter have the right to make out of the same lump of clay some pottery for noble purposes and some for common use?

It is perhaps best to respect Paul's inspired words without reducing to an abstract principle or sanitized theological proposition the struggle that his readers (and he too?) must have felt. The specific issue that gave rise to Romans 9 is the inclusion of the Gentiles into God's family and the rejection of some Jews (those who do not believe in Christ; see esp. the citation of Old Testament passages in vv. 25–29). The ultimate answer to God's apparent lack of consistency in judging people is given by Paul: God can do as he pleases.

I sometimes wonder whether the tension in Scripture between free will and predestination is not there for a purpose. Perhaps it is not a riddle to be solved (i.e., "Which is the 'correct' view?"). Its purpose may be to remind us of how distant our thoughts are from the Lord's. How God deals with the world and with his people is ultimately far beyond our reckoning. It could not be otherwise. Already in the opening chapters of Exodus this tension is introduced: "Pharaoh won't let you go unless I show my power; I will harden Pharaoh's heart so that he won't respond properly to my display of power." No one can read these words and not feel his or her mental categories about God and life shaken a bit. The sovereign Lord does as he wills.

Related to this notion of sovereignty is the sonship theme discussed above. God is sovereign and does as he wills, but this is not an abstract, baseless kind of sovereignty. What drives God is the love he has as father for a son. This may be seen, for example, in Isaiah 64:8:

Yet, O LORD, you are our *Father*.
    We are the clay, you are the *potter;*
    we are all the work of your hand.

God's role as potter is not to be divorced from his role as Father; "potter" does not mean "tyrant." Rather, he does as he wills as a *father* acting for the good of his children.

Let us think for a moment of how parents treat their children. How often is the charge leveled against us by our children, "That's not fair"? I hear this all the time from my own children, and try as I might, I can never get them to understand the old parental stand-by line: "I'm doing it for your own good." But it is absolutely true! In Exodus 4:18—31, such a scenario seems to be played out on the way at the lodging place (vv. 24—26). Although I have no intention of sweeping away the tensions and ambiguities of this passage, I contend that God's "attack" actually affords Moses an opportunity to correct his mistake. Had God wanted to bring swift retribution on Moses, he could have, but he didn't. In this regard it is tempting to read verse 24 as an indication that God was not fully committed to bringing about Moses' demise: The Hebrew literally says, "He sought (*baqaš*) to kill him" rather than the NIV's "he was about to kill him."[23] Hence, 4:24—26 may be more a story of a lesson learned, father to son, than a narrowly aborted attempt by a capricious God to kill Moses.

But there is something missing in drawing together God's role as potter and father. Can the two be brought together so easily? Saying that God is both potter and father to Moses or Israel is one thing, but what of Pharaoh? Certainly God is not father to him. When we grow angry with our children and punish them, they do not cease being our children. We do not drive them off or kill them. Moreover, we certainly don't punish children outside of our family. But this is precisely what God seems to be doing. His role as potter goes beyond his fatherly treatment of his family Israel; he is sovereign over all creation.

This is precisely what troubles us so, and we arrive back at the beginning of the problem. How can we understand a God who does as he pleases, at times apparently completely out of sync with the rules of conduct that we take for granted every day? For Christians, focusing our attention on how God is *our* potter/father is perhaps the most concrete way of addressing the issue. It is not given to Christians to fathom the depths of the mind of God. Perhaps we should be less concerned with how God's sovereignty works in general and more concerned with how it relates to us. In the end we may finally have the mind of Paul (Rom. 11:33—36):

---

23. See R. Allen, "The 'Bloody Bridegroom,'" 265.

Oh, the depth of the riches of the wisdom and knowledge of God!
How unsearchable his judgments,
and his paths beyond tracing out!
"Who has known the mind of the Lord?
Or who has been his counselor?"
"Who has ever given to God,
that God should repay him?"
For from him and through him and to him are all things.
To him be the glory forever! Amen.

GOD IS OUR FATHER. That we are God's children and he is our Father is not something to be taken for granted. As John writes, "How *great* is the love the Father has lavished on us, that we should be called children of God" (1 John 3:1). It is truly a wonderful thing that God is our Father. Many in our world today, however, think of it as a burden. For some, fatherhood is thought to be not only an oppressive notion that is offensive to women, but the notion of God as Father is a mere product of ancient Israel's social (patriarchal) setting and has little value for present-day reality. Rather than an indication of how God loves his people, "father" has become a hated symbol for some or an abstract academic term for others.

Part of the problem that some today have with referring to God as Father and thinking of themselves as children of God is that they have endured painful and horrible experiences with their own fathers. While I was in graduate school, I met a woman in the photocopying room (where it seems I spent most of my graduate years!). She was at an adjoining copier. I decided to strike up a conversation with her: "What are you working on?" She turned to me with a look of both preoccupation and a bit of agitation. She proceeded to tell me that she was working on a passage in one of the Gospels (I can't remember the details), which, she argued, indicated that God cannot and should not be referred to as "Father," since people who have suffered abuse by their fathers would be unable to relate positively to this image. Part of me wanted to debate her. Another part of me, however, was more patient. The Holy Spirit muzzled me, and I listened to what she was saying. It turned out that she was abused by her father. It stands to reason that she would have some barriers to overcome if she were to think of God as her Father.

Despite the reality of her terrible experiences, however, there is something vital that is missing in her way of thinking. She has not caught on to the wonder of *God* as her Father. True, her earthly father violated the sacred trust between a father and his child. The mistake this woman made, however, was in projecting these failures onto *God* as Father. Rather than measuring God by what her earthly father had done, she should be measuring her earthly father by the character of her heavenly Father—a standard by which an earthly father would have come up damnably short.

I am not suggesting that this would have been easy for her at this point in her life, but it is certainly the place to start. She should not reject the notion of God as Father because of the behavior of her earthly father. She should look to the biblical picture of God the Father as her inspiration for what the father-daughter relationship can really mean. She would see perhaps, in time, that God as Father is a good thing and not something to be avoided. She would learn that the fatherhood of God is precisely that element that is designed to bring us closer to God rather than repel us from him.

Our world is sinful; we distort what is good. But the Bible presents us with an image of God's fatherhood that is intended to transcend our experiences and transform our minds and hearts (Rom. 12:2). Perhaps one day this woman, who has suffered much, will learn that as a child of the heavenly Father she is loved by the Father with a love that is pure, holy, and ever faithful. She will learn that her heavenly Father zealously guards and cares for his children, that her heavenly Father is precisely the refuge she should run to in her struggles rather than avoid.

Being a son, as we have seen, entails certain responsibilities in addition to √ privileges. As children of earthly parents, we are taught to obey and respect our elders. There is, in a word, a relationship between parent and child; it is a two-way street. This is also what we find in our relationship to God the Father. We come into the family of God by being born anew by his grace, or to use Paul's image, we are adopted (Rom. 8:15, 23).

Once we are claimed as God's own—in other words, once we enter into that relationship—we begin to bear greater and greater responsibility within that relationship. Like parents of earthly children, we do not expect a three-year-old to assume the obligations of a ten-year-old. Nevertheless, any child, at least after a certain age, is expected to be a cooperative and contributing member of the family. This notion of responsibility lies behind the biblical idea of covenant responsibility. Israel is redeemed from Egypt. Following upon that historical act, God impresses on them the necessity to serve him and him alone.

Liberation theology. In recent years a popular theological movement, both in American and Latin American countries, has been "liberation theology." This is no mere academic movement. In fact, most Americans who are tuned in to their culture can see occasional, albeit veiled, references to it. Although there are differing nuances of liberation theology (varying from theologian to theologian or from issue to issue), what they all have in common is the notion that God is, without qualification, on the side of the oppressed and that relief from oppression is the true goal of all Christian work. Appeal is commonly made to the Exodus as support: The Israelites were enslaved by an oppressive political force, and God came to destroy this force and set his people free. Now, most everyone agrees that God is not for oppression, nor does he approve of injustice, whether political, cultural, judicial, or private. In fact, liberation theology has been a healthy reminder to evangelicals that God is not simply concerned with matters of personal piety, but also with broader societal sins.

What liberation theologians tend to neglect, however, is the theological context in which the Exodus occurs. (1) The assumption is often made that, according to Exodus, God is *always* оіn the side of the oppressed. But the focus of the book of Exodus is the oppression of *Israel, God's firstborn son*. There is an element of truth to their assertion, since elsewhere God cautions the Israelites not to oppress aliens living among them (e.g., Ex. 23:9); that is, God seems to show concern for more than just Israelite oppression. Nevertheless, Exodus is not a story of how God hates oppression and will go to great lengths to deliver the oppressed. Rather, it is a story of how great the Father's love is for the son. In other words, Israel is not redeemed simply because it is *oppressed*, but because Israel is God's *firstborn son*.

(2) Looking back at Exodus 1, the ultimate sin of Pharaoh is not so much in enslaving the Israelites. Although this is truly a terrible thing and provides the final motivation for deliverance, Pharaoh's ultimate sin is in working against the creation mandate (see comments under Ex. 1). Pharaoh's sin is only peripherally against Israel; the truly offended party is God.

(3) Liberation theology tends to overlook the real purpose for which Israel was delivered. Moses does not say, "Let my people go," but "Let my people go, *so that they may worship me in the desert* " (7:16).[24] As Jon Levenson puts it, the Exodus is more a story of "repatriation than emancipation. . . . It is a movement from one form of servitude to another."[25] The point of the Exodus is lost when we reduce it to a story of liberation from slavery, as if it can be applied to any oppressed people who wish "freedom."[26] The point of the Exodus is not freedom. It is about God's calling his own people back to him

---

24. This point is forcefully made by J. D. Levenson, "Liberation Theology and the Exodus," *Midstream* 35/7 (1989): 30–36.

25. Ibid., 34, 35.

26. The fact that the post-Exodus Israelite society made provisions for slavery, class distinctions, and other societal differences should be enough to demonstrate that Exodus does not paint a picture of a God who is "against oppression" (ibid., 32).

in order that they might enter into a relationship, one in which Father and children are obligated to each other.

> The limitation on Israelite slavery is owing to YHWH's prior claim upon them: He, and none other, is their master, and the "jealous God" will share their service with no one else. To speak of this subtle and paradoxical theology as one of "liberation" is to miss the paradox that lies at the heart of the Exodus: Israel's *liberation* from degrading bondage is a function of their *subjugation* to YHWH their God. The Exodus is not only a road out of Egypt; it is also a road to Mount Sinai.[27]

This understanding of the purpose of the Exodus is not only the proper backdrop from which to understand current theological trends, but also the proper framework in which to view our Christian lives. An issue with which every Christian struggles is the relationship between grace and works. On the one extreme (although I must admit that I have met few people like this), you have those who say that since we are saved by grace, it doesn't matter what we do. Grace is what saves us; hence, it is what keeps us saved. Since we do not become Christians by our works, our works are also irrelevant to the Christian life. Although passages such as Romans 5:1–11 and Ephesians 2:8–10 may be (wrongly) appealed to in support of such thinking, it clearly ignores Paul's own warnings against having this mindset (Rom. 6:1–23). The other extreme is to accentuate the need for good works to such a degree that the grace of God is lost sight of. Here, James is often called upon in support (e.g., James 1:23–25; 2:14–26).

Both extremes miss the message of Exodus and the gospel. Works are most certainly not irrelevant to the Christian life. We are all obliged by God to bear the fruit of the Spirit (Gal. 5:22–26). The New Testament letters as a whole are concerned to encourage and admonish believers with respect to proper *conduct* precisely in view of the fact that they have been saved by *grace*. Grace and works are not antithetical; the latter flows from the former. When God calls us to be his sons and daughters, he calls us to be obedient children whose *actions* exemplify the reality of the presence of God's grace in our lives.

Conversely, and this is probably the area that more Christians struggle with, we should not so maximize the importance of works that we forget God's grace, which is the proper basis from which to view our works. Here Romans 5:9–10 is truly a comfort to us:

> Since we have now been justified by his blood, how much more shall we be saved from God's wrath through him! For if, when we were

---

27. Ibid., 35.

God's enemies, we were reconciled to him through the death of his Son, how much more, having been reconciled, shall we be saved through his life!

We are saved by grace, and now that we are saved, the risen Christ, the firstborn among many brothers and sisters (Rom. 8:29), continues to be at work in us. As James says, "faith without deeds is dead" (James 2:26). But our deeds are performed within the context of the Father-child relationship with God, a relationship we have had secured for us by virtue of our relationship to Christ, the true Son of God. This has significant ramifications for how we view the Christian life. We do not simply work, we work in Christ. We do not labor only for Christ, but in Christ and by his power.

The point is that we need not be paralyzed by whether we have done enough today or whether our works are good enough. In one sense they are never good enough. But in another, more important sense, we labor not on our own but in Christ. This gives us a measure of security—not complacency, but comfort knowing that, as we read in Romans 5, God continues to be on our side after we have been brought into his family. Our ultimate security is to be found in the work of Christ on the cross and in the empty tomb, and not on how we have performed today. This is not because performance is irrelevant, but because the just penalty for the shortcomings of our actions or our failure to act has been put on Christ's shoulders, not ours. In short, we labor not so that God will be pleased with us. That was dealt with on the cross. Rather, God *is* pleased with us. We labor now because we *are* in God's family.

I hear so often how well-intentioned Christians feel guilty for not having their devotions that morning, or that their devotions were not long enough or sincere enough. Guilt gets a bad rap in our day, and Christians are absolutely correct in pointing out that guilt is a proper feeling to have when one is disobedient to God. Yet for Christians, our guilt for not "doing" what we ought needs to be tempered by a knowledge that we are God's children and he is our Father. If my children do something wrong, I want them to feel guilty, but I do not want them to be paralyzed with guilt. Nor do I want them to be guilty about silly things. They need to learn which things are worthy of guilt and which are not.

But most important, I want my children to realize that no matter what they have done, no matter how much guilt they feel, and however much that guilt may affect the nature of our relationship for the time being, it will never sever that most essential tie: I am their father, they are my children. That will never change. They will never stop being my children, no matter what they do. My wife and I try hard to provide a home environment where that knowledge forms the basis from which they view their own actions as members of

as if it's a command.

our family. However gracious we are to our children, we know that the God of the Exodus is, in Christ, more gracious still with us.

Why bother trying? God tips his hand in Exodus 4:18–31. He is in control of the process. He shows this by how he treats Pharaoh: At times Pharaoh hardens his own heart, at other times God does it for him. Certainly, God's complete sovereignty in bringing Israel out of Egypt is meant to convey a sense of security that the Israelites would have. God will treat Israel's enemies as he pleases. Israel has nothing to fear concerning this great nation that once held them under its thumb. The problem, however, is the apparent capriciousness of God. Why is he not consistent in his dealings? Moreover, it is not too difficult to project God's dealings with Pharaoh onto other things. Will God also deal as "sovereignly" with his own people? Is this not the point of the potter/clay passages, particularly as they are drawn into Paul's argument in Romans 9:19–21?

We have before us in Exodus hints of the recurring problem in Scripture called by various names: election, predestination, or divine sovereignty. This problem crosses the boundaries erected by the various theological camps. No Christian will deny that God can and does do as he pleases. Yet no Christian, however committed to notions of God's absolute direction of even the most minute details of affairs, can escape the tension between God's sovereignty and the repeated biblical admonitions and warnings to walk in God's ways. If God is as sovereign as Exodus 4:22 seems to imply, the question is naturally raised: "Why should I bother to try? If everything is under God's 'control,' what is there left for me to do?"

As mentioned above, there are few theological issues that inspire as much heated debate as the relationship between sovereignty and free will. For some, predestination is the key that unlocks the victorious Christian life. For others, it is a destructive doctrine that robs the Christian life of any force or meaning. Few remain neutral. If readers are hoping to find a solution to this problem in these few sentences, they need read no further, for they will be disappointed. What I will attempt, however, is to draw out a few salient items that may help to put the issue in a more concrete context for Christians who endeavor to live godly lives.

(1) We must remember that election, or sovereignty, is never an abstract notion. Common arguments against election that I have heard include, "I guess God predestined what kind of tie I would put on today," or, "Are you trying to tell me that God predestined that crack in the sidewalk and that I would trip over that crack!?" As the old joke goes: What did the Calvinist say after he fell down the stairs? "I'm glad that's over with!"[28] Of course, most of

---

28. Of course, this must be tempered with the Arminian response, "What did I do to deserve this?"

these objections are not meant to be taken wholly seriously, but the basic thrust remains: How does God's sovereignty actually, practically, play out in the details of our lives?

This is a question that the Bible does not address. The Bible is not concerned to reveal fully the mysteries of God's dealings with his creation. The notion of God's sovereignty in the Bible is always connected specifically to one issue: the deliverance of God's people. Although this raises a host of other concerns (e.g., are we saved by God's choice without any input on our own?), understanding the salvation context of sovereignty at least puts us on the proper starting point for discussing the issue and how it might affect our lives. Burdening our hearts and minds with abstract implications of sovereignty, something the Bible itself does not entertain, will unnecessarily detract us from the focus the Bible gives to the issue.

(2) However uncomfortable we all feel from time to time with election and its implications, we must remember that the biblical writers do not seem to share that feeling of discomfort. Though the issue is mysterious, it is not presented as a burden in the Bible. This is not to say that it is easily accepted. Paul's protracted argument in Romans 9 may indicate that not only his readers but perhaps Paul himself felt the need to engage the issue more closely. For Paul, the end result of any such internal struggle with sovereignty results in praise (11:33–36). For Job, it ends in humility (Job 42:1–6). Sovereignty is a blessing rather than a hindrance. I am not saying that *understanding* how sovereignty works is a blessing, but that it *is* a blessing regardless of how little we understand.

The Lord holds us in his arms. He is the truly loving Father who cares for us, his children in Christ. Can we really hope for anything better than this? What recourse do we have? Partial sovereignty? It is good to be under the Lord's care. What such an understanding of sovereignty engenders in us is actually a sense of freedom, the knowledge that we are God's children and that we are somehow under his sovereign gaze—no matter what. Sovereignty means that in our everyday lives, we can go forth and act boldly without fear that our constant missteps or imperfections will catch the Lord by surprise and tear us away from him.

(3) However much we try to make sense of sovereignty and incorporate it into our theological systems (as I have just tried to do!), we must remember that it is ultimately a great and humbling mystery. To understand how it works is to peer into the heart of God. I remember so little of my college years, which is no one's fault but my own, but one conversation stands out in my mind. An older classmate and I were discussing the issue of sovereignty and free will and I said, "At the very least we have to accept the basic notion that either one or the other is true. Both cannot be right." My wiser

friend responded, "Why?" I blurted out a comment or two about God needing to be logically consistent, or something like that, but that response
seemed as shallow then as it does now. We should not forget the tension that
Exodus and other portions of Scripture set up. We should not assume that ✓
God conforms to our ways of thinking.

Is this not a recurring theme in the Bible that God's ways are not our
ways? Perhaps part of the value of the tension between predestination and
free will is not found in solving the problem, as if it is a riddle God put in
Scripture to occupy our intellectual energy, but in our standing back in awe
of a God who is so much greater than we can understand. The hope is that
we would go forth with this knowledge (or better, lack of knowledge) and
live humble lives, trusting in the Lord all the more because of the depth of
the riches of his wisdom and knowledge.

Exodus 5:1–21

AFTERWARD MOSES AND Aaron went to Pharaoh and said, "This is what the LORD, the God of Israel, says: 'Let my people go, so that they may hold a festival to me in the desert.'"

²Pharaoh said, "Who is the LORD, that I should obey him and let Israel go? I do not know the LORD and I will not let Israel go."

³Then they said, "The God of the Hebrews has met with us. Now let us take a three-day journey into the desert to offer sacrifices to the LORD our God, or he may strike us with plagues or with the sword."

⁴But the king of Egypt said, "Moses and Aaron, why are you taking the people away from their labor? Get back to your work!" ⁵Then Pharaoh said, "Look, the people of the land are now numerous, and you are stopping them from working."

⁶That same day Pharaoh gave this order to the slave drivers and foremen in charge of the people: ⁷"You are no longer to supply the people with straw for making bricks; let them go and gather their own straw. ⁸But require them to make the same number of bricks as before; don't reduce the quota. They are lazy; that is why they are crying out, 'Let us go and sacrifice to our God.' ⁹Make the work harder for the men so that they keep working and pay no attention to lies."

¹⁰Then the slave drivers and the foremen went out and said to the people, "This is what Pharaoh says: 'I will not give you any more straw. ¹¹Go and get your own straw wherever you can find it, but your work will not be reduced at all.'" ¹²So the people scattered all over Egypt to gather stubble to use for straw. ¹³The slave drivers kept pressing them, saying, "Complete the work required of you for each day, just as when you had straw." ¹⁴The Israelite foremen appointed by Pharaoh's slave drivers were beaten and were asked, "Why didn't you meet your quota of bricks yesterday or today, as before?"

¹⁵Then the Israelite foremen went and appealed to Pharaoh: "Why have you treated your servants this way?

¹⁶Your servants are given no straw, yet we are told, 'Make bricks!' Your servants are being beaten, but the fault is with your own people."

¹⁷Pharaoh said, "Lazy, that's what you are—lazy! That is why you keep saying, 'Let us go and sacrifice to the LORD.' ¹⁸Now get to work. You will not be given any straw, yet you must produce your full quota of bricks."

¹⁹The Israelite foremen realized they were in trouble when they were told, "You are not to reduce the number of bricks required of you for each day." ²⁰When they left Pharaoh, they found Moses and Aaron waiting to meet them, ²¹and they said, "May the LORD look upon you and judge you! You have made us a stench to Pharaoh and his officials and have put a sword in their hand to kill us."

MOSES RETURNS TO EGYPT and is now ready to carry out the task that God has specifically chosen for him. We expect a quick, cataclysmic end to Pharaoh's destructive plan. But this is not what happens. In this section things get worse before they get better. Is this supposed to happen? Did not God say that he would be with Moses and teach him what to say (4:12)? To the detached observer, it looks as if God is still disinterested in Israel's affairs, and the ramblings of an old man and his brother before Pharaoh are not only ineffective, but counterproductive. What is going on?

After Moses and Aaron perform the signs before the Israelites (4:29–31), they appear before Pharaoh.[1] They are confident. They are bold. God has appeared to Moses and given him the authority to do this. Moreover, the Israelites are convinced of the role Moses is to play (4:29–31), which, as we remember, is one misgiving Moses had earlier (3:12–20). Moses is on a roll, and we can rightly expect him to march into Pharaoh's court with confidence. It is, after all, God who is speaking to Pharaoh, since Moses is "God" to Aaron and Aaron is Moses' mouth (4:16). The long period of Egyptian oppression is about to end with but a command from Moses' mouth. They

---

1. As we have seen so often in the opening chapters of Exodus, various details of these events are not provided. How much time elapsed between Moses' meeting with the Israelites and his audience with Pharaoh? How did he get in to see Pharaoh in the first place? Did he barge in? Was he granted an audience?

proclaim,[2] "This is what the LORD, the God of Israel, says." Nothing they could have said would have displayed more authority and confidence.

This opening line may be more familiar to us as the recurring refrain in the prophetic books, "Thus saith the LORD." Moses and Aaron march in and declare that they are God's ambassadors, and in so doing put plainly before Pharaoh that any slight against their message is nothing less than a slight against the one who sent the messengers. Surely, Pharaoh must listen!

Two elements of this opening sally are worth mentioning. (1) The precise content of the command given to Pharaoh is somewhat curious. They mention a *festival* to be celebrated in the desert. The command given by God in 3:18, however, is for the Israelites to take a three-day journey into the desert in order to perform *sacrifices*. One must not, however, draw too sharp a distinction between 5:1 and 3:18, as if Moses is here uttering a command that is contrary to 3:18, since the festival to be celebrated certainly entailed sacrifices. Yet, is it not striking that the first words out of the mouths of Moses and Aaron do not adhere strictly to what God commanded Moses to say? To be sure, he does get around to it two verses later (5:3 = 3:18; perhaps he learned his lesson after the first rebuff in v. 2). Still, his initial utterance is not exactly what God told Moses to say in his confrontation with Pharaoh. We will return to this below.

(2) Note, too, that according to 3:18, Moses *and the elders* are to go before Pharaoh to declare their God-given independence. But where are the elders? They do not so much as set foot in Pharaoh's court, here or anywhere else in Exodus. One can argue, I suppose, that we should assume their presence, but the absence of any mention of the elders elsewhere in the narrative suggests otherwise.[3] We have, then, two specific elements of 3:18 that are missing.

One might suggest that Moses' negligence in fulfilling God's command of 3:18 with scrupulous attention to detail contributes to Pharaoh's negative reaction in 5:2. In other words, had Moses done as he was told by taking the elders and giving the proper command, God would have brought the

---

2. Verse 1 does say that Moses and Aaron speak to Pharaoh. This should hardly be taken literally, however, as if they both speak in unison or that they may have alternated in their address. We should understand this to mean, at least for now, that they both confront Pharaoh while Aaron is the one who does the talking (4:10–17). In keeping with the Exodus narrative itself, however, I will sometimes refer to Moses as the speaker, since Moses addresses Pharaoh regularly in the plague narrative. The possible significance of Moses as speaker rather than Aaron will be discussed at an appropriate juncture below.

3. Jewish tradition, for example, recognizes the difficulty in reconciling 3:18 and 5:1, and explains the elders' absence as due to their loss of nerve. They intend to go with Moses but, on the way, they lose nerve and drop out one by one (Sarna, *Exodus*, 27; cf. *Ex. Rab.* 5.17). This tradition is obviously aimed at exonerating Moses, i.e., he *did* take the elders with him, but they reneged on their own account.

Israelites out of Egypt right then and there. This seems unlikely, however, particularly in light of 3:18–20. Already there God hints that Pharaoh will not immediately release the people, for only a display of his power will do the trick. It is, therefore, best not to invest too much meaning in these curious details (or lack of details!) in 5:1. The point of this narrative is certainly not how Moses is unfaithful to God's initial instruction and the consequences thereof. Rather, the point is Pharaoh's hardness of heart and God's miraculous deliverance of his beloved people.

Perhaps nowhere is Pharaoh's hardness of heart demonstrated more clearly than in the first words he utters in the Exodus narrative: "Who is the LORD?" In time, of course, Pharaoh will have this question answered for him more pointedly than he ever imagined, and as such, Pharaoh's question foreshadows the irony of Israel's escape from his grasp.[4] Moreover, verse 2 gives us a further glimpse into the true conflict that drives the subsequent chapters. As we saw in chapter 1, the true battle in Exodus is not between the Israelites and Pharaoh, nor even between Moses and Pharaoh. Rather, it is between the God of Israel and Pharaoh. In chapter 1, the previous Pharaoh (his death is mentioned in 2:23) sinned not so much in enslaving the Israelites. Enslavement is merely one of three solutions Pharaoh attempted in response to a bigger problem: "The Israelites were fruitful and multiplied greatly" (1:7).

The Israelites have been fulfilling God's creation mandate, and the biblical writer's aim is to present Pharaoh as one whose ultimate purpose is to oppose God. Pharaoh's role as an anti-God figure becomes clearer here in 5:2: "Who is *he*, this God you are talking about?" Likewise, the previous Pharaoh is said not to have "known" Joseph (1:8), which, as we have seen, is not to say that he was ignorant of his own country's history, but that he acted in willful disregard of what Joseph had previously done for Egypt's benefit.

What, then, are we to make of Pharaoh's question to Moses in 5:2? Is this an honest question? Should we expect Pharaoh to have known who Yahweh is? Pharaoh's question is not simply a request for more information. Again, one of the points of this narrative is to demonstrate Pharaoh's hardness of heart. Pharaoh does not keep the Israelites under lock and key because he doesn't know who Yahweh is, but because he does not *know* Yahweh, meaning he does not accord him any respect. At the very least, he should recognize as a matter of diplomacy the God of these slave people, just as he recognizes the many gods of the Egyptian pantheon and the gods of other nations around him. Pharaoh's response is disrespectful and sarcastic. He is, with disastrous consequences, positioning himself to do battle with this

---

4. As Fretheim puts it, God's goal is that Pharaoh will "know" (*Exodus*, 86; cf. 7:17; 8:10, 22; 9:14, 29; 10:2; 11:7; 14:4, 18).

so-called "God of Israel." Pharaoh here counterattacks: Yahweh's messengers are not even given a hearing.

Things are clearly not working out as Moses anticipated. He responds to Pharaoh's rebuff by rewording the command, this time (v. 3) in words that more directly echo 3:18. As stated above, the three-day journey should not be thought of as a lesser request, as if Moses says, "OK, if you won't let us go, Pharaoh, how about just a three-day trip into the desert to make some sacrifices? We promise we'll be back." Moses is not cowering here, as some suggest.[5] Remember that the three-day journey is specifically what God had told Moses to say to Pharaoh, and, as we saw in 3:18, Yahweh does not have merely a weekend retreat in mind.

As mentioned earlier, the predominant scholarly view is that "three-day" indicates not the time away from Egypt, but the approximate time it would take to get to the proper site for the celebration without in any way implying that a return to Egypt is in view.[6] Verse 3, then, is not a cowering response on Moses' part, who, after Pharaoh's rebuff, is willing to settle for the next best thing. The requests of verses 1 and 3 are not really different, since the feast in the desert (v. 1) implies a journey into the desert (v. 3).[7] Rather, Moses is now spelling out more clearly the request of verse 1. Moses, inspired perhaps with confidence by the foregoing events, simply cannot believe that Pharaoh is not capitulating immediately to his demand in verse 1. Thus he says: "Read my lips; perhaps I didn't make myself clear. It is *God* who met with us.[8] *He* came to us with this message. *God* is speaking to you now, not two old men."

There is a lot of wisdom in this approach to the issue at hand, and it should be given due consideration. Nevertheless, there is another twist to this scenario that should also be kept in mind. As we will later see in 14:1–5, Pharaoh is utterly surprised to find out that the Israelites have *fled*. As I will spell out in more detail there, Pharaoh's surprise that the Israelites have left makes little sense since he is the one who gave the order (12:31–32). I suggest, therefore, that Pharaoh's surprise is not that they left, but in his sudden awareness that they are not coming back. In 12:31 Pharaoh tells them to leave and "worship the LORD *as you have requested.*" That request was a three-day journey. This presents us with one possible reason for why the journey is termed a three-day affair: to entice the Egyptians to follow the Israelites, thus resulting in their death. As we will see more clearly below, perhaps

---

5. See, e.g., Cassuto, *Commentary on Exodus*, 66; Sarna, *Exodus*, 28.

6. Cate, *Exodus*, 40; Jacob, *Exodus*, 125; Plastaras, *The God of Exodus*, 116, n. 23.

7. See Driver, *Book of Exodus*, 34–35.

8. The Hebrew phrase here can also be translated, "God is on our side" (Niphal of the verb *qaraʾ* plus the preposition *ʿal*). This would further strengthen Moses' reprimand.

God's intention is not to bring Egypt to the point of repentance, but to harden them in order to bring on them the full force of his anger.

In light of this, the irony of the final phrase of verse 3 should not be lost. If Pharaoh does not release the Israelites, "he may strike us with plagues or with the sword." Moses promises dire consequences for not heeding God's command. Although "plagues and sword" is a stock biblical phrase that represents "conventional symbols of divine judgment,"[9] in the context of the Exodus, the reference to "plagues" is too striking to miss. The Hebrew word for "plague" (*deber*) is used again in 9:3 and 15 (plague on livestock and plague of hail).[10] This is not Moses' begging Pharaoh: "Let us go or God will deal severely with *us*, the Israelites." It is, at least on the level of the narrative, a veiled threat: "Let us go or God will become angry with *us*, including you."

Kings, however, do not respond well to threats, and Moses' command is not even considered for a moment. "I'm a busy man, Moses and Aaron, and you're wasting my time and the people's. Now, get back to your work" (vv. 4–5).[11] Here, too, as we have seen in 1:9, Pharaoh seems fixated on the large number of slaves he has. In chapter 1, the growing number of Israelites was an occasion for panic. As we recall, the first pharaoh attempted three schemes to reduce their population: slavery, midwives killing newborn males, and newborn males being thrown into the Nile. This pharaoh, however, seems to have grown quite comfortable with these large numbers. He has seen what the first pharaoh did not: A large number of slaves is to his advantage, not his disadvantage. A growing slave population is not to be reduced but exploited.

But one similarity between the two pharaohs remains: Both are working against God's creation mandate—the first pharaoh by means of open conflict, the second by more subtle means. This pharaoh's eagerness to further his godless claim on the lives of this growing population is made more explicit beginning in verse 6. He, on that very same day, gives a command to counter the divine command just given to him through Moses. From now on, the Israelite slaves will have to gather their own straw to make their quota of

---

9. Sarna, *Exodus*, 28, n. 7.

10. Elsewhere in Exodus, the root *ngp* is used to describe plagues (8:2 [MT 7:27]; 12:23, 27).

11. Houtman suggests that the reference to *your* work in 5:4 may presume the presence of the elders with Moses and Aaron, since Moses and Aaron never work (*Exodus*, 1:466–67). Admittedly, telling Moses and Aaron to get back to work is problematic, but having the elders present would not necessarily make much more sense, since Pharaoh's intention is to have the people as a whole get back to work—not just the elders. The command to Moses and Aaron should be understood as a command given to the people through Moses. The matter is clarified in the second part of v. 5: "*their* work," meaning the people's.

bricks. This is no random decree, but one calculated to drive a wedge between Moses and the people.[12]

This is a level of resistance that Moses did not expect. The obstacles he must negotiate are not simply the people's disbelief or the Egyptians' hostility, but Pharaoh's clever, political maneuver to instill internal conflict. The people have apparently begun to find some glimmer of hope in Moses' promise of deliverance. To discredit the message, Pharaoh slings mud at the messenger: Moses is a liar (v. 9). Moreover, he discredits the people by misconstruing their complaint: They are *crying out* (s^cq) because they are lazy (v. 8). As we have seen (e.g., 2:23; 3:7), the Israelites are crying out (s^cq or its equivalent z^cq) because of their slavery, not because they are lazy. But from Pharaoh's point of view, they are *his* people; they have no right to complain. Yet it is precisely their cry that their God has heard and that moves him to action. By belittling the Israelites' pain and suffering, Pharaoh is positioning himself even further into direct conflict with the God who cares about his people.

The result of Pharaoh's latest decree is that the Israelites must work harder. Such is Pharaoh's intent, and it serves as yet another element in his handling of the Israelite slaves that pits him squarely against their God. His command, ironically, is that the Israelites be made to work harder whereas God commands that they should not work at all. Pharaoh does not simply reject and disobey God's command ("keep working"), he counters it with yet an even more severe measure ("work *more*"). Specifically, Pharaoh says he wants to make their "work harder" (v. 9). Some commentators have rightly picked up on the significance of this phrase. In Hebrew, the phrase is made up of two words, *tikbad ha^cabodah*, which may be translated "let the work become [more] severe." The verb *tikbad* is from the root *kbd*, the verb used elsewhere in the Exodus narrative to describe Pharaoh's hardness of heart.[13]

The irony, of course, is that as Pharaoh punishes Israel by making the people work "hard," his own heart is "hardened," which results in *his* punishment—the plagues and the Red Sea incident. The word *^cabodah*, meaning "work" or "service," is also ironic. In 4:23, God tells Moses that he is to command Pharaoh, "Let my son [Israel] go, so he may *worship* me." The verb "worship" is a translation of *^cbd*, the same root we find in *^cabodah*. In other words, Pharaoh and Yahweh are both competing, so to speak, with each other: Whom will Israel "serve"?[14]

This battle of sovereigns continues in verse 10, when the slave drivers and foremen give the Israelites the bad news. They preface their message by say-

---

12. Fretheim, *Exodus*, 85; Childs, *Book of Exodus*, 106.
13. Sarna, *Exodus*, 29, n. 14.
14. Fretheim, *Exodus*, 83.

ing, "This is what Pharaoh says." The wording is surely not accidental but a deliberate echo of 5:1 and 4:22: "This is what the LORD says."[15] Yahweh gives the command to release the Israelites, but Pharaoh, the "false god," commands that they stay—and he even increases their labor to boot.

Verses 13–14 then tell us that the Israelite foremen, who are responsible for making sure the daily quota of bricks does not diminish, are beaten by their Egyptian slave drivers. This is quite a twist. Would not the Israelite foremen have expected the Egyptians to beat the slaves, who actually do the work, rather than the foremen? The foremen are understandably taken aback by this and go to Pharaoh, thinking, perhaps, that some mistake had been made, some breakdown in communication in the chain of command (vv. 15–16). They say, in effect, "Why are you beating *us?* *Your* people are the ones who have stopped supplying us with straw. It's their fault. If anything, beat them."

Here (v. 15) the root *ṣ'q* ("cry out") is used for a second time in this passage (see v. 8). The NIV says that the Israelite foremen "appealed" to Pharaoh, which is certainly an acceptable translation, but it misses some of the force of the encounter. Once again, oppressed Israelites "cry out" because of their oppression, and once again, Pharaoh does not listen. Yet it is precisely these cries that Yahweh, the God of Israel, has heard and will soon act on (2:23; 3:7).

Pharaoh not only refuses to heed their cry but he mocks them as well. He repeats his accusation of verse 8: "Lazy, that's what you are—lazy" (v. 17). This is a wholly inadequate response to the foremen's argument. All they are saying is that *they* should not be beaten because the people are not given sufficient straw, but Pharaoh talks right past them. Clearly, the lines of communication between Pharaoh and the slaves are not open. Moses' abrupt, disrespectful (in Pharaoh's eyes) command at the beginning of this chapter has so incensed the king of Egypt that he turns a deaf ear and now borders on the irrational. Is this not a picture of Pharaoh's "hard heart"? His stubbornness and refusal to face the facts will be augmented in later chapters, but we see it already here. Refusal to let the Israelites go is, to a certain extent, perfectly understandable from Pharaoh's point of view. Should he just be expected to let them march out the door?

But his response is much more villainous than that. He has not only made their work harder by providing no straw, but he also rubs salt in their wounds by accusing them of bringing their own problems on themselves: "You are lazy." Pharaoh has completely turned his back on the Israelites (which is not to say that he was ever concerned for their welfare!). He shows his true

---

15. Both phrases begin *koh 'amar,* "Thus says."

colors. Pharaoh is not a neutral figure, but opposes the Israelites and their God. *He* is truly "absent," whereas the God of Exodus 1 only seems that way. Pharaoh has cut off all communication between himself and the people. He simply tells them to get back to work (v. 18).

In this verse, too, the Hebrew wording is significant, for Pharaoh's words will come back to haunt him later. His command is "Go, work" (Heb., *ləku ʿibdu*), ordering the Israelites to go back to making bricks. But this is not the last time Pharaoh utters this command. He does so later in the Exodus narrative, but then as a defeated ruler who finally acquiesces to Moses' command: *ləku ʿibdu ʾet-yhwh* , "Go, serve/worship Yahweh" (see 10:8, 11, 24; 12:31).[16]

But for now, Pharaoh's strategy of disparaging Moses' reputation among the people has worked. The messenger of God, Moses—who saw God on the holy mountain, was chosen for this very purpose, was assured of God's presence throughout his ordeal, and by God's help, has proven his calling to the elders and people of Israel—is now perilously close to seeing his entire mission evaporate before his eyes. The foremen leave Pharaoh's presence, perhaps dumbfounded, and see Moses and Aaron waiting to meet them. Immediately, the foremen turn on them and pronounce a curse on them ("May the LORD look upon you and judge you!" v. 21).

Note the irony here. Have they forgotten so quickly that it is Pharaoh who enslaved them and who is responsible for this latest insane decree? Have they also forgotten Moses' display of power in 4:30, whereby they became convinced of the authority with which he was vested? The plan of deliverance seems to be falling apart at the seams. How ironic it is to call God's judgment down on the very one whom he has chosen to deliver his people!

The Hebrew of verse 20 also hints at the magnitude of the foremen's ire against Moses. The NIV says that they "found" Moses and Aaron. The Hebrew verb, however, is from the root *pgʿ*, which can also mean "to strike, afflict." This is how the verb was used in verse 3, where Moses tells Pharaoh that unless he lets the Israelites go, God will "strike [his people] with plagues or with the sword." This verbal correspondence should not be pressed too far, but, in the context of 5:1–21, it suggests the alacrity with which the foremen pounce on Moses and Aaron.

In the closing verses of this section, therefore, the grumbling theme reemerges. Moses expects, and perhaps rightly so, to be greeted with open arms by the slaves he has come to lead out of bondage, but they turn on him instead. Yet can we blame them? Their situation is admittedly harsher now that Moses has come. The Israelites' reaction here to Moses is indicative of

---

16. Sarna, *Exodus*, 30, n. 18.

their own hardness of heart toward not only Moses but the God who has come to save them, which subsequent chapters will make clear.

The parting shot given by the foremen is curious, to say the least. It is bad enough that they ask God to bring down his judgment on Moses. But they also say, "You have made us a stench to Pharaoh and his officials and have put a sword in their hand to kill us" (v. 21). Is this really fair? The Israelites had been a stench to Pharaoh long before Moses came on the scene (cf. ch. 1). It was not Moses who put a sword in the Egyptian's hand to kill them. In fact, Moses' own life was threatened at birth (ch. 2). He is not the cause of their problems, but a participant in those problems. The foremen have it backward: This Moses, whom they treat so disrespectfully now, is not the reason for their oppression, but God's instrument to end that oppression.

THIS PASSAGE ACTS as a bridge between the narrative of Moses' commission by Yahweh on Mount Horeb and the beginning of the deliverance from Egypt. It is a prelude of sorts, but one that the reader might not have expected. Any resistance to Moses' leadership was supposedly anticipated in Moses' dialogue with God on the mountain in chapters 3–4. So what is happening here? The preceding discussion yields several suggestions.

The enemies of God's people are enemies of God. The narrative's use of certain words hints that Pharaoh's actions pit him squarely against Israel's God. Pharaoh is an "anti-God" figure, a fact already seen in Exodus 1. Pharaoh here demands the people's allegiance despite Yahweh's claim on them. But such posturing is not unique to the pharaoh of the Exodus. Are not the enemies of God's people always in such a state? We already see this seed sown in Genesis 3. The serpent tries to trick the woman into eating of the fruit from the tree of the knowledge of good and evil by placing himself in a position of hostility toward God: "Did God really say. . . ?" (3:1). But Satan is not simply hostile toward God. He is, by questioning God's word, attempting to replace God's authority with his own. The results are disastrous.

Sennacherib's attempted capture of Jerusalem (2 Kings 18:17–37; 2 Chron. 32:9–19; Isa. 36:1–22) proceeds along a similar vein. In 701 B.C., Sennacherib, the king of Assyria, sent a delegation to Jerusalem with the news that he was on his way to capture the city. His field commander speaks for him, not unlike Moses or a prophet speaking on God's behalf. He tries to convince the Israelites to give up without a fight. His rhetorical strategy, reminiscent of the serpent in the garden, is to use God's words against him. It is no use, he says, to depend on God; it was *his* high places and altars that

Hezekiah had foolishly removed (2 Kings 18:22). The irony, of course, is that Hezekiah was actually obedient to God in removing the high places.

The field commander continues twisting God's words: "Furthermore, have I come to attack and destroy this place without word from the LORD? The LORD himself told me to march against this country and destroy it" (2 Kings 18:25). Sennacherib seeks to convince the Israelites of their impending doom not simply by flexing his muscles, but by pitting his word against Yahweh's. Indeed, he himself claims to speak for Yahweh. In doing so, Sennacherib, perhaps unwittingly, declares opposition not simply against this one city, Jerusalem, but against God. This is, in fact, what Isaiah himself prophesies (19:21–23a):

> The Virgin Daughter of Zion
>> despises you and mocks you.
> The Daughter of Jerusalem
>> tosses her head as you flee.
> Who is it you have insulted and blasphemed?
>> Against whom have you raised your voice
> and lifted up your eyes in pride?
>> Against the Holy One of Israel!
> By your messengers
>> you have heaped insults on the Lord.

The results of such presumptuousness, for both the serpent and Sennacherib, are sudden: The serpent is cursed forever (Gen. 3:14–15) and Sennacherib falls dead in his pagan temple. A similar fate awaits Pharaoh here.

In the Old Testament, Satan is not an overtly predominant player in Israel's affairs. Although he does make an occasional appearance,[17] his role in the lives of God's people is spelled out more clearly in the pages of the New Testament. Satan is the enemy of all God's people. He is and has always been the ultimate source for opposition against them and the ultimate inspiration for any who pit their own authority against that of Yahweh.

It was Satan who, when God was poised at the threshold of the climax of his redemptive plan in Christ, attempted to subvert God's plan by pitting his own authority against God's. At the outset of Jesus' ministry Satan tempts Jesus to abandon his mission (Matt. 4:1–11; Luke 4:1–13). He does so, as we have seen in the cases mentioned above, by employing "God-talk." He twists Scripture—in this case Psalm 91:11–12—to tempt Jesus not to trust in his Father. Satan's pride in dealing with Christ, the new Moses, is simply a more

---

17. For example, David was incited by Satan to number his fighting men (1 Chron. 21:1). Satan accuses Job before God in Job 1:6–12.

pronounced version of Pharaoh's in Exodus 5: "Who is this Yahweh? Don't listen to him, listen to me. Thus says Pharaoh. . . ."

As Christians are aware, Satan is the enemy not only of our Lord but of his people. He is the prowling predator of which the apostle Peter speaks (1 Peter 5:8). Satan's effectiveness is due, at least in part, to his ability to deceive: He "masquerades as an angel of light" (2 Cor. 11:14). Note the beast and the dragon, who are the Satan/anti-God figures in Revelation. They are persuasive because they imitate God's speech and power (Rev. 13:1—18). In doing so, the beast blasphemes God (13:6); he attempts to mislead God's people by usurping God's authority.

This perspective brings out more clearly Pharaoh's portrayal in Exodus as an anti-God figure. He, too, is against God's people, trying to deceive them by pitting his word and authority against that of Yahweh. He uses God-talk that directly opposes what God intends for the Israelite slaves. Just as Moses proves victorious over Pharaoh's pride, Christ, our Moses, is victorious over the deceptions and attacks of the primal false god, Satan. Our Lord's death and resurrection are the final blow to any hope of Satan to keep God's people in slavery to sin.

God's presence does not guarantee immediate results. Exodus 5:1—21 also shows us that God's direct involvement in the affairs of his people does not guarantee immediate results. We have seen this already in chapters 1—2 with respect to God's apparent absence from his people, but the present passage puts a different spin on the issue. It is not that God appears to be absent but then comes in the nick of time to save. Here, he has already spoken; through Moses, he has promised to be present with his people. But when push comes to shove, when confronting Pharaoh as he was commanded, Moses suddenly finds himself behind the eight ball.

We should remember that the problem here is not so much that Pharaoh refuses to let the Israelites go. God said that would happen (3:19). Rather, the problem is that the people, whom Moses had just won over to his side (4:29—31), begin to grumble. They are worse off after the initial confrontation than before, and as a result, the *people* begin to resist Moses, and the whole plan begins to unravel before his eyes. One would expect Pharaoh to be less than receptive to Moses' words, but the Israelites' reaction is disconcerting to say the least.

When God finally announces his presence with and blessing on his people, things may actually appear to get worse before they get better. In the Old Testament, one need only think of the life of Abraham. God promises him children more numerous than the sand on the seashore, but Abraham must endure much before he and Sarah receive the promised child. Approximately ten years pass (see Gen. 16:3) since Abraham received the promise of offspring in 12:1–3, but that promise is not yet realized. In frustration Sarah tries to force the promise by giving her servant Hagar to Abraham as a wife, but this is not what God had in mind.

A number of years later, when Abraham is ninety-nine years old, God promises again that he and Sarah will have a child (Gen. 17:15–22; 18:9–15). The following year they finally realize the promise and name their boy Isaac. Such a delay in receiving a promise is not what one would have expected after the triumphant announcement of 12:1–3. We can see the frustration of Abraham and Sarah both in the Hagar episode and in their open disbelief (17:17; 18:12).

In fact, the entire covenant narrative of Genesis 15 should be understood not as a step of faith on Abraham's part, but as his need to see some concrete evidence that God will finally keep his word. One senses already in 15:2–3 Abraham's struggles with doubt: "I know, Lord, that you said I would have an heir. But where is he? I haven't seen him yet." God then assures him that he will, in due time, have a son as an heir, and Abraham believes (15:6).

The topic then turns to the second part of the promise: land. God reiterates this in Genesis 15:7: "I am the LORD, who brought you out of Ur of the Chaldeans to give you this land to take possession of it." But now Abraham chimes in (almost interrupts), "How can I know?" (v. 8). It is as if he is saying, "I have already seen how you 'fulfill' promises. What assurance can you give me now that this land promise will happen any quicker than the seed promise?" In reading the Abraham narrative, we should not overlook this struggle on his part. He is beginning to have doubts here in chapter 15. Why does God delay?

But Abraham's struggles do not end with the birth of Isaac in Genesis 21. As we have seen in Exodus 5:1–21, although God's promise is delayed, the realization of that promise can sometimes (appear to) make a bad situation worse. After all their yearning for a child, Abraham is told to do the unthinkable: sacrifice him (Gen. 22:1–19). It would have been better had he never been born. In the end, of course, the sacrifice is aborted and Abraham is blessed (22:15–18), but the more immediate point should not be lost: For a time, God's increased presence in and involvement with Abraham's life produces challenges he has not expected.

The same lesson is apparent in the life of Joseph. He is the favorite of his father (Gen. 37:3–4). That fact, plus Joseph's dreams that predict his eventual supremacy over his brothers, cause them to be jealous. Hence, Joseph's "blessing" takes a bad turn when he is sold by his brothers into slavery and lands in Egypt (37:12–36). Yet the Lord is clearly with Joseph in Egypt. He is put in charge of Potiphar's (an official of Pharaoh) house (39:1–6). The brothers' vindictiveness has turned out to be a wonderful boon for Joseph.

But then Potiphar's wife falsely accuses Joseph of attempted rape (39:11–20), and Joseph is thrown in prison. Is this how God blesses—rescuing Joseph from the obscurity of slavery only to have him thrown into prison for remaining obedient to him? Should not God's blessing look different?

For Joseph, as for Abraham, things turn worse before they get better, although in the end God's ultimate purposes are brought into view (Gen. 50:20). Without pressing the issue here, it is worth mentioning once again how in wisdom literature and the Psalms biblical writers struggle with reconciling their supposed privileged standing with God as Israelites and the daily turmoil of their lives (e.g., Ps. 73; see Contemporary Significance section of Ex. 1:1–22).

Who is it in the Bible who, more than any other, receives God's absolute imprimatur and who was sent by God for a special mission of deliverance? It is only Christ of whom the Father said, "This is my Son, whom I love; with him I am well pleased" (Matt. 3:17). What greater stamp of approval can anyone receive? Yet Christ's ministry, as that of Moses, is beset with resistance, both from outside and from within. Would not one expect complete capitulation in the face of God's Son who has finally come? But, as we read in John 1:10, even though he made the world, "the world did not recognize him" (see also the parable of the tenants, e.g., Matt. 21:33–44). God's presence is with him more than with any who have come before, but even that does not guarantee the swift, immediate fulfillment of God's plan.

Early on in Jesus' ministry he commands his disciples to preach the gospel to "the lost sheep of Israel" (Matt. 10:6). But after meeting with continued resistance, Jesus tells the parable of the wedding banquet (22:1–14). Now his call is not to be restricted to Israel (the invited guests) but to outsiders as well (those on the street corners). In this regard, the learned religious leaders of Jesus' day, the Pharisees, offer the strongest resistance to Jesus' work. This is somewhat of an unexpected twist. They of all people should know better; they are the experts in the Scriptures and should be able to discern in Christ the authority of the Father. But Jesus also experiences resistance from his sometimes dimwitted disciples. This is even less excusable, for they are on his side. They have witnessed firsthand his many signs and wonders; yet, as the Gospels tell us, they continually demonstrate how far they are from grasping the gravity of the redemptive-historical reality in which they have been privileged to participate.

As Christ meets with opposition, so too do the apostles. Paul's letters, for example, show clear evidence of resistance on the part of those whose teachings or practices subvert the purpose for which he was called (e.g., Galatians, 1 and 2 Corinthians). Has not Paul been commissioned by Christ himself to be an apostle to the Gentiles (Gal. 1:11–24)? Why, then, can he not simply go from town to town, wave his Bible around (so to speak), and see the masses converted in droves to unwaveringly pure lives and sound doctrine?

The same holds true for the church as a whole. The Holy Spirit is, as Paul states a number of times, a "deposit" and "guarantee" or "firstfruits" of future, ultimate blessing (Rom. 8:23; 2 Cor. 1:22; 5:5; Eph. 1:13–14). There is no richer sign of blessing for God's people than the immediate presence of the Holy Spirit in the lives of believers. Yet even this richest of all blessings does not guarantee that our service to the Lord will not take unexpected turns and twists.[18] In fact, as Peter reminds us, "Dear friends, do not be surprised at the painful trial you are suffering, as though something strange were happening to you" (1 Peter 4:12).

God, by his Spirit, is truly present with his people in a way now that is only glimpsed at in Old Testament times. The Spirit of God actually dwells in us (1 Cor. 3:16; 6:19), and we are united with Christ in his death and resurrection (Rom. 6:5). Yet even for the church, which enjoys such intimacy with God, we have experiences like Moses before Pharaoh; we are positive we are obeying God's command, but struggles persist. In fact, it seems we struggle not despite our intimacy with God, but precisely because of it.

"WE ARE THEREFORE CHRIST'S AMBASSADORS" (2 Cor. 5:20). Exodus 5:1–21 teaches that resistance to God's messenger is resistance to God himself. As Christians, we are, to use Paul's words, "Christ's ambassadors, as though God were making his appeal through us." The King has commissioned his people to make his appeal of reconciliation to the world (see 5:18–21). We, therefore, like Moses long before, are "God" to the world; we speak on his behalf. We, like Moses and the prophets, proclaim to a dead world, "This is what the Lord says."

Do we understand the magnitude of this calling? By reconciling us to himself, God has also allowed us to participate in his continuing work of reconciliation. We are not bystanders who are merely "saved." Rather, the Lord puts us to work, and we labor with him toward a glorious goal. God actually entrusts *us* to carry out, by the power of his indwelling Spirit, the ministry of reconciliation that cost him his own Son. We would do well, then, to remember just what we are doing when we bring the good news to others. We are not the origin and source of the message. Indeed, *we* are not the ones speaking. It is God "making *his* appeal through us."

---

18. Here we see some overlap with two themes discussed earlier: patience in view of God's apparent absence (Ex. 1) and patience under suffering (discussed under 2:1–10).

One common obstacle to evangelism is timidity—most Christians have struggled with this, myself included. Timidity is, it seems to me, not so much a lack of nerve as a misdirection of focus from God to ourselves. It is forgetting that we are merely the messengers through whom God makes his appeal. "Should I say something? What if they make fun of me? What if they ignore me and walk away? The risk is too great." This is Moses talking.

Most of us have shown similar apprehension at certain times. I am not suggesting here that "real" Christians go marching forth happily to any battle they are called to fight, while "immature" Christians waver in periods of doubt and lack of confidence. What I am saying, however, is that the risks we may feel in bringing the gospel to a fallen world are put into their proper perspective when we see that evangelism—that is, being Christ's ambassadors—means, in the words of John the Baptist, "He must become greater; I must become less" (John 3:30).

Evangelism, properly executed, is not accompanied by timidity, but not so much because the evangelist has confidence in herself or himself (a debilitating trait for Christians), but because the evangelist's focus shifts from the messenger to the originator of the message. This is what eventually enables Moses to march into Pharaoh's court: not a conviction about his own newfound preaching skills, but a boldness that comes from knowing and being known by God. The message we preach, then, is not our own. Nor are we somehow indispensable in bringing this message to others. We are, rather, the most privileged of God's creation to be given this most honorable task of being coworkers with God himself to reconcile the world.

The other end of the spectrum is pride. Some of us suffer not from timidity but from being enamored by the sound of our own voice. We do not remember that since the message is from God, any success we experience is due to his supervision and not our own skills, knowledge, or technique. There is no place for pride in being Christ's ambassadors. We have all met or heard preachers of the gospel who are arrogant (although how to define that word may differ from person to person), brash, and brazen, ready to demonstrate their skills of persuasion as soon as the door is cracked open. It is always tempting to focus so much on ourselves and our own abilities that little room is left for the awe that should accompany the task we have been given. Sometimes, by his mercy, the Lord allows us to fail to remind us of our role in his plans.

I remember a high school experience of mine. I was a recent convert (in a manner of speaking, not unlike Moses after his Mount Horeb experience) and, being emboldened perhaps by my own recent submission to the gospel, the matter appeared clear-cut, so I assumed that others would have a similar reaction. Hence, I did what so many new converts have done: I cornered people, raised my voice a little, and insisted they have the same conversion experience as I had. My focus was rarely on the supernatural power of God to change people's lives, but on my own cleverness, my "strategy" in taking as many prisoners as I could.

In one instance, I was playing miniature golf with a friend, sharing the gospel with her between putts. Toward the beginning of the game, I pronounced that if I would win, she would have to come to church with me. She, foolishly, took the bet, not realizing that I had squadrons of angels ready to divert her ball from the cup while keeping me well under par for the afternoon. "There was no way that she can beat me now. God will make me win, since he certainly wants her to come to church with me." I was intoxicated by my own strategic brilliance.

This story has a predictable ending: She beat me by one stroke. I couldn't understand what went wrong. I was just doing what I *knew* God wanted me to do. What I should have remembered is that the message is from God, not my own cunning. I should have thought less about my own strategy and more of simply talking about Jesus, proclaiming *him* and acknowledging the Spirit's superintendence and sovereign timing.

A related matter, apparent here in Exodus 5:1–21, is nonreceptivity on the part of those who hear the message. In light of the examples of Moses and even Jesus himself, this should come as no surprise. The message will often fall on deaf ears. This is part of what it means to bring God's message to a world that does not know him. This is what Christ's ambassadors are to expect. At such times, we must remember that rejection of the gospel is not rejection of *us*. From a limited point of view, of course, we feel reproached, but we are reproached precisely because we are in Christ, for our identity is in him. The ultimate offended party is God.

Furthermore, rejection comes not at the hands of neutral bystanders, simply weighing the options and assessing the strengths and weaknesses of what *we* have to say and thus, perhaps, "choosing Christ." They are, rather, rebels who suppress the truth, imagining that they actually have something of value to add to what the Lord has already said. They, like Pharaoh, pit their own words and thoughts against those of God. A fallen world is rebellious at heart.

With this in mind, I am often surprised by how some Christians react in the face of the world's rejection of the gospel. The world's nonreceptivity to the gospel is, after all, a basic fact we face all the time. One example that struck a particular cord with me a number of years ago concerns the well-known controversy surrounding the film version of Nikos Kazantzakis's 1960 novel, *The Last Temptation of Christ*. This movie clearly portrayed Christ in a way that, to say the least, had little to do with the Christ of the New Testament.

It is telling that the reaction of many evangelicals was complete shock, as if such a thing were unthinkable. Is it? I remember one flyer urging all true Christians to boycott the movie and register, by letter or phone calls, how "offended" we were. Offended? Tell me something I *don't* know! Christians are offended every day, and *The Last Temptation of Christ* is not an isolated, or even a particularly gripping, example of this. Rejection of the gospel is part of the territory. Frankly, I doubt if "offense" is a proper reaction for Christians. Offense implies some injury to one's person, but as we have seen above, *we* are not the ones offended. This may be how the world reacts, but our message is from the Lord. Perhaps a better strategy would have been not to focus on our own feelings about the movie ("*I* don't like it; *I* don't like what it says about Christ; it makes *me* feel uncomfortable or offended") but on the true Christ that the movie never came close to portraying.

Another issue concerns Christians and the public schools. As a parent of three young children, I am not at all encouraged by some elements of public education today. My list of concerns includes intellectual, social, and spiritual matters. Different Christian parents handle their concerns in different ways. Some choose to home-school, others send their children to private schools, while still others remain in the system, perhaps to maintain a witness for Christ where it is so sorely needed (for the record, as I write this, each of our three children is in one of these settings). Others take a more aggressive route. They work to have laws passed that, for example, allow for displaying the Ten Commandments in hallways or that disallow certain views to be taught.

My purpose here is not to pass judgment on this latter group, for they apparently see an urgency I do not. My point is that when their message falls on deaf ears, they become angry, offended, and outraged. Picket lines form, television cameras begin to roll, and sound bites are captured with picketers referring to our founding fathers and their plan to have Jesus in every classroom. I am not suggesting here that we should leave everything as it is and not challenge the system. The problem is in thinking that our views "ought" to be given a fair hearing in the free market of ideas, that we somehow deserve to be heard because we are Christians or perhaps because we have a notion of the Christian "roots" of America. Then, when the message is not heard, we grow angry and even militant.

It remains an inescapable fact that our world today is no more receptive to God's will than the Egypt of Pharaoh's day. Our reaction to opposition should not be outrage, as if *we* are the ones offended, or surprise, as if American hearts are somehow less rebellious toward God. Rather, our reaction should be one of godliness and patience, knowing that the message belongs to the Lord and he will set things aright. We must rise above the fray, the plans and schemes of humanity, with a godly confidence that comes only from knowing Christ and being known by him.

One final related thought may be particularly relevant to new Christians and those who are just beginning their ministries: Rejection is hard to take. Many recent seminary graduates naively enter their first position with stars in their eyes, convinced that their difficult years of training are behind them and now they can begin to "do" ministry. It doesn't take long before they begin wishing that their biggest problems were language exams and exegetical papers. Resistance, as Exodus 5:1–21 reminds us, can come not only from the outside but also from within, from God's own people. Evangelistic programs don't work as well as anticipated. Ministries oriented to the congregation are met with skepticism and complaints. Moses, too, was bold at the outset of his ministry after his initial encounter with God on Mount Horeb, and he met considerable resistance both from without and within. But Moses was soon to learn that he was merely the messenger and that *his* "ministry" was really the Lord's work.

Likewise, young Christians sometimes approach their newfound faith with a childlike vigor. This is normal and to be expected. But this youthfulness must be properly discipled by more experienced Christians. How many Christians have lived the parable of the sower? Their enthusiasm for the gospel wanes in time and their fruit withers in shallow, rocky soil. They must be taken under wing and reminded again and again that there is nothing that endures in our Christian lives but the grace of God. When we meet resistance from friends and family, it is time to channel our enthusiasm into a more mature form of spirituality: patience and a quiet heart. It is time to learn, as did Moses and countless saints throughout the Bible, the meaning of the often repeated but seldom understood phrase: "God is in control." It is this lesson that Moses begins to learn in the following passage.

Exodus 5:22–7:7

MOSES RETURNED TO the LORD and said, "O LORD, why have you brought trouble upon this people? Is this why you sent me? ²³Ever since I went to Pharaoh to speak in your name, he has brought trouble upon this people, and you have not rescued your people at all."

^{6:1}Then the LORD said to Moses, "Now you will see what I will do to Pharaoh: Because of my mighty hand he will let them go; because of my mighty hand he will drive them out of his country."

²God also said to Moses, "I am the LORD. ³I appeared to Abraham, to Isaac and to Jacob as God Almighty, but by my name the LORD I did not make myself known to them. ⁴I also established my covenant with them to give them the land of Canaan, where they lived as aliens. ⁵Moreover, I have heard the groaning of the Israelites, whom the Egyptians are enslaving, and I have remembered my covenant.

⁶"Therefore, say to the Israelites: 'I am the LORD, and I will bring you out from under the yoke of the Egyptians. I will free you from being slaves to them, and I will redeem you with an outstretched arm and with mighty acts of judgment. ⁷I will take you as my own people, and I will be your God. Then you will know that I am the LORD your God, who brought you out from under the yoke of the Egyptians. ⁸And I will bring you to the land I swore with uplifted hand to give to Abraham, to Isaac and to Jacob. I will give it to you as a possession. I am the LORD.'"

⁹Moses reported this to the Israelites, but they did not listen to him because of their discouragement and cruel bondage.

¹⁰Then the LORD said to Moses, ¹¹"Go, tell Pharaoh king of Egypt to let the Israelites go out of his country."

¹²But Moses said to the LORD, "If the Israelites will not listen to me, why would Pharaoh listen to me, since I speak with faltering lips?"

¹³Now the LORD spoke to Moses and Aaron about the Israelites and Pharaoh king of Egypt, and he commanded them to bring the Israelites out of Egypt.

[14]These were the heads of their families:

The sons of Reuben the firstborn son of Israel were Hanoch and Pallu, Hezron and Carmi. These were the clans of Reuben.

[15]The sons of Simeon were Jemuel, Jamin, Ohad, Jakin, Zohar and Shaul the son of a Canaanite woman. These were the clans of Simeon.

[16]These were the names of the sons of Levi according to their records: Gershon, Kohath and Merari. Levi lived 137 years.

[17]The sons of Gershon, by clans, were Libni and Shimei.

[18]The sons of Kohath were Amram, Izhar, Hebron and Uzziel. Kohath lived 133 years.

[19]The sons of Merari were Mahli and Mushi.

These were the clans of Levi according to their records.

[20]Amram married his father's sister Jochebed, who bore him Aaron and Moses. Amram lived 137 years.

[21]The sons of Izhar were Korah, Nepheg and Zicri.

[22]The sons of Uzziel were Mishael, Elzaphan and Sithri.

[23]Aaron married Elisheba, daughter of Amminadab and sister of Nahshon, and she bore him Nadab and Abihu, Eleazar and Ithamar.

[24]The sons of Korah were Assir, Elkanah and Abiasaph. These were the Korahite clans.

[25]Eleazar son of Aaron married one of the daughters of Putiel, and she bore him Phinehas.

These were the heads of the Levite families, clan by clan.

[26]It was this same Aaron and Moses to whom the LORD said, "Bring the Israelites out of Egypt by their divisions." [27]They were the ones who spoke to Pharaoh king of Egypt about bringing the Israelites out of Egypt. It was the same Moses and Aaron.

[28]Now when the LORD spoke to Moses in Egypt, [29]he said to him, "I am the LORD. Tell Pharaoh king of Egypt everything I tell you."

[30]But Moses said to the LORD, "Since I speak with faltering lips, why would Pharaoh listen to me?"

[7:1]Then the LORD said to Moses, "See, I have made you like God to Pharaoh, and your brother Aaron will be your prophet. ²You are to say everything I command you, and your brother Aaron is to tell Pharaoh to let the Israelites go out of his country. ³But I will harden Pharaoh's heart, and though I multiply my miraculous signs and wonders in Egypt, ⁴he will not listen to you. Then I will lay my hand on Egypt and with mighty acts of judgment I will bring out my divisions, my people the Israelites. ⁵And the Egyptians will know that I am the LORD when I stretch out my hand against Egypt and bring the Israelites out of it."

⁶Moses and Aaron did just as the LORD commanded them. ⁷Moses was eighty years old and Aaron eighty-three when they spoke to Pharaoh.

EXODUS 5:22—7:7 MAY be justly summarized as a second conversation that Moses has with the Lord, paralleling to a certain degree the previous conversation between them on Mount Horeb (3:1—4:17). Both conversations pertain to Moses' claim to be insufficient for the task he has been given and God's promise that he will indeed be with him; each closes with a confrontation with Pharaoh. Yet, this second conversation is not merely a repetition of 3:1—4:17. This, after all, follows Moses' first, failed, confrontation with Pharaoh. The purpose of 5:22—7:7 is to move us further along to the realization of God's plan of deliverance, and it does so precisely by drawing out, reiterating, and nuancing certain elements of the first conversation.

God (Again) Promises Deliverance (5:22—6:12)

THE SECTION BEGINS with Moses seemingly at the end of his rope. He is exasperated. After the dual defeat of the previous verses (both Pharaoh and the Israelites want nothing to do with him), he "returns" to the Lord. It is not clear precisely what this means. Did he physically return to Mount Horeb? This is unlikely, especially since no return journey is mentioned. Did he "return" to God in prayer?[1] This is possible, since a conversation between him and God follows. Still, *prayer* is not what the text actually says. Moreover, the previous conversation between Moses and God was not a prayer, so why should we think this *return* to Yahweh should be described so? We are struck, once again, by the fact that the biblical writer is not

---

1. See Sarna, *Exodus*, 30.

concerned to tell us the details of the circumstances surrounding this conversation. What is vital is simply the fact that the conversation takes place—and what is said.

As Moses returns to God, he asks why he has brought this evil on the people, as if to say: "You are to blame, God. Why are you making my job so much harder?" His complaint here is reminiscent of the foremen's complaint to Pharaoh in verse 15: "Why did *you* do this?" It also follows closely upon the complaint the Israelites give to Moses in verse 21: "*You* are to blame, Moses." Everyone seems to be looking for someone to blame. Moses' complaint in verse 22 is just one more in a series of complaints and shows that his grasp of the situation has not yet transcended that of the other parties involved, despite the fact that he has earlier had the privilege of receiving instructions directly from Yahweh. At this juncture, Moses is not yet the stalwart leader he later becomes. He still has much to learn about the God who is unwavering in keeping his promise to Abraham, Isaac, and Jacob.

Here, in effect, Moses is calling into question God's character. God said he was planning to bring the Israelites out of Egypt with Moses as his chosen vessel to bring it about. For now, however, things seem to be skidding out of control, and Moses concludes that God is actually bringing trouble on them. His complete exasperation comes across in the second part of verse 22: "Why *in the world* have you sent me?"[2]

Moses is undone; his focus is on the disastrous outcome of his first encounter with Pharaoh, not on the character of the God who has called him. The most vital lesson of the Mount Horeb experience, "I will be with you" *despite* Pharaoh's hard heart, has not yet sunk in. Moses has not yet learned that there is more at stake here than how *he* is doing. God's character is at stake; he has a promise to keep to Abraham, Isaac, and Jacob.

In chapter 6, the Lord responds to Moses' complaint: "*Now* you will see what I will do to Pharaoh" (6:1). Although "now" may simply preface the following remark, as is common in both Hebrew and English,[3] it seems to take on a temporal nuance in this context. *Now* is the right time for God to show *his* great saving power. Moses is confused and despondent, the people have all but turned their backs on him, and Pharaoh's pride is increasing by the minute. It is at this point in the unfolding drama that God responds: "*Now* look at what *I* will do." We have already seen what Moses has done. We

---

2. This nuance of the Hebrew *lamah zeh* is effectively lost in the NIV. The demonstrative adjective *zeh* when following the interrogative serves to intensify the interrogative (*IBHS*, 312–13, 323–24). See also Houtman's translation, "Why did you ever send me?" (*Exodus*, 1:497).

3. Consider, for example, the following English sentences: "Now, what I want to say is . . . ," or "Now, I don't know about that."

have also seen what Pharaoh, the anti-God figure, has done. Now it is God's turn to act.

God's response to Moses recalls three prominent elements of their previous conversation:

- v. 2: I am Yahweh (see 3:14)
- vv. 3–4: I am the God of the patriarchs (see 3:6, 15–17)
- v. 5: I have heard your complaint (see 3:7 [and 2:24–25])

By repeating these vital elements, God is saying to Moses, "Let's try it again, but this time listen closely. This is who I am; I am Yahweh [v. 2]. I made a promise to the patriarchs that I have every intention of keeping [vv. 3–4]. I know what is happening, and I am now poised to do something about it [v. 5]. So, stand back and watch."

No discussion of this passage can pass by verse 3, which, along with 3:14–15, is one of the more difficult, controversial, and widely discussed verses in the entire book. According to the mainstream of critical scholarship, 6:3 is all but impossible to reconcile with 3:14, since both seem to *reveal* God's name, Yahweh, for the first time: "I appeared to Abraham, to Isaac and to Jacob as God Almighty, but by my name the LORD I did not make myself known to them."

How can God reveal his name to Moses twice? Critical scholarship has essentially concluded, with some variation, that these two passages come from different, independent sources.[4] It is argued that in 3:14–15, God's name "Yahweh" is being revealed according to the "E" source, while in 6:3 it is being revealed according to the "Priestly" (or "P") source, typically dated to the postexilic period. According to the theory, the author of "P" held that *El-Shaddai*[5] was the name by which the patriarchs knew their God, but "Yahweh" is a *new* name, just now given to Moses. In other words, 3:14–15 and 6:3 are two *parallel* but *different* and *mutually exclusive* versions of the *revelation* of God's name "Yahweh" to Moses. These two versions were simply placed near each other in the Exodus story by an editor of some sort, who apparently was not bothered to have two contradictory episodes in his book.

The issues involved are numerous, and a full discussion of this approach to understanding 3:14–15 and 6:3 would take us far beyond our purpose here. Still, it is worth distilling the responses that have been given to this

---

4. I am referring here again to the well-known "Documentary Hypothesis," mentioned in the discussion of 3:14.

5. The NIV has "God Almighty," which is one possible translation of the Hebrew ʾel šadday. The precise meaning of this term is not clear, but neither is it crucial for discussing the matter at hand.

approach.[6] It seems to me that, inasmuch as 3:14–15 is not the revelation of God's name (see comments), neither is 6:3. One point that argues against the documentary approach, both here and in 3:14–15, is that if "Yahweh" is a *new* name, the force of the argument seems to be lost.[7] In other words, if the purpose of the constant references to the patriarchs in the opening chapters in Exodus is to establish a *connection* to the past, what purpose would there be for such an *absolute contrast* between the names by which that God was known?

The traditional answer to the documentary approach is in my view correct: Exodus 6:3 does not say that God is now giving a *new* name, but that God's name is now going to be *fully* known; that is, the *significance* of the name is going to be understood at this most pivotal time in Israel's history.[8] Verse 3, then, may be paraphrased as follows:

> I appeared to Abraham, Isaac, and Jacob, but only partially—in the capacity of El Shaddai. But who I am fully, which is what my name Yahweh captures, I did not make myself known to them. This is made known first only now, to you, the Exodus generation, who will witness my mighty saving power.

There is, to be sure, a distinction between the age in which Moses lived and that of the patriarchs, but it is one of emphasis and degree rather than kind. Exodus 6:3 does create some distance between the God of the Exodus and the God of the patriarchs: Now God's character as a saving God is to be fully revealed. Nevertheless, what 3:14–15 and 6:3 demonstrate is not the newness of the divine *name*, but the centrality of the Exodus as the event by which God's salvation, and hence his salvation name, "Yahweh," is fully known. To make it merely an issue of knowing someone's name is trivial and anticlimactic.

We see here the degree to which the two conversations between Moses and God follow a similar progression. Both the first meeting on Mount Horeb and this conversation involve a complaint on Moses' part, which is answered

---

6. My observations on 6:3 are informed to a certain extent by the following works (as well as others): the commentaries by Sarna, Childs, and Cassuto; E. A. Martens, *God's Design: A Focus on Old Testament Theology* (Grand Rapids: Baker, 1986), 11–20; W. R. Garr, "The Grammar and Interpretation of Exodus 6:3," *JBL* 111 (1992): 385–408; S. D. Glisson, "Exodus 6:3 in Pentateuchal Criticism," *ResQ* 28 (1985–86): 135–43; G. E. Whitney, "Alternate Interpretations of *loʾ* in Exodus 6:3 and Jeremiah 7:22," *WTJ* 48 (1986): 151–59; R. D. Wilson, "Critical Notes on Exodus VI 3," *PTR* 22 (1924): 108–19. This list of secondary sources is no more than a sampling of the generous amount of activity that this verse has engendered.

7. My comments on 3:14–15 above are relevant here as well. I will not repeat them in full.

8. See Sarna, *Exodus*, 31. He cites Isa. 52:6 and Jer. 16:21 in support. See also Fretheim, *Exodus*, 92. Childs cites the commentaries of Rashi and Ibn Ezra (medieval Jewish commentators) and Calvin, among others, as proponents of this view (*Book of Exodus*, 112).

by God. And that answer reaffirms his character, a character that is best exhibited by his name: Yahweh, the saving God, the God of the patriarchs.[9]

Armed, then, with this reaffirmation of God's character and his presence with Moses and the Israelites, Moses is again sent back. His first step is to revisit the Israelites, just as he did in 4:29–31, in an effort to reestablish the trust broken in the previous passage. Moses is to speak God's promise to them, that he will "bring out" the Israelites, "free" them from slavery, and "redeem" them (v. 6). The end result is that (1) they will become the people of God, (2) Yahweh will be their God, and (3) they will *know* that Yahweh has delivered them (v. 7).

This third point is particularly important for at least two reasons. For one thing, it helps put 6:3 in its proper perspective. By being delivered from Egypt, the Israelites will come to *know* God in a way that the patriarchs did not. Also, the Israelites will know that "I am the LORD your God." The refrain "I am Yahweh [the LORD]" is familiar to us from the previous encounter between Moses and the Lord on Mount Horeb (see also 6:2, 8, 29; 7:5). Clearly, the focus of God's message to the Israelites is on who *he* is, and their assessment of the situation must be based squarely on that immovable fact.

The reaction of the Israelites, however, is not unlike that of Moses at the beginning of the passage: They will not be fooled again. Once again the Israelites are grumbling in the face of God's mercy.[10] Their present reality dictates what they think God can and cannot do; they do "not listen to him because of their discouragement and cruel bondage" (v. 9).

But inasmuch as the Israelites have not yet learned their lesson, apparently neither has Moses. The Lord tells him to go once more to Pharaoh (v. 10), but Moses responds (can we really blame him?), as it were: "It's no use, LORD. If my own people won't listen, what makes you think Pharaoh will? Besides, I speak with faltering lips." In a certain sense, we reach here the nadir of Moses' despondence, for he falls back on the same excuse that God answered in the previous meeting (4:11–17). Does Moses really think it will work this time? Here is no evidence of Moses' humility but of his continued inability to see past the end of his nose.

The Genealogy (6:13–27)

AT THIS POINT in the narrative we read a genealogy of Moses and Aaron (6:13–27). This striking element raises a number of questions. What is it doing here, especially since it seems to disrupt the flow of the narrative.

---

9. For a similar view, see Moberly, *The Old Testament of the Old Testament*, 26–35.
10. See also 14:10–31; 15:22–25; 16:1–36; 17:1–7; 32:1–33:6.

Does it really need to be there? Verses 28–30 may help bring us closer to answering such questions. Verses 10–12 and 28–30 surround the genealogy. Moreover, verses 28–30 essentially repeat verses 10–12. In both passages God gives Moses the order to go to Pharaoh and both times Moses reminds God, somewhat feebly, that he has a problem speaking.

These two passages are not separate events, but one and the same. That is, verses 28–30 repeat verses 10–12 in an effort to "frame" the genealogy. Hence, this repetition shows that the "insertion" of the genealogy here is purposeful. What is that purpose? Verses 26–27 provide the answer: It establishes the pedigree of Moses and Aaron—or perhaps more accurately, of Aaron. Both are of the tribe of Levi.

But this purpose raises two further questions: (1) Why is their Levite heritage so important, and (2) why is it so important to place it at *this* juncture in the narrative? A close, though brief, look at this genealogy may help us arrive at some answers.

In verse 13, one gets the impression that the genealogy to follow will be a more or less complete genealogy of the Israelites as a whole: "Now the LORD spoke to Moses and Aaron about the Israelites and Pharaoh king of Egypt, and he commanded them to bring the *Israelites* out of Egypt." And the list begins by mentioning Reuben and Simeon (vv. 14–15), the two oldest of the twelve sons of Jacob (see also Gen. 46:8ff.). Thus, the genealogy begins in an ordinary way.

The next name to appear is Levi, the third son of Jacob and Leah, but the emphasis placed on this son becomes quickly apparent. The remainder of the genealogy traces Levi's descendants exclusively, to the fifth generation, with the primary focus being not Moses but Aaron, as can be seen in the following diagram (this diagram streamlines the genealogy in order to allow its focus to stand out more clearly):

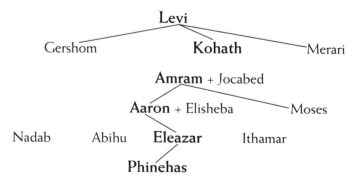

Although other names are mentioned, the clear focus of the genealogy is the levitical lineage from Levi to Phinehas, with Aaron standing in the midway position. This is not to say, however, that the genealogy is to be understood wood-enly.[11] Rather, there is strong indication that this, like other biblical genealogies, is telescoped. For example, according to Genesis 46:11, Kohath is one of the sons of Levi who made the initial journey into Egypt. Hence, there must have been about a 350-year span between Kohath and Moses (since the entire stay in Egypt was 430 years and Moses was 80 at the time of the Exodus; Ex. 7:7; 12:40—41), which makes it unlikely that Kohath is Moses' great-uncle. One should not con-clude, however, that this genealogy is thus faulty or inaccurate. Rather, it is pre-cisely the nonliteralness of the genealogy that suggests a purposefulness and a *theological* significance for the manner in which it is presented here.

What is the significance of this genealogy in this context? For one thing, it extends back to the patriarchal period. Thus, we see once again the con-nection with the past that the writer of Exodus is so concerned to underscore throughout his book. To put it another way, the reference to the patriarchal period highlights the ancient purposefulness of God and his plan to redeem Israel.[12] Moreover, the genealogy ends with the grandson of Aaron, Phine-has, a fact that suggests that the author's view is not only past but future as well. By providing this wide-ranging genealogy, at least one purpose of the author is to place the Exodus event in its broad historical perspective: God's purpose reaches backward and forward.

The termination of the genealogy with Phinehas is also significant, but it does not afford an easy explanation. Phinehas is a highly regarded figure in the Old Testament. In Numbers 25:1—17, he is the one who turns God's anger away from the Israelites by killing an Israelite and his Midianite wife (Zimri and Cozbi).[13] The result of his actions is that God makes a "covenant of peace" with him (25:12), meaning, "He and his descendants will have a covenant of a lasting priesthood, because he was zealous for the honor of his God and made atonement for the Israelites" (v. 13). In Joshua 22:1—34, Phine-has is among those who successfully intervene to avoid war when the east-ern tribes build an altar at Geliloth. Perhaps the significance of Phinehas as the termination point for this genealogy is to draw attention to the covenant faithfulness of the line of Levi to Phinehas, which includes Aaron.

---

11. But see Cassuto, *Commentary on Exodus*, 85—87.

12. Sarna comments, "Because a genealogy inherently symbolizes vigor and continuity, its presence here also injects a reassuring note into the otherwise despondent mood. . . . A detailed analysis of the content of the genealogy discloses careful design and purpose" (*Exodus*, 33).

13. The issue here is clearly more than simply marrying a foreign woman, since Moses himself married Zipporah, daughter of Reuel, priest of Midian (2:15—21). This episode concerns sexual immorality in the context of spiritual seduction. Phinehas's actions are extolled in Ps. 106:30—31.

The question remains, however, why the focus of this genealogy should be Aaron rather than Moses. The context of this passage may help point us in the right direction. Aaron and Moses have been working in tandem (see 4:14). In the present passage, too, the verses that frame the genealogy (6:13 and 26) mention both Moses and Aaron. In fact, in verse 26, Aaron is mentioned first. The point of this genealogy *in this context* seems to be to establish Aaron as a worthy partner in the deliverance of Israel from Egypt, particularly in his role as Moses' mouthpiece—a role reiterated in 6:28–7:7.[14]

Verse 12 brings this into sharper focus. The point at which the genealogy "interrupts" the conversation between Moses and God is where Moses, once again, complains about his difficulty in speaking. In 4:14–16, when Moses makes this complaint, Aaron is designated to help. In an effort to provide the reader with some rationale for such a choice, the genealogy, quite logically, is placed here. By the time we get to the end of the genealogy, Aaron's pedigree is firmly established and the stage is set for the series of encounters with Pharaoh that will eventually lead to the release of the Israelites. Yet, to anticipate a point we will treat later on, it is most curious why, after such an apology for Aaron, he seems to take on a relatively inactive role throughout the plague narrative, which is precisely where we would expect him to become more prominent.

Aaron Speaks for Moses (6:28–7:7)

IN 6:28–30, THE author picks up where he left off before the genealogy, repeating verses 10–12. The emphasis is again placed on God's decisive role in bringing the Israelites out of Egypt. The Lord addresses Moses by announcing yet again, "I am the LORD." Moses is only to tell Pharaoh what God tells him to say. Moses' reiteration of the complaint he gave in 4:10, which is also mentioned in 6:12 and of which the reader is no doubt tiring by this point, is answered by God a final time.

But there is one significant difference between God's response to Moses here and that given in 4:15–16. In their first conversation on Mount Horeb, God tells Moses that he will be God to *Aaron*. Here the roles played by Moses and Aaron are presented differently: Moses is to be God directly to *Pharaoh* (7:1). That is, Moses will be an authority figure to Pharaoh rather than

---

14. For some scholarly works that treat the functions of biblical genealogies in general, see G. A. Rendsburg, "The Internal Consistency and Historical Reliability of the Biblical Genealogies," *VT* 40 (1990): 185–206; R. R. Wilson, *Genealogy and History in the Biblical World* (New Haven: Yale Univ. Press, 1977). Both these works deal more with the historicity of genealogies, Wilson being more skeptical than Rendsburg, but they are nevertheless thoughtful and interesting studies. Rendsburg's article does treat Ex. 6 specifically (albeit briefly), whereas Wilson's does not.

just to Aaron. We may think of this as an extra dose of power that God bestows on Moses for the purpose of confronting the king of Egypt. The halting dismissal that Pharaoh gave the first time will not be repeated. From now on, albeit not all at once, Pharaoh, too, will know that Moses is God's representative and is therefore someone to be reckoned with.

The point of 7:1–5 is similar to 3:18–22: God gives Moses a preview of coming attractions. Moses and Aaron are to go to Pharaoh to demand the Israelites' release, but God will make Pharaoh resistant to complying with this request. Instead, he will use this as an opportunity to show Egypt *his* might. Hence, this second conversation with Moses ends by repeating the theme that has formed the backbone of the first six chapters of Exodus: the focus of Exodus is Yahweh. *He* is now poised to do a great thing for Israel. He promised the patriarchs he would, and he will not allow his honor to be trampled by Pharaoh. Rather, he will toy with this "mighty" nation and its godlike king, and by doing so will leave no doubt that it is he who fights the battle (7:5).

God is more interested in Israel's vindication and Egypt's punishment than Moses has been giving him credit for, for it is God's honor that is ultimately being vindicated. Perhaps the great irony of all this, as we will see later, is that whereas Egypt learns this lesson in most decisive terms, it is Israel, the people whom God came to deliver, who are so slow to understand what God has done.

Exodus 3:1–7:7 as a whole forms a large unit that is unified by a central theme: The God of Israel is in control. The main way in which this theme is presented is by the reiteration of the divine name in 3:14–15 and 6:3 and the recurring reference to God being the "I AM." Despite apparent setbacks, the game plan has not changed. Moses and the Israelites may be panicking, but God is steady and sure, for the outcome is never in doubt. Moses and Aaron should understand the recurring setbacks they experience by Pharaoh's repeated refusals as being well within the parameters of God's plan of deliverance.

Bridging Contexts

REVIEW OF THEMES **and the writer's manner of expression.** Before we look at the unique themes of this passage, it is worthwhile to pause and mention a number of elements in 5:22–7:7 that have already surfaced in previous passages.

(1) Consider the *manner* in which the author of Exodus tells the story. One pattern in his approach that has been easy to discern is the streamlined manner in which he presents the material. As we have noted again and again, the author is not concerned to give all the details of the events—he is not writing an exhaustive history or a journalistic account of Israel's release from

Egypt (in fact, no history writing, ancient or modern, is ever exhaustive or neutral). Rather, he is writing a theological account of that event. As a result, our exploration of this (and any other) book of the Old Testament should similarly be concerned, sooner or later, to uncover its *theological* significance rather than the details or background matters, whether geographical or historical, that the account itself does not provide.

This is not to say, of course, that the historical setting of the book is irrelevant, only that uncovering some of these specifics should not be the focus of reading Exodus. In 5:22–7:7, for example, the focus of the genealogy is the line of Levi extending to Phinehas with Aaron at the center. This is its main concern. It is the biblical narratives themselves that drive us to look for the overarching meaning of the passage. This is one reason why we focus on theological themes in the Bridging Contexts sections.

(2) Though this point is more subtle, we should note that throughout the previous chapters the author has presented a complex moral portrait of his characters, Moses in particular. He is the chosen instrument of Israel's redemption, but at the same time a refugee from justice and a stubborn recipient of God's plan. The Exodus narrative presents Moses neither as an ideal moral figure to be emulated nor as a rogue to be shunned.

This narrative does not intend to present Moses as a moral paradigm for present-day (or ancient) readers. There is no exhortation to "be like Moses" when he humbly removes his sandals in God's presence (3:5), nor to "not be like Moses" when he questions God's integrity (5:22–23). Rather, Moses, like so many of the major figures in the Old Testament, is a complex character. As we continue reading—not only in Exodus but throughout the remaining books of the Pentateuch—we see a *progression* in Moses' self-understanding and in his relationship to God. It is precisely the varied moral portrait of Moses in these early chapters that is one of the factors that pushes us to read the story in its broader context. This, too, is another reason why I prefer to place the passages under discussion in ever-widening circles of canonical reflection.

(3) There are also a number of themes from previous passages that are revisited in 5:22–7:7. Exodus, like so much of Old Testament narrative, is a repetitive book, where themes are reiterated, developed, and expanded. Hence, each passage does not necessarily have its own theological theme or themes distinct from the rest of the book. Rather, the same themes come into play at various points, often with increased emphasis or added dimensions.

We have already seen that the reference to the patriarchs (6:3) and the inclusion of the genealogy (6:13–27) reiterate the writer's desire to maintain a connection to the past, that present events can only be understood in the fullest historical context. The theme of grumbling is already hinted at in

2:11–14, but becomes an undercurrent of sorts in both conversations between Moses and God: The people grumble against Moses and Moses grumbles against God. This theme intensifies throughout the book and the Pentateuch, culminating in the forty-year desert purge and Moses' preclusion from entering the Promised Land. God's sovereign control of circumstances despite appearances (e.g., ch. 1) also receives considerable treatment in 5:22–7:7.

In fact, with the reiteration of the divine name in 3:14–15 and 6:3 and the recurring refrain "I am the LORD," we may say that we have a reached a high-water point in this theme. The focus turns more and more to God and what he will do, and the reader is left with the expectation of imminent action. Ultimately, this complex of themes in Exodus converge on one central notion, that the mighty God loves his people and will display that love by saving them.

Moses as God. One striking element in this section is 7:1, which, like 4:16, refers to Moses as God. Of course, this is in no way intended to suggest that Moses actually becomes the God of Israel, the Creator of heaven and earth. Still, it will not do to lessen the impact of this statement. Exodus 7:1 does not say that Yahweh will make Moses "like" God to Pharaoh (as the NIV has it), but, rather straightforward, that he will make Moses God to Pharaoh.[15] This is, however, not a statement of some divine metamorphosis. Rather, the point is that Moses will be God *functionally* both to Pharaoh and to the Israelites.

It may be helpful here to understand this through Pharaoh's eyes. In Egyptian royal ideology, the pharaoh was considered to be a divine being. So by calling Moses God, Yahweh is beating Pharaoh at his own game.[16] It is not the king of Egypt who is god; rather, it is this shepherd and leader of slaves who is God. And this Moses-God defeats Pharaoh in a manner that leaves no doubt as to the true nature and source of his power: He controls the elements, bugs, livestock, fire from heaven, and the water of the sea; he even has authority over life and death. Moses is not simply *like* God to Pharaoh. He truly *is* God *to Pharaoh* in that God is acting through Moses.[17]

Not only is Moses God to Pharaoh; he is also God to the Israelites. Although this point is not explicitly mentioned in the text, it is certainly implied in the role that Moses is to play in delivering the Israelites. In 5:22–7:7, Moses is, for the second time, privy to God's self-disclosure. He

---

15. The Hebrew phrase in 7:1 is different from 4:16. The latter uses the idiom "to be" (*hayah*) plus the preposition *l* while the former uses the root "to give" (*natan*). The meaning, however, is essentially the same.

16. This approach to the text is also hinted at in rabbinic literature, e.g., *Exodus Rabbah* 8.2: "Go and make him that made himself a god an abomination in the world, because he exalted himself."

17. This imagery is unfortunately lost in the NIV.

announces to Moses what he intends to do: Israel will be delivered and Moses will be his instrument to bring that about. Moses is the one through whom God brings salvation to Israel. God does not simply act; he acts *through* Moses. Later, on Mount Sinai (chs. 20–23), he does not simply speak; he speaks *through* Moses.

Moses' role as "God" is unique to this point in the Old Testament. But from a theological and canonical point of view, Moses' close association with God should be seen not as an arbitrary spasm of divine empowerment, but as a striking episode in the type of intimacy that God intended to have with all humanity but that was lost in the garden. Adam and Eve enjoyed as close a union with God as any people ever did. Specifically relevant to this context is Adam and Eve as image-bearers of God (Gen. 1:27). Further, they were given dominion over all of creation (1:26; cf. Adam's naming the animals in 2:19–20). As "rulers" of creation, Adam and Eve exhibited their image-bearing role most clearly.

From this perspective we may think of Moses as God as a striking example of "Adam-like" activity. Moses' acting like God is not so much a comment on his elevation to some superhuman status. It is, rather, a sad comment on the "subhuman" status to which the rest of humanity—in this case, the Israelites—have sunk because of Adam's sin. From this canonical perspective, Moses is not *super*human, but *truly* human—he is a new Adam. His true humanity is displayed precisely in his intimacy with God.

In this sense, Moses is called by God to mediate God's image to the enslaved Israelites. The Israelites are themselves dominated by the Egyptians, led by Pharaoh, the false image-bearer. But God plans for them to be delivered from their condition and brought back to intimacy with him. This intimacy is already displayed in the person of Moses, through whom God will not only save the Israelites but will later, on Mount Sinai, reveal his will to them for how this intimacy can be sustained—that is, the law and the tabernacle, expressions of God's holiness.

Any Old Testament figure who mediates God to the people is in some sense performing a similar image-bearing role. We have already seen elsewhere that prophets, priests, and kings represent God to the people. The clearest parallel with Moses is to be found with the prophets, since they, too, bring a message of salvation to the Israelites and a message of judgment to Israel's enemies, and, when needed, to rebellious Israel herself.[18] Priests mediate God to the people by maintaining the intimacy between God and his people through the ritual of sacrifice, by which Israel's sins are atoned for. In other words, like Moses, the priests mediate salvation or deliverance to the people.

---

18. Note, too, that Moses is explicitly referred to as a prophet in Deut. 18:15 and 34:10.

Moses as God, then, is a powerful reminder of what was lost in the garden, but likewise of what is to come in Israel's history as embodied by prophets, priests, and kings. Moses is the most striking Old Testament example of regaining the glory that humanity once had in the garden as the bearers of God's image. He is also the paradigm for subsequent image-bearers.

Moses as God is not just a trick used to stump Pharaoh, nor is it merely hyperbole. It is a profound theological statement that takes us from the garden to the cross. Few Christians can read 4:16 and 7:1 without having their thoughts turn quickly to Jesus, *the* God-Man. Moses' role as God is a typological foreshadowing of Jesus, who is God. In this sense, Moses' divine function is similar to what we have seen in conjunction with 3:2 and the angel of the Lord. Both figures serve to draw us to a fuller understanding of the significance of Jesus. The angel is not the preincarnate Christ in the Old Testament, nor is Moses in 4:16 and 7:1. What these figures represent, rather, are partial hints of what we, living in postresurrection reality, are privy to. Christ truly is God, not just in a functional sense as we have seen with Moses, but in his essence. As such, he can fully mediate both God's word and salvation to us.

Christ is the one who is able fully to restore our image-bearing right as human beings. He is the true "image of the invisible God" (Col. 1:15). He embodies the glory of humanity that was lost in the garden, since he is without sin or blemish. In a manner of speaking, Christ embodies what it means to be truly human—not so much by his frailty and other "human" characteristics (which we think of when we consider Christ's humanity), but by his exemplifying what God intended for humanity: perfect image-bearers. Christ fulfills the ideal hinted at in the life of Moses and the other Old Testament mediators. Jesus saves us not simply so that we can have a "relationship" with God, but so that the intimacy between God and humanity, lost in the Fall, can be restored. As Christians, we participate in nothing less than the first installment of the reversal of the Fall, which was inaugurated at the resurrection of Christ and will be complete at his return.

A witness to the nations. Yahweh is the God of the Israelites. But he is not simply a local god, as were so many of the gods of the ancient Near Eastern world. Rather, he is with his people wherever they go. He was with Abraham as he left his homeland of Ur in Mesopotamia. He was with the patriarchs during their travels throughout Canaan. He also accompanied the Israelites during their lengthy stay in Egypt, first accompanying Joseph during his enforced exile, and then the Israelites as they went from citizens to slaves. It matters not where his people are; he is with them.

From an Egyptian perspective, the God of Israel had no business intruding on Egyptian soil. They had their own gods; why would they need a foreign god, particularly one who allowed his patrons to become slaves? Yet Yahweh is no "foreign" God. He is the Creator and Sustainer of all the earth, including the mighty land of Egypt. At least part of the purpose behind God's mighty acts in Egypt is to display just that: The God of Israel is the true God and his act of salvation will bring this to light for all to see. We see this throughout the Exodus story; for example: "And the Egyptians will know that I am the LORD when I stretch out my hand against Egypt and bring the Israelites out of it" (7:5; see also 7:17; 8:22; 9:29). To say that Yahweh is the God of the *Israelites* should not be mistaken as an indication of his limited power. It indicates instead the special relationship he has with Israel, his chosen people.

Even though God in the Old Testament has a special relationship with the Israelites, his salvation of his people has far-reaching implications. God is zealous to display his glory and might to the nations and to creation as a whole. His purpose for choosing a *particular* race of people is, somewhat iron-ically, to show his ownership over *everything*. We see this in prophetic litera-ture, where the nations that surround the Israelites, however powerful and fearsome they may be, are nothing more than pawns in Yahweh's hand. They are used ultimately for Israel's benefit, and in the end, these nations will come to know the true God for who he really is.

In some cases, this newfound knowledge will result in a saving knowledge of God (see Isa. 19:16–25). This prophecy speaks of a time when Egypt and Assyria will, along with Israel, be a blessing on the earth and "will worship together" (v. 23; see also Zeph. 2:11). Is this prophecy to be taken literally, or do these nations represent the non-Israelite, Gentile, world? I am strongly inclined toward the latter (particularly since biblical "Assyria" no longer exists as a national entity), with its fulfillment coming with the death and resur-rection of Christ.

Elsewhere in prophetic literature we see various oracles delivered against the nations.[19] In Yahweh's dealings with Israel, God has something to say to all peoples, and that message can be one of judgment (as we see in Exodus). God judges these nations to a large extent because of their hostile stance toward Israel, his people. The end result is an implicit recognition, if not confession, by the nations that Yahweh is God. Thus, when God delivers Israel from oppressive circumstances, his glory is revealed not only to Israel but to the nations as well. This point is made with great force in Isaiah 40:3–5, where Israel's deliverance from Babylon is drawing near. God is coming to bring them across the desert back to their homeland (vv. 3–4). In doing so,

---

19. The primary oracles against the nations are found in Isa. 13:1–24:23; Jer. 46:1–51:64; Ezek. 25:1–32:32; Amos 1:3–2:3; Zeph. 1:14–2:15.

"the glory of the LORD will be revealed, and *all mankind* together will see it" (v. 5; see also 52:10).

Yet prophecies such as this do not serve primarily as warnings to the nations of God's impending activity. They are words of encouragement to Israel, for whom the machinations of the world powers often seem overwhelming. The words of the prophets, after all, were likely not handed over for consideration to the respective rulers of the nations. They were intended for the Israelites themselves, so that, when the smoke and dust of political intrigue had settled, God's people could look back and declare his faithfulness to them. "Do you not know? Have you not heard? Has it not been told you from the beginning?" (Isa. 40:21).

Christ's coming does not signify the beginning of God's "universal" appeal to humanity as distinct from the Old Testament's more restricted scope. It is a common misconception of the Old Testament that God's glance is directed solely toward Israel. To be sure, the inclusion of the Gentiles is a more dominant theme in the New Testament, but this emphasis is not to be contrasted absolutely to the Old Testament. It is, rather, the fuller realization of the universalism that is implied, even promised (see Isa. 19:16–25), in the Old Testament.

In fact, Luke 3:4–6 quotes Isaiah 40:3–5 (cf. above). With Christ's birth, God's salvation has fully come and will truly be seen by "all mankind." The deliverance of Israel from Babylon in Isaiah 40 is a prelude, a foreshadowing, of God's final salvation sealed by the resurrection of Christ. The nations will witness God's ultimate act of salvation.[20]

The point of this universal appeal is not that the inclusion of the Gentiles means the abandonment of God's promises to Israel, but that the Gentiles, by virtue of their union with the risen Christ, now partake in those blessings. The inclusion of the Gentiles into God's family is the ultimate witness of the nations to God's salvific power. All Gentiles united to Christ have also been grafted into the "branch" (Israel; see Rom. 11:11–24) and, hence, are the fulfillment of the universalistic promise of God through the Old Testament prophets.

The resurrection of Christ has far-reaching implications. It is not simply a one-time display of God's power over death. Nor is it simply a powerful vindication of Christ's status as God's Son. It is *the* great act of salvation, whereby God displays once and for all his purpose for humanity. This was not done in secret but in public. Armed with the power of the resurrected Christ, the apostles went out and proclaimed the gospel to the nations in fulfillment of a command from the resurrected Christ: "You will be my witnesses in Jerusalem, and

---

20. See also the comments in the introduction concerning Isa. 49:8 and its use by Paul in 2 Cor. 6:2.

in all Judea and Samaria, and to the ends of the earth" (Acts 1:8). God's mighty acts in the Exodus generation were primarily to bring judgment on the Egyptians. They would know God as a result—not as a savior but as a destroyer. The oracles against the nations likewise bear a tone of judgment, although throughout we catch glimpses of God's overarching plan for them.

The focus of the New Testament is the inclusion of the nations into the family of God through faith in the risen Christ. The final result will be that all people in all ages, whether in Christ or not, will acknowledge the Lord as the one who raised Christ from the dead. "At the name of Jesus every knee [will] bow, in heaven and on earth and under the earth, and every tongue confess that Jesus Christ is Lord, to the glory of God the Father" (Phil. 2:10–11; cf. Isa. 45:23). The nations have witnessed the gospel of Christ. All the world acknowledges him as Lord. The author of the play, as C. S. Lewis puts it, has come out on stage and received the acclaim that is his due. The play is over. God's purpose is accomplished.

BEARING THE IMAGE of God. It is perhaps easy to empathize with Moses in 5:22–7:7. God has called him to a special task, yet in following God he faces severe discouragement. One can hardly blame Moses' exasperation in 5:22–23. It seems natural for us to allow setbacks to affect how we live out the Christian life—even how we view our relationship to God himself. Yet, the Lord often pushes us, as he did Moses, to reach limits we thought impossible.

As Christians, we have been re-created in God's image. In our union with the Son, we, like him, are true image-bearers. Although not yet fully, we *truly* reflect the image-bearing status that was lost in the garden but that will once again be fully realized in eternity. Such knowledge ought to have an effect on how we live from day to day. It seems an almost natural tendency among the Christians I know (including myself!) to follow the pattern of Moses rather than that of Christ. We have doubts regarding our status as being re-created by the Father, in Christ, for a glorious purpose. We are known by God. He gives us a new start, a fresh beginning, but that high reality does not always translate well in our contact with the world in which we live.

To be human is not to be frail, weak, or rebellious. These are marks of sin. To be human means to be the pinnacle of God's creation. It is only after he created humanity that God said "very good" (Gen. 1:31). It was humans alone whom God created in his image (1:27). People were intended all along to be God-like in the world, to have intimate communion with him, and, therefore, to have authority over the rest of creation, to "fill the earth and subdue it" (1:28).

We should thus resist with great boldness trends that devalue the marvel and wonder of what it means to be human. How often have we heard someone excuse his or her actions with the disclaimer, "I'm only human"? There is nothing "only" about being human. Being human means having a great capacity for love, joy, energy, justice, work, accomplishments, charity—a capacity for anything God-like. Our shortcomings are not the result of being human, but of our sinful nature that has tarnished true humanity.

One contemporary issue that reflects such a distorted view of humanity is animal rights advocacy. In my estimation, this currently popular issue is the logical flip side of such a low view of humanity. Although any reasonable person would freely acknowledge that the abuse and cruel treatment of animals is wrong, the argument for "animal rights" is often made on the basis of the supposed link between humans and animals. Even leaving aside the complicated issue of the theory of evolution, which some argue supports an elevated view of the value of animal life (or, conversely, the devaluation of human life), there is a prevalent notion today that animals are our brothers and sisters, that we must learn to live in harmony with them, that they have the right to occupy our planet as much as we do, and that any activity on our part that infringes on their right to exist is wrong.

There are a number of obvious difficulties with animal rights advocacy. Again, in the language of Genesis 1:28, as humans in God's image, God has given us authority over the animal kingdom. Authority does not mean abuse, of course; these two are often equated in our world. Authority in the biblical sense is a God-like authority, an image-bearing authority. It exercises authority with wisdom, compassion, and justice. The creatures God created are *entrusted* to our care, but they are not on the same level as God's crowning creative act, humanity, which bears his image. Of course, this perspective does not settle the many ethical questions that arise. For example, is it right to experiment on animals to develop new drugs? What about new cosmetics? Is it okay to wear mink? If not, why do we wear leather shoes and jackets? The point here is not to solve these questions but to suggest a proper foundation for discussing them.

Being human is precious, but it is something that our world takes for granted. It is ironic that in the midst of our "culture of narcissism," to use Christopher Lasch's famous phrase, we are so unreflective of the utter awe and wonder that being human should inspire.[21] We are self-centered, but

---

21. Christopher Lasch, *The Culture of Narcissism: American Life in an Age of Diminishing Expectations* (New York: Warner, 1979). This is a curious irony in our culture. We are self-centered and narcissistic while at the same time entertaining the subhuman understanding of what it means to be human.

the self we are centered on is a sorry substitute. It is our humanness that, of all the wonders of God's creation, shouts loudest to us that we are not an accident of the random convergence of cosmic forces. We are here by design. We are here for a purpose. And that purpose is not to make the world a better place to live, however admirable such efforts may be. It is ultimately not to help our fellow human beings or contribute to society. These things are not so much wrong as superficial.

Our ultimate purpose is here to reflect the glory and image of God, and any philosophy, worldview, international summit, or government program that falls short of that purpose is "subhuman." Whatever benefits such activities may bring, they will ultimately not set captives free or bring true joy. God's purpose for his creation is far beyond the expectations of the world. As Christians, therefore, we have the obligation and privilege of telling a fallen world, "Be all you can be." We are the instruments used by God to bring the gospel to them, a gospel that does not just save sinners—barely—but that is intended to blow apart the present system and replace it with one that is holy and lasting. Indeed, that process has already begun—the tomb is empty.

"Being God" to others. Such an understanding of humanity should instill confidence in us, both in how we view our relationship to God and in how we relate to the world in which we live. Moses' doubts as reflected in 5:22– 7:7, however much empathy we may feel, are wrong. We have often heard the argument for boldness in evangelism: "You may be the only Bible they ever see." Taking our cue from our passage, we should take this a step further: You may be the only "God" they see. Or, perhaps more accurately, you may be the *first* God they see. As people re-created in God's image, as true image-bearers, we are the means by which the news of God's salvation spreads.

Rarely (if ever) does one repent of one's sins by watching a sunset or by some other attempt at communing with nature. The primary way God has ordained to bring others onto the path of being a restored image-bearer is through words, through communication, and this normally involves some form of human contact. This is the purpose behind the mystery of the Incarnation: For God to reach us, he became like us. Christians, in whom the image of God has been restored in Christ, are the ideal means to spread God's Word. It is not verbal manipulation or finely crafted arguments. It is the whole person's life, so thoroughly re-created in God's image, that bears witness to the world, that draws people to the kingdom.

There is more to being a witness to Christ than quoting Bible verses and refraining from certain filthy habits. As Christ's brothers and sisters, we are God to the world. Our goal is to be a part of that process that brings the world (those with whom the Lord places us) back to its Edenic glory. The extent to which that goal is realized is, of course, the Lord's doing, not ours.

Still, we labor toward that end. Put otherwise, we reflect God's image to a world in which that image has been corrupted by the effects of sin. The ways in which we perform this role, the ways in which we, like Moses, act as "witnesses to the nations," are varied and diverse.

If I may speak from recent personal experience, the ways in which we are called upon to be God to the world are often subtle and challenging. I have been coaching my son's Little League team for several years. As I write this, one particularly "memorable" season ended—mercifully—just a few days ago (let's just say we didn't come in first place!). Every Little League coach knows the nearly impossible challenge he or she faces: field a team that won't get blown off the field but give every child a chance to play and develop as people and players. Unfortunately, when you do the one, you rarely succeed in the other. But as you step back from the competitive fray, you begin to see the children under your charge more than simply as players with varying degrees of ability who may or may not help you win. You see children from broken homes, children with difficulty following directions, children with abilities that help them excel in areas other than the baseball diamond.

You see, in a word, *people* created in God's image but who, because of the Fall, reflect that image in a distorted way. Long after these children have outgrown their cleats and lost their gloves, long after the standings and statistics have been forgotten, these children, these people, will still exist—either as distorted image-bearers or as completed image-bearers. For all I know, as I sit in the dugout and make up the lineups and contemplate who will and will not play, I may be the only completed image-bearer they or their parents have ever known. My knowledge of my role as image-bearer, as "God" to my Little League team, should form the motivating factor in how I treat them. As always, such knowledge does not determine the precise decisions I make (e.g., would it be best for all involved if I insert a weak player into a demanding, stressful situation?). The point is not so much the decisions themselves as it is the approach I take to making those decisions.

Another recent incident involves an episode of nearly universal suburban appeal: neighbor problems. Neighbors do not always get along. Often such problems are a matter of differing perspectives and can be exacerbated by poor communication. The details are not important here, but, in my mind, a simple and workable problem has escalated beyond what the issue warrants. Accusations have begun to fly our way, even a little gossip. No amount of reasoned discussion is helping. In fact, discussion at this point seems out of the picture.

How should I and my wife handle this situation? It is *very* tempting to fire back by starting some gossip ourselves. How tempting it has been to forget that they are not Christians and that we are! More than once I have come close to alerting our other neighbors as to what is happening in order to get them on our side. Also, more than once I have been tempted to answer their accusations one-by-one and tell them "what I really think" of them.

But I am God to them. This does not mean that I am a doormat and I take their tactics without any response. But as God, what do I do? My wife and I decided to resist what comes naturally to us: to counter their gossip with our own, to be rude or give them the "silent treatment," to find things that they do that we don't like and make problems for them (revenge). Rather, we have decided on two strategies. The first is to speak to them face-to-face about the fact that we do not think the way they are handling the situation is proper. We are not angry, vengeful, or combative. We simply tell them that if they have a legitimate complaint, they should come to us directly and not talk about us to the neighbors. Second, we are killing them with kindness. In the midst of an awkward situation, we are going out of our way to greet them when we see them, to pick up their trash cans when they blow over, to cut their small patch of grass that borders our property directly but that is out of the way for them.

Our approach is to think of the long term. We may be the only God they know. They know we are believers, and they (perhaps the other neighbors as well) are watching. The Lord has delivered us from our sins and put us in this situation so that we might "witness to the nations" how thorough and far-reaching his might is. We are to act in such a way that even through our frailties, God's power and love may be seen, that they may know that there is another way to behave, that God's purpose is to bring them to a higher level of existence, that is, to make them fully human, completed image-bearers.

All of life is ready to be used by the Lord to bear witness and bring glory to himself. He makes us God to the people around us so that they may know the great and awesome mystery—their Creator is their Savior. This situation has reminded me to be alert in whatever situation I find myself. How am I, here and now, even where I least expect it, to be God in this situation?

Our passage has much to teach us, and these thoughts only scratch the surface. Personally, I have been moved by Calvin's diagnosis of the significance of this portion of Exodus. I would like to end this discussion with his insights.

> It was, indeed, possible for God to overwhelm him [Pharaoh] at once, by a single nod, so that he should even fall down dead at the very sight of Moses; but ... as he will himself presently declare, He, *in the first place*, chose more clearly to lay open His power; for if Pharaoh had either voluntarily yielded, or had been overcome without effort, the glory of the victory would not have been so illustrious. *In the second place*, He wished this monument to exist of His singular love towards

His elect people; for by contending so perseveringly and so forcibly against the obstinacy of this most powerful king, He gave no doubtful proof of his love towards his Church. *In the third place*, He wished to accustom His servants in all ages to patience, lest they should faint in their minds, if He does not immediately answer their prayers, and, at every moment, relieve them from their distresses. *In the fourth place*, He wished to shew that, against all the strivings and devices of Satan, against the madness of the ungodly, and all worldly hindrances, His hand must always prevail; and to leave us no room to doubt, but that whatever we see opposing us will at length be overcome by him. *In the fifth place*, by detecting the illusions of Satan and the magicians, He would render His Church more wary, that she might carefully watch against such devices, and that her faith might continue invincible against all the machinations of error. *Finally*, He would convince Pharaoh and the Egyptians that their folly was not to be excused by any pretense of ignorance; and, at the same time, by this example, He would shew us how horrible a darkness possesses the minds of the reprobate, when He has deprived them of the light of His Spirit. These things must be attentively observed in the course of the narrative, if we desire to profit by it.[22]

---

22. Calvin, *Four Last Books of Moses*, 112–13.

Exodus 7:8–10:29

🔥

Introduction: The Plague Narrative As a Whole

THE PLAGUE NARRATIVE spans several chapters in Exodus. In keeping with the intention of this commentary series, however, it seems best not to treat this lengthy narrative in a series of briefer segments, either grouping some of the plagues together or treating each one individually. The ultimate purpose of this commentary is to point the reader toward the application of the passage in question, specifically a decidedly Christian application. It would be awkward, for example, to make a distinction between the plague of gnats and the plague of flies in both the Bridging Contexts and Contemporary Significance sections. The significance of the plague narrative is to be found in its overarching theology and its Christological perspective.

Consequently, the approach taken here (also taken elsewhere in this commentary, e.g., in the Book of the Covenant [20:22–23:19] and the tabernacle sections [25:1–31:18; 35:1–40:33]) will be to treat smaller sections of the narrative individually under Original Meaning. In the case of the plagues I will take them one at a time. Each plague has its own concerns, and they differ from each another in certain details. Then under the Bridging Contexts and Contemporary Significance sections, I will discuss the narrative as a whole. Such an approach should not be misunderstood as an attempt to slight these sections of Exodus. Quite the opposite: It is my hope that this method of organizing the material will help to maintain the theological integrity of the narrative—something the text itself demands—and, thereby, lead to a more judicious and helpful application of its contents.

I have also decided, contrary to popular convention, to treat the tenth plague separately from the first nine,[1] for several reasons. (1) Plagues 1–9 are prelude to the coming deliverance that has been anticipated since the beginning of the book. These are even organized so that the reader can treat them as three groups of three (see chart below under the third plague). These plagues do not lead directly to the release from Egypt, but they set up that event and hence are appropriately treated separately. The tenth plague, however, is clearly the climax of this portion of the book—indeed, of the book as a whole to this point—for here the long-awaited release from Egypt comes.

(2) Moreover, the account of the tenth plague is much longer than that of the other nine. Properly considered, it spans chapters 11, 12, and most of 13. Chapters 12–13 deal mainly with the Passover and the Feast of Unleav-

---

1. Although I am by no means the first to do so. See Houtman, *Exodus*, 2:17–21.

ened Bread, but these festivals are no mere dead rituals. They are, rather, the symbolic representation of the powerful deed that God has just performed: the death of the Egyptian firstborn, which leads directly to the release of Israel from Egypt.

The following chart introduces the plagues in such a way that highlights some of the differences among them.[2] Although detailed discussion of the tenth plague will wait for the next chapter, it is included in the chart on page 194 for sake of comparison and completeness.

IN ADDITION TO the discussion of the first nine plagues, I am including comments on the sign that was performed before Pharaoh, turning the staff into a snake. Although not a plague, it obviously sets up the plague narrative, has many of the characteristics of a plague, and serves as a prologue for what is to come.[3]

Preview of the Plagues: The Snake (7:8–13)

[8]The LORD said to Moses and Aaron, [9]"When Pharaoh says to you, 'Perform a miracle,' then say to Aaron, 'Take your staff and throw it down before Pharaoh,' and it will become a snake."

[10]So Moses and Aaron went to Pharaoh and did just as the LORD commanded. Aaron threw his staff down in front of Pharaoh and his officials, and it became a snake. [11]Pharaoh then summoned wise men and sorcerers, and the Egyptian magicians also did the same things by their secret arts: [12]Each one threw down his staff and it became a snake. But Aaron's staff swallowed up their staffs. [13]Yet Pharaoh's heart became hard and he would not listen to them, just as the LORD had said.

Changing his staff into a snake is one of the three signs that God showed to Moses during their first conversation on Mount Horeb (4:1–9; the other two signs are leprosy and changing water from the Nile into blood). It is not clear how these signs were to function. For example, were they to be used to convince the Israelites or the Egyptians of God's power? Clearly 3:13 and 4:1–5 imply the former (cf. 4:30: "He [Aaron] also performed the signs before the people"). But why, then, was this sign performed before Pharaoh

---

2. Similar charts may be found in A. M. Cartun, "'Who Knows Ten?' The Structural and Symbolic Use of Numbers in the Ten Plagues: Exodus 7:14–13:16," *USQR* 45 (1991): 107; N. Sarna, *Exploring Exodus*, 76.

3. See Durham, *Exodus*, 89.

plague	magicians reproduce plague	magicians or court beg	Pharaoh begs/ capitulates	Pharaoh hardens heart[a]	Pharaoh's heart is/ becomes hard	God hardens Pharaoh's heart[b]	distinction between Israel and Egypt	early morning confrontation	con- frontation in palace	Aaron's staff	Moses' staff
[Snake][c]	X				X					X	
Nile	X				X			X		X	
Frogs	X		X	X					X	X	
Gnats		X			X					X	
Flies			X	X			X	X			
Livestock					X		X		X		
Boils		X				X					
Hail			X	X			X	X			
Locusts			X			X			X		X
Darkness			X			X	X				X
Firstborn			X[d]			X[e]	X				X

a. Snake and plagues 1 and 3 use the Hebrew word *ḥazaq* to describe the hardening of Pharaoh's heart. Plagues 2, 4, 5, and 7 use *kabad*.

b. The Hebrew word used throughout is *ḥazaq*.

c. I include the incident of the snake because of its similarity to some of the plagues. It is not a plague itself but a preview of the plagues (see below).

d. See 12:31–32.

e. See 14:4.

and his court? If it is assumed that the three signs were to be performed also before the Egyptians (a point not made in the text), why is there no mention of the leprosy sign? Some commentators suggest that the sixth plague (boils) fulfills this sign, but that is hardly convincing. Moreover, changing the water to blood is not given as a *sign* to Pharaoh but is the first plague, which commences after the sign of the snake has been ignored.

Perhaps one approach to this problem is to treat the water to blood not as the first plague but as the last sign. This would at least yield two signs of the three being performed plus nine plagues. The difficulty with this, however, is that there is no indication in 8:1–15 (the plague of frogs) that the water to blood incident is the second sign and the frogs the first plague. That is, there is nothing in this narrative that suggests, "The signs have not worked, so let's proceed with the plagues." If anything, there is strong similarity in the way the water to blood and the frogs plagues are presented; the one simply follows the other.

If we try to lay aside our "biblical memory" and simply read the text before us, it becomes increasingly difficult to make a convincing argument for where the signs stop and the plagues begin. Perhaps the most convincing argument for the water to blood being the first plague is that it is actually a plague (!), something that the snake incident is not. But if this is the case, the question is raised why the water to blood seems to be treated as a *sign* in 4:8–9.

A close look at 4:8–9 may yield a solution. Yahweh tells Moses that if the Israelites do not listen to the first two signs (staff into a snake and leprosy), then he is to take some water from the Nile and turn it into blood. The text does not say that if his people do not listen to the first two signs, then he is to perform a *third* sign. In fact, the word "sign" seems to be assiduously avoided. Perhaps, then, there are only two signs, not three. This is a possible interpretation of 4:1–10, but, I must admit, it seems overly subtle. The clear implication of 4:30 is that the three "signs" given to Moses in the previous passage (4:1–10) were performed before the Israelites.

Hence, there is some confusion generated by the biblical text. In the final analysis it is best simply to say that there is a fairly smooth transition from sign to plague beginning in 7:8.[4] Also, I suggest that the snake, leprosy, and water to blood were *three signs* for the Israelites, which were performed in 4:30. Only one of these signs was performed before the Egyptians (7:8–13). The water to blood, although merely a sign for the Israelites, is

---

4. D. J. McCarthy, however, argues that the staff to snake episode is the first plague and the plague of darkness is the last plague. Exodus 11 (plague of death) and the subsequent chapters should be separated from the preceding narrative ("Plagues and Sea of Reeds: Exodus 5–14," *JBL* 85 [1966]: 137–58; "Moses' Dealings With Pharaoh: Ex 7,8–10,27," *CBQ* 27 [1965]: 336–47).

a plague for the Egyptians. This is not a problem, since it was only considered a *sign* for the Israelites.

In 7:8–13, then, Aaron and Moses confront Pharaoh with God's power. The initial audience with Pharaoh (5:1–21) did not go as well as they had hoped, but things will be different now. Aaron casts his staff before Pharaoh and it turns into a snake. Pharaoh's magicians duplicate the feat, but Aaron's snake swallows those of the magicians.

A number of elements are worth considering here, but the overarching point is clear: This encounter is an initial sparring between rival gods. This one brief incident embodies the main elements of the ten plagues that follow: God shows his power and Pharaoh resists the obvious conclusion that he is no match for the God of Israel. He should concede victory to Yahweh. But he does not, which will yield disastrous circumstances.

Hence, this passage summarizes the battle between Yahweh and Pharaoh that follows. It gives us a snapshot of the drama to unfold and of the final victory that will be won. This is the significance of Aaron's staff *swallowing* those of Pharaoh's magicians. The Hebrew word translated "to swallow" (*balaʿ*) is used in Exodus only here and in 15:12, where the sea swallows up the Egyptian army.[5] The final demise of the Egyptians is already hinted at in 7:12. Pharaoh does not heed the warning now, nor will he later.

Several elements of this narrative require explanation. (1) Whose staff is being used? In 4:17, the staff to be used to perform the signs belongs to Moses. But here in 7:9, Moses is to tell Aaron, "Take *your* staff and throw down it before Pharaoh." In fact, this sign plus the first three plagues are all performed through Aaron's staff; Moses' staff does not become the operative agent until plagues seven through nine.[6] This almost free interchange between Moses and Aaron likely reflects the close working relationship described in 4:14–17 and 6:28–7:5. Also, the genealogy of Aaron in 6:13–27 in part justifies Aaron's status in the ensuing plague narrative.

(2) The act of turning the staff into a snake (vv. 9–10) requires no explanation, since this was commanded in 4:2–5. It seems odd, however, that a different word is used for "snake" (*tannin*) in this passage from what was used before (*naḥaš* in 4:3).[7] But we should note that 7:9–10 is the execution of what Yahweh ordered in 4:3. Hence, it is necessary to identify the terms, at least to some extent. It is unlikely that an animal other than a snake of some sort is meant. But why the change in terms? Why not be consistent? This may sim-

---

5. Fretheim, *Exodus*, 113.

6. Ibid., 106. In the 9th plague, only Moses' "hand" is mentioned rather than the staff (compare this to 9:22–23 and 10:12–13). I do not think this is a significant variation.

7. Scholars such as Durham (*Exodus*, 91) argue for a special significance in this change of term. He suggests that a more "monstrous" reptile is meant here.

ply be a case of a biblical writer modifying his terms for the sake of aesthetic appeal. Such practice is common in all literature, and we should not expect any author to maintain strict consistency.

On the other hand, might there be some theological significance to these terms? I think so. While the alternation in words for "snake" does not indicate that their *historical* referents are different, the writer may be making a *theological* point. One way of looking at this is to connect this passage with creation, which we have seen throughout the opening chapters of Exodus and will continue to see in the Exodus narratives. The term *naḥaš* is used also in Genesis 3:1, referring to the serpent that tempted Eve in the garden; *tannin* is used in 1:21.

More important, *tannin* in the Old Testament as well as in the ancient Near East represents the chaotic forces of nature that God conquers at creation. According to the ancient worldview (cf. Gen. 1), creation means the power of God giving order to chaos. The staff of Aaron, then, as it swallows the *tannin* of Pharaoh, is another example of this theme.[8] The king represents an anti-God, anti-creation force, which the true God conquers.

(3) Why, of all the signs to give at the outset, should turning a staff into a snake be the one? One possible explanation, of course, is to maintain the creation connection. Another explanation (but by no means mutually exclusive of the first) is the fact that snakes represent Egyptian power.[9] The pharaonic headdress, so famous from such popular images as King Tut's coffin, looks like a cobra. For Aaron's staff to turn into a snake is nothing less than a direct challenge to Pharaoh's power.[10] His magicians counter this attack by duplicating the feat, but their snakes are swallowed in the process. In this sense, the swallowing of the snakes is a striking illustration to all present of what Israel's God thinks of Pharaoh's might.

(4) The theological significance of turning a staff into a snake is that, like the plagues to follow, it is a manipulation of nature. God battles Egypt by controlling creation; it does his bidding. This sign and the ten plagues display one by one Pharaoh's impotence, despite his grandiose self-image and Yahweh's unquestionable and unconquerable might.

The battle between Yahweh and Pharaoh is joined. By calling together his "wise men and sorcerers, and ... magicians,"[11] Pharaoh intends a great show of force. What should not be lost, however, is the distinction between

---

8. See also Fretheim, *Exodus*, 113–14.

9. See Hoffmeier, *Israel in Egypt*, 154–55.

10. It is interesting to note that in Ezek. 29:3, Pharaoh himself is called *tannin*.

11. The Hebrew word translated "magician" (*ḥarṭummim*) is likely of Egyptian derivation and refers to a priest of some sort engaged in magical rituals (J. Quaegebeur, "The Egyptian Equivalent of Biblical Ḥarṭummîm," *Pharaonic Egypt: The Bible and Christianity*, ed. S. Israelit-Groll [Jerusalem: Magnes, 1985], 163–64).

the parties and how that force is enacted. Aaron and Moses are not magicians. They do not rely on "secret arts" (v. 11), as do Pharaoh's magicians, and the turning of Aaron's staff into a snake is no trick. They do not conjure; they obey. God told Moses to throw down the staff and it would turn into a snake. This is what was done, and this is what happened. In fact, Aaron's staff seems to act on its own;[12] it follows God's plan. Pharaoh needs magicians to perform his trick; Yahweh needs no such mediation.[13]

This is a real encounter between Yahweh and Pharaoh, albeit an encounter that Yahweh easily wins. Does this, then, suggest that such magic displayed by Pharaoh's magicians actually happened? It is worth noting that the text itself does not indicate that the magicians' countermove was any less real or "miraculous" than Aaron's staff turning into a snake. Naturalistic explanations have been proposed—for example, that the magicians were able to induce a state of catalepsy in the snakes, whereby they became rigid and behaved in a trance-like state.[14] But naturalistic explanations do not do justice to the theological integrity of the narrative.

The text does not imply that the magicians' feat was not real or that it was a mere parlor trick. In fact, to argue that this exchange between Yahweh and Pharaoh is nothing more than snakes in a state of catalepsy not only diminishes the *real* power conflict here, but upends the narrative thrust. The text states clearly that the staffs become snakes. It is not our place to "explain" incidents such as this in ways that are more in harmony with our modern "sensibilities." It is striking to me how conservative scholars reject naturalistic explanations for the ten plagues or drying up of the Red Sea, but then argue (against the text) for a naturalistic explanation for staffs turning into snakes.

Perhaps the central point of this passage is that counterfeit power, although real power, is not lasting power, and neither the Israelites nor the Egyptians should be fooled by appearances. Unfortunately, this lesson is not readily learned. For Pharaoh, the lesson is learned too late. For the Israelites, this lesson is one they will have to learn and relearn in the coming years.

First Plague: Water to Blood (7:14–25)

[14]Then the LORD said to Moses, "Pharaoh's heart is
unyielding; he refuses to let the people go. [15]Go to Pharaoh

---

12. See Sarna, *Exodus*, 37.

13. There are clear similarities between this episode and the confrontation between Elijah and the priests of Baal in 1 Kings 18:16–46.

14. See Currid, "The Egyptian Setting of the 'Serpent': Confrontation in Exodus 7,8–13," *BZ* 39 (1995): 206–8.

in the morning as he goes out to the water. Wait on the
bank of the Nile to meet him, and take in your hand the
staff that was changed into a snake. [16]Then say to him, 'The
LORD, the God of the Hebrews, has sent me to say to you:
Let my people go, so that they may worship me in the
desert. But until now you have not listened. [17]This is what
the LORD says: By this you will know that I am the LORD:
With the staff that is in my hand I will strike the water of
the Nile, and it will be changed into blood. [18]The fish in the
Nile will die, and the river will stink; the Egyptians will not
be able to drink its water.'"

[19]The LORD said to Moses, "Tell Aaron, 'Take your staff
and stretch out your hand over the waters of Egypt—over the
streams and canals, over the ponds and all the reservoirs '—
and they will turn to blood. Blood will be everywhere in
Egypt, even in the wooden buckets and stone jars."

[20]Moses and Aaron did just as the LORD had commanded.
He raised his staff in the presence of Pharaoh and his officials
and struck the water of the Nile, and all the water was
changed into blood. [21]The fish in the Nile died, and the river
smelled so bad that the Egyptians could not drink its water.
Blood was everywhere in Egypt.

[22]But the Egyptian magicians did the same things by their
secret arts, and Pharaoh's heart became hard; he would not
listen to Moses and Aaron, just as the LORD had said.
[23]Instead, he turned and went into his palace, and did not
take even this to heart. [24]And all the Egyptians dug along
the Nile to get drinking water, because they could not drink
the water of the river.

[25]Seven days passed after the LORD struck the Nile.

(1) The first question that may come to mind is why this is the first plague.
Is there something significant about changing the waters of the Nile into
blood that would make it the first act of God's judgment on Egypt? Consider
the following. (a) The parallelism between this plague and the death of the
Egyptian army in the Red Sea (chs. 14—15) should not be lost. The beginning and end of Israel's deliverance concerns a mighty act of God relating to
water. In other words, the first plague and the Red Sea incident serve as a narrative frame for the story of deliverance.

(b) The plague on the Nile should also be connected to chapter 1. It is fitting that the means by which the first pharaoh tried to exterminate the Israelite

threat—casting them into the Nile (1:22)—should now become a source of trouble for the Egyptians. The Nile has turned on them, so to speak.[15]

(c) Egypt's greatness as a civilization was wholly dependent on the life-giving waters of the Nile. An attack on the Nile was nothing less than an attack on Egypt itself. It is, in other words, an omen of things to come, and in this sense fits nicely with (a) above. The first plague is both a swift retribution for the previous attempt to kill the Israelite male children and a jarring preview of Egypt's ultimate fate. The waters of the Nile will no longer bring security and prosperity to Egypt; they will rather be the cause of Egypt's destruction. The miraculous blood of the first plague will soon become the blood of Egyptian soldiers in the Red Sea.

(d) The Nile was personified and worshiped as a god in Egypt.[16] An attack on the Nile is in effect an attack on Egypt's gods and, hence, reflects the conflict that drives the Exodus narrative as a whole. The fight is not between Israel and Pharaoh, nor even between Moses and Pharaoh; it is between God and Pharaoh. Pharaoh, as we have seen in chapter 1, is an anti-God character in Exodus. In fact, he himself was thought to enjoy some type of divine/human "blend." The attack on the Nile is the attack of the true God on false ones.

However one might seek to understand the significance of the first plague, it is clearly a significant moment! It is off the mark to say with one commentator that the first three plagues were "little more than a softening-up process, a major nuisance but little more."[17] If the previous sign (staff to a snake) served as a preview of the ensuing plagues, the plague on the Nile was the first toll of the bell that signaled Egypt's demise. Judgment has come.

(2) We should also discuss a question that surfaces with each of the ten plagues, indeed, with any miraculous event in Scripture: Did this really happen, or, if so, was it an act of God or simply a natural occurrence? Treating these difficult questions fully would take us far from the Exodus story, but a word or two is in order here. Although some biblical scholars dismiss outright an event such as water turning to blood as mere fantasy, others admit to its historicity but attribute to it a naturalistic explanation. A common approach is to see the blood of the Nile as an interpretation of the sediment

---

15. The apocryphal book Wisdom of Solomon (likely written somewhere between 100 B.C. and A.D. 50) speaks of the first plague as a "rebuke for the decree to slay the infants" in Ex. 1 (Wisd. Sol. 11:5–7).

16. The name of the god is Hapi (see Sarna, *Exodus*, 39). D. P. Silverman points out, more correctly, that it was not the Nile itself that was personified but the yearly inundation of the Nile that was so important to Egypt's agriculture ("Divinity and Deities in Ancient Egypt," *Religion in Ancient Egypt: Gods, Myths, and Personal Practice*, ed. B. E. Shafer et al. [Ithaca: Cornell Univ. Press, 1991], 34).

17. H. L. Ellison, *Exodus* (Philadelphia: Westminster, 1982), 51.

of red earth that occasionally discolors the water.[18] Such an explanation is suggested by the conservative Jewish scholar U. Cassuto (known best perhaps for his vigorous defense of the Mosaic authorship of the Pentateuch). He writes that the water *resembled* blood.[19] There are at least two points that commend such an explanation. If this was a natural, even common, phenomenon, we can understand why it has no effect on Pharaoh. Moreover, "blood" is sometimes used figuratively in the Bible (e.g., Joel 2:31; Rev. 6:12), so it need not necessarily be taken literally here.

Yet a simple answer to this problem does not easily present itself. True, God can use a natural phenomenon for his own holy purpose. In other words, the Nile turning red *like* blood is no less an act of God simply because such a phenomenon is said to have occurred before. If God brings about an earthquake, it is no less God's doing simply because earthquakes do occur. We sometimes too quickly make a distinction between a natural phenomenon and an act of God. Such bifurcation of reality into "sacred and secular" did not exist for ancient Israelites.

Nevertheless, this act is said to happen "in the presence of Pharaoh" (v. 20). The dramatic, even instantaneous nature of this act is striking. A naturalistic explanation does not do justice to the theological thrust of this passage. Further, Pharaoh's response to Moses is to get his magicians to work on duplicating this feat (which they do!). Were this merely a natural phenomenon, Pharaoh could simply have countered, "But this happens all the time, Moses! Can't your God do any better than this?" But the fact that the magicians had to appeal to their "secret arts" (v. 22) suggests that there was more here than red sediment pouring into the Nile.

Perhaps the most straightforward solution to this problem is to acknowledge that even if the blood can be explained as a natural phenomenon (itself a debatable point), the fact that this phenomenon happened *at God's command* is the central concern of the biblical writer. The point is not so much what happened to the Nile, but that it happened as an explicit act of judgment by God on the Egyptians. The purpose of this plague—indeed, the entire confrontation between Moses and Pharaoh—is so that Egypt will know that "I am the LORD" (v. 17; cf. 7:5).

(3) A third question that presents itself to the reader of this narrative has to do with the extent of the plague: Was *all* the water of Egypt turned to blood? This is certainly the impression that one gets from verse 19 of the NIV:

---

18. There is Egyptian literary evidence for the Nile becoming "blood." Some scholars mention the oxygen imbalance that results from such sediment, which results in the death and subsequent stench of water life (Sarna, *Exodus*, 38–39; idem, *Exploring Exodus*, 70–71).

19. Cassuto, *Commentary on Exodus*, 97–98.

> The LORD said to Moses, "Tell Aaron, 'Take your staff and stretch
> out your hand over the *waters of Egypt*—over the streams and canals,
> over the ponds and all the reservoirs'—and they will turn to blood.
> Blood will be *everywhere* in Egypt, even in the wooden buckets and
> stone jars." (See also v. 21.)

Yet if this were the case, we face two difficulties. (a) This plague (along
with the second two) is reproduced by Egypt's magicians. Where would they
have found the water to turn to blood if all the water had already been turned
to blood by Moses and Aaron? (b) Verse 25 seems to imply that the plague
lasts seven days. Are we to understand that the Israelites, too, have no water
to drink during this time? True, perhaps they are given some miraculous provision of water, but this is hardly a detail the writer would neglect to mention, especially since such a distinction between Israel and Egypt is made
explicit in plagues 4, 5, 7, 9, and 10.

A closer look at verse 19, however, helps resolve this tension. The Hebrew
of the relevant portion of the verse reads: "Stretch out your hand over the
waters of Egypt, over *their* streams, over *their* canals, and over *their* ponds, and
over *their* reservoirs." The use of the third person masculine plural suffix (not
reflected in the NIV) seems to specify that it is the *Egyptians* who will be
affected by the plague. Moreover, the Hebrew does not explicitly say that
water in "wooden buckets and stone jars" was turned to blood. The last portion of verse 19 simply says, "And there was blood in all the land of Egypt,
in wood [plural] and in stones." The Hebrew is a bit awkward and has inspired
some scholarly discussion, but the water stored in *vessels* of any sort is not actually mentioned. True, the plurals "wood" and "stone" could imply vessels
made of those materials, but this is by no means a necessary or even reasonable conclusion.

A number of alternate explanations have been suggested, including: wood
and stone bled; sap from trees and springs from the clefts of rocks became
blood; idols made of wood and stone bled;[20] water inside of wood and stone
buildings turned to blood. Sarna offers what I think is the best explanation:
The phrase "wood and stones" is parallel to the preceding phrase "in all the
land of Egypt."[21] In other words, it is just another way of saying "there was
blood all over the place." Moreover, the NIV's "blood will be everywhere in
Egypt" is just one possible translation of the Hebrew. It is just as plausible to
say, "There will be blood throughout the land of Egypt"; in other words, no
part of the land will be unaffected by the plague. This does not necessarily
imply that every last drop of water will become blood for seven solid days.

---

20. This is Cassuto's suggestion (ibid., 98–99).
21. Sarna, *Exodus*, 39.

Such a perspective on the extent of the plague also helps make sense of verse 24: "And all the Egyptians dug along the Nile to get drinking water, because they could not drink the water of the river." It should not be assumed that their excavation efforts are unsuccessful. It is perfectly reasonable to assume that although the Nile waters turn to blood, ground water does not. It seems, therefore, that the extent of the first plague is limited so as to affect the Egyptians and their source of strength and vitality, the Nile (and its tributaries).

(4) One final question concerns the "reservoirs" in verse 19. It has already been mentioned that the creation theme is clearly present in the Exodus story (see 1:7; 2:2, and comments). Relevant here is the use of *miqweh* in verse 19 referring to the "collection" of water into one place and in Genesis 1:10 (the "gathering" of the waters under the sky into one place). Although it is rarely wise to base sweeping arguments on uses of single words, the Exodus narrative does display clear creation overtones throughout.[22] In this broad theological context, the use of *miqweh* here is certainly reminiscent of its use in Genesis.

In a manner of speaking, the adverse condition of the "gathered" waters in Exodus 7:19 (they are turned to blood) may be considered an example of "creation reversal." The order God introduced to chaos in Genesis 1 is now yielding, as far as the Egyptians are concerned, to chaos once again.[23] In fact, the plagues and the Red Sea incident are nothing less than a series of creation reversals: God is unleashing his creative forces on Egypt for punishment, but employing those same forces for Israel's benefit. This culminates in the parting of the Red Sea where God, in a new act of creation, once again divides the water from the land (cf. Gen. 1:9–10), only to bring those waters crashing down on the Egyptians while the Israelites march safely across.[24]

Second Plague: Frogs (8:1–15)[25]

8:1 Then the LORD said to Moses, "Go to Pharaoh and say to him, 'This is what the LORD says: Let my people go, so that they may worship me. ²If you refuse to let them go, I will plague

---

22. Moreover, the noun *miqweh* occurs only nine times in the Old Testament, three times in the Pentateuch.

23. Egyptian religion had a strong notion of cosmic order called *Maʿat*, which suggests that these creation reversals would have spoken powerfully to them as well as to the Israelites (Hoffmeier, *Israel in Egypt*, 151).

24. An informative overview of the creation theme in the ten plagues is Z. Zevit, "Three Ways to Look at the Ten Plagues," *Bible Review* (June 1990): 16–23, 42. He concludes: "Through the plagues the Lord demonstrated that he was the God of creation" (22).

25. The Hebrew versification for this plague is 7:26–8:11. References to specific verses will be given according to the English.

your whole country with frogs. ³The Nile will teem with frogs. They will come up into your palace and your bedroom and onto your bed, into the houses of your officials and on your people, and into your ovens and kneading troughs. ⁴The frogs will go up on you and your people and all your officials.'"

⁵Then the LORD said to Moses, "Tell Aaron, 'Stretch out your hand with your staff over the streams and canals and ponds, and make frogs come up on the land of Egypt.'"

⁶So Aaron stretched out his hand over the waters of Egypt, and the frogs came up and covered the land. ⁷But the magicians did the same things by their secret arts; they also made frogs come up on the land of Egypt.

⁸Pharaoh summoned Moses and Aaron and said, "Pray to the LORD to take the frogs away from me and my people, and I will let your people go to offer sacrifices to the LORD."

⁹Moses said to Pharaoh, "I leave to you the honor of setting the time for me to pray for you and your officials and your people that you and your houses may be rid of the frogs, except for those that remain in the Nile."

¹⁰"Tomorrow," Pharaoh said.

Moses replied, "It will be as you say, so that you may know there is no one like the LORD our God. ¹¹The frogs will leave you and your houses, your officials and your people; they will remain only in the Nile."

¹²After Moses and Aaron left Pharaoh, Moses cried out to the LORD about the frogs he had brought on Pharaoh. ¹³And the LORD did what Moses asked. The frogs died in the houses, in the courtyards and in the fields. ¹⁴They were piled into heaps, and the land reeked of them. ¹⁵But when Pharaoh saw that there was relief, he hardened his heart and would not listen to Moses and Aaron, just as the LORD had said.

Once again Moses goes to Pharaoh fully armed with God's power in order to announce the coming of the second plague: "This is what the LORD says" (8:1). One distinctive mark of the frog plague when compared to the first plague and the preceding sign is that here Moses warns Pharaoh of the coming catastrophe if he does not heed the command to let the people go. Turning the Nile into blood should have convinced Pharaoh to comply.

This is also the first plague that involves the animal kingdom. Plagues 1 and 9 affect the elements (water and the sun) whereas plagues 2, 3, 4, and 8 unleash the animal kingdom on human victims. Turning the animal kingdom against humanity is, as we have seen with the first plague, a reversal of creation. In the ideal pattern of creation, humanity is to have dominion over the animals (Gen. 1:28). The "chaotic" behavior of animals in these plagues is God's measured unleashing of "anti-creation" forces on the helpless Egyptians. In this respect, the use of the Hebrew term *šaraṣ*, to teem, also calls to mind creation in Genesis. The teeming of God's creatures was originally something good, something that exhibited God's creative work (1:20–21). But now this chaotic, *teeming* mass of frogs (Ex. 8:3) is a destructive abundance.[26]

The frogs are not just here and there, but everywhere, throughout the entire country (v. 2). They are in every nook and cranny: in homes, in bedrooms, even in ovens and kneading troughs (vv. 3–4). Such a scene should not evoke images of cute little animals popping out of sock drawers or cushy slippers. Rather, the environmental effects would be disastrous.[27] They are clearly a threat to the sanitary preparation of food. And when they begin dying (vv. 13–14), their rotting bodies not only send up a horrible odor but also pose a public health catastrophe.

As with the first plague, the relevance of frogs is usually thought to reflect a polemic against Egyptian religion. Heqet (also spelled Heqt, Hekt, Heket, or Heqat), a goddess of childbirth, is depicted in Egyptian art with the head of a frog. Although perhaps we cannot make a direct connection between all ten plagues and the specific gods of the Egyptian pantheon, such a connection seems justified here.[28] A plague of frogs can be understood as an attack on the Egyptian fertility goddess for the Egyptians' previous attempt at eradicating the Israelites' male infant population (Ex. 1).[29] Furthermore, note that the frogs come from the Nile and its associated waters (8:5; cf. 7:19). The Nile, therefore, is the source of the first two plagues, which is fitting retribution to Pharaoh for attempting to use the Nile against the Israelites. In light of this, it is best not to think of this plague as presenting merely a "nuisance and annoyance" to the Egyptians.[30] It is, like the first plague, a pointed theological statement: Yahweh is bigger than the gods of Egypt and will unleash the forces of creation to drive this point home.

---

26. The connection with Gen. 1:20–21 is also brought out by Zevit, "Three Ways to Look at the Ten Plagues," 22, and Cassuto, *Commentary on Exodus*, 101.

27. See Fretheim, *Exodus*, 116.

28. See Zevit, "Three Ways to Look at the Ten Plagues," 21. No Egyptian gods seem to correspond to the third, fourth, and sixth plagues. Durham (*Exodus*, 104) and Hoffmeier (*Israel in Egypt*, 150) remain somewhat skeptical of any connection between the plagues and Egyptian gods, though Hoffmeier does suggest that the ninth plague is a polemic against the sun god Re or Atum (ibid., 151).

29. Sarna, *Exodus*, 40.

30. Childs, *Book of Exodus*, 155.

This is only the second plague, but it is the last one that Pharaoh's magicians are able to reproduce. But what purpose is there for them to do so? Would not duplicating this plague severely add to Egypt's misery?! Apart from the recurring question of how Pharaoh's magicians are able to make "frogs come up on the land of Egypt" (8:7), it is somewhat curious why they choose to increase the number of frogs rather than rid Egypt of this menace.[31] Furthermore, it is after the magicians have their turn that Pharaoh asks Moses to make the plague stop. Apparently, this double dose of frogs is too much for him, for why else does he ask for help after demonstrating that his magicians can duplicate the feat?

With the second plague we see the first sign of Pharaoh's weakness. He sees that Israel's God, despite his magicians' ability to mimic the plague, is a power to be reckoned with. But if Pharaoh is now convinced by the plague of *Yahweh's* might, why does he capitulate only after his magicians produce frogs on their own? It may be that Pharaoh has recognized not only that God has the power to produce frogs, but that *only* God has the power to get rid of them. Note that in the plagues narrative, the cessation of the plagues is as much a sign of God's power as the plagues themselves. Pharaoh now sees the great problem he has and goes to the only source of help—not his magicians but the God of Israel. To show the king the extent of Yahweh's might, Moses gives him the choice of when the plague will stop—"Tomorrow."[32] This timing demonstrates to Pharaoh that this is no trick manipulated by Moses, no bit of magic contrived to pull the wool over his eyes. Pharaoh gladly takes Moses up on the offer (v. 10).

Verse 9 is unusual when seen in the context of the plagues narrative as a whole: Moses addresses Pharaoh directly (cf. 8:1, where God tells Moses, "Go to Pharaoh and say to him . . ."; also cf. 7:16). The issue here is that previous conversations between God and Moses make it clear that Aaron is to be the spokesman to Pharaoh, relaying to Pharaoh the word of God given to Moses (see esp. 7:2). How should the command in 7:2 be understood in light of the obvious speaking role that Moses now seems to hold? Note too that as the narrative unfolds, Aaron's role diminishes and Moses' increases, and in fact, much of the theology of the narrative is played out precisely in the interchanges between Moses and Pharaoh.

There is no obvious solution to this problem, and facile attempts should not be made to explain it away. Perhaps having Aaron as a spokesman was only a temporary concession on God's part. Once the action starts, in the heat of battle, God throws Moses into the fray, and, as God has planned all along,

---

31. Cate suggests that this is meant to be humorous (*Exodus*, 91).

32. The Hebrew here may mean "tomorrow," as we have it in the NIV, or "as soon as possible" (Houtman, *Exodus*, 2:49–50; Cassuto, *Commentary on Exodus*, 103; Durham, *Exodus*, 105).

he rises to the occasion and performs his prophetic task admirably. Such an explanation, however, is not confirmed by any text in Exodus. In any case, it does demonstrate God's sovereignty over Moses. God's choice of a messenger is a good one, despite feelings (real or feigned) of his own inadequacies. God, like a father, takes Moses by the hand at first and says, "OK, OK, don't worry. I'll have Aaron help you." But like a father who knows his own son's abilities better than the son himself, God nudges Moses into the very situation he fears most. In all this, it becomes apparent how fully in control God is in bringing Israel out of Egypt. He has his way with Pharaoh *and* Moses, to harden the one but to build up the other.

Moses intercedes for Pharaoh and God listens to Moses, his messenger. The frogs die more or less right where they are. They are piled into heaps and begin to stink.[33] This should be a lesson for Pharaoh: "We're serious, Pharaoh. We'll play ball if you will." But at this stage in the narrative, the final outcome is to be expected: Pharaoh hardens his heart. He brushes off God's salvation. The confidence he had earlier in his own power has started to wear down, but he quickly forgets his weakness. As soon as the plague is out of sight, it is also out of mind. Yahweh's second display of his control over creation is not enough to convince the king of Egypt that he is no match. But in the end, we will see that Pharaoh's reluctance to capitulate is less a result of his own stubbornness and more a result of God's desire to keep him pinned against the ropes, long after the bell should have rung. God will not allow Pharaoh to quit so easily.

Third Plague: Gnats (8:16–19)[34]

[16]Then the LORD said to Moses, "Tell Aaron, 'Stretch out your staff and strike the dust of the ground,' and throughout the land of Egypt the dust will become gnats." [17]They did this, and when Aaron stretched out his hand with the staff and struck the dust of the ground, gnats came upon men and animals. All the dust throughout the land of Egypt became gnats. [18]But when the magicians tried to produce gnats by their secret arts, they could not. And the gnats were on men and animals.

[19]The magicians said to Pharaoh, "This is the finger of God." But Pharaoh's heart was hard and he would not listen, just as the LORD had said.

---

33. Note that the first plague also results in the stench of death (7:21). In a way, the deliverance is no better than the plague itself. Also, T. Fretheim reminds us that the heap of frogs in 8:14 will later be called to mind when we see the mass of Egyptian soldiers lying dead on the shore; they, too, come up from the water (Fretheim, *Exodus*, 117).

34. The Hebrew versification is 8:12–15.

This plague differs from the previous two in that it comes upon us abruptly. This is the first plague without any sort of introduction; it simply happens. This is not haphazard but reflects the structure of the plague narrative as a whole. In terms of its literary structure, the plagues are divided in to three groups of three (plagues 1 through 9), with the tenth plague forming the climax.[35] Each series of three has the same pattern:

	plague	forewarning	time of warning	instruction formula
first series	1. blood	yes	"in the morning"	"Station yourself"
	2. frogs	yes	none	"Go to Pharaoh"
	3. gnats	none	none	none
second series	4. flies	yes	"in the morning"	"Station yourself"
	5. livestock	yes	none	"Go to Pharaoh"
	6. boils	none	none	none
third series	7. hail	yes	"in the morning"	"Station yourself"
	8. locusts	yes	none	"Go to Pharaoh"
	9. darkness	none	none	none
climax	10. death of firstborn	yes	none	none

As this chart indicates, for the last plague of each series (plagues 3, 6, and 9) there is no forewarning, time of warning, or instruction formula. Likewise, the first plague of each series occurs "in the morning." This pattern at the very least indicates a purposefulness on the part of the writer in how the plagues are presented. In other words, as Sarna reminds us, the plagues account has a "didactic and theological purpose, not a historiographic one."[36] This in no way implies that the plagues did not happen, but only that the manner in which they are presented betrays a motivation on the part of the writer that goes beyond the mere presentation of "brute facts."[37] These cycles hit Pharaoh like regular, unrelenting waves of judgment. The last plague in each series is a final, quick blow following upon the heels of the king's stubbornness.

---

35. The following information is summarized by Sarna (*Exploring Exodus*, 76), although recognition of this literary pattern goes back to rabbinic writings. See also Cassuto, *Commentary on Exodus*, 92–93; Sarna, *Exodus*, 38.

36. Sarna, *Exploring Exodus*, 77.

37. Similar observations were made in connection with Moses' birth narrative and the Sargon epic (see comments on 2:10).

The plague of gnats receives the shortest account. The precise identity of the insect has been a subject of debate, but it is certainly some sort of nagging, pesky insect like lice or gnats.[38] The significance of these creatures may be more in where they come from than in what they are. Plagues 2, 3, and 4 are pests that come from the water, dust, and air, respectively. In other words, they come from the three sectors of the ecosystem—water, land, and air. Further significance may be attached to dust as the origin of this plague. There may be a connection with the use of "dust" in Genesis 3:19 ("for dust you are and to dust you will return"). Dust, in this sense, represents death (see also Job 17:16; 21:26; Ps. 22:29; Isa. 26:19). These gnats are more than a nagging discomfort; they are "a sign of human mortality."[39] The dust, to which all flesh must return, becomes an instrument that speeds the Egyptians on toward that inexorable end.[40]

As in the first plague (7:19), Moses fulfills his role as "God" to Aaron (see 4:16): The Lord gives a directive to Moses, which he in turn is to give to Aaron.[41] Aaron's role is highlighted in this third plague for the last time. Henceforth, he will no longer speak to Pharaoh, nor will his staff be used to enact the plague (8:16—17). To paraphrase the New Testament expression, from here on out "Aaron must decrease and Moses must increase."

This is also the first plague that Pharaoh's magicians are unable to reproduce, which raises the obvious question: Why? If they were able to reproduce the first two plagues, why not this one? Why are they able to produce frogs from the water but not gnats from the dust? Ellison's explanation, that gnats are too small to be manipulated by magicians, does not help.[42] The

---

38. For the various options, see Houtman, *Exodus*, 1:138–39; 2:52–53; Fretheim, *Exodus*, 118; Hyatt, *Exodus*, 110.

39. Fretheim, *Exodus*, 56. Z. Zevit takes the Genesis connection further by arguing that the "lice correspond to the crawling creatures (*remes* [sic]) that come forth from the earth in Genesis 1:24" ("Three Ways to Look at the Ten Plagues," 22). Although I am sympathetic to Zevit's argument, it may not be best to tease the Genesis connection to the third plague in this way, particularly since the word *remes* does not appear in the plague narrative. A more legitimate way of seeing the Genesis connection is in terms of the divine command-fulfillment pattern that we see throughout the plague narrative and in Genesis 1: God speaks and it happens (Plastaras, *The God of Exodus*, 127–28).

40. With Cassuto, it seems that v. 17 should be understood as hyperbole. Are we to think that every speck of dust becomes a gnat and that no dust remains in Egypt? This type of expression, so common to the Hebrew idiom, merely conveys the fact of a tremendous, incalculable number of these pesky insects in Egypt.

41. It is worth noting that the second plague corresponds more to 7:1, where Moses is said to be "God to Pharaoh": The Lord gives Moses a directive that he is to bring to Pharaoh directly.

42. Ellison, *Exodus*, 47.

proper answer is to be found perhaps not in the types of creatures but from where they originate. The first two plagues concern the water, which is the life and power of Egypt, politically, economically, and religiously. The gnats, however, come from the dust of the earth, which is not the Egyptian "power source." Their magic and secret arts are empowered by the Nile, but with the third plague, the magicians are out of their element.

The God of Israel is the God of all nature. The magicians of Egypt, however, are not able to reproduce the plague because the power of their gods is limited. Having defeated the power of Egypt on the only level playing ground they have, Yahweh now expands his show of power beyond the comfort zone of their magic powers. This plague, therefore, represents a movement toward a deeper display of the might of Israel's God.

The magicians recognize that they are in over their heads by confessing, "This is the finger of God" (v. 19). The Hebrew is somewhat ambiguous, however. It may simply mean, "This is the finger of *a god*." In other words, this is not necessarily a confession on their part that Yahweh has done this. Rather, they may simply be saying, "This is too big for us," or, "This is no trick." In any event, this plague does represent a movement *toward* recognition of Yahweh as the mighty God, which is, in the words of the Exodus narrative itself, one of the central purposes for the plagues (e.g., 7:5). The irony is that this movement toward recognition at least on Pharaoh's part is what God, by his sovereignty, ultimately impedes.

This account ends with no mention of the cessation of the plague. This is a curious element in this report. True, there is no cessation reported for the fifth plague either, but the death of the animals is its own cessation. Likewise, the sixth plague does not report that the boils ceased tormenting the Egyptians. In view of the fact that the cessation of the plagues is explicitly mentioned everywhere else, the lack of such mention for plagues 3 and 6 may suggest that they have a more lasting effect. The gnats "seem now to be a way of life" for the Egyptians.[43]

Precisely how long these plagues last, however, is not to be discerned from the texts themselves. Are gnats swarming and boils festering until the Israelites leave Egypt? No one knows. It may be that these two plagues are of longer duration than the others. Significant, too, may be that both plagues 3 and 6 are the final plagues of the first two series (see chart above). They are perhaps intended to be a lasting reminder of the previous series of plagues throughout the subsequent series. This may explain why the ninth plague is said to cease (it lasts for only three days, 10:22), since there is no subsequent series with which to overlap.

---

43. Fretheim, *Exodus*, 119.

Fourth Plague: Flies (8:20–32)[44]

²⁰Then the LORD said to Moses, "Get up early in the morning and confront Pharaoh as he goes to the water and say to him, 'This is what the LORD says: Let my people go, so that they may worship me. ²¹If you do not let my people go, I will send swarms of flies on you and your officials, on your people and into your houses. The houses of the Egyptians will be full of flies, and even the ground where they are.

²²'''But on that day I will deal differently with the land of Goshen, where my people live; no swarms of flies will be there, so that you will know that I, the LORD, am in this land. ²³I will make a distinction between my people and your people. This miraculous sign will occur tomorrow.'''

²⁴And the LORD did this. Dense swarms of flies poured into Pharaoh's palace and into the houses of his officials, and throughout Egypt the land was ruined by the flies.

²⁵Then Pharaoh summoned Moses and Aaron and said, "Go, sacrifice to your God here in the land."

²⁶But Moses said, "That would not be right. The sacrifices we offer the LORD our God would be detestable to the Egyptians. And if we offer sacrifices that are detestable in their eyes, will they not stone us? ²⁷We must take a three-day journey into the desert to offer sacrifices to the LORD our God, as he commands us."

²⁸Pharaoh said, "I will let you go to offer sacrifices to the LORD your God in the desert, but you must not go very far. Now pray for me."

²⁹Moses answered, "As soon as I leave you, I will pray to the LORD, and tomorrow the flies will leave Pharaoh and his officials and his people. Only be sure that Pharaoh does not act deceitfully again by not letting the people go to offer sacrifices to the LORD."

³⁰Then Moses left Pharaoh and prayed to the LORD, ³¹and the LORD did what Moses asked: The flies left Pharaoh and his officials and his people; not a fly remained. ³²But this time also Pharaoh hardened his heart and would not let the people go.

The fourth plague begins the second series of plagues (4, 5, and 6; see chart above). A number of elements in this plague recall the first plague and,

---

44. The Hebrew versification is 8:16–28.

hence, support the notion of a purposeful presentation of the plagues. In both the first and fourth plagues Moses is said to go out *in the morning* and *confront* Pharaoh as he is *going out to the water* (7:15; 8:20). Also, both 7:16 and 8:21 employ a play on the Hebrew root *šlḥ*, which is lost in the NIV. This word is used in Exodus to refer to the release from Egypt (e.g., 8:20, "Let my people go"). In 7:16, Moses announces, "The LORD, the God of the Hebrews, has sent [*šlḥ*] me to say to you: Let my people go [*šlḥ*]." The wordplay in 8:21 takes on a more threatening tone: "If you do not let my people go [*šlḥ*], I will send [*šlḥ*] swarms of flies on you." It is as if Moses is telling Pharaoh, "Listen. One of us is going to 'šlḥ.' Why don't you make it easy on yourself and *šlḥ* the people so that I don't have to *šlḥ* the flies on you."

The identity of the creatures employed by God in this plague is not entirely clear, but a fly of some sort is nearly universally accepted.[45] It is unlikely that this represents a polemic against Egyptian religion, since no god was thus depicted.[46] Of more significance is that this plague is from the air, whereas the previous two are of the water (where the Egyptian magicians exercised power) and earth (cf. comments above). God shows the extent of his power by releasing on Egypt creatures from the dust and air as well.

Some commentators see in this plague another connection to creation. Zevit, for example, argues that these creatures correspond to the "flying creatures" mentioned in Genesis 1:20–22.[47] This is worth considering, albeit cautiously, since there is no verbal overlap between this plague and Genesis. In fact, the flying creatures of Genesis 1 are probably birds, not insects. If a creation connection is to be sought here, it is more likely in the recurring pattern of the plague narrative as a whole. Each plague reintroduces chaos into the order of creation. Creatures that were made for and to be ruled by humanity are unleashed upon humanity, bringing destruction and death.

There are a number of "firsts" that occur in the fourth plague. (1) As distinct from the first three plagues, no staff is involved in bringing about the swarm of flies (the entire second series is done without a staff). A staff is reintroduced in plagues 7, 8, and 9, but there it is Moses' staff rather than Aaron's. It should be remembered that the magicians used staffs as well. Perhaps the significance of this is to give a direct display of God's power that does not have to be "conjured up" (from the perspective of the Egyptian

---

45. The commentaries routinely suggest some sort of a biting fly (a dog-fly). Houtman, however, prefers not to restrict the term so, and simply translates it "vermin" (*Exodus*, 2:58).

46. Zevit, "Three Ways to Look at the Ten Plagues," 21. Durham connects this plague to Beelzebub ("lord of the flies"), but not to the Egyptian pantheon, an unlikely suggestion (*Exodus*, 117).

47. Zevit, "Three Ways to Look at the Ten Plagues," 22.

magicians) by the use of a staff. This truly is a more potent display of God's creative power: He merely speaks and it is so (cf. Gen. 1).

(2) This is also the first plague to make a distinction between God's people and the people of Pharaoh. Yahweh makes it clear that the Israelites are "my people," whereas the Egyptians are "your [Pharaoh's] people" (vv. 21, 23). This distinction is maintained throughout the remainder of the plagues (except for the locust plague), either explicitly or implicitly, and culminates in the tenth plague, where the "destroyer" sees the blood of the Passover lamb on the doorframes of the Israelites and passes them by. The distinction between the two peoples is finally played out in the Red Sea, where the Israelites safely pass through the very same water that crashes down on the Egyptians and brings them to their doom. God unleashes his creation power for the benefit of Israel but for Egypt's destruction.

This turn of events is a fitting retribution for Egypt's actions in chapter 1, where Pharaoh's attempt to exterminate the fruitful Israelites was tantamount to an attack on Israel's God and his creation mandate. Furthermore, this distinction between the two peoples is not just to save the Israelites but to display God's might to the Egyptians. This is explicit in verse 22: "so that you will know that I, the LORD, am in this land." This is not a hope that Egypt will turn and be saved. Rather, it is simply that the Egyptians may know that the God of Israel is no foreigner on Egyptian soil, that he is here, in their country, and that he will divide it up as he pleases. And it is not just God's power in the plagues that displays his glory, but his election of Israel as a special people.

(3) Another "first" of this plague is that the flies bring destruction to the land. What the NIV translates as "ruined" in verse 24 is from the Hebrew root *šḥt*. This is a strong word that is used also in 12:23 for the "destroyer." The previous plagues, although significant in their own right, do not wreak the havoc that this plague does. Yahweh intends to destroy the land. This first plague of the second series deepens the cycle of destruction. It takes Yahweh's judgment to a new level by giving a preview of the ultimate outcome—the ruining of Egypt at the Red Sea.

Pharaoh's response to this plague is predictable in light of the Exodus story as a whole, but no less numbing. This is the second time that he calls to Moses and Aaron and gives in to Yahweh's might (see 8:8), but, as before, he will change his mind and maintain his stubborn stance. Pharaoh does capitulate, but his motive appears to be halfhearted: He will allow the Israelites to sacrifice, but they must remain in Egypt to do so (v. 25). Such a thing is never what Moses or God intended, and Pharaoh knows it as early as 5:3.

Still, Moses' response to Pharaoh raises an eyebrow. One would expect him to say, "No, Pharaoh, you know perfectly well that our God, who is bringing such destruction on you, requires us to leave the land." Instead,

Moses' response in verse 26 seems to be, "Oh, no. We don't want to offend the Egyptians' religious sensibilities. They might stone us as a result." What a curious thing to say! Has not God just shown his might four times? Could not Moses, backed by the full power of God's display of force, have responded more directly than this?

Or perhaps Moses is simply displaying political diplomacy by providing Pharaoh a way to save face: "Oh no, Pharaoh. We couldn't *possibly* think of sacrificing here, what with the offense it would give you." I do not think, however, that Moses would have felt the necessity of such political niceties in view of the recent turn of events. It is best to see that Moses is sparring with Pharaoh here, that he is matching Pharaoh's cleverness. In verse 25, Pharaoh slyly gives the impression that he is giving in, but then slips into the deal a clause in fine print restricting them to the land of Egypt.[48] In this light, Moses' response is to point out the foolishness of Pharaoh's own proposed solution; *he* would be causing the offense for his own religion.

In other words, rather than doing a polite political dance with Pharaoh, Moses is saying: "Don't even try it, Pharaoh. You know as well as I that if we even tried to sacrifice to our God on Egyptian soil, which you believe is home to your gods, the Egyptians will stone us to death. We're a little more clever than that! You think you can give the appearance of letting us have our way, but the end result plays right into your hands! Forget it! No deal! We're leaving just as we said we were. It's all or nothing."

Pharaoh sees that his subtle maneuver has not worked. Still, he wants to hold on: "OK, go ahead. Just don't go too far" (cf. v. 28). He wants to let them go, but he cannot. Perhaps he intends to chase after them quickly, and the closer they are to Egypt the easier it will be. It is interesting that Moses does not respond directly to Pharaoh's new request (v. 29). Perhaps it is absurd enough not to justify a response. Even in his renewed capitulation, as halfhearted as it is, the hardness of Pharaoh's heart can be seen: "*I* will let you go to offer sacrifices" (v. 28). Pharaoh's repentance is only on the surface.[49] He has not yet learned that it is in Yahweh's power to let the people go and that, when all is said and done, his role in Israel's release is not significant. Later, God will harden Pharaoh's heart to make that point painfully clear.

Nevertheless, Moses prays a second time for the cessation of the plague (see 8:8). As we see throughout the narrative, the cessation of the plague is

---

48. W. H. Gispen, *Exodus* (The Bible Student's Commentary; Grand Rapids: Zondervan, 1982), 93.

49. There is, perhaps, a hint of exasperation in the Hebrew: "Pharaoh hardened his heart even [*gam*] this time" (v. 32).

as much a display of Yahweh's might (and correspondingly of Pharaoh's impotence) as the plague itself. The cessation of the plague is after all an act of re-creation, where once again God restores the order of Genesis 1.

Fifth Plague: On Livestock (9:1–7)

9:1Then the LORD said to Moses, "Go to Pharaoh and say to him, 'This is what the LORD, the God of the Hebrews, says: "Let my people go, so that they may worship me." 2If you refuse to let them go and continue to hold them back, 3the hand of the LORD will bring a terrible plague on your livestock in the field—on your horses and donkeys and camels and on your cattle and sheep and goats. 4But the LORD will make a distinction between the livestock of Israel and that of Egypt, so that no animal belonging to the Israelites will die.'"

5The LORD set a time and said, "Tomorrow the LORD will do this in the land." 6And the next day the LORD did it: All the livestock of the Egyptians died, but not one animal belonging to the Israelites died. 7Pharaoh sent men to investigate and found that not even one of the animals of the Israelites had died. Yet his heart was unyielding and he would not let the people go.

This second plague of the second series of three has certain elements similar to plagues 2 and 8 (see 8:1; 10:1; also, see chart on p. 208)—specifically, God's command to Moses to "go" to Pharaoh. Again, no staff is involved here: Moses need only speak to Pharaoh and the plague happens (see comments on plague 2). Also, as with the second plague, Pharaoh is not given a chance to think it over and repent (though cf. perhaps "tomorrow" in 9:5). The narrative moves quickly from the announcement of the plague to its occurrence. Perhaps we have here an abbreviated account of an extended conversation.[50]

Having just wreaked havoc on Egypt, Moses returns to Pharaoh and proclaims the now familiar phrase, "This is what the LORD ... says" (*koh 'amar yhwh*). The wills of the two rival gods (Pharaoh and Yahweh) continue to clash, only now the hope is that the last plague will have beaten some sense into Egypt's king. It does not. Whereas God's "finger" (8:19) brought about the plague of gnats, the force of his "hand" is now about to come on the Egyptians.

The "hand" of God to deliver the Israelites is a common term in Exodus (e.g., 3:19; 6:1; 13:3) and is normally associated with some mighty act of judgment. This is the first plague in which this term is used, and it concerns the first plague that directly causes death; that is, it is the first plague directed

---

50. Houtman, *Exodus*, 2:72.

against created things (plagues 2, 3, and 4 *used* created things). As such, it serves as a harbinger of worse things to come, a pattern of death that culminates in the tenth plague and the failed crossing of the Red Sea by the Egyptian army. More precisely, the tenth plague is once again said to include Egypt's animals (11:5; 12:29). The curtain has already begun to go down on Egypt's comedy of errors.

The precise nature of the fifth plague itself is not specified, but that is not important. The narrative's focus is clearly on what was afflicted: Egypt's livestock.[51] Perhaps this is a polemic against Egyptian religion, since Hathor, the mother and sky goddess, was depicted as a cow,[52] in which case we see another psychological blow to Pharaoh's perceived source of strength. Some also see a continuation of the creation reversal theme: Animals that were once given to humans for the purpose of being ruled by them (Gen. 1:26) are now taken from them.[53]

As with the previous plague, a distinction is made between Egypt and Israel. God's people are protected so that their livestock escape the plague. In light of this, naturalistic explanations for the plague (e.g., anthrax caused by the rotting corpses of frogs) are not as helpful as they might at first appear, since the protection of the Israelites' animals would still be left unexplained.[54]

A problem routinely discussed concerns the reference to *all* the livestock of Egypt having died (v. 6). If all the animals died, how can animals be mentioned later (e.g., 9:9, 19)? Probably the writer does not expect the reader to take this "all" literally.[55] It is possible to appeal to 9:3, where only the livestock "in the field" are specified, but is this too subtle a reading? Moreover, such a solution still does not account sufficiently for the absolute language of verse 6 ("*All* the livestock of the Egyptians died, but *not one animal* belonging to the Israelites died"; see also v. 7). Neither can appeal be made to the differing vocabulary of 9:9, where *b'hemah* is used rather than *miqneh* in 9:1—

---

51. See Sarna for a helpful discussion of the possibly anachronistic mention of camels in 9:3 (*Exodus*, 44).

52. Zevit, "Three Ways to Look at the Ten Plagues," 21. See also Gispen, *Exodus*, 96.

53. Zevit, "Three Ways to Look at the Ten Plagues," 22. Houtman, however, questions such a connection (*Exodus*, 2:70).

54. See Durham, *Exodus*, 118.

55. Houtman does take it literally. The question of how there can be livestock again so quickly in Egypt does not, in Houtman's opinion, concern the writer, and, hence, should not concern us (*Exodus*, 2:69—70). This solution, however, raises more questions than it answers. Problems such as this are often adduced as evidence for multiple sources in the Pentateuch (i.e., the Documentary Hypothesis; see Hyatt, *Exodus*, 115). Conflicting sources were supposedly combined by an editor into one document. Why, however, an author of a source would necessarily be completely consistent, but an editor, apparently, would feel no need to smooth out such inconsistencies, is rarely discussed by advocates of this theory.

7. If anything, *bᵉhemah* is a general term that includes *miqneh*. Also, 9:19 uses first *miqneh* and then *bᵉhemah*. The use of "all" in 9:6 seems to be nothing more than hyperbole (cf. also 7:19–21; 8:2, 17);[56] it simply means "a lot."

Pharaoh, in an act that betrays a diminishing self-confidence, has his people check to see whether what Moses promised has happened (v. 7). The Hebrew of verse 7 is ambiguous. It does not start out "Pharaoh sent men to investigate," as the NIV has it. The Hebrew simply has "Pharaoh sent" (there is no object to the verb). The NIV has, in my opinion, correctly surmised the sense, but the translation obscures a wonderful play on words. The verb "sent" is once again a form of *šlḥ*, which was used earlier in wordplays (see comments on 8:21). Moses demands that Pharaoh let the Israelites go (*šlḥ*, v. 1). Well, Pharaoh does *šlḥ* in verse 7, but instead of "sending" the Israelites on their way, he "sends" people to investigate whether Moses' threat comes through. He intends to keep the Israelites under his thumb. Pharaoh still does not give in. The writer describes his stubbornness[57] with irony and even a hint of mockery.

Sixth Plague: Boils (9:8–12)

[8]Then the LORD said to Moses and Aaron, "Take handfuls of soot from a furnace and have Moses toss it into the air in the presence of Pharaoh. [9]It will become fine dust over the whole land of Egypt, and festering boils will break out on men and animals throughout the land."

[10]So they took soot from a furnace and stood before Pharaoh. Moses tossed it into the air, and festering boils broke out on men and animals. [11]The magicians could not stand before Moses because of the boils that were on them and on all the Egyptians. [12]But the LORD hardened Pharaoh's heart and he would not listen to Moses and Aaron, just as the LORD had said to Moses.

This is the third plague of the second series, and as with plague 3, it is narrated with no announcement, warning, or chance for debate (see chart on p. 208). Perhaps since words have had no effect on Pharaoh, none are

---

56. See Cassuto, *Commentary on Exodus*, 111; Fretheim, *Exodus*, 121; Plastaras, *The God of Exodus*, 5, 131.

57. There is an interesting interchange in the Exodus narrative concerning the hardening of Pharaoh's heart (see chart at the beginning of this chapter). Plagues 1, 3, 5, and 7 say "Pharaoh's heart was/became hard." Plagues 2 and 4 say "Pharaoh hardened his heart." In Plagues 6, 8, and 9, it is God who hardens Pharaoh's heart. I see no significant difference between the first two expressions.

wasted.[58] Yet subsequent plagues do record an exchange of words between Moses and Pharaoh. So, if words have had no effect, why are they used again later? Whether the terseness used here reflects the actual event or the writer's decision is of no importance.

Most significant is the fact that it is the first real demonstration to the Egyptians that their lives are in danger. Heretofore it has been pesky frogs and insects or plagues on livestock. Now humans bear the brunt of God's judgment. This plague represents a concrete step toward the ultimate, irrevocable outcome, the death of the firstborn and of the Egyptian army in the sea.

The point of origin of this plague is new. It is not water, dust, or air, but the dust from a kiln. Cassuto's view is insightful as well as sensitive to the "measure-for-measure" theme we have seen throughout the narrative: Taking soot from the kiln is poetic justice for the kiln-baked bricks the Israelites had to make as Pharaoh's slaves.[59] Once again, the Egyptians get what they deserve.

The nature of the plague is said to be "festering boils." Whatever type of skin problem this may be, it is certainly uncomfortable and likely painful. Zevit suggests, somewhat tentatively, that there may be a veiled polemic against Egyptian religion, since skin diseases of nearly any kind mean ritual impurity.[60] That this plague affects only the Egyptians (see v. 11) may indicate a further mockery of Egypt's gods, and, conversely, a statement of Yahweh's supremacy. This is driven home further in view of the magicians' inability not only to reproduce the plague, but even to stand before Moses (v. 11).[61] The obvious contrast should not be missed with verse 10, where Moses and Aaron "stand before" Pharaoh and scatter the soot into the air. The magicians have lost their power, but Moses and Aaron are far from done. The magicians have been unmasked and exposed, and their magic cannot even save *them*. The effects of the plagues are moving closer to the power center.

This plague marks another turning point, for here is the first time that Pharaoh's refusal to heed the sign is attributed to *Yahweh's* hardening of Pharaoh's heart.[62] This, of course, is not unexpected, for verse 12 ends with the familiar refrain, "just as the LORD had said to Moses." The reference is to

---

58. Houtman, *Exodus*, 2:73–74.

59. Cassuto, *Commentary on Exodus*, 112–13. Houtman, however, feel this is too subtle an interpretation (*Exodus*, 2:77).

60. Zevit, "Three Ways to Look at the Ten Plagues," 22.

61. The text is not clear whether this inability results from their physical discomfort or a demoralizing awareness of their own impotence. Perhaps this ambiguity is purposeful.

62. Helpful overviews on the various issues concerning the hardening of Pharaoh's heart may be found in Fretheim, *Exodus*, 96–103; Childs, *Book of Exodus*, 170–75; Plastaras, *The God of Exodus*, 133–37. For more technical and critical discussions, see R. R. Wilson, "The Hardening of Pharaoh's Heart," *CBQ* 41 (1979): 18–36.

4:21, where Yahweh reveals to Moses, far in advance of the onset of the plagues, his intention to make Pharaoh a mere tool of his redemptive plan. No attempt should be made to "reconcile" Yahweh's hardening of Pharaoh's heart (plagues 6, 8, 9, 10) with statements in the other plagues that Pharaoh hardened his own heart.

The tension cannot be resolved in a facile manner by suggesting, for example, that Pharaoh has already demonstrated his recalcitrance, so Yahweh merely helps the process along, or that he is doing what Pharaoh would have done on his own anyway. Rather, 9:12 is a striking reminder of what God has been trying to teach Moses and Israel since the beginning of the Exodus episode: He is in *complete* control. However Pharaoh *might* have reacted given the chance is not brought into the discussion. He is not even given that chance. Yahweh hardens his heart. It is best to allow the tension of the text to remain.

Seventh Plague: Hail (9:13–35)

[13]Then the LORD said to Moses, "Get up early in the morning, confront Pharaoh and say to him, 'This is what the LORD, the God of the Hebrews, says: Let my people go, so that they may worship me, [14]or this time I will send the full force of my plagues against you and against your officials and your people, so you may know that there is no one like me in all the earth. [15]For by now I could have stretched out my hand and struck you and your people with a plague that would have wiped you off the earth. [16]But I have raised you up for this very purpose, that I might show you my power and that my name might be proclaimed in all the earth. [17]You still set yourself against my people and will not let them go. [18]Therefore, at this time tomorrow I will send the worst hailstorm that has ever fallen on Egypt, from the day it was founded till now. [19]Give an order now to bring your livestock and everything you have in the field to a place of shelter, because the hail will fall on every man and animal that has not been brought in and is still out in the field, and they will die.'"

[20]Those officials of Pharaoh who feared the word of the LORD hurried to bring their slaves and their livestock inside. [21]But those who ignored the word of the LORD left their slaves and livestock in the field.

[22]Then the LORD said to Moses, "Stretch out your hand toward the sky so that hail will fall all over Egypt—on men and animals and on everything growing in the fields of Egypt."

²³When Moses stretched out his staff toward the sky, the
LORD sent thunder and hail, and lightning flashed down to the
ground. So the LORD rained hail on the land of Egypt; ²⁴hail
fell and lightning flashed back and forth. It was the worst
storm in all the land of Egypt since it had become a nation.
²⁵Throughout Egypt hail struck everything in the fields—both
men and animals; it beat down everything growing in the
fields and stripped every tree. ²⁶The only place it did not hail
was the land of Goshen, where the Israelites were.

²⁷Then Pharaoh summoned Moses and Aaron. "This time I
have sinned," he said to them. "The LORD is in the right, and I
and my people are in the wrong. ²⁸Pray to the LORD, for we
have had enough thunder and hail. I will let you go; you don't
have to stay any longer."

²⁹Moses replied, "When I have gone out of the city, I will
spread out my hands in prayer to the LORD. The thunder will
stop and there will be no more hail, so you may know that the
earth is the LORD's. ³⁰But I know that you and your officials
still do not fear the LORD God."

³¹(The flax and barley were destroyed, since the barley had
headed and the flax was in bloom. ³²The wheat and spelt,
however, were not destroyed, because they ripen later.)

³³Then Moses left Pharaoh and went out of the city. He
spread out his hands toward the LORD; the thunder and hail
stopped, and the rain no longer poured down on the land.
³⁴When Pharaoh saw that the rain and hail and thunder had
stopped, he sinned again: He and his officials hardened their
hearts. ³⁵So Pharaoh's heart was hard and he would not let the
Israelites go, just as the LORD had said through Moses.

The seventh plague begins the third series of plagues (see plagues 1 and
4, both of which begin with a morning confrontation; see chart on p. 208).
This plague is recounted in greater length than any of the other nine and acts
as a climax of sorts for what has heretofore transpired. Now Pharaoh is to feel
the "full force" of God's power. The Hebrew of verse 14 reads literally: "I am
about to send *all* (*kol*) my signs to your heart." As we have seen elsewhere,
"all" clearly cannot mean each and every, and the NIV translation ("full force")
seems a good way to get the thought across.[63] The narrative is reaching a
higher plateau of devastation. The heavens themselves are to be unleashed

---

63. See also Gispen, *Exodus*, 99. Some commentators understand "all" to refer to the
remainder of the plagues (plagues 7–10), which is a reasonable option (Sarna, *Exodus*, 146).

against Egypt. The elements are obeying their Creator, even to the point where God can specify the target of his destruction (see v. 26).

This show of frightening power should have finally convinced Pharaoh to release the Israelite slaves. God's purpose throughout the plagues is to make Pharaoh bow to him, that is, to make him "know" the true God. This purpose is reiterated in verse 14 with, possibly, one twist: God's scope now extends beyond Egypt and includes the earth as a whole.

What is unique to this plague is that now Moses lets Pharaoh in on a secret, one the readers have been privy to from the outset, saying in effect: "By now I could[64] have wiped you off the face of the earth. The reason I haven't is because I am using you to spread the word throughout the world that I am God. Understand this well, Pharaoh: *You* are serving *my* purpose" (vv. 15–16). The end of verse 16 refers to God's reputation being proclaimed "in all the earth" (cf. vv. 14, 29). God's purpose in the Exodus has worldwide implications. There is more at work here than simply liberating a band of oppressed slaves from Egypt. Pharaoh is, unfortunately for him, involved in something far bigger than he understands or has planned for.

The nature of the seventh plague itself is significant. Hail is often associated with an act of judgment on God's part (Josh. 10:11; Ps. 18:12; Isa. 28:2, 17; 30:30; Ezek. 13:11–13; 38:22). In fact, weather disturbances of a variety of sorts often represent theophanic language—that is, not just that God is judging, but that God is present. Thunderstorms with lightning, for example, are commonly used in this way in the Old Testament (Ex. 19:16–19; Ps. 18:13–14; Hab. 3:11). In other words, the plague of hail is an intensification of judgment on Egypt, an intensification that will continue for the rest of the plagues. Verse 23 broadens the theophanic language to include thunder and "fire" (probably lightning[65]), which makes clearer the tone of divine judgment on Egypt.[66] In this respect, the theophanic language may also represent a polemic against Egyptian gods, who were similarly represented.[67]

---

64. The word "could" is not a separate word in Hebrew but is inferred from the context. In view of this ambiguity, some commentators have argued that it should be translated "should" (i.e., "This is what you deserve, Pharaoh"). See Fretheim, *Exodus*, 124; Cassuto, *Commentary on Exodus*, 116; Durham, *Exodus*, 124–25. It seems, however, that this does not do full justice to the conjunction *ʾulam*, which normally means "however" (see *IBHS*, 668–73, esp. 671–73).

65. See, for example, Cate, *Exodus*, 57; Gispen, *Exodus*, 102.

66. The sudden mention of "rain" in v. 33 is abrupt. Is the hail of v. 23 meant? If so, why not simply say so? It is not entirely clear how this phenomenon coincides with the flow of the narrative to this point.

67. The god Seth manifested himself in the wind and storms (Zevit, "Three Ways to Look at the Ten Plagues," 21).

For the first time in our narrative, Pharaoh is offered some chance of protection. He is advised to "give an order" (*šlḥ*) that the livestock be brought inside for safety. Once again the author makes a play on this Hebrew word (see comments on 8:21; 9:7). The point of the pun here is that Moses is nudging Pharaoh along to get him to *šlḥ* something! If not the Israelites, then perhaps he will "send" his own livestock to safety.

Some have remarked that this chance of escape is a sign of God's mercy in the midst of his judgment, not unlike Noah's ark. But this hardly seems to be the case. For one thing, the ark is rescuing the *righteous* remnant from God's judgment. Moreover, if this were the case, then God's compassion is certainly short-lived, since no way out is offered for the remaining three plagues. It is better to see this as a test for Pharaoh, to see if he will take steps to comply with Yahweh's warning and thus tacitly acknowledge Yahweh's authority.[68] No mention is made whether Pharaoh heeds Moses' advice; only those who fear "the word of the LORD" respond to Moses' warning (v. 20).[69] Such laconic prose serves to highlight Pharaoh's stubbornness.

When the plague finally arrives, the hail hurts not only human beings and animals, but "everything[70] growing in the fields of Egypt" (v. 22). Some have seen here, and rightly so, an allusion to creation and Genesis 1:11–12. The word for vegetation in Exodus 9:22 is *ʿēseb*, the same word used in Genesis, and it comes upon the reader unexpectedly. As in the following plague (locusts), mention is made of the effects of the plague on vegetation, and as such it seems to suggest another creation reversal.[71] The world of plants is being undone here.

According to verse 25, the hail "beat down everything growing in the fields and stripped every tree." The Hebrew is even more forceful. The vegetation is said to be "struck" (*nkh*), a word used elsewhere in Exodus with reference to the plagues. Also, the word used to describe the effects of the plague on the trees is a form of the root *šbr*, which is better rendered "smash" than "strip."[72] The mention of the destruction of vegetation may also be a

---

68. Houtman, *Exodus*, 2:90.

69. These "God-fearers" may be those who make up the "mixed crowd" (NRSV) that leaves Egypt with the Israelites (see 12:38; NIV has "many other people").

70. Here again the Hebrew uses the word *kol* (all), which may be hyperbole or a reference to all *available* vegetation (see comments on 9:6). The latter solution is suggested by vv. 31–32, which indicates that only some of the vegetation is harmed; vv. 31–32 also explain how some vegetation remains for the locusts (10:5).

71. Zevit, "Three Ways to Look at the Ten Plagues," 22–23.

72. The verb is Piel in v. 25. The same word is used in 32:19 for the smashing of the stone tablets that contained the Ten Commandments.

veiled reprisal for the Israelites' being made to gather their own straw for making bricks in chapter 5.[73]

Verse 27 brings us to the point we have been expecting—what appears as a truly heartfelt capitulation by Pharaoh. Is this true repentance? He confesses that he has sinned and that "I and my people are in the wrong." Pharaoh seems to begin to understand the core problem. This is his first real compliance with Moses' commands without any strings attached; he seems to be making progress. Verse 27 gives us another pun on the verb *šlḥ* (see comments on 9:7, 19), for here he "sends" for Moses and Aaron. The reader is left wondering when Pharaoh will capitulate fully by taking the final step and "send" all the Israelites away so they can worship the God who is bringing these mighty plagues against him.

However authentic this repentance seems to be at first blush, it is certainly short-lived (and perhaps therefore not authentic). No sooner does the plague cease than Pharaoh "sins again"[74] (v. 34) by hardening his heart to the lesson he really should have learned long ago: He cannot compete with Israel's God. Moses, in a strong show of force that under normal circumstances would have sealed his own fate, calls Pharaoh a liar (v. 30). He anticipates what has now become Pharaoh's predictable cycle of behavior: Say one thing and do another.[75] Note once again that neither Moses nor his God are taken by surprise by Pharaoh's tactic. In fact, as we have seen in 9:12 (cf. also 9:16), Pharaoh's stubbornness is by God's design.

Eighth Plague: Locusts (10:1–20)

[10:1]Then the LORD said to Moses, "Go to Pharaoh, for I have hardened his heart and the hearts of his officials so that I may perform these miraculous signs of mine among them [2]that you may tell your children and grandchildren how I dealt

---

73. Houtman, *Exodus*, 2:84–85. Zevit also suggests that a polemic against Egyptian gods may be at work here, since both Isis and Min were connected to the yearly crop cycle. As Zevit puts it, "Min is an especially likely candidate for these two plagues [hail and locusts] because the notations in Exodus 9:31 indicate that the first plague came as the flax and barley were about to be harvested, but before the wheat and spelt had matured. A widely celebrated 'Coming out of Min' was celebrated in Egypt at the beginning of the harvest. These plagues, in effect, devastated Min's coming-out party" ("Three Ways to Look at the Ten Plagues," 21).

74. The use of the root *ḥaṭaʾ* (to sin) in both Pharaoh's "confession" of sin in v. 27 and his change of heart, referred to as sin in v. 34, draws the reader's attention to make some comparison between the two. The insincerity of the former is suggested by how quickly Pharaoh can fall into sin again.

75. Verse 35 seems to be a concerted attempt on the part of the writer to emphasize Moses' perceptive grasp of the events. It is the only plague in which Pharaoh's hardened heart is said to occur "just as the LORD had said *through Moses.*" Vv. 31–32 is a parenthetical comment designed to explain the existence of crops in 10:5 (Sarna, *Exodus*, 47).

harshly with the Egyptians and how I performed my signs among them, and that you may know that I am the LORD."

³So Moses and Aaron went to Pharaoh and said to him, "This is what the LORD, the God of the Hebrews, says: 'How long will you refuse to humble yourself before me? Let my people go, so that they may worship me. ⁴If you refuse to let them go, I will bring locusts into your country tomorrow. ⁵They will cover the face of the ground so that it cannot be seen. They will devour what little you have left after the hail, including every tree that is growing in your fields. ⁶They will fill your houses and those of all your officials and all the Egyptians—something neither your fathers nor your forefathers have ever seen from the day they settled in this land till now.'" Then Moses turned and left Pharaoh.

⁷Pharaoh's officials said to him, "How long will this man be a snare to us? Let the people go, so that they may worship the LORD their God. Do you not yet realize that Egypt is ruined?"

⁸Then Moses and Aaron were brought back to Pharaoh. "Go, worship the LORD your God," he said. "But just who will be going?"

⁹Moses answered, "We will go with our young and old, with our sons and daughters, and with our flocks and herds, because we are to celebrate a festival to the LORD."

¹⁰Pharaoh said, "The LORD be with you—if I let you go, along with your women and children! Clearly you are bent on evil. ¹¹No! Have only the men go; and worship the LORD, since that's what you have been asking for." Then Moses and Aaron were driven out of Pharaoh's presence.

¹²And the LORD said to Moses, "Stretch out your hand over Egypt so that locusts will swarm over the land and devour everything growing in the fields, everything left by the hail."

¹³So Moses stretched out his staff over Egypt, and the LORD made an east wind blow across the land all that day and all that night. By morning the wind had brought the locusts; ¹⁴they invaded all Egypt and settled down in every area of the country in great numbers. Never before had there been such a plague of locusts, nor will there ever be again. ¹⁵They covered all the ground until it was black. They devoured all that was left after the hail—everything growing in the fields and the fruit on the trees. Nothing green remained on tree or plant in all the land of Egypt.

¹⁶Pharaoh quickly summoned Moses and Aaron and said, "I have sinned against the LORD your God and against you. ¹⁷Now forgive my sin once more and pray to the LORD your God to take this deadly plague away from me."

¹⁸Moses then left Pharaoh and prayed to the LORD. ¹⁹And the LORD changed the wind to a very strong west wind, which caught up the locusts and carried them into the Red Sea. Not a locust was left anywhere in Egypt. ²⁰But the LORD hardened Pharaoh's heart, and he would not let the Israelites go.

The locust plague is the second plague of the third series and, like the previous plague, is another lengthy account. The final three plagues take the judgment cycle to a higher and irreversible level. In these plagues, there is no chance that Pharaoh will change his heart. In fact, the eighth plague begins by telling us this much: Yahweh has hardened Pharaoh's heart (10:1). The outcome of this and the following two encounters is never in doubt. Pharaoh is a rag doll in God's hands, and he is about to witness the irrevocable finale. The process is proceeding as Israel's God has designed it, and Pharaoh is helpless to do anything about it.

The plagues of hail and of locusts are similar in two respects: Both wreak widespread devastation on human beings, animals, and crops, and both represent forms of judgment common to other parts of Scripture. The former has already been discussed in conjunction with the previous plague. As for the latter, God occasionally uses locusts for judgment (e.g., Joel 1–2).[76] The devastation of crops by locusts may represent a polemic against Egyptian religion.[77]

Also, as with the plague of hail, a number of elements recall the creation narrative in Genesis. The trees that "grow" in the fields are devastated by the locusts (v. 5). The Hebrew word translated "grow" is *samaḥ*, which also appears in Genesis 2:5. In Exodus 10:12 and 15, we see the root *ʿeseb* (green plants; see 9:22). Moreover, 10:15 also has two more words that strengthen this creation connection: *pᵉri* (fruit) and *yereq* (green). The former is also found in Genesis 1:11 and the latter in 1:30. Once again, creation reversal is taking place. This connection, I again suggest, is central to the theological thrust of the narrative.[78]

---

76. See also Deut. 28:38; Amos 4:9; 7:1–3. Sometimes armies are compared to locusts as instruments of God's judgment (e.g., Isa. 33:4; Jer. 51:14).

77. See remarks above under the 7th plague. See also Cate, *Exodus*, 59; Zevit, "Three Ways to Look at the Ten Plagues," 21.

78. In this context the writer's use of the word "to fill" (*mlʾ*) also seems significant. The locusts (10:6) and flies (8:21) "fill" Egypt, perhaps in retribution for the Egyptians objecting to the Israelites "filling" the land in 1:7.

The locust plague provides connections not only to what has been but to what will come. (1) The locusts come on the land by an east wind (v. 13); an east wind also causes the Red Sea to part (14:21). We have, in other words, a preview of coming attractions. (2) The fact that the locusts meet their demise in the Red Sea clearly alludes to the drowning of the Egyptian army in 14:28. Even the language of 10:19 and 14:28 is similar, for both include the phrase "not one survived."[79] (3) The "deadly plague" from which Pharaoh asks Moses for relief (v. 17) foreshadows the tenth plague, the death of the firstborn. (4) The blackness (*ḥšk*) caused by the locusts in verse 15 anticipates the plague of darkness that soon follows (see *ḥošek* in 10:21—22).[80] We see, then, the final three mighty acts of God (plagues 9, 10, and the Red Sea incident) all anticipated in the plague of locusts.[81]

This locust plague brings to light another purpose of the plagues, one that has been hinted at previously but has not yet been given clear expression: not merely so that the Egyptians may "know" God, but so that future generations of Israelites may know him as well (v. 2). Thus, the broader purpose of the Exodus is slowly being unveiled, a point that will be made even more strongly in the Passover narrative (12:1—30; 13:1—16). God's actions in Egypt with the Exodus generation are not meant to be kept secret. They must be told and remembered in future generations. Nor is it simply that the whole earth may know of Yahweh now. Rather, even those not yet born will "remember" what God has done here. God's redemptive purposes reach out much further than the Exodus generation.

The hardening of Pharaoh's heart (v. 1) is played out throughout the account of this plague. After Moses announces the plague, he and Aaron simply leave Pharaoh's presence without giving him any chance to respond. The time for discussion is over. God has hardened Pharaoh's heart. His sorry state stands in sharp contrast to the desire on the part of his court officials to let the Israelites go (v. 7). Pharaoh is the last to catch on. His magicians abandoned him long ago (8:19); now his court officials ask "how long," a clear echo of the words Moses and Aaron are told to bring to Pharaoh in verse 3. This turn of events also serves to move the focal point of God's judgment to where the readers have anticipated since the beginning of the book: to Pharaoh, the anti-God figure of the book. The con-

---

79. Cassuto, *Commentary on Exodus*, 128—29.

80. The NIV here says that the locusts "covered all the ground *until it was black.*" This is one possible translation, but it obscures the obvious verbal link between 10:15 and 10:21—22. Furthermore, the Hebrew can also mean that there are so many locusts that they blot out the sun and, thus, make the earth "dark."

81. "Darkness" also connects this plague back to creation (see comments on the ninth plague).

frontation between the true God and the false one is now beginning to draw to a climax.

In a certain sense, however, Pharaoh is making measured progress. Here, for the first time, he says he will actually allow the Israelites to leave Egypt— at least, the men (v. 11), presumably because only men were needed to fulfill religious obligations. It should be remembered that what Moses, by God's command, has been calling for is a three-day journey into the desert in order to sacrifice to Yahweh (see 5:3). Might not this have contributed to Pharaoh's notion that only men need to be released? In fact, he is clever. He seems to call Moses' bluff by asking him who would be going (10:8).

When Moses responds that everybody is to leave, Pharaoh is understandably upset (vv. 10–11). From his perspective, it seems as if Moses is trying to pull a fast one on him. All along this request to sacrifice seems to have been nothing more than a ploy. But have we not here perhaps begun to see the ultimate purpose for requesting the three-day journey to sacrifice?

Clearly, God's purpose all along is to get Israel out of Egypt, never to return. But Pharaoh is given only part of the reason: a journey to sacrifice. As difficult as this may be for modern readers to accept, it seems that God has set Pharaoh up. It has taken now eight plagues for Pharaoh to acquiesce to Moses' request to allow the Israelites to go sacrifice to their God. But at precisely this moment, when, according to Pharaoh's perspective, the judgments should have ceased, God's full intention is made known to Pharaoh, and this contributes to the hardening of his heart—which is exactly what God wants to do with him in the first place. God is making a mockery of the king of Egypt. He is trapped in a divine plot with unexpected twists and turns, and there is no way out. His reaction, then, is not only understandable, but perfectly expected because it is ordained by God. Thus, when Moses and Aaron leave Pharaoh's presence, they are not humiliated[82] but triumphant in the knowledge that God's plan is working itself out.

This unprecedented event of locust plague (v. 14; see also 10:6) brings Pharaoh to his knees. He quickly calls[83] for Moses and Aaron and confesses, once again, that he has sinned (vv. 16–17). Whether such a confession is truly heartfelt is hardly a debatable point. Although the intensity level of the plagues is rising, Pharaoh is up to the same old tricks. He asks for another chance. Perhaps it is in a moment of panic. Perhaps he really thinks he means it this time. Such questions are beside the point, however. God has hardened his heart, so it is certain that whether this confession is real or feigned, the result will be the same. Still, Moses prays for the plague to be removed, and it is—not for

---

82. Such is the opinion of Houtman, *Exodus*, 2:100.
83. Pharaoh also "calls" (*qrʾ*) for Moses and Aaron in 8:8 and for the last time in 12:31.

Pharaoh to repent but in order to give him another chance to see God's might. When the locusts are gone, God again hardens Pharaoh's heart.

Ninth Plague: Darkness (10:21–29)

[21]Then the LORD said to Moses, "Stretch out your hand toward the sky so that darkness will spread over Egypt—darkness that can be felt." [22]So Moses stretched out his hand toward the sky, and total darkness covered all Egypt for three days. [23]No one could see anyone else or leave his place for three days. Yet all the Israelites had light in the places where they lived.

[24]Then Pharaoh summoned Moses and said, "Go, worship the LORD. Even your women and children may go with you; only leave your flocks and herds behind."

[25]But Moses said, "You must allow us to have sacrifices and burnt offerings to present to the LORD our God. [26]Our livestock too must go with us; not a hoof is to be left behind. We have to use some of them in worshiping the LORD our God, and until we get there we will not know what we are to use to worship the LORD."

[27]But the LORD hardened Pharaoh's heart, and he was not willing to let them go. [28]Pharaoh said to Moses, "Get out of my sight! Make sure you do not appear before me again! The day you see my face you will die."

[29]"Just as you say," Moses replied, "I will never appear before you again."

The ninth plague is the penultimate blow before the final punishments meted out in the tenth plague and the Red Sea incident. This is the third plague of the third series, and, like plagues 3 and 6, it comes with no announcement or delay.

That this plague is darkness is significant. (1) As noted above, this affliction was already intimated in the eighth plague (see comments on 10:15). (2) A plague of darkness is almost certainly intended to be understood as a polemic against an Egyptian solar deity, possibly Re, a common sun god throughout Egypt's history.[84] For the God of Israelite slaves to have his way with such a powerful Egyptian god would send a clear message. This would speak to Pharaoh even more directly, since Egyptian kings were sometimes

---

84. There is routine agreement on this point: Zevit, "Three Ways to Look at the Ten Plagues," 21; Ellison, *Exodus*, 58; Cate, *Exodus*, 61; Durham, *Exodus*, 126; Sarna, *Exodus*, 51.

referred to as the son of Re.[85] (3) More significant, especially in light of the plague narrative as a whole, is the connection between this plague and creation. Darkness is a "chaos" word. It was the first thing God brought under control by introducing light in Genesis 1:3. A reintroduction of darkness brings creation back to its chaotic beginnings, which is a signal to the Egyptians of what awaits them at the sea.[86]

But this creation reversal does not affect the Israelites (v. 23). Once again, creation does not work against the Israelites but for them. The phrase "there was light" (lit.) at the end of verse 23 is an almost unmistakable echo of Genesis 1:3, "Let there be light."[87] Inasmuch as darkness represents chaos, it also represents death (see 1 Sam. 2:9; Job 15:30; 17:13; 18:18; Ps. 88:12, 18; 143:3), in which case the ninth plague serves to anticipate the next two acts of destruction, both of which bring death to the Egyptians. In view of the theological significance of this plague, discussions concerning natural explanations for the darkness are beside the point.[88]

Pharaoh once again seems to capitulate, but this time with one seemingly inconsequential stipulation: They are to leave the animals behind. It is these animals, however, that have been preserved for some reason from the effects of some of the previous plagues. Why would Yahweh simply abandon them now? Moreover, this is likely a ploy by Pharaoh to get the people to return. It is not the case that he needs these animals, but that he knows the Israelites do. How long would they survive without them? Pharaoh does not have an affection for animals; rather, he wants some security that the people will have to rush back.

Furthermore, as Moses points out correctly, if also diplomatically, such a request cannot be reconciled with Pharaoh's concession to allow the Israelites to leave and worship their God (v. 24), for without livestock, there is no worship of Yahweh. In other words, without the animals, their release is no release at all. The very purpose for leaving Egypt, we have been told repeatedly throughout the narrative, is so the Israelites can worship the Lord. Thus, Pharaoh's compliance with Moses' request fails to appreciate the reason for the request at its very heart.

Pharaoh receives no chance for rebuttal. Moses explains why the animals must come along, but Pharaoh is cut off from speaking his mind: God

---

85. Shafer, ed., *Religion in Ancient Egypt*, 59, 65, 97, 100, 109.

86. Darkness is used in a similar way elsewhere in the Old Testament, including Deut. 28:29; Isa. 8:22; 13:10; 59:9; Joel 2:2, 10; Amos 5:20; Zeph. 1:15. See esp. Ezek. 32:7–8, which speaks of the eventual destruction of the pharaoh of Ezekiel's day and is described in terms reminiscent of the ninth plague.

87. Both phrases are made up of a form of the verb *hayah* (to be) plus *ʾor* (light).

88. See Houtman, *Exodus*, 2:120–21; Gispen, *Exodus*, 109; Hyatt, *Exodus*, 126; Cassuto, *Commentary on Exodus*, 129; Sarna, *Exodus*, 50–51.

hardens his heart (v. 27). How he may have responded if left to his own is not the point, nor should we become preoccupied with reconciling such decisive action on God's part to our own images of how a fair God should behave. God is bringing this contest between himself and Egypt's king to a speedy resolution.

At this point, Moses and Pharaoh part company for what appears to be the last time (but see 12:31). Pharaoh, ironically, cuts off the only means of salvation he has by banishing Moses from his presence forever. Of course, this too is according to God's plan. By having Pharaoh cast Moses out of his presence, God is in effect casting Pharaoh out of his presence. If the end were ever in doubt, it is no longer so. Later, Pharaoh's pronouncement (v. 28) will come back to haunt him. He and Moses will meet again at the Red Sea, but it is not Moses who dies, but Egypt.

CREATION IN SERVICE of redemption. These nine plagues against Egypt are not just a display of God flexing his muscles. They are, as we have seen, the unleashing of God's creative forces against the enemies of God's people (and therefore the enemies of God himself). In the abstract one can imagine God using a variety of other means to bring Egypt to its knees, ways that have biblical precedent elsewhere. He could have sent an angel dressed in armor and girded with sword. He could have used a foreign army as his pawn to plunder. But this was not the tactic he takes. He chooses, rather, to fight with weapons that no one but he has at his disposal and that only he can command. After all, what defense is there against the forces of creation itself? This series of attacks on Egypt removes all doubt as to who the victor will be.

It has already been mentioned that the reason God chooses such a means of punishment is due, at least in part, to the nature of the crime perpetrated against Israel, namely, Pharaoh's posing as an anti-God force whose decree in chapter 1 is nothing less than a challenge to God's creation mandate in Genesis 1. Furthermore, throughout Scripture there is a close relationship between creation and salvation; when God saves, it is a re-creation of sorts. This is why the narrative of the departure from Egypt—the central, paradigmatic salvation event in the Old Testament—is permeated with creation language. Whatever hints of this creation-salvation connection we see in early chapters of Exodus are given clearer expression in the narrative of the plagues and reach their pinnacle in chapter 14 and the parting of the Red Sea.

With the departure of Israel from Egypt, Israel has a new beginning. This is where the *nation* of Israel truly has its start. From now on it will be a recognizable national entity, much like the surrounding nations. Israel will have its own God and accompanying religious trappings, its own system of law, its own land, and, eventually, its own king (though the monarchy does not begin for several hundred years). When seen in this light it is no surprise that creation plays an active role in Israel's emancipation.

Creation is at God's command both to deliver his people and to destroy his enemies. The plagues are creation reversals: Animals harm rather than serve humanity; light ceases and darkness takes over; waters become a source of death rather than life; the climax of Genesis 1 is the creation of humans on the last day, whereas the climax of the plagues is the destruction of human beings in the last plague. The plagues do not run rampant, however. They eventually cease, and each cessation is another display of God's creative power. He once again restores order to chaos as he did "in the beginning": The waters are restored, the pesky insects and animals retreat. Each plague is a reminder of the supreme power of God who holds chaos at bay, but who, if he chooses, will step aside and allow the chaos to plague his enemies.

The Exodus narrative is not alone in linking creation and salvation. In fact, on the pages of the Old Testament creation often "goes ballistic" when God seeks to punish or save. Perhaps the most obvious example is the Flood. This is the first creation reversal, and (the force of this observation should not be lost) it appears in the Genesis narrative only moments after the majesty of the creation itself (see comments on ch. 14 for further discussion of the Flood).

Prophetic literature frequently states how God is in complete command of his creation and uses it to effect his goals. The description of such events bears strong similarity to the plague narrative. God's judgment on Babylon, for example, will be accompanied by celestial upheaval: "The stars of heaven and their constellations will not show their light. The rising sun will be darkened and the moon will not give its light" (Isa. 13:10; see also Joel 2:10, 31). "I will make the heavens tremble; and the earth will shake from its place" (Isa. 13:13). The nations, who are likened to "the raging sea," God simply rebukes and they "flee far away" (17:13).

Prophecies against Egypt in particular are imbued with allusions to the Exodus, although many of these allusions refer more specifically to the crossing of the sea than to the plagues (Isa. 19:5–6, an allusion to the stinking waters of Egypt after the first plague; see also Jer. 46 and Ezek. 29–32). Hail and locusts are often signs of God's judgment on Israel's enemies (Josh. 10:11; Isa. 28:2; 30:30; Ezek. 38:22; Joel 1:4; Hag. 2:17).

It is hard not to think of the events surrounding the Exodus as providing a paradigm for subsequent acts of deliverance by God. We will examine later (see comments on Ex. 14) how the Exodus pattern as a whole is appealed to at a number of crucial junctures in redemptive history, specifically the return from

Babylon and the coming of Christ. But even in these brief examples we see, in a manner reminiscent of the plagues, God's use of creation as he pronounces judgment. Note especially the ironic twist of Joel 1:4, where the object of God's creation-reversal anger is not the wicked nations, but unrepentant Israel. Although they are the beneficiaries of the creation reversals in Exodus, Israel is not immune from the punishment once intended for her oppressors.

We do not do justice to this theme if we limit our observations to those passages that echo the specific language of the plague narrative. The famous encounter between Elijah and the prophets of Baal on Mount Carmel is another example (1 Kings 18:16–46). This story, too, is about the power of Israel's God versus a foreign god (Baal, the Canaanite storm god). It is Yahweh, the true God, who shows control over the elements by bringing fire down from heaven (reminiscent of the lightning of the plague of hail, esp. since the Hebrew word in Exodus for lightning is "fire") to ignite the water-saturated altar (see also Num. 11:1–3, where fire from heaven is directed against the grumbling Israelites).

Another example is the famous incident of the sun standing still in Joshua 10:1–15.[89] The net result was Israel's victory over Adoni-Zedek and the proclamation, "Surely the LORD was fighting for Israel" (10:14), a conclusion at which the Egyptians also arrive in Exodus 14:25. Again, both instances could have been handled differently. The warrior God could have mounted his chariot and swept the enemy away with his mighty sword. But he took another approach, one that allows those present, on both sides of the conflict, to reflect on the power of the only God.

More closely associated with the Exodus is the miraculous provision of manna, quail, and water from the rock (Ex. 16:1–17:7; Num. 11:4–35; 20:1–13). The normal exigencies that accompany desert travel (lack of food and water) present no barrier to the God of creation. Just as he is capable of casting darkness over light and turning water into blood, he can make the skies rain quail, the dew of the earth bring forth bread, and water come from a most unlikely source, rocks. Like some of the plagues, these examples show that it is not simply a matter of God *using* creation to serve his ends. He is rather *suspending* the normal operations of his creation to show that he is Lord of all—and all this to benefit his beloved people: Fire consumes water, the earth yields bread, there is darkness during daytime, and water becomes blood. Creation serves its Maker by behaving in ways that are contrary to all reason and expectation.

---

89. An insightful discussion of this passage is J. H. Walton, "Joshua 10:12–15 and the Mesopotamian Celestial Omen Texts," in *Faith, History, and Tradition: Old Testament Historiography in Its Near Eastern Context*, ed. A. R. Millard, J. K. Hoffmeier, and D. W. Baker (Winona Lake, Ind.: Eisenbrauns, 1994), 181–90.

In view of the connection between creation and salvation in the Old Testament, the presence of creation language with respect to the coming of Christ seems obvious. As Exodus is the paradigmatic salvific event in the Old Testament and serves as a paradigm for other redemptive acts, the coming of Christ is the climactic salvific event; thus, we see creation behaving in ways that resemble the passages mentioned above. At the beginning of his earthly life, creation announces Christ's birth through a special star that leads the Magi to him. His first miracle involves changing the natural properties of water and making it wine. This is no mere trick to impress the witnesses or to show them how special he is. This is, rather, a first hint at what Jesus' life and death are meant to do: turn creation upside down.

Like Moses, Jesus has command over the elements. He walks on water; he commands the storms to cease; he provides a miraculous supply of fish and bread; he makes a fig tree wither. These well-known incidents show that he, like the God of the Exodus, has creation at his disposal. He can command it at will to serve whatever purpose he has in mind. That he is able to do these things is nothing less than a clear indication that the God of the Old Testament is walking among his people, once again manipulating the created order to bring blessing and relief to his people. Christ has the entire created order at his disposal. It is of him that Paul wrote, "All things were created by him and for him" (Col. 1:16). This is the Christ who came to change the hearts of people.

At Jesus' death we see an inversion of this theme. The Gospel writers tell us that darkness came over the earth, the earth shook, and rocks split (Matt. 27:51; Luke 23:44). Here, too, creation signals the deliverance of God's people, but only by means of the punishment of God's Son, against whom God's anger is directed. He bears in his body the punishment God formerly inflicted on the enemies of his people, such as Egypt and Babylon. Now Christ has become the enemy of God. With his death, God is on the move for the last time. He has come to bring his people out of bondage, at whatever the cost. Creation bears witness to this fact.

Even the resurrection of Christ takes on a new dimension when seen in light of this theme: It is the ultimate creation reversal. God has control over that most intractable of the laws of creation. When people die, they are dead. But even death is of no account to God. The power that controls the elements can break into the very core of human mortality and bring life from death. Our knees should shake.

The book of Revelation remains a difficult and controversial book to interpret. Without wishing to enter the fray, I would suggest that we are on safe ground when we say that this book is a highly symbolic work that deals with the final, ultimate victory of Christ over sin and death and with God's bringing all of history to its final goal, edenic blessing in the presence of the Lamb. John's vision is filled with allusions to plagues and creation upheavals, a point to which Jesus himself seems to hint (e.g., Mark 13:24–25). The angel's warning to the church at Laodicea is prefaced as being "the words of the Amen, the faithful and true witness, the ruler of God's creation" (Rev. 3:14). These believers are to heed his warning, since creation is at his disposal.

The seven seals and the seven trumpets (6:1–17; 8:1–9:21; 11:15–19) allude to well-known biblical descriptions of cosmic cataclysm. The third seal upsets the agricultural cycle. In the fourth seal, plague and wild animals contribute to the death of over a fourth of the population. The sixth seal brings us a blackened sun, stars falling from the sky, the sky rolling up like a scroll, and the removal of mountains and islands.

The first trumpet brings hail and fire mixed with blood, which destroy a third of the earth, trees, and grass. With the second trumpet a huge blazing mountain is hurled into the sea, bringing great maritime destruction, not the least of which is the sea turning to blood, a clear reminder of the first plague. The third trumpet signals the star Wormwood, turning sweet waters to bitter (a reversal of Ex. 15:22–27?). With the fourth trumpet, the sun is once again darkened, along with the moon and stars. The fifth trumpet brings darkness and locusts; the latter receive power to agonize the enemies of God (those without his seal on their foreheads). The sixth trumpet brings plagues of fire, smoke, and sulfur to kill a third of humankind. With the seventh trumpet, heaven is opened, and lightning, rumblings, thunder, an earthquake, and hailstorms occur.

The seven bowls of God's wrath (16:1–21) largely repeat the symbolism of the previous sevenfold series of judgments: sores break out; the seas, rivers, and springs turn to blood; the sun alternatively scorches and is darkened; lightning, thunder, and earthquakes take place. We even see frogs (v. 13) and the drying up of waters (v. 12).

It is, in my view, beside the point to invest energy in defending the literalness of these descriptions. They are powerful, symbolic descriptions of ultimate reality, which, not surprisingly, utilize biblical themes and images that had become part of the first-century Jew's religious worldview. God's final judgment on his enemies will bear no mere coincidental resemblance to his other acts of judgment in the Old Testament (the Exodus in particular). In this sense, the power God displays at the Exodus is a foretaste of the forces he will use to bring about his judgment. The symbolism of Revelation is a not cheap, nonliteral representation of what God "really" did in Exodus. If anything, the opposite is the case: Exodus is a down payment and earthly depiction of the final cataclysm, one that is so powerful, so ultimate, so final, that it can only be described in a manner reminiscent of these earlier earthly acts.

At the consummation, when all is set aright, creation will be intimately involved. Perhaps this is in part what Paul is driving at in Romans 8:18–27. The most relevant portion is verses 18–23:

> I consider that our present sufferings are not worth comparing with the glory that will be revealed in us. The *creation waits in eager expectation* for the sons of God to be revealed. For the creation was subjected to frustration, not by its own choice, but by the will of the one who subjected it, in hope that the *creation itself will be liberated* from its bondage to decay and brought into the glorious freedom of the children of God.
>
> We know that the whole *creation has been groaning* as in the pains of childbirth right up to the present time. Not only so, but we ourselves, who have the firstfruits of the Spirit, groan inwardly as we wait eagerly for our adoption as sons, the redemption of our bodies. (italics added)

Creation is "waiting" for God to move; it yearns to be "liberated"; it "groans" for the end. Creation has always figured into God's plans whenever he appeared on the scene. And in the end, it will once again—finally—be so. Creation will participate in the final act of redemption, and thus will itself experience liberation from the bondage to decay in which it has been held. It is perhaps in this broadest of contexts that the participation of creation with salvation should be understood. Creation has a vested interest in the outcome. All things will be made new. Redemption and re-creation are two sides of the same coin.

 THE PLAGUES AND YOU. As mentioned at the outset of this section, it seems to me that there is little *literal* contemporary significance in the nine plagues recounted in Exodus 7:8–10:29. We are not Israelites, and we are not oppressed by Egypt. We must resist the temptation to "apply" the plague narrative by ascribing to God's judgment any natural catastrophe or other similar disasters that happen along and fit them into our personal views of how God acts. We all know of individuals—some well-intentioned, some charlatans—who cram the earthquakes, floods, and diseases that occur regularly and have always been so much a part of our world, into pet end-times theologies. But God does not speak to us as he did to Moses and bring about natural calamities to punish our enemies. In fact, those who claim special knowledge and predict such things are rightly dismissed as overzealous literalists at best and crackpots at worst.

Nor will the lesson of the plagues be found in distilling moralistic principles. It certainly misses the point to argue, as one commentator does, that one of the lessons of the plague narrative is to caution us against making vows that we have no intention of keeping—a reference to Pharaoh's recurring change of heart. Such an approach is problematic, not only because the text itself gives no indication whether Pharaoh's promise to let the Israelites go was intended to be sincere, but especially because the point of the hardening episodes is to drive home in no uncertain terms that Yahweh is in complete control of the process of Israel's release.

Whatever approach we may take to understanding the plague narrative, its intention is certainly not to teach the Israelites, "Don't be like Pharaoh." Something much more fundamental, much more significant, is happening here. The story of the plagues is not telling us about a bad man, Pharaoh, whose example we are to avoid. Nor is it a morality play with Moses as the positive example of how to act, since he himself does not rise to saintly status in the narrative.

The key to applying the plagues is found in struggling with the theology of the plagues and how the significance of that theology is given fuller expression in the person and work of Jesus Christ. The answers are not straightforward and obvious. It takes study, contemplation, and patience. We must look again and again at what this theme has to tell us about the nature of God and how we, in Christ, are to respond to that God.

On one level, we apply this theme simply by saying, "Wow!" We should not feel short-changed if our understanding of a passage does not translate directly into some overt, specific behavior. The point of the plagues for today is not so much in what *we* do with it, but in having our hearts and minds opened to what *God* has done and thereby understanding *him* better. Who else but the supreme judge of the universe can make the heavens and the earth do his bidding?

I know I have the tendency to read over the Exodus story without considering thoughtfully the implications of what God is capable of doing. When we read that old story of frogs, gnats, rivers turning to blood, and so forth, perhaps scenes of the famous movie *The Ten Commandments* come to mind. We are so familiar with it that we do not allow it to strike us deeply, which is the effect it had some three thousand years ago. At the end of the day, when the masks come off and we are left to our own conscience, do we really believe in the God that the biblical narrative is presenting to us? Do we believe that this God is somehow connected to his people several thousand years removed from these events?

This story was not taken for granted by the generations of Israelites living after the Exodus. It was rather intended to be a gripping reminder of who God is. In the final analysis, the story of the plagues is not about what God does to save *you*, or perhaps even so much a story of how he saved

Israel. It is about God, period; for when all is said and done, we all need to be reminded of *him* now and then. The question, then, to ask of our passage is not, "What does this have to do with me?" We must at least first ask, "What does this tell me about who God is?"

Perhaps the application is, in a word, doxological. We praise, that is, worship God for his fearful might and great love, both of which he has employed for the sake of his beloved children. Praising God is not a lesser form of application. Rather, it is what so much of the Bible is driving us toward. It is the goal of redemption itself—not to feel self-important by being part of God's club, but to turn ourselves away from our sinful inclination toward self-centeredness and toward God. This, I suggest, is how the ancient Israelites properly "applied" the plagues (e.g., see the Song at the Sea in Ex. 15 and Ps. 105). They saw what God had done for them, and they fell back in awe—and they remembered.

This is why a moralistic reading of the story falls far short of the mark. The Israelites came to know God better by what he had done, and it is this knowledge that formed the basis for their morality. When our hearts and minds are imbued with a personal knowledge of our Creator, proper morality will follow. Our actions flow from who we are at our very core. And who we are is determined by whom we worship—whether God, the world, or ourselves. The plague narrative—indeed, the book of Exodus and the entire Bible—is a call to worship the true God, and it calls us to that goal by telling us who he is.

There are a number of elements in the plague narrative that strike me in particular as I seek to know God better through his Word. It is the recognition that personal salvation, however important, is only part of the big picture. God's purposes are broader than what we sometimes think in modern, evangelical America. The nature of the plagues helps us catch a glimpse of that broader purpose. They are, as we have seen, not just muscle flexing. Rather, God arms himself with creation to bring creation itself to its ultimate goal. Our salvation is a *part* of that goal. I am not for one moment diminishing the importance of the atoning work of Christ in reconciling fallen *humanity* to the holy God. The point here, however, is that we miss something of the wonder of our own salvation if we do not see it in light of the grand scope of salvation. In the plagues, God manipulates the created order and thereby reaches back to the dawn of time and ahead to the consummation—the death, resurrection, and return of Christ. And he does this ultimately for his glory, not for ours.

Our redemption is a piece, albeit a large piece, of a puzzle that extends beyond our personal eternal state. It is about the restoration—re-creation, if you will—of what was lost in the Garden of Eden. This is why salvation, whether the deliverance from Egypt or through the death and resurrection of Christ, is often described in creation language. The coming of Christ re-creates humanity, and this re-creation is part of a plan that has the widest of possible implications. Jesus came to inaugurate a new world order, which he called the kingdom of God. It is an order in which all creation will eventually be restored to the glory God intended at the beginning.

Another element, touched on earlier but more prominent in the plague narrative, is the fact that God has complete control in the process of salvation. We should be careful not to try to fit these passages too neatly into our theological constructs, as if God's sovereignty can be tamed (!). This goes for people of all theological stripes, whether Calvinist or Arminian. The almost playfulness with which God handles Pharaoh despite his apparent repentance, and the determination with which he brings Israel out of Egypt despite their less than full support, should give everyone reason to pause.

Who is this all-loving, merciful God who, rather than fanning Pharaoh's nascent obedience into a flame, seems to direct him in a completely opposite direction? Who is this God who chooses a people for himself, through no merit of their own, and then determines to mold them into his own image despite their repeated shortcomings and rebellions? A proper reaction to reading this story is simply to sit back and shake our heads in disbelief. God is beyond our understanding.

A tension that all Christians deal with sooner or later is having an understanding of God while at the same time recognizing that he is always open to directions that we have not anticipated. We feel this tension acutely, for example, when we find ourselves coming to grips with an understanding of a doctrinal issue that at an earlier time we would have found problematic or unorthodox. This tension is often difficult to hold in balance, but it is one that all Christians must try to respect. Knowledge of God is a powerful commodity, which is why it is so susceptible to abuse. It is always a temptation to think that you "understand" who God is and how he works. God has revealed himself to us, to be sure, and most clearly in his Son, but too often the wonder of his revelation is reduced to a narrow dogmatism that has everything in its place. It is the kind of faith that favors heated theological debate rather than unity in love.

For some, it seems that all the mysteries of the gospel and life have been entrusted to *them*. This is not just a danger for famous Christian thinkers (or cult leaders!) who make their livelihood from expounding the deep mysteries of the gospel, but for everyone. We all know Christians like this and, if we are honest, we would admit to similar transgressions. Yet there are others for whom the Christian life is shrouded in mystery to the point that dogma is an intrusion. Although theological systems have been exploited to the detriment of the gospel, it is also true that eschewing any sort of theological system can be detrimental to one's faith. Such a view emphasizes the mystery of the gospel so that its revelatory content is not taken seriously.

The lessons of the plague narrative are a merciful slap in the face to both these extremes. The plagues are revelation. They are not done in private, but for all the world to see. They tell us, in no uncertain terms, who God is and what he can do. But God's dealings with Pharaoh are also beyond our understanding. They cannot be contained in a series of tidy propositions handed down like a math formula or grocery list. We have in the Bible at once the openness of God and his hiddenness. The paradox we see hinted at already in the plagues is fully embodied in Christ, for the fullness of God dwells in him (Col. 1:19), but he is also like us in every way (Heb. 2:17).

All those who "have come to share in Christ" (Heb. 3:14) share in this tension, and we would do well to keep this in mind as we journey toward a deeper knowledge of Almighty God. God is in our midst, yet he is beyond us. We should be humble in our knowledge, for we are dealing with a God of boundless depth, who has creation at his fingertips. But we must also be bold in our limited understanding, for the same God has gone to great lengths to make himself known to us.

Exodus 11:1–13:16

ᶹ

NOW THE Lord had said to Moses, "I will bring one more plague on Pharaoh and on Egypt. After that, he will let you go from here, and when he does, he will drive you out completely. ²Tell the people that men and women alike are to ask their neighbors for articles of silver and gold." ³(The LORD made the Egyptians favorably disposed toward the people, and Moses himself was highly regarded in Egypt by Pharaoh's officials and by the people.)

⁴So Moses said, "This is what the LORD says: 'About midnight I will go throughout Egypt. ⁵Every firstborn son in Egypt will die, from the firstborn son of Pharaoh, who sits on the throne, to the firstborn son of the slave girl, who is at her hand mill, and all the firstborn of the cattle as well. ⁶There will be loud wailing throughout Egypt—worse than there has ever been or ever will be again. ⁷But among the Israelites not a dog will bark at any man or animal.' Then you will know that the LORD makes a distinction between Egypt and Israel. ⁸All these officials of yours will come to me, bowing down before me and saying, 'Go, you and all the people who follow you!' After that I will leave." Then Moses, hot with anger, left Pharaoh.

⁹The LORD had said to Moses, "Pharaoh will refuse to listen to you—so that my wonders may be multiplied in Egypt." ¹⁰Moses and Aaron performed all these wonders before Pharaoh, but the LORD hardened Pharaoh's heart, and he would not let the Israelites go out of his country.

¹²:¹The LORD said to Moses and Aaron in Egypt, ²"This month is to be for you the first month, the first month of your year. ³Tell the whole community of Israel that on the tenth day of this month each man is to take a lamb for his family, one for each household. ⁴If any household is too small for a whole lamb, they must share one with their nearest neighbor, having taken into account the number of people there are. You are to determine the amount of lamb needed in accordance with what each person will eat. ⁵The animals you choose must be year-old males without defect, and you may take them from the sheep or the goats. ⁶Take care of them

until the fourteenth day of the month, when all the people of the community of Israel must slaughter them at twilight. ⁷Then they are to take some of the blood and put it on the sides and tops of the doorframes of the houses where they eat the lambs. ⁸That same night they are to eat the meat roasted over the fire, along with bitter herbs, and bread made without yeast. ⁹Do not eat the meat raw or cooked in water, but roast it over the fire—head, legs and inner parts. ¹⁰Do not leave any of it till morning; if some is left till morning, you must burn it. ¹¹This is how you are to eat it: with your cloak tucked into your belt, your sandals on your feet and your staff in your hand. Eat it in haste; it is the LORD's Passover.

¹²"On that same night I will pass through Egypt and strike down every firstborn—both men and animals—and I will bring judgment on all the gods of Egypt. I am the LORD. ¹³The blood will be a sign for you on the houses where you are; and when I see the blood, I will pass over you. No destructive plague will touch you when I strike Egypt.

¹⁴"This is a day you are to commemorate; for the generations to come you shall celebrate it as a festival to the LORD— a lasting ordinance. ¹⁵For seven days you are to eat bread made without yeast. On the first day remove the yeast from your houses, for whoever eats anything with yeast in it from the first day through the seventh must be cut off from Israel. ¹⁶On the first day hold a sacred assembly, and another one on the seventh day. Do no work at all on these days, except to prepare food for everyone to eat—that is all you may do.

¹⁷"Celebrate the Feast of Unleavened Bread, because it was on this very day that I brought your divisions out of Egypt. Celebrate this day as a lasting ordinance for the generations to come. ¹⁸In the first month you are to eat bread made without yeast, from the evening of the fourteenth day until the evening of the twenty-first day. ¹⁹For seven days no yeast is to be found in your houses. And whoever eats anything with yeast in it must be cut off from the community of Israel, whether he is an alien or native-born. ²⁰Eat nothing made with yeast. Wherever you live, you must eat unleavened bread."

²¹Then Moses summoned all the elders of Israel and said to them, "Go at once and select the animals for your families and slaughter the Passover lamb. ²²Take a bunch of hyssop, dip it into the blood in the basin and put some of the blood on the

top and on both sides of the doorframe. Not one of you shall go out the door of his house until morning. ²³When the LORD goes through the land to strike down the Egyptians, he will see the blood on the top and sides of the doorframe and will pass over that doorway, and he will not permit the destroyer to enter your houses and strike you down.

²⁴"Obey these instructions as a lasting ordinance for you and your descendants. ²⁵When you enter the land that the LORD will give you as he promised, observe this ceremony. ²⁶And when your children ask you, 'What does this ceremony mean to you?' ²⁷then tell them, 'It is the Passover sacrifice to the LORD, who passed over the houses of the Israelites in Egypt and spared our homes when he struck down the Egyptians.'" Then the people bowed down and worshiped. ²⁸The Israelites did just what the LORD commanded Moses and Aaron.

²⁹At midnight the LORD struck down all the firstborn in Egypt, from the firstborn of Pharaoh, who sat on the throne, to the firstborn of the prisoner, who was in the dungeon, and the firstborn of all the livestock as well. ³⁰Pharaoh and all his officials and all the Egyptians got up during the night, and there was loud wailing in Egypt, for there was not a house without someone dead.

³¹During the night Pharaoh summoned Moses and Aaron and said, "Up! Leave my people, you and the Israelites! Go, worship the LORD as you have requested. ³²Take your flocks and herds, as you have said, and go. And also bless me."

³³The Egyptians urged the people to hurry and leave the country. "For otherwise," they said, "we will all die!" ³⁴So the people took their dough before the yeast was added, and carried it on their shoulders in kneading troughs wrapped in clothing. ³⁵The Israelites did as Moses instructed and asked the Egyptians for articles of silver and gold and for clothing. ³⁶The LORD had made the Egyptians favorably disposed toward the people, and they gave them what they asked for; so they plundered the Egyptians.

³⁷The Israelites journeyed from Rameses to Succoth. There were about six hundred thousand men on foot, besides women and children. ³⁸Many other people went up with them, as well as large droves of livestock, both flocks and herds. ³⁹With the dough they had brought from Egypt, they baked cakes of unleavened bread. The dough was without yeast

because they had been driven out of Egypt and did not have time to prepare food for themselves.

⁴⁰Now the length of time the Israelite people lived in Egypt was 430 years. ⁴¹At the end of the 430 years, to the very day, all the LORD's divisions left Egypt. ⁴²Because the LORD kept vigil that night to bring them out of Egypt, on this night all the Israelites are to keep vigil to honor the LORD for the generations to come.

⁴³The LORD said to Moses and Aaron, "These are the regulations for the Passover:

No foreigner is to eat of it. ⁴⁴Any slave you have bought may eat of it after you have circumcised him, ⁴⁵but a temporary resident and a hired worker may not eat of it.

⁴⁶"It must be eaten inside one house; take none of the meat outside the house. Do not break any of the bones. ⁴⁷The whole community of Israel must celebrate it.

⁴⁸"An alien living among you who wants to celebrate the LORD's Passover must have all the males in his household circumcised; then he may take part like one born in the land. No uncircumcised male may eat of it. ⁴⁹The same law applies to the native-born and to the alien living among you."

⁵⁰All the Israelites did just what the LORD had commanded Moses and Aaron. ⁵¹And on that very day the LORD brought the Israelites out of Egypt by their divisions.

¹³:¹The LORD said to Moses, ²"Consecrate to me every first-born male. The first offspring of every womb among the Israelites belongs to me, whether man or animal."

³Then Moses said to the people, "Commemorate this day, the day you came out of Egypt, out of the land of slavery, because the LORD brought you out of it with a mighty hand. Eat nothing containing yeast. ⁴Today, in the month of Abib, you are leaving. ⁵When the LORD brings you into the land of the Canaanites, Hittites, Amorites, Hivites and Jebusites—the land he swore to your forefathers to give you, a land flowing with milk and honey—you are to observe this ceremony in this month: ⁶For seven days eat bread made without yeast and on the seventh day hold a festival to the LORD. ⁷Eat unleavened bread during those seven days; nothing with yeast in it is to be seen among you, nor shall any yeast be seen anywhere within your borders. ⁸On that day tell your son, 'I do this because of what the LORD did for me when I came out of

Egypt.' ⁹This observance will be for you like a sign on your hand and a reminder on your forehead that the law of the LORD is to be on your lips. For the LORD brought you out of Egypt with his mighty hand. ¹⁰You must keep this ordinance at the appointed time year after year.

¹¹"After the LORD brings you into the land of the Canaanites and gives it to you, as he promised on oath to you and your forefathers, ¹²you are to give over to the LORD the first offspring of every womb. All the firstborn males of your livestock belong to the LORD. ¹³Redeem with a lamb every firstborn donkey, but if you do not redeem it, break its neck. Redeem every firstborn among your sons.

¹⁴"In days to come, when your son asks you, 'What does this mean?' say to him, 'With a mighty hand the LORD brought us out of Egypt, out of the land of slavery. ¹⁵When Pharaoh stubbornly refused to let us go, the LORD killed every firstborn in Egypt, both man and animal. This is why I sacrifice to the LORD the first male offspring of every womb and redeem each of my firstborn sons.' ¹⁶And it will be like a sign on your hand and a symbol on your forehead that the LORD brought us out of Egypt with his mighty hand."

PROPERLY CONSIDERED, THIS entire section deals with the tenth plague. The accounts of the previous nine plagues typically include (with exceptions noted in the previous section) not only the announcement of the plague, but also its execution, its effect, and Pharaoh's reaction. Exodus 11:1–10 announces the tenth plague, but its execution and the distinction made between the Egyptians and the Israelites (Passover) do not come until 12:29–30. For the result of the plague, which is Pharaoh's release of the Israelites, we must wait until 12:31–42.

More important, the regulations for the Passover and Feast of Unleavened Bread (12:1–28, 43–51) and the laws concerning the consecration of the firstborn (13:1–16) are not an excursus or a digression, nor are they merely legal baggage tacked onto the narrative of the departure from Egypt. Rather, these regulations are integrally related to this plague. It is contrary to the flow of the narrative to subdivide this section into smaller units.

The problem this leaves us with, however, is that, like the nine plagues treated in the previous section, the narrative of the tenth plague is a large chunk of text to use as a basis for a Sunday sermon. Although probably one will not read and preach on this entire section at one time (it is certainly suitable for a series of Bible studies or Sunday school classes), the integrity of the *theology* of this plague, which should form the basis for any sermon or lesson, would be lost, or at least misplaced, if it is not treated together. The inspired text does not always easily conform to a neat thirty-minute exposition. It is better if we conform our expectations to the text rather than the other way around.

The Announcement of the Tenth Plague (11:1–10)

THE TENTH PLAGUE is the climax of the plague narrative, as God himself announces: "I will bring one more plague" (11:1). The announcement of this plague should be read in light of 4:21–23, where God had previously told Moses what would ultimately happen to Egypt. This also helps make sense of the fact that Moses and Pharaoh apparently have a conversation in 11:4–8 after they have both vowed that they will never see each other again (10:28–29). The NIV correctly translates the verb of verse 1 as a pluperfect, "Now the LORD *had said* to Moses," that is, previously in 4:21–23. The conversation between Moses and Pharaoh that follows is, therefore, simply a continuation of the conversation of 10:24–29. It is as if, while leaving, Moses turns to Pharaoh and says, "Oh yes, one more thing before I go." With the announcement of the tenth plague, the confrontation between the two is ended. They will meet once again, but only for Pharaoh to capitulate fully to Moses' demand to release the Israelites (12:31–32).

But this plague is not an afterthought. It is the mighty act of God that finally results directly in the Israelites' departure from Egypt, which is the goal to which the narrative has been leading. It is the only plague for which there is no hope of reversal. It is the final blow for which God has been setting Pharaoh up since his first encounter with Moses.

The significance of this plague may be seen in part that Pharaoh is considered a son of the sun god Re in Egyptian religion—a fact that lends some continuity between the ninth and tenth plagues. This plague can be construed as an attack on Pharaoh's power. Zevit adds that it may also be an implicit attack on Osiris, the Egyptian god of the dead.[1] Yahweh demonstrates by killing the firstborn Egyptians that he, unlike the son of god Pharaoh, is the true God, the one who truly has power over death and life. A final hint that the tenth plague is a polemic against Egyptian religion may perhaps be seen at the end of verse 5, with explicit mention made that the cattle, too, will be affected, since cattle were "objects of Egyptian veneration."[2]

---

1. Zevit, "Three Ways to Look at the Ten Plagues," 21.
2. Sarna, *Exodus*, 52.

In addition to the connection with the ninth plague, the death of the Egyptian firstborn takes us back to the first chapter of Exodus. In 11:4, Moses warns Pharaoh that God is coming[3] at midnight to kill the firstborn of Egypt. This is clearly retribution for Pharaoh's attempt to kill the male children of Israel in chapter 1. His decree was ultimately not against *Israel's* children, but against *God's* children. God will now respond in kind by putting to death the firstborn children of Egypt. God's decree, like Pharaoh's, will even affect the "firstborn son of the slave girl" (v. 5). He will make no distinction. Even "innocent bystanders," such as lowly servants, will feel the sting of death.

So thorough and devastating will God's action be that the Egyptians will beg the Israelites to leave. Moreover, they will be "favorably disposed" toward them,[4] so that God's people will leave with more than what they came with. Now it will be Egypt's turn to "cry" because of *their* oppression (the use of *ṣᵉᶜaqah* [cry] in v. 6 is an echo of Israel's cry in 3:7). Among the Israelites, however, not even a barking dog will be heard. The tenth plague is clearly a "measure-for-measure" punishment.

Verses 9—10 summarize both what has gone before and what will soon come about. Pharaoh's heart has been hardened by God *for the very purpose* that the Lord's "wonders may be multiplied in Egypt" (v. 9). What is about to happen will fulfill his plan on a level much deeper than simply retribution for the king's actions. Rather, Pharaoh is being used by God. His actions have been scripted so that God can execute his plan.

Regulations for the Passover and Feast of Unleavened Bread (12:1–28)

THE DRAMA OF the departure from Egypt gives way to what seems like a liturgical interlude. But, as noted above, this is much more than an aside or an intrusion of legal, ritualistic mumbo jumbo. It is the institution of a powerful, everlasting observance whereby God's love for his people Israel will be remembered—indeed, reenacted—until the end of time. These verses go into considerable detail concerning the Passover meal and the Feast of Unleavened Bread, the week-long festival that follows Passover after the Israelites have settled in the land.

---

3. In 12:23, reference is made to "the destroyer" rather than simply to God. The plague is apparently personified. The reference is not, however, to an "angel of death," as this character is commonly named. No such character is mentioned in the narrative.

4. What this means is not entirely clear. Does it mean that the Egyptians now "like" the Israelites? Are they merely sympathetic? Gispen suggests that they respond in "servile fear" (*Exodus*, 112).

The purpose of these celebrations is clearly for the benefit of those generations who did not participate in the Exodus itself, a trajectory already hinted at in 10:2 (referring to the children and grandchildren of the Exodus generation—a point repeated throughout chapters 12–13). Yahweh's acts on behalf of his people are never meant to be anything less than acts that transcend time and space. There is more to the Exodus than simply delivering slaves from Egypt. God's field of vision is far and broad.

When one takes a step back and looks at these rituals afresh, ignoring if possible years of familiarity, they are strange indeed. At a specifically prescribed time, every household is to observe scrupulously a series of regulations concerning the celebration of the Passover meal. It is to be observed on what has become the first month, the *new* first month (Abib; cf. 13:4).[5] The deliverance from Egypt is a new beginning for Israel; from now on, every glance at the calendar will remind them of this fact. It also provides a connection to Genesis and creation. At the Exodus, God's people are being "re-created"; they are starting over with a fresh slate.[6]

At this prescribed time, each household is to take a one-year-old male lamb, without defect.[7] If any house is too small to consume an entire lamb, neighbors are to share. Moreover, the blood of the young lamb is to be drained into a basin (12:22), a hyssop branch is to be dipped into it, and the tops and sides of the doorframes are to be painted with the blood. This will be a sign that the occupants of that house are placing themselves under God's protection and so will be spared.

Furthermore, they are to "roast" the meat and eat it with "bitter herbs" (12:8) and "bread made without yeast" (12:15). In other words, raw or boiled meat should not be eaten. The significance of bitter herbs is not made explicit, although it is tempting to see in them a reminder of the "bitter" service of the Israelites in 1:14 (the Hebrew root *mrr*, bitter, is used in both places). We are

---

5. Abib is the first month of the sacred calendar; its name is of Canaanite origin. Elsewhere the same month is referred to as Nisan (Neh. 2:1; Est. 3:7), which is of Babylonian origin.

6. Such an approach to understanding Ex. 12:1–2 enjoys ancient support. The Samaritan work *Memar Marqah* (a lengthy midrash on Moses and the Exodus, dating perhaps to the second to the fourth century A.D.) is just one example of the close relationship between creation and deliverance. Commenting explicitly on Ex. 12:1–2 we read: " ... the beginning of the months is made like The Beginning [*b'rešit*, which is the first word in Gen. 1:1], which was made the start of creation" (J. MacDonald, *Memar Marqah: The Teaching of Marqah* [BZAW 84; Berlin: Alfred Töpelmann, 1963], 2:31).

7. This regulation seems to suggest that God deserves the best of the flock. One can easily imagine an ancient Israelite's temptation to keep the best for himself and offer a less desirable animal to God. Such an offering, according to Lev. 22:18–25, is unacceptable. Still, the specific reasons for *why* such animals are unacceptable are not made explicit.

told of the symbolic significance of the bread made without yeast: The journey is to be made in haste, so there is no time to let the dough rise (see also
12:17—20). This meal is to be called "Passover" (*pesaḥ*), while it is being celebrated, God will bring judgment on Egypt and their gods (12:12).

Such a celebration may be strange to our ears, but it was to become the
defining ritual in Jewish self-identity. Even though the regulations listed here
for the Passover and Feast may seem somewhat cryptic, the Exodus generation apparently needed no further clarification. This has led scholars to argue
that these celebrations were not *founded* as a response to the tenth plague
and the departure from Egypt, but were *adaptations* of cultic rituals that preceded this generation, that is, festivals that were celebrated by seminomadic
Semitic peoples at various places and times and adapted *on the basis of the Exodus experience.* Such an understanding makes a certain degree of sense of the
biblical evidence, for sacrifice and other rituals were commonplace in the
ancient world. There may indeed have been a certain preunderstanding on
the part of the Israelites within which these regulations made sense.

In fact, even the name "Passover" argues for the meal's antiquity. The
meaning of the word is not entirely clear here.[8] It is used elsewhere in the Old
Testament for being lame or limping. Is this what the word means in Exodus
12? Or should it be translated "to skip," which seems somewhat of a compromise between its more common meaning and that assumed in the
"Passover" narrative? The root also exists outside of the Old Testament. In
Akkadian it is used in the sense of appeasing.[9] Some argue that the cultic overtones of this meaning fit better with the significance of the Passover meal in
Exodus (the blood on the door posts appeased God's wrath). Still others
argue that protection does more justice to the original sense of the word.[10]
It is reasonable to argue, as many do, that *pesaḥ* came to be called "Passover"
in view of what God in fact did that fateful night: He passed the Israelite
houses by/over, thereby protecting them.

This possibility that these central rituals in Israelite religion were adaptations of preexisting ancient Near Eastern rituals should not be dismissed too
readily, nor should it be a cause for concern. True, understanding them *merely*
as reflexes of ancient Near Eastern custom is incorrect, for such a view fails
to account for the theological significance attached to them.[11] Still, it is not

---

8. The noun form is used in 12:11, the verb form in 12:13, 23.

9. See Plastaras, *The God of Exodus*, 150–51.

10. T. F. Glasson, "The 'Passover,' a Misnomer: The Meaning of the Verb *Pasach*," *JTS*
ns 10 (1959): 79–84. M. G. Kline argues that the better translation is to "hover over" or
"cover over" ("The Feast of Cover-Over," *JETS* 37 [1994]: 497–510).

11. T. D. Alexander, "The Passover Sacrifice," *Sacrifice in the Bible*, ed. R. T. Beckwith and
M. J. Selman (Grand Rapids: Baker, 1995), 16–18.

too difficult to see Israelites transforming an ancient Near Eastern ritual, under God's direction, for their own particular purposes. This is given even more credence when we remember that a transformation of the Passover is precisely what Jesus did when he instituted the Last Supper (see Bridging Contexts section below).

The focus of this section of Exodus, however, is not simply on the regulations. This celebration is to be a lasting, eternal ordinance. Passover is not just an event, and it is not just for one night. The Israelites from now on are to remember this night, impress it on their collective consciousness, and pass it on to their children (12:26–27). It is a reminder not just of what God has done but of what he continues to do. In fact, it is more than simply remembering: Passover is a night of "watching," as we read later in 12:42. Israelites are forevermore to "keep vigil to honor the LORD," even as he "kept vigil that night" to deliver them from slavery. By celebrating the Passover and the Feast, God's people in some mysterious sense participate in the Exodus themselves, a point that is still remembered in Passover celebrations to this day: "In every generation a man must so regard himself as if he came forth himself out of Egypt."[12]

Not just the rituals themselves but the regulations too are clearly future-oriented. The first Passover was celebrated in haste (v. 11) on the same night in which God struck the Egyptian firstborn (v. 12). The Feast, however, calls for an extended festival, lasting seven days (vv. 15, 19). Such a command clearly has future generations in mind, since a *hasty* Passover that entails a *seven-day* Feast to follow makes little sense. The future orientation of the writer is evident.

The Departure From Egypt (12:29–42)

THE LENGTHY, REPETITIVE account of the regulations for the Passover and the Feast of Unleavened Bread gives way once again to the narrative of the departure from Egypt.[13] As with the accounts of the other plagues, we are told that God's threat is made good (vv. 29–30). Loud wailing (*seʿaqah*, see v. 6; also 3:6) is heard throughout Egypt. This prompts Pharaoh, once again, to call for Israel's release (vv. 31–32). He has done so before (9:27–28; 10:16), but here there is a new sense of urgency, for he calls to them at night, right then and there, without a moment to lose, saying as it were: "Just get out! Take what you want, but just get out!"

This is total capitulation on Pharaoh's part. Even the people "urge" the Israelites to leave at once (v. 33), which they do, but not before they plunder

---

12. *m. Pesaḥim* 10:5 (H. Danby, *The Mishnah* [Oxford: Clarendon, 1933], 151).

13. As Fretheim rightly puts it, "Liturgical material flows into the event and away from it" (*Exodus*, 136).

the Egyptians. The precise nature of this plundering has been debated since before the time of Christ. Some consider it was improper for Israelites, a holy people, to plunder anyone, even the Egyptians. Some, however, retort that any material gain the Israelites might receive is a fitting reward for their years of abject slavery.[14] The general thrust of this statement should not be lost, however: The Israelites march out of Egypt through the front door, with dignity—not like dogs crawling through the back fence, but like God's people. This exaltation of Israel is another humiliation for Egypt.

It is important to note that bread made without yeast is mentioned again in verses 34 and 39. The repetition of the regulations for both the Passover and the Feast throughout 12:1—28, in addition to Israel's obedience in following the commands regarding the unleavened bread, underscore how inextricably bound the rituals are to the departure itself. This is especially striking in verses 37—42, which at first glance seem simply to summarize the initial stages of Israel's departure (vv. 37—38) and the length of Israel's stay in Egypt as a whole (vv. 40—41). This summary is twice "interrupted" by remarking how faithfully the Israelites follow their new rituals. The theology of this narrative will not allow us to separate the departure from Egypt from the rituals that remind the people of the lasting significance of that event.

Two numbers are mentioned in this summary statement, both of which have engendered discussion. (1) We are told that "six hundred thousand men" leave, not including women and children (v. 37). This number is probably not symbolic, but a round number for 603,550 (38:26; see also Num. 1:46).[15] Most commentators, however, mention that such a large number would require a total population of roughly two million, a number that the archaeological data do not support. So, is this number inaccurate, an exaggeration designed to bolster Israelite morale? N. Sarna offers an interesting solution, arguing that the number represents an accurate, historical picture, but of the population at the time of the united monarchy.[16] Like most of Sarna's observations, this is worthy of thoughtful consideration, but it is not clear how this solution supports the historicity of Exodus 12:37, since there the six hundred thousand are clearly connected to the departure from Egypt.

---

14. This ancient tradition may be found, e.g., in *Jub.* 48:18 (2d cent. B.C.), Philo's *De vita Mosis* 1.141 (late 1st cent. B.C. to early 1st century A.D.), and Ezekiel the Tragedian's *Exagoge* 162—66 (late 2d century B.C.).

15. A balanced treatment on the problem of large numbers in the Old Testament is D. M. Fouts, "A Defense of the Hyperbolic Interpretation of Large Numbers in the Old Testament," *JETS* 40 (1997): 377—87.

16. *Exodus*, 62. See also Sarna's *Exploring Exodus*, 94—102. Durham also includes a discussion of the problem (*Exodus*, 171—72).

If anything, Sarna's solution reminds us just how difficult this number is to reconcile with our notions of historical accuracy. That a large number of Israelites departs is expected, since it was their rapid growth that caused Pharaoh to panic in the first place (ch. 1). But what are we to make of this number? It seems best for us to remain agnostic on this matter.

(2) The second number is the 430-year stay in Egypt. Is this an exact number? It seems so, since the four hundred years spoken of in Genesis 15:13 (cf. Acts 7:6) is most likely a round number. Note too the emphatic point made that the Israelites left Egypt 430 years "to the very day" after they entered (Ex. 12:41). But if this is an exact number, it raises the question why a round number six hundred thousand has just been used above. We have come to expect our author to use nonliteral numbers. Recall, too, the genealogy of chapter 6, which refers to four generations from Levi to Aaron—clearly an example of a telescoped genealogy. When all is said and done, how these numbers are to be understood is not clear.[17]

Additional Regulations (12:43–13:16)

IN 12:43–49 WE are given additional Passover regulations. Here again the narrative of the departure is interwoven with liturgical stipulations. The regulations concerning foreigners seem to reflect the fact that non-Israelites left Egypt along with the Israelites (see 12:38: "Many other people went up with them").[18] The Hebrew word translated "other people" is *ʿereb*, which likely indicates an ethnic mixture of peoples. Non-Israelites are not excluded from the meal simply on the basis of their ethnicity. They must, however, put themselves under the sign of the covenant (i.e., circumcision) in order to participate.

We have here an attractive mixture of exclusivism and, ultimately, universalism. This is another hint that God's purpose for bringing the Israelites out of Egypt is for a broader purpose. Although God has throughout made a distinction between the Israelites and the Egyptians, those who are willing may nevertheless partake of this holy celebration, thus forming a "mixed crowd" (12:38, NRSV). The appeal to circumcision also emphasizes that, although the meal is to be celebrated inside the home, it is more properly considered a community affair. This is not private worship. It is a community of believers bound by circumcision to their covenant God.

---

17. A more detailed discussion of this issue, in addition to those found in the commentaries, may be found in P. J. Ray Jr., "The Duration of the Israelite Sojourn in Egypt," *AUSS* 24 (1986): 231–48.

18. J. Hoffmeier argues that this mixed crowd may have included non-Israelites enslaved by the Egyptians after the so-called Hyksos expulsion around 1550 B.C. ("The Evangelical Contribution to Understanding the [Early] History of Ancient Israel in Recent Scholarship," *BBR* 7 [1997]: 84).

The regulations concerning foreigners clearly pertain to the Israelites only after they have left Egypt. Like so much of this chapter, these regulations are future-oriented. For example, mention of foreign slaves, temporary residents, and hired workers is not applicable to the Israelites while they are slaves themselves. In light of this, 12:50–51 does not seem to refer to Israel's obedience regarding the regulations that are given immediately before. Rather, this statement seems intended as an object lesson for *future* generations, for whom the foregoing regulations are actually relevant. Future generations, looking back at the forebears' obedience, are expected to follow suit, a factor that may suggest a point in time in which this narrative was written down in its final form.[19]

After the reiteration and expansion of the Passover regulations in 12:43–49, 13:1–16 reiterates and expands on the regulations concerning the Feast of Unleavened Bread (vv. 3–10) and the future consecration of the firstborn (vv. 11–16). However redundant such repetition may seem to us, these regulations form the heart of the Exodus story. This section specifies that the new first month is the month of Abib (12:2), corresponding to our late March and early April. Verse 5 articulates what has been hinted at earlier, that these more detailed regulations are for future generations: "When the LORD brings you into the land of the Canaanites ... you are to observe this ceremony in this month." They do not enter the land for another forty years, and when they do, only Joshua and Caleb are left from those who witnessed the Exodus.

The Feast of Unleavened Bread is to be scrupulously observed, and its meaning is to be impressed on the children from generation to generation. The ceremony will be "like a sign on your hand and a reminder on your forehead" (v. 9). It will be a mark, for all to see, of who they are. This statement gave rise to the use of phylacteries (see Matt. 23:5), which are still used by observant Jews today.[20] They are always to remember who they are—or better, *whose* they are. Israel's identity is a function of what God has done for them.

Likewise, after they enter the land, they must be careful to consecrate to God the firstborn of every womb in Israel, whether human or animal, a point made plain later in 22:29–30. We should understand this ritual in light of the tenth plague itself: Israel as God's son (see 4:22) was redeemed (delivered from Egypt) by the death of Egypt's firstborn sons. There is also a parallel between the tenth plague and the mention of the donkey in 13:13. Rather than being

---

19. The Passover, however, is celebrated again one year after the Exodus (Num. 9:1–14). Like the first Passover, this celebration, since it occurred before the settlement of the land, cannot have followed the full extent of the regulations.

20. See also Deut. 6:8–9. Phylacteries are small leather boxes tied to the forehead and left arm. In these boxes are strips of parchment on which are written Ex. 13:1–16; Deut. 6:4–6 (the famous "Shema"); and 11:13–21.

sacrificed itself, a donkey is to be redeemed (replaced) with the sacrifice of a lamb, just as Israel was redeemed (replaced) with the blood of a lamb. In fact, the parallel can be taken a step further. We may think of the Egyptian firstborn as "redeeming" (replacing) the Israelites (for more on this, see the Bridging Contexts section).

The point is that the firstborn of every womb belongs to God, but in the case of the Israelites he will not claim his right fully; a substitute will take their place. These ceremonies are to be observed through all generations as a reminder, in this case a graphic reminder, of the lengths God will go to save his children—his firstborn son, Israel. We see, then, a hint of what becomes clearer almost fifteen hundred years later on a cross near Jerusalem: Life comes from death, or better, life can *only* come from death. The tenth plague was not a divine temper tantrum where God flexes his muscles before the Egyptians and really lets them have it. It is the necessary implementation of a redemptive pattern, one that requires death as a means to fuller life. The consecration of the firstborn, therefore, is a reminder of the once-for-all substitutionary death of the beloved firstborn son who is to come.

GOD'S RIGHT TO THE FIRSTBORN. The tenth plague and the ensuing departure from Egypt are to be seared into the Israelites' memories for "generations to come" (12:14). The purpose of the Passover and Feast of Unleavened Bread is not a one-time celebration but a provision for the future. This future orientation can be seen by the fact that Passover and the Feast are recorded in subsequent Old Testament passages. In Numbers 9:1–5, the Israelites celebrated the Passover in the Sinai desert one year after the Exodus, thus fulfilling the commands outlined in Exodus 12 to observe the ritual on a yearly basis. The Passover regulations are reiterated in Leviticus 23:4–8; Numbers 28:16–25; and Deuteronomy 16:1–8, but there is no other record of any celebration of the meal until the entrance into the Promised Land, about forty years later.

The rebellion of the Israelites in the desert (Num. 14) prompts Yahweh to make that generation wander through the desert until every adult member has died, except for Caleb and Joshua. During this period of God's wrath, the celebration of Passover would certainly have been out of place. Joshua 5:10 records the first Passover celebration after the forty-year desert wandering. It coincides with the crossing of the Jordan River (Josh. 3–4), where, as in the Exodus, a body of water parts to allow the Israelites to pass through to a new beginning.

Deuteronomy 16:1–8 seems to represent a shift in how the Passover is to be celebrated, for the meal is to be observed in "the place the LORD will choose as a dwelling for his Name" (16:2)—that is, in the temple in Jerusalem. The meal has moved from a family observance in homes to a pilgrimage feast that requires all Israelites to come to Jerusalem (see, as examples, 2 Chron. 30:1–31:1, during Hezekiah's day [715–686 B.C.], and 2 Kings 23:21–23; 2 Chron. 35:1–19, during the time of Josiah [640–609 B.C.]). Second Kings 23:22 observes that the Passover as it was celebrated by Josiah had not taken place "since the days of the judges who led Israel, nor throughout the days of the kings of Israel and the kings of Judah," a comment indicating the scrupulousness with which Josiah attempted to adhere to the Mosaic regulations of Deuteronomy. The next recorded Passover occurs in Ezra 6:19–22 (516 B.C.), after the return from Babylonian exile and the rebuilding of the temple.

In other words, despite the various twists and turns we find in the Old Testament,[21] the Passover celebration is recorded in passages that reflect various stages in Israel's journey from Egypt, to Canaan, to the Exile, and back to her homeland. Passover and the accompanying Feast of Unleavened Bread remained an abiding feature in Israel's relationship with the God of the Exodus, a means whereby the people would remember what God had done for them. It was a celebration of Israel's redemption from Egypt, which they ought not to forget, for their departure constituted the inception of their existence as a nation.

Nor must Israel forget the terrible means by which that redemption was enacted. The sacrifice of the Passover lamb is a constant reminder to Israel that their life came from death. They must also remember that the firstborn of the womb belongs to God. It is his by right and he may do with it as he pleases. The "destroyer" (i.e., the tenth plague) was not a random type of punishment; it was directed against the *Egyptian firstborn*. This is significant. Not only was the tenth plague a payback for Pharaoh's decree to kill the Israelite children in chapter 1, but it was God's exercising his divine right over the firstborn. The Passover is not *simply* a matter of a lamb replacing the Israelites' firstborn. It is also God purchasing, so to speak, the redemption of his firstborn son Israel through the death of the Egyptian firstborn, since it was precisely this catastrophe that led Pharaoh to call for Israel's release.

---

21. A side-by-side comparison of the various passages that treat the Passover regulations reveals a number of divergences. A discussion of this phenomenon would take us far from our topic. Most commentaries deal with this at some level; see esp. A. J. Saldarini, *Jesus and Passover* (New York: Paulist, 1984), 1–15.

There is a further dimension of this ritual that warrants discussion. The destroyer's mission was blind to ethnic distinctions. Had an Israelite family not painted its doorway with the lamb's blood, the destroyer would have killed the firstborn of that household. It was on the basis of the blood, and only on that basis, that the destroyer made the distinction between Israel and Egypt. In other words, the divine right to the firstborn extended to all Israel (see 22:29–30), but that right should not be understood as some vague sense of ownership. God had the right to express his ownership over Israel by killing their firstborn as well. This, it must be admitted in view of the context of this narrative, is the full understanding of what it means for the firstborn to "belong" to God.

And this is why the consecration of the firstborn (13:1, 11–13) is integrally related to the celebration of Passover. Israel is to be redeemed from Egypt, but that redemption requires blood. Both the death of the Egyptian firstborn and the blood of the lamb on the doorposts symbolize God's ownership of the firstborn and his provision to protect his own firstborn son, Israel. Hence, the ritual of redeeming every firstborn donkey with a lamb symbolically represents what God did for Israel in the tenth plague: The firstborn belongs to God and must be bought with a price.

The Passover is the concrete manifestation of a pattern of divine conduct reflected elsewhere in Scripture: The redemption of the firstborn son can only come through death.[22] The idea of "Passover" is not restricted to explicit references to or celebrations of the meal itself. Rather, the *ritual* of Passover finds *narrative* expression at various places in the Old Testament.

The famous story of the binding of Isaac (Gen. 22) illustrates the point. This is an obvious instance of a substitute "sacrifice" being made on behalf of Isaac. Isaac, of course, is the beloved son of Abraham (22:2), and the last-minute intervention of the angel delivers Isaac from death at his own father's hand. This story, if allowed to speak on its own terms, is alarming and should raise a number of questions in our minds. Note that God *commands* Abraham to *sacrifice* Isaac. This is not a false command. Too often we approach this text with the preunderstanding that, since child sacrifice is clearly forbidden elsewhere in Scripture, God cannot possibly mean what he seems to mean. Yet, it *is* a command, and Abraham proceeds *dutifully* to carry it out.

When we read this story in light of the Passover (and vice-versa), we begin to understand what may have motivated the God of Israel to behave

---

22. A stimulating discussion of this theme in the Old Testament, New Testament, and rabbinic literature may be found in Jon D. Levenson, *The Death and Resurrection of the Beloved Son* (New Haven: Yale Univ. Press, 1993). Much of my own thinking has been prompted by Levenson's thoughts.

in this way. The simple fact, once again, is that the firstborn is his by right, a fact stated plainly in Exodus 22:29, "You must give me the first-born of your sons." This command refers to both human offspring and animals, as the following verse implies: "Do the same with your cattle and your sheep" (v. 30). This right extends beyond human and animal off-spring to include the produce of the land, which is why the ancient Israelites had a Feast of Firstfruits, in which the initial harvest was given to God (Lev. 23:9–14). Everything "firstborn" belongs to God and must be given over to him.

God's command to Abraham in Genesis 22 is thus well within his pattern of conduct. In this context we see the heinousness of Pharaoh's decree in Exodus 1 more clearly. By wanting to kill Israel's male children, Pharaoh is not simply killing God's people or reducing the number of potential rebels. The children whom Pharaoh has killed include the *firstborn* of Israel, God's prop-erty, those who will later be shown to be special to God and who belong to him exclusively. By having them thrown into the Nile, Pharaoh is, as we have seen elsewhere, setting himself up as a god-figure. He is doing no less than usurping Yahweh's right to the firstborn.

The episode of the sacrifice of Isaac makes sense only if there is a *real* possibility that the command be carried out. Abraham is commended for fearing God (Gen. 22:12), and, as Jon Levenson puts it, "it is Abraham's *will-ingness to sacrifice his son* that verifies his fear of God."[23] This also helps makes sense of the apparent ease with which Abraham seems to accept the com-mand. This is not to say that it would be easy for him, but that, as far as Abraham is concerned, the thought of God commanding such a thing is perfectly within his right and character. The redemption of Isaac by the ram (22:13), therefore, should be understood as the means by which God exer-cises his right to have Isaac for his own: by offering a replacement.

God's right to the firstborn is what gives meaning to both Genesis 22 and the tenth plague: Israel is God's firstborn, beloved son (Ex. 4:21–23), and he delivers his son from certain death. And he does so not sim-ply by picking the Israelites up and carrying them out of Egypt. The means of their redemption follows a set pattern that culminates in the death of the Egyptian firstborn in the tenth plague, as symbolized by the blood of the lamb.

Another example of this theme concerns the dedication of the Levites to God. According to Numbers 8:5–26, the Levites are to take the place of the firstborn Israelite males (esp. vv. 16–19). True, the passage does not spell out explicitly what it would mean for the Israelite males to be "given" to God and

---

23. Ibid., 13 (his emphasis).

thus in what sense the Levites are taking their place.[24] But the reason the Levites take the place of the firstborn sons is the assumption that the firstborn is God's by right, and in order for God to relinquish that right, a substitute must be provided. In the case of Isaac it is a sacrificial ram. In the case of the Israelite males, it is the Levites who are in charge of the sacrificial system. In the Exodus, God's beloved firstborn son, Israel as a whole, is redeemed through the death of the firstborn of the Egyptians, an event to be commemorated through all time by the yearly, ritualistic sacrifice of a lamb at Passover.

Such an understanding of Passover helps give some sense to that strangest of passages, Exodus 4:24–26, discussed earlier. It is perhaps no accident that the place where Israel's status as firstborn son is propounded (4:21–23) is followed by the circumcision at the lodging place in 4:24–26. The general point to be kept in mind is that through the blood of Moses' son, his circumcision, Moses escapes death. What unites this story and the Passover is that blood is necessary to circumvent a sure death. The story at the lodging place, as noted above, is a preview of sorts of the Passover and release from Egypt. Already here the pattern is hinted at: Without blood, God's purposes will not go forth. The departure from Egypt will not be without a price; a sacrifice will have to be made.

Passover has remained an important, indeed defining, element in Judaism through the centuries. It is likewise with Christianity. There are clear reflexes of the Passover and the consecration of the firstborn in the New Testament.

(1) The Gospel writers closely associate the Last Supper with the Passover.[25] As the Passover was to be a lasting ritualistic representation of God's deliverance of Israel from bondage, the Last Supper is to be a lasting reminder of God's final act of deliverance from a bondage more terrible than slavery to a human despot. This last meal with Jesus' disciples must be seen

---

24. Much of Levenson's book argues that child sacrifice, although forbidden in the Old Testament, was an accepted practice at some early time in Israel's history, reflexes of which can be seen in such stories as the binding of Isaac and the sacrifice of Jephthah's daughter (Judg. 11:29–40). The consecration of the Levites is another example, according to Levenson, of the *transformation* in Judaism of the ritual of the sacrifice of the firstborn son. Levenson's thesis is provocative and well argued, but in-depth interaction is out of place here.

25. Matthew, Mark, and Luke seem to equate the two, since they indicate that the crucifixion occurred on the next day, which was Passover. Hence, the meal the night before, on the day of preparation, was the Passover meal. John, by contrast, indicates that Jesus' crucifixion occurs on the day of preparation, i.e., the day before the Passover, thus putting the meal on the *previous* day, the day before the preparation. In this case, the Last Supper would not have been the Passover meal specifically. Many scholars also hold that at the precise moment at which Jesus was dying on the cross in John, the Passover lamb was being sacrificed in the temple. Despite these differences among the Gospels, it is clear that the writers see some theological connection between the two meals.

in light of his death and resurrection, which follow immediately, just as the Exodus followed the Passover meal. There is no lamb at this meal, however, for Christ is the Lamb, something we are told already at the beginning of his earthly ministry (John 1:29). Rather than the typical diet of lamb and bitter herbs, this consummate Passover meal consists of bread and wine, which represent the body and blood of Christ, the new Lamb. Now that the final Passover Lamb has come, a new meal with new elements is in order.

Moreover, this last meal points not only to the imminent sacrifice of the Lamb of God, but to a future meal, an end-time banquet that will celebrate the final victory of the sacrificed and risen Lamb (Mark 14:25). Israel's redemption, going back to the evening of the tenth plague, begins with a meal and is destined to end so.

(2) The sacrifice of Christ also fulfills the other important element of this theme, the consecration of the beloved firstborn son. Christ is the only Son of his Father. He, like Israel, is the firstborn son in whom the Father's favor rests (cf. Mark 1:11). But here we note an important twist. In the Old Testament it is the beloved son who is redeemed through a substitution of some sort. But Christ, the firstborn Son, is the *means* of redemption. It is in Christ that God actually claims *fully* his right to the firstborn son—he belongs to God. By sacrificing the firstborn Son of God, God's redemption of Israel is now complete.

The great irony is that the *true* firstborn Son is not protected as was Israel, but he has become the enemy of God, as was Egypt. In his death, God's firstborn Son is more like Egypt than Israel in that he bears God's wrath. But three days later he rises to exaltation to fulfill another purpose, the exaltation of Israel. Through this special Son, God fulfills another purpose, the redemption not of Israel the firstborn, but of Israel the "lateborn" (as Levenson puts it). With Christ's death and resurrection the true spiritual pedigree of God's people comes to light. The people of God are *not* firstborn, but they *become* firstborn through their union with Christ, the true firstborn Son.

This exaltation theme is true of God's people even in the Old Testament, as we see already at Israel's beginning. Jacob is not the firstborn of Isaac. Yet he is exalted in God's eyes by choice. The nation of Israel is named after the younger brother of Esau (Gen. 32:28), whom God favors and exalts over the older brother. This is not an isolated theme in the Old Testament. The list of "lateborn" sons who are favored by God reads like a "who's who" of biblical characters: Abel, Isaac, Jacob (Israel), Joseph, David, Gideon, Solomon, to name just a few. Each of these was other than firstborn but was exalted over older siblings for one reason or another.

The death of Christ, the firstborn Son, is what allows God's people, the lateborn son, to be raised to the primary status of the firstborn son. This is why Christ is referred to as the "firstfruits of those who have fallen asleep" (1 Cor. 15:20; cf. also Rom. 8:29, where he is called the "firstborn among many brothers"). The resurrection is the first installment of what is waiting for us. It is by his resurrection that we have become *co-heirs* with Christ; in other words, we have become, like Christ, firstborn children. Redemption is about election, the election of a people who are not firstborn, who are not of any favored status, and the sacrificial death of the true firstborn Son, through whom these lateborn people are adopted to receive the status of the firstborn. The Passover blessing of Israel has been extended to the world. All those who are in Christ, the Passover Lamb, have become God's children.

THE POWER OF RITUAL. The most obvious point of application of the Passover is instituted by Christ himself and concerns the church as a whole: the regular celebration of the Lord's Supper by Christians around the world and through all time. This is not the place to enter into a prolonged discussion of the nature of the Lord's Supper and the most faithful way to celebrate it. Christians have disagreed for centuries about whether the elements are in some mysterious sense the actual body and blood of Christ, merely represent Christ, or serve simply as reminders of Christ. Also, the frequency of the celebration of the Lord's Supper continues to be discussed. In the congregation of which I am a member and serve as an elder, the topic has once again come up whether it is most biblical to serve Communion weekly, monthly, or quarterly. Indeed, if the Passover model is to be followed woodenly, an argument could be made for yearly communion (!), but this does not do justice to the New Testament's transformation of the ritual.

The church's redemption from her "slavery" is a weekly one. Every Sunday we remember the death and resurrection of Christ, our Passover Lamb, so it would seem appropriate to commemorate this redemptive reality by joining it to the appropriate ritual, the Lord's Supper. Jesus, unfortunately, did not make explicit how often we are to "do this in remembrance of me" (Luke 22:19), so it is certainly the wisest course of action not to be dogmatic here.

The broader, more basic aspect should be kept in the foreground. As we celebrate the Lord's Supper, we are celebrating our redemption through Christ and the glory that awaits us. But we should also remember that the Lord's Supper is itself a fulfillment of that Israelite meal at an earlier stage of God's redemptive work. By partaking in Communion, we are participating in the effects of God's redemptive work that he began to execute in

Israel's day and that came to completion on Easter Sunday. It seems, then, that we, like the Israelites, in celebrating the Lord's Supper, are not merely *remembering* what God has done. By partaking of the body and blood of Christ, we are, in some mysterious sense, participating in his death and resurrection.

Like successive generations of Jews called to think of themselves as participating in the Exodus, so, too, does the church participate in the work of Christ by virtue of her union with him. This, of course, is a theological participation, but that does not make it an abstract one. The reality of the church's new, resurrected life in Christ is so powerful, so real, that that fact can only be fittingly branded onto our hearts through an outward act, a symbol, in which we physically participate. The Lord's Supper is not *merely* a symbol of our union with the resurrected Christ, something that is nice to do but is really a "less real" representation of some other reality. It is a ritual *founded by Christ*, in which we as believers bear witness to ourselves and the world that we *are* one.

However individual congregations and denominations work out the particulars, the Lord's Supper is serious business. This is why it is good practice to remind us of what we are doing and for whom the meal is intended. It is not something to be taken lightly by those who are in Christ, nor should it be taken at all by those who do not know him. It is a redemptive meal. I must confess wholeheartedly that I need to be reminded of what the Lord's Supper is and why we partake. We do so not simply because Christ commanded it and we *have* to do it. It goes deeper. We must understand *why* Christ commanded it. It is something that in principle God's people have been doing since that great redemptive act in the Old Testament, the Exodus, and it receives its fuller significance in Christ. Communion is the symbolic representation of the fact that we, in Christ, stand at the highest mountain peak of God's redemptive plan.

Some have argued that the clear debt the Lord's Supper owes to the Passover suggests that this is fruitful common ground for discussing Jewish-Christian relations. I know people on both sides of the equation who are working to understand better the religion of the other. It is, I can say from my own experience (much of my graduate work was under the direction of Jewish scholars), an emotional, complicated, and even unsettling discussion. I do not want to complicate the issue further by making a few reductionistic statements here. Still, I would want to argue that, however much the Lord's Supper and Passover have obvious theological overlap, they cannot be considered so "common" that their distinctives become blurred. For one thing, to suggest that the Lord's Supper can be seen as a point of contact between Christianity and Judaism, since the former arose out of the latter is like arguing that the Jewish Passover should be a point of contact with Canaanite religion, its own likely source (see discussion above).[26]

Nevertheless, it is vital to a proper understanding of the Lord's Supper to see it as a *transformation* of the Passover more than simply as a Christian reflection of Passover. Judaism and Christianity are, after all, two different religions despite their common heritage. Nothing is gained and everything is lost if we obliterate those aspects of the Lord's Supper that make it distinctly Christian—that is, those things that it does not and cannot share with Judaism, namely, a celebration of redemption not only through the God who sent plagues to Egypt, but also through the God who raised Christ from the dead. Although the Lord's Supper is not distinctly Christian in terms of its origins, it is quintessentially Christian in terms of its meaning.

Perhaps the greatest source of commonality between Passover and the Lord's Supper lies in their future orientation: Neither meal is merely for the historical moment in which it was first instituted. These rituals are to be observed for successive generations. Although this is not a constant refrain in the Lord's Supper (the narrative is much briefer than with Passover), Jesus' command that the meal be done in remembrance of him (Luke 22:19) suggests as much. Moreover, the eschatological references in Luke 22:16 and 18 (which refer to the coming of the kingdom of God) imply a continued observance until such time (see also 1 Cor. 11:17–34).

One thing we can learn from this is the importance the Bible places on ritual. The Old Testament repeatedly refers to teaching Israelite children who God is and what he has done.[27] This teaching occurs in the context of ritual, whether it concerns the keeping of the law or the regular observance of Passover. Ritual breeds familiarity. It seeps into one's subconscious and, however subtly, begins to exert a formative influence.

I am reminded here of a graduate school experience that has made a lasting impression on me. I was amazed to see that my Jewish professors had the Pentateuch memorized completely in Hebrew, as well as large portions of the rest of the Old Testament. When asked about a particular passage, one of my professors would pause momentarily, look up at the ceiling, and then recite the passage from memory. I finally asked him how he could memorize so much of the Hebrew Bible. The reason was that from his childhood he had chanted (sung) the Torah in the synagogue. His pause after being asked a question was

---

26. Of course, one would not want to take this argument too far, since there is another, more basic connection between Christianity and Judaism that is not shared between Judaism and Canaanite polytheism: They share the same God.

27. See Ex. 12:26–27; 13:14; Deut. 6:7–9, 20; 32:7; Josh. 4:6. Also important here are those psalms that recount God's past actions, presumably for the benefit of future generations who need to be taught (e.g., Ps. 44; 105; 106).

to chant the passage to himself before he repeated it to the class in prose form! Memorization through chant is not something that happens by means of a mnemonic trick or an interactive Bible CD for your PC to make it "easy." It is gained only through repetition, particularly during one's formative years.

The influence of the familiar on our lives is something that advertisers never forget. The point of advertising is to capitalize on real needs or to create needs and then to provide a product to fill that need. This symbiotic relationship between the perception of need and the perception that that need is filled by purchasing a particular product does not happen by chance. Advertisers work hard at finding out why we spend our money the way we do. The seemingly endless *repetition* of the same commercials is designed not simply to present a product for our consideration. Rather, they are attempting to do nothing less than create a world in which their product holds an important, if not central, place. I am certain that most conservative Christians in America would have an easier time recalling ten commercial jingles by heart, perhaps ones they have not heard for twenty or thirty years, than ten psalms (or five, or three, or one).

Repetition and familiarity work. What is repeated becomes familiar, and this becomes a part of us. Our own culture understands this, but alas, not always the church. Far too many equate ritual with spiritual dryness.[28] True, ritual and liturgy can be dead—even using the terms can raise hackles—but only when the significance and power of those rituals are forgotten. Spiritual death is not a property of ritual itself. To the contrary, ritual has always been and will always be a means of securing for future generations the power and reality of the gospel.

The one ritual that is clearly instituted in the New Testament, and which follows closely upon its rich Old Testament counterpart, is the Lord's Supper. It is a powerful ritual. When we celebrate the Lord's Supper, we are to think of ourselves as "participating" in Christ. We are to understand ourselves as "being there"—not physically, nor even in our imaginations, but in the most powerful way, theologically. Again, this is not "theology" understood as an abstract, academic concept, a subject in school. It is the means by which we are connected to Christ through the centuries as a person who once instituted the meal with his small group of followers. So too, whenever we celebrate the same meal, we are part of the group.

---

28. Gary M. Burge has written a thoughtful article on the necessity of ritual in worship ("Are Evangelicals Missing God at Church? Why So Many Are Rediscovering Worship in Other Traditions," *Christianity Today* [October 6, 1997], 20–27). Burge correctly points out that there seems to be a shift, especially among younger people, to rediscover the importance of liturgy, a phenomenon that is sparking interest, for example, in the Greek Orthodox Church.

Ritual is important because it affects us on a level deeper than other things can. We do not always appreciate this in our world today (although, again, advertisers do). In our secular world, despite deft use of its own kind of "rituals," religious symbols and rituals are seen as poor substitutes for ultimate reality, a relic of a bygone, prescientific age, a crutch for those who cannot come to terms with the notion that "what's real is what you see." Sadly, this is not only something we see in the secular world, but in the church as well. Perhaps it is the stress on personal salvation and one's *own* personal experience of Christ that must be initiated without the mediation of rituals of the past. But the Lord's Supper teaches the exact opposite: Rituals are good, and they are instituted and used by God to "connect" his people with him. We learn through ritual that the church is not just made up of individuals, but is a corporate body. It is not just about personal salvation, but a group of people, the people of God, who are bound to one another and to the faithful through the generations.

One must be careful not to extend the principle of ritual haphazardly beyond this specific example of the New Testament, but one point comes to mind that seems appropriate. In my church, as in many today, we have had some sensitive discussions concerning worship style, particularly the type of music to use in the worship service. As everyone with experience in this subject knows, the matter is complex and requires great patience and love on the part of all involved. The two general poles of the debate can be justly summarized: (1) Traditional worship and older hymns are tried and true and therefore more conducive to worship; (2) contemporary worship and newer songs are more conducive to worship because they connect better to the people where they are.

I admit there are nuances of opinion between these poles. But both extremes should be avoided. Those who espouse the former view have forgotten that something is not good simply because it has been done for a long time.[29] If its meaning has been forgotten, it is transformed quickly from ritual, which is something good, into dead ritual. Likewise, we do not celebrate the Lord's Supper *simply* because it is something that Christians do. There is a deeper purpose behind the act, and understanding that purpose allows us to connect with the ritual itself.

Those who hold to the other opinion, however, are more prevalent in this discussion. Many of this group are younger believers who have had secular upbringings, and, consequently, have not been taught an appreciation of the past. Others may have been brought up in Christian homes, but where tradition was equated with dead ritualism. Hence, any talk of the importance

---

29. Even the great hymns of the church were "contemporary" at one time or another!

of tradition falls on rocky soil or connotes "dryness." They have never seen the *vitality* that can come from a proper respect for tradition, one that does not adhere slavishly to the things of the past, but respects that God's Spirit has been speaking to his people in all generations. Perhaps the former group should learn the same lesson, that since God does have every generation of believers close to his heart, new is not necessarily bad.

Ritual is vital for the life of the church, and the regular, thoughtful celebration of the Lord's Supper is the most concrete reminder of that fact. The principle Christ enacted in the Lord's Supper should be cautiously applied to the life of the church in other areas, while allowing fully for differences of opinion in how that principle should be applied. But whatever is done, the church should have in its view successive generations of believers. We must think ahead, as we are taught to do in the Passover and Lord's Supper. The purpose of ritual is not simply to maintain tradition for its own sake, but, like the Lord's Supper, to drive home in our hearts the experience of being united with the risen Christ. This can be accomplished in a variety of ways, which is reflected in the differing traditions among the various Christian denominations.

Catechism, for instance, was important in my own upbringing. It impressed on me that I am part of a line of believers that extends back for centuries and even millennia. We memorized, among other things, the Nicene and Apostles' Creeds, those great confessions of faith that have withstood the test of time and are recited every Sunday throughout the world. Of course, nothing can lend itself more quickly to dead ritualism than the rote droning of a congregation's recitation of "God of God, Light of Light, Very God of Very God," but this is not the necessary outcome of maintaining rituals.

When we turn to the topic of the application of Passover, attention must be given to 1 Corinthians 5:7–8, for it is here that Paul himself hints, albeit briefly, at this very matter:

> Get rid of the old yeast that you may be a new batch without yeast—as you really are. For Christ, our Passover lamb, has been sacrificed. Therefore let us keep the Festival, not with the old yeast, the yeast of malice and wickedness, but with bread without yeast, the bread of sincerity and truth.

The context of this passage concerns the expulsion of an immoral Christian from the church in Corinth. The influence of one such person on the others is like yeast that works through and leavens the entire batch of dough (the rest of the church). The basis for expelling the immoral brother is the fact that Christ, the Passover Lamb, has been sacrificed. In keeping with the regulations in Exodus 12, the Feast of Unleavened Bread follows immediately upon the Passover meal. The analogy Paul is making is that the sacrifice of Christ is in the past, and the church now is in the process of celebrating the Feast of Unleavened Bread, which, to complete Paul's analogy, should be characterized by moral purity (no yeast).

Yet this is no simple moralism on Paul's part. He is not telling them to give it their best try to live right. If that were the case, he would be using a strange passage to support such a notion! Rather, the basis for their morality is twofold: Christ's death has atoned for their sin and, perhaps more important, in Christ, the people are *already* a new batch without yeast. They are to act like what they are, which is not the result of their own efforts but the result of Christ's efforts.

I do not think Paul's (nearly allegorical?) use of the Passover exhausts all the theological significance of the Passover or the Lord's Supper, nor is it entirely clear why to make this particular moral point he employs the Passover in support. The general point, however, is clear: What Christ has done on the cross, which the Gospel writers tie overtly to Passover, should influence how we live. This, like so many of Paul's arguments, is not crystal clear in its details, but the main thrust rings true.

As we celebrate the Feast of Unleavened Bread every day, in the wake of the sacrifice of the Passover Lamb, we must be ever vigilant to maintain the high standard of conduct to which we, as co-heirs with Christ, are called. In the same way as the Israelites were faithful to carry on their backs batches of dough without yeast as they left Egypt, we are to be mindful of the haste with which we have left the Egypt of sin and death and remain obedient to the God who gave his beloved firstborn Son to be our Passover Lamb.

Exodus 13:17–14:31

W HEN PHARAOH LET the people go, God did not lead them on the road through the Philistine country, though that was shorter. For God said, "If they face war, they might change their minds and return to Egypt." ¹⁸So God led the people around by the desert road toward the Red Sea. The Israelites went up out of Egypt armed for battle.

¹⁹Moses took the bones of Joseph with him because Joseph had made the sons of Israel swear an oath. He had said, "God will surely come to your aid, and then you must carry my bones up with you from this place."

²⁰After leaving Succoth they camped at Etham on the edge of the desert. ²¹By day the LORD went ahead of them in a pillar of cloud to guide them on their way and by night in a pillar of fire to give them light, so that they could travel by day or night. ²²Neither the pillar of cloud by day nor the pillar of fire by night left its place in front of the people.

^{14:1}Then the LORD said to Moses, ²"Tell the Israelites to turn back and encamp near Pi Hahiroth, between Migdol and the sea. They are to encamp by the sea, directly opposite Baal Zephon. ³Pharaoh will think, 'The Israelites are wandering around the land in confusion, hemmed in by the desert.' ⁴And I will harden Pharaoh's heart, and he will pursue them. But I will gain glory for myself through Pharaoh and all his army, and the Egyptians will know that I am the LORD." So the Israelites did this.

⁵When the king of Egypt was told that the people had fled, Pharaoh and his officials changed their minds about them and said, "What have we done? We have let the Israelites go and have lost their services!" ⁶So he had his chariot made ready and took his army with him. ⁷He took six hundred of the best chariots, along with all the other chariots of Egypt, with officers over all of them. ⁸The LORD hardened the heart of Pharaoh king of Egypt, so that he pursued the Israelites, who were marching out boldly. ⁹The Egyptians—all Pharaoh's horses and chariots, horsemen and troops—pursued the Israelites and overtook them as they camped by the sea near Pi Hahiroth, opposite Baal Zephon.

¹⁰As Pharaoh approached, the Israelites looked up, and there were the Egyptians, marching after them. They were terrified and cried out to the LORD. ¹¹They said to Moses, "Was it because there were no graves in Egypt that you brought us to the desert to die? What have you done to us by bringing us out of Egypt? ¹²Didn't we say to you in Egypt, 'Leave us alone; let us serve the Egyptians'? It would have been better for us to serve the Egyptians than to die in the desert!"

¹³Moses answered the people, "Do not be afraid. Stand firm and you will see the deliverance the LORD will bring you today. The Egyptians you see today you will never see again. ¹⁴The LORD will fight for you; you need only to be still."

¹⁵Then the LORD said to Moses, "Why are you crying out to me? Tell the Israelites to move on. ¹⁶Raise your staff and stretch out your hand over the sea to divide the water so that the Israelites can go through the sea on dry ground. ¹⁷I will harden the hearts of the Egyptians so that they will go in after them. And I will gain glory through Pharaoh and all his army, through his chariots and his horsemen. ¹⁸The Egyptians will know that I am the LORD when I gain glory through Pharaoh, his chariots and his horsemen."

¹⁹Then the angel of God, who had been traveling in front of Israel's army, withdrew and went behind them. The pillar of cloud also moved from in front and stood behind them, ²⁰coming between the armies of Egypt and Israel. Throughout the night the cloud brought darkness to the one side and light to the other side; so neither went near the other all night long.

²¹Then Moses stretched out his hand over the sea, and all that night the LORD drove the sea back with a strong east wind and turned it into dry land. The waters were divided, ²²and the Israelites went through the sea on dry ground, with a wall of water on their right and on their left.

²³The Egyptians pursued them, and all Pharaoh's horses and chariots and horsemen followed them into the sea. ²⁴During the last watch of the night the LORD looked down from the pillar of fire and cloud at the Egyptian army and threw it into confusion. ²⁵He made the wheels of their chariots come off so that they had difficulty driving. And the Egyptians said, "Let's get away from the Israelites! The LORD is fighting for them against Egypt."

²⁶Then the LORD said to Moses, "Stretch out your hand over the sea so that the waters may flow back over the Egyptians and their chariots and horsemen." ²⁷Moses stretched out his hand over the sea, and at daybreak the sea went back to its place. The Egyptians were fleeing toward it, and the LORD swept them into the sea. ²⁸The water flowed back and covered the chariots and horsemen—the entire army of Pharaoh that had followed the Israelites into the sea. Not one of them survived.

²⁹But the Israelites went through the sea on dry ground, with a wall of water on their right and on their left. ³⁰That day the LORD saved Israel from the hands of the Egyptians, and Israel saw the Egyptians lying dead on the shore. ³¹And when the Israelites saw the great power the LORD displayed against the Egyptians, the people feared the LORD and put their trust in him and in Moses his servant.

FINALLY, THE ISRAELITES leave Egypt! This passage brings us to the end of Egyptian rule over Israel and to the climax to which the first fourteen chapters have been leading us. This section resumes the narrative of the departure from Egypt after the liturgical "interlude" of 12:1–13:16.[1] From now forward, Egypt will never again have the stranglehold over God's people that it once had. The mighty enemy of Israel will play a far less central role for the remainder of Israel's history. Israel's attention will be directed toward the kings surrounding Canaan, the Canaanite peoples themselves, and more important, the mighty nations of Assyria and Babylon. Hence, this passage tells not only of the end of Israel's servitude to Egypt and the beginning of her servitude to Yahweh, it tells of the beginning of Israel itself, from a band of slaves to a nation.

Exodus 13:17–22 sets the stage for the drama in chapter 14. Pharaoh has let the people go. The use of the verb *šlḥ* (to release, let go) in verse 17 is surely intentional. It is what Moses has been demanding of Pharaoh from the very beginning of their confrontation (5:1) and what God said would happen as far back as 3:20 (see comments on 8:21; 9:7). Indeed, 13:17 brings us to the threshold of the consummation of God's deliverance of Israel.

---

1. The mention of Succoth in 13:20 is a clear echo of 12:37. Hence, 13:17 picks up where we left off in 12:37. It is worth emphasizing again that the regulations of 12:1–13:16 are not an intrusion or interruption into the story, but play a vital role in the significance of the story itself.

The story takes an unexpected twist, however. God leads the Israelites on a path that they may not have expected—the longer route rather than the shorter.[2] The reason stated is that the shorter route will bring them into military conflict with the Philistines. Yahweh does not want the Israelites to become discouraged and change their minds, so he has them avoid this region entirely. But why, after such an irresistible display of power in Egypt, does the possibility of armed conflict give God such pause for thought (if we can even speak this way)? Can he not continue fighting for Israel and use such military engagement as another source of *encouragement* for the Israelites?

In one sense, the subsequent narrative makes clear that the circuitous route taken by the Israelites is one of the things that gives Egypt the impetus to follow, though this is not the reason given in 13:17. They are not led through the desert in order to inspire Egyptian confidence but to avoid war. But again, why? Also, why avoid war now only to see it a mere two months later (17:8–16)? Does God feel the Israelites have had enough excitement for one day? Is it a display of his care for his young flock that not too much testing can be expected of them so early in their journey? All this is speculation and probably not fruitful to discuss. Moreover, such suggestions do not take into account the fact that this alternate route will quickly result in a much *greater* test of their faith (being hemmed in by the sea) than open conflict with the Philistines might have.

Another strange phrase is that the Israelites march out "armed for battle" (v. 18). What sense does this phrase make in the context, since verse 17 tells us that God wants to *avoid* war. The fact of the matter is that the Hebrew word translated in the NIV as "armed for battle" has posed problems for interpreters and translators throughout history, and its meaning is still uncertain.[3] Some ancient versions do have "armed" (e.g., Targum Onkelos), but this translation is far from certain. Reading "armed," however, does help make sense of the fact that the Israelites are apparently well armed by the time they fight the Amalekites in chapter 17; this is no doubt one reason why interpreters since intertestamental times have understood 13:18 as "armed for battle." Nevertheless, the context of this passage is decidedly nonmilitary, so a reference to an armed departure is somewhat odd, to say the least.

---

2. The question of the exact route taken by the Israelites and the point at which they cross the sea (indeed, the question of *which* body of water they cross) is largely a matter of speculation and will not detain us here. See the discussions in the commentaries, e.g., Hyatt, *Exodus,* 156–61; Gispen, *Exodus,* 136–38; Durham, *Exodus,* 185; Sarna, *Exodus,* 68–69; idem, *Exploring Exodus,* 103–10.

3. For example, the Septuagint avoids the military connotations by reading "in the fifth generation."

Moreover, were the Israelites given weapons by the Egyptians upon their departure? Some see in 12:36 a veiled reference to such a scenario, but this is cryptic at best. Some ancient interpreters have attempted to solve the problem of where Israel got her weapons by suggesting that they stripped the Egyptians of their armor after their bodies washed up on the shore (see 14:30). Clearly, the Israelites must have gotten their arms from somewhere, but the text does not tell us where. I suggest with other commentators that the military overtones should not be stressed, and we should settle for a less specific translation, such as "in an orderly fashion."[4]

It is significant that the move forward out of Egypt does not commence without a look backward: Moses remembers to take the bones of Joseph with them, thus fulfilling the patriarch's wish that his bones be taken to Canaan when the Israelites leave Egypt (Gen. 50:24–25). As we have seen throughout these chapters, Exodus is vitally connected to Genesis. God delivers Israel from Egypt not because they somehow deserve it, but because he has a promise to keep to Abraham and the other patriarchs (e.g., Ex. 2:24). Here we have another reminder that the departure from Egypt is part of a larger plan that God has been orchestrating for hundreds of years and that is now coming to its climax (see Deut. 7:7–8).

Inasmuch as the reference to Joseph's bones is a reminder of the past, so too is the mention of the pillar of cloud and of fire in 13:21–22. Although this is the first time we encounter these phenomena, which will become prominent throughout the desert period, we have had a hint of them in 3:2 with the burning bush. Hence, we arrive at a partial understanding of the significance of the burning bush: It is another element in the early chapters of Exodus that presages the subsequent events of the Exodus. The burning bush is a theophany, that is, a manifestation of God's presence with his people. The pillars of cloud and fire take us to the next level of intensity of God's presence with his people, an intensity that will reach its climax at Mount Sinai, where that presence will be too much for the people to bear (20:18–19). For now, the presence of God in the cloud and fire is meant to be unbearable not for the Israelites but for the Egyptians, as the subsequent narrative makes clear.[5]

With 14:1, the narrative shifts back to the action at hand. The departure from Egypt takes another unexpected turn. One would think after all the

---

4. For this view, see Houtman, *Exodus*, 2:251–52.

5. As with so many other phenomena in Exodus, some commentators seek a naturalistic explanation for the cloud and fire. For a discussion of these explanations see Houtman, *Exodus*, 2:255; Sarna, *Exploring Exodus*, 110–13. Some of these explanations include: smoke and fire signals carried by troops at the head of their procession; a dust cloud; a volcano. A more technical discussion may be found in Thomas W. Mann, "The Pillar of Cloud in the Reed Sea Narrative," *JBL* 90 (1971): 15–30.

Israelites have gone through that a speedy, painless, undelayed departure would be in order (especially since God himself ordered the departure to be hasty [12:11]). But God is not finished with the Egyptians yet. He devises what by common military standards is a foolish strategy: March the Israelites toward the sea, leaving them no escape route. Then entice Pharaoh to follow the Israelites so he and Pharaoh can engage in one final battle, one that will show Pharaoh who is truly God.

In fact, to make sure that this strategy will work, God does what he has done several times before during the plagues: He hardens Pharaoh's heart (14:4). Everything Pharaoh does—his previous decisions to let the Israelites go, the hardening of his heart not to let them go, his final decision to let them go, the retracting of that decision we see here, and finally the death of the Egyptian army in the sea—it is all in God's hands. God does not so much predict Pharaoh's move as force the move himself. Like a master chess player, God induces Pharaoh to move his king into checkmate, and he doesn't even realize it.

The paradox of God's plan to harden Pharaoh's heart and of the latter's decision to pursue begins in 14:5. Pharaoh regrets having let his slaves go. His concern should remind us of his predecessor's initial response to the growing numbers of Israelites: He enslaves them (1:11). This strategy appears to have been a boon for Pharaoh, and he is understandably reluctant to let them go. What is intriguing in this passage, however, is the dialogue that precedes Pharaoh's pursuit. Why does he need to be told (v. 5) that the Israelites have left? Had he not given the order himself? Is this news to him, or does the report merely jar him into realizing what is happening? Moreover, why does the realization that releasing the Israelites means losing his slaves come as such a surprise to him? "What have we done?" he responds in verse 5.

The likely answer to both of these issues is that Pharaoh apparently expects the Israelites to go only on a three-day journey, which is what Moses asked for from the beginning and which Pharaoh probably means in 12:31 when he finally gives the command to go. Although the text does not spell this out, it is reasonable to conclude that after three days have elapsed, Pharaoh is told that "the people . . . *fled*" (v. 5), meaning that they have kept right on going.[6] The three days are up, and it finally dawns on Pharaoh what is happening. If this is the proper understanding of the scenario, the purpose of proposing to Pharaoh a three-day journey from the outset becomes clear. It was never God's intention to take the Israelites on a three-day journey anywhere, even though this is what Moses is commanded to tell Pharaoh. The purpose of this ruse, however, is to entice Egypt to follow the Israelites,

---

6. On this view, see Sarna, *Exodus*, 71.

thus resulting in their death in the sea and allowing Egypt's punishment to come full circle: They are drowned in the sea for drowning the Israelite children in the Nile.

The thought that the Israelites will not come back is too much for Pharaoh, so he chases them. He musters all his power. He calls the best and brightest of Egypt's troops (v. 7). The irony, of course, is that Pharaoh has gone to fight Israel's God, the God of the plagues, with mere chariots, horsemen, and troops (v. 9). These may be the best of the best, but they will prove of no avail. Whatever dissension in the ranks there may have been earlier (e.g., 10:7) is now gone. They *all* pursue (14:9). God's punishment, like the tenth plague, makes no distinction among the Egyptians. They will all get what is coming to them. They arrive near Pi Hahiroth along the route the Israelites have taken. Things are proceeding according to God's design.

But this turn of events comes as a great shock to the Israelites. It is clear to the reader that Pharaoh's pursuit will end badly for him, but Israel is not made privy to God's purpose for taking the long way out of Egypt.[7] The Israelites, contrary to God's plan, are expecting a carefree jaunt out of Egypt. The last thing they expect is to pause for a moment at the sea, and then turn around and see the Egyptians in hot pursuit, camped within easy striking distance. So, in one sense one can hardly blame the Israelites for reacting the way they do in verses 10–14: "They were terrified and cried out to the LORD" (v. 10).

Still, their moment of panic is not painted by the author in a sympathetic light. There is, for one thing, a significance attached to the use of the word "cry out." This is the same word we have seen before (*sa'aq*), first in 3:6. The story of the Exodus is proof to the Israelites that God *has* heard their cry. The sudden reiteration of that cry, so soon after they have witnessed God's mighty acts in the plagues, is nothing less than capitulation to the appearance of their immediate circumstances, of which the events of the previous thirteen chapters should have cured them. This quick, almost embarrassing mood change by the Israelites is the first installment of the grumbling theme, hinted at as early as 2:11–14, that will characterize much of Israel's behavior throughout the desert period to follow, and to which we will have ample opportunity to return.

The people's specific outcry is also startling. Apparently they were quite happy as slaves in Egypt, and their blindness to God's might leads them to think of only two options: slavery in Egypt or death in the desert (v. 12). This

---

7. The NIV translation of 13:17 implies that God *spoke*, i.e., announced, his plan to take the long way out of Egypt, but this is based on an overly literal translation of the Hebrew verb *'amar*, which often means "to think," i.e., to say to oneself. The text itself does not indicate in any way that God announced his plan openly, or even that he told Moses privately.

hyperbolic response is more of a temper tantrum than a cry for help. At the first sight of trouble, they are willing to march straight back to Egypt, ignoring the mighty acts of God that have brought them out in the first place. With Pharaoh in hot pursuit, they do not give a second thought to the promise God made to the patriarchs. They still have not learned that God's purpose for bringing them out of Egypt is not simply to save *them*, but to maintain his covenant tie to *all* his people, past, present, and future. They have still not learned that *their* circumstances are not the final standard on which to view the work of God.

The precise wording of the outcry in verse 12 is not found anywhere in the preceding narrative. It is possible that this specific complaint was made earlier but simply not recorded (perhaps hinted at in 5:21). But why would this be the case? Whether or not the complaint itself was actually made, the fact that it was not previously recorded adds to the startling effect this response has on the reader. Moses is blindsided.

It is in this context of the Israelites' faithlessness in light of what God has done that we should understand verse 14: "The LORD will fight for you; you need only to be still." This is not, as is suggested by a number of translations (including the NIV) and commentaries, a word of comfort.[8] Moses is not saying, "There, there. Don't worry. God will take care of you. You'll see. Be calm." Rather, this is a terse, impatient command on Moses' part. In Hebrew, the last part of the verse is a mere two Hebrew words, which are best translated as "You be quiet!" or better, "Shut up!"[9] This is no word of comfort but an angry denouncement of Israel's paper-thin faith.

One's thoughts turn immediately to a similar episode in Numbers 20:9—11, where, in response to Israelite murmuring about lack of water, Moses becomes extremely angry and strikes the rock instead of speaking to it. Exodus 14:10—14 is the first such episode where Israel's lack of faith brings upon them Moses' anger. This lack of trust in light of the plague narrative is startling, and perhaps it is meant to be. It is a harbinger of things to come.

Verse 15 is one of the oddest twists in Exodus and has been a topic of discussion by interpreters since before the time of Christ. Why is it, after the *Israelites* cry out in verse 14 and Moses rebukes *them* for their lack of faith, that *Moses* is reprimanded by God for crying out? Some commentators suggest

---

8. See Sarna, *Exodus*, 72: Moses "calms them and assuages their fear."

9. Perhaps the closest biblical parallel to 14:14 is 2 Kings 18:36, where the same Hebrew root (ḥrš) is used. The Israelites did not respond to the threats of Sennacherib's commander: "The people *kept silent;* they did not answer him, because the king had commanded, 'Do not answer him'" (pers. trans.). Here, as we see in Ex. 14:14, ḥrš is used to describe the people's silence in response to their leader's command to be quiet. See also Gen. 24:21; 1 Sam. 10:27; Jer. 38:27. This root consistently denotes the absence of speech rather than peaceful calmness.

that Moses' cry, although not recorded, must certainly have happened, otherwise God's rebuke makes no sense.[10] This view must be given due consideration, since, as we have seen elsewhere, the narrative does not fill in all the gaps. Yet, this gap is baffling if we are expected to supply such a fundamental incident in order for the passage to make sense.

like Jesus

I suggest another approach to this problem. We have seen earlier in Exodus that Moses is a representative of his people. In chapter 2, for example, in his "persecution" at the hands of Pharaoh and in his flight from Egypt, Moses embodies what all Israel will soon come to experience. There is a close identification between Moses and the people he is leading, and this identification becomes even more obvious in the subsequent chapters. He is "one" with them, and as such, he can represent the people to God. He is the mediator who connects the people to God (e.g., 32:9–14). What we see in 14:15, then, is one reflex of this close identification between Moses and the Israelites: Their guilt becomes his.

What makes the rebuke of verse 15 unusual as well is the fact that it is over so quickly. It is a curt rebuff and the action resumes. God is now going to give the final display of his power. In the face of a seemingly hopeless situation, God will do something that must have been completely unexpected. He tells Moses to raise his staff so that the water will be divided and the Israelites can walk through on dry ground (v. 16). Once again, as in the plagues, the elements obey Moses' command to bring deliverance for the Israelites but punishment for the Egyptians.

As we have seen repeatedly, the plagues are God's employing the forces of creation against Pharaoh and his people. They are reversals of creation; that is, what was done in Genesis 1 is undone in the plagues. The parting of the water at Moses' command is the ultimate creation reversal. In Genesis 1:9, the seas *come together* and separate themselves from the dry land. Here, the seas are *split open* to expose the land beneath. In both episodes, the result is that "dry land" appears, though in Exodus this has a different purpose. In Genesis 1, the dry land brings forth the myriad of creatures who will live there.

death for Egyptians, but life for Israel

So too in Exodus, the dry land will give life to the Israelites. For the Egyptians, however, this act of "creation" is reversed, for it brings death, not life. As such, it is not just a creation reversal, but the ultimate payback for Pharaoh's attempt to kill the Israelite firstborn in the waters of the Nile.

To ensure that this is indeed payback time, God says he will harden the hearts of the Egyptians. He is preparing them not just to follow the Israelites, but to die. Verses 17–18 are largely repetitive of verse 4. The ultimate goal of the Egyptians' tragic end is that (1) God will be glorified, that is, he will

---

10. See, for example, Durham, *Exodus*, 192; Sarna, *Exodus*, 72.

use them to bring glory to himself, and (2) the Egyptians will know that "I am the LORD" through the death of their soldiers in the sea.

It may be difficult for people living in the modern world to understand how God can be "glorified" by killing his enemies, but this sentiment should not obscure what is clearly the case here. In fact, passages such as this have led many to think of the God of the Old Testament as a God of "wrath" while the God of the New Testament is a God of grace and love. Of course, even a cursory knowledge of both Testaments quickly dissolves such a view, since there is plenty of grace in the Old Testament, even toward the enemies of God (e.g., Isa. 19:16–25), and a good bit of wrath in the New Testament (e.g., Matt. 8:12; Rev. 14:14–20). God is not as tame as we would like him to be.

In verse 19 we meet, somewhat unexpectedly, "the angel of God." Who is this figure? We get a hint from 13:21, where we read that the LORD went ahead of the Israelites in the pillars of cloud and fire. The fact that the angel of 14:19 is said to perform the same function leads to the conclusion that he is a concrete manifestation of God's presence with his people. We are thus drawn back to 3:2, where we first meet an angelic representative of Yahweh, also manifest in fire (the burning bush; see the comments on 3:1–10 for the identity of this figure). Thus, Israel's redemption from Egypt begins and ends on a similar note: the appearance of a heavenly messenger, closely identified with Yahweh. His role in 3:2 is to announce the coming salvation; in 14:19–20 he is a presence in the salvation itself. His role is to keep the two camps[11] separate, presumably to keep the Egyptians from attacking the Israelites (although this is not explicit).

But why wait until daytime? Why not just finish off the Egyptians right away? Perhaps it is to create suspense, but this just begs the question: Why create suspense? Most likely the fact that the cloud brings *darkness* to Egypt but light to Israel (presumably the pillar of fire) is a reminder of the ninth plague and, hence, should have been a clear sign to Pharaoh of what is about to happen. A brief journey into his short-term memory should have alerted Pharaoh what happened the last time Egypt was swallowed in darkness but Israel had light: Soon after God killed the Egyptian firstborn. This period of darkness will also be followed by a mass killing, against which the tenth plague will pale in comparison.

Verse 21 brings together a number of other statements in Exodus. In verse 16, Moses is told to raise his staff to divide the water. Verse 21 begins in the same way, "Moses stretched out his hand"; but then we read that the LORD is the one who does the parting. Who, then, is responsible for the parting of

---

11. The NIV translates the Hebrew as "army." This is one possible meaning, but I prefer "camp," since it is debatable whether the Israelites can be pictured as an army poised for battle. If anything, as mentioned above, 13:17 paints a very different picture.

the sea? The simple answer, of course, is that God is working through Moses. But on a deeper level, at various stages in the book thus far, there is ambiguity concerning who is acting, Moses or God. As early as 3:7—10 we read that *God* has "come down to rescue" the Israelites (v. 8), but also that God is sending *Moses* to "bring my people the Israelites out of Egypt" (v. 10). Similarly in 13:17, *God* is leading the people out of Egypt despite the fact that we are repeatedly reminded that God has raised up *Moses* for this very purpose. In other words, God and Moses act almost as if they have interchangeable roles. To be sure, they are not equated, but they are closely identified.[12]

As the mediator between the people and God, Moses takes on characteristics of both. As we have noted regarding 14:15, he "participates" in their grumbling, even though he himself rebukes the grumbling. Elsewhere he is clothed in glory, as when he commands the elements, thus highlighting his more "divine" attributes. He is even called "God" in 4:16 and 7:1. The ambiguity is not a result of poor writing or sloppy thinking. It is a window into the manner in which God has brought Israel back to himself. Indeed, it is a hint of how God will once again, more than a millennium later, save "Israel" through one who identifies both with the people and with God.

The parting of the sea is described in an unusual manner: a result of "a strong east wind" (v. 21). The mention of what appears to be a "natural cause" for the parting of the sea brings us back to discussions regarding the nature of the plagues, whether they can be explained as natural phenomena. Mention of an east wind seems to encourage such a view, and, in fact, has inspired many scholars to accent this element, even at the expense of the miraculous.[13] What is clear, however, is that the ancient Israelites did not view the parting of the sea in either-or categories.

The natural-supernatural dichotomy, we must remember, is essentially a modern invention. No Israelite, or inhabitant of the ancient Near Eastern

---

12. The question of who is ultimately responsible for the parting of the sea and the subsequent death of the Egyptians is a question dealt with, not surprisingly, in rabbinic sources, specifically *Mekilta Beshallach* 5.58—79. This tradition is also fully retold in L. Ginzberg, *The Legends of the Jews*, trans. H. Szold (15th ed.; Philadelphia: Jewish Publication Society of America, 1988), 3:18—20. Commenting on the *Mekilta*, D. Boyarin writes that Ex. 14:21 is "problematic from the point of view of the narrative logic. If Moses has been empowered to split the sea with his hand, as implied by God's command to him in the previous verse, 'stretch out your hand over the sea and split it,' then why does God intervene directly and perform the splitting himself?" (*Intertextuality and the Reading of Midrash* [Bloomington: Indiana Univ. Press, 1990], 96). For a similar analysis, see the Pseudepigraphon *Biblical Antiquities* 10:5—6 (J. H. Charlesworth, ed., *The Old Testament Pseudepigrapha* [Garden City, N.Y.: Doubleday, 1983], 2:317). See also the discussion by S. Loewenstamm, *The Evolution of the Exodus Tradition*, trans. B. J. Schwartz (Jerusalem: Magnes, 1992), 280—91.

13. See the discussion by Houtman, *Exodus*, 2:236—38.

world for that matter, would have considered that God's acts and everyday occurrences are incompatible. To see the east wind as a veiled reference to some sort of "naturalness" in the parting of the sea is, to say the least, an overly subtle and thoroughly anachronistic reading of the text. God does not need to alter the laws of nature in order to act; he can make use of them.[14]

The sea is parted and the Egyptians follow in pursuit, hardened against the horrible end that surely awaits them. But they finally grasp that all hope is lost, for in their pursuit, God throws the Egyptians "into confusion" (v. 24). This is not mere intellectual confusion, as if they are confused about what course of action to take. This is a *terrifying* confusion, and it takes the form of wheel trouble (v. 25)—most likely either that their wheels come off or that they get stuck in the muddy road that once was the bottom of the Red Sea.[15]

However we try to understand this, we should not lose sight of the fact that this tactic hits the Egyptians at their symbol of power—their mighty chariots—which earlier struck fear into the Israelites. It is precisely that element that God mockingly derails. There they are, stuck in the middle of the sea, unable to proceed or retreat, and it finally dawns on them that they are, literally, in over their heads. In what is an almost comic confession in light of the preceding fourteen chapters, their wooden brains finally draw the obvious conclusion, "Let's get away from the Israelites! The LORD is fighting for them against Egypt" (v. 25).

This comedy soon turns tragic. Within moments the sea, at Moses' command, comes crashing down on the Egyptians. When he stretches out his hand—the one holding the staff, which had been with him since the beginning (see v. 16)—an amazing thing happens (v. 27):

> Moses stretched out his hand over the sea, and at daybreak the sea went back to its place. The Egyptians were fleeing toward it, and the Lord swept them into the sea.

It seems as if the Egyptians make a beeline *for* the sea, apparently after the parted waters have already begun to return to their former state.[16] After the sea returns to its normal state, they keep on marching into it! They are totally

---

14. See Cassuto, *Commentary on Exodus*, 168.

15. One might also envision seaweed or reeds wrapping around the axles to slow the wheels down. See John H. Stek, "What Happened to the Chariot Wheels of Exod 14:25?" *JBL* 105 (1986): 293–94.

16. It is difficult to read the sequence of the Hebrew of v. 27 in any other way. The Egyptians are not fleeing *from* the sea in an effort to get out; rather, they were fleeing *toward* it. The Samaritan Pentateuch, apparently in an attempt to alleviate this awkwardness, has the Egyptians "retreating" *from* the sea. One can also argue that the "it" should be translated "him," so that the Egyptian army is still pursuing Moses in this hopeless situation.

confused. And as they approach the water, God ensures victory by "sweeping" them in; last-minute escape is impossible. The entire army is killed; "not one of them survived" (v. 28). Egypt has finally paid the ultimate price for the ultimate transgression. Their king has been contending with God, thinking that he was his equal. He set out to destroy God's beloved son, Israel. Now, finally, once mighty Egypt understands that this was a mistake.[17]

Verses 29–31 end the narrative of the departure from Egypt. Although the events will be recounted in poetic form in chapter 15, these verses form the conclusion to what has been a climactic, whirlwind series of events that end four hundred years of Israelite stay on foreign soil. The Egyptians perish while the Israelites pass through the sea on dry ground. The Egyptians prove no match for the God of Israel, and the fact that they are washed up on the shore, in plain view of all, is proof to the Israelites that their escape is now complete. The Egyptian might that they have so feared now gives way to a display of God's own power.

This contrast between Egypt's might and Israel's is lost in the NIV, but it comes through in Hebrew. In verse 30, the NIV reports that the Israelites have been saved "from the hands of the Egyptians." The Hebrew is actually singular ("hand," *yad*), and the biblical idiom is best translated "from the *power* of the Egyptians.*" This is in fact how the NIV handles the same idiom in verse 31: "The Israelites saw the *great power* [*yad*] the LORD displayed." The Israelites are then moved to fear God and to trust both him and Moses. This is trust that was broken in verses 10–12, when the Israelites murmured against God and Moses by saying that they liked their odds better in Egypt than being hemmed in at the sea. The hand of Egypt is no match for the hand of God.

The redemption of the Israelites has been accomplished. The promise to the patriarchs—at least the first installment of that promise—has been kept. Egypt is in their rearview mirror, and the people are about to embark on the second stage of their journey. They have left their service to Pharaoh and are now on the way toward a new service to Yahweh, a new life as a people with their own land and national identity. The next stop on this journey is the foot of Mount Horeb (Sinai), where God will make plain to them what is expected of them, now that he has graciously brought them out of slavery and death. There is some trouble along the way, however (see chs. 15–17), and these incidents will soon prove indicative of the people's poor response to God's love. Still, the end is always in God's sight and his plan will not be thwarted.

---

17. It has been a point of discussion since ancient times whether Pharaoh himself drowned in the sea. Verse 28 seems to restrict the reference to the army, without including Pharaoh. On the other hand, if we understand the Red Sea incident, at least in part, as retribution for Pharaoh's edict in ch. 1, it would only be fitting that Pharaoh be included among the dead. The text does not furnish us with unambiguous information on this issue.

Bridging Contexts

THERE ARE A NUMBER OF THEMES in 13:17–14:31 that we have seen earlier. For example, God "does the unexpected" by leading the Israelites on a circuitous route out of Egypt. This, to all observers, becomes a great cause for peril, but God uses this unexpected means to bring an even greater salvation to his people. The murmuring theme, which we have seen as early as chapter 2, comes into greater prominence in 14:10–14, but further discussion of this theme will wait for chapter 16. We have also glimpsed briefly at the divine warrior theme in Exodus. Earlier hints at this theme come to a climax in the defeat of the Egyptian army, for here God is truly fighting for Israel (14:14). But since this theme has been touched on earlier, I will treat a different theme here, one that proves central not only to this book but to many in the broad sweep of Scripture.

Exodus as a paradigm of salvation. The Exodus is the inception of Israel's existence as a people. It does not simply deliver them from slavery. It is also the event that forms them, that gives them their beginning. Since it is the foundational event in Israel's history, it should come as little surprise that it becomes a paradigm for understanding other acts of deliverance throughout their history and into the New Testament era.[18]

There are, for example, a number of instances in the Old Testament where the Exodus is appealed to or alluded to in the context of some other act of deliverance. The first example is Joshua 3–4, the crossing of the Jordan, ✓ which took place a generation later. That this story is meant to be understood in light of the crossing of the Red Sea needs little elaboration. Here, too, the Israelites are encamped by a body of water (3:1) that they are about to cross. They are led this time, however, not by pillars of cloud and fire but by another manifestation of God's presence, the ark of the covenant (3:3). As Moses did in Exodus 14:13–14, Joshua promises the people direct divine intervention in their imminent journey (Josh. 3:5). In fact, the purpose of this miracle is to give the people further confidence in God's might (3:7–13). The most obvious parallel, of course, is the parting of the water (3:13–17).

But there is a further element of this episode that parallels the Exodus. After the crossing of the Jordan, we read of an incident that brings to mind immediately the Passover ritual. Each of the leaders of the twelve tribes takes a stone from the middle of the Jordan and builds a pile at the point at which they step out of the river (Josh. 4:4–7). This pile is to serve as a sign for *future generations* so that they, too, will know what God did for Israel. Like the

---

18. F. F. Bruce provides a helpful treatment of the Exodus theme in general, which supplements nicely the one here. See *The New Testament Development of Old Testament Themes* (Grand Rapids: Eerdmans, 1968), 32–50.

Passover, the crossing of the Jordan is tied closely to a concrete acting-out of the events themselves, all for the purpose of ensuring that Israel's descendants "forever" (4:7) will remember what God has done.

The central purpose of this crossing of the Jordan seems to be to confirm God's presence with Joshua "as I was with Moses" (Josh. 3:7), so that the Israelites will revere Joshua "just as they had revered Moses" (4:14). In one sense, the point of this is simply to verify God's continued presence with his people in the person of Joshua after Moses' death. But the parallel runs deeper. With the demise of the Exodus generation, the obvious problem that faces the Israelites is the essential lack of firsthand experience of what God has done, the danger being that God's relationship with his redeemed people will not be as real to successive generations.[19]

The crossing of the Jordan, then, is not simply another display of God's power, but another Exodus, a *reenactment* of the Red Sea crossing. It is, in other words, itself a ritual of sorts. This second generation does not have a particularly stellar pedigree to look back on. Their parents, except for Joshua and Caleb, have not set a faithful example. The parting of the Jordan, then, allows this second generation to "participate" in that first great act of deliverance, to experience what their fathers and mothers experienced. It is a concrete display that God is still with his people, that the God of Moses and the plagues and the passage through the Red Sea is the same God of Joshua and the community about to take possession of the land. Of course the parting of water will not be repeated for every successive generation, but the foundational event at the Red Sea becomes a predominant paradigm for subsequent events.

We see this, for example, in 1 Samuel 4–6 with respect to the capture of the ark by the Philistines. The presence of the ark in Philistine territory brings great harm to them, and they are eventually eager to rid themselves of this nuisance. The initial stubbornness on the part of the Philistines to recognize the cause of their predicament, despite their apparent confession to the contrary in 4:7–8, is condemned by their own priests and diviners in 6:6: "Why do you harden your hearts as the Egyptians and Pharaoh did? When he [God] treated them harshly, did they not send the Israelites out so they could go on their way?"

As with the crossing of the Jordan, the ark represents God's presence (hence the people's desire to have the ark with them in battle in 1 Sam. 4:3), but that presence with Israel's enemies does not bring deliverance but destruction. Is this not the lesson of the Exodus? The Philistine priests and diviners

---

19. According to Num. 14:29, only those Israelites under the age of twenty about a year after the Exodus survived the forty-year desert experience. Apart from Joshua and Caleb, none living in the days of the Jordan crossing were mature witnesses of the Exodus.

are perceptive enough to point this out. Their warning is not merely a haphazard appeal to a great past event where God called down judgment on wicked people. If that were the case, there were other incidents to draw upon (e.g., the Flood, Sodom). Rather, the priests employ Exodus language, which leads to the conclusion that the defeat of the Philistines should be understood as another Exodus-type event. God's presence among an impure people that seeks to harm his people will bring pain and affliction. The Philistines learn, as did Pharaoh before them, that Israel's God is not to be taken lightly.

Of the other allusions and references to the Exodus in the Old Testament, some more subtle than others, most worthy of mention is the book of Isaiah. The Exodus theme is of vital importance for Isaiah, particularly after chapter 40.[20] Leaving aside the matter of authorship (irrelevant for this discussion), Isaiah 40—66 is clearly written with Israel's deliverance from Babylon in mind.[21] Isaiah wants his readers to understand this release as another Exodus. We have already glanced at 43:16—17 in conjunction to Exodus 1, but it bears repeating here:

> This is what the LORD says—
>   he who made a way through the sea,
>   a path through the mighty waters,
> who drew out the chariots and horses,
>   the army and reinforcements together,
> and they lay there, never to rise again,
>   extinguished, snuffed out like a wick.

The context of this passage is Israel's unfaithfulness contrasted to God's mercy. He promises in Isaiah 43:14 that he will bring Israel out of Babylon despite their forgetfulness of who he is; verses 16—17 remind them of this. It is no accident that the imminent release from Babylon is juxtaposed so closely to the Exodus. God is in effect telling the people, "I've done it before and I'll do it again." The departure from Babylon will be another Exodus.[22]

---

20. This is not to say that Isa. 1—39 makes no reference to the Exodus. The mention of "a cloud of smoke by day and a glow of flaming fire by night" in 4:5 is just one example.

21. That the Babylonian exile forms the proper backdrop for Isa. 40—66 is beyond debate. The question, however, at least in modern times, is whether this Babylonian context results from the fact that these chapters are *written* near the end of this period (mid to late sixth century, the so-called "Second Isaiah"), or whether they are prophetic and thus written by the "First Isaiah" of Jerusalem (eighth century). This issue has no bearing on the topic at hand.

22. Another use of the Exodus tradition, which will not be treated here, concerns God's victory over the Assyrians (e.g., Mic. 7:15—17; Zech. 10:8—12).

The parallels between the Babylonian exile and Israel's slavery in Egypt are straightforward. In both situations the people find themselves on foreign soil, held against their will and needing divine intervention for deliverance. The references in Isaiah, therefore, to the Exodus are to be expected. But the analogy goes beyond this surface similarity. There is a theological connection between the two events that binds them not only to each other, but back to the dawn of history, to Genesis 1. In both events God is pictured as displaying his might in ways that resemble what he had previously done at creation. Isaiah 51:9–10 may serve as an illustration:

> Awake, awake! Clothe yourself with strength,
> O arm of the LORD;
> awake, as in days gone by,
> as in generations of old.
> Was it not you who cut *Rahab* to pieces,
> who pierced that monster through?
> Was it not you who *dried up the sea*,
> the waters of the great deep,
> who made a *road in the depths* of the sea
> so that the redeemed might cross over? (italics added)

As in Isaiah 43:16–17, the prophet is appealing to the past, to God's acts "in days gone by," "in generations of old." This past act is certainly the Exodus, references to which are easy to spot in the second half of the passage. But is this the only past act to which Isaiah refers? No. He refers to "Rahab" in the first part of the passage. What is this?

According to ancient Near Eastern creation stories, the world was created out of conflict, part of which was the subduing of a god associated with water and depicted as a sea monster of some sort. Rahab is one name of this creature.[23] It was necessary to tame this creature in order to create the inhabitable world. The sea, in other words, was a symbol of *chaos*, which had to be controlled for the *order* of the created world to exist. The particular god that won the struggle, that is, the creator of the habitable world, was elevated to supreme status in the pantheon. Although these specifics of the ancient Near Eastern story do not seem to come into play in the Old Testament, the story as a whole is used by a number of biblical writers to serve their own theological purposes.

Isaiah is one such writer. In Isaiah 51:9 he says that it is *Yahweh* who won this "struggle" against Rahab. It is he who "cut Rahab to pieces" and thus

---

23. Another well-known name is Leviathan. These figures appear in a number of Old Testament passages (e.g., Ps. 89:10). The name we find in the Babylonian creation story *Enuma Elish* is Tiamat; in Canaanite religion, Yam.

tamed the chaotic waters. Thus we see the connection between the slaying of Rahab and the dividing of the waters of the Red Sea. For Isaiah, the power God displayed over the Red Sea is another slaying of Rahab. The significance of these two events goes beyond mere analogy. According to the ancient myth, the creator-god *subdued* the sea, but this left open the possibility of chaos breaking through now and then. When seen in this light, the parting of the Red Sea may be thought of as a *continuation* of this cosmic battle between Yahweh and Rahab.[24]

This also explains the identification between Rahab, the mythic sea monster, and Egypt, such as what we find in Isaiah 30:7 and Psalm 87:4. Egypt, and particularly Pharaoh, is seen as a chaotic force bent on encroaching upon God's created order. We have already seen this in Exodus 1–14. The biblical writer styles Pharaoh not simply as a king but as an anti-God figure, whose purpose is to keep the Israelites from fulfilling their creation mandate to be "fruitful and multiply" (ch. 1). Pharaoh's actions pit him against the Creator-God. So, as fitting punishment, Yahweh unleashes a series of plagues against him, which are reversals of creation. These punishments are the reintroduction of a watery chaos into creation by God himself, and as such they are a dose of Pharaoh's own medicine for wanting to reverse the creation blessing. The death of the Egyptians in the Red Sea is the final installment of this struggle between the true God and the monster Rahab/Egypt, where, once again, the waters are tamed.

The use of water to punish, indeed destroy, Egypt/Rahab is, therefore, not arbitrary but takes us back to the dawn of time. There is more at stake in the Exodus than the deliverance of one people at one point on the historical timeline. It is, at least according to Isaiah 51:9–10, a reflex of an ancient cosmic battle, one over which Yahweh has complete control but which he allows to surface from time to time.

This connection between the Exodus and the waters of creation also helps bring to light the relevance of another event important for understanding the Exodus: the Flood in Genesis 6–9. We have already seen this theme hinted at in Exodus 2:3, where Moses as an infant is a new Noah, placed in an "ark" coated with tar and pitch.[25] This is no mere entertaining allusion to a past event. Moses' deliverance from the waters of the Nile is to be seen as a second Noah story, another deliverance from chaotic waters. As

---

24. I should be careful here to point out that this in no way implies that there actually was a battle between the God of Israel and other gods. The biblical writer is merely employing the imagery that formed the cultural and religious backdrop of the ancient world for his own specific purposes.

25. See comments on Ex. 2:1–10.

Noah's deliverance inaugurated a new beginning for God's people, Moses' flood-like deliverance at the beginning of his life foreshadows Israel's flood-like deliverance in Exodus 14.

Furthermore, the waters of the Flood themselves are not just a haphazard display of might, for God could have chosen a variety of ways to destroy the earth—but he chose water. The unleashing of the waters above and below the earth is a creation reversal, just as the plagues and the Red Sea incident are. God allowed the chaotic forces of the sea, which he had earlier tamed, to undo his created order, at least for the time being. Both the Flood and the Exodus revisit creation with destructive (chaotic) results for God's enemies. These same waters, however, in both instances, bring new life for those in God's favor.

This discussion of the connection between the Exodus and what has gone on before brings to mind other important connections between Exodus and Genesis. As Exodus was to become a paradigm for *subsequent* acts of deliverance, it is also the event that brings a sense of unity to a number of *previous* episodes in Genesis. There are, in other words, a number of mini-exoduses throughout Genesis, and those familiar with the story of Israel's deliverance from Egypt will find hints of this in the life of Abraham, specifically Genesis 12:10–20. It is not too daring to see here a foreshadowing of Israel's own experience later under another Pharaoh, especially if we keep in mind that Moses, too, in the opening chapters of Exodus foreshadows Israel's subsequent experience. As Israel was threatened by Pharaoh but then miraculously delivered by God, so, too, was Abraham. We even read in Genesis 12:17 that God "inflicted serious diseases on Pharaoh and his household," clearly a hint of the plagues under Pharaoh. This affliction causes Pharaoh to order Abraham to leave (12:19), which bears the unmistakable echo of the other Pharaoh's similar order in Exodus 12:31–32. Abraham even leaves Egypt with great wealth, as did the Israelites under Moses.[26]

Abraham's trek into and out of Egypt is clearly a taste of things to come. Joseph also experiences the same trek. He, like the Israelites, goes down into Egypt as a slave but emerges triumphant by God's continued presence with him. The Joseph story is not just filler to explain how the Israelites enter into Egypt. It is also a mini-exodus as he, like Abraham and Isaac, embodies the future experience of his ancestors. The Abraham story is a clue to God's pattern of activity that leads us to the climactic event of the Exodus.

In other words, the release of Israelite slaves from Egypt is not so much a series of similar stories, but *one grand story told in a number of similar ways*. In Gen-

---

26. Compare Ex. 3:22 and 12:36 to Gen. 13:1 (and 26:12–16). A thorough discussion of parallels between these episodes would take us far afield, but even a quick comparison makes the obvious connection clear.

esis Yahweh is not only the Creator-God, he is also the Deliverer-God. As we have seen on various occasions, creation and salvation are closely tied. Consequently, perhaps it is not too much a stretch to see the expulsion of Adam and Eve from Eden in similar terms. This is the first and paradigmatic exile from God's presence into hostile territory. The Garden of Eden is the promised land that God's people are forced to leave, but to which they long to return. One of the earlier installments on the fulfillment of this promised return is the conquest of Canaan, the "Promised Land," where the Israelites enjoy God's presence. The final return to Eden, however, will have to wait for the truly climactic act of deliverance, the final victory of the Lamb over the forces of chaos as told in Revelation.

The Exodus was in mind already in Genesis. To put it somewhat boldly, Genesis was written for the purpose of bringing us to Exodus. This close connection has led many scholars to conclude, correctly, that Genesis was written in light of the Exodus, that is, from the reflective stance of Israel's deliverance from slavery. This is why the writer has made such a point of emphasizing the Egypt connection in Genesis, namely, that Egypt is a place that needs to be gotten out of, by God's help, for the sake of preserving God's people.[27]

We see, then, that a look *back* from Exodus into Genesis actually leads us *forward* to a time when the ideal situation of the early chapters of Genesis, paradise, will again reign. It is, I contend, the Exodus—more accurately, the close connection between Exodus and creation—that gives shape to much of the Bible. I am not arguing that it is *the* biblical theme under which all others should be subsumed. But in one sense the Bible as a whole can be summarized as the story of God's intervening to bring his chosen people out of a foreign, hostile place and back to the chosen land, back to Eden.

The full depth of this pattern of divine activity becomes clear through the person and work of Christ. Exodus continues to serve as a paradigm for salvation in the New Testament. The person and mission of Christ recall unmistakably Israel's deliverance from Egypt. There are many examples of the Exodus theme in the New Testament, so we cannot do a thorough treatment here (the Gospel of John is particularly rich in Exodus imagery), but a number of examples will suffice.

We begin with Matthew's use of Hosea 11:1 in Matthew 2:15. Matthew is clearly drawing on an analogy between Christ and the Israelites. As God

---

27. I should state plainly that this "after-the-fact" writing of Genesis has no bearing whatsoever on any specific view of pentateuchal authorship. To have written Genesis from the perspective of Exodus could have been done shortly after the Exodus (by Moses) or centuries later during the monarchy, as some suggest.

called the *Israelites* out of Egypt, so, too, did God call *Christ* out of Egypt as a boy. From this we can draw the conclusion that Christ in some sense is to be understood as living out Israel's experience, in a way similar to how the patriarchs and Moses foreshadow the Egypt experience of Israel. Matthew 2:15 differs from this, however, in that Christ does not foreshadow Israel, but Israel somehow foreshadows Christ. Christ, to put it a bit differently, is the final, concrete focal point for Israel's experience. He is the "ultimate Israel," which is demonstrated by the fact that Jesus, like Israel, *came out of Egypt*.[28] And in the same way that Moses' personal Exodus experiences in the opening chapters of this book foreshadow Israel's subsequent experience, Christ's "Exodus" as a child is a preview of the subsequent Exodus that his people will make, the Exodus for which he is the new Moses.

So Christ is not only the new Israel coming out of Egypt, but the new Moses leading them. The story of Jesus' transfiguration as told in Luke 9:28–36 bears this out. As Jesus' death in Jerusalem draws near, he goes up to a mountain to pray. As he does so, he changes somehow (v. 29), and Moses and Elijah appear with him. The three have a conversation, the significance of which is lost in English translations. According to verse 31, "They spoke about his *departure*, which he was about to bring to fulfillment at Jerusalem." The Greek word for "departure" is *exodos*. Although the plain sense of this expression refers to Jesus' upcoming death in Jerusalem, it is giving Luke too little credit not to see here a theologically potent reference to the Exodus.

In other words, Jesus is not just discussing with Moses and Elijah his death, but the *significance* of his death, which is nicely summarized by *exodos*. Jesus' death is his departure, his Exodus, from this life to the next. He is a new Moses, leading the way for God's people to a new mode of existence. He is a new Moses, leading God's people to a new chosen land.

Perhaps nowhere in the New Testament is the "new Moses" theme more explicit than in Hebrews 3:1–6, where Moses and Christ are compared as deliverers.[29] The writer here employs a rather difficult analogy to explain the superiority of Christ over Moses (esp. v. 3). The main point, however, should not be lost in the details: In order to argue for Jesus' superiority over Moses, the writer assumes a connection between the two. Jesus is a new and better Moses.

The reasons for this assertion are clarified in what follows (Heb. 4:1–13). It is through Christ (the new Moses) that we as the church (the new Israel) gain entrance into heaven (the new Promised Land). Christ has come

---

28. The fact that Jesus is the new Israel may also be seen in the fact that he is called God's son, a title given also to Israel in the Old Testament (e.g., Ex. 4:22; Hos. 11:1).

29. For parallels between Moses and Christ, see comments on 2:1–10.

to complete what the first Moses could not do and what Joshua had to do in his stead: not only deliver the people out of Egypt but bring them into Canaan. The writer of Hebrews does not extend the analogy to its fullest extent, but the possibility is attractive: Jesus is the new Moses who has come to deliver his people from a country more oppressive than Egypt (the present world order characterized by sin, death, and eternal separation from God) and governed by a ruler far worse than Pharaoh (Satan).[30]

The parallels between Moses and Jesus extend beyond the departure from Egypt and include incidents in Israel's desert experience (the giving of manna and the law); these will be discussed at the appropriate point in subsequent chapters. But for now, I wish to discuss one more parallel—the one alluded to by Paul in 1 Corinthians 10:1–13. For our purposes, the relevant portion is verses 1–2:

> For I do not want you to be ignorant of the fact, brothers, that our fore-fathers were all *under the cloud* and that they all *passed through the sea*. They were all baptized into Moses in the cloud and in the sea. (italics added)

Paul is recalling the Exodus for the benefit of his Christian audience (a point made explicit in v. 11). The Israelites who experienced the Exodus were "under the cloud"; that is, they were guided and protected by God in the form of the pillar of cloud, and it was by that guidance that they "passed through the sea." The unusual part of this passage, however, is the reference to baptism. What does it mean that the Israelites "were all baptized into Moses"?

This is not an easy question to answer. But at the very least, Paul is drawing an analogy between what happened to the Israelites at the sea and what happens to Christians at baptism. By being baptized, the Christian is giving expression to the fact that he or she, in Christ, is leaving behind an old way of life—a life of bondage to sin and death—and entering a new mode of existence (cf. Rom. 6:3–4, that we are baptized into the death of Christ and are buried, but then also raised to a new life). In other words, Christian baptism is the process whereby we undergo our own Exodus, leaving this world and joining another way of life under Christ's leadership and authority.

This, perhaps, is Paul's point about Israel's passage through the sea. That, too, was a kind of baptism, where God's people left an old way of life and began another under Moses' leadership. The Red Sea incident became for Paul a powerful, theologically rich forecast of our final deliverance in Christ. We, like the Israelites, have passed through a sea of sorts. We have begun a

---

30. See Philip E. Hughes, *A Commentary of the Epistle to the Hebrews* (Grand Rapids: Eerdmans, 1977), 135–36.

new life, a new mode of existence in a new land, with God as supreme ruler. We are living in an ultimate spiritual sense what the Israelites experienced in a physical way.

The Exodus theme in the New Testament reaches its final stage in the book of Revelation. The coming of Christ, the new Moses, and the deliverance he has achieved for his people through his death and resurrection are in actuality the first stage of a two-stage process. The final stage of this Exodus journey will take place at his second coming. Revelation speaks a great deal about the destruction of "Babylon." This is certainly not meant to represent any one city, much less the literal city of Babylon, but the present world order as a whole. The status that Egypt achieved in the Old Testament as the ultimate symbol of worldly opposition to God was supplanted during the postexilic and intertestamental period by Babylon. And for generations of Jews living in the shadows cast by this horrific event, it stands to reason that the exile to Babylon inspired them to use this nation as a shorthand representation for any major opposition to God. We have already seen how Isaiah draws the forceful analogy between Egypt and Babylon. The writer of Revelation, then, stands in a strong tradition in his use of Babylon.

The destruction of God's enemies in Revelation is marked by a series of plagues and disasters that are clearly reminiscent of the plagues against Egypt (see Bridging Contexts section of 7:8–10:29). When this world order, with its oppression against God's people, is brought to an end, it will be the final act of judgment against God's enemies who dare harm his servants. In the end, Babylon will, like Pharaoh and his army before them, meet a violent end, like a huge millstone thrown "into the sea" (Rev. 18:21). Babylon will meet a watery death, in symbolic terms, and the final Exodus will be complete.

The final scene in Revelation brings us to the end of the present world and the beginning of the next. What Christians have been privy to in a spiritual sense since the resurrection will be brought to a new level. There will be a new heaven and earth, but, curiously enough, no sea (Rev. 21:1). What, we might ask, does God have against the sea? As noted above, it represents chaos, and in saying so we find ourselves coming full circle in our discussion.

The Exodus ends in the same way it began, not in Egypt some 1,500 years before Christ, but at the cosmic conflict between Yahweh and the sea. Here, in God's new creation, there will be no place for chaos. There is only order. There is a new heaven and a new earth. A new Jerusalem will come down from heaven shining, like Eden, in all its pristine, pre-Fall brilliance. Its dimensions will be laid out in geometric perfection, and it will be reserved only for those "whose names are written in the Lamb's book of life" (Rev. 21:27). Chaos will be defeated fully, and God's people will find themselves back where their first ancestors began, in paradise, complete with river and tree of life (22:1–2). Christ is truly the Alpha and Omega. At the end of history we find ourselves at its beginning.

THE EXODUS AND YOU. The importance of the Exodus theme in the Bible would seem to have tremendous potential for contemporary application. But this application is not as straightforward as it may at first appear. True, the significance of the Exodus cannot be more obvious or more central to the very essence of what it means to be "in Christ." It is aptly summed up by Jesus' words in John 5:24: We have *"crossed over* from death to life."* When Jesus spoke these words, he was not likely thinking of the Exodus, but the image is still appropriate. As Christians, we have crossed over from our slavery to sin and death to a new beginning as God's people, in subjection to him. We who are in Christ have moved out of one country and into another (or more accurately, we are moving toward another country), which itself is a preview of our entrance to the heavenly country that awaits us. The application of the Exodus theme to our lives could not be more central.

Moreover, the significance of the Exodus for today's Christians is no different from what it has been for the past two millennia. The sea through which the church has passed has remained parted since the coming of Christ and will not go "back to its place" (Ex. 14:27) until our world comes to an end. Wherever men and women come to a saving knowledge of the one Lord Jesus Christ, wherever children raised in Christian homes reach the age at which they make the faith of their parents their own, the Exodus in its fullest, most sublime sense is happening. The meaning of the Exodus for Christians today, therefore, is to be understood in light of our relationship to Christ, the new Moses. It is a story of salvation in Christ, for this is how the New Testament writers have already claimed this theme for us.

But what of a personal, concrete application of the Exodus? What can we learn from this event with respect to conducting our lives from day to day? This is a more difficult question, but in the end, I would suggest that it is probably not a question the Exodus story is prepared to answer. For one thing, the application of the Exodus, understood in the manner just noted, *is* personal, concrete, and practical. It is as practical as you can get! Perhaps we can say that it is not so much that *we* apply the Exodus to our lives, but that the Exodus is applied *to us.*

The significance of the Exodus for us is not found in what we do with it, but in what God has done for us already. We have missed the theological point of the story if we reduce its grand theological message to a number of moral lessons, such as "Be faithful in a tight fix," or, "Don't fear tough times, just 'be still' and let God take care of you." Of course, these are good things to remember (and difficult to do!), but the question here is whether the point of the *Exodus story* is to teach us these things. I think not. The Exodus story is not a pep talk for when we go through trying circumstances, to teach us that God will win *our* battles for us. Rather, if anything, it is a pep talk to remind us that God *has* won *the* battle. All of our daily battles, which are real and matter to God, should be seen in this overarching context.

There are many personal situations in which we want God's help. We may find ourselves in a job or at school, for example, where people make fun of us because of our faith. Perhaps our faith even keeps us from making legitimate advances or getting promotions. So we ask God to help. Perhaps we ask him to give us a new job or to punish those who are making our lives difficult. These requests may or may not be legitimate (depending on the circumstances), but the question is whether it is legitimate to call on the *Exodus* paradigm in such cases.

Can we say to God, "You delivered the Israelites out of Egypt. Now do the same for me"? Generally speaking, such an application of the Exodus is not legitimate. This story itself, especially within the context of the reflexes of this theme throughout Scripture, shows that a direct line should not be drawn from Egypt in the middle of the second millennium B.C. to our own day. We are not to draw the hasty conclusion that the Exodus is about God's saving of oppressed peoples and then simply equate our own situation of "oppression" with that of the Israelites. To do so is to miss the rich theology of this event. To put it another way, it is a mistake to think of the Exodus as initiating a general pattern that is then to be applied to a variety of subsequent, specific circumstances.

But does not Isaiah do precisely this when he applies the Exodus to the Babylonian exile? A closer look at Isaiah's use of the Exodus, as well as the use of Exodus elsewhere in Scripture, shows the opposite. Exodus is not the initiation of a general pattern with subsequent, concrete applications. Rather, it is itself a particular application of a general pattern that, as we have seen in the Bridging Contexts section, extends from creation to consummation: God is calling people out from one type of existence to another. This process is one of salvation, and in the end it is God who battles for us and defeats the forces of chaos that wish to harm us.

This sort of theological grasp of the significance of the Exodus will keep us from calling any bad-hair day we may happen to have a personal "Egypt," and any person we don't happen to like our "Pharaoh." It should also keep us from getting disappointed in God when our expected "deliverance" does not come. Even more profound examples of Christian suffering are not "Exodus" situations. We do not see New Testament authors enlisting the Exodus paradigm when speaking of intense personal suffering: "God will deliver you from your suffering as he did the Israelites from Egypt." Such suffering is not something so much to be gotten out of as to be patiently endured—and even something to be thankful for (e.g., Col. 1:24; James 1:2–4; 1 Peter 4:12–19). This is not a "get out of suffering at all costs" mentality. We pray for suffering to end, of course, but, when it is over, it is not as if the Exodus has happened personally for us.

What God did for Israel some 3,500 years ago is not something we can do with as we please. It is not a story about Israel as much as a story about God and about who he is. It is not a story that will be duplicated in the lives of individual Christians anytime they get into trouble, but a story that gives us a glimpse of the underlying battle between God and evil, well beyond our circumstances, a battle that has eternal ramifications. The fact of the matter is that whatever circumstances we find ourselves in, we must remember not that we are *awaiting* God's deliverance, but that that deliverance has *already come*, in Christ. We are not to say, "What I am going through is like Israel's Egypt experience," but "My Egypt is behind me. I am on the other side of the sea, so how am I expected to behave?" Those portions of the book of Exodus that are most relevant for our lives, in other words, are to be found in subsequent chapters.

One particularly important contemporary misapplication of the Exodus story is liberation theology (see also comments in the Contemporary Significance section of Ex. 4:18–31).[31] The basic thrust behind liberation theology is to see in the Exodus an essentially *sociopolitical* event that can then be transposed to any situation where one people is oppressed by another.

> Israel grasped a liberating sense of God and an essential value in its own vocation, namely freedom.... We are now enjoined to prolong the exodus event because it was not an event solely for the Hebrews but rather the manifestation of a liberative plan of God for all peoples ... an unfinished historical project.[32]

This is not an atypical sentiment in liberation circles, but it is, as we noted earlier, a fundamental misunderstanding of the significance of Israel's

---

31. See Jon D. Levenson, "Liberation Theology and the Exodus," *Midstream* 35/7 (1989): 30–36; idem, "Exodus and Liberation," *Horizons in Biblical Theology* 13 (1991): 134–74. Some examples of works that espouse a liberation theology perspective are G. Gutierrez, *A Theology of Liberation* (Maryknoll, N.Y.: Orbis, 1973); J. S. Croatto, *Exodus: A Hermeneutic of Freedom* (Maryknoll, N.Y.: Orbis, 1981); G. V. Pixley, *On Exodus: A Liberation Perspective* (Maryknoll, N.Y.: Orbis, 1987); B. van Iersel and A. Weiler, eds., *Exodus—A Lasting Paradigm* (Edinburgh: T. & T. Clark, 1987).

32. Croatto, *Exodus: A Hermeneutic of Freedom*, 28, 15 (cited in Levenson, "Exodus and Liberation," 134).

deliverance from Egypt. Israel's liberation from Egypt was a religious statement; God was claiming his right over Israel, to take his people out from
under Pharaoh's rule and put them under his own rule. Exodus is not the
story of Israel's *release* from Egypt, as if they now can go their merry way and
build a Marxist-like utopia. Rather, they have left one form of slavery in
order that they may be *free* to enter *another form of slavery*, to Yahweh. It is a journey that does not merely take them *out* of Egypt, but *to* Mount Sinai and the
law. Liberation theologians' use of the Exodus to support a wholly unshack-
led political freedom runs contrary to the story they are attempting to appropriate.[33]

The Exodus is not a story of liberation in the sense in which many use it
today, but a story of salvation. This is not to say, to be sure, that the Bible
does not speak to the issue of "man's inhumanity to man." The Exodus, however, when all is said and done, is not the story of mere politics any more than
it is a story of our own personal troubles. It is, rather, the foundational event
in Israel's existence as a people before God. The means by which God brings
them into existence is one manifestation of God's pattern of conduct that
extends well beyond any specific historical instances. It is a pattern of conduct that is given its most concrete manifestation in the death and resurrection of the new Moses and the countless numbers who have and will follow
him across the sea.

Any attempt to apply the Exodus to contemporary situations that does not
first struggle with this Christological dimension, let alone the religious dimension in general, is ignoring the decidedly theological essence of the Old Testament story as well as the specifically Christian interpretation given to the
Exodus by Christ and the New Testament writers.

---

33. Levenson aptly summarizes the threefold message of the Exodus: enthronement of Yahweh as Israel's king, the making of a covenant bond between God and the people, and the dedication (consecration) of the people to God's service ("Exodus and Liberation," 148–60).

Exodus 15:1–21

THEN MOSES AND the Israelites sang this song to the LORD:

"I will sing to the LORD,
    for he is highly exalted.
The horse and its rider
    he has hurled into the sea.
² The LORD is my strength and my song;
    he has become my salvation.
He is my God, and I will praise him,
    my father's God, and I will exalt him.
³ The LORD is a warrior;
    the LORD is his name.
⁴ Pharaoh's chariots and his army
    he has hurled into the sea.
The best of Pharaoh's officers
    are drowned in the Red Sea.
⁵ The deep waters have covered them;
    they sank to the depths like a stone.

⁶ "Your right hand, O LORD,
    was majestic in power.
Your right hand, O LORD,
    shattered the enemy.
⁷ In the greatness of your majesty
    you threw down those who opposed you.
You unleashed your burning anger;
    it consumed them like stubble.
⁸ By the blast of your nostrils
    the waters piled up.
The surging waters stood firm like a wall;
    the deep waters congealed in the heart of the sea.

⁹ "The enemy boasted,
    'I will pursue, I will overtake them.
I will divide the spoils;
    I will gorge myself on them.
I will draw my sword

and my hand will destroy them.'
¹⁰ But you blew with your breath,
 and the sea covered them.
They sank like lead
 in the mighty waters.

¹¹ "Who among the gods is like you, O LORD?
 Who is like you—
 majestic in holiness,
 awesome in glory,
 working wonders?
¹² You stretched out your right hand
 and the earth swallowed them.

¹³ "In your unfailing love you will lead
 the people you have redeemed.
 In your strength you will guide them
 to your holy dwelling.
¹⁴ The nations will hear and tremble;
 anguish will grip the people of Philistia.
¹⁵ The chiefs of Edom will be terrified,
 the leaders of Moab will be seized with trembling,
 the people of Canaan will melt away;
¹⁶ terror and dread will fall upon them.
 By the power of your arm
 they will be as still as a stone—
 until your people pass by, O LORD,
 until the people you bought pass by.
¹⁷ You will bring them in and plant them
 on the mountain of your inheritance—
 the place, O LORD, you made for your dwelling,
 the sanctuary, O Lord, your hands established.
¹⁸ The LORD will reign
 for ever and ever."

¹⁹When Pharaoh's horses, chariots and horsemen went into the sea, the LORD brought the waters of the sea back over them, but the Israelites walked through the sea on dry ground. ²⁰Then Miriam the prophetess, Aaron's sister, took a tambourine in her hand, and all the women followed her, with tambourines and dancing. ²¹Miriam sang to them:

"Sing to the LORD,
    for he is highly exalted.
The horse and its rider
    he has hurled into the sea."

THIS PORTION OF EXODUS has received a fair amount of scholarly attention relative to other portions of the book. It is a song that the Israelites sing after crossing the Red Sea in response to what God has just done, which is the chronological point made in 15:1, *"Then* Moses and the Israelites sang. . . ." The song has been given various names, including "The Song of Moses and Miriam," "The Song of Miriam," and "The Song of Moses" (although Deut. 32:1–43 is usually reserved for this latter title). The best title, in my view, is the one that has been used in the history of Jewish interpretation: "The Song at the Sea." The reason for the variety of titles has to do with the ambiguities that surround the opening and closing of the song.

According to 15:1 the song is sung by "Moses and the Israelites." In verses 20–21, however, Miriam and the women do the singing. This has led to some discussion concerning the identity of the singers and the nature of the song itself. The song that Miriam and the women sing begins the same way as the song Moses and the Israelites sing (cf. v. 21 to v. 1). What are we to make of this? Are we to assume that the song in its entirety (not just the first line) is sung by the women in response to the singing of the men in verses 1–18, sort of an antiphonal song?

This is possible, although the gender distinction may not be as clear-cut as it seems at first glance. Note that "Moses and the Israelites" (v. 1; lit., "sons of Israel") should not necessarily be restricted to men, especially since the Hebrew phrase "sons of Israel" (*bᵉne yiśraʾel*) is used throughout Exodus and the Old Testament to refer to the nation as a whole irrespective of gender. Perhaps it is best to think of the women (especially Miriam) singing after the company as a whole has sung the song. That a woman does the singing in verse 21 should be no cause for surprise, since elsewhere in the Old Testament women sing after great military victories (e.g., 1 Sam. 18:6–7). The question here, however, is whether men and women sing antiphonally, which is by no means certain.[1]

---

1. Verse 21, however, may lend itself toward the antiphony explanation. Miriam is said to sing "to them," the Hebrew being the masculine plural suffix (*lahem*). In other words, this may be a response to the song the *men* have just gotten done singing. Hebrew pronouns rarely warrant such close reading, however. There is no neuter pronoun, so, when a group of men and women are referred to, the masculine plural pronoun is regularly used.

Another version of the antiphonal explanation is inspired by verse 1. The use of the singular "I will sing" has given rise to the theory that the song is sung antiphonally: first *Moses* sings (indicated by the first person pronoun "I") and the Israelites respond.[2] In other words, Moses sings, "I will sing to the LORD, for he is highly exalted," and the people respond, "The horse and its rider he has hurled into the sea," and so forth. This antiphonal explanation breaks down quickly, however, since the singular does not alternate neatly throughout the song. Moreover, it is overreading the text to think that the use of the singular in verses 1–2 indicates that only one person is singing. Many psalms are in the singular but were no doubt intended for corporate use (e.g., Ps. 89:1; 101:1; 108:1), as with many hymns sung in churches today.[3]

The identity of the singers, the manner in which the song is sung, and its title should not detain us. Regardless of these ambiguities, this is certainly a song sung after the crossing of the Red Sea. It is a song of victory to Yahweh (v. 1) and about Yahweh; it is a response to what he has done. But God is extolled not for the general deed of bringing the Israelites out of Egypt (as we might expect), but for something specific, namely, destroying the Egyptian army in the sea. This is the clear focus of the song.

The practical results of this act are twofold: (1) The surrounding nations will fear God (vv. 14–16), and (2) God will bring his people safely to his dwelling (v. 17). There is, with the possible exception of the ambiguous mention of "wonders" in verse 11,[4] no reference to the plagues or to Israel's release from slavery. To be sure, these things are assumed and form the backdrop from which to view the song, but they do not come into play here. This song has a different purpose: to praise God's destruction of his enemies. It is a poetic rendering of the narrative of the death of Egypt's army described toward the end of chapter 14.

Perhaps more important, it is also the gateway to what will be the focus of attention for the remainder of the book. It reminds the reader not only of what has just transpired, but gives a glimpse of what will soon take place. It takes us, at least on one level (see discussion below), from the Red Sea to the foot of Mount Sinai. It is the bridge that closes the first half of the book and begins the second half. After we leave this passage, Egypt will remain in Israel's rearview mirror and her desert wandering will have begun.

---

2. See Sarna, *Exodus*, 77.

3. Gispen even argues that the singulars in vv. 1–2 indicate that Moses is the one who wrote the song (*Exodus*, 146–47). But whoever wrote it, the singular is not germane to the discussion.

4. The reference to "wonders" may tie this notion more explicitly to the plagues, since in 3:20, where God announces to Moses the coming plagues, the same root is used (pl°).

The main theme of the song, God's victory over the Egyptian army, is introduced in verse 1: "The LORD ... is highly exalted." Why? "The horse and its rider he has hurled into the sea." How does such a description of the death of the Egyptians (being *hurled* into the sea; see also v. 4) square with chapter 14, where they are *covered* with the water on their way to the other side? This is not as much of a discrepancy as one might think. For one thing, we must respect the rights of a biblical author—any author, for that matter— to portray events in such a way that will produce the desired effect, especially in a poetic description.

If we go through this song, as many have done, with a fine-toothed comb, looking for possible discrepancies with the narrative of chapter 14, we will find them;[5] but in doing so we will have misread the song. It is a modern Western penchant to require complete "consistency" between accounts, but the biblical authors are not so concerned. We must resist the temptation to impose our own modern expectations on a text, which ancient texts are not always prepared to shoulder.[6]

The song, as we have also frequently seen in chapters 1–14, is tied to Genesis. Verse 2 speaks of "my father's God."[7] This likely refers to God's covenant fidelity to the patriarchs (see 2:24), although, admittedly, the singular "father's" is not the way one would expect this to be expressed. The other option is to read "father's" as a reference to the more recent ancestors of the Exodus generation, perhaps even one's biological parents, but this would be anticlimactic, to say the least.[8] The purpose of verse 2 seems to be to tie those crossing the

---

5. Verses 4–5, for example, have the Egyptians *thrown* into the sea and *sinking like a stone*. One might argue that this is a different picture than having the sea close in upon the Egyptians. See also v. 10, where the Egyptians "sink like lead." At first glance, the most obvious example is found in v. 12. How is it that the "earth" can swallow the Egyptians where it is the "sea" that drowned them? But even this apparently obvious discrepancy cannot be pressed too far. There are a number of instances in the OT where "earth" (*'ereṣ*) clearly refers to the underworld, ancient Israel's conception of the abode of the dead, essentially identical to Sheol. Verse 12 simply means that God "stretched out his hand" and the Egyptians died, i.e., were "swallowed" by the underworld. See N. J. Tromp, *Primitive Conceptions of Death and the Nether World in the Old Testament* (BibOr 21; Rome: Pontifical Biblical Institute, 1969), 25–26.

6. Having said this, however, the description of v. 1 may fit well with 14:27, where we read that the Egyptians are "swept" into the sea. Hence, 15:1 may either be a general description of the helpless demise of the Egyptians or a reference to the sweeping of the army into the sea as discussed above. Houtman adds that the Egyptian army may have been thrown down into the sea while they were making their way across (*Exodus*, 2:278).

7. The word for "LORD" here is the relatively infrequent *yah*. It is a shortened form of the tetragrammaton YHWH (Yahweh). Although not common by itself, it is a common element in many biblical names, such as "Jeremi*ah*," "Zephani*ah*," and the well-known phrase "halleluj*ah*."

8. According to this scheme, each person singing the song would be referring to his or her father.

sea with those who have gone long before and who worship the same God. The Song at the Sea, in other words, is not only a bridge connecting the two halves of the book of Exodus. It reaches back further to remind the reader yet again of God's overarching purpose for bringing the Israelites out of Egypt.

We see another Genesis connection in verses 5 and 8. The "deep waters" are a translation of *t'homot*, which is the plural form of the word used in Genesis 1:2 to describe the primordial "deep" (*t'hom*). In other words, the Red Sea is described in Exodus 15 in a manner reminiscent of the chaotic waters that God tamed at creation. The Red Sea has become "The Sea."

This song as a whole is a textbook example of the divine warrior imagery so prevalent in the Old Testament. It is *Yahweh* who has hurled the Egyptians into the sea (15:1, 4). He is a warrior (v. 3), who extends his right hand and "shatters the enemy" (v. 6; see also v. 9). This particular use of divine warrior imagery further serves to tie together the crossing of the sea with the primordial battle against chaos. The enemy God slays at the sea is Egypt, an act that clearly reflects the slaying of the primordial enemy sea. Egypt is God's enemy (v. 7), a Rahab figure, and as such is merely a concrete personification of an age-old nemesis (see comments on 13:17–14:31).[9] This does not make Egypt any less real. On the contrary, as a manifestation of chaos, this is reality at its core! Egypt is a real enemy to God's people, an enemy whom God has destroyed. And Israel should never forget that Egypt is the enemy of God—though, as we noted in 14:10–14, Israel has already forgotten and will forget again.

Verse 8 raises a number of matters of interest. The description of the state of the sea during the crossing seems overtly in line with that given in chapter 14: The waters "piled up," which certainly calls to mind the image of two walls of water in 14:22. The "congealing" of the waters mentioned at the end of 15:8 evokes a similar image: The sea condenses or hardens on either side of the dry path that appeared in its midst. What is stranger, perhaps, is the reference to the nostril blast in the first part of 15:8. This is not at odds with the "strong east wind" given in 14:21 as the cause of the sea's parting. Rather, 15:8 and 14:22 are two sides of the same coin. The issue here is the same one we have seen repeatedly in the plagues: Is this event a result of natural phenomena or an intervention into the natural order by God?

This example illustrates wonderfully that to ask such a question is foreign to the way ancient Israelites understood the relationship between God and

---

9. Verse 7 may also employ a pun on the verb *šlḥ* (to release, let go). Throughout the plague narrative, this word refers to Israel's release from Egypt (see comments on 8:21; 9:7). Pharaoh finally agrees to "release" the Israelites, but here it is God who "releases" (NIV "unleashed") his anger against Egypt.

nature. Israel's God shows his mastery over creation not always by super-vening natural processes, but by using them for his own purpose. To put it another way, the parting of the sea is miraculous precisely *because* it is the result of a strong east wind, and God's snorting is a poetic way of communicating this message. This is a powerful image, and we should not think that ancient writers were any less adept at using such imagery than we are. To call the wind a nostril blast is to say that the wind is *his*. It is his to command as easily as we breath in and out.

Verse 11 continues another topic addressed throughout the plague nar-rative: God's defeat of the Egyptians is likewise a defeat of their gods. "Who among the gods is like you, O LORD?" Should we understand this comment as an affirmation that Yahweh did indeed defeat the gods of Egypt, or is it hyperbolic, that is, that there were no such thing as Egyptian gods, so verse 11 poses an unreal condition? This is a huge question, and to answer it prop-erly would take us far from the confines of Exodus 15.

Yet to answer it briefly, it seems to me that the former is the more likely option. The idol polemic running through the plague narrative was not a sus-pended, hypothetical polemic, as we modern readers might assume it to be. The ancient world was imbued with polytheism, and the power of the true God of Israel is expressed in a manner that the ancient mind would have readily understood. We must remember the polytheistic environment in which the Israelites have just spent over four hundred years! Surely, the effects of such an environment would have made itself felt on generations of Israelites who lived, worked, raised families, and tried to make sense out of what their God was doing to them.

Perhaps an analogy can be drawn from another time in Israel's history. After Alexander the Great's conquest of the ancient Near East in the latter part of the fourth century B.C., Greek became the common language and Hellenism began to exert its influence on Jewish thinking. The Jews did not lose their sense of identity and history during this time—quite the opposite. But they did begin to understand and express their identity in ways that sounded—well—more and more Greek. This interface of the two cultures caused tremendous strain and strife, a fact that much of the intertestamen-tal literature records for us, but the point here is that Greek thinking began to seep into the worldview of a Semitic people.

Closer to home, we see a similar situation in the first commandment: "You shall have no other gods before me" (20:3). We will come back to this below, but it stands to reason that God, at the initial stages of Israel's journey as his people, would address them in a way they would recognize. Acceptance of a multiplicity of gods was a ubiquitous element in the world in which the Israelites lived, not only generally in the ancient Near East, but most acutely in Egypt.

We should not read into this passage later idol polemics, such as we find in Isaiah 44:6–20, into Exodus 15:11 or 20:3. The passage in Isaiah (and other prophets) reflects a more mature time in Israel's understanding of who God is, that there truly are no other gods. But at the beginning of Israel's life in God's presence, God, like a father leading his young child by the hand, reveals himself slowly, not all at once. Israel is to learn just who their God is, but it will take time. So, for now, God's defeat of Egypt is a defeat of Egypt's gods.

Verses 1–12 recount the destruction of the Egyptians. Verse 13 introduces the purpose for which the Israelites have been permitted to escape the doomed Egyptian army: God "redeemed" his people in order to lead them to his "holy dwelling." What is the identity of this dwelling? Three options, all of which are amply illustrated in the Old Testament, present themselves: Sinai, the Promised Land of Canaan, and the temple. Mount Sinai would seem to be the most convincing. It is the next stop on their journey, the destination that has been previously announced (3:12), and the Israelites would likely have this place on their minds. But the Promised Land has also been announced as the ultimate destination (3:8, 17). Nor should the temple be ignored as an option, since the word for "dwelling" (*naweh*) in 15:13 is also used elsewhere to refer to the temple (e.g., Isa. 33:20).

Perhaps verse 17 offers some help. There we read that God will plant the Israelites on the "mountain of your [God's] inheritance." Does this refer to Mount Sinai? Not necessarily. The temple was also located on a mountain, Mount Zion. Mention of a "sanctuary" (*miqqᵉdaš*) at the end of the verse would seem to support this conclusion, as does "dwelling" (*makon*; see 1 Kings 8:13; 2 Chron. 6:2; Isa. 4:5; 18:4). Also "inheritance" is not necessarily a reference to the Promised Land, but may refer to the temple, perhaps including Jerusalem (see Ps. 79:1).

In the final analysis, however, it poses a false dilemma to have to choose among these three options, as if they are mutually exclusive. In a manner of speaking, they all meld together. Mount Sinai is God's holy dwelling, but he will choose to move his holy presence to live among the Israelites, first in the moveable tabernacle and then in the temple. Mount Sinai and Mount Zion (Jerusalem) are integrally related. So, too, is the land of Canaan. This is no mere patch of land, but God's permanent gift to his people, within which will be his glory and presence. We can say that God is bringing his people out of Egypt in order that he might be present with them, and that presence will be manifest in "sacred space" that takes three forms. God's self-revelation at Sinai is, although itself a frighteningly powerful reality, a prelude to the permanence of his presence in the land and the temple.

The building of the temple under Solomon several hundred years later can then be seen for what it is. It is the culminating stage in which God's presence will abide with his people. For the ancient Israelites, the building of the temple was not an afterthought, nor was it, like church buildings today, "a nice thing to have but you don't really need it." Jerusalem and the temple are where God chooses to make his dwelling. It is his house. As we will see with respect to the tabernacle (the forerunner to the temple), it is more than simply a place where God chooses to dwell. It is constructed in such a way that brings to mind God's first earthly dwelling with his people, Eden—the first "temple." And Eden itself represents God's heavenly throne room, where God's presence is most full.

The allusion to the temple raises another issue. Is this reference not anachronistic, since the temple will not be built until several hundred years after the crossing of the sea? This has led some scholars to conclude that the Song at the Sea was written either in whole or in part well after the events themselves. Such a theory also seems to be supported by verses 14–16. One should not glance over the fact that verses 14–15 mention the Philistines, Edomites, Moabites, and Canaanites. These are peoples with which Israel will not come into contact until well after they leave Sinai. In fact, the Philistines and Canaanites will not be encountered for at least another forty years. What compounds the problem is the fact that the picture presented in verses 14–16, one of fearful, servile capitulation by the nations, does not seem to square well with the account of Israel's struggles with these people recorded in Joshua and Judges.

(1) There are a number of ways to look at the issue of anachronism. This may simply be a matter of prophecy, in which case God is giving his people a preview of what is to come. Although altercations with other nations are likely not foremost on their minds as they step out of the sea, this may be a glimpse of the future, that other nations will fare no better than the Egyptians.[10] Such an explanation would yield a progressive structure to the song as a whole. It begins in the past with praise to God for what he *has done* and ends with the future defeat of other nations, the entrance into the land, and the eventual building of the temple.

But this explanation is not without its own problems. For one thing, the verb tenses in Hebrew are somewhat ambiguous. There are two main forms that Hebrew verbs take, commonly referred to as the *perfect* and *imperfect*. At the risk of giving a crass oversimplification, the perfect form is often (but by no means always) used in Hebrew to indicate past tense while the imperfect is often used to indicate future tense. These forms, however, in and of themselves, do not indicate tense. The particular tense any verb in Hebrew has is determined by a number of other factors (syntactical and contextual), none of which (thankfully) will be discussed here.

---

10. The nations will be "still as a stone" (v. 16), just as the Egyptians sank "like a stone" (v. 5).

Why this abbreviated Hebrew lesson? Throughout the song, there is an alternation of perfect and imperfect forms. And although these forms alternate, *both the perfect and imperfect are consistently used to express the past tense.* A good example is verses 7–8:

> ⁷In the greatness of your majesty
> you *threw down* those who opposed you.
> You *unleashed* your burning anger;
> it *consumed* them like stubble.
> ⁸By the blast of your nostrils
> the waters *piled up*.
> The surging waters *stood firm* like a wall;
> the deep waters *congealed* in the heart of the sea. (italics added)

There are six verbs (italicized) in these two verses, all of which clearly refer to the past, the defeat of the Egyptians. The verbs in verse 7, however, are in the imperfect while the verbs of verse 8 are in the perfect. Verbal form, in other words, is not the definitive indicator of the tense with which that verb should be translated.

This has implications for translating verses 13–17. In the NIV the verbs of these verses are translated in the future tense *even though the same alternation of perfect and imperfect forms exists here as in verses 1–12.* There is, in other words, no grammatical indication that a shift in tense has taken place. If the same alternation of verbal forms appears in verses 13–17 as in verses 1–12, why should the verbs in the two sections be treated any differently in translation? One reason, of course, is that the events described in verses 13–17 are in the future *from the point of view of the crossing of the sea*—hence the future tense seems warranted! But here we get to the crux of the matter: On what basis can one assume that these are future events with respect to the *writing* of the song? They are certainly future from the point of view of those crossing the sea, but might it be the case that the song, at least as we have it here, was written later?

The question simply is this: Is it correct to assume that the song was written in its entirety soon after the crossing of the sea? This is possible in the abstract, but verbal forms that appear throughout this song militate against such a view. Why switch in translation suddenly from the past tense in verses 12 ("You *stretched out* [perfect] your right hand and the earth *swallowed* [imperfect] them"), only to revert to the future in verses 13–17? The following reproduces the NIV's translation of verses 13–17. Perfect verbs are underlined and imperfects are in italics:

> ¹³"In your unfailing love you *will lead*
> the people you <u>have redeemed</u>.

In your strength you <u>will guide</u> them
    to your holy dwelling.
¹⁴The nations <u>will hear</u> and *tremble;*
    anguish <u>will grip</u> the people of Philistia.
¹⁵The chiefs of Edom <u>will be terrified</u>,
    the leaders of Moab *will be seized* with trembling,
the people of Canaan <u>will melt away;</u>
¹⁶ terror and dread *will fall* upon them.
By the power of your arm
    they *will be as still* as a stone—
until your people *pass by*, O LORD,
    until the people you <u>bought</u> *pass by*.
¹⁷You *will bring them in* and *plant* them
    on the mountain of your inheritance—
the place, O LORD, you <u>made</u> for your dwelling,
    the sanctuary, O Lord, your hands <u>established</u>.

The translation of Hebrew verbs is tricky business, especially in poetry. But the point to be made here is that the subject matter of verses 1–12 is clearly in the past. Verses 13–17 exhibit the same alternation of verbal forms as we find in verses 1–12. If, therefore, verses 1–12 are past, the same should perhaps be said for verses 13–17.

To make such an assertion is not to deny the reality of prophecy in the Old Testament. God certainly could have inspired a song that refers to events that have not yet happened. The point is simply, *what will the text allow us to conclude?* The grammar does not lend itself easily to making a sudden shift to the future in verses 13–17. Nor does it mean that the Israelites do not sing a song after crossing the sea. But should not the grammar of the text be allowed at least to invite us to consider the possibility that the song *as we have it* comes from a later time?

What I am suggesting is that the *written version of the poem as we have it* is the product of the mature reflection on the crossing of the sea from the point of view of those who have not only the Exodus but also the Conquest behind them. Moses and the Israelites *did* sing the Song at the Sea, but the inspired version of that song, the one that achieved canonical status, gives us, the readers of today, the added benefit of seeing how the significance of the Exodus was understood and celebrated by Israelites who lived some time after the initial event itself.[11] Most important perhaps, placing such a song, with its

---

11. This is not to deny the widely held scholarly conclusion that the Song at the Sea is one of the earliest pieces of Hebrew poetry, likely dating to the thirteenth century B.C. See Hoffmeier, *Israel in Egypt*, 201–3. For a brief bibliography on the scholarly discussion see ibid., 216, n. 16.

---

allusions to subsequent events, in the context of the crossing of the sea apparently does not present a problem for the biblical author. However odd this may seem to us, we see once again that our expectations should not exert undue influence in how we approach, and what we see in, the biblical data.

(2) The second issue relative to anachronism concerns the manner in which the nations are depicted in verses 14–16. They seem to fall like dominoes at the sight of the Israelites. They are "as a stone" until the Israelites have safely passed by. But this does not seem to square with other biblical descriptions. Edom, for example, does not exactly quake in its boots in Numbers 20:14–21. In fact, they stand up against Israel and deny them passage through their country on the way to Canaan. Not only does Moab not tremble, but they seduce Israel into idolatry (25:1–18). As for the Philistines and Canaanites, their protracted struggles with Israel are amply recounted in a number of places in the Old Testament. What are we to make of this?

This is not nearly as difficult an issue as it might appear. For one thing, if we are right in placing the final form of the song some time after the Conquest, this may simply be an example of later Israelites looking back not so much at Israel's initial encounters with these peoples but at the ultimate result. For the time did come when these particular peoples no longer posed any threat to the Israelites (that role was to be taken over by the Assyrians and later the Babylonians).

Another explanation, and one that is more satisfying to me (although the two are not mutually exclusive), is to see in verses 14–16 an idealized description of Israel's encounter with her enemies. To say "idealized" is not to say "fictitious." Rather, it gives us a bird's-eye view—or more accurately, a God's-eye view—of the struggle. To say that the nations shook with fear is not to ignore those passages where the opposite seems to be the case, but to transcend them. The Old Testament is blunt in recounting the struggles and defeats the Israelites encounter with respect to the peoples around them. But it is just as quick to remind them that the ultimate concern rises above these particulars.

The parade example of this is the differing descriptions of the Conquest in Joshua and Judges. Judges makes much of Israel's protracted struggles with the Canaanites. In fact, a mark of Judges is the insistence that the expulsion of the Canaanites was not complete, but that they linger (see Judg. 1:19–36). This is what causes the problems that lead to the need for God to raise up the judges, who were military leaders called upon to lead the Israelites against their Canaanite oppressors. Although Joshua is certainly not devoid of such struggles, its emphasis is clearly on the systematic finality of the Conquest.

These differences in perspective are certainly not insuperable, as a number of scholars have maintained. They are not contradictory, but they do give different perspectives because their authors have different goals in mind. The distinction between Joshua and Judges is similar to the other "synoptic problems" we see in Scripture, namely, the relationship between Chronicles and Samuel/Kings and the relationship of the Gospels to each other. What is important to keep in mind for all of these examples is to respect their differences and even to suggest motives that may account for these differences. These differences are theological. Judges has as a constant refrain the sins of the people in disobeying God, which leads to their oppression. Joshua, on the other hand, recounts the Conquest in order to highlight the smooth transition from Moses' leadership to that of Joshua; that is, God is with Joshua as he was with Moses.[12]

This difference in perspective, I suggest, is analogous to what we see in Exodus 15:14—16. The writer of this song has a different view from what we see elsewhere in the Old Testament because his purpose is different: He is teaching the Israelites to look at their circumstances from the ultimate frame of reference, God's point of view, rather than from their own. It is a poetic expression of what we have seen in narrative form in 14:14: "The LORD will fight for you." The battle is God's; hence, from his vantage point, there is no struggle. To use the imagery of Psalm 2, even though the nations rage and conspire—and however disheartening this may be for those experiencing it—God sits in heaven and laughs. Even though the Edomites, Moabites, Philistines, and Canaanites confront the Israelites with military strength, they tremble and melt.

Throughout her history, checkered with stressful relationships against overpowering foes, Israel is constantly reminded to keep her focus on the God who rules these circumstances, not on the circumstances themselves. This is a lesson Israel will learn only imperfectly, yet God never grows tired of teaching it. We find this lesson taught in the Song at the Sea. The battle is the Lord's and is therefore ultimately cosmic. The end is never in doubt.

The song concludes in a most fitting way (v. 18). The rule of God is eternal, and if the Israelites are to learn anything from the death of the Egyptians, it is that the Exodus story is about more than the Exodus. It must be understood, in the words of Terence Fretheim, "in terms of the worldwide purposes of a Creator God who is about the business of setting a chaotic, oppressive world straight."[13] The Exodus is about God and who he is. The focus of the song is not on what happens to the Israelites or the Egyptians, but on God,

---

12. With respect to the Exodus, a side-by-side reading of Psalms 105 and 106 is of interest. Both recount the departure from Egypt, but Psalm 105 has no interest in mentioning the people's rebellion (cf. Ex. 14:10—14). Psalm 106, on the other hand, seems to be concerned with nothing other than these rebellions (Ps. 106:6—15).

13. Fretheim, *Exodus*, 165.

who "will reign for ever and ever." The deliverance of the Israelites is an act in this cosmic drama, a drama that transcends the particulars of the world while at the same time being directly involved in that world.

God's eternal reign is seen not apart from the world, as if God is detached from his creation, but precisely through what he does in space and time. These events are designed to teach God's people, then and now, to look beyond events themselves. The song is about the victory of God.

This passage concludes, as noted above, with the song as it is sung by Miriam (her first explicit mention in Exodus). Verse 19 essentially recapitulates the events of chapter 14, and this is followed by the song of Miriam in verses 20—21. This sequence is interesting. In the same way that the song of verses 1—18 follows the events of chapter 14, the song of verses 20—21 follows the events described in verse 19.

It does seem as if this song of Miriam is a response to the song just sung in verses 1—18. What function does it play in the context? It may be, as Fretheim points out, that this female song highlights the importance of women in the story, so prominent in chapters 1—2.[14] I do not think, however, that this view represents the thrust of its purpose. The author could simply have recorded the song once (vv. 1—18) and made some notation at the outset that it was sung by the Israelites and then followed (if the antiphonal explanation has any value here) by the women. So why record the opening line of the song a second time in verse 21?

It is not recorded a second time simply because it happened. There are many things that "happen" to the Exodus generation, but not everything is recorded. If anything describes the nature of Old Testament narrative, it is economy of speech. The problem readers throughout history have regularly encountered in the Old Testament is not too much information but too little! So, when something is repeated like this, there is a reason for it. The authors are selective. So why select this? The text itself, of course, rarely makes explicit what that reason might be. Nevertheless, it is appropriate to suggest possibilities, particularly if they are in keeping with things we have seen elsewhere in the book.

Hence, I suggest that the repetition of the song in verse 21 is another look toward the future, as we have seen in the Passover regulations and even in verses 1—18 (esp. vv. 14—16). The song is recorded not merely to preserve some artifact from the past, but to bring the past to bear on the present. We have already noted that verses 1—18 make this fairly explicit, since these verses mention events that are only relevant for future generations. We have also seen this with respect to the Passover: It is future-oriented. Something

---

14. Ibid., 161.

similar is happening here with the Song at the Sea. Built into Scripture is the notion that the song should be repeated.[15] The fact that it is repeated so soon after its premiere performance hints that it should be sung not just once more, but again and again. We have, in other words, a reminder of the liturgical and ritualistic function of the song. It is a repeated celebration of God's deliverance, of which God's people must be reminded continually.

Bridging Contexts

SONGS OF REDEMPTION. There are a number of themes in this passage we have already considered: the divine warrior, the creation connection, and looking at one's situation from God's point of view rather than our own. Each section of this book does not have its own unique theme that can be conveniently isolated from the surrounding story. Rather, its many themes overlap. Hence, it is only fitting to be selective as to which themes will be discussed at each turn.

The theme we will focus on here is both theological (as is every theme) and literary: the role of song in redemptive history. When the sweep of Scripture as a whole is taken into account, it is not surprising to see the Israelites singing at the sea. Singing is what God's people do in response to what he has done for them. Many of the Psalms, for example, praise God not in the abstract but for some concrete act of deliverance, whether on a personal or a national level. The author of Psalm 40, after recounting how God gave him "a firm place to stand" (40:2), writes, "He put a new song in my mouth, a hymn of praise to our God" (v. 3; for similar expressions, see 28:7; 33:3; 69:30; 96:1; 98:1; 144:9; 149:1). In fact, the book of Psalms as a whole may be thought of as Israel's melodic response to who God is and what he has done.

Exodus 15, however, is not just another psalm. It differs in that it occurs in a narrative context. It is a break in the action, so to speak—a hymnic interlude in the midst of a story of deliverance. We see this same phenomenon elsewhere in the Old Testament. Numbers 21:17–18, for example, is a song praising God for his provision of water in the desert (see v. 16), an issue that was certainly on Israel's mind for the duration of the desert journey (see Ex. 15:22–27; 17:1–7). The similarity between Numbers 21:17–18 and Exodus 15:1–18 extends beyond the mere fact of the singing of a song. In Hebrew, the introductions to both are strikingly similar.

---

15. Note that in contrast to 15:1 ("I will sing"), Miriam's song begins *šîru* ("sing," a pl. imperative; cf. also Ps. 96:1–2; 105:2). This is a formulaic call to worship, through which Miriam is inviting (or even commanding) the Israelites, and hence the readers of this book, to sing of Yahweh's Exodus deliverance.

Exodus 15:1	*ʾaz yašir–mošeh ubᵉne yiśraʾel ʾet–hašširah hazzoʾt*
Numbers 21:17	*ʾaz yašir yiśraʾel ʾet–hašširah hazzoʾt*
Trans.	"Then sang [Moses and] the Israelites this song."

The only difference between these two is that Moses is explicitly mentioned as a singer in the first song. (He is clearly implied as a singer in Numbers 21.) The main point is that God is with the Israelites in the desert as he was with them in their departure from Egypt. In one instance he has brought them through the water; in the other he has provided them water to drink. On both occasions of deliverance, the people respond in song.

A particularly close parallel to Exodus 15 is Judges 5. Judges 4 recounts the death of Sisera, commander of the army of Canaan, and the defeat of Jabin, Canaan's king. Judges 5 is the song sung by Deborah and Barak in response to this act of deliverance. Like Exodus 15, its content is what has just been described in narrative form in the previous chapter (although some of the details are different, as is also the case in Ex. 15).[16] The main point to stress here is that the type of song we see in Exodus 15 is not unique to the Old Testament. Songs are means by which God is praised for his saving acts.

Another close parallel to Exodus 15 is 2 Samuel 22:1–51 (also Ps. 18:1–50). This song, too, is set in the context of a narrative, although no one specific act of deliverance is in mind. Rather, it is likely a song sung toward the end of David's life (his last words are recounted in 2 Sam. 23), praising God for his deliverance in a variety of circumstances. As 22:1 puts it:

> David sang to the LORD the words of this song [*hašširah hazzoʾt;* see Ex. 15:1] when the Lord delivered him from the hand of all his enemies and from the hand of Saul.

The general structure of the song is reminiscent of the Song at the Sea. David's song is much longer than Exodus 15, so we should expect it to exhibit a greater variety than Moses' song. For example, in 2 Samuel 22:21–30 David recounts his own righteousness as the basis for God's deliverance of him, a theme missing from Exodus 15. Still, the general focus of the song is on God's faithfulness in defeating David's enemies. It begins with praise to Yahweh, as does Exodus 15, and ends with a statement of eternal perpetuity, which reminds the reader that God's deliverance extends beyond the circumstances that prompted the song in the first place. Both songs recognize that specific instances of God's deliverance have far-reaching ramifications.

---

16. For extended comparisons between these two songs, see, e.g., A. J. Hauser, "Two Songs of Victory: A Comparison of Exodus 15 and Judges 5," *Directions in Biblical Hebrew Poetry*, ed. E. R. Follis (JSOTSup 40; Sheffield: JSOT, 1987), 265–84.

As to the imagery of David's song, a number of elements call to mind Exodus 15. We read about David's deliverance in terms of cosmic upheavals: earthquakes, dark clouds, rain, and lightning (2 Sam. 22:8–20). The Exodus, of course, is the story of the grand cosmic upheaval, with the chaotic waters parting to provide a safe passage for God's people. David describes his deliverance in similar terms in verses 16–20:

> The valleys of the sea were exposed
> > and the foundations of the earth laid bare
> at the rebuke of the LORD,
> > at the blast of breath from his nostrils.
> He reached down from on high and took hold of me;
> > he drew me out of deep waters.
> He rescued me from my powerful enemy,
> > from my foes, who were too strong for me.
> They confronted me in the day of my disaster,
> > but the LORD was my support.
> He brought me out into a spacious place;
> > he rescued me because he delighted in me.

Such imagery is obviously not to be taken literally. These are purposeful allusions to the Exodus. As king of Israel and leader of his people, David is extolling God for his Exodus-like victory against the enemies of God's people. God pulled David out of the "deep waters" and brought him to a "spacious place."

Furthermore, in 2 Samuel 22:44–46 we find a statement that echoes Exodus 15:14–16 concerning the attitude of the nations regarding Israel:

> You have delivered me from the attacks of my people;
> > you have preserved me as the head of nations.
> People I did not know are subject to me,
> > and foreigners come cringing to me;
> > as soon as they hear me, they obey me.
> They all lose heart;
> > they come trembling from their strongholds.

It is not clear to what specific event or events David might be referring, but the confident description of his enemies' abject fear of him seems to fit better an ideal state, as we saw with Exodus 15:14–16, than with each and every detail of David's military exploits. The degree of David's success against his enemies was certainly not uniform, but the above verses give a divine perspective (or perhaps in this case, the perspective from the end of David's life) on the ultimate status of the nations when confronted with God's power.

In discussing 13:17–14:31, we noted the close theological relationship between the Exodus and the return from exile in Babylon. Both are acts of God's deliverance of his people from captivity in a foreign land. Another area where these two great events overlap is in the singing of a song. In Isaiah 42:9, for example, the prophet declares that God is about to do a "new thing" for his people (see also 43:19)—the deliverance of Israel from Babylon. What follows in 42:10–17 is a "new song" that God's people are to offer him for this great act that will soon come to pass. The song praises God for his victory over his enemies in a manner reminiscent of Exodus 15:

> The LORD will march out like a mighty man,
>   like a warrior[17] he will stir up his zeal;
> with a shout he will raise the battle cry
>   and will triumph over his enemies. (Isa. 42:13)
> I will lay waste the mountains and hills
>   and dry up all their vegetation;
> I will turn rivers into islands
>   and dry up the pools.
> I will lead the blind by ways they have not known,
>   along unfamiliar paths I will guide them;
> I will turn the darkness into light before them
>   and make the rough places smooth. (Isa. 42:15–16)

Whether such imagery was an intentional allusion to the Exodus in Isaiah's mind is impossible to tell. Certainly the references to cosmic upheavals, drying up of waters, leading along unfamiliar paths, and light in the midst of darkness (pillar of fire?) would trigger the Exodus in any careful reader's mind.

In Isaiah 44:23 we read of the cosmos itself joining in the singing:

> Sing for joy, O heavens, for the LORD has done this;
>   shout aloud, O earth beneath.
> Burst into song, you mountains,
>   you forests and all your trees,
> for the LORD has redeemed Jacob,
>   he displays his glory in Israel.[18]

It is perhaps fitting that this great act of deliverance is accompanied by cosmic participation in singing praise to God. God used the cosmos to bring destruction to his enemies, whether the Egyptians or the Babylonians: mountains shake and waters dry up and form walls that come crashing down. We

---

17. It is worth noting that the term for "warrior" in Isa. 42:13 is the same used in Ex. 15:3.
18. Similar expressions are found in Isa. 49:13 and 55:12.

should recall here again the succession of ten cosmic upheavals, the plagues. Creation has been God's tool for destroying his enemies, but now it has ceased being an instrument of punishment and joins in jubilant praise to God.

One final Old Testament example of this praise theme is Hannah's prayer in 1 Samuel 2:1–10.[19] Although a prayer (see v. 1), we can include it for a number of reasons. For one thing, the categories of prayer and song are not mutually exclusive. The Psalms, for example, are prayers, but many of them are also introduced with directions as to their musical accompaniment (e.g., Ps. 4; 6; 39; 40; 51; 54; 55; 61; 67; 76). Hannah's prayer is not just a spontaneous, one-time prayer in our sense of the word. Its highly poetic structure indicates that it came to have abiding significance. Moreover, the words of Hannah in the canonical form of the prayer have a strong song-like quality. Moreover, the manner in which it is recorded suggests that it had a liturgical significance for the Israelites.

The main point for bringing 1 Samuel 2:1–10 into this discussion is clear: It is a song of praise to Yahweh for yet another act of deliverance, namely, God's granting Hannah a child despite her apparent barrenness. When God gives her a child, whom she names Samuel, she keeps her promise and gives her son over to a lifetime of service to God. The content of the song that follows is interesting. Having just been "delivered" by God through her child, she praises God: "My mouth boasts over my enemies" (v. 1). Just how we are to understand this somewhat unexpected reference to "enemies" is hard to tell. Perhaps it refers to those who had ridiculed her for her barrenness (e.g., the rival wife Peninnah, cf. 1:2, 7), though the remainder of the song is not easy to reconcile with the events of chapter 1.

Reference to "warriors" in 1 Samuel 2:4 brings to mind another state of affairs. Hannah's song is not just a thankful mother responding to God's faithfulness. Rather, it introduces a number of themes that will be played out in 1 and 2 Samuel.[20] More broadly considered, it is another victory song extolling God's might in the midst of seemingly insurmountable odds. God has once again come to the aid of his people, and singing is the proper response.

---

19. Other songs that could be considered are Deut. 32:1–43; Isa. 38:9–20; Dan. 2:20–23; Jonah 2:2–9. Two recent treatments of these and other songs in narrative contexts are S. P. Weitzman, *Song and Story in Biblical Narrative: The History of a Literary Convention in Ancient Israel* (Bloomington: Indiana Univ. Press, 1997), and J. W. Watts, *Psalm and Story: Inset Hymns in Hebrew Narrative* (JSOTSup 139; Sheffield: JSOT Press, 1992).

20. Scholars have long noted the overlap between Hannah's song and David's song in 2 Sam. 22, discussed above. The two songs are intended to frame the narrative spanning the birth of Samuel to the death of David. More specifically, God's humbling of the proud and arrogant (1 Sam. 2:3) finds ample confirmation in the lives of several characters in 1 and 2 Samuel: Saul, Nabal, Goliath, Amnon, and Absalom, just to name a few.

Hannah's song, in addition to being a personal reflection, extends well beyond the bounds of her private experience. The birth of this child is the initial act of God in installing his chosen king over Israel. This one birth has national implications. To put it another way, the act by which God "delivers" Hannah (cf. again 1 Sam. 2:1) is ultimately intended to deliver the entire nation. It is through Samuel's ministry that God bypasses Saul and chooses David as his representative in governing his people. It is through Samuel's mediation that, to use the words of Psalm 2:7, the king has become God's son, and God his father.

Understood in this sense, it is no surprise that Hannah's song is often viewed in close connection to Mary's song in Luke 1:46–55. Not unlike Hannah, Mary has a child through unexpected circumstances. During Mary's visit to her relative Elizabeth, she recites words that, like Hannah's, have an unmistakable song-like quality. The strongest similarity between them is that they both praise God for things that extend well beyond the bounds of the birth of a child. True, part of Mary's song concerns God's dealings with her individually (vv. 46–49), but this quickly crosses over to images that have a more far-reaching significance (vv. 50–55). In fact, the song ends with a reference to Abraham and God's covenant promise to be faithful:

He has helped his servant Israel,
    remembering to be merciful
to Abraham and his descendants forever,
    even as he said to our fathers.

The theological similarities between these two songs should not be lost. What is most important to point out here, however, is that both acts of redemption (which have personal and national ramifications) are celebrated in song. Just as God's acts of deliverance in the Old Testament are often accompanied by song, it is fitting that Christ's coming should be as well.

Our theme comes to a climax, as do so many biblical themes, in the last book of the Bible. Revelation 5:9 and 14:3 record a "new song" sung to the Lamb. I do not understand these passages to refer to the end time, to Christ's second coming. I see them rather as a picture of present reality: Christ is sitting on his throne and his people sing praise to him. In the case of 5:9, the singers are the four living creatures and the twenty-four elders (5:8), the latter likely representing the heavenly saints.[21] The song of 14:3 is sung by the 144,000, who represent true believers. The main point once again is that

---

21. M. Wilcock takes these figures to represent "God's people and God's world" (*The Message of Revelation: I Saw Heaven Opened* [Leicester, England/Downers Grove, Ill.: InterVarsity, 1975], 68).

God is praised in song because of his deliverance. Specifically, it is the Lamb who is praised in these songs. He alone is worthy to open the seals of the scroll, thus unleashing the judgments of God beginning in chapter 6, because he was "slain," thereby purchasing "men for God from every tribe and language and people and nation" (5:9).

The deliverance in view here is not national redemption, such as we have in Exodus 15 and the other Old Testament examples mentioned above, but reconciliation to God. The song continues in Revelation 5:12, and now the creatures and elders are joined by countless angels:

Worthy is the Lamb, who was slain,
to receive power and wealth and wisdom and strength
and honor and glory and praise!

A moment later, every creature in heaven, earth, under the earth, and in the sea joins in the singing (Rev. 5:13–14). The song sung by oppressed Israelites in the Old Testament is now universal, for Christ has come, and through him all creation is brought back to God. The song ends, as does the Song at the Sea, with the announcement that God will reign forever and ever.

That deliverance is clearly the theme of this new song is seen not only in Revelation 5:9–14 but also in 14:1–5. The 144,000 are the only ones who can learn the song, for it is they who have been "purchased from among men" (14:4). It is a song to be sung only by the redeemed.

The clearest reflex of Exodus 15 in the New Testament is found in Revelation 15:3–4, which is called "the song of Moses the servant of God and the song of the Lamb" (v. 3). This song is much shorter than Exodus 15, but they share at least three elements. (1) The focus is on God and what he has done, his "great and marvelous" deeds (Rev. 15:3). (2) God's lasting rule is extolled ("King of the ages," v. 3). (3) Verse 4 focuses on one important element of the Song at the Sea, namely, the recognition on the part of the nations that God is to be feared. In fact, this is an element that appears in a number of the songs we have seen. The redeemed sing to God for what he has done in purchasing them, and they alone are to be those who join in the song.

But the topic of the song is not merely salvation, but God's universal rule that will sooner or later be recognized by all the nations. This element reiterates a point we have seen from time to time in previous sections: God's act in delivering his people is never simply a matter of saving a small group of people from a bad situation. It is also a means by which he asserts his right of rule over all creation. This notion is prominent not only here and in Exodus 15, but in Hannah's song as well, which quickly moves the reader to consider the God of Hannah as the one whose reach extends to "the ends of the earth" (1 Sam. 2:10).

Contemporary Significance

"SING PSALMS, HYMNS and spiritual songs with gratitude in your hearts to God" (Col. 3:16). Singing has universal appeal. The Creator made us that way. We sing for different reasons. Sometimes we are happy, other times miserable. Sometimes we know why we sing, other times it just comes out. We sing to remember good times and to take our minds off bad times. Singing changes our moods as well as simply reflects them. What we sing can have a tremendous influence in how we subsequently think or behave. Song can enter portals of our being that prose and logic cannot. The capacity to sing and to react to song is part of the human experience, so much so that without it, we would truly be less than human.

Singing is such a characteristically human trait because it is divine as well. I do not know whether God sings,[22] but he has certainly woven song into the fabric of creation. It is a means not only of reflecting or changing our moods, but it is also a means by which we "connect" with God, or to put it in more traditional language, it is a means by which we worship God. We do not have an "order of worship" anywhere in the Bible, although there are sufficient clues as to the types of things that probably went on in both Old and New Testament worship. But by God's good will, we do have a fairly extensive record of one thing they most certainly did: singing. The Bible records a lot of singing; there is even an entire book devoted to the subject (Psalms).

What we see in Exodus 15 and the other songs discussed above is worship, pure and simple. Most Christians I know, including myself, find worship to be a frustratingly elusive thing. It is something we know we are supposed to do, but often we just can't seem to get a handle on it. It is something we are supposed to feel like doing, but, to be honest, we would often rather be off doing something else. But this is where these songs can help us.

Although neither I nor anyone else can prove the point, I do not think that the songs of the Old Testament were spontaneous outpourings of worship quickly jotted down and then preserved in a glass jar for future generations to gawk at. They are rather models for worship. They were written down precisely so that they could be pondered, studied, and reflected on— and not just for ancient Israelites, but for those who live in the light of the resurrection of God's Son. They are not trophies on a mantel but inspired examples, not so much because they have to be followed word for word, but because they give us a glimpse of who God is and, therefore, what our proper stance toward him should be.

---

22. I am reminded, for example, of C. S. Lewis's description of the creation of Narnia (as told in *The Magician's Nephew*), where Aslan creates Narnia by singing. Likewise, J. R. R. Tolkien's account of the creation of the world by Ilúvatar in *The Silmarillion* is also through music.

One thing that strikes me about the biblical songs we have discussed is the lack of focus on oneself. And any attention that is paid to the one uttering the song (as in the case of Mary's song) quickly recedes into the background to let the true focus of the song come through—praise to the Lord. Songs in Scripture are about what God has done for his people. Although many psalms offer praise to God for more "abstract" things (though that is hardly a fair characterization), such as his creation, this is not the case for the songs examined here. They are songs filled with thanksgiving, gratitude, awe, and power because God has shown himself to be mighty in some situation, and his might is to be recognized throughout all the earth. To put it another way, these songs are thoroughly theocentric. Our worship of God in song should be equally theocentric and, ever since Easter morning, Christocentric as well.

I resist with all my heart making simplistic, blanket statements, but the biblical model for "hymnic worship," as we may call it, should cause us to think long and hard about the state of music in the church today. Different kinds of music reflect different personalities and create different kinds of moods, and it is a hopeless task to get any ten people to agree on what kinds are and are not appropriate for worship. My point here, however, has little to do with the musical dimension, but with the content of the songs.

Does worship really happen when stanza after stanza of a hymn or other type of song focuses on the personal status of the worshiper rather than the nature, character, and acts of God? I have become more sensitive to this over the years. When I hear myself singing "I," "me," or "we" too often, I begin thinking that our emphasis at that moment is misplaced. I am not suggesting that songs in worship should make *no* reference to the worshiper. I am simply suggesting that we remain in an "analytical" (but not judgmental) mode in order better to discern what is right and what is wrong in how we worship God.[23]

At the risk of getting too specific, allow me to provide an example.

Jesus, we just want to thank You (3x)
Thank You for being so good.

Jesus, we just want to praise You (3x)
Praise you for being so good.

Jesus, we just want to tell You (3x)
We love You for being so good.

---

23. Of course, I am assuming (and assuming that the reader is assuming!) that "right and wrong" are serviceable categories to talk about worship. This is not to say, however—and this is a point worth emphasizing—that right and wrong are always easy to discern.

Savior, we just want to serve You (3x)
Serve You for being so good.

Jesus, we know you are coming (3x)
Take us to live in Your home.[24]

The point here is not the quality of the music or the question of whether repetition is an aid or hindrance to worship. (It could be both. Ps. 119, for example, is very repetitive.) Nor am I addressing whether such a song would be profitable in a setting other than a worshipful one. But the focus of this song is clear: It is on the worshipers, on what *we* are doing (thanking, praising, telling, serving, knowing). Again, this is not to say that there should be no mention of the worshiper. That would be equally ridiculous. Even the Song at the Sea begins, "*I* will sing to the LORD." The difference, however, is that this biblical song shifts quickly to the object of praise, God, rather than lingering on the one giving the praise. I am not saying the above song is not appropriate for worship and should be excluded from the hymnal. Still, when I look at the songs of old—not just the hymns of recent centuries, but of the Old Testament—I cannot help but wonder if we could do better.

There is another aspect of this hymn that stands in stark contrast to the biblical examples. It is, for all intents and purposes, devoid of any specific content. Why is Jesus good? Is such a basis for praise too vague? Another example will make the point even clearer.

Jesus is the sweetest name I know,
And He's just the same as His lovely name,
And that's the reason I love Him so;
Oh, Jesus is the sweetest name I know.[25]

Again, I am not saying that such songs should not be sung, but it does raise some questions. *Why* is Jesus' name so "sweet"? And just what is a "sweet" name? I am not calling for a full-blown, Latin oration every time we open our mouths in song. Different levels of content are appropriate for different Christians. It is a matter of wisdom rather than applying black-and-white categories that will contribute to the discussion. But when I think of how praise is offered to God in the Bible, there is more meat to them. Skimming the biblical songs we have looked at above shows the types of things God is praised for: his universal rule, power, eternality, incomparability, love, faithfulness to his people, and coming universal recognition.

---

24. The hymn is called "Jesus, We Just Want to Thank You," written by Gloria and William Gaither. The text as it is here is taken from *The Hymnal for Worship and Celebration* (Waco, Tex.: Word, 1986), number 98.

25. "Jesus Is the Sweetest Name I Know," *The Hymnal for Worship and Celebration*, number 95.

It is not too much, I am sure, to expect the church's worship of God to be thoughtful, biblical,[26] and awe-inspiring. Our natural tendency throughout the week is to focus on ourselves. This should not be the case for Christians when we gather together in order to worship God; rather, we should make a decided effort to turn from ourselves and toward him who is truly worthy not just of our attention but of our adoration. It is perhaps in this context that we can come to a deeper understanding of passages such as Colossians 3:16: "Let the word of Christ dwell in you richly as you teach and admonish one another with all wisdom, and as you sing psalms, hymns and spiritual songs with gratitude in your hearts to God."

The "word of Christ," which we can safely equate with Scripture, is to dwell in us richly, not only as we teach and admonish each other, but as we *sing* to God "with gratitude" in our hearts. We show this gratitude by making the focus of our singing the nature and work of God in calling us to be his own. We need constant reminders of who God is and what he has done. What we sing should, like the biblical examples, reflect these things.

This is all the more true in light of our high calling in Christ. We participate in an act of God that is far greater than the Exodus, for it is God's climactic act of deliverance. Focusing our attention in worship relentlessly on God is not mundane nor tedious. Rather, it places the focus where it ought to be. This is the great "content" that is the acceptable form of worship for the church, not only in its teaching, preaching, and missions statements, but also in its music. We do not sing in worship to reflect our moods any more than our sermons and Sunday school lessons should reflect our pet theories on the gospel. Rather, quite bluntly, we sing in an effort to take us *away* from what we think and draw us toward what we ought to think, feel, experience. We sing to create a mood more than to reflect one.

This is why the content of what we sing is so vital. Our songs are, like the songs of the Bible, reminders of who God is and what he has done. This is not to say that only one type of song fits this description—for example, the "classic" hymns of the church. To argue as I have done is not to close off discussion on the subject because the issue is now settled. Rather, the discussion can truly be opened when we have all agreed at the outset that, like the biblical examples, who we sing to and what we sing about is a matter worthy of constant reflection and spiritual energy.

---

26. Which is not the same as being biblicistic, e.g., only singing from the Psalms or only reproducing precise biblical wording.

Exodus 15:22–17:7

〜

THEN MOSES LED Israel from the Red Sea and they went into the Desert of Shur. For three days they traveled in the desert without finding water. ²³When they came to Marah, they could not drink its water because it was bitter. (That is why the place is called Marah.) ²⁴So the people grumbled against Moses, saying, "What are we to drink?"

²⁵Then Moses cried out to the LORD, and the LORD showed him a piece of wood. He threw it into the water, and the water became sweet.

There the LORD made a decree and a law for them, and there he tested them. ²⁶He said, "If you listen carefully to the voice of the LORD your God and do what is right in his eyes, if you pay attention to his commands and keep all his decrees, I will not bring on you any of the diseases I brought on the Egyptians, for I am the LORD, who heals you."

²⁷Then they came to Elim, where there were twelve springs and seventy palm trees, and they camped there near the water.

¹⁶:¹The whole Israelite community set out from Elim and came to the Desert of Sin, which is between Elim and Sinai, on the fifteenth day of the second month after they had come out of Egypt. ²In the desert the whole community grumbled against Moses and Aaron. ³The Israelites said to them, "If only we had died by the LORD's hand in Egypt! There we sat around pots of meat and ate all the food we wanted, but you have brought us out into this desert to starve this entire assembly to death."

⁴Then the LORD said to Moses, "I will rain down bread from heaven for you. The people are to go out each day and gather enough for that day. In this way I will test them and see whether they will follow my instructions. ⁵On the sixth day they are to prepare what they bring in, and that is to be twice as much as they gather on the other days."

⁶So Moses and Aaron said to all the Israelites, "In the evening you will know that it was the LORD who brought you out of Egypt, ⁷and in the morning you will see the glory of the LORD, because he has heard your grumbling against him. Who are we, that you should grumble against us?" ⁸Moses

also said, "You will know that it was the LORD when he gives you meat to eat in the evening and all the bread you want in the morning, because he has heard your grumbling against him. Who are we? You are not grumbling against us, but against the LORD."

⁹Then Moses told Aaron, "Say to the entire Israelite community, 'Come before the LORD, for he has heard your grumbling.'"

¹⁰While Aaron was speaking to the whole Israelite community, they looked toward the desert, and there was the glory of the LORD appearing in the cloud.

¹¹The LORD said to Moses, ¹²"I have heard the grumbling of the Israelites. Tell them, 'At twilight you will eat meat, and in the morning you will be filled with bread. Then you will know that I am the LORD your God.'"

¹³That evening quail came and covered the camp, and in the morning there was a layer of dew around the camp. ¹⁴When the dew was gone, thin flakes like frost on the ground appeared on the desert floor. ¹⁵When the Israelites saw it, they said to each other, "What is it?" For they did not know what it was.

Moses said to them, "It is the bread the LORD has given you to eat. ¹⁶This is what the LORD has commanded: 'Each one is to gather as much as he needs. Take an omer for each person you have in your tent.'"

¹⁷The Israelites did as they were told; some gathered much, some little. ¹⁸And when they measured it by the omer, he who gathered much did not have too much, and he who gathered little did not have too little. Each one gathered as much as he needed.

¹⁹Then Moses said to them, "No one is to keep any of it until morning."

²⁰However, some of them paid no attention to Moses; they kept part of it until morning, but it was full of maggots and began to smell. So Moses was angry with them.

²¹Each morning everyone gathered as much as he needed, and when the sun grew hot, it melted away. ²²On the sixth day, they gathered twice as much—two omers for each person—and the leaders of the community came and reported this to Moses. ²³He said to them, "This is what the LORD commanded: 'Tomorrow is to be a day of rest, a holy Sabbath to

the LORD. So bake what you want to bake and boil what you want to boil. Save whatever is left and keep it until morning.'"

²⁴So they saved it until morning, as Moses commanded, and it did not stink or get maggots in it. ²⁵"Eat it today," Moses said, "because today is a Sabbath to the LORD. You will not find any of it on the ground today. ²⁶Six days you are to gather it, but on the seventh day, the Sabbath, there will not be any."

²⁷Nevertheless, some of the people went out on the seventh day to gather it, but they found none. ²⁸Then the LORD said to Moses, "How long will you refuse to keep my commands and my instructions? ²⁹Bear in mind that the LORD has given you the Sabbath; that is why on the sixth day he gives you bread for two days. Everyone is to stay where he is on the seventh day; no one is to go out." ³⁰So the people rested on the seventh day.

³¹The people of Israel called the bread manna. It was white like coriander seed and tasted like wafers made with honey. ³²Moses said, "This is what the LORD has commanded: 'Take an omer of manna and keep it for the generations to come, so they can see the bread I gave you to eat in the desert when I brought you out of Egypt.'"

³³So Moses said to Aaron, "Take a jar and put an omer of manna in it. Then place it before the LORD to be kept for the generations to come."

³⁴As the LORD commanded Moses, Aaron put the manna in front of the Testimony, that it might be kept. ³⁵The Israelites ate manna forty years, until they came to a land that was settled; they ate manna until they reached the border of Canaan.

³⁶(An omer is one tenth of an ephah.)

¹⁷:¹The whole Israelite community set out from the Desert of Sin, traveling from place to place as the LORD commanded. They camped at Rephidim, but there was no water for the people to drink. ²So they quarreled with Moses and said, "Give us water to drink."

Moses replied, "Why do you quarrel with me? Why do you put the LORD to the test?"

³But the people were thirsty for water there, and they grumbled against Moses. They said, "Why did you bring us up out of Egypt to make us and our children and livestock die of thirst?"

⁴Then Moses cried out to the LORD, "What am I to do with these people? They are almost ready to stone me."

⁵The LORD answered Moses, "Walk on ahead of the people. Take with you some of the elders of Israel and take in your hand the staff with which you struck the Nile, and go. ⁶I will stand there before you by the rock at Horeb. Strike the rock, and water will come out of it for the people to drink." So Moses did this in the sight of the elders of Israel. ⁷And he called the place Massah and Meribah because the Israelites quarreled and because they tested the LORD saying, "Is the LORD among us or not?"

Original Meaning

FOR REASONS ONCE AGAIN determined by the narrative, we must treat a lengthy passage as a unit. Exodus 15:22–17:7 are three stories that should be taken together. All three deal with the Israelites' grumbling because of a lack of elements vital to their survival in the desert. The first and third stories concern the supply of water, the second with the issue of food.[1]

This section is the first of the desert narratives. Israel has crossed the Red Sea and remains in the desert for the remainder of the Pentateuch. Not until Joshua 3 do they cross the Jordan into Canaan. To use an analogy, if Israel's departure from Egypt is her "birth," she is now in her period of infancy,[2] the beginning where God is taking his people by the hand and teaching them patiently and lovingly about who he is and what he has in store for them. These stories, therefore, are not just about the murmuring of God's people, but God's care for them.[3]

Still, these three rapid-fire stories of rebellion in the desert stagger the imagination. Perhaps they are meant to. No sooner do the Israelites leave Egypt under the most miraculous of circumstances than they, within one month of their

---

1. The battle against the Amalekites (17:8–16) could also be included in this section, since it is a fourth desert incident that precedes the actual approach to Mount Sinai. I have chosen to treat it separately, however, since 15:22–17:7 deal with issues of food and water in the desert. The battle with the Amalekites is of a different order and thus merits separate treatment even though there is some theological overlap.

2. Fretheim prefers to line up this period of Israel's existence with adolescence (*Exodus*, 171). Neither analogy should be pressed too far, but I prefer to use the term "adolescent" to describe the more insidious rebellions during the period of the judges. I can imagine parents of teenagers agreeing wholeheartedly.

3. See also Gowan, *Theology in Exodus*, 170.

departure, lapse into an old pattern. They again use their own perception of their circumstances as the standard by which to base reality. They still have not learned that even though they are in a desert with no food or water, God is above their circumstances. So, they grumble. But God uses their grumbling as an occasion not to punish his people, but to teach them something about himself.

Throughout these stories we see echoes of Egypt and the plagues to remind them of what has happened. But this passage also gives glimpses of what is to come. A number of elements of these stories foreshadow Sinai, that pivotal and climactic scene in Israel's history where the Israelites will receive the law and instructions for building the tabernacle.

Water at Marah (15:22–27)

THIS FIRST STORY concerns the provision of water at Marah. We are not given all the details of the itinerary (see Num. 33 for more detail), but it seems that three days have passed since the Israelites have crossed the sea. Might this be an echo of the three-day journey mentioned as far back as 3:18? Perhaps the three days have come and gone and, with no festival in sight, the Israelites become despondent. Moreover, for these three days they have had no water. Only a short time earlier they may have been thinking that they would be perfectly happy never to see another drop again. Now, however, the harsh realities of a desert march set in, and they begin to fear that they may die of thirst. Then, when they finally do come to water, they find it is "bitter," which is the meaning of the Hebrew word Marah.[4] Thus, the grumbling against Moses begins: "What are we to drink?"[5]

Moses responds in a manner familiar to us; he "cries out" (15:25)—the same way the Israelites earlier responded to their oppression in Egypt. God, in turn, responds in a manner reminiscent of the plagues and the Exodus: He performs another water miracle. While some commentaries try to find a correspondence between the type of wood Moses uses and its possible chemical properties and medicinal qualities, such an approach misses the theological point of the narrative. A suitable "natural" explanation is hardly what the narrative intends for us to grasp.

The wood thrown into the water reminds us of the wood of the staff that Moses used to perform the two great water miracles of the departure

---

4. Incidentally, I suggest here that the bitter waters of Marah are an intentional echo of the Israelites' bitter lives under Egyptian rule (see 1:14). Perhaps the waters of Marah are a reminder of where they have just been.

5. Houtman's translation, although not really supported by the Hebrew, in my opinion comes closer to the exasperation the Israelites must have felt: "There is no way we can drink this stuff" (Houtman, *Exodus*, 2:306).

narrative: the first plague and the parting of the sea. Here we have another example of God's control over chaotic waters as he had twice done in Egypt. Waters that could have brought death to God's people behave in a manner contrary to their nature and work for Israel's good. The connection to the events in Egypt is made explicit in verse 26: If the Israelites obey God's commands and decrees, they will be spared the diseases that inflicted the Egyptians. The sweetening of the bitter water evokes images of what God did in Egypt, particularly when he turned the "sweet" waters of the Nile into blood. By performing what is essentially the opposite miracle here, God is showing his continued faithfulness to *his* people despite apparent evidence to the contrary.

What do the "commands" and "decrees" mentioned in verse 26 refer to? What are the Israelites to do in order to avoid the diseases that befell Egypt? Sarna suggests that God gave some laws here that have not been recorded and are now lost to us.[6] What makes this comment more startling is the fact that the law does not become an issue until chapter 19, when the Israelites arrive at Sinai. Is it not then that the law is finally given to Israel?

The reference to commands and decrees at this stage in the journey is admittedly vague, but consider these two approaches. (1) We should not assume that Israel had no law until Sinai. This seems especially true in 16:23, where the Sabbath day is mentioned explicitly for the first time in the Old Testament. Although the command to keep the Sabbath is explicitly given only in 20:8–11 (the fourth commandment), this does not mean that God's will for his people to keep the Sabbath was unheard of until then.

It is reasonable to assume that the Ten Commandments as they are given on Mount Sinai are not new but a reiteration of things that the Israelites (and probably other ancient Near Eastern peoples) already knew. After all, are we to think that the command to honor one's parents or the prohibitions against stealing, murder, or adultery are unheard of before Sinai? The Israelites most likely have known something of God's law before Sinai, even though we are not told what they know or how they come to know it. Exodus 15:26 should be similarly understood.

(2) Another approach sees in this reference to commands and decrees a foreshadowing of Sinai. As the water miracle evokes images of the past, the reference to law gives a glimpse of the future. What God is telling his people at this crucial juncture in their young life as a people is: "Stick to me and you will never relive the horrors of Egypt again. If you ignore my law, although you will not return to Egypt physically, you will be treated as they were." The first thing that Israel does after crossing the sea is to rebel by not

6. Sarna, *Exodus*, 85.

trusting in God's goodness. An Egypt-like fate awaits them if they continue down this course. God's threat is severe, but it is precisely so at the outset of their relationship together. For the climactic expression of the centrality of obeying God's commands we must wait until chapters 20–24.

As the reference to commands foreshadows Sinai, the reference to "Elim" foreshadows another climactic event in Israel's existence: entrance into the Promised Land. I do not see the trek to the fresh springs of Elim as a concession to Israel's sinfulness, as Calvin sees it.[7] It is rather another glimpse of what is to come, the lush land of Canaan, the land God promised to the patriarchs and which he has prepared for his people. The numbers twelve and seventy should probably be seen as numbers of completion: The Israelites have plenty of springs for water (perhaps one for each tribe) and palm trees for shade. Elim is a reversal of the desert environment and a foretaste of things to come.

Manna and Quail (16:1–36)

THE REVERSAL AT Elim is only temporary, however. Eventually the foretaste of paradise ends and the people again find themselves on the arduous journey toward Sinai (16:1). But, surely, having just seen again God's care for them, rebellion is now out of the question, right? Wrong! A mere month has passed since the departure from Egypt. Is their memory so short? They have just witnessed God's Exodus-like provision of water in the desert. Still, they arrive in the desert of Sin[8] and immediately begin grumbling against Moses and Aaron.

The Israelites bring what is an absurd charge against their leaders, well in keeping with the absurdity of this passage as a whole: "You have brought us out into this desert to starve this entire assembly to death" (16:3).[9] Only the most callused heart or the most stupid mind could conceive of such a ridiculous charge. The only thing more surprising, perhaps, is the response God gives. Rather than punish them, he rains down bread from heaven (v. 4). If any need convincing of the grace of God in the Old Testament, they need only to look here!

---

7. Calvin, *Four Last Books of Moses*, 267.

8. Sin and Sinai are as similar in Hebrew as they are in English (*sin* and *sinay*, respectively). It seems likely to me that with the arrival at Sin we have here another glimpse forward to Sinai. Rebellion accompanies both.

9. Many commentators have picked up on the fact that the cattle would have provided an ample supply of food; hence, their situation was not as dire as they make it out to be. Yet, as a number of other commentators have rightly pointed out, cattle were an important commodity in the ancient world, which is why they were often used as a measure of one's wealth and a barometer of God's blessing. Cattle would be needed upon entering the land, so the Israelites would not have eaten them in the desert.

Without any hint of anger or malice, God provides for his people again, but with one minor provision. They are only to gather as much bread as they need for each day. This is a test, a point explicitly made in 16:4, to see if they will follow God's instructions.[10] In view of Israel's behavior thus far, a test is certainly in order. This provision, like the mention of law in 15:25–26, also serves to foreshadow the giving of the law at Sinai. God is testing the Israelites to see whether they will follow "my instructions [*torah*]." This Hebrew word calls to mind the law given at Sinai. Torah can mean more than just the Sinaitic legal material. It is a fluid term, but in this context there seems to be an intentional multivalence.

Verses 5 and 24–30 refer to the Sabbath as the motivating factor for gathering twice as much bread on the sixth day. As mentioned above, this is the first reference to the Sabbath in the Old Testament, an indication that it is already known before its official promulgation in 20:8–11. This, too, is another indication that the narrative, at least in part, is preparing us for the events at Mount Sinai. Note also the nature of this Sabbath command. It is not simply that the Sabbath is "observed" by the Israelites in that *they* refrain from gathering food. Rather, it is *God* who refrains from supplying the food. It is *he* who ceases working, so that no manna or quail is to be found. Some of the Israelites break the command not by actually gathering food but merely by attempting to do so. Keeping the Sabbath is something God does and the Israelites are expected to follow suit. This pattern is rooted in creation itself: The Israelites rest because God did.

The main purpose of sending manna and quail is certainly not just to test the Israelites or simply to fill their stomachs. It is rather to teach them something about God, or as verse 6 puts it, so that the Israelites will "know that it was the LORD who brought you out of Egypt" (see also v. 12). That the Israelites will "know" is another echo of the departure narrative. God is not yet finished teaching his people who he is. In fact, he has hardly begun.

It is also in this context that Moses addresses the grumbling of his fellow Israelites. They have complained to Moses and Aaron, but Moses reminds them that their real complaint is against God (vv. 7–8). He is the one they are distrusting and even mocking by their display of thanklessness. God responds again by giving the people another glimpse of his Exodus might. There, out in the desert, they see "the glory of the LORD appearing in the

---

10. One element to this test is worthy of discussion but will not detain us here. Why does God need to test them to see whether they will obey? Does he not know already? Is his knowledge limited? The fact is that God is often painted in a similar way in the Old Testament (see the parade examples in Gen. 22:12 and Job 1:1–2:10). The Old Testament portrait of God is very human at times.

cloud" (v. 10). The last time the Lord appeared in a cloud was in 14:24 as they were making their way through the sea. The cloud was then a sign of God's presence with and protection of his people, just as it is now.

Reference to the cloud is also a glimpse of what is to come. The book of Exodus ends with the *cloud* covering the Tent of Meeting and God's *glory* (*kabod*) filling the tabernacle (40:34). God's glory appearing to them in the cloud (16:10) foreshadows both Sinai and the building of the tabernacle, where the cloud and the glory become more prominent.

Thus, with a view both to the past and the future, God provides bread in the morning and quail at night. Quail was common enough in those regions, but the bread is another matter. Morning dew yields to snow-like flakes, and this is supposedly bread to eat. The people are reasonably surprised. Their initial response is to ask: "What is it?" (v. 15). The Hebrew for this question is *man hu⁾*, which partly explains the name "manna," first seen in verse 31.[11]

Most important is the fact that this food is God's gift to his people. All he asks is that they gather only as much as they need for one day and not keep any until the next morning (v. 16). This gracious provision of food is not to be hoarded, but God is to be trusted anew every day, a lesson they will have to learn for their long trek in the desert and their life as a nation thereafter. Israel is to be kept in a perpetual state of dependence. After all, God has brought them out of Egypt so that they may "serve" him. They must learn that as servants of God, they are bound to trust in his good pleasure.

As might be expected, not everyone obeys God's simple instructions to gather only what they need (v. 20). This, too, foreshadows future events, in particular the "golden calf" episode (ch. 32), where God's giving of his law is likewise accompanied by rebellion. Hence, the Sabbath command hinted at in 16:4–5 is reiterated and expanded. Moses spells out for them that because the seventh day is the Sabbath, there will be no manna or quail for them to gather; God is "resting." They are to follow suit by not going out to gather any food. Thus, in order to have food on the Sabbath, the Israelites must gather twice as much on the day before. But if the food spoils overnight, how is the surplus to be kept edible? They are to bake and boil it (v. 23).[12]

---

11. Actually, v. 31 has simply *man* (the "a" is pronounced as in "father"). It is not clear how the term *manna* came from the Hebrew. The LXX has *man* here, though it has *manna* in such places as Num. 11:6, 7, 9; Deut. 8:3, 16; the New Testament has *manna* (John 6:31, 49; Heb. 9:4; Rev. 2:17).

12. Contrary to the NIV, this is not a suggestion but a command. A better way of translating v. 23 is, "Bake what you *should* bake and boil what you *should* boil." In other words, whatever is "bakeable," i.e., the manna, bake it so it keeps. Whatever is "boilable," i.e., the quail meat, boil it so it keeps.

Some of the Israelites do not see the necessity of obeying the God who has saved them, and they go out on the Sabbath anyway. This second act of disobedience is met with a stunning rebuke by God: "How long will you refuse to keep my commands and my instructions" (v. 28). This pattern becomes commonplace throughout the trek in the desert: rebellion in the face of God's clear commands. The reference to God's commands *for Israel* comes up quite suddenly. The focus of previous chapters has been on Pharaoh's obedience to God's commands, not Israel's. But God has won the battle against Pharaoh. The Israelites are his people now, and he wastes little time reminding them of that fact. Lack of obedience will have dire consequences.

The only previous time Moses uttered a similar phrase to 16:28 was to Pharaoh in 10:3: "How long will you refuse to humble yourself before me?" Is God's patience with his people here already reaching its limit? Is the Israelites' stubbornness so similar to Pharaoh's that it warrants a similar rebuke? This is another warning to Israel that in their grumbling they are in danger of becoming more like Egypt than the holy people God has called them to be.

Although talk of the quail recedes to the background, the manna takes on added significance (vv. 33–36). (1) It is evidently tasty. This is no rice cake or Communion wafer. It tastes like honey, which is one of the elements that make the Promised Land so attractive (see 3:8, 17; 13:5; 33:3). Hence, the manna seems to be a foretaste (literally) of the blessings of Canaan. (2) Some of the manna is to be kept (an omer, i.e., about two quarts) in a jar as a perpetual reminder to future generations that God brought the Israelites out of Egypt. Like the previous meal of Passover and Unleavened Bread, this meal is future-oriented. We see again that God acts in ways that have far-reaching purposes. The point here is not simply to fill their stomachs but to teach his people something that will be passed on for generations.

Verses 34–35 are significant because of a sudden and anachronistic reference to the "Testimony" (i.e., the ark of the Testimony, which is not built until 37:1–9). Any doubt of the anachronism of these verses is put away in 16:35: "The Israelites ate manna forty years, until they came to a land that was settled; they ate manna until they reached the border of Canaan." Clearly, this comment was written after the forty years in the desert were over and the people had "settled" in the land (i.e., after Josh. 5:10–12, when eating manna ceased).

Whatever one may think of the authorship of Exodus in general, Moses did not write these words. This is no veiled prophecy but a backward look to the desert era from the perspective of someone who lived at the very least sometime after Moses died. Are these two verses merely editorial additions updating a Mosaic work, or are statements such as this (along with, e.g., the Unleavened Bread regulations in 12:14—20[13]) clues as to the authorship of the whole? As interesting as this question is, it need not detain us here, for that would divert attention from the theological focus of the narrative.

Verse 36 should not be passed over too quickly. The omer is already mentioned in verse 16, but here the writer adds the explanation that "an omer is one tenth of an ephah" ("omer" is mentioned in the Old Testament only in 16:16, 18, 22, 32, 33, 36). This verse is part of the post-Mosaic summary begun in verse 34. I suggest this was penned at a time when an omer was no longer a popular measurement, hence the need for an explanation. By contrast the ephah is used over thirty times in the Old Testament, often in places where an omer could have been used.[14] Yet note also that even though verse 36 suggests a date of *authorship* well after the time of Moses, the reference to an omer and the need to explain it argue for the *story's* antiquity.

Water From the Rock at Rephidim (17:1–7)

THE THIRD REBELLION episode is the famous incident at Rephidim of getting water from the rock (17:1–7). Rephidim is the Israelites' last stop on their way to Sinai, and here they again complain to God about the lack of water. To have two similar episodes so close to each other in the narrative points out the absurdity of Israel's lack of trust in God. Like Pharaoh before them, how many times do they need to see God work before they understand? They still do not see that he has their best interests in mind, that he has moved mightily from the time of the patriarchs to come to this moment, and he will not let a little thing like a water supply stand in the way.

Still, the people complain. Actually, the word in verse 2 is "quarrel," which is somewhat stronger than "grumble" (used in the other episodes and in v. 3 here).[15] As before, Moses responds by reminding the people that a complaint against him is really a complaint against God. But Moses seems to be at the end of his rope. He "cries out," as he did in 15:25 (again, reminiscent of Israel's cries while in bondage), to God with a complaint of his own (17:4): "What am I to do with these people?" He has just told the Israelites that their complaint is *not* against him but against God. Yet when

---

13. There are a number of correspondences between the manna passage and the Passover and Feast of Unleavened Bread, but these largely come across only in Hebrew. See Houtman, *Exodus*, 2:324.

14. See, e.g., Lev. 5:11; 6:20; 19:36; Num. 5:15; 28:5; Judg. 6:19; Ruth 2:17; 1 Sam. 1:24; 17:17; Isa. 5:10; Ezek. 45:10, 11, 13, 24; 46:5, 7, 11, 14; Mic. 6:10.

15. Sarna, *Exodus*, 94.

he turns to God, his focus is directed toward himself. Is Moses still harboring doubts about his mission?

But God does not become angry with Moses here. He is as patient with him as he is with the others. Moses is instructed to walk ahead to Horeb with some of the elders and strike a rock with the staff with which he struck the Nile (17:5–6). The imagery is obvious. The water from the rock[16] is another Exodus-like event: A staff touches water and the people are saved. The power that has brought the Israelites out of Egypt is the same power that is sustaining them in the desert and that will bring them, eventually, safely into the land God promised to Abraham. It shows that Yahweh is Lord of the desert as he has also shown himself to be Lord of Egypt. The desert is a hostile place, as was Egypt, but both are at God's command.

We should note too that this rock is located at (or near) Horeb.[17] This indicates that Horeb (Sinai) is not far from Rephidim, since the people are able to partake of the water but still be located in Rephidim (where the battle with the Amalekites takes place). Yet the reference to Horeb is more than just a random geographical notation. Like the other rebellion stories, this one brings us closer to Sinai. In fact, this time it is mentioned. The final destination is not only getting closer for the Israelites, it also becomes clearer for the readers. And whereas the manna in the jar is to remind the people of God's goodness, the name of this place is to remind them of their own lack of trust: "Massah and Meribah" (v. 7) means "testing and quarreling." This, of course, is not just a reminder for them but, like the manna, for generations to come.

We have in this passage three stories of grumbling and complaining, which are lovingly and patiently answered by God. Israel's rebellion against God is both sudden and sustained. The reader can only wonder why he puts up with it. But he does put up with it because he has the full picture in mind. His promises to the patriarchs will not be thwarted by anyone—neither by Pharaoh nor even by the Israelites themselves. He keeps his people on track. We must remember that their relationship with God is still in its infancy. Despite all they have seen, perhaps they still need a clearer picture of the holy God who has called them into being. That clearer picture is soon to come on Mount Sinai in chapter 20, but two other episodes must first be addressed.

---

16. A similar incident is narrated in Num. 20:1–13. This is theologically significant. These two events happen near the beginning and end of the desert period. In other words, they "frame" this period, indicating that as a whole this is characterized as a period of rebellion (see P. Enns, "Creation and Re-creation: Psalm 95 and Its Interpretation in Hebrews," *WTJ* 55 [1993]: 255–80).

17. The Hebrew can be read either way.

GOD'S PEOPLE IN THE DESERT. The desert is a difficult time for the Israelites. It is easy to condemn them as faithless, but I suspect that many of us would not have fared much better. Life was hard in Egypt, but it must seem harder still in the uncharted desert through which they are traveling. It is not an easy place for them to live, not only because of their harsh surroundings, but also because their only recourse in a barren land is to trust God completely. And if the Bible teaches us anything about human nature, it is that total trust and obedience are rare even in the most godly person.

The desert is a theme that comes up repeatedly in the Bible. The present passage sets up certain parameters within which we are to look at this theme. At least three prominent elements play off of each other and give definition to the way in which the desert is presented: grumbling, God's gracious provision in response to that grumbling, and God's testing of his people. These three are not to be isolated from one another but help give this passage its shape.

(1) Exodus 15:22—17:7 is, if anything, a story of Israel's grumbling (complaining, quarreling) against God. Complaint is not always a bad thing in the Old Testament. For example, many of the psalms are complaints by God's people who wonder why God has abandoned them (see Ps. 64:1; 142:1; cf. also Hab. 2:1). But the complaining here is different. It is *rebellious* complaining, not such as we see in the psalms, where the psalmist is truly at the end of his rope and calls *to God* precisely *because* he has some faith in him (however tenuous it may be at the time). Here, however, the desert community grumbles or murmurs *to a third party against God* (or God's chosen leader) because of *lack* of faith. At the first sign of difficulty or perceived inequity on God's part, they turn away from him with an attitude of contempt. God does not chide his children for honest doubts, but this is not what is meant by "grumbling" here.

The grumbling we see in 15:22—17:7 is, somewhat stunningly, revisited in Numbers 11:1—35, where the Israelites again complain for lack of food. They are tired of manna and want meat to eat. Although the events of that chapter are similar to those in Exodus 16, Numbers 11 is not merely a retelling of those same events. That complaint happens shortly after the Israelites leave Mount Sinai (10:11), two years after they have left Egypt. The events of Exodus 16 occur in the second month after they have left Egypt, that is, two years *before* Numbers 11.

In Numbers 11, therefore, we have a second series of complaints against God. This chapter assumes that manna has been in steady supply for those two years, but that quail was only intermittent at best (a point not explicitly made in Ex. 16). The people want meat, which is just what God gives them once again. But this time it is no gracious provision but a punishment. They will have enough meat to eat—more than enough. Soon it will come out of their nostrils and they will hate the very sight of it (Num. 11:20). We have moved on to another level of meaning with respect to the desert theme: It is starting to become a place of punishment rather than a gracious supply of food and water, a place where God shows his care for his people.

This dimension of the desert theme reaches a climax of sorts in Numbers 14, 16, and 17. With chapter 14 we are still only about two years into the desert journey.[18] Here the grumbling of God's people reaches a level where God reacts in a way that would have been unthinkable in the Exodus narrative. All those twenty years old or older will not be permitted to enter the land. They will be made to wander in the desert until the last rebel is dead (14:26–35). Surely we have hit the low point in Israel's once victorious march to Canaan. By human standards, the entire plan seems to be hanging by a frayed thread.

(2) But this is not the case. Exodus 15:22–17:7 also testifies to God's gracious provision for his people despite their lack of trust. It would be wrong to think of the desert, even as it is presented in Numbers, as an unexpected twist in God's plan to bring his people to Canaan. It is not a time when God temporarily loses his control over the events. The story about Elim in 15:27 is in part designed to rid us of that notion. God shows his control and power over the desert. It, too, is "his country," and his people are as safe there as anywhere else. It is the place where God comes to his people to provide for them.

(3) God also tests his people in the desert. The word "test" no doubt conjures up images in our minds of pop quizzes or IRS audits, but this is not what the concept means in the Old Testament. God is not a professor looking to "fail" his people at the first wrong answer. He is not putting them in an unbearable situation because he is looking for an excuse to do them in. These are his people, after all, whom he has redeemed from Egypt. The desert tests

---

18. Again, Num. 10:11 put us in the second month of the second year after leaving Egypt. The next date given is the cryptic "first month" mentioned in 20:1. The events that follow (specifically, the death of Aaron in 20:22–29) and comparison to 33:38 make it likely that the events of ch. 20 and following happen somewhere near the close of the forty-year period. The events between chs. 15–19 occur during the intervening thirty-eight years; it is difficult to be more specific than this. Information given in the expanded itinerary in Num. 33:3–49 combined with the retelling of these events in Deut. 1:1–2:23 puts the rebellion of Num. 14 (Kadesh Barnea) around the two-year mark. The relative date of the rebellion of Num. 16 is more difficult to determine. It is also worth mentioning that at this point, Israel had "tested" God ten times (Num. 14:22). This may be reminiscent of the ten plagues, where Pharaoh "tested" God ten times by not letting the Israelites go.

are not trials for the Israelites to prove that they are somehow "worthy" of God. Such thinking misunderstands not only the Exodus narrative but the theology of the Old Testament. God does not redeem Israel from Egypt for any reason other than his own sense of fidelity to the promise he made to the patriarchs. It is not that the Israelites are now "good enough" to be worthy of his attention.

The purpose of the desert tests are succinctly summarized in Exodus 20:20: "Moses said to the people, 'Do not be afraid. God has come to test you, so that the fear of God will be with you to keep you from sinning.'" God tests his people for *their* benefit, not for his own. It is through passing and failing these tests that God's people learn the nature of the obedience that he requires of them. Exodus 15:22–17:7 records the first series of tests that the Israelites are to go through, and we should note the nature that this testing takes on: (a) "Pay attention to his commands and keep all his decrees" (15:26); (b) trust God daily by gathering only what you need (16:4, 16); and (c) keep the Sabbath (16:5, 24–30).

These are apparently vital lessons for God's people to learn at this stage of their journey (both physical and spiritual). It is not so much that God is testing them to see whether they will keep the Sabbath, for example. On a certain level of the narrative that is part of it, but there is a deeper lesson being taught. God wants to produce in his people a deepening relationship with him as their covenant God so that they will better understand the importance of keeping the Sabbath, the other commands, and the need to trust him daily. In other words, they are being taught how to obey God. This is what it means for God to test his people. The problem is not so much that the Israelites "fail" the test, but that *they* turn around and put *God* to the test (17:7).

By testing the Israelites, God is teaching them. This is why at this initial stage in their journey he responds to their complaint not with fire (see Num. 11:1–3) but with the gracious provision of water and food. We should not lose sight that God responds to the Israelites in Exodus 15:22–17:7 with barely a hint of retribution. His only harsh words in this passage are in 16:28, which are certainly threatening, but this is all we hear of him. God's anger, to put it another way, is not the focus.

But this forbearance on God's part seems to come to an end in the book of Numbers. Now he does not just speak stern words but enacts punishments as well. The desert has taken on a very different feel. Whereas it was once a place where Israel could see God's care for them, it is now a place of his wrath. A victory march has become a death march—or nearly so, were it not for the grace of God, which once again rises to the occasion. For they do not all die. A core is left: Joshua, Caleb, and all those under the age of twenty at the time of the rebellion at Kadesh in Numbers 14. What was to be a brief journey through a barren land has become a trial by fire, a process of purification wherein God's people are being prepared to enter the land at last.

Subsequent reflections in the Bible on the desert period reflect the transition we see from Exodus to Numbers. A number of passages in the Old Testament describe the desert in a positive way, as the place where God came to meet his people and escort them to Canaan, the place where God demonstrated to all his special care for his special people:

> There [in the desert] you saw how the LORD your God carried you, as a father carries his son, all the way you went until you reached this place. (Deut. 1:31)

> Therefore I am now going to allure her; I will lead her into the desert and speak tenderly to her. (Hos. 2:14)

> For forty years you sustained them in the desert; they lacked nothing, their clothes did not wear out nor did their feet become swollen. (Neh. 9:21)

These passages speak of the desert period as one in which God showed his love for his people, as a father for his child and as a husband for his bride.[19] The desert was a positive place where God's love for Israel was the focus.

Such an understanding of the desert is also carried through in Isaiah with respect to the departure from Babylon. As we have noted in other chapters, the departure from Babylon is a second Exodus for God's people. Isaiah typically depicts the desert as a place of refuge, where God will meet his people and bring them back home. It is not a hostile place but the way back to Canaan, with God marching alongside of them:

> A voice of one calling:
> "In the desert prepare
>   the way for the LORD;
> make straight in the wilderness
>   a highway for our God." (Isa. 40:3)

> See, I am doing a new thing!
>   Now it springs up; do you not perceive it?
> I am making a way in the desert
>   and streams in the wasteland.
> The wild animals honor me,
>   the jackals and the owls,
> because I provide water in the desert

---

19. See also Ps. 78:52; 105:41; Jer. 2:6; Hos. 13:5.

> and streams in the wasteland,
> to give drink to my people, my chosen,
>> the people I formed for myself
>> that they may proclaim my praise. (43:19–21)

Other Old Testament passages, however, have a different view of the desert, a view more in line with that given in Numbers. The element that is highlighted in these passages is Israel's rebellion in the desert despite God's care for them. The desert is used as a constant reminder and object lesson for God's people not to harden their hearts:

> He split the rocks in the desert
>> and gave them water as abundant as the seas;
> he brought streams out of a rocky crag
>> and made water flow down like rivers.
> But they continued to sin against him,
>> rebelling in the desert against the Most High.
> They willfully put God to the test
>> by demanding the food they craved.
> They spoke against God, saying,
>> "Can God spread a table in the desert?
> When he struck the rock, water gushed out,
>> and streams flowed abundantly.
> But can he also give us food?
>> Can he supply meat for his people?"
> When the LORD heard them, he was very angry.... (Ps. 78:15–21; see
>> also v. 40)

> In the desert they gave in to their craving;
>> in the wasteland they put God to the test. (Ps. 106:14)[20]

Certainly the reason why the Old Testament itself reflects such diverse opinion on the characterization of the desert period is due to the diversity in the Pentateuch itself. Thus, a dual lesson is to be learned: comfort and trust in God's blessing, and punishment in the face of constant rebellion. Israel's desert experience had both.

Both of these summaries of the desert experience are also reflected in the New Testament. There are a number of echoes of the Exodus experience in the Gospel of John, some of which have already been mentioned in other contexts in this commentary. Particularly relevant here is the feeding of the five thousand (6:1–15) and Jesus as the "bread of life" (6:25–59).

---

20. See also Ps. 95:8; Ezek. 20:13–36.

The feeding of the five thousand can be understood on a number of different levels. One of those levels is as a provision of food similar to the manna incident. Here Christ miraculously provides food for a mass of people who have been following him. There is even a "test" involved (John 6:6). By providing bread and meat (like manna and quail?), Jesus is not just filling their stomachs but teaching them about who he is. He is their source of life, who will take care of them as they wander through life. This is not just a random trick Jesus has pulled, like the magicians of Pharaoh's court, to show the people how powerful he is. It is rather a display of power and love as God had done for Israel centuries earlier. Thus, by learning this lesson, the people will know that they are not "to work for food that spoils [like manna left overnight], but for food that endures to eternal life, which the Son of Man will give you" (6:27).

Jesus' "bread of life" speech is even more explicit. The crowd that has witnessed the feeding miracle are intent on following him. They find him and begin to discuss with him what God requires of them. Jesus tells them that they are "to believe in the one he has sent" (John 6:29). But the people require a sign to prove to them that Jesus is worthy of such attention. After all, as they argue in verse 31, Moses gave *his* people a sign, bread from heaven. What is Jesus' proof? Jesus responds (vv. 32–33):

> I tell you the truth, it is not Moses who has given you the bread from heaven, but it is my Father who gives you the true bread from heaven. For the bread of God is he who comes down from heaven and gives life to the world.

The benefits to those who "eat" this bread from heaven are greater than for those who ate the manna: They will never hunger nor thirst again, and they will be raised up at the last day (vv. 35, 40).

But how does the crowd respond? They grumble (John 6:41, 43). Even some of the disciples grumble to the point where they stop following him (vv. 61–66). How ironic! Jesus, the true bread, *has* come and the people *respond* by grumbling. Whereas the Israelites grumbled because they had no bread, the crowd grumbles because they do. Even though this bread far exceeds anyone's expectations—it gives eternal life, not simply filling one's stomach to live another day—they will have none of it. But it is the only means by which they have any hope to live. In the same way as the manna was the only food to keep the Israelites alive another day, Christ, the bread from heaven, is now the only way to life eternal. We may also presume in Jesus' use of this desert story that he saw a ready analogy between the Israelites in their desert wandering and the people of his day, a point to which we will return shortly.

The desert motif in John may be traced further to include John 7:37–39. Jesus has already introduced the notion of "thirst" in 6:35, which reflects the miraculous giving of water in Exodus 15:22–27 and 17:1–7. He is the bread *and* the water of Israel's desert experience. This is made more explicit in John 7:37–39.

On the last and greatest day of the Feast, Jesus stood and said in a loud voice, "If anyone is thirsty, let him come to me and drink. Whoever believes in me, as the Scripture has said, streams of living water will flow from within him." By this he meant the Spirit, whom those who believed in him were later to receive. Up to that time the Spirit had not been given, since Jesus had not yet been glorified.

What is particularly interesting here is the equation of the "living water" with the Spirit given at Pentecost. Paul likewise speaks of the manna as "spiritual food" in 1 Corinthians 10:3, which doesn't mean "food for spiritual people" but food that is of the Spirit. This is also what Revelation 2:17 seems to be pointing toward, although in a more directly eschatological sense ("To him who overcomes, I will give some of the hidden manna"). This, then, gives us a proper perspective from which to apply the desert motif to our lives (see below).

Other New Testament passages highlight the negative side of the desert experience. One of those is 1 Corinthians 10:5–11:

Nevertheless, God was not pleased with most of them; their bodies were scattered over the desert.

Now these things occurred as examples to keep us from setting our hearts on evil things as they did. Do not be idolaters, as some of them were; as it is written: "The people sat down to eat and drink and got up to indulge in pagan revelry." We should not commit sexual immorality, as some of them did—and in one day twenty-three thousand of them died. We should not test the Lord, as some of them did—and were killed by snakes. And do not grumble, as some of them did—and were killed by the destroying angel.

These things happened to them as examples and were written down as warnings for us, on whom the fulfillment of the ages has come.

The lesson to be learned from Israel's rebellions in the desert is that the church should not follow their example. In view of Christ's coming, such grumbling is unthinkable. It seems obvious that for Paul's admonition to be effective, one must assume a certain analogy between Israel and the church. Specifically, for Israel's desert experience to be a fitting warning for the church, Paul understands the church to be in some sort of "desert" setting too.

This analogy is precisely what we find explicated in greater detail in Hebrews 3:1—4:11. This is a complex passage, but the main contours are plain. Hebrews 3:1—6 provide the basis for understanding the subsequent citation of Psalm 95:7—11. The writer of this book explains that Jesus is a new Moses and that, therefore, Jesus' people, the church, are the "new Israel."

With this in mind the writer proceeds to expound Psalm 95:7—11 in Hebrews 3:7—4:11. In its original context, Psalm 95 is a warning to Israel not to rebel as the Exodus community had done. This psalm explicitly draws on the events of the desert wanderings.[21] It was during their period of desert wandering that Israel rebelled.

The point is this: In order for the rebellions of Israel's desert wanderings to provide the basis for a warning to the church (see esp. Heb. 3:12—19), the writer must understand the church to be in an analogous period of desert wandering. If we look at this passage through 4:11, the analogy extends further: Both Israel and the church have been led out of oppression of some sort by a divinely appointed leader. The goal of that Exodus was to bring God's people to their final rest. For Israel this rest was the land of Canaan; for the church it is a spiritual and eternal rest.

But *in the meantime*, both communities are in an extended period of desert wandering. For the church, it is not just individual Christian lives that are "in the desert." The entire church age is analogous to the forty-year period of our Israelite ancestors. We who have been redeemed through the death and resurrection of Christ, our Moses, are on the way to our final rest. While we are on that journey, the Old Testament warnings pertaining to Israel's desert wandering apply to us as well.

There is one significant difference, however, between the church's desert and Israel's, and Hebrews' citation of Psalm 95 brings this out nicely.[22] The relevant portion is 95:7b—10a:

> Today, if you hear his voice,
>> do not harden your hearts
> as you did at Meribah,
>> as you did that day at Massah in the desert,
> where your fathers tested and tried me,
>> though they had seen what I did.
> *For forty years I was angry* with that generation. (italics added)

---

21. In fact, the events of Meribah and Massah are most likely in mind. In Heb. 3:8, the words "rebellion" and "testing" are translations of the Hebrew Meribah and Massah. Hebrews is here following the LXX.

22. For what follows, a fuller treatment may be found in Enns, "Creation and Re-creation," 255—80.

Here, "forty years" is characterized by God's anger. The manner in which Hebrews cites this portion of Psalm 95 introduces a slight, but theologically powerful change:

> Today, if you hear his voice,
>   do not harden your hearts
> as you did in the rebellion,
>   during the time of testing in the desert,
> where your fathers tested and tried me
>   and *for forty years saw what I did.*
> *That is why* I was angry with that generation,
>   and I said, "Their hearts are always going astray,
>   and they have not known my ways." (Heb. 3:7—10; italics added)

By inserting one small word, the Greek *dio* (translated "That is why" in the NIV), the author of Hebrews has introduced a shift in the psalm's meaning. Now, the "forty years" characterizes the period during which Israel "saw what I did," and anger is what *follows* this forty-year period. He does this to make a gripping theological point in his application of this psalm to the life of the church. If the church age is analogous to the forty-year period, it is inappropriate to characterize it as the period of *wrath* as it was for Israel. Christ has come! The climax of redemptive history is here. This is not a period of wrath, but, as the writer correctly puts it, the period in which we see God's activity ("for forty years saw what I did"): The lame are healed, the dead are raised, throngs of Jews and Gentiles are worshiping the Savior.

That such an exegetical move on Hebrews' part is wholly intentional is seen in Hebrews 3:17, where he does refer to the forty-year period as one of anger ("and with whom was he *angry for forty years?*"). Why does he flip-flop between these two citations of Psalm 95? Because in Hebrews 3:9—10 he is applying the psalm to the *church*, whereas in 3:17 he is referring to *Israel's* desert wandering. Although this author's use of Psalm 95 may raise a number of issues regarding the appropriate use of the Old Testament in the life of the church, we should not lose sight of the overarching lesson to be learned here. The church is the new Israel as it exists in its own type of desert wandering. Our Egypt of sin and death is behind us. Our Moses, unlike the first Moses, has entered before us into the promised rest, and we are soon to follow.

It was, of course, Joshua and not Moses who brought the Israelites into Canaan. Hence, Christ is the "true" Moses who completes the mission. And by bringing his church into "Canaan," Christ is not only fulfilling the role of Moses but also that which Joshua performed. In fact, Joshua's role, according to Hebrews 4:8–11, is merely a prelude to the final rest to be given by the final "Joshua," who is Christ. So, we are in our desert wanderings. Hence, "Today, if you hear his voice, do not harden your hearts" (3:15; 4:7).

THE CHRISTIAN'S DESERT WANDERING. The desert period of the Exodus community is ours as well, but, as we have seen in Hebrews 3:9–10, with a slight twist. This is no period of wrath but one of untold blessing, for we are privy to the "fullness of time," the climax of God's redemptive plan. We are in a privileged position of living in the age in which the kingdom of God has indeed already come in Christ, although we still await its final implementation at his second coming. Still, grumbling and complaining as our Israelite ancestors did remains a live option for us. And thus we must make every effort to guard against this in view of the clearer vision we have of God's goodness that is ours by virtue of the Spirit who dwells in us. Indeed, it is precisely because of the Spirit's indwelling that we are able to resist.

If all we learn from this passage is "don't be a grumbler," we will miss the riches it holds for us as we walk through the desert. The lessons we learn from Exodus 15:22–17:7 must be set in the context of the completed work of Christ, as I have attempted to do in the Bridging Contexts section. What remains is to point out two avenues of Christian application.

(1) We see that the desert is "hostile" territory. As a popular song puts it, "This world is not my home." This is true. We are merely passing through on a journey. This is not to say that the world is necessarily antithetical to God. This is still *God's* world. It belongs to him, and he is still very much in control of his creation, although in ways not always clear to us. Just as the desert posed no barrier for God to act mightily on behalf of his people (he provided water and food), the desert in which we live is fully at God's disposal as well.

Our view toward the world in which we live should balance the knowledge that it belongs to God, but it is not our final resting place. We should take comfort in the fact that we, even here, are God's special people, but we should not become too comfortable where we are. We are to trust God fully while we are here (unlike the Israelites) while at the same time not allowing our current circumstances to define ultimate reality. Our gaze must always be not on where we are but on where we are going.

(2) We must be continually on guard against our all-too-common penchant for judging our circumstances by our "stomachs." This is precisely what the Israelites in the desert were guilty of. We must ask, "Why did they not trust God to help them, especially after all they had seen him do already?" The answer is not simply "lack of faith." That is far too vague. One must ask

why they lacked faith. The reason why they behaved the way they did is actually transparent, not because the text itself makes it explicit but because Israel's error in the desert is the sin common to us all, and the one from which so many of our sins derive: self-centeredness.

Throughout Exodus we have seen Israel's inclination for defining their situation in terms of their own perceptions. Whether it is lack of straw for making bricks or the advancing Egyptian army at the shores of the Red Sea, the Israelites did not respond in a way that we would expect people who have witnessed God's mighty acts to respond.

All around us is the ever-present temptation to see ourselves as the center of the universe. What we see on television in particular trains us to think that our perceived "needs," whether it be a new toothpaste, a car, razor, beer, deodorant, nice clothes, or whatever, are to be met as quickly as possible. In fact, we are told that we have a right to those things. Nothing is more important than meeting our perceived needs.

The way of the cross is different. We are being trained in righteousness to be able to rid our minds of perceived needs and their immediate gratification and to turn our glance outward (or upward) toward Canaan and the God who is determined to get us there. It is an arduous training process. We are in a hostile environment in which the gospel is attacked, not simply by such superficial avenues as political agendas or New Age theories, but in subtle and simple ways that have always been at the core of human misery. Christians cannot forget—in fact, this must be the center of our self-understanding—that Christ and Christ alone is our bread and water. He is our true need. Unlike what the world offers, he truly fills us up with bread and water that lead to eternal life, not junk food that tastes good for the moment but does us no good whatsoever.

We must not judge our circumstances by how we see them but by how God wants us to see them. He is teaching us to look at the big picture rather than our own narrow, doomed version of that picture. But seeing only our version of things is so natural to us! We were born that way.

I still remember a heated debate at our dinner table some time back between my youngest child (then age four and a half) and my oldest (age ten). Several years earlier we lived in suburban Boston, and one of our favorite family activities was visiting the Public Garden and riding the swan boats (known to children the world over through Robert McClosky's *Make Way for Duck-lings*). Now, Sophie, my four-and-a-half-year-old, was only one year old when we left the Boston area. She doesn't remember riding on the boats (or anything else for that matter).

At dinner, my son Erich, the ten-year-old, made the tactical error of reminiscing about the fun *all* of us had on the swan boats. Sophie, of course, insisted that she never rode them. Erich, having the advantage of a bigger perspective than Sophie, rejoined that she most certainly *did* ride them, to which Sophie responded in the predictable manner until the whole thing escalated well beyond what my wife and I thought was warranted. Erich's final threat was to produce pictures of us all smiling on the swan boats.

At this point Sophie responded in a very interesting way. "But Erich, I don't *remember* being on the swan boats." It was clear what she meant by that. Since the event was not within her sphere of perception, it did not happen. Her grasp of the situation defined reality for her. Although we all eventually grow up physically, our spiritual development often lags behind. Christ's goal for his people is to lead us to greater knowledge of him, which leads to a more sober understanding of our own puny perspectives.

We are Christians called to a higher life, but the things we want, the things we work for and strive after, are often no different from those around us. We accept the needs that our world tells us to have. Our gods are our stomachs, to paraphrase Paul (Phil. 3:19). It is a wonderful breakthrough in Christian maturity when the Lord teaches us to *examine* these needs to see whether they are from God or not. Many Christians in America struggle with material issues. How many of us have not said things like the following: "I have this sofa, but I would like a nicer one." "This house is adequate, but we need a bigger one." "My income allows us to live fine, but if only I made $10,000 more a year, that would make all the difference."

How difficult it is for us to learn the lesson that Paul himself had to learn (Phil. 4:11–13):

> I have learned to be content whatever the circumstances. I know what it is to be in need, and I know what it is to have plenty. I have learned the secret of being content in any and every situation, whether well fed or hungry, whether living in plenty or in want. I can do everything through him who gives me strength.

We go through our own desert experiences honed in on our own lacks and desires, but wholly oblivious to the new creations we are in Christ. After all we have seen God do in our lives, not the least of which is giving us a new life, we still harbor the notion, "But if I only had this or that, then things would be OK."

There is nothing wrong with praying for a new house or a better income. There is no virtue in being "antimaterialistic"; God gives us all things. But there is that fine line that is sometimes so faint to us, but so thick and clear to God, between seeking the Lord's guidance in these matters with simple trust, knowing that our perceptions of what we need are not always pure, and seeking these things because we feel that we just *cannot* be happy without them, that they will meet some deep emotional need. The fact is that they will not meet those needs. If anything, it will make things worse. A free person is one who is content *whatever* the circumstances, because he or she knows that the big picture is more than the clothes on our back.

Jesus himself addressed this issue in words that are as relevant to us today as they would have been for the Israelites at the beginning of their desert journey (Matt. 6:30–32):

> Will [God] not much more clothe you, O you of little faith? So do not worry, saying, "What shall we eat?" or "What shall we drink?" or "What shall we wear?" For the pagans run after all these things, and your heavenly Father knows that you need them.

Did the Israelites really think that they were being led out into the desert to die? Apparently, this *is* what they thought. And it is easy to see why: They did not look past themselves and their own needs, so they turned their frustration toward Moses and God. All they could see was that their needs, right then and there, were not being met. As foolish as their actions may seem to us, my guess is that many of us may have more in common with the Israelites than we like to admit.

The good news, of course, is that Christ does not let go of us during our desert march. He has bought us at a great price and at least *he* keeps things in perspective for us. To use the language of the desert narrative, he is *testing* us. Again, this is not an occasional spot check to see if we *really* mean business. It is Christ knowing full well that, when push comes to shove, we *don't* mean business, but he is there to train us to do so. Sometimes I have noticed that he uses our perceived needs as a means for teaching us this lesson. The Lord, by his grace, sometimes allows us to experience the fruit of our own self-centeredness in order to impress on us how fleeting such a focus really is. These times of testing are a great gift from God. He is moving us to a deeper understanding of what life is *really* about.

For example, it is easy to get caught up in the flow of "upward mobility." This is not something reserved for yuppies. The love of money is something nearly everyone, in every age (see 1 Tim. 6:6–10) struggles with. Whenever this happens to me, which seems to be quite often lately, it takes a lot of effort to seek the Lord's guidance to be able to look at the matter clearly.

Not long ago our family was in the throes of a significant decision: whether to move into a nicer house or stay where we are. This decision process began, quite imperceptibly, as a feeling of dissatisfaction with our present situation. This dissatisfaction arose from a mental picture we had of the *ideal* house we wanted. The question, of course, is where this mental picture came from. I don't really know, but most likely from subtle, implicit comparisons I have made all my life between what I have and what others have. So, our decision to put the house on the market became an obsession of sorts. It became the center of what we felt we *needed* to make our lives complete, although I was much too sophisticated to ever let on that this was the case!

As it turns out, the Lord has been using even this mundane situation to test us, that is, to teach us about himself and what it means to be a servant of God. As I write this, it has been over a year since our house first went on the market, and during that time we have learned, slowly but surely, some things about ourselves that we don't particularly like. Why was I so irritable and so quick to complain to God that "all we want is a house"? More important, we are learning that God has in store for us much more than we imagine. He knows what we *need*. His goal is to conform us to the image of Christ so that we begin to understand what real needs are, what gives us true, lasting happiness.

I wish I could say that I had a vision or an angel came to me in a dream, telling me what God's will is, but this is not what happened. Through a series of experiences and observations, as subtle as those false perceptions that started us down that road to begin with, we are beginning to see, to understand, that God cares for us more than we give him credit for. And he shows this care not by giving us what we want, but by using what *we* want to teach us how to want *him* more. It is a gift from God to be able to say with one's whole heart, "I trust the Lord to do what is best." It is a gift he is willing to give.

When we rise above the din of our self-centered world, we can begin to make a difference in our world to those around us. What message are we passing on to our children if we make it our passion to listen to those grumbling voices inside us that tell us we are not complete unless something is added to us? I cannot help but think that a life of contentment, which is a life that trusts in God, when it is truly lived out, will have a lasting impact on those around us.

It is important for us to be examples of piety to others. Not in a superficial moralistic sense, for that is far too simple, but in the sense that one is so much a servant of God that he or she will go wherever the Lord leads. That trust in God is not fleeting but the bedrock on which life's everyday decisions are to be made.

Exodus 17:8–16

THE AMALEKITES CAME and attacked the Israelites at
Rephidim. ⁹Moses said to Joshua, "Choose some of our
men and go out to fight the Amalekites. Tomorrow I
will stand on top of the hill with the staff of God in my hands."

¹⁰So Joshua fought the Amalekites as Moses had ordered,
and Moses, Aaron and Hur went to the top of the hill. ¹¹As
long as Moses held up his hands, the Israelites were winning,
but whenever he lowered his hands, the Amalekites were winning. ¹²When Moses' hands grew tired, they took a stone and
put it under him and he sat on it. Aaron and Hur held his
hands up—one on one side, one on the other—so that his
hands remained steady till sunset. ¹³So Joshua overcame the
Amalekite army with the sword.

¹⁴Then the LORD said to Moses, "Write this on a scroll as
something to be remembered and make sure that Joshua hears
it, because I will completely blot out the memory of Amalek
from under heaven."

¹⁵Moses built an altar and called it The LORD is my Banner.
¹⁶He said, "For hands were lifted up to the throne of the
LORD. The LORD will be at war against the Amalekites from
generation to generation."

Original Meaning

ALTHOUGH THIS PASSAGE recounts another act of
deliverance in the desert, it is treated separately
from the previous three stories. The concern here
is not over food or water in a barren land, but a
military exploit. The attack of the Israelites by the Amalekites is the first
such military encounter for the recently freed slaves, though it will not be the
last. After they leave Sinai and for the remainder of their existence as a nation,
wars and battles with the surrounding nations will be commonplace.

The mention of this battle here in the narrative performs a specific theological function. Just as certain elements in the previous passage foreshadow
events in Israel's near future (Sinai and the giving of the law), the battle with
the Amalekites foreshadows the ultimate goal toward which God is bringing his newly freed people: the conquest of Canaan. In fact, in Numbers 13–
14, the presence of the Amalekites is one of the causes for the Israelites to

have doubts about God's promise to take the land. It is striking that their defeat here in Exodus 17 has no bearing on the people's perception of their situation two years later.

This story also helps to underscore the lesson the people should have learned from the previous events, that grumbling about Moses and his leadership is not only lacking in trust, it is dangerous. Israel's real enemies should not be from within, for there are plenty on the outside to worry about. The defeat of the Egyptian army at the sea did not end outside hostility toward Israel. Egypt only tried to prevent their departure. Now the Amalekites are poised to prevent their arrival at Sinai and Canaan. If they succeed, the Exodus may just as well have never happened.

The Amalekites are a mysterious people. They were certainly desert dwellers, but the only information we have about them is from the Old Testament itself.[1] We meet them first somewhat abruptly in Genesis 14:7. Later we come upon a certain Amalek, who is said to be the grandson of Esau (36:12, 16). Presumably Amalek is the ancestor of the people named after him.[2] In fact, the word translated "Amalekites" in Exodus 17:8, 13, 14, and 16 of the NIV is actually "Amalek": The Israelites battle "Amalek," meaning the people, the Amalekites.

But this piece of information does not clear up who these people are. When we meet them in Exodus 17, we only learn of their apparently unprovoked attack on the Israelites. The memory of this brutal attack was ingrained on Israel's collective memory (Deut. 25:17, 19; cf. Num. 24:20). We meet them a third time as the Israelites are exploring the land of Canaan on what should have been the end of their desert march (Num. 13:29; 14:25, 43, 45). The Amalekites, along with other peoples, discourage the Israelites from seizing the land, which results in a prolonged desert march of an extra thirty-eight years.

The struggles of the Israelites with the Amalekites do not end, however, after crossing the Jordan. They actively stand in their way (Judg. 3:13; 6:3, 33; 7:12; 10:12). They are not defeated until Saul's campaign recorded in 1 Samuel 15, although David has to finish the job later (1 Sam. 30), since Saul spares "Agag king of the Amalekites" (15:8, 20, 32) and keeps some of the spoils for himself. They are not heard from again apart from a reference to "Haman the Agagite" in Esther 3:1, which likely indicates that Haman was

---

1. A helpful summary of what little we know of the Amalekites may be found in G. L. Mattingly, "Amalek," *ABD*, 1:169–71.

2. It also seems that the mention of the Amalekites in Gen. 14:7, i.e., before the time of Esau and the birth of Amalek, is an indication that the writing of Gen. 14, in whole or in part, reflects a later time. Perhaps the reference to the "territory of the Amalekites" was the writer's way of making the past events of Gen. 14 more intelligible to his readers.

of Amalekite ancestry. We have no more information on who exactly these people were. Nevertheless, the Amalekites were a well-known, recurring threat to Israel's well-being. The original audience of Exodus 17:8–16 needs no further introduction to these people.

A number of elements of the Exodus story are mentioned here for the first time. In verse 9 Joshua is referred to. It is striking that he appears here so matter-of-factly, as if he is a well-known character by this time. His name appears four times in this brief passage.[3] This suggests that he needs no introduction to Israelite readers. As we have seen throughout Exodus, the writer tells the story at times in an abbreviated manner, either because the information is not vital to his interests or because the information is so well known.

Joshua's appearance here foreshadows the many military encounters the Israelites will have later on, especially during the Conquest. Since Joshua will be leading the Israelites at that time, it is only fitting that he be prominently displayed here. Moses could just as well have, at God's command, struck the Amalekites with some disease or plague as he did Egypt. He could have climbed the hill with his staff, waved it around a few times, and made the Amalekites go away. But this is not what happens. Rather, Joshua is told to pick some good fighters and meet them in the battlefield. God commands that *they* now fight, not apart from God to be sure (see vv. 11–12), but that they fight nevertheless. Introduced here is a taste of what will occupy much of Israel's time and resources until the Babylonian exile—war.

Three other elements in verse 9 are also theologically significant: "Tomorrow" Moses will climb a "hill" with "the staff of God in [his] hand." (1) Why wait until "tomorrow"? Throughout Exodus "tomorrow" represents the time in which God will act to punish Israel's enemies. We saw this in the plague narrative (8:23, 29; 9:5, 18; 10:4). Most recently the word was used in 16:23 with respect to Israel's gathering of bread on the sixth day in anticipation of the Sabbath. In other words, tomorrow is when something "big" happens.[4] That the defeat of the Amalekites is to take place "tomorrow" signals to the reader that this is another redemptive event. It is a plague on another of Israel's enemies.

(2) This is reinforced by the use of the "staff," which was present in the plague narrative. Through Moses' staff God worked great acts to bring Israel out of Egypt, not the least of which was the parting of the sea. The defeat of the Amalekites will be another act of deliverance by the God of the Exodus, and thus it is fitting for the staff to play a role in this.

---

3. Apart from ch. 17, Joshua's name appears three more times in Exodus: 24:13; 32:17; 33:11. The last reference is the only one to indicate that Joshua is Moses' aide and the son of Nun.

4. The word is also used in Ex. 32:5. After the altar for the golden calf was built, Aaron announces, "Tomorrow there will be a festival to the LORD." Mimicking this language highlights Israel's contemptuousness in attempting to sanctify their own sinful worship.

(3) As "tomorrow" and the "staff" are a look backward, "hill" is a look forward. Within two chapters, Moses will again stand on the top of another "hill," Mount Sinai, to hear what God will do for his people. Like the hints of the giving of the law we saw in the previous passage, this passage prepares us further for the climactic encounter between God and his people.

In verse 10, we read that Joshua obeys Moses' command to fight the Amalekites. This is another hint of what is to come. It is precisely Joshua's obedience that makes him a fitting successor to Moses (see Num. 27:12–23; Deut. 31:14; 34:9). As the Pentateuch progresses, Joshua's obedience is often contrasted to the disobedience of the Israelites.

Verse 10 also gives another name that has to this point not been mentioned: Hur (see also 24:14, where he is again mentioned along with Aaron). He is the son of Caleb and the grandfather of Bezalel (1 Chron. 2:19–20; this same genealogy is given in Ex. 31:2; 35:30; 38:22).[5] If the Hur of Exodus 17 (where no genealogy is given) is the same one referred to later in Exodus and 1 Chronicles, we have another significant foreshadowing in our passage. Bezalel, Hur's grandson, is one of the builders of the tabernacle, which is the topic for most of Exodus 25–40. His mention here may be hinting at what will dominate most of the second half of the book.

Verses 11–13 recount one of the more unusual events in this book. Moses goes up to the top of the hill and raises his hands. As long as his hands are up, the Israelites prevail in the battle. Whenever they drop from fatigue, the Amalekites gain the upper hand (no pun intended). Finally, to ensure that his hands remain in the correct position, Aaron and Hur hold Moses' hands up until sunset. This brings total victory to the Israelites.[6]

Several questions surface in our minds. Most important, the text does not tell us what Moses' raised hands are supposed to represent. Does he raise them in *prayer*? This is often assumed to be the case, but why doesn't the text say so? It is true that the raising of hands is a common Semitic posture for prayer,[7] but why are no words spoken? Exodus 9:29 can be adduced in support of the prayer explanation ("When I have gone out of the city, I will spread out my hands in prayer to the LORD"), but why does 9:29 mention prayer whereas 17:11 does not? Furthermore, if it is prayer, why does the course of battle shift whenever his hands drop? Are we to understand that the act of praying only occurs when hands are raised? This seems unlikely.

---

5. We should note here that this is not the Caleb who served as a spy in Canaan, who is listed as the son of Jephunneh (Num. 32:12).

6. Verse 13 in the NIV says, "Joshua overcame the Amalekite army *with the sword*." The Hebrew is literally "with the mouth of the sword." This is a common idiom (e.g., in Judges) and can be translated "mercilessly" or "harshly." The clear notion is that Israel's victory is total.

7. Sarna, *Exploring Exodus*, 122.

Some commentaries suggest this is some sort of "magical" feat performed by Moses, perhaps some power emanating from the staff.[8] Others assign to Moses' gesture a psychological explanation, that his raised hands are a sign of encouragement to the troops. Neither explanation seems satisfying. Nowhere else do we find a hint of "magic" in Moses' acts on behalf of the people. The psychological explanation seems too desperate. But can a better explanation be found? To be frank, no proposed explanation is problem-free. This problem is a classic example of what interpreters run into when attempting to explain a cryptic text.[9]

But let me give several thoughts to keep in mind as we continue the age-old discussion of the meaning of this story. (1) As with the other "abrupt" elements of this passage (e.g., the mention of Joshua and Hur), we should assume that the ancient Israelites understood what this meant. Of course, this does not help *us*, but at least the solutions we pose should be more or less in keeping with what ancient readers may have been able to accept.

(2) The important thing to keep in mind is not necessarily what Moses does but the result it has. Moses' strange act focuses our attention not so much on the battlefield but on the hill. Is it not somewhat striking that the battle itself is not referred to, only the result? The hill is where the battle is truly won. It is not the case that *God* earlier defeated the Egyptian army but now the *Israelites* must muster troops on their own against the Amalekites. The battle is God's here too. They must remember this as they engage more and more frequently in battles with other peoples.

(3) This next point is more subtle. This is not the first time Moses raises his hands to heaven before God acts on behalf of his people. We have already seen this with respect to the hail (9:22), the locusts (10:12), and the parting of the sea (14:16). In fact, hail and locusts are plagues that are also announced as to occur "tomorrow" (9:18; 10:4; cf. 17:9 here). I suggest that this incident should be seen, at least in some sense, as analogous to the power of God displayed in the plagues. Since the raising of Moses' staff was crucial in Israel's departure from Egypt, it is fitting that the Amalekites, Israel's new enemy, be defeated by a similar display of power. This does not, of course, settle the issue of why the battle shifts when Moses drops his hands. Why must Moses keep his hands raised all day? Commentators throughout history have not been bashful about offering suggestions. Perhaps, as others have suggested, it is a

---

8. See Houtman, *Exodus*, 2:383—84.

9. I have, however, found helpful the discussion by C. L. Meyers (*The Tabernacle Menorah: A Synthetic Study of a Symbol From the Biblical Cult* [ASORDS 2; Missoula, Mont.: Scholars, 1976], 144—48). Meyers argues that the "staff of God" is a symbol of God's presence. More specifically, it is a "portable tree." Trees are known to have had such symbolic significance in the ancient Near East.

lesson in "team play": The Israelites need to begin working with Moses rather than against him.

Calvin offers a suggestion that, I must admit, I passed over quickly at first. To summarize, he thinks that this represents how God delegates authority to ministers.[10] I admit that this can easily be dismissed as reading ecclesiastical structures into the Old Testament. Exodus 17:8—16 should not be adduced as a proof text for the status of the ordained ministry (and I am not convinced Calvin is doing this). But the broader context of this passage puts Calvin's suggestion in a different light. In the very next chapter we read of the delegation of certain of Moses' responsibilities, at Jethro's suggestion, to some of the elders of the community. They are to help Moses when his tasks become too heavy for him. I do not want to push the matter too far, but it is plausible to understand Hur's and Aaron's helping of Moses as another foreshadowing of things to come: the division of labor in chapter 18.

There is another important first in verse 14. It is one of only a few places in the Pentateuch where Moses is said to "write." Here he is to record the battle with the Amalekites. The precise words he writes, however, are not given. Is it the precise content of 17:8—16? If so, should we then presume that he does *not* write the surrounding material, since no such command to write is given there?[11] It is more likely that the actual words Moses writes on the scroll are not available to us. All the writer of Exodus does is refer to the fact that Moses recorded the event somewhere else. Perhaps he does not have access to the words themselves.

Why Moses writes, however, is clearer to discern. It is another foreshadow of Sinai, where Moses will again be instructed to write at God's command. Moreover, he writes so that Israel will remember what God has done for Israel in the desert (this is also the function of the altar in v. 15). Hence, like Passover and the names Marah, Meribah, and Massah encountered earlier, the focus here is on future generations and their memory of God's past acts. What the NIV translates "something to be remembered" in verse 14 is a single word in Hebrew, *zikkaron* (see also Deut. 25:17). Another translation of this word is "memorial."

In Exodus, *zikkaron* has already appeared in 12:14 (NIV, "to commemorate") and 13:9, and it will occur later in 28:12, 29; 30:16; 39:7. The first passage concerns the Feast of Unleavened Bread, which is to be a lasting "memorial" of the Exodus. The latter two passages concern the "memorial stones" to be worn on Aaron's ephod as he enters the Holy Place in the

---

10. Calvin, *Four Last Books of Moses*, 292–93.

11. Moses is recorded as having written very little in the Pentateuch (see Ex. 24:4; 34:27–28). According to the Pentateuch itself, Moses is essentially responsible for recording the legal material, 17:14 being the exception.

tabernacle. That the words on the scroll in 17:14 are also a "memorial" suggests, once again, that this passage has both a backward and forward glance. The memory of the Amalekite defeat is connected to other "memorials" the Israelites are to have.

The writer also employs a pun in his use of *zikkaron*. Whereas the defeat of the Amalekites is to be a memorial, all "memory of Amalek" is to be blotted out. The Hebrew word for "memory" is *zeker*, from the same root as *zikkaron*. But this raises a question: When exactly was their memory "blotted out"? For one thing, verse 16 seems to imply the opposite, that not only will their memory not be blotted out but that the struggle between the two peoples will last "from generation to generation," a Hebrew idiom implying a lengthy period of time. But it seems that it is precisely *because* the Amalekites will cease to exist that a memorial of some kind is needed, to keep the lesson alive for Israel.

Perhaps the reference is to the events of 1 Samuel 15 and 30. As noted above, in chapter 15 Saul is to destroy completely the Amalekites, but he only does a partial job. In chapter 30, David makes the defeat complete. Already in Deuteronomy 25:17–19 is a clear indication that one of Israel's prerogatives after they are settled in the land is to finish the Amalekites for good:

> Remember what the Amalekites did to you along the way when you came out of Egypt. When you were weary and worn out, they met you on your journey and cut off all who were lagging behind; they had no fear of God. When the LORD your God gives you rest from all the enemies around you in the land he is giving you to possess as an inheritance, you shall blot out the memory of Amalek from under heaven. Do not forget!

It seems best to understand the reference to blotting out the Amalekites in Exodus 17:14 as God's promise of what he will eventually do through Saul and David. Perhaps the events of verses 8–16 do not actually bring an end to these peoples, only their sound defeat and the promise of their inevitable demise.

Another question concerns why God plans such cataclysmic destruction on a relatively insignificant group of desert dwellers. Why not simply beat them at Rephidim and move on without needing to come back later to finish the job? Doesn't God go a bit overboard here? Perhaps, but might this not be an indication of the special care God gives to his people? One can understand this incident as a clear display of the extent to which God protects his people. Moreover, this is not the first example of God "going ballistic" in the book of Exodus. Egypt, too, met a horrible and irrevocable end. If God treated Egypt the way he did, a people who tried to prevent Israel's deliverance, should we not also expect God to treat the Amalekites in a similar manner, since these people are trying to prevent their going any further?

Reference to an altar in verse 15 is another foreshadow of later events. Moses is commanded to build another altar in 20:24–26, and he builds one at the foot of Mount Sinai in 24:4. Instructions for building an altar for burnt offerings (27:1–8; 38:1–7) and incense (37:25–28) are also given, and there are frequent references to altars in chapters 29–31, 35, and 38–40. In the final chapter of the book (ch. 40), altars are mentioned no less than nine times, and over a hundred times from Leviticus through Deuteronomy. The altar at Rephidim is the first altar Moses builds, and as such it serves as a hint of the importance altars will take on throughout the remainder of the book and the Pentateuch.

This altar also connects Moses to the past. It was common practice for the patriarchs to set up altars as memorials of some sort (although a name is associated only with the altars mentioned in Gen. 33:20 and 35:7). The purpose of the altar here is not for sacrifice but, in keeping with the meaning of verse 14, a means by which Israel will remember what God has done for them in the desert. Hence, like the writing in the scroll in verse 14 and several other acts in the previous chapters, the view here is once again toward the future.

The name of the altar (v. 15) and the significance attached to that name (v. 16) have generated a fair amount of discussion. The name, "The LORD is my Banner," seems straightforward enough, but it is not entirely clear what it means. Most likely "banner" is a military term, indicating a signal of some sort or a call to arms. As Houtman puts it, "With his own mouth Moses declares that his battle against Amalek . . . was conducted under YHWH's aegis."[12] To put it another way, this is divine warrior language, a theme we have seen throughout Exodus, particularly at the Red Sea, and one we will see throughout Israel's history.

The explanation given to the name, however, is far more cryptic. The NIV has, "For hands were lifted up to the throne of the LORD." The Hebrew is difficult, particularly the word translated "throne." The Hebrew is *kes*, which appears only here in the Old Testament. Most commentators take it as a shortened form of *kisse'* (or *kisseh*), the common word for "throne."

Assuming this to be correct, the rest is still not clear. Literally, the Hebrew reads "hand upon/against the throne of Yah."[13] Perhaps "hand" refers to the Amalekites' show of force against God's throne, since "hand" in the Old Testament commonly refers to military power. Or perhaps "hand" refers to Moses' raised hands upon or toward Yahweh's throne (see vv. 11–13). But if

---

12. Houtman, *Exodus*, 2:390.
13. Yah is merely a short form of Yahweh.

this is the case, why is "hand" singular in verse 16 but plural in verses 12–13?[14] In light of the fact that the number of Hebrew nouns should not always be handled woodenly in English, it seems most reasonable to conclude that verse 16 refers to Moses' outstretched hands that shape the content of the narrative as a whole.

We have, then, in this passage the final dilemma out of which God must deliver his people before their arrival at Mount Sinai. The stories in Exodus are not disconnected stories. They all serve to remind the people of what has gone before and what will soon come to pass. Exodus 15:22–17:16 as a whole reminds Israel of who God is and what he expects of his people. After one more narrative (the appointment of the elders in ch. 18), we finally find the Israelites at God's holy mountain, where the remainder of the book takes place.

A CRYPTIC PASSAGE. This is a somewhat puzzling passage, and I readily admit it is difficult to know how to handle it properly. As I have suggested elsewhere, it is tempting (and would be easy) to reduce the book of Exodus to a number of moralistic themes. This is particularly the case for this passage. For example, it would be easy to say something like, "God will come to your aid and completely destroy your enemies whenever they attack you," or, "Remember to thank God when he helps you."

It is not that such sentiments as these are necessarily "wrong," but the question is whether this is what the present passage is designed to do. Indeed, it is appropriate to ask whether the Bible at all is made for such a purpose. We can readily see the shortcomings of such an approach. If we distill from this passage that "God will help you in your time of need" and elevate it to a timeless principle applicable to the church, what are we to make of those many other passages suggesting that "sometimes God doesn't come to your physical aid"?

There is something deeper happening in the Bible than the immediate application of surface "teachings" to our own private circumstances. The whole point of a specifically Christian interpretation of the Old Testament is to see passages such as this ultimately within the context of God's culminating salvation in Christ. This is not simply a matter of looking for hints of the gospel here (although that is certainly part of it). It is also allowing this passage to surprise us about who God is and allowing that understanding to affect our understanding of the gospel.

---

14. Curiously, "hand" is singular in the Hebrew of v. 11, but this poses a text-critical problem that should not be exploited to connect the "hand" of v. 11 with the "hand" of v. 16.

A number of things in this passage are worth discussing. Before doing so, however, I would like to mention one Christological approach that has been popular, in varying forms, throughout the history of the church. This line of interpretation has tended to equate specific elements of our passage with supposed New Testament counterparts.[15] According to this scheme, Moses' raised hands foreshadow Christ's hanging on the cross. The hill on which Moses stands is Golgotha. Hur and Aaron, who help on either side of Moses, represent the two thieves crucified alongside Jesus. Joshua also represents Christ because he chose men to fight as Christ chose disciples to "fight."

In one sense, such an interpretation seems a bit excessive. A Christological approach to Old Testament interpretation does not mean making one-to-one correspondences between elements of a passage and the New Testament (see the Introduction; this point will become more important below in our discussion of the tabernacle and its furnishings and articles). The process, as I have tried to show up to this point, is more subtle. Nevertheless, the Christian interpreters who have handled this passage in the way outlined above were not fools! They had reasons for doing what they did. At least one of those reasons is the firm conviction that being a Christian in union with the risen Christ should make a difference in how the Old Testament is read. With this I heartily agree, and so I look at such interpretations with an eye toward what I can learn from them rather than simply dismissing them as fanciful.

Another reason that led these interpreters to handle Scripture the way they did was the general interpretive climate in which they lived, that is, what was commonly accepted as good interpretive practice. For example, allegory, although generally scorned in our day, was not only popular and generally accepted throughout the early church and medieval periods, but in some circles represented the pinnacle of biblical interpretation.

But leaving those matters to the side, one of the reasons why I do not favor this type of reading is that it reduces the art of Christological interpretation to a mechanical process, one that requires little reflection and contemplation—sort of a hermeneutical "Where's Waldo?" Although the ultimate meaning of any Old Testament passage is to bring us to a fuller understanding of the risen Christ and our relationship to him, this is not done by "finding" Jesus in the Old Testament in a superficial way.

This is not to say, however, that the Christological message of any Old Testament passage is necessarily obvious or natural. As the New Testament writers demonstrate again and again, a Christological sense is to be achieved

---

15. Helpful summaries may be found in Houtman, *Exodus*, 2:383–84; Childs, *Book of Exodus*, 316–17.

by a thoughtful and *creative* interaction with what God was revealing about himself at the time the Old Testament passage was first written and how that original message is played out, either directly or indirectly, in Scripture. We see throughout the pages of the New Testament that the bearing of certain Old Testament passages on Christ is not the first thing that might come to mind. Reading the Old Testament as a Christian book requires subtlety and a commitment to the centrality of Christ in interpretation.

In this sense, to say that Moses' raised hands point to Christ's raised hands on the cross is both right and wrong, depending on how you understand the phrase "point to." On the one hand, it is wrong in the "mechanical" sense. Moses' hands are raised, supposedly *high* toward heaven. But if we are to be mechanical, let's be consistent. Christ's hands were not pointed up but were stretched *out* on the cross. What is gained by equating the two? Is every Old Testament character who stands on a hill and raises his hands above the waist a foreshadow of Christ? Also, the only things in common between Hur and Aaron and the two thieves are that they are both "two" and that they are on either side of the key figure. But have we really advanced a Christological understanding of 17:8—16 by saying that Hur and Aaron, who support Moses, "point to" two thieves crucified next to Jesus, one of whom mocks him?

On the other hand—and this is the point well worth remembering—we can quickly see some justification for this type of interpretation. Were not Moses' raised hands on the hill the very thing that brought deliverance to his people? Might the approach taken by early Christian interpreters, as hopelessly naive as it may seem on the surface, actually point toward a subtle and profound theological connection between Moses and Christ? We must still keep in mind what we have seen time and time again throughout the pages of Exodus, and what these early interpreters no doubt saw as well: Christ, in his life, death, and resurrection, truly is a fulfillment of the type of ministry Moses had. This is "fulfillment"—not simply in a literal, predictive-prophetic, one-to-one sense, but in a grand sense. It is a crystallization, clarification, and culmination of the redemptive realities of the ancient Israelites. Hence, we *should* see Christ here somehow.

But the question still remains: "How exactly are we to see Christ here?" My answer to this question is not just one simple answer. The plain meaning of Scripture is clear enough, but like the God who inspired it, it is also deep and unfathomable. We do not all find the same thing even when we are looking in the same place, and this passage is a good example. Let me suggest that Moses' raised hands should be seen as another example of Exodus power. His hands and staff are raised here as they were before in several of the plagues and in the parting of the sea.

There are a number of echoes in this passage of what God has done through Moses previously, so it seems straightforward to look at this incident as another example of God's power saving his people. It is another "Exodus," to be understood in connection with all that has gone before. Hence, this passage should be understood Christologically in the context of the part it plays in the complex of events in Exodus. But what should we make of the two helpers, Hur and Aaron? Well, do we *have* to make anything of them? Whatever we do, I do not think they are to be equated with the thieves.[16] A Christological reading of any other Old Testament passage does not depend on assigning some element from the Gospels to every detail.

Rather than asking how Christ "fulfills" this or that detail, perhaps we should take a step back and ask questions that this passage raises about the nature of God. Why do raised hands have such an effect on how God directs the course of the battle?[17] What do we learn about God, who promises the complete destruction of a desert people for an act that could easily have been punished some other way? What can we learn from the scroll and the altar about what God expects of his people? Perhaps the answers to these questions do not drive us neatly to some "fulfillment" in Christ. They may, however, drive us more deeply in our knowledge of God, which will help us know our Savior in ways we had not expected.

With respect to the raised hands, I am content to stick with the explanation that I have suggested above, but also to allow the mysterious and unexpected elements of this incident to stand as they are. I am often struck in Scripture by how many things defy explanation. Perhaps they are meant to be so. How often do we read a story and say to ourselves, "Why would God behave in such a way?" Despite the explanations we attempt (including my own), the simple fact remains that we are not explicitly told what Moses was doing when he raised his hands. More important, we do not know why the *position* of his hands had the effect they did.

This for me is the really gnawing element in this passage. If there were an explicit command in this passage from God that Moses should do such

---

16. However, I would invite you to look at the treatment of this passage in Plastaras, *The God of Exodus*, 297–99. Plastaras argues on the basis of a number of Old Testament and New Testament passages that, according to John 19:18, the two criminals are to be seen as allusions to Aaron and Hur. Plastaras's argument is brief, but it is subtle and deserves to be taken seriously. His view illustrates what I have suggested above, that there may be a variety of ways at coming at this problem.

17. I have no problem assuming that it is God who directs the course of the battle. That is essentially the point of vv. 14–16. To argue otherwise is to imply that there is some sort of "magic" involved in Moses' gesture. This is to be rejected not simply on the basis of how *we* might object to such a notion. Rather, the point is that this would be out of touch with the tenor of Exodus as a whole.

and such, at least we could say he was following orders (although this would simply throw the question back on God). Also, it appears as if Moses does not need an explanation. He seems to understand what sort of an effect his actions will have. There is no query on Aaron's or Hur's part as to why Moses is raising his hands. They simply see what happens when he lets his hands down and spring into action. In acknowledging some level of puzzlement over this, we join a throng of interpreters who have worked on this passage for well over two millennia.

The Amalekites: prelude to final victory. The complete and seemingly exaggerated destruction of the Amalekites should be seen first in the context of the destruction of the Egyptians. Their utter defeat begs to be compared to what happened to Egypt. This is true even though the Amalekites are not wiped out as the Egyptians were at the sea. We must remember that both the Amalekites and the Egyptians live to fight another day. Both, too, will prove to be a thorn in Israel's side at other junctures in Israel's history. The main similarity here is the decisiveness with which both enemies, within two chapters of each other, are defeated.

This is also another example of the divine warrior theme we have encountered elsewhere in Exodus. When God goes to battle against his enemies or the enemies of his people, he takes it personally. We see hints of this already in Genesis with the Flood and the destruction of Sodom and Gomorrah. Egypt's death in the sea, as we have seen, is another Flood-like event. The Conquest of the land will entail the complete destruction of the peoples currently inhabiting the land, a point made clear in Deuteronomy 7:1–6.[18] Eventually, all God enemies will be utterly destroyed, as we are reminded by the psalmists and prophets (e.g., Ps. 21:10; 94:10; Isa. 34:2; Zech. 12:1–9). These incidents involve us in a larger topic of the "wrath" of God in the Old Testament and how this is to be "balanced" with what appears to many to be a more "open-door policy" in the New Testament.

It is certainly true that God in the Old Testament exhibits wrath. But we must keep two things in mind. (1) God shows his wrath against the nations because they are attempting to get in the way of his redemptive plan. Israel is not just another nation. This tiny people is the vehicle God has chosen through which he will redeem humanity and all of creation. Israel's redemption is Phase One of that redemptive plan, and thus he guards that plan with jealousy. I admit that this does not solve the problem entirely. For example, why could God not simply bring these other nations along to an increased

---

18. See esp. v. 2: "and when the LORD your God has delivered them over to you and you have defeated them, then you must destroy them totally. Make no treaty with them, and show them no mercy."

understanding of himself rather than destroy them? Or why could he not have made the Amalekites favorably disposed toward the Israelites and avoid the conflicts altogether? I do not know. But at the very least we should try to understand God's "extreme" behavior in the context of redemption as a whole. Sometimes the only way we can accept reasons for why God acts as he does is by faith.

(2) It is false to think of the "God of the Old Testament" (even the term should be repulsive to Christians) as a God of wrath, whereas the God of the New Testament is one of grace and patience. Even a surface reading of the Bible puts such a notion to rest. The Old Testament is replete with evidence of God's patience and grace with the nations. Moreover, the New Testament is hardly devoid of God's wrath. His plan to destroy the enemies of his people is no less apparent there. In fact, from a certain perspective the intensity increases. We don't see the walls of Jericho toppling or godless people dropping like flies. But we do see the power of Satan, the true enemy of God and his people, crumbling daily. God's warring activity is now directed at him, full blast! The victory has been secured at the resurrection of Christ and will be completed at his second coming.

A number of thoughtful theologians have compared this to the end of the Second World War in Europe. For all intents and purposes, the decisive battle was fought and the war won by the Allies at D-Day, although the final victory did not come until V-Day.[19] We are living between D-Day and V-Day. The resurrection assures the final outcome. As Paul puts it, "And having disarmed the powers and authorities, he made a public spectacle of them, triumphing over them by the cross" (Col. 2:15).

The final victory over God's enemies is depicted in Revelation. The fall of Babylon is an apocalyptic description not of the destruction of one nation but of all opposition to God, which is spearheaded by Satan. In the final world order described in Revelation 21–22, there will be no place for any opposition to God. All will be made right, and God's people will live in his presence free from any hostility. Their foes have been utterly vanquished.

Revelation brings up another angle to this theme that should be mentioned, albeit briefly. The nations of Babylon and Egypt (for the latter, see Rev. 11:9) take on a more-than-literal persona. As mentioned above, Babylon represents all opposition to God, that is, the domain of Satan. We find the same thing throughout the intertestamental period, not only with respect to Babylon and Egypt, but Edom and other nations as well. The Amalekites

---

19. This analogy was coined by the Swiss theologian Oscar Cullmann (*Christ and Time*, trans. F. V. Filson [London: SCM, 1962]). For a helpful summary of Cullmann's position, see A. Hoekema, *The Bible and the Future* (Grand Rapids: Eerdmans, 1979), 301–6.

are not mentioned in the New Testament, but it is worth pausing to consider whether we should not think of them in a similar manner.

The Amalekites arrive on the scene at a crucial point in Israel's history. They come on the scene again in the book of Esther, with a similar agenda in mind, the extermination of the Jewish people.[20] So, although there is no explicit New Testament reference to the Amalekites as representing God's enemies,[21] their role in redemptive history is similar to that of the more frequently mentioned countries. I am merely suggesting here that we assign to the Amalekites a similar role. They, along with Babylon and the other nations in their opposition to Israel, are merely prelude to the ultimate battle being waged between the forces of God and those of Satan. They are players in a larger drama. They are early reflexes of a battle that meets its initial defeat at the empty tomb and will meet its final defeat at the Second Coming.

Memorials to the Lord. The final theme to be considered in this section is the role of the altar and the scroll as memorials of God's redemptive acts. We should note at the outset that the altar Moses builds here is not an altar of sacrifice. It may presage the sacrificial altars that assume a prominent role for the remainder of the Pentateuch, but this is not the function of the altar mentioned in 17:15. Along with others in the Old Testament, this one is a tangible reminder to whoever passes it of what God has done. These nonsacrificial altars were built in response to some appearance, announcement, or act of God, at stages of redemptive significance.

It is likely that already in Genesis 12:6–7 we have an altar built as a reminder, perhaps not so much of what God did but of what he promised to do:

> Abram traveled through the land as far as the site of the great tree of Moreh at Shechem. At that time the Canaanites were in the land. The LORD appeared to Abram and said, "To your offspring I will give this land." So he built an altar there to the LORD, who had appeared to him.

The significance of the altars in Genesis 12:8, 13:4, 18 is likely similar. These are places where Abraham "called on the name of the LORD." It is doubtful whether sacrifices were offered on these altars, for when sacrifices took place, the Old Testament usually makes this explicit (e.g., 22:9–10). Another altar of note for the patriarchs is the one Isaac builds as a response to God's

---

20. As mentioned earlier, "Haman the Agagite" in Est. 3:1 is usually understood to indicate Haman's Amalekite ancestry.

21. One possible hint in the NT is King Herod, who was out to destroy the Christ (Matt. 2). Herod is an Idumean, which is a descendant of Esau (the words "Idumean" and "Edom" are related). The conflict between Esau and Jacob, of which Amalek is one expression (cf. Gen. 36:15–16), permeates the Bible (cf. also Obad.; Mal. 1:2).

appearance to him (26:25). Jacob too builds two altars (33:20; 35:1–7), the first of which has a name (as does that of Ex. 17:15): "El Elohe Israel" (which likely means "El is the God of Israel," or perhaps "God, the God of Israel"). Genesis 35:7 also cites a name, "El Bethel" ("God of Bethel"; Bethel itself mean "house of God"), though this seems to refer to the area rather than to the altar.

After we read of Moses' altar in Exodus 17:15, most if not all of the altars from this point on take on a decidedly sacrificial function. It is fair to say, then, that "The LORD is my Banner" is the last in a line of altars that were erected solely as a memorial of God's redemptive activity (though cf. Josh. 22:34; Judg. 6:24). It should come as no surprise that altars are not prominently mentioned in the New Testament. They appear mainly in descriptions of the Old Testament sacrificial system (1 Cor. 10:18; Heb. 7:13; 9:4) or with respect to practices current in Jesus' day (Matt. 5:23–24).

No explicit reason is given for why altars as memorials cease in the New Testament, but I suggest it has to do with the transformation of all of Israel's symbols and practices in light of the resurrection. God has left his final mark in the empty tomb and the indwelling of the Holy Spirit in and among his people. From now on, God is not to be remembered by passing altars of stone in the region of Judea. God's people will spread his good news throughout every land and people. Moreover, since the purpose of these altars in the Old Testament was to memorialize an event of some redemptive significance, we have the empty tomb as the Christian memorial. It is the act of God on which all subsequent acts are based.

The defeat of the Amalekites is memorialized not only in stone but also on a scroll. As noted above, Exodus 17:14 is the first reference in the Old Testament to writing on a scroll, but it will not be the last. The reasons for such a common practice in the Old Testament is obvious. Ever since the invention of writing, there has been no more efficient and transportable means of communication than writing of some sort, whether on stone, potsherds, scrolls, or, by the second century A.D., codices. If God wants his people to remember something, a good way of doing it is by writing it down, carrying it around, and handing it down to the next generation.

That the apostles maintained this practice of writing down God's deeds is obvious. The life and ministry of Christ and the acts and writings of some of the apostles are recorded in what Christians have come to call the New Testament. God has always committed to writing moments of redemptive significance.

The significance of both the altar and the scroll in Exodus 17 is that God wants to be remembered and known at some future time when the mere memory of the act itself may grow dim. He therefore provides his people with memorials to keep that memory alive. But this is not simply nostalgia. God has a redemptive plan, in which his people are participants, so he takes steps to assure that who he is and what he has done are always before them. We see, then, that the altar and the scroll perform a similar function to that of the Passover in chapters 12—13 and the Song at the Sea in chapter 15. God's view is never merely on the present, but also on the future. With every redemptive act, he has future generations in mind. In a manner of speaking, the great memorial left for the church is his Word, which reminds us of who God is and what he has done. It should be our companion until we leave this life and see the culmination of his plan.

THE BATTLES IN **our lives.** The defeat of the Amalekites is not simply an isolated battle from Israel's past. It is an early manifestation of a grander and more basic battle, one that comes to a head on the cross and in the empty tomb. It is one battle that is part of a bigger picture. This is the proper perspective from which to apply the defeat of the Amalekites to our lives. The true identity of the enemies of God's people has finally been unmasked. They are not tribes or nations, kings or princes. They are a spiritual entity, and they have been defeated already. The battle against the "Amalekites" that was to last "from generation to generation" (17:16) has finally come to an end.

This is the good news of the gospel: Christ has triumphed over Satan. As a Christmas hymn ("Break Forth, O Beauteous Heavenly Light") puts it, "the power of Satan breaking, our peace eternal making." Yet, as we all know, despite the fact that Satan has lost, the battle rages on every moment we spend on this earth. It is within this grand spiritual perspective that our daily battles must be viewed. Our battles, as Paul said, are against "powers" and "authorities," against spiritual figures who intend on making us fit for darkness rather than light (Eph. 6:10—12). We are at war daily, so, as good soldiers, we must be on guard.

Against whom do we fight these daily battles? We must be careful here not to label as "spiritual enemies" those that are not. Our enemies are not people whom we happen to find annoying or disrupting, such as mean bosses or politicians we don't like. Early on in our marriage, my wife and I had a landlady who refused to fix our living room ceiling after it caved in from the weight of downed branches. This was a vexing experience, and it took several weeks before we were able to part company and be compensated for our losses. In the midst of this situation a well-meaning but misguided friend of ours cited Psalm 60:12 as words of encouragement: "With God we will gain the victory, and he will trample down our enemies."

Now, we may have had a heated disagreement with our landlady about the roof, but this certainly does not qualify her as our "enemy" in a biblical sense. Our enemies are those whose actions have *redemptive significance*. It is far too easy to pick people with whom we may have some disagreement and fancy that they are our enemies. We do not battle primarily against people who want to cheat us, affect our political system in ways we disagree with, or who want to put shows on television that shouldn't be there. Many of us should stand up against those types of things, but those who purport such devious views are not the "Amalekites in our lives."

The real enemies we must guard against are those who can seriously affect our spiritual state, and such enemies (it has been my experience) are rarely easy to label by political, social, and even theological titles. Spiritual warfare is a subtle business. Perhaps this is why Paul admonishes us to put on the armor of God for protection all around, not to fight against earthly forces, but to "take [our] stand against the devil's schemes. For our struggle is not against flesh and blood, but against the rulers, against the authorities, against the powers of this dark world and against the spiritual forces of evil in the heavenly realms" (Eph. 6:11–12). The weapons he lists are for engaging in spiritual battle: belt of truth, breastplate of righteousness, shield of faith, helmet of salvation, sword of the Spirit (vv. 14–17). Above all is prayer (v. 18). He offers no strategies for gaining social or political influence. These are not the fronts where the battle rages.

Our battle is truly spiritual, and it occurs in the many situations we encounter every day that vie for our attention and attempt to make us less fit for heaven. One of the best books of the twentieth century that I know to plumb the depths of this battle is the popular work by C. S. Lewis, *The Screwtape Letters*. This book is a collection of fictitious letters written by Screwtape, a demon who is a head-tempter, to his nephew Wormwood, a tempter-in-training. The letters give advice from Screwtape for how Wormwood should deal with his "patient," a man who has recently become a Christian and who is assigned to Wormwood to make him fit for hell.

This little book is full of penetrating insights into the nature of spiritual warfare. I have found particularly helpful Lewis's grasp of how *subtle* this battle is. The battle is all around us, and it is waged in many unexpected and barely perceptible ways: the friendships we keep, fear of the future, the words we use with our spouses and children that show our self-centeredness, our avoidance of prayer, the corruption of simple pleasures that God has given us, and so forth.

In other words, the battle does not concern the grand, obvious things that we sometimes think of: the direction our country is headed in or the state of the church at large. How many of our Christian leaders in our own day have focused on these things only to have the shallowness of their own spirituality exposed by some scandal! The true nature of the battle is best seen in the quiet of our own hearts where two powers are fighting for control.

But it is precisely here that we must remember the larger picture. The *daily* battles to be won must be seen within the context of the *cosmic* battle that Christ has already won. We see this in principle already in Exodus 17:8—16: The protracted battles between the Israelites and the Amalekites (17:16) must be seen in light of their initial, crushing defeat (17:13) and the fact that their ultimate annihilation is never in doubt (17:14). Again, the analogy of D-Day and V-Day is apt. We battle against spiritual powers today not simply with the belief that victory is in sight, but that the victory has already in principle been truly achieved by Christ, our warrior.[22]

Living memorials. The application of the altar and the scroll should also be understood ultimately from the point of view of the redemptive significance of the cross and the empty tomb. Of course, we do not go around building altars to memorialize what God has done nor do we record redemptive events in writing. These biblical activities were part of God's redemptive plan and have come to their final expression in Christ. Hence, we do not mimic these things because we are the recipients, the beneficiaries, of the culmination of God's redemptive work throughout the Old Testament. Christ *has come.*

Thus, there are no more altars to be built to remind people of who God is and the steps he has taken to redeem his people. The cross and the empty tomb suffice. And we are living, roaming "memorials" who can attest to the world of God's goodness in Christ. We are not being "biblical" if we find some modern analogue for the altars that Moses and the patriarchs built. We are truly biblical when we see how what these altars represent—lasting testimonies to God's acts—find their clearest and most concrete expression in what God has done in Christ.

The same goes for the scroll. The writing that took place in the Old Testament of the events and commands of God, are, in a word, authoritative. They were meant to convey God's truth for generations to come. Christians today may keep prayer journals or diaries (good practices, in my opinion), but these are not the same thing as writing authoritative words meant to convey the work and nature of God to peoples of all nations and races and through all time.

Let me suggest two ways in which these elements may be applied to our lives. (1) As I just indicated, God has recorded in the Bible the redemptively

---

22. If I have any criticism of Lewis, it is on this matter. For my tastes, he does not emphasize enough that, in principle, the battle is lost for Wormwood before it even begins. Of course, the reason for this omission is likely the fact that the letters are written from the perspective of demons who are themselves ignorant about a good number of things, a point that Screwtape himself begrudgingly admits on a number of occasions.

significant events. Nothing can be added to this. It is up to us to put this scroll of remembrance before ourselves and our children so that we too may come to know better the God we worship. We are to teach it and meditate on it, for it offers us the most valuable lesson of all, that God loves his people and has taken great measures to make them fit for heaven.

(2) Perhaps, too, we can make an application on a more personal level. Like Moses and the patriarchs, we all have moments in our lives when we can look back and clearly see God's presence. Again, this is not the same thing as when Abraham or Moses saw God's hand in *their* lives. They were actors in the unfolding drama of God's redemptive plan. Their lives were significant from a redemptive-historical point of view whereas ours are not. But this is certainly not to say that God does not work in our lives! We all have "markers" in our lives that attest to God's presence—"Ebenezers," to use the biblical term. This word comes from 1 Samuel 7:12: "Then Samuel took a stone and set it up between Mizpah and Shen. He named it Ebenezer, saying, 'Thus far has the LORD helped us.'" Ebenezer in Hebrew means "stone of help," and it commemorated God's help in defeating the Philistines.

So, in the famous hymn "Come, Thou Fount of Every Blessing," we read in the second stanza, "Here I raise mine Ebenezer, Hither by Thy help I'm come." We, too, have such markers we have set up in our lives to remind us of God's presence. I can easily look back on a number of circumstances that I had no control over whatsoever and (I suspect precisely for that reason) worked out better than I had ever imagined: the grace God has given me in my family, the inexplicable turn of events that brought me to graduate school and my present teaching position, the many doors that were closed for me that in retrospect desperately needed to stay closed despite my efforts to open them.

As I look back on some of these things, I can see that they are much more than detached memories or warm feelings of times when things went well for me. They are not simply reminiscences but towers of granite in my memory that remind me not of my own accomplishments but of God's. They, too, are in an extended sense redemptively significant events. That is, they are not random nor do they result in making us better people or more productive members of society. Rather, God designs and uses such events to shape us into creatures that resemble more and more the risen Christ. They are places where God meets us in the desert wanderings of our lives to prepare us for the ultimate goal he has destined us for. They are the "altars" of our lives with names of their own: "I remember the time when God saw to it that we had a decent place to live"; "I remember when God gave me the strength to resist the temptation to fall into sin."

In fact, there is no time in our lives when God is not working for our good (cf. Rom. 8:28). Every moment we breathe the air of this world is a personal memorial to God's presence, if we only learn to look at it that way. As I write this it is nearly New Year's Day 1998, and the local paper has been carrying a story on drunk driving from various perspectives (police check points, bartenders' responsibilities to check excess drinking, etc.). The latest story is from the perspective of people who have lost family members to drunk drivers in past New Year's Eves. One comment struck me. It was from a father who lost his only child, a twenty-three-year-old daughter, to a drunken fool behind the wheel of a car. He said, "I have nothing but bitterness in my heart. I will never be happy again." Any parent can well imagine his heartache.

I shudder to think what my reaction would be in the same situation. I would hope, however, that it would be different. If God is always with us and if every moment is a memorial to his presence, should there not also be some hope that eventually we will see God more clearly even in the most tragic of life's turns and twists? I do not want to dismiss this father's agony and anger, but I am trying to look at it from the point of view of the resurrection, which perhaps he does not share. Doesn't Jesus somehow make a difference, even here—*especially* here? By contrast, I think of mature Christians I have known who have suffered much and I cannot help but notice the difference. It may take time, but we should eventually reach a point where we can look back and say, "I see God was there, too. I have come to know him more clearly as a result."

This is not a crutch to make life more bearable. This is staring square in the eye the worst this life has to offer and saying, "God is still with me. This has a higher purpose. Here, too, I raise my Ebenezer."

Exodus 18:1–27

NOW JETHRO, THE priest of Midian and father-in-law of Moses, heard of everything God had done for Moses and for his people Israel, and how the LORD had brought Israel out of Egypt.

2After Moses had sent away his wife Zipporah, his father-in-law Jethro received her 3and her two sons. One son was named Gershom, for Moses said, "I have become an alien in a foreign land"; 4and the other was named Eliezer, for he said, "My father's God was my helper; he saved me from the sword of Pharaoh."

5Jethro, Moses' father-in-law, together with Moses' sons and wife, came to him in the desert, where he was camped near the mountain of God. 6Jethro had sent word to him, "I, your father-in-law Jethro, am coming to you with your wife and her two sons."

7So Moses went out to meet his father-in-law and bowed down and kissed him. They greeted each other and then went into the tent. 8Moses told his father-in-law about everything the LORD had done to Pharaoh and the Egyptians for Israel's sake and about all the hardships they had met along the way and how the LORD had saved them.

9Jethro was delighted to hear about all the good things the LORD had done for Israel in rescuing them from the hand of the Egyptians. 10He said, "Praise be to the LORD, who rescued you from the hand of the Egyptians and of Pharaoh, and who rescued the people from the hand of the Egyptians. 11Now I know that the LORD is greater than all other gods, for he did this to those who had treated Israel arrogantly." 12Then Jethro, Moses' father-in-law, brought a burnt offering and other sacrifices to God, and Aaron came with all the elders of Israel to eat bread with Moses' father-in-law in the presence of God.

13The next day Moses took his seat to serve as judge for the people, and they stood around him from morning till evening. 14When his father-in-law saw all that Moses was doing for the people, he said, "What is this you are doing for the people? Why do you alone sit as judge, while all these people stand around you from morning till evening?"

¹⁵Moses answered him, "Because the people come to me to seek God's will. ¹⁶Whenever they have a dispute, it is brought to me, and I decide between the parties and inform them of God's decrees and laws."

¹⁷Moses' father-in-law replied, "What you are doing is not good. ¹⁸You and these people who come to you will only wear yourselves out. The work is too heavy for you; you cannot handle it alone. ¹⁹Listen now to me and I will give you some advice, and may God be with you. You must be the people's representative before God and bring their disputes to him. ²⁰Teach them the decrees and laws, and show them the way to live and the duties they are to perform. ²¹But select capable men from all the people—men who fear God, trustworthy men who hate dishonest gain—and appoint them as officials over thousands, hundreds, fifties and tens. ²²Have them serve as judges for the people at all times, but have them bring every difficult case to you; the simple cases they can decide themselves. That will make your load lighter, because they will share it with you. ²³If you do this and God so commands, you will be able to stand the strain, and all these people will go home satisfied."

²⁴Moses listened to his father-in-law and did everything he said. ²⁵He chose capable men from all Israel and made them leaders of the people, officials over thousands, hundreds, fifties and tens. ²⁶They served as judges for the people at all times. The difficult cases they brought to Moses, but the simple ones they decided themselves.

²⁷Then Moses sent his father-in-law on his way, and Jethro returned to his own country.

Original Meaning

BEFORE WE ARRIVE at Mount Sinai and the culminating scene of the Exodus, the author records a story of Jethro's visit to Moses. It may seem strange to have this story in the flow of the narrative. Why does a Midianite priest figure so prominently? The general content of this chapter seems clear enough: Verses 1–12 recount Jethro's acknowledgment of the God of Moses and verses 13–27 Moses' father-in-law's advice to him about dividing the labor. The real question is why this story is told at all. Why, if the biblical writer has such a penchant for brevity, did he not make at best a passing remark about a family reunion in the desert and proceed with haste to the giving of the law at Sinai?

For one thing, the existence of this record suggests the historicity of such an encounter. It is unlikely that such a story would have been woven out of whole cloth and inserted here. But apart from this issue, chapter 18 is purposefully situated in the context of the book. As Cassuto has outlined,[1] there is a striking degree of lexical overlap between this episode and the Amalekite episode in chapter 17. The overlap is even clearer in Hebrew, but the English will make the general point well enough (italics indicate overlap).

- In 17:8, the Amalekites *came* and *attacked;* in 18:5–7, Jethro *comes* and *greets.*
- In both 17:9 and 18:25, men are *chosen* for some specific task.
- In 17:12, Moses *sits* on a stone; in 18:13 he *sits* to judge. Moreover, both activities are said to commence on the *next day* (17:9; 18:13) and last *all day* until evening (17:12; 18:13–14).
- In both 17:12 and 18:18 Moses is said to be *tired,* with help provided in each instance.

Such overlap indicates a connection between the two stories, as several commentators have noted.[2] Jethro the Midianite's encounter with Moses in the desert stands in contrast to the "greeting" he and the Israelites received from the Amalekites. Moreover, as we will see, a number of elements of the story connect it to both earlier and later portions of Exodus.

Jethro's Acknowledgment of the God of Moses (18:1–12)

THE WORD OF Yahweh's victory over Egypt has spread so as to reach Jethro's ears. Unlike the nations of 15:14–16 who tremble at such news, Jethro is attracted to it, and so he comes to Moses. How does this news reach him? This information is not given. Perhaps Zipporah, Moses' wife, has told him. If so, this also poses a handy solution to another dilemma, noted earlier. According to 4:20, Moses took his family with him to Egypt after leaving Midian. Yet here in 18:2, Zipporah returns after having been "sent away."

When was she sent away? There is no clear answer to this question, and it seems best to admit we do not know because the narrative does not tell us— a phenomenon any reader of Exodus and the Old Testament as a whole must get used to. Perhaps Moses sent them away before the plagues so as to protect his family from Pharaoh's wrath.[3] Or conversely, as Calvin argues, she may have been sent away after the Israelites have been delivered from Egypt, since Moses would certainly have had his own family present to witness God's

---

1. Cassuto, *Commentary on Exodus,* 212.
2. Ibid., 211–12; Sarna, *Exploring Exodus,* 128–29.
3. Durham, *Exodus,* 221.

mighty act.[4] Or again, perhaps after the Amalekite battle, Moses sent Zipporah to relay the news to her father. According to this scenario, she took her children too, and we can presume that others may have gone with her. But all in all, we have to admit the highly conjectural nature of all such solutions.

Rather than focus on how Zipporah came to be sent away, I prefer to look at verses 2–4 as a whole. These verses are much more than simply a family reunion in the desert, as some commentators have argued. Rather, they form a concrete reminder to the readers of where Moses *and the Israelites* have been. This is why the names of the sons are mentioned. We meet again Gershom, who is a reminder not only that Moses was a foreigner in Midian (see 2:22), but that the Israelites experienced a similar alienation in Egypt. And here for the first and only time we meet Eliezer,[5] meaning "my God is helper." He is a reminder of deliverance, not only for Moses but for Israel. True, Moses says he named him thus because "he [God] saved *me* from the sword of Pharaoh" (18:4), but the application of this significance of this name to Israel as a whole is too obvious to miss.[6] This is why the writer mentions the second son's name while leaving, for example, the name of the Pharaoh of the Exodus a total mystery.

Verse 5 raises an interesting problem. How can the Israelites be "near the mountain of God" when they do not arrive until 19:1–2? In fact, the Hebrew is even more problematic. It does not say *near* the mountain but simply says "the mountain of God," leaving it to the reader to supply the appropriate preposition. Some have argued that chapter 18 is displaced and that the actions here occur after the arrival at Sinai. The reason the story is placed here is to provide a fitting contrast between the Midianites here and the Amalekites of 17:8–16 (cf. above). I concur that this contrast between the Amalekites and the Midianites exists, but too much is made of the reference to the mountain of God in verse 5. After all, the story of the water from the rock at Rephidim (see comments on 17:1–7) has indicated that the Israelites are already near Horeb.

Another issue linked with the displacement theory is provided by Numbers 11:16–17 and Deuteronomy 1:6–18. There, elders are chosen to ease Moses' burden *after* the departure from Sinai. I think it best, however, not to feel a pressing need to harmonize these accounts. Perhaps they are relating

---

4. Calvin, *Four Last Books of Moses,* 297.

5. He is mentioned in the genealogies in 1 Chron. 23:15, 17; 26:25, but we are given no additional information. He is not to be confused with Eleazar, who is the third son of Aaron (see Ex. 6:23–25) and figures more prominently in other Old Testament narratives.

6. The personal situation to which "the sword of Pharaoh" likely refers is 2:11–15 (Sarna, *Exodus,* 98). In addition, I take the phrase as a metonymy for the Exodus, thus applying the phrase to Israel's experience as a whole.

two separate instances of Moses' dividing the labor (note that Jethro is not mentioned in either Num. 11 or Deut. 1). Of course, this raises the question of why such a thing would have occurred twice, but this is beyond our scope here. The reference to "the mountain of God" in Exodus 18:5 both describes the Israelites' relative location and foreshadows what is now about to command our full attention: the revelation at Sinai of God's law and the tabernacle.

The meeting between Moses and Jethro in verses 7–8 should jar our memory a bit. Moses here experiences a second reunion with a family member in the desert (cf. the reunion with Aaron in 4:27–28). Moses kisses his father-in-law, just as earlier he kissed Aaron. There is a fine literary (chiastic) symmetry here. As Moses had earlier met the Lord at Mount Horeb and then left, meeting Aaron in the desert, here he meets another relative, which is then followed by the climactic encounter with God on the mountain. Also, 4:28 parallels somewhat 18:8–9: In both places, Moses recounts "everything" God has done or said.

Upon hearing the news of God's mighty acts in Egypt, Jethro praises God. What is happening here? Is he a convert to "Yahwism"? Perhaps so, but at the very least we can say that he has had a shift in thinking based on what God has done for Israel, ironically a realization that Israel itself is often slow to learn. Jethro's confession "now I know" (v. 11) is standard Exodus language (see 6:7; 7:5; 8:10; 9:29). Although neither the Egyptians nor the Amalekites get it, Jethro, the Midianite, has learned the lesson of the Exodus: "The LORD is greater than all other gods."

This is, I suggest, the central theological point of this chapter, and it gives us a good hint of why this story should be included in Israel's saga at all. Midian is the one nation that gives a proper response to God's deliverance of his own people. God's dealings with Pharaoh were so that "my name might be proclaimed in all the earth" (9:16). The Hebrew word for "proclaim" is *sipper*, which is used also in 18:8 (translated "told" in the NIV). But it is Jethro, not Pharaoh or the Amalekites, who gives the proper response: praise.

The reference to "a burnt offering and other sacrifices" (v. 12) should not be passed over too quickly. This is the first "sacrifice in the desert" to which Moses referred in his earlier audiences with Pharaoh (3:18; 5:3; 8:27). Exodus 10:25 is especially relevant, since there burnt offerings and sacrifices are mentioned together: "You must allow us to have sacrifices and burnt offerings to present to the LORD our God." This is what begins to happen in 18:12. Of course, this is not the last sacrifice. In 20:24 and throughout the remainder of the book, we have many references to sacrifices. Moreover, 18:12 should not be thought of as the fulfillment of 10:25, but perhaps as a first installment on the importance placed on sacrifice in subsequent chapters.

We should also note that this sacrifice presumably takes place in "the tent" (v. 7; likely Moses' tent), and that a show of hospitality is to be expected. Yet some have remarked that this may be a portable sanctuary of some sort.[7] In fact, the ambiguity of the phrase "the tent" may be purposeful so as to suggest either option. In any case, that a sacrifice occurs is significant. It is clearly another forward look to the supreme cultic site, the tabernacle of chapters 25–40.

Note also the meal that Jethro, Moses, Aaron, and the elders have "in the presence of God" (v. 12). One unusual element is the bread (Heb. *leḥem*, the common word for bread). Where does this bread came from? A few short chapters earlier, it seemed necessary for God to provide manna from heaven or else the Israelites would starve (16:3). Is manna (their main food during the desert years; cf. Josh. 5:11–12) meant here?[8] If so, one would think it would be made clear. Perhaps Jethro has brought the bread with him, or at least the ingredients to bake bread. Or are we to assume that the Israelites themselves have the ingredients handy to bake bread? If so, their earlier complaint makes no sense. This element of the story is difficult to explain.

Beyond the matter of bread, the meal has a number of theological implications for how we understand this stage of the story. Note that this is not the first meal referred to in Exodus. The most recent meal is the Passover, which takes place on the eve of Israel's deliverance. In both cases, a meal precedes a climactic redemptive event. More important, this is not the first meal Moses and Jethro have together, for in 2:20 they also eat *leḥem*. This first meal, from the point of view of the flow of the narrative, occurred just before Moses' first encounter with God on Mount Horeb (ch. 3). This second meal immediately precedes Moses' second and climactic encounter with God on Mount Sinai. Clearly, the author is aiming at literary symmetry.

But what precisely does this meal signify? This is more difficult to determine. There are essentially two options: Either this is a covenant or treaty meal[9] between Moses and Jethro, or it is not. A meal was a typical way of ratifying a treaty or covenant in the Old Testament (e.g., Gen. 26:30; 31:54). Further, such a meal seems to be in view between God and his people in Exodus 24:11, after the giving of the law. Others, however, argue that this is not an official treaty meal, but simply "a festive meal to the praise of God."[10]

Little is gained by pressing one option over the other. The fact that they partake of a meal together is certainly theologically significant in that it pro-

---

7. Fretheim, *Exodus*, 196.

8. Calvin thinks manna is the bread referred to (*Four Last Books of Moses*, 301).

9. This is ably argued by a number of scholars, including Y. Avishur, "Treaty Terminology in the Moses-Jethro Story," *AO* 6 (1988): 139–47; A. Cody, "Exodus 18,12: Jethro Accepts a Covenant With the Israelites," *Bib* 49 (1968): 153–66.

10. Houtman, *Exodus*, 2:412.

vides a further hint of what is to come in 24:11, and this is true whether or not this particular meal with Jethro is actually covenantal. The events recorded in 18:9–12 unmistakably echo things that came before and that will come later. This seemingly superfluous meeting between Moses and Jethro gives the writer an opportunity to draw together a number of theological threads before we reach Mount Sinai.

Jethro's Advice to Moses (18:13–27)

VERSES 13–27 RECORD the second topic of this chapter, Jethro's advice to Moses to divide the labor of judging the people's disputes. Moses is said to "judge" (v. 13), which in context means arbitrating legal issues between parties based on the standard of "God's decrees and laws" (v. 16). We have here another transparent hint of the more detailed legal administration of Sinai. One may well ask how they could have known God's laws and decrees before Sinai, but we have seen this problem earlier with respect to the "commands and decrees" of 15:26 and the Sabbath law of 16:5, 23, 25–26, 29–30, which, as we argued, must have been common knowledge at the time. The "giving" of the law at Sinai is not the first time Israel hears of God's laws, but is the codification and explicit promulgation of those laws (allowing, of course, for the imposition of additional laws at Sinai).

This adjudication between parties proves too much for Moses. He is dead tired after keeping up the pace all day. Jethro sees what is happening to his son-in-law and offers sound advice: Get some help. Moses is in over his head, and things cannot go on like this for long. In my view, this harsh reality gives some perspective to the Sinai legislation. At least one purpose of codifying the law is so that everyone will know firsthand right from wrong. The Ten Commandments and the Book of the Covenant (21:2–23:19) are not ornaments for Moses' legal bookshelf. They are meant to be put before the people directly. This does not diminish Moses' importance, it merely gives people a more direct knowledge of God's will.

The advice Jethro gives is a much-needed remedy to a problematic situation. From one perspective, Jethro is returning a favor. In 2:16–20, Moses comes to Jethro's aid by driving away the shepherds from the well. Now, Jethro comes to Moses' aid. It is worth noting again that both incidents are accompanied by a meal and both acts of kindness result in making "shepherding" more effective—for the former the shepherding of a flock, for the latter the shepherding of God's people. (That Moses is shepherding his people is already hinted at in 3:1 and made explicit in such places as Ps. 77:20.)

Jethro's advice (18:17–23) is fairly detailed and may indicate that he had experience in these matters, being a priest. (1) Moses is to have superiority over his chosen helpers in that he is the "people's representative before God" and is to "teach" the people God's laws (vv. 19–20). (2) Moses is to "select capable men," each of whom is to act as judge over an assigned group of people for the "simple" cases (vv. 21–22); Moses will get only the "difficult" ones (v. 22). Separating the difficult from simple cases presumes a standard by which to make such a decision. What that standard is we are not told, but this lends further credence to the fact that Israel's legal self-consciousness must have developed somewhat before Sinai.

Note also the qualifications of these judges. They are to be "men who fear God, trustworthy men who hate dishonest gain" (v. 21). What is significant here is both what is stated and what is not. The explicit reference to dishonest gain anticipates a common temptation of leadership, namely, bribery—one that will rear its head repeatedly throughout Israel's history (e.g., 1 Sam. 8:3; Jer. 22:17). Some of the qualifications cited in Numbers 11:16 and Deuteronomy 1:9–18 are not mentioned here, however: people who are known, respected, and, above all, wise and understanding. The qualifications of Exodus 18:21 are simple in comparison. As noted above, what is recorded in Exodus 18 and Numbers 11/Deuteronomy 1 are likely two separate events, with unique circumstances that demand their own set of qualifications.

Moses listens to his father-in-law and puts the plan into operation; we can assume it works well (vv. 24–26). It seems that the reason why Moses obeys Jethro is not to be polite or to try it to see if it works.[11] Rather, as a number of commentators have mentioned, Jethro's advice is also God's command.[12] Verse 23 of the NIV has, "If you do this *and God so commands*, you will be able to stand the strain," which assumes that the second clause (in italics) is part of the protasis (the "if" clause). This may be the case, but it makes more sense to read this clause as Jethro adding "punch" to his advice: "If you do this— God commands you—you will be able to stand the strain." By dividing the labor, Moses was following God's order given through Jethro.

That God can use a Midianite in this special capacity should come as no surprise to those familiar with similar instances in prophetic literature (e.g., the role of Cyrus in Isa. 44:28; 45:1, 13). But more puzzling is why *Moses* needs to have advice given to him through such channels. He is God's chosen instrument. He is on an intimate basis with God. Why does God not simply *reveal* to Moses directly that a division of labor is necessary, as he has been doing since chapter 3? To be honest, I do not know. It is worth noting,

---

11. Calvin argues that this is a sign of Moses' modesty (*Four Last Books of Moses*, 307–8). I do not think modesty is a sufficient motive for Moses to institute a new scheme for shepherding God's people through the desert.

12. Houtman, *Exodus*, 2:420–21; Fretheim, *Exodus*, 199.

however, that this does not seem to bother God or the biblical writer. It seems most prudent here simply to observe *that* it happens rather than to try to explain *why*.

Jethro and Moses part company in verse 27, as they had done earlier in 4:19–20, but now for the last time. Presumably Moses' family remains behind, since Gershom's descendants serve as priests (Judg. 18:30), although Zipporah is not mentioned again. Interestingly, according to Numbers 12:1, Moses had a Cushite wife. This may be a second wife in addition to Zipporah, or a wife after the death of Zipporah (not recorded); any suggestion is conjecture. The fact that 18:27 stresses that *"Jethro returned"* should, I feel, be taken at face value: he and he alone.

As we come to the close of this chapter, we, like the Israelites, are prepared to approach God at Mount Sinai. A number of elements of chapter 18 have provided further hints of this climactic event, as have other passages since the beginning of the book.

Bridging Contexts

GOD'S PLAN FOR THE NATIONS. Ever since God chose a particular people through whom to work his grand plan of reconciliation, the question has come up, "What about the other nations?" This question begins to be answered directly in Exodus 18 with Jethro's acknowledgment of the God of Moses as "greater than all other gods" (v. 11).

Although the Midianites are presented in a most positive light in this chapter, this is not the case elsewhere in Scripture. These descendants of Abraham (Gen. 25:2) first come on the scene in the Joseph story as the merchants who sell Joseph to Potiphar (37:28, 36). Perhaps already here we catch a glimpse of the type of relationship Midian and Israel will come to have.

They later become a serious opposition and threat to Israel. Their elders, along with those of the Moabites, serve as Balak's messengers to lure Balaam to curse Israel by promise of financial gain (Num. 22:7ff.). Their opposition to Israel comes to a head in 25:1–18. The marriage of the Israelite (Zimri) with a Midianite (Cozbi) prompts Phinehas to kill them both. The matter cannot be made more plain than in 25:17: "Treat the Midianites as enemies and kill them." They are mentioned again in a negative light in Joshua 13:21, almost in passing, with reference to Moses' defeat of Sihon told in Numbers 21:21–31. The final significant mention of Midianites is in Judges 6–7, where they are Israel's enemies and are soundly defeated by Gideon.

Israel's attitude toward the Midianites comes to a stunning climax in Isaiah 10:26: "The LORD Almighty will lash them with a whip, as when he struck down Midian at the rock of Oreb; and he will raise his staff over the waters, as he did in Egypt." When compared to Exodus 18, Isaiah 10:26 presents a sharply contrasting view of Midian. Whereas Midian was at first a great help to Israel after their deliverance from Egypt (as opposed to the Amalekites), they are now lumped into the same category as the Egyptians, Israel's arch-enemies. Such is Midian's fate. But in Exodus 18 at least, Israel and Midian are allies, and the Midianites serve as models of how nations ought to respond to Israel's God, in contrast to Egypt and the Amalekites.

We see once again that God's reach, even at this stage of Israel's infancy, is broader than simply saving Israel. That the nations acknowledge God as the only God is a recurring theme in the Old Testament. It is not true that the Old Testament is "exclusivistic" whereas the New Testament is "universalistic."[13] The nations are always on God's mind. Already in Genesis 17:5–6, the broader implications of Abraham's election are made explicit:

> No longer will you be called Abram; your name will be Abraham, for I have made you a father of many nations. I will make you very fruitful; I will make nations of you, and kings will come from you.[14]

Clearly the purpose of Israel's election transcends the well-being of one particular people.

This theme, however, is not fully developed in the Old Testament. This fact likely inspires the charge that the Old Testament is exclusivistic. We have hints, perhaps, in the Exodus story with the "many other people" (12:38) and the confession of Pharaoh's officials (10:7). A clearer demonstration of this principle is the book of Ruth. Ruth was a Moabite,[15] who became a direct ancestor of none other than King David. What is remarkable about this, among other things, is the apparently unqualified statement in Deuteronomy 23:3 that neither Ammonites not Moabites would ever be allowed access to "the assembly of the LORD." In any event, God will include non-Israelite peoples in his plans; he is not just the God of one particular people.

A similar universalistic scenario is played out in the story of Naaman, the commander of the army of the king of Aram (2 Kings 5). Naaman has leprosy. He hears of Elisha's power, and so he goes to him in the hope of being cured, which is what happens after washing seven times in the Jordan. Naaman responds in words reminiscent of Jethro's confession: "Now I know that there is no God in all the world except in Israel" (v. 15). This confession can be excused for its naiveté (God is not just "in Israel"), for it is true and hon-

---

13. The meaning of "universalistic" here and elsewhere in this chapter is not that all will be saved, but that salvation is not restricted to any single ethnic group.

14. See also Gen. 12:1–3; 17:16; 35:11; 48:19.

15. The close connection between Moab and Midian is worth pointing out here (Num. 22:7).

est nevertheless. He, not unlike Jethro, bears witness to God's saving power and thus acknowledges him as the true God.

A final passage worth mentioning here is Isaiah 19:18–25. Isaiah sees a time when even Egypt, Israel's great and first national enemy, will come to know God. Egypt will be punished for her oppression of Israel, but in the end "they will acknowledge the LORD" (v. 21) and "turn" to him (v. 22). The interest God takes in bringing the nations to a saving knowledge of him can be seen in the mercy shown even to Egypt. What makes this act of mercy stand out all the more is the otherwise harsh context of judgment against the nations in Isaiah 13–21.

Even this brief survey of the Old Testament shows us that God's acts concerning Israel have redemptive ramifications for the nations as well as for his people. Such ramifications, of course, are not automatic, but are accompanied by a confession on the part of these nations that the God of Israel is the one true God.

When we get to this point in the discussion, we have arrived at one of the central tenets of the gospel itself. Christ has made all nations one by grafting them into Israel (Rom. 11:11–24). It is not that the nations take on a "separate but equal" status over against Israel in God's redemptive plan, but all nations may participate fully in that redemption since they can now become *part of* Israel. They are partakers of that redemption insofar as they acknowledge not simply the God of Israel, but God's Son. And, unlike Jethro, the nations now acknowledge God's deliverance not simply for an ethnic entity, but for themselves. The clear strand of universalism in the Old Testament becomes prominent in the gospel.

This point is made in a number of New Testament passages. In Romans 4, for example, Paul presents Abraham as having been justified by faith. Since faith brought him into right standing with God, he is fit to be the "father of many nations" (vv. 17–18). This is how Paul understands Genesis 17:5: Abraham will father many nations—not in the sense of physical offspring, but in the spiritual sense, "those who are of the faith of Abraham" (Rom. 4:16).[16] Paul capitalizes on the universalism inherent in the very beginning of Israel's story and argues that it has come to pass truly only in light of the coming of Christ.

Perhaps nowhere is this emphasis more obvious than in the Great Commission (Matt. 28:19–20):

> Therefore go and make disciples of *all nations*, baptizing them in the name of the Father and of the Son and of the Holy Spirit, and teaching

---

16. Essentially the same point is made in Gal. 3:29.

them to obey everything I have commanded you. And surely I am with you always, to the very end of the age. (italics added)

This theme was alluded to earlier in Matthew, as in 12:18–21:

Here is my servant whom I have chosen,
      the one I love, in whom I delight;
I will put my Spirit on him,
      and he will proclaim justice *to the nations*.
He will not quarrel or cry out;
      no one will hear his voice in the streets.
A bruised reed he will not break,
      and a smoldering wick he will not snuff out,
till he leads justice to victory.
      In his name *the nations* will put their hope. (italics added)

Matthew here quotes Isaiah 42:1–4. Jesus' mission is fully in keeping with the trajectory set in the Old Testament. That the gospel is to be preached to the nations (Mark 13:10) is not an afterthought, but part of God's redemptive plan from the beginning.

The missionary activities of the early church as recorded in Acts show us the implementation of this universalistic plan. Paul in particular was chosen by God for the singular purpose of bringing the gospel to the Gentiles (Acts 9:15; 10:45; 11:1, 18; 13:47–48; 15:7). It is not, nor was it ever intended, in either Old or New Testament, to be the private message of any one national entity. God's news is for all who acknowledge him.

Finally, this same point is made repeatedly in Revelation. As noted elsewhere in this commentary, Revelation is a book that describes not just the future, but the reality of the present Christian life in light of the resurrection of Christ. Part of that reality is the fact that God and the Lamb are made known to all the nations. The blood of the Lamb has "purchased men for God from every tribe and language and people and nation" (Rev. 5:9). Around the throne, John sees "a great multitude that no one could count, from every nation, tribe, people and language" (7:9; see also 14:6). Note also 15:4, since it is similar to what we see happening in Exodus:

Who will not fear you, O Lord,
      and bring glory to your name?
For you alone are holy.
All nations will come and worship before you,
      for your righteous acts have been revealed. (italics added)

The nations will worship the God of Israel because God's "righteous acts" have been revealed. In other words, they see what God does and their response is to worship. Jethro has a similar response because God's righteous acts at the sea have come to his attention.

The inclusion of the Gentiles comes to a climax in the final two chapters of Revelation. The new Jerusalem will not need a temple or the sun or moon. The presence of God is light enough. And the nations and the kings of the earth will walk by this light (Rev. 21:24). And in 22:2, the leaves of the tree of life are "for the healing of the nations."

It is precisely here, in the final pages of God's Word, that we come back to a theme enunciated with Abraham and that begins to come to concrete (although proleptic) expression in Jethro's confession. God created the world and it was good. Through the fall of our first parents, the world was "subjected to frustration" (Rom. 8:20). It is nothing less than the world that God has come to redeem. In the Old Testament this began to be accomplished through the chosen people, the children of Abraham. In the New Testament, this purpose is fully accomplished through the chosen Son, Christ, in whom God is preparing Abraham's spiritual children.

The law written on their hearts. Exodus 18:13–26 is not just a story of Moses receiving some helpful advice from an in-law. The bigger question is, "What does Moses need help doing?" There is more to this story—any biblical story—than meets the eye. Exodus 18 is as much a theological statement as anything else in the book. It is not simply reporting events, but reporting them with a purpose.

The flow of the narrative is plain. The people want to know what must be done in order to settle their disputes; they are coming "to seek God's will" (v. 15). Apparently, they have no clear way of knowing what that is. So, for the time being, it is up to Moses to tell them, and this, as we have seen, proves too taxing for him. Jethro suggests a solution to ease the burden by increasing the number of judges. This is fine for now, but within a few chapters another solution will be presented. Rather than increasing the number of judges, at Mount Sinai, the people themselves will become directly aware of what God requires of them by the written publication of the law (chs. 20–23). Hence, when we look below the surface of the story, the problem exposed here is not simply Moses' frailty, but the people's.

This concern is not just in chapter 18 but elsewhere in the Old Testament. God is in the process of raising a people, as a father raises his child, to know him. One gets to know God not simply by having a written copy of the law on one's bookshelf, but by having the law in one's heart. This is the goal toward which God is stretching his people. Simply having the law in their possession is not enough, as we will see soon enough in the golden calf episode (ch. 32). It needs to become a part of a person. What is at stake is not simply knowledge *about* God in an academic or detached sense, but actually knowing *him*. The law is not some legalistic mumbo jumbo but the expression of God's will and character to his people. Hence, in order to know God, that law that comes from God's "inner being" must be *in* us.

This is the refrain we find in Deuteronomy. Moses reiterates and recounts the law to the Israelites nearly forty years after Sinai. Over that intervening time, Israel has amounted to little more than a complete failure, or nearly so were it not for the grace of God. But now, standing at the brink of the Promised Land, the people are reminded of the law (Deut. 6:6—9):

> These commandments that I give you today are to be upon your hearts. Impress them on your children. Talk about them when you sit at home and when you walk along the road, when you lie down and when you get up. Tie them as symbols on your hands and bind them on your foreheads. Write them on the doorframes of your houses and on your gates.

While the law was not merely external at Sinai, now all of a sudden it must be on the heart. The hard lessons learned during the desert wandering period have struck a cord with the Israelites, and so the need is felt to emphasize the proper "location" of the law: within you, on your heart (see also Deut. 11:18; 30:14; 32:46—47).

This theme finds recurring expression in the Psalms. For example:

> The law of his God is in his heart;
>   his feet do not slip. (Ps. 37:31)

> I desire to do your will, O my God;
>   your law is within my heart. (Ps. 40:8)

Psalm 119, the longest psalm (176 verses), is essentially dedicated to this theme, that God's law is truly "inside" the psalmist. It is a part of him, or as he says in verse 11: "I have hidden your word in my heart that I might not sin against you." The last part of that verse is important, not just for understanding this psalm but this theme as a whole: The purpose for having the law on one's heart is so that proper behavior may follow. It is not just to have a warm feeling about God, but to have that warm knowledge of God translate into action. This, too, is the focus of Exodus 18:13—26: The people want to know God's will so they can act accordingly.

Although there are a good number of other passages that we could look at with great profit, we move to Jeremiah 31:33, a passage that takes on added significance in the New Testament. The passage is found in the context of a stunning declaration by Jeremiah, which runs from verses 31—40. The time is coming when God will make a "new covenant" (v. 31) with his people, the character of which is to be contrasted with that made with Israel's forefathers, "when I took them by the hand to lead them out of Egypt" (v. 32)—in other words, the covenant at Mount Sinai. The nature of this contrast is seen at the end of verse 32: "because they broke my covenant." This situation will be remedied in the manner cited in verse 33: "I will put my law in their minds and write it on their hearts."

Jeremiah does not see the Sinai covenant as essentially useless because it was written, and therefore in desperate need of being superceded by a more "spiritual" version of the law, one written on the heart. Such a perspective ignores the witness of the Old Testament itself as described above, the necessity of having the law on one's heart. In other words, this is no preview of a supposed law-grace dichotomy. Rather, Jeremiah is saying that the covenant with Israel at Sinai will be taken to an even greater level of intimacy; it will be "taken to heart" even more deeply. In other words, we have here a glimpse of the ultimate realization of what the law all along has required—heart assent.

As is well known, Jeremiah 31:31–34 is cited in Hebrews 8:8–12. This is because in Christ the new covenant has come. Again, this new covenant is not to be contrasted *absolutely* with the old. It is rather a heightening and full realization of what the Old Testament had always required. God wants us, all of us. He wants our devotion. He did not come to us as a man to make us good people, but to restore our fallen image. Christians now have in them not the law in a legalistic sense. What we have is the indwelling of the Holy Spirit, who will guide us in the proper path and enable us to have a true heart for God.

This is what Jesus was zeroing in on in the Sermon on the Mount.

> Blessed are the *pure in heart*, for they will see God. (Matt. 5:8)
>
> But I tell you that anyone who looks at a woman lustfully has already committed adultery with her in his *heart*. (5:28)
>
> For where your treasure is, there your *heart* will be also. (6:21)

Throughout the Gospels, Jesus makes it clear that it is the heart that he is after (e.g., Matt. 13:15, 19; 15:8, 18–19, and parallels). We should not think of statements such as these as innovations. Jesus is calling the people back to the standard of morality that the Old Testament itself calls for, a message that may have been obscured in the religious climate of his day.

God's purpose has always been to make a people who have an intimate knowledge of him, a knowledge of the heart that leads to proper behavior, not simply knowing about God. Exodus 18 is the first concrete step God uses to give his people such knowledge. But although Moses is their model and leader, his ministry is temporary. Having the law on their hearts will come to an even grander expression for those who are bound to God by virtue of their union with the risen Christ, the supreme minister of the covenant.

TELL OF WHAT the Lord has done. As Exodus 18 shows us, the nations are part of God's plan. This is no less true today. No, this is not going to be a pep talk for overseas missions. Rather, I wish to stress that the response of the nations to God's acts, as seen adumbrated in Jethro's response, has *already* happened. The church is universal. The call to preach the gospel "in Jerusalem, and in all Judea and Samaria, and to the ends of the earth" (Acts 1:8) has come to pass. Belief in the God of Israel is no longer located in the tiny strip of land in the Middle East. Nothing more needs to be done for God's general purpose to bring the gospel to all the world to be "accomplished." This is *not* to say that missionary activity can cease!! It means that the dividing wall of hostility between the Jews and Gentiles has been broken down because of the resurrection of Christ (Eph. 2:14–18). The gospel now goes freely to the whole world.

In this sense, most Christians today can identify with Jethro more than Moses and the Israelites! Unless one is of Jewish heritage, he or she is also of a Gentile nation that, to use Paul's analogy in Romans 11:11–24, has been grafted into Israel, the branch. Theologically speaking, the Great Commission has been fully obeyed, which, again, does not mean that missionary activity can cease. Such a thing does not even enter the mind of a true follower of Christ. The nations are still being called into God's kingdom, and we take part in that.

But the application of Exodus 18 should not be restricted to bringing the gospel to virgin soil. The fact remains that the gospel is "out there" for all the world to see. And we, as faithful followers of Christ, are a part of that outward movement of the gospel to the nations not just when we board a plane for a Third World country or send a check to a mission organization. We also bring the good news to the nations when we talk to our neighbors and the people we see every day. As we do this, more and more of the "nations" are being brought into "Israel." This "mixed crowd" (to use the language of 12:38, NRSV) is increasing. It is called the church.

The nations come to a knowledge of God today, as they have always done, by hearing (Rom. 10:14–15). Specifically, it is by hearing about God and his acts. For the church age, of course, the message is how God is reconciling the world to himself in Christ (2 Cor. 5:19–21). It is also relating to others how he acts in our lives, how he is turning us into Christ-like beings.

The message the church is to give to the nations should focus on God. But we all know that is not always the case. When our witness to the gospel begins to sound a little too much like "Look how together I am. Wow, don't you want to be like me!?" we have strayed from the path. Nor should it be,

"Come to our church because we are growing. We have a variety of ministries to meet your needs. Our pastor is a motivating and gifted preacher; he will change your life."

Few are this blatant, but there is a subtle difference between "Look what *God has done* in my life" and "Look what God has done *in my life*"; between "Look how *God is moving* here" and "Look how God is moving *here*." Even the most mature believers, who can serve as examples (cf. Phil. 3:17) for us to follow, are not to be the main focus. Imitating such godly people should never turn into idolizing them. It is our natural tendency to center on our own efforts and accomplishments, but the cause of the gospel demands that we lose ourselves entirely, that we get out of the way and let the glory of God and the wonder of the gospel shine to all the nations. Then they, like Jethro, will be "delighted to hear about all the good things the LORD had done for Israel" (Ex. 18:9).

The law and the Christian life. That we would have the law of God written on our hearts is the victorious Christian life. Such a statement should not seem too strange to us. I suspect that some negative reactions might result from the word "law": "Are we not beyond that? Isn't the law dead?" I am not using "law" here as a list of commands. This is not even what it means in the Old Testament. Even there it refers to much more than a moral checklist. For example, Psalm 78 helps us broaden our understanding of what "law" means. This psalm gives an overview of Israel's history, predominantly the Exodus; verse 4 makes the didactic purpose of the psalm clear:

> We will not hide them from their children;
> > we will tell the next generation
> the praiseworthy deeds of the LORD,
> > his power, and the wonders he has done.

What is of interest for us is verse 1, which sets the tone for the entire psalm:

> O my people, hear my *teaching*;
> > listen to the words of my mouth.

The word translated "teaching" (correctly) is the Hebrew word *torah*, which is often simply spelled "Torah" in English. This is the word commonly used for law, especially the law given at Sinai. But here Torah refers to *narrative* portions of the Pentateuch.

This is also the case in Deuteronomy 1:5. We read that "east of the Jordan in the territory of Moab, Moses began to expound this *law*, saying...." What follows is not an exposition of the Ten Commandments or some other legal material but, from 1:6 to 4:43, a review of the major *events* of the Exodus community. In other words, law once again includes narrative.

Law is more than precepts. Even in the Old Testament, it encompasses Israel's *story*, what God has done to and through his people. In this sense, law is much more than we normally take it to mean, all that antiquated, legalistic stuff that Christ has annulled. Law in the broader sense is the expression of God's character. It is his story of how he cares for his people.

In other words, to have the law on our hearts is to know God, which ultimately means to have his grace clearly imprinted in us. This is an essential element to living the Christian life. If the law is just an external law to be obeyed, the result is disastrous: a form of piety without the substance. There is plenty of "pharisaism" in the church, that is, the notion that being a Christian means trusting in Jesus for your salvation *and* having the correct view or displaying the proper behavior concerning certain issues. This is not unlike the problem with the Judaizers that Paul had, for example, in Galatia. Certain people there argued that to be a Christian you needed Jesus *and* circumcision. But the essence of the gospel is that there is no "and."

Still, we all know people—indeed, we likely struggle with this ourselves—who are suspicious of the legitimacy of someone's claim to be a Christian on the basis of observed behaviors or opinions that *they* do not agree with. The list of grievances is long and well known. "I know he *says* he is a Christian, *but* his hair is too long; he smokes; he has a wine cellar; he watches *The Simpsons*; he goes to the mall on Sundays; he is active in social issues; his political views are different from mine." If we are honest with ourselves, I suspect that all of us have our own checklist.

Let me make it perfectly clear that I am not suggesting that external behavior is irrelevant. Nor do I mean to paint with the same brush everyone who might disapprove of certain behaviors. Quite the contrary. Even in Exodus 18 knowing God's will was for the express purpose of *behaving* correctly. But the type of person I am describing here is different. This person is petty, suspicious, and judgmental, someone who thinks that true spirituality can be reduced to a number of easily identifiable behaviors that *he or she* considers proper. Part of the gospel is that we who have the law written on our hearts are free from such a debilitating view of life.

One of my best loved Christian friends is a man who feels that drinking wine is not a thing Christians should do, whereas I feel this view does not have scriptural support. We have come to different conclusions on this matter. But he does not think I am any less a true follower of Christ because I do not share his view. For him, the law is on the heart and not merely a checklist to see if someone walks the straight and narrow. I am often struck by the zeal of these "checklist" Christians. Their zeal blinds them to their own arrogance, sense of superiority, and judgmentalism, all of which are clear markers that the law of God is *not* written on their hearts.

Unlike the Israelites of Exodus 18, the law, in Christ, is truly written on our hearts. But like the Israelites, we still need to discern daily what God wants us to do. It is not always easy to know what God requires of us, especially since the Bible does not tell us what to do in each and every situation. It is not a morality manual with an index we flip through to find the answers for all of life's problems. It does not tell us, as I read in one strongly conservative publication years ago, whether it is OK to go to the circus or what movies we can or cannot go to. And even when the Bible seems to speak directly to our situation, we must still patiently discern whether that biblical precept or example is truly relevant. For example, should we seek contact with sinners on the basis of 1 Corinthians 9:22 or Matthew 9:9–13, or keep away from them on the basis of 1 Corinthians 5:11?

It is precisely these kinds of concerns that led to the massive legal literature of Judaism, the best known of which are the Mishnah and the two Talmuds. For example, the Bible says, "Remember the Sabbath day by keeping it holy." Fair enough, but this raises a number of questions. What does "keep" mean? What is considered "work"? Can I cook a meal on the Sabbath? Can I rescue an animal trapped in a ditch? In other words, *how* is this command to be kept? Christians have similar concerns, and some of our efforts to answer these questions share a striking degree of similarity to their Jewish counterparts. How should Christians keep the Sabbath? (Or should it be Sunday? Or do they need to keep it at all?) Can I watch a football game but not a double-header? Should I attend the evening service? And so forth.

What it means for the law to be written on our hearts is not that we automatically know what to do in every situation. Sometimes we do, but sometimes we must be patient in our judgments by seeking the Lord's guidance. Other times we must seek the advice of respected Christian friends. It is only those who do not have the law written on their hearts who think that God's will is easily discernible. That God has put the law on our hearts means, if anything, that our wills *are being* conformed to his own because, as we live day by day and struggle in our decisions, we are getting to know him more and more. We learn to lean toward him, as a flower leans toward the light. It is in the process of this desire to do right that we seek God with our whole hearts. We seek him because we, like the Israelites, want to do his will. And because of the spirit of Christ dwelling in us, that quest is never in vain.

Exodus 19:1–25

I N THE THIRD month after the Israelites left Egypt—on the very day—they came to the Desert of Sinai. ²After they set out from Rephidim, they entered the Desert of Sinai, and Israel camped there in the desert in front of the mountain.

³Then Moses went up to God, and the LORD called to him from the mountain and said, "This is what you are to say to the house of Jacob and what you are to tell the people of Israel: ⁴'You yourselves have seen what I did to Egypt, and how I carried you on eagles' wings and brought you to myself. ⁵Now if you obey me fully and keep my covenant, then out of all nations you will be my treasured possession. Although the whole earth is mine, ⁶you will be for me a kingdom of priests and a holy nation.' These are the words you are to speak to the Israelites."

⁷So Moses went back and summoned the elders of the people and set before them all the words the LORD had commanded him to speak. ⁸The people all responded together, "We will do everything the LORD has said." So Moses brought their answer back to the LORD.

⁹The LORD said to Moses, "I am going to come to you in a dense cloud, so that the people will hear me speaking with you and will always put their trust in you." Then Moses told the LORD what the people had said.

¹⁰And the LORD said to Moses, "Go to the people and consecrate them today and tomorrow. Have them wash their clothes ¹¹and be ready by the third day, because on that day the LORD will come down on Mount Sinai in the sight of all the people. ¹²Put limits for the people around the mountain and tell them, 'Be careful that you do not go up the mountain or touch the foot of it. Whoever touches the mountain shall surely be put to death. ¹³He shall surely be stoned or shot with arrows; not a hand is to be laid on him. Whether man or animal, he shall not be permitted to live.' Only when the ram's horn sounds a long blast may they go up to the mountain."

¹⁴After Moses had gone down the mountain to the people, he consecrated them, and they washed their clothes. ¹⁵Then he said to the people, "Prepare yourselves for the third day. Abstain from sexual relations."

¹⁶On the morning of the third day there was thunder and lightning, with a thick cloud over the mountain, and a very loud trumpet blast. Everyone in the camp trembled. ¹⁷Then Moses led the people out of the camp to meet with God, and they stood at the foot of the mountain. ¹⁸Mount Sinai was covered with smoke, because the LORD descended on it in fire. The smoke billowed up from it like smoke from a furnace, the whole mountain trembled violently, ¹⁹and the sound of the trumpet grew louder and louder. Then Moses spoke and the voice of God answered him.

²⁰The LORD descended to the top of Mount Sinai and called Moses to the top of the mountain. So Moses went up ²¹and the LORD said to him, "Go down and warn the people so they do not force their way through to see the LORD and many of them perish. ²²Even the priests, who approach the LORD, must consecrate themselves, or the LORD will break out against them."

²³Moses said to the LORD, "The people cannot come up Mount Sinai, because you yourself warned us, 'Put limits around the mountain and set it apart as holy.'"

²⁴The LORD replied, "Go down and bring Aaron up with you. But the priests and the people must not force their way through to come up to the LORD, or he will break out against them."

²⁵So Moses went down to the people and told them.

Original Meaning

THE IMPORTANCE OF the law in chapters 20–23 should not cause us to pass over quickly chapter 19. It is here that God's promise to Moses in 3:12 is fulfilled: "And God said, 'I will be with you. And this will be the sign to you that it is I who have sent you: When you have brought the people out of Egypt, you will worship God on this mountain.'" Moses' journey has come full circle. He met God on Mount Horeb in chapter 3, and he has now returned to him with the recently redeemed Israelites. As one commentator put it, Israel is now "transformed into a worshipping people of God."[1] Israel will remain at Mount Sinai for almost one year, a scene that will take the writer fifty-nine chapters to describe (they depart in Num. 10:11).[2] What will this lengthy (from a narrative point of view) stage in Israel's journey bring them?

The Israelites arrive and set up camp in 19:1–2. Immediately Moses climbs the mountain to God (v. 3). This will not be his last trip. Although the narrative is not entirely clear, he apparently makes three such treks in chapter 19 (vv. 3–7, 8–14, 20–25). God's words on this first trip (vv. 4–6) are among the most important in the book to this point—words intended not just for him but for "the house of Jacob . . . the people of Israel" (v. 3). In other words, Moses ascends the mountain not simply to commune with God, but to bring God's message back down to the people. He is the one through whom God is going to teach the people about who he is. The first phase of Moses' assignment is completed: He brought God's people out of Egypt and to the foot of the mountain. Now the second stage begins.

God's first speech to Israel is a simple message: remember. This is the basic content of verse 4. At the beginning of God's self-disclosure to them, the Israelites are to think back to what he has done in destroying Egypt and bringing them to himself. One memorable phrase is that they have been carried to God "on eagles' wings." This can be understood in a dual sense here. (1) Eagles are depicted elsewhere in the Old Testament as birds that care for the weak. The central passage for this is Deuteronomy 32:9–11:

> For the LORD's portion is his people,
>> Jacob his allotted inheritance.
> In a desert land he found him,
>> in a barren and howling waste.
> He shielded him and cared for him;
>> he guarded him as the apple of his eye,
> *like an eagle* that stirs up its nest
>> and hovers over its young,
> that spreads its wings to catch them
>> and carries them on its pinions. (italics added)

Israel's deliverance from Egypt is like an eagle swooping down to hover over its young and carrying them off to safety. (2) Eagles are also fierce birds of

---

1. W. J. Dumbrell, "The Prospect of Unconditionality in the Sinaitic Covenant," *Israel's Apostasy and Restoration: Essays in Honor of Roland K. Harrison*, ed., A. Gileadi (Grand Rapids: Baker, 1988), 144.

2. We are told in Ex. 19:1 that the Israelites arrive at Mount Sinai three months to the day after they have left Egypt. In Num. 10:11, they leave Mount Sinai "on the twentieth day of the second month of the second year," about ten days short of a twelve-month stay.

prey (e.g., Deut. 28:49; Jer. 4:13; 48:40; 49:22). Such imagery is also fitting for Exodus 19:4, for God behaved as a fierce predator with respect to Egypt in order to carry Israel to safety.[3]

Not only are the Israelites to remember what God has done, but that memory is to motivate them to *obey* (v. 5). Their movement to the mountain is not a free ride; something is expected of them. But having said this, I must make something else clear: That Israel's faithfulness to the covenant is required should in no way be understood to mean that Israel worked for her salvation in the Old Testament. This entire scene at the mountain and the subsequent laws are predicated on verse 4, what *God has done*. The Israelites are not to keep the law in order for God to save them. They have already been saved; God has brought them out of Egypt. The law he now gives is the subsequent stage in Israel's developing relationship with God. It is what is expected of a people *already* redeemed. It is law, but it is based on the prior establishment of the relationship between them by God's good pleasure. The people do not earn their salvation; but once saved, they are obligated to act in a manner worthy of their high calling. This is true in the New Testament as well (see Eph. 4:1; 2 Thess. 1:11).

What is the nature of the "covenant" that the Israelites are to keep (v. 5)? Which covenant is meant? Most commentators understand that the covenant here is what will be revealed in the following chapters, that is, God's law. Such thinking is understandable, but I am convinced that this is not the case. W. Dumbrell has argued convincingly that "covenant" in verse 5 does not refer to what is about to transpire, but what has gone on before, namely, the covenant with the patriarchs.[4] This should not seem odd to us in light of the continual backward glances the writer of Exodus gives. Particularly important is 2:24–25, a passage mentioned a number of times but worth repeating:

> God heard their groaning and he remembered his *covenant* with Abraham, with Isaac and with Jacob. So God looked on the Israelites and was concerned about them. (italics added)

We will never properly understand the Exodus if we forget the connection to the patriarchs, which is foundational to the book's message. The Exodus is about God's keeping a promise he made to Abraham. What is about to transpire on Mount Sinai is *not* a new covenant, but the continuation and

---

3. It is worth mentioning here that Isaiah describes Israel's deliverance from Babylon in similar imagery. "Even youths grow tired and weary, and young men stumble and fall; but those who hope in the LORD will renew their strength. They will *soar on wings like eagles*; they will run and not grow weary, they will walk and not be faint" (Isa. 40:30–31, italics added).

4. W. J. Dumbrell, *Creation and Covenant: A Theology of Old Testament Covenants* (Nashville: Thomas Nelson, 1984), 80–90.

deepening of an existing covenant, the covenant God made with Israel's ancestors long ago. Hence, the giving of the law does not represent the initiation of God's relationship with his people but a heightening of that relationship.

This is similar to what we have seen in chapters 3 and 6 and the "revelation" of the divine name Yahweh. God was not adding a piece of information that the patriarchs did not have, but reminding Moses and the Israelites of the name that was used throughout the patriarchal period and that bound them to the God of Abraham, Isaac, and Jacob. The clause "keep my covenant" is a call to Israel to remain faithful to the covenant initiated with Abraham—the covenant that will be given greater substance in the following chapters.

Note especially the three consequences of Israel's obedience (vv. 5–6): Israel will be a treasured possession, a kingdom of priests, and a holy nation. This is the heart of the message Moses is to bring to the people. The long wait is over. God has finally spoken to his people. We should not underestimate the significance of these expressions.

(1) A "treasured possession" (Heb. *segullah*) can mean a number of things; here it means that Israel is royal property (cf. a similar use of the word in 1 Chron. 29:3).[5] Moreover, they are God's purely by virtue of his own will and desire. Note the phrase "the whole earth is mine" (Ex. 19:5); the Lord can do as he pleases, and it has pleased him to make Israel his treasured possession. They have done nothing to deserve it. They are simply his special possession; he has already shown this to be the case by bringing them out of Egypt and destroying their enemies.

(2) Israel is a "kingdom of priests." This title appears nowhere else in the Old Testament and is therefore a bit difficult to pin down. What is also somewhat strange is that the priesthood in Israel has not been established yet, so what does God mean by designating his people in this way? To refer to Israel as a kingdom of priests does not imply that we should think of priesthood in the developed, cultic sense we see later (e.g., chs. 28–29). Yet we must remember that even though the Israelite priesthood proper was not inaugurated until after chapter 19, this is not to say that priesthood was a new idea for them. There is no record of Israel's having performed a priestly role before 19:5, but they have had plenty of contact with other peoples with priests (e.g., Gen. 14:18; 41:45, 50; 46:20; 47:22, 26; Ex. 2:16; 3:1; 18:1).

Moreover, the patriarchs performed "priestly" duties when they sacrificed (e.g., Gen. 15:10–11). Israel, simply by living in the ancient world, knew very well what priests were and how they functioned. As we saw with the Sabbath law in chapter 16, the law promulgated on Sinai does not necessarily *intro-*

---

5. Ibid., 85–86.

duce a concept, but reinforces it or gives it a new definition. "Kingdom of priests," therefore, is not an anachronism. Rather, it is a statement of the manner in which God will use Israel with respect to the rest of the nations.

(3) This is where the third phrase, "holy nation," comes in. Both "kingdom of priests" and "holy nation" are to be taken together, if not as identical then at least as clearly supporting each other. As a kingdom of priests, Israel is set apart (which is what "holy" means) from the other nations. Israel is different, since she is a "treasured possession." This is God's peculiar people, and so they will be separate. But Israel is not separate in the sense of living in isolation from the other nations. As holy and priestly, Israel is the means by which God will, as his plan unfolds more and more, *bring the nations to have knowledge of him.*

By describing Israel as he does in verse 6, God is not just making a statement about Israel's new inner character as a special and separate people. He is also making a statement about the *international implications* of Israel's favored status. This is the significance of the Hebrew word for "nation": *goy*, a term normally reserved for nations other than Israel. It is used, however, in Genesis 12:2 in the midst of God's promise to Abraham to make him a "great nation." The use of this same word here signals that this scene on the mountain is to be seen in conjunction with God's promise to Abraham. It also highlights Israel's role as a *goy* among the many other *goyim* (nations) of the world. Israel is a holy and priestly nation that God has chosen to work through to bring about his broad, far-reaching plan.

Moses descends the mountain for the first time and tells the elders (whom we first met in 3:16) what is required of them (19:7–8). Presumably he has some sort of private meeting with them, since this message is not announced generally to the people. The fact that the people as a whole respond in verse 8 indicates that the instructions to the elders are passed on in some form to the people. They respond with an unqualified "yes." We will see, however, that much of Israel's subsequent history falls far short of this enthusiastic and perhaps well-intentioned assent.

Moses goes back up the mountain and brings Israel's answer to the Lord (v. 8b); their second conversation is recorded in verses 9–13. Verse 9 reiterates the issue of trust we have seen elsewhere in Exodus, notably with the manna, quail, and water incidents in chapters 16–17. In order to obviate any subsequent opposition to Moses, God will speak to Moses directly out of the cloud in the hearing of the people. The cloud, of course, is an image we have seen before (13:21–22; 14:19–20, 24; 16:10) and will see again at the climax of the covenant stipulations (24:15–18) and at the end of the book (40:34–38). It is a sign of God's presence—an awe-inspiring, frightening presence. Israel will soon be privy to the private conversation Moses had with God in chapter 3. It is important to God that Israel learn to trust Moses, the mediator. He is the link between his own glory, which no one may gaze upon, and the people he has come to deliver.

Verses 10–13 relate another set of instructions: The Israelites are to prepare themselves to approach the mountain and meet their God. To do so, they must be consecrated by Moses. Just how he is to do this is not stated. Elsewhere in Exodus consecration pertains to an act of setting apart for special service to God (28:3, 38, 41; 29:1, 21). This fits well with the notion of Israel's being a "holy nation" and "kingdom of priests" (19:6): They are set apart for God's service. In fact, both the adjective "holy" and the verb "consecrate" are derived from the same root, *qdš*. But this only speaks to the *purpose* of the consecration, not the *means* by which it is to happen.

Perhaps 13:2 and 13 give some perspective here. There God instructed that the firstborn of Israel be consecrated or set apart (v. 2, *qaddeš*) by a sacrifice. Perhaps this is what is meant in 19:10, although the writer does not fill in this gap for us. One could equate consecration and washing of clothes (cf. 19:14), but such an explanation is inadequate. Consecration is something done to the Israelites by Moses, while washing the clothes is something they do themselves. Consecration is no doubt an important act, since it involves preparing the people to meet God. But it is precisely for this reason that the lack of specificity is so perplexing for modern readers.

Not only is the nature of the consecration ambiguous, but one also wonders why God requires them to wash their clothes. Once again, we can only speculate. Perhaps washing clothes is analogous to Moses' removing his shoes in God's presence in 3:5; they are to be in God's holy presence. Or perhaps Houtman is correct in suggesting it is symbolic of personal uncleanness.[6] But we should not feel the need to dig too deeply here. We have another gap in the story that makes what was no doubt clear for the ancient readers a bit of a mystery to us. Note too that as with other elements of the book, the washing of one's clothes becomes commonplace later in the Pentateuch.[7] Hence, this reference foreshadows a later, more explicitly spelled-out ceremonial duty.

While we do not know the meaning of washing the clothes, we do know that the Israelites cannot simply come as they are. They are about to do something that no other nation has ever done—to meet their heavenly King and listen to his voice. They are given two days to prepare themselves, and part of that preparation involved the outward act of washing their clothes. Perhaps this is a sign of respect.

---

6. Houtman, *Exodus*, 2:450. Another possibility is that this washing foreshadows the function of the bronze basin in 30:17–21 and 38:8.

7. See Lev. 11–17; Num. 8:7, 21; 19:7–21; 31:24.

But meeting God does not mean marching up to the top of the mountain as Moses does. To go up, they must wait for the blast of the ram's horn (v. 13). Any premature advance, whether by man or animal, will result in death by stoning or being shot by arrows, lest the perpetrators themselves be touched by those carrying out the sentence! This is a serious matter. It is striking that these people, whom God loves and has compassion on, are guided to this holy place to meet their God, and yet upon their arrival are kept at arm's length. It is like receiving an exclusive invitation to a Presidential dinner at the White House only to be kept waiting a few hours outside the gates on Pennsylvania Avenue. The fact that limits are placed around the mountain accents the holiness of God's dwelling. You do not simply walk up to it in street clothes and chat with the occupant. The way is barred. You must prepare yourself first, and then you must wait until the occupant is willing to receive you.

This sanctity of the mountain is expressed in its tripartite division, which a number of commentators (going back at least to the Middle Ages) have compared to the tripartite structure of the tabernacle,[8] hinted at more clearly in 24:1—2:

> Then he said to Moses, "Come up to the LORD, you and Aaron, Nadab and Abihu, and seventy of the elders of Israel. You are to worship at a distance, but Moses alone is to approach the LORD; the others must not come near. And the people may not come up with him."

According to this division, the top of the mountain, to which Moses alone has access, corresponds to the Most Holy Place. Aaron, Nadab, Abihu, and the seventy elders have access to the mountain but not its summit; this corresponds to the Holy Place. The rest of the people stay at the foot of the mountain, which corresponds to the outer court where the laity gather.

This is a helpful connection. Even if this tripartite division is not crystal clear, the fact that only some people have access to certain portions of the mountain certainly foreshadows the more highly structured divisions of the tabernacle, which dominate most of the second half of the book. It also highlights the fact that the tabernacle itself is an earthly reflection of God's heavenly abode. In other words, the mountain does not mirror the tabernacle; the structure of the tabernacle is patterned after the mountain.

Moses comes back down the mountain and carries out God's orders. He consecrates the people, and they wash their clothes. But Moses seems to add a command: They are to abstain from sexual relations (v. 15). This command was not given in verses 10–13, so why does Moses add it? Nowhere else in the Old Testament does God require such across-the-board abstinence.

---

8. See Sarna, *Exodus*, 105.

Only where deviant sexual behavior or cleanliness issues are concerned is sex disallowed (cf. Lev. 18 and 20). Hence, this command is unique and calls for some sort of explanation.

It is not a question whether such a command is improper in the abstract. Although a temporary prohibition against sex seems unprecedented, it may be that "three days of preparation and self-restraint allow time for sober reflection."[9] From this perspective, the sentiment to abstain from sexual relations certainly makes sense. But this is not the point. Why does Moses give this command if Yahweh did not speak it? Well, perhaps God did say it, but it wasn't recorded. But this answer raises the question why it wasn't recorded. Was it too obvious or too incidental? If the latter, why does Moses mention it later? And why would the writer allow such an obvious disjunction between verses 10–14 and verse 15? Perhaps Sarna is correct that the fact that it is not mentioned in verses 10–13 makes its inclusion in verse 15 all the more striking, so as to draw the reader's attention to it. But then the question remains: Why do sexual relations need to be singled out? In the final analysis, an obvious explanation eludes us.

Having been consecrated, the people are now ready to meet God. But it is certainly not anything they may have expected. If we imagine the scene, particularly if you have ever been trapped outside in an open area during a strong thunderstorm, Israel's reaction is understandable. Not only are they surrounded by thunder, lightning, and thick clouds (standard theophany language), but by a loud trumpet blast, too. At these they tremble. Israel, after a process that has taken several months, finally sees the author of her salvation and fears. If they go on to forget repeatedly God's goodness to them in bringing them out of Egypt, they should at least have burned this terrible sight into their minds—but this, too, is soon forgotten.

This trumpet blast signals to the people to approach God (cf. v. 13), which they do, coming to the foot of the mountain (vv. 16–17). Now the mountain is covered with smoke, which we are told in verse 18 is caused by the Lord's fiery presence. Again, one cannot but think of Exodus 3 and Moses' initial encounter with God where he appeared to Moses in the burning bush. Israel is now participating in the experience of Moses, their mediator. In response to this, it is not just the people who tremble but the mountain itself. This is not an uncommon phenomenon used to describe God's presence (see Ps. 18:7; 97:5; 104:32; 144:5).

To add to the drama, the trumpet keeps getting louder (Ex. 19:19). The climax of the scene comes when Moses and God converse, thus fulfilling what was promised in verse 9. Unfortunately, we are not told what they

---

9. Ibid.

speak about. It is clear that verses 20–25 do not represent the content of this discussion, since it is further information Moses is to bring to the people. Apparently, all the people need to hear is that Moses and God do speak to each other.

Verses 20–25 pose a number of difficult questions that have occupied scholars for many centuries. Does verse 20 describe a second descent of God after the one mentioned in verse 18? This would be rather awkward. Rather, it seems that verse 20 merely repeats what happened in verse 18 to make it clear in what context Moses ascends the mountain. In other words, verse 20 is saying, as it were: "Now, the LORD descended to the top of the Mount Sinai (as you already know from v. 18), and it is here that he called Moses to the top in order to speak with him." At the end of verse 19, Moses is still at the foot of the mountain with the rest of the Israelites. But now the descended God calls to him, and Moses goes up.

God's command to Moses in verses 21–22 is difficult to understand fully in the context. After Moses goes up on the mountain, God tells him right away to go back down and tell the people to do something he has essentially already told them—to warn the people not to force their way through. But is this not the point of placing the limits around the mountain in verses 12–13? In fact, this is the meaning of Moses' rejoinder in verse 23: "LORD, you just told us that!"

Nevertheless, there is a difference between the command of verses 12–13 and that of verses 21–22. In the former, the Israelites are to keep away until the trumpet sounds. In the latter, the trumpet has already sounded. Has not permission, therefore, been given to advance? If so, why the warning in verses 21–22 not to? If it were not for Moses' rejoinder in verse 23, which unequivocally states that the two warnings are one and the same, I would be tempted to argue that verses 21–22 are *additional* commands aimed at keeping the people from *forcing* their way through after the trumpet has blown; but Moses' response does not allow us this option. I am not sure how to put these two factors together.

What compounds the difficult nature of this passage is the reference to priests in verse 22. This is the first reference to Israelite priests in the Old Testament. Officially, the priesthood is not established until chapter 28. So, where do they come from? Do the Israelites have "priests" in a looser sense of the word before they are officially established? Some commentators reconcile this difficulty by suggesting that the elders or young men function as priests at this stage.[10] We should not dismiss this too quickly, especially in light of 24:5 (which has young men sacrificing). Still, nowhere are these

---

10. For example, see Cassuto, *Commentary on Exodus*, 234.

men called *priests*, the term used here. Perhaps this passage assumes the official priesthood of chapter 28 and following, but that would throw the entire scene at Mount Sinai into chronological disarray.

It is tempting to suggest that this overt reference to Israelite priests is another hint of what is to come, a device we have seen the writer use throughout Exodus. But such a solution suffers from one fatal flaw. When we take verses 23 and 24 together, clearly the *people* and the *priests*, who are both subject to the prohibition, are assumed to be at the foot of the mountain *now*. The scenario goes like this:

(1) Moses goes to the top of the mountain, leaving the people behind (vv. 12, 20). At this point there is no mention of priests.
(2) God first warns Moses not to let the people force their way through (v. 21).
(3) He then warns Moses that the priests must be consecrated before approaching him (v. 22). As we have seen in verse 10, the precise nature of this consecration is not made explicit, at least not until chapter 29.[11]
(4) Moses responds that the command to put limits around the mountain (cited in vv. 12–13) makes this most recent command superfluous (v. 23). Moses only refers here to *people* not being allowed to approach. This may suggest that Moses ignores the prohibition against the priests in verse 22 because they, unlike the people, are not yet present. They will only be present after the priesthood has been established later on. However. . . .
(5) Verse 24 seems to obviate this option. God tells Moses to go down and address the people *and the priests*. Hence, the reference to priests in verses 22 and 24 is not a foreshadowing, but is descriptive of something actually active at the time. There are priests at the foot of Mount Sinai in chapter 19.

I am as confused by this chapter as by any other in Exodus. I see only two possible solutions. Either priests of some sort exist before the official establishment of the priesthood, or portions of this chapter are chronologically displaced. I should add, however, that neither option should cause too much distress. For one thing—and this is so true of the book as a whole—although there is confusion for us in some areas, many elements come through loud and clear. We should not lose sight of the forest for the trees. If we look past

---

11. In fact, I suggest that the consecration of the priests here at the base of the mountain foreshadows the consecration of the priests before they are to enter the tabernacle (ch. 29). Again, the tabernacle is a reflection of the mountain.

the confusion, we will see that God repeats essentially the same warning three times (vv. 12–13, 21–22, 24).

Does God find it necessary or beneficial to do so? I think so. Humanly speaking, God has the "right" to be suspicious of Israel's conduct. He has already seen how they react in times of stress (cf. the incidents at the Red Sea and with food and water shortages). He knows they are prone to rebellion. But the topic here is meeting God, and the penalty for misconduct is death. In this respect, the triple warning makes good sense. And whatever else we might say, what always fascinates me is that these types of things do not seem to bother the biblical writer. Obviously, this passage is not prepared to answer the types of questions we are posing here (even though it is the passage itself that, at least for us, raises these questions!).

One final element of this passage should be mentioned. Aaron is referred to specifically in verse 24 as being allowed to ascend the mountain with Moses. We have not seen such privileged status for Aaron since before Moses returned to Egypt from Midian. It was at Moses' first encounter with God that Aaron was singled out for special service: he would be Moses' mouthpiece (chs. 3–4). Moreover, the genealogy of 6:14–25 focused on Aaron, thus preparing the reader for the important role he would play. We now see another installment of this in 19:24: Aaron alone can accompany Moses. This also fits with the "tripartite" division of the mountain suggested above. Of the descendants of Levi only Aaron's line may enter the Most Holy Place (see Lev. 16). Aaron's ascent up the mountain with Moses prepares us for what is to come.

Verse 25 reports Moses' third descent down the mountain. He again reports to the people what God has said. The Israelites have been reminded of what God has done for them, encouraged by their privileged status as his special people, exhorted to keep the covenant, and given a lesson in what it means to be in God's holy presence. These things have prepared them to listen to the words of God, to hear the laws their holy God requires of them, which will further define them as servants of God, both now and for generations to come.

Bridging Contexts

"A CHOSEN PEOPLE, a royal priesthood, a holy nation, a people belonging to God" (1 Peter 2:9). In God's first official encounter with his redeemed people, he refers to them as a treasured possession, a kingdom of priests, and a holy nation. Although these terms are unique to this passage, the ideas they entail are not. God has chosen a people to be separate from the rest of the world, not just so that they can "belong" to him in some private sense, but in order that they be used by him for a special purpose. Exodus 19:5–6 is a crystallization of a pattern seen elsewhere in the Old Testament up to this point. It is also a pattern that will continue to come to fuller expression as Israel's story, both in terms of its triumphs and failures, unfolds.

We have already seen briefly that Israel's special status in 19:5–6 is not an innovation but continues God's promise to Abraham. When God called Abraham (Gen. 12:1–3), he made it clear that the patriarch's privilege extended beyond his own progeny to the nations as a whole: "and all peoples on earth will be blessed through you" (v. 3). This universal element in Abraham's call does not come to the foreground through much of the subsequent narrative, where the emphasis is on Abraham's offspring rather than on the nations. Still, it is only through Abraham's seed that the blessings to the peoples will be realized. Hence, even though the problem of barrenness quickly becomes the dominant topic, this is not to say that the far-reaching goal of God announced in 12:3 is forgotten or takes a back seat. The seed is not merely for Abraham's benefit, nor does Sarah's barrenness merely afford an opportunity for God to perform a miracle. It is the process whereby God's plan will be fulfilled.

We can push this back a step to include the story of Noah and the Flood. This is much more than simply a story of sin and punishment, although it is certainly that as well. It is also a story of eventual blessing to the world through Noah and his offspring. We see this in the covenant God makes with Noah, in which he promises never again to flood the earth and destroy its inhabitants (Gen. 9:1–17). This covenant is established with Noah and his descendants *and* with all living creatures. The benefits of this covenant will be felt for generations to come—not simply by Noah and his family, but by all creatures of the earth. Like Abraham, Noah was delivered from a situation not just for personal benefit but for the benefit of those who come after him. Everyone may see the rainbow and remember how they benefit from God's mercy to Noah.

The role played by Abraham and Noah with respect to the world as a whole achieves a heightened state of clarity in Exodus 19:5–6. It is here, in earnest, on Mount Sinai, that the full implementation of God's plan of world redemption begins to be seen. The annunciation of this ideal, however, is followed by repeated failure on the part of God's people, his treasured possession, to feel the full weight of that high calling. As we so often see in the Old Testament, whereas God has created a people to be the means of reconciling the nations, by their disobedient conduct they become rather a byword and an object of ridicule by the nations. We see this as early as 32:25 in the golden calf incident: "Moses saw that the people were running wild and that Aaron had let them get out of control and so become a laughingstock to their enemies."

Rather than redeeming the nations, Israel, by rejecting the God who saved her, becomes a laughingstock. As a result the nations will be less attracted to the true God than before. The same theme is represented in a number of Old Testament passages (e.g., 1 Kings 9:6–9; Ps. 44:13–14; Jer. 24:9; Ezek. 5:14–15; 14:8; 22:4; 23:10), all of which describe Israel's disobedience to God, which leads to their reproach by the peoples of the world.

Israel's obedience or disobedience to God's covenant stipulations has implications beyond simply that of Israel's relationship to God, that is, blessing or curse. It has ramifications for the outworking of God's redemptive plan for the world. We see this even in the Exile, where Israel felt the full weight of the consequences of her disobedience. God promised to bring the remnant of Israel back to the land, which would renew his universal purpose in calling Israel:

> It is too small a thing for you to be my servant
>> to restore the tribes of Jacob
>> and bring back those of Israel I have kept.
> I will also make you a *light for the Gentiles,*
>> that you may bring my salvation to the *ends of the earth.* (Isa. 49:6,
>> italics added)

Even during the darkest period in Israel's history, when her own release from captivity posed the most pressing concern, God reminded his people of the broader implications of their release—to bring salvation to the ends of the earth.

The ideal of Exodus 19:5–6 comes to fruition in two senses in the New Testament: in terms of the person and work of Christ and in terms of the church. (1) As we have already seen in a number of places, Christ himself is the fulfillment of God's intention for Israel (e.g., he is God's Son, as was Israel in Ex. 4:22–23). He is also the fulfillment of 19:5–6. That is, Christ is God's "treasured possession," his "kingdom of priests," and his "holy nation" in the sense that through him the universal call to the nations is finally and fully put into effect. Christ is "a light for revelation to the Gentiles" (Luke 2:32, borrowing language from Isa. 49:6; cf. also 42:6; 51:4). He fulfills this role for the very reason Israel did not: He is perfectly obedient to God.

In attempting to fulfill this role, Israel stumbled along for hundreds of years, never quite reaching the mark. With the death and resurrection of Christ, however, we begin to see how truly far-reaching God's promise to Abraham was. Now, indeed, all nations will be blessed, but not through Abraham and his earthly offspring, but through the true Israel, the true Son of God in whom the promise to Abraham finds its final expression.

(2) The church is also a light to the Gentiles. In fact, it is precisely because Christ is the light that the church, by virtue of her union with the risen

Christ, also fulfills this role. In Acts 13:47, Paul and Barnabas cite Isaiah 49:6 in the context of Jews' jealousy at seeing so many Gentiles coming to hear them speak in the synagogue. They remind the Jews that this phenomenon, to which their hard hearts are so resistant, is nothing less than the culmination of God's purpose announced in the Old Testament: "For this is what the Lord has commanded us: 'I have made you a light for the Gentiles, that you may bring salvation to the ends of the earth.'"

The "us" referred to here is no doubt the apostles, the nucleus of the soon-to-be expanding church, in their role of spreading the gospel to the Gentiles. The apostles are to preach the gospel to the Gentiles so that the doors of the church may be opened to people other than Jews, something that the Jews of Pisidian Antioch find objectionable. But the word is to go to the Gentiles, in part because it was first rejected by the Jews (v. 46) but also because this has been God's plan all along.

A New Testament passage that interacts more directly with Exodus 19:5–6 is 1 Peter 2:4–10 (esp. v. 9).[12] This passage describes the blessing of the church as God's chosen people, and it does so by alluding to a number of Old Testament passages that in their respective contexts are descriptive of Israel: Isaiah 8:14; 28:16; Psalm 118:22; Hosea 1:6, 9; 2:1, 23. First Peter 2:9 is a clear reference to Exodus 19:5–6: "But you are a chosen people, a royal priesthood, a holy nation, a people belonging to God, that you may declare the praises of him who called you out of darkness into his wonderful light."

The point Peter is making here seems obvious. The blessed status assigned to Israel in the Old Testament is now the property of the church, the true and final Israel. The promise made to Abraham—that the nations will be blessed through him and his offspring—has been fulfilled in the final and unqualified inclusion of the Gentiles into God's family.

Now, Peter's emphasis in his use of Exodus 19:5–6 is not so much on the new Israel's role of bringing blessing to the nations of the world. His emphasis, rather, is in distinguishing the church as a distinct, separate people in order to motivate them to live godly lives (1 Peter 2:11–12).[13] But this is not to say that the evangelistic role of the church as a "holy nation" and a "kingdom of priests" is not in view. To the contrary, Peter stresses the evangelistic implications of such godly living: "Live such good lives *among the pagans* that,

---

12. Some helpful treatments of this passage include A. T. M. Cheung, "The Priest As the Redeemed Man: A Biblical-Theological Study of the Priesthood," *JETS* 29 (1986): 265–75; T. D. Lea, "The Priesthood of All Christians According to the New Testament," *Southwestern Journal of Theology* 30 (1988): 15–21.

13. A similar emphasis can be seen in Rev. 1:6 and 5:10.

though they accuse you of doing wrong, they may see your good deeds and *glorify God* on the day he visits us" (v. 12, italics added).

The reason they are to live "as aliens and strangers in the world" (1 Peter 2:11) is so that the world might no longer be strangers to the gospel. In other words, in living lives that are "holy" to God, in the sense of being separate from the world (which is precisely the point at which the Israelites failed), the church fulfills its divinely appointed duty of being "light to the Gentiles." The task is now given to the church as a whole and to individuals to be holy in order that others might also one day be redeemed.

"Prepare to meet your God, O Israel" (Amos 4:12). Our passage records Israel's first encounter with God *as a nation*. True, they have seen God at work in bringing them out of Egypt, something they will need to be reminded of from time to time. They also know the ancient stories of how God dealt with the patriarchs. Still, it is here on Mount Sinai that the Israelites are formally "introduced" to their God. Judging by their reaction, they may have gotten more than they bargained for.

Approaching God is a serious matter. This is why it must be done only on God's terms. Even the Israelites, whom God has just delivered from Egypt, whom God calls his "son," cannot simply walk up to him as they please. There are certain rules and regulations that must be followed. In Exodus 19, these rules are essentially two: consecration and waiting for the trumpet. As we have seen, precisely what consecration involves is not clear, although it does pertain to some means whereby the Israelites are "set apart." Presumably there is some ceremonial process whereby they are "changed" in order to be prepared to meet God. Moreover, part of this preparation includes the washing of clothes, another act that invites a number of explanations but without a definitive solution.

Rather than focusing on the precise nature of the consecration process, it is more profitable to point out that *something* has to occur before the Israelites can approach God. Israel is at the beginning of its existence as a nation before God. With the arrival at Mount Sinai, they are entering into a new stage of redemptive history, where God forms a nation to be used for a broader purpose. They are about to see God more clearly than others ever have. It is worth noting that neither Abraham nor Noah have a similar preparatory period. They are simply called by God because they are deemed somehow "worthy."[14] But now God's people are on his holy mountain, where his Spirit dwells, the place that will form the basic blueprint for both the tabernacle and the temple. At this heightened stage in redemptive history,

---

14. Noah is called blameless in Gen. 6:9. Abraham receives no such designation. He is simply called to leave his homeland.

when Israel's exalted role in the drama of redemption is being revealed more clearly, it is necessary for them to have a clearer glimpse of God. But such a clearer glimpse cannot be attained lightly.

Even Moses has a preparation period of sorts; he too must do something before he can approach God: remove his sandals (3:5). Such an understanding of Moses' initial encounter with God fits well with what we have seen throughout the opening chapters of Exodus, that Moses' experiences in Egypt and Midian parallel and foreshadow Israel's experiences later in the book.

Another well-known biblical figure with a similar experience at a decisive juncture in redemptive history is Isaiah. In his vision of God, high and exalted on the throne (Isa. 6), the prophet does not see God "straight"—there is a strong element of imagery in the vision; it is a powerful and unsettling gaze into God *seated on his throne*. To put it another way, we are in the control room for the universe. Or to use an image more appropriate for the Old Testament, we are in the most inner holy place of the heavenly sanctuary. This is Isaiah's Mount Sinai experience.

Isaiah does not receive this vision because of anything he has done. In fact, his fearful response in Isaiah 6:5 suggests the opposite, that he was worthy only of death. "'Woe to me!' I cried. 'I am ruined! For I am a man of unclean lips, and I live among a people of unclean lips, and my eyes have seen the King, the LORD Almighty.'"

The reason the prophet is given a vision of such gravity is because he must deliver a message of great gravity. His ministry will be far-reaching. His prophecies will bring him to the threshold of a number of events of profound redemptive significance. These include three crises involving the superpower of the day, Assyria.[15] For our purposes, a fourth crisis is more important: the deportation of the southern kingdom by the Babylonians in the early sixth century B.C. and their return under the Persian ruler Cyrus in 538 B.C. The message Isaiah is to bring to the people is one of God's wrath and punishment because of their sin, which will result in their exile into foreign land. But that does not mean that God is finished with his people. He will also bring a remnant out of Babylon with which to form a new beginning.

The parallels between Babylon and Egypt have been mentioned elsewhere in this commentary, and here we see another. With each successive unfolding of God's redemptive plan comes a clearer vision of God. And

---

15. The crises with Assyria include (1) the triple threat of 735–733 B.C. that involved not just Assyria but also Damascus and the northern kingdom of Israel (Isa. 7ff.); (2) the conquest of the northern kingdom by the Assyrians in 722 B.C.; (3) Sennacherib's unsuccessful attack on Jerusalem in 701 B.C. (chs. 36–39).

that vision necessitates some process of consecration, or perhaps better, purification, on the part of the people. In Isaiah's case, it is a fearful vision of God and the taking away of his sin by being touched on the lips by the live coal from the altar (Isa. 6:6–7). In Israel's case at Mount Sinai, it is consecration and washing. With Moses, it was a burning bush and removal of his sandals.

Isaiah's fearful response is also anticipated in Exodus 19. The cause for Israel's fear, even panic, is, as in Isaiah, an unsettling glimpse of God. In Exodus 19, this glimpse is manifest in "thunder and lightning, with a thick cloud over the mountain, and a very loud trumpet blast" (v. 16). We have already discussed how cosmic disturbances are a standard manner of describing an appearance of God in the Old Testament.

An added element in Exodus 19 is the trumpet blast. Trumpet blasts are common in the Bible. They are used for various purposes: calling troops to battle (Josh. 6; 1 Sam. 13:3), signaling to break camp and set out on a journey (Num. 10:2–10), and worshiping (Lev. 23:24; 25:9; 1 Chron. 13:8; 15:24, 28; 16:6; Ezra 3:10). A heavenly trumpet blast such as we have in Exodus 19:16, however, can also be a sign that God is coming to his people. Perhaps the clearest example of this in the Old Testament beyond the present passage is Zechariah 9:14–15a:

> Then the LORD will appear over them;
>> his arrow will flash like lightning.
> The Sovereign LORD will sound the trumpet;
>> he will march in the storms of the south,
>> and the LORD Almighty will shield them.

The context of this passage concerns the coming of Zion's king (vv. 9–13), a passage teeming with messianic allusions (see Matt. 21:5; John 12:15). It is with the appearance of this king that the sovereign Lord will sound the trumpet. The prophet, however dimly, catches a glimpse of a climactic redemptive event: The King is coming.

It is no surprise, therefore, that we read about a heavenly trumpet blast in several places of the New Testament where God comes to his people in a way he has not done before. The first reference is in Matthew 24:31, in Jesus' Mount of Olives discourse. Regardless of whether his words here pertain to the end of the world or to some other "nonfinal" cataclysmic event (e.g., the fall of Jerusalem in A.D. 70), this event is an unequivocal act of God involving the Son of Man. Accompanying this event are various celestial signs (vv. 29–30) and a "loud trumpet call" (v. 31). The purpose of that call is apparently to announce the gathering of God's "elect from the four winds, from one end of the heavens to the other." Although the text does not draw this out further, presumably the elect are gathered for the purpose of meeting the "Son of Man coming on the clouds of the sky" (v. 30).

The well-known last trumpet of 1 Corinthians 15:52 is also relevant here,[16] where Paul speaks of the raising of the dead at the blast of the last trumpet (see also 1 Thess. 4:16). The precise interpretation of this future event, in combination with several other New Testament passages, continues to be a matter of debate. Does it refer to the Second Coming and the end of the world[17] or to a prior period when God's people will be taken up to meet Christ in the air, which is to be followed by the (earthly?) reign of Christ and his church? I am only too happy to step around the intricacies of the debate in the church over eschatology. The point to be made here is that, as in Exodus 19, the meeting of God and his people is announced with a trumpet blast. We can go so far as to say that Exodus 19, as the first such example in all Scripture, is a "preview of coming attractions."

One thing that is missing from the New Testament examples discussed above is the notion of fear. In the Old Testament, such a shocking revelation of God caused a great trembling on the part of the recipients. But this is not the case in the New Testament. The reasons for this are made clear in Hebrews 12:18–24:

> You have not come to a mountain that can be touched and that is burning with fire; to darkness, gloom and storm; to a trumpet blast or to such a voice speaking words that those who heard it begged that no further word be spoken to them, because they could not bear what was commanded: "If even an animal touches the mountain, it must be stoned." The sight was so terrifying that Moses said, "I am trembling with fear."
>
> But you have come to Mount Zion, to the heavenly Jerusalem, the city of the living God. You have come to thousands upon thousands of angels in joyful assembly, to the church of the firstborn, whose names are written in heaven. You have come to God, the judge of all men, to the spirits of righteous men made perfect, to Jesus the mediator of a new covenant, and to the sprinkled blood that speaks a better word than the blood of Abel.

We do not fear because we as Christians have arrived at another mountain, not Mount Sinai but Mount Zion, the heavenly Jerusalem. Not only this

---

16. Some equate the trumpet of Matt. 24:31 with this trumpet, which would settle the question of whether the Olivet Discourse concerns the end of the world. I have no strong opinion on the matter, nor is it crucial here.

17. This seems to be the case with Rev. 11:15–19, the seventh trumpet. This passage has a number of things in common with Ex. 19, not simply the trumpet blast (v. 15) but the cosmic upheavals (v. 19).

but we have come to angels and heavenly saints, to God himself and to his Son, Jesus, the mediator. We do not fear because we, even now, are given access to God in heaven—not on an earthly mountain, but on his heavenly throne. We, like Isaiah, see the Lord high and exalted on his throne, but a trembling fear does not come upon us. Why? Because, as Hebrews explains elsewhere in the book, Christ the mediator, by his once-for-all sacrifice (Heb. 7:27; 9:26; 10:10), intercedes for us (2:17; 4:14–16; 7:24–25). We, therefore, "have confidence to enter the Most Holy Place" (10:19).

The factor that makes the difference between the New Testament saint and the Old Testament saint is the work of Christ. This is not to say that we enter into his intimate presence casually, without reverence. But it does mean that, since the death and resurrection of Christ, we enter into that presence with a degree of joy, thanksgiving, and confidence, which were wholly lacking in Exodus 19 and Isaiah 6, for we know that we are without sin before God and have been reconciled to God through Christ. As Moses consecrated the people in Exodus 19 to prepare their approach to God, we are consecrated by virtue of our relationship to the risen Christ. The difference is that our present consecration fully prepares us for the awesome encounter, whereas Moses' consecration did not. This is the disjunction between the two eras in redemptive history that the author of Hebrews so patiently explains.

SALT OF THE **earth, light of the world (Matt. 5:13–16).** First Peter 2:4–12 is not interested in making an abstract connection between Israel and the church. The purpose of making the equation is for practical reasons. The church as the new Israel is to exhibit impeccable behavior, which is what Old Testament Israel essentially failed to do. But by fulfilling this God-given mandate to be holy, we not only designate ourselves as "different" from the world, but the world will now also take notice, thus being drawn to "glorify God on the day he visits us" (v. 12). The intention of God to reconcile the world to himself through a select and holy people, a plan first announced in Genesis 12:1–3 and more clearly in Exodus 19:5–6, and that has come to a climax in the death and resurrection of Christ, is something God is still working out. As instruments of God's plan, we are to live holy lives before God *and humanity*. This is a just summary of the path that all Christians are to walk. Both elements are crucial.

(1) We are truly a chosen people, holy and regal. We are to be different from the world around us. This has always been true of God's people. Israel had a number of specific regulations to obey, regulations that served the primary purpose of making sure they were fully cognizant of how separate they

were from the world around them. These laws covered everything from having only Yahweh as their God (Ex. 20:3–6) to not cooking a young goat in its mother's milk (23:19).

(2) Such separateness is also a mark of God's people today. True, we are not subject to the same laws as Israel was, particularly since Christ came to fulfill the law (Matt. 5:17). But this is not to say that the church has no moral obligations, and 1 Peter 2:4–12 (along with the many hortatory passages of the New Testament, such as Matt. 5–7; Rom. 12–15; Eph. 4–6) is a reminder of that fact. Much of the New Testament, particularly the letters, is directly concerned with how believers ought to *behave* in light of the resurrection.

As a separate people belonging to God, we should never shy away from being mindful of the things we ought and ought not to do. I was once asked by a friend, who was not married, whether I thought it was OK for him to sleep with a woman with whom he was in a fairly serious relationship, likely leading to marriage. Of course, my answer was no, but as we discussed the matter more fully, his argument began to center around this line of thinking: "But if I am a Christian, won't God forgive me anyway?" Such is not a new way of thinking. In fact, this is what Paul anticipated in Romans 6:1–2: "What shall we say, then? Shall we go on sinning so that grace may increase? By no means! We died to sin; how can we live in it any longer?"

One danger of the great gift of God's grace is that, since he saved us while we were in our sin, sinning further should have no effect on us. There is truth in this statement. As Paul puts it in 5:10: "For if, when we were God's enemies, we were reconciled to him through the death of his Son, how much more, having been reconciled, shall we be saved through his life!" Note, however, that this passage addresses the peace and joy that believers have, not only in the grace of God to save, but also in the grace that sustains every believer every day. Romans 6, by contrast, addresses a different issue, one raised in Paul's mind on the basis of possible misunderstandings of Romans 5. Being saved by grace and being daily kept in God's family by grace do not mean that sinning is of no consequence. In fact the opposite is true. Being saved by grace means we have died to sin and entered a new life (6:4) where sinning should be repulsive to us. This is why the New Testament does not shy away from giving us a healthy dose of commandments and moral directives.

There are many things that Christians should and should not do. Our *behavior*, not just the "belief system" we may adhere to, is, if not the most important, then at least the most visible means by which we distinguish ourselves from those who have not been raised with Christ and united with him (Rom. 6:5). We should never forget that what is required of us, *precisely because we are saved by grace*, is a high moral standard of thought and action that for many outside the kingdom of God is incomprehensible. We are neither saved by these actions nor do we "remain saved" by them. Rather, obedience to God reflects the fact that our citizenship is in heaven, that he is training us to transcend the present world even though we still occupy its space. It is what is expected of us, for God is forming us into creatures that this world cannot fully grasp.

But being separate from the world is never merely so for its own sake. It is never meant to be a display of otherness for no purpose. Rather, as we see in Exodus 19 and 1 Peter 2, we are to be wholly separate from the world precisely in order to better serve the world. We have been given the wonderful task of going back and invading the world from which we are taken in an effort to bring the good news of the resurrected life to those still dead in sin. To paraphrase Paul's language, we died *to* sin in order to be effective witnesses to those still dead *in* sin.

Christian morality must always maintain this perspective. If not, it can turn into dead legalism. In my experience, this is a much greater danger for Christians than the opposite extreme (that our actions don't matter). Our otherness as Christians certainly makes an absolute distinction between us and the world, but only as it defines our nature. We are different types of beings: one raised in union with the living Christ, the other not. But that absolute distinction does not extend to the *ministry* that God has called us all to. That ministry is, as Christ puts it in Matthew 5:13—16, one of being salt and light in the world:

> You are the salt of the earth. But if the salt loses its saltiness, how can it be made salty again? It is no longer good for anything, except to be thrown out and trampled by men.
>
> You are the light of the world. A city on a hill cannot be hidden. Neither do people light a lamp and put it under a bowl. Instead they put it on its stand, and it gives light to everyone in the house. In the same way, let your light shine before men, that they may see your good deeds and praise your Father in heaven.

God's intent in raising Christ from the dead is not merely to get us into heaven, but to use us to raise others up from death. God has masterminded an "alien invasion" of the world. We who are in Christ are "from above." Our citizenship is in heaven, since we have been raised with Christ. We are, therefore, ideally suited to set examples to the world of how life is to be lived.

We set such examples in a variety of ways. But it is certainly much more than "I don't smoke, I don't chew, I don't go with girls who do." The example we set is not by lauding our morality over others but by humbly being light and salt to world—that is, by demonstrating in no uncertain terms, by our words and our actions, that we are of a different pedigree, a holy race. It is, in a manner of speaking, the clearest proof of the existence of God—not a logical and scintillating exegetical argument, not forceful rhetoric, but pure, humble, godly lives lived in the shadow of the cross and in the brilliant glow of the resurrection. By living such lives we show the world that the gospel works. It is not just words or a great idea, it changes us from the inside out and makes us into creatures whose behavior is inexplicable.

As I write this, I recently attended a funeral in suburban Philadelphia for two young students from Westminster Seminary who were killed by a drunk driver. Don and Buddy were twenty-six years old, loved by hundreds (as the overflow crowd attested to), whose lives and families radiated the love of Christ in a way that is far too rare in our world. I have been to Christian funerals and to non-Christian funerals. There is no comparison between the two. The one is darkened by false hopes and hollow words, the other by the sobering reality that although something is terribly wrong in this world—death reminds us of this—God in Christ has defeated death, and we trust in his covenant promise to raise the dead on the final day.

If the gospel works at all, it must work here, when we stand as it were on the edge of the universe, looking out into complete darkness and hopelessness. If the gospel means anything, it must show it here—or nowhere at all. What I saw at the funeral, as I have seen before, is that the gospel does indeed work. What was almost stunning, however, was in how this was shown.

The young widows each stood in turn and addressed the church. They expressed their thankfulness to God, despite heavy hearts, for being faithful and not letting go of them. They spoke of their resolve that this tragic event was also, somehow, in God's control and that he would remain their loving heavenly Father. They were not naive. They were as sober as any two people I have ever heard. They were not acting or putting on a false front. In fact, it is precisely in the midst of such sadness that you find out what people are really made of. Christ was not a crutch these two women leaned on to make everything all right. Rather, their union with Christ defined who they were at their very core, in any and every circumstance. And then, one by one, friends and family came to the open microphone and expressed both their sadness and their simple trust in God their Father.

This is an example of living godly lives. The young widows did not "hold up" well at the funeral. Rather, God held them up. In doing so they did not merely demonstrate for its own sake how different they were. Rather, this demonstration was "slam dunk" in the world's face. By their behavior, they bore witness to the fact that God exists, that he must be wonderful indeed, that Christ marched through death's door, that he pronounced victory, and that he has passed this on to those who are his own.

Those of us in the church that day felt the weight of the gospel. The local media took notice too. The major networks were all there. The wives were interviewed two days earlier. As one correspondent put it at the close of her segment, "These are very special women." Yes, they are. True, they did not at that point understand why, though that process had begun. The wives, by their behavior, played a role of being a light to the nations.

This is admittedly an extreme example, but this is precisely why I have used it. We are called to be God's holy people in any and every circumstance, both the big and the not-so-big. We are to behave correctly even in the day-to-day things that may not seem so important. Our mission to the world remains the same despite the circumstances. We befriend unpopular and outcast people. We come quickly and unselfishly to the help of people around us. We do not let ourselves become obsessed with the types of things others around us are obsessed with: success, money, power—in all their many forms. We are unafraid to be unrecognized or even humiliated when, by the world's standards, we ought to assert ourselves more. Others take credit for your work, for example, but you keep quiet.

In acting this way, you are being holy and separate, and sooner or later someone, somewhere, in one way or another, will notice and perhaps admire you for it. They will then be forced to look in the face of God who has trained you to behave that way. How they respond to such behavior is not for you to determine. That is God's doing. But you, as God's servant, have done faithfully what is expected of you.

"We know what it is to fear the Lord" (2 Cor. 5:11). In Exodus 19 we read of the people's fear in approaching God. The author of Hebrews, as we have seen, draws explicitly on this passage and concludes that the opposite is now true in light of the coming of Christ. I would like to discuss briefly this contrast.

As 2 Corinthians 5:11 shows, this contrast is not between the New Testament and the Old, but within the New Testament itself (see, e.g., 1 Peter 2:17). Both elements are true, and we should not elevate one over the other: We are to fear God and not fear him. How does this work? This is difficult to answer, and I cannot give "three easy steps to fearing God properly." But both extremes are being played out in the lives of people I have known.

We all know people who seem to live with a constant threat of God's retribution over them. It may be rarely articulated, but a dark cloud seems to follow them wherever they go. I myself see this cloud looming over the horizon of my life every now and then, and it is a battle to beat it back. There is in all of us, either deep down or at the surface, a tendency to think that we have to "do enough" to keep in God's favor, a thought so contrary to the basic thrust of the gospel that one wonders why we cannot simply put it to rest once and for all. "I didn't have my devotions today" or "I had them but not long enough." "I haven't witnessed to enough people this week." "I missed church for no good reason."

Let me stress again that I am *not* suggesting that behavior is irrelevant! The comments on the previous pages say the opposite. But fear of our right standing with God *has been dealt with* on the cross and in the empty tomb. In this sense, there is no fear on our part. To paraphrase Romans 5:10 cited above, "We didn't do anything to get saved, so there is nothing we can do to keep us saved." The Christian life is not one lived in fear.

Nevertheless, I see another extreme,[18] both in others around me and in myself as well. This is the "God is your pal" approach to the Christian life: confidence without reverence. What prevents me from sounding pious in this regard is the fact that I understand this way of life only too well. Are we sometimes too casual in our approach to reading Scripture on a regular basis? Do we come to church without the awesome sense that we, as a collective people of God, are coming to worship the one who saved us from sin and death? We all do this, so I need not elaborate.

Exodus 19 is a clear reminder that the God we meet with regularly, by virtue of the intercessory work of the risen Christ and into whose presence we have confidence to come, is the Creator of everything. He is fearful, threatening, unsettling, all-powerful, all-knowing. He is, to use the well-known expression of the beaver in C. S. Lewis's classic children's book *The Lion, the Witch and the Wardrobe*, not safe but good. He is both someone to be feared and the one who has traversed the universe to meet us where we are, in the form of a human being, born of a woman, who bore our sin in his own body and who loves us dearly. It is perhaps, in the end, a paradox well worth maintaining: We fear him because he is good; we see his goodness because we fear him.

---

18. In labeling these as two extremes, I am not suggesting that any one person will only exhibit a tendency toward one or the other. The two are mixed in all of us.

Exodus 20:1–21

❧

AND GOD SPOKE all these words:

²"I am the LORD your God, who brought you out of Egypt, out of the land of slavery.

³"You shall have no other gods before me.

⁴"You shall not make for yourself an idol in the form of anything in heaven above or on the earth beneath or in the waters below. ⁵You shall not bow down to them or worship them; for I, the LORD your God, am a jealous God, punishing the children for the sin of the fathers to the third and fourth generation of those who hate me, ⁶but showing love to a thousand generations of those who love me and keep my commandments.

⁷"You shall not misuse the name of the LORD your God, for the LORD will not hold anyone guiltless who misuses his name.

⁸"Remember the Sabbath day by keeping it holy. ⁹Six days you shall labor and do all your work, ¹⁰but the seventh day is a Sabbath to the LORD your God. On it you shall not do any work, neither you, nor your son or daughter, nor your manservant or maidservant, nor your animals, nor the alien within your gates. ¹¹For in six days the LORD made the heavens and the earth, the sea, and all that is in them, but he rested on the seventh day. Therefore the LORD blessed the Sabbath day and made it holy.

¹²"Honor your father and your mother, so that you may live long in the land the LORD your God is giving you.

¹³"You shall not murder.

¹⁴"You shall not commit adultery.

¹⁵"You shall not steal.

¹⁶"You shall not give false testimony against your neighbor.

¹⁷"You shall not covet your neighbor's house. You shall not covet your neighbor's wife, or his manservant or

maidservant, his ox or donkey, or anything that
belongs to your neighbor."

¹⁸When the people saw the thunder and lightning and
heard the trumpet and saw the mountain in smoke, they trembled with fear. They stayed at a distance ¹⁹and said to Moses,
"Speak to us yourself and we will listen. But do not have God
speak to us or we will die."

²⁰Moses said to the people, "Do not be afraid. God has
come to test you, so that the fear of God will be with you to
keep you from sinning."

²¹The people remained at a distance, while Moses
approached the thick darkness where God was.

WITH THE POSSIBLE EXCEPTION of some of the stories in Genesis or Psalm 23, we come to what may
be the most widely known portion of Scripture in
all of the Old Testament, the Ten Command-
ments.[1] These verses have been read, pondered, and memorized more than
almost any others. Even on the popular level in today's supposed post-Chris-
tian culture, the average person on the street has at least some passing
acquaintance with what these laws contain and from where they originated.

The passage to be treated here includes the epilogue to the Ten Commandments (vv. 18–21). Although not part of the Decalogue themselves,
these verses are clearly to be understood as connected with it (note how 20:22
begins: "Then the LORD said to Moses," which implies that a new dialogue has
begun). Hence, we should take verses 18–21 with verses 1–17. Still, the
abruptness of verse 18 raises its own questions, to which we will return below.

The issues surrounding the Ten Commandments are complex, and many
scholars have written on them. Some of these issues are as follows:[2]

---

1. They are also referred to in our day as the Decalogue (lit., "ten words"; Heb. ᶜᵃśeret had-
dᵉbarim). This is actually a more accurate title, since this phrase appears in Ex. 34:28; Deut.
4:13; 10:4.

2. For those interested in these varied topics, I suggest the following works as a point of
departure. W. Harrelson, *The Ten Commandments and Human Rights* (OBT; Philadelphia: Fortress,
1980); E. Nielsen, *The Ten Commandments in New Perspective: A Traditio-Historical Approach* (SBT, Second Series, 7; Naperville, Ill.: Allenson, 1968); J. J. Stamm and M. E. Andrew, *The Ten Commandments in Recent Research* (SBT, Second Series, 2; Naperville, Ill.: Allenson, 1967); B. Z. Segal,
ed., *The Ten Commandments As Reflected in Tradition and Literature Throughout the Ages* (Jerusalem:
Magnes, 1985); W. Johnstone, "'The Ten Commandments': Some Recent Interpretations," *Exp-
Tim* 100 (1989): 453–59; R. F. Collins, "Ten Commandments," *ABD*, 6:383–87.

- What is the relationship between the Ten Commandments as they are given in Exodus 20:2–17 and in Deuteronomy 5:6–21, particularly in view of the fact that the two lists do not agree in every detail?
- What is the relationship between the Decalogue and other similar lists of laws in the Old Testament (e.g., Ex. 34:4–26)?
- To what extent are ancient Near Eastern legal codes relevant, especially the supposedly close parallels with the Hittite treaty formula, for understanding the origin and development of the Ten Commandments?
- Are these laws uniquely Israelite?
- What is their "original form" (were they originally shorter, especially the fourth commandment, with additions added over time)?
- To what extent, if any, are these laws Mosaic?
- How should the commandments be numbered, and why are there ten?

We will not treat these issues here systematically, but only as they become relevant when we look at each commandment individually.

We must keep in mind at the outset that the Decalogue is no mere list of laws given in the abstract. It is given by God to a people he has just redeemed. They reflect the manner in which his people are to be "holy" (cf. ch. 19). It is, therefore, safe to say that these laws are more than simply good rules to live by. They show us something of the nature of God, and for this they deserve our close attention. We see in them not simply "what we must do" but what God is like.

Following Fretheim and others, we can take this thought a step further. The giving of these commands is not simply the introduction of rules that help us hold society together—to make us good citizens, as it were. Rather, it "integrates cosmic order and social order ... [the] means by which the divine ordering of chaos at the cosmic level is actualized in the social sphere, whereby God's will is done on earth as it is in heaven."[3] The giving of the law, in other words, is an act of re-creation. It therefore continues a theme we have encountered throughout the book.

The Setting and Prologue (20:1–2)

VERSE 1 POSES a number of puzzles. When precisely does God speak "all these words"? The problem is that 19:25 has Moses coming back down the mountain to speak with the people. Are we to presume that Moses then goes back up, even though a return trip is not mentioned?[4] Here it may be helpful to bring 20:18 into the discussion. This verse is worded closely to 19:16

---

3. Fretheim, *Exodus*, 204.
4. This may be suggested by 19:24: "Go down and *bring Aaron up with you*."

(thunder, lightning, trumpet, smoke/cloud), which suggests that both refer to the same event; that is, 20:18 resumes the action of 19:16 after the "interlude" of the Ten Commandments. This suggests that the Decalogue was given to Moses sometime *before* his descent in 19:25.

If so, the reason for separating the Ten Commandments from their narrative context would no doubt be to give them greater emphasis, and their resumption of the mountain scene in 20:18 would alert us to this fact. This solution has certain advantages, but in the end may be inadequate, for it makes it difficult to put together the entire complex of events from the end of 19:25 through 20:26 (try it and see!).

Untangling all this is a bit much, which is why this has caused so much scholarly activity. Another solution is simplest of all. Since 19:25 has Moses descending and 20:21 has him ascending, perhaps the intervening material (20:2–17) is spoken by God to Moses and all the people at the foot of the mountain. We must remember that the people are not permitted to ascend the mountain. The people's reaction in verse 19, "speak to us yourself," implies that they have just heard God speaking in verses 2–17; they ask Moses to make sure this doesn't happen again. This is a solution I am willing to live with, for the time being at least, although this, too, may prove difficult to maintain at every point throughout Exodus. As we will see, Moses' ascents and descents of Mount Sinai are a challenge to keep straight.

Verse 2 is not a commandment itself, but is a prologue that properly sets up the frame of mind from which all the commandments, indeed all of Israel's existence, should be viewed. It reminds Israel *who God is and what he has done.* It begins with another "I am Yahweh" assertion (see 6:6; 7:5; also, later, 29:46).[5] This God has brought the Israelites out of Egypt. The relationship between them has already been established. Now they are to learn what a redeemed life should look like. The law, in other words, is connected to grace. It is based on God's gracious act of saving his people; it is not a condition of becoming God's people, for that has already happened in the Exodus. They now receive rules for holy living, so they can become more and more God's holy people. This is what God wants for them (see comments on 19:5–6).

In light of this, we can appreciate how inadequate it is to refer to Moses as the "lawgiver" of Israel, as is commonly done. This is not wrong, but it tells only part of the story. Moses does not actually *give* the law, he relays it. The Lawgiver is God himself—giving the people a piece of himself, a glimpse into

---

5. The Hebrew is *'anoki YHWH*. It is also possible to translate the first three words of v. 2 as "I, Yahweh, am your God."

the divine mind and will. "Morality is the expression of the divine will."[6] It is a major, concrete step in Israel's journey toward getting to know their God better and better.

The Ten Commandments (20:3–17)

WE COME, THEN, to the Ten Commandments themselves. To be honest, so much thoughtful work has been done on them over the centuries that I hesitate adding my own comments to this "great cloud of witnesses." I will take the commandments one at a time without feeling an obligation to treat them fully. For more information, please consult the works cited in the footnotes. I will focus on some elements that I have found particularly relevant for forming a picture of how they may have been understood by the ancient Israelites.

(1) *First commandment (v. 3)*. This command follows naturally the prologue (v. 2). Because Yahweh is the Savior of Israel, Israel is to have no other gods. It is not so much the case that Israel "owes" it to God. It is more a matter of Yahweh's demonstrating his incomparable might and love, his faithfulness to the promises he made to his people beginning with Abraham. This is not payback for God's deliverance; rather, God is worthy.

This command also sets Israel apart from the surrounding nations in a manner that would be immediately striking to them. In distinction to every other people of the ancient world, they are to worship one and only God, Yahweh. In this way, Israel's uniqueness, her absolute "holiness" and separateness vis-à-vis the surrounding nations, is broadcast loud and clear. The appeal to have one God, of course, is to Israel alone. It is they who are to be different. Eventually this allegiance to the one true God will become the confession of the other nations. But for that to happen, the elect of God must first learn the lesson: There is no other god but Yahweh.

The phrasing of this commandment helps us see how the ancient Israelites may have understood it. It is striking to me that verse 3 does not say, "There *are* no other gods before me, therefore do not worship them." It simply says, "You shall *have* no other gods before me." Some have suggested that the first commandment is not an explicitly monotheistic statement but a command to be monolatrous. (Monotheism is the belief that there *is* only one God; monolatry implies the existence of more than one god, but we must worship only one.)

As foreign and "idolatrous" as this may seem to our ears, there is something to be said for interpreting verse 3 in the latter way. From a grammatical

---

6. Sarna, *Exploring Exodus*, 142.

point of view, this seems to be what the text is saying. The Hebrew idiom *hayah l^e* suggests language similar to forming a covenant or entering marriage.[7] In other words, "Your allegiance, Israel, is to one God." Of course, one can argue that the nonexistence of other gods is *assumed*. But is it? Besides the fact that the ancient world was replete with religious systems that supported a vast array of gods and goddesses, we must remember that Israel had just spent several hundred years in Egypt, living among a polytheistic people.

I am certainly not suggesting that verse 3 *teaches* the existence of a multiplicity of gods, nor am I suggesting that Israel is correct in assuming such a state of affairs. Rather, here, in Israel's infancy, God is teaching them about himself in a way that speaks to them most directly. He is not yet declaring with blazing clarity that he and he alone is the only God in the universe. For such a declaration we will have to wait for another stage in Israel's journey (e.g., Isa. 40:18—20; 44:9—22). For now, God speaks in a manner that his infant people can readily identify with. He is not giving them the entire story at once, and he is certainly not launching a religious discourse on the merits of monotheism.

We should remember, too, what God did in Egypt. As we have seen, the plagues and the crossing of the sea were concrete demonstrations to the Israelites that their God *defeated* the gods of Egypt, declaring them impotent against his might. The conclusion is never drawn, however, that these gods do not exist. He simply says to Israel, "Look at what I did to the gods of Egypt. I beat them at their own game, on their own turf. I and I alone am worthy of worship." This first commandment gets to the heart of what it means to be God's people, not only in terms of what the Israelites have left, but also in terms of where they are going—to another polytheistic land, Canaan. When they get there, they are to remember what their God does to those, both divine and human, who oppose him.[8]

This first commandment is a fitting way to begin. It is the basis from which the other nine derive their meaning. If the prologue provides the motivation for obeying the commandments, the first commandment provides the conceptual framework from which the others are to be understood. Yahweh alone is God, and he is speaking to the people who belong to him.

(2) *Second commandment (vv. 4—6).* This commandment goes into greater detail than the first, and it seems to follow it logically. But its meaning is not entirely clear. The basic prohibition is against making an idol in the form of

---

7. Sarna, *Exodus*, 109.

8. Although the matter can certainly be debated, I see Ps. 29:1 and 95:3 as being well in line with the train of thought I am developing here. The latter says, "For the LORD is *the great God*, the great King *above all gods*" (italics added). Such an elevation of Yahweh seems to assume a true comparison is worth making.

any created thing. But does "idol" refer to an idol of one of the gods spoken of in verse 3, or does it include any sort of representation of Yahweh himself? The commandment certainly entails at least the former. Idols that the Israelites had seen were idols of other gods, a ubiquitous ancient custom. The second commandment, therefore, is to be understood within the framework of the first.[9] It expands the first, which is why the first two commandments have sometimes been thought of as one.[10] The Israelites are not to worship other gods; therefore, they are not to make any idol of any kind. They are not to represent these other gods by any earthly, created form.

But are we to conclude that this prohibition allows the Israelites to make idols of Yahweh? Absolutely not! Part of this command is also to prevent Israel from identifying the true God with any created thing. To identify God with any created thing is merely one step from thinking of God in terms of that image. It would be creating God in the image of his creation, which would put Israel's God on par with the gods of the nations.[11] Thus, I suggest that this command has a twofold thrust: Israel is not to do as other peoples do by worshiping the idols of *their gods*, nor are they to do as other nations do by worshiping their *own God* that way.

This command is longer than the first, for it includes a threat to those who disobey and a promise to those who obey. God is jealous for his people to remain truly faithful to him. When that jealousy is roused through disobedience, it leads to punishment; but when roused through obedience, the result is blessing. This jealous God will "visit" (*paqad*) the sin of the fathers upon future generations. The verb *paqad* has heretofore been used to describe God's visitation of Israel as an act of punishment toward Egypt (3:16; 4:31; 13:19). Now, in a striking reversal, God will "visit" Israel if they disobey this command. A lot is at stake in Israel's fidelity in not making idols.

As for the punishment, the fact that children might suffer for their parents' actions (which is what v. 5 implies; see also 34:7) is contrary to explicit

---

9. Childs, *Book of Exodus*, 405.

10. See Harrelson, *The Ten Commandments*, 47. Combining the first two commandments necessitates making two commands of the commandment on coveting in order to yield a total of ten. Harrelson cites Augustine and the Lutheran tradition as examples of this. Judaism has likewise combined the first two commandments but derives the number ten by making the preamble ("I am the LORD your God") the first commandment.

11. Although I am not fully convinced, this may be what is happening in the golden calf episode (ch. 32). The Israelites sin in fashioning an image of *Yahweh* and declaring that this *created* thing is the god who brought them out of Egypt. This is also the meaning behind 1 Kings 12:28–29, which is clearly dependent on Ex. 32 to the extent that the words of 32:4 are almost exactly reproduced in 1 Kings 12:28. Jeroboam makes idols in an effort to secure his political power. His intent is for these idols to be understood as representing Yahweh and not some new god, since this would hardly have achieved his political ends.

statements made elsewhere in the Old Testament (e.g., Deut. 24:16; Ezek. 18:4). The former reads, "Fathers shall not be put to death for their children, nor children put to death for their fathers; each is to die for his own sin." Sarna suggests, with typical honesty, that "the intensification of the problem of evil led to revision of this view,"[12] an approach even made explicit in the Talmud. In other words, the ideal of 20:5 could not be carried through because Israel became too sinful. No one would be left.

As unsatisfying as this solution seems to me, I am hard pressed to think of a better one. I do not want to argue that God doesn't really mean what he says here. In fact, the threat of punishment may be more severe than a surface reading of verse 5 lets on. "Third and fourth generation" need not be taken literally. For example, the refrain in Amos 1–2 ("for *three* sins . . . even for *four*") is not to be understood as literally only "three or four" sins. It means simply for all their *many* sins. Moreover, the blessing of Exodus 20:6 going to "thousands of generations" likewise means more than just literally thousands, but a lot, perhaps even never-ending.[13]

In view of this, it seems that the second commandment is teaching that *both* obedience *and* disobedience have far-reaching implications for Israel's life as God's covenant people. If they disobey, the effects will be felt for a long, long time.[14]

But this still does not answer the question concerning the contradiction between this command and Deuteronomy 24:16 and Ezekiel 18:4. How can this be reconciled? Or can it? As I mentioned above, Sarna's explanation is not out of the question. I would suggest (and only suggest) an alternative, however. Both Deuteronomy 24:16 and Ezekiel 18:4 refer specifically to acts of the individual, crimes apparently punishable by death. Also, the reciprocity in these passages goes both ways: The father will not die because of the children, and the children will not die for the father. The intent of Exodus 20:5–6 seems less intensive. It communicates the fact that the degree to which Israel obeys the commandments—in this case, the second commandment—will affect the long-term vibrancy and health of the community. In other words, I take this to be a statement of corporate responsibility, that

---

12. Sarna, *Exodus*, 110.

13. Durham says it refers to "an innumerable descendency" (*Exodus*, 287). Durham, however, takes this as a contrast to the punishment of v. 5, which is of limited duration, thus taking "third and fourth generation" literally.

14. The notes to the *NIV Study Bible* suggest that "third and fourth generation" refers to a particular household, i.e., an extended family living under one roof. If I read the note correctly, this offers another solution, but it is too speculative to be of definitive help (do we know that three to four generations lived under one roof?). Moreover, since the blessing of v. 6 extends over time, it is best to understand the punishment in v. 5 in the same way.

the disobedience of one or a few (see Josh. 7) affects the whole, not of literal blood descendants paying for their father's sins.

(3) *Third commandment (v. 7).* What's in a name? Plenty. The name of God, the tetragrammaton YHWH, is *God's* name. It is the name whose significance was patiently explained to Moses in chapters 3–4. It is the name whose very mention connected the Exodus community to the patriarchs. It is God's salvation name (3:15; 6:6; 15:3), and as such must be treated with highest respect. Even today, many Jews make no attempt to use or even pronounce the name, referring to God simply as *Hashem* (Heb. for "the name"). And since it is God's name, it is an indication of the intimacy between God and his people. Other nations may refer to him as God or the God of Israel, but not as Yahweh.[15] This is the name by which Israel, the saved people of God, his treasured possession, his holy people, know him. This is why his name is to be treated with utmost respect.

But what specifically is prohibited in the third commandment? Opinions vary. It may mean to use the name flippantly, pointlessly—the Hebrew root *šaw*, translated "misuse" in the NIV. This root is used again in 23:1, where it seems to mean "false" (as in a false report spread about someone). If we may transport that meaning to here (which is by no means automatically legitimate), it may suggest that the third commandment prohibits saying something false about God, something untrue that compromises his honor.

Others suggest that this commandment refers not to saying something false about God, but using the name in a harmful way towards others, that is, using God's name to curse others.[16] In the end, this is a command that contains a fair amount of ambiguity. Durham's comments come as close as any to stating the general principle behind the commandment.

> The third commandment is directed not toward Yahweh's protection, but toward Israel's. Yahweh's name . . . must be honored, blessed, praised, celebrated, invoked, pronounced, and so shared. To treat Yahweh's name with disrespect is to treat his gift lightly, to undermine his power, to scorn his Presence, and to misrepresent to the family of humankind his very nature as "The One Who Always Is."[17]

The Jewish practice throughout history of not at all pronouncing YHWH is no doubt a safeguard against any possibility of breaking this commandment. Its ambiguity perpetuates zealous adherence.

---

15. Yahweh is the popular vocalization of YHWH, but this does not represent with any confidence the way in which ancient Israelites may have pronounced it (if they pronounced it at all).

16. Harrelson, *The Ten Commandments*, 73; *ABD*, 6:385.

17. Durham, *Exodus*, 288. The capitalized phrase with which Durham ends this quotation is his rendering of "I AM WHO I AM" in Ex. 3:14.

(4) *Fourth commandment (vv.* 8—11*).* This and the fifth commandment are the only two positive commands among the ten. This one is given in three parts: the command itself (v. 8), specification of what it means to keep the commandment (vv. 9—10), and the reason for the commandment (v. 11). The apparent emphasis placed on this commandment, suggested by its length, is in harmony with the foreshadowing of this commandment in 16:26 as well as the reiteration of the importance of the Sabbath in 31:12—17 and 35:1—3 (see comments). Clearly, the issue of the Sabbath is of special concern for the writer.

As for the commandment itself, the Israelites are told to "remember" the Sabbath day. This is not merely a cognitive exercise, any more than remembering your wedding anniversary means simply recalling it. As any forgetful husband can well attest, some concrete demonstration of remembrance is expected. Biblical remembrance requires action. In Exodus, we have seen this already in 2:24 and 6:5, where God remembers Israel in their slavery. There, too, remembering means more than just recalling that the Israelites are slaves. It means delivering them from Egypt. Likewise, by remembering the Sabbath, the Israelites are no doubt required to act in a certain way, a notion supported not only by the alternate phrasing of Deuteronomy 5:12 ("observe"), but by the explicit instructions that follow in Exodus 20:9—10.

The actual phrasing of the commandment is also worth noting. The NIV has, "Remember the Sabbath day *by keeping it holy.*" The Hebrew, however, suggests an alternate translation: "in order to keep it holy" (*l*ᵉ*qaddᵉšo*). I take the *lamed* preposition (*l*ᵉ) to indicate purpose, that is, "in order to."[18] The NIV translation equates "remembering" and "keeping holy," that is, the latter explains the former. I suggest, however, that the explanation for the commandment is addressed in verses 9—10. "Keeping holy" should better be understood as the resulting effect of remembering. "By remembering the Sabbath, Israel, you are treating the day as separate from the other six days. You are treating it as holy."

But how should this remembering and hallowing of the day be done? This is answered in verses 9—10. Work six days, but on the seventh no one in the Israelite community—not even servants, animals, or aliens[19]—is to work. But what is work? This question, unfortunately, the commandment

---

18. This, too, is Durham's understanding, as his translation indicates: "Remember the sabbath day, to set it apart for holiness" (*Exodus*, 276).

19. It is not entirely clear how relevant reference to servants and aliens would be to a desert community. Are we to understand that the Israelites, so soon after their release from Egypt, had servants? The idea is not in and of itself unlikely, but an explanation of Israel's social structures at this stage in their journey would help round out the picture. The reference to "aliens" is not as puzzling. Non-Israelites were included in the Exodus community, as 12:38 suggests.

does not answer. We do not know whether the ancient Israelites understood it completely either.

The history of Judaism has gone to great lengths to specify precisely what requirements are involved here. Jeremiah 17:22, 24 seem to add some specificity (no loads are to be brought through the city gates on the Sabbath), but this can hardly be understood as other than a specific application of this commandment. Likewise, in Exodus 16:26 the rules about gathering manna do not help us in answering the question of what types of things are and are not covered. In 23:10–11 the law of the Sabbath day is applied to the "Sabbath year" (leave the land unplowed in the seventh year), but this does not help us understand the manner in which the Sabbath day should be observed. In 23:12 the Sabbath command is simply repeated with no further elaboration. The question of how the Israelites were to keep the Sabbath has baffled interpreters for centuries and will not be answered here.

Verse 10 hints at a possible humanitarian motive for the Sabbath—to allow servants and others to rest—although the commandment as given in Deuteronomy 5:14–15 makes this motive much more explicit and central. But even if a similar motive is suggested in Exodus 20:10, the explicit motive given in verse 11 is dominant. The pattern of six days of work followed by one day of rest is to be maintained by the Israelites because this is the pattern of creation. Their "work week" is a reflection of the original work week. Whatever else we might glean from this pattern, one thing is striking especially in light of the author's use of the creation theme throughout Exodus: Israel's day-to-day life is a re-creation. God saved Israel to be a new creation community whereby all things would become new.

This is a reconnection with the Garden of Eden as Israel sits poised to enter the land of Canaan, the new garden. As God ordered the universe in Genesis 1, he is now giving Israel order in its existence amid the chaos of the world around them. By resting on the seventh day, Israel is not just following God's command, but actually following God's lead. They are doing what he himself did first. This pattern, therefore, is not a burden but a delight and high honor. By ceasing his own work on the seventh day, God declared it to be different, separate—or, as the commandment puts it, "holy." The Israelites, too, are to "keep it holy" (v. 8) by remembering it.

The first four commandments concern our conduct toward God; the remaining six concern our conduct toward others. But we should not force too sharp a distinction between these two foci, as if the first four are "religious" and the last six "social" or "ethical." The laws concerning conduct toward others are still commands *from God*. They are still his laws, so that breaking any commandment, even one against a fellow Israelite, is an offense toward God. That is, there is no sphere in ancient Israelite life that is "secular."

A twofold division of the law may be suggested by the fact that there were two tablets (cf. 34:1), but such a common view is not problem-free. For one thing, the fourth commandment already contains both "social" and "religious" dimensions, so the hard and fast division is not so clear-cut. Moreover, we are nowhere told what exactly was written on the two tablets. The popular assumption is that the first four commandments were written on the first tablet and the last six on the second, but this is nowhere stated or even implied in the Old Testament. Some have suggested that all ten were on each of the two (i.e., Moses received two copies). This suggestion is based on an analogy with Hittite legal treaties, where two copies of a treaty were made, one for each party. Douma considers this option too speculative, particularly since *both* tablets were deposited in the ark (Deut. 10:1–5).[20] It seems best to leave this matter open.

One thing that is striking about the latter six commandments is their relative brevity, a point that leads to a number of interpretive challenges, especially an ambiguity about precisely how they are to be obeyed. This is not a factor exclusive to these six. We have seen already that the third and fourth commandments are not very explicit either. But the ambiguity of these six commandments is exacerbated precisely because they are so brief.

(5) *Fifth commandment (v. 12)*. Fretheim suggests that the commandment to honor one's parents is the first one of the second table because it is the most basic of human relationships.[21] Even if we assume a four/six division of the commandments (cf. above), this is not entirely convincing. One might think that marriage is "more basic," especially in view of Genesis 2:20–24. Perhaps the parent/child relationship is basic in another way. It is the most potent human analogy for understanding Israel's relationship to God, especially since Israel is God's son (Ex. 4:22–23). In any case, such deliberation is speculative.

Many have suggested over the long history of interpretation that honoring "your father and your mother" necessarily extends to other people of authority in the community. This seems somewhat justifiable in light of the fact that the titles "father" and "mother" were applied to individuals other than parents (e.g., Judg. 5:7; 1 Sam. 24:11; 2 Kings 5:13). But expanding the areas of

---

20. J. Douma, *The Ten Commandments: Manual for the Christian Life* (Phillipsburg, N.J.: Presbyterian & Reformed, 1996), 11.

21. Fretheim, *Exodus*, 231. According to Durham, the position of this commandment relative to the others is due to the fact that "this relationship is the beginning of society, the inevitable point of departure for every human relationship" (*Exodus*, 290). The point is well worth considering, but I remain skeptical of the primacy of the parent/child relationship over the husband/wife relationship. If there is any sense in the order of these commandments, I feel that another way must be found.

application does not help us in understanding the essence of the command itself. Various questions arise: What does "honor" of one's parents mean? Does it mean doing what they say no matter what? What if the parents are wrong? Is there ever a time when children outgrow this commandment?

In light of the ambiguity of this and other commandments, it seems to me that we may be asking too much from them. The Ten Commandments are consistently ambiguous, and I suggest this is not just the case for us but for the ancient Israelites themselves. The purpose of the Ten Commandments is to tell us God's "pattern of conduct." They reveal to the Israelites a bit of who God is, knowledge that must translate into appropriate behavior on their part. In other words, as glimpses into the nature of God and his relationship with his people, the Ten Commandments are not exhaustive pieces of legislation that account for each and every contingency and possibility. They are to be obeyed, but as to *how*, that is a matter of continual reflection by the Israelites as they continue to live and grow in the shadow of God's love and protection. Examples of specific applications of these commandments are found in chapters 21–23.

As Paul notes in Ephesians 6:2, this is "the first commandment with a promise." Honoring one's parents means long life in the land. But this should not be understood in an individual sense. In other words, dishonoring one's parents does not mean that a child (whether young or old) will die before his or her time. Rather, the reference to length of stay in the land is a warning to the Israelites as a whole (cf. Deut. 4:40; 5:32–33), a fact that underscores just how important this command is. By breaking God's commands, the people will jeopardize their possession of the land God has given them. This "promise" is not personal blessing, but a blessing for a people to possess a land under God's rule and thus become a light to the nations.

(6) *Sixth commandment (v. 13).* The next four commandments are briefer than the fifth. They contain no explanation or threat of consequences. In each, the general gist is clear enough, but they defy a definitive, fuller explication.

A prohibition against murder is nothing new. Murder was reprehensible before this command was given, not only in the Pentateuch as far back as the story of Cain and Abel but in the ancient Near Eastern world as well. This is another reminder that the Ten Commandments were not new, but reiterations of what was known on some level before.

The command clearly does not mean that *any* taking of a human life is wrong. Killing is something both God and the Israelites, by God's approval, do throughout the Old Testament. So what is meant here? Only "wrongful" killing of another? If so, what does that mean? What of unintentional killing? Does it pertain only to the killing of human beings, or are animals included in the prohibition? Perhaps only the killing of fellow Israelites is in view. A number of specific situations are addressed in 21:12–36, but they can hardly be thought to be exhaustive. The full implications of this command are made explicit neither here nor in the chapters that follow.

The Hebrew word translated "murder" in the NIV (*raṣaḥ*) is a common one in the Old Testament. It is a restricted term, generally referring to the killing of someone who is not an "enemy" of the people. In other words, it is not used in contexts of war or just punishment for a crime.[22] It can, however, refer to unintentional killing (e.g., Deut. 4:41–43), a circumstance in which "murder" is not an appropriate term. Thus, perhaps, murder is not as straightforward a translation as might be assumed. If the circularity is not too frustrating, at the very least we can state that there is legitimate and illegitimate killing in the Old Testament and that this commandment refers to any type of killing that God disallows. Just what that means is, again, a matter of wise reflection on the part of the Israelite leaders.

Life is something that the God of Israel does not treat lightly, and it is thus incumbent on his people to behave likewise. W. Harrelson puts the entire matter in a helpful perspective:

> In short, the sixth commandment stakes out the claim of God over all life and serves notice to all human beings—but especially those who claim the biblical heritage as binding upon them—that God's claim upon life is to be given priority in the decisions taken by a community of its individual members.[23]

To what extent we can extrapolate from this commandment the full manner in which the Israelites are obliged to obey remains a matter of ongoing debate.

(7) *Seventh commandment (v. 14)*. Whereas the fifth commandment treats one vital human relationship, this commandment treats another, that between husband and wife. Yet even this is not as straightforward as it might seem at first blush. How did the ancient Israelites understand adultery? It seems that this sin is committed when and only when a *married* or *betrothed woman* is involved.[24] A married or unmarried man who had sexual relations with an unmarried woman had not committed adultery, although this is not to say that there were no consequences of such actions (see Gen. 38; Judg. 16). In such cases, the man would normally be expected to marry the woman (see Ex. 22:16–17). If he already had a wife, he would acquire a second one, since polygamy is not prohibited in the Old Testament.

---

22. The only exception to this is Num. 35:30, where it refers to punishment for a guilty party. It is never used in contexts of battle. See Stamm and Andrew, *The Ten Commandments*, 99.

23. Harrelson, *The Ten Commandments*, 121–22 (he discusses the entire matter on pp. 107–22).

24. Ibid., 123; see also Sarna, *Exodus*, 114.

The focus of the command is physical adultery. True, Jesus later will reveal that the full implications of this commandment includes adultery in the mind, but that is not in view here. God wants the physical intimacy of the marriage bond to be maintained. To say that such a nonspiritual understanding of adultery minimizes the command is not justified, as anyone who has been harmed by adultery can attest. Maintaining the physical sanctity of marriage is a central element in the maintenance of social cohesion, which is not a small consideration in light of Israel's impending entrance into the land, but it is also an earthly symbol of the intimacy between God and his people. This is why failing to obey Yahweh is described as adultery in Hosea 1–3.

(8) *Eighth commandment (v. 15).* This commandment is developed somewhat in chapters 21–22. Although the references to stealing are not exhaustive in these chapters, it does give us a framework from which to understand how the Israelites may have heard this command. Stealing includes kidnapping (21:16) in addition to taking animals (22:1, 12) and material things (22:7). Clearly the Israelites have some notion of ownership and rightful property for such a command to make sense. Stealing from one's "neighbor," as with the seventh commandment, is a threat to society. It breeds distrust and strife. Little explanation is given perhaps because little is needed.

(9) *Ninth commandment (v. 16).* Giving "false testimony" (ʿed šeqer) is explained, at least in part, in 23:1–2, 6–8, where the context is clearly legal. It refers not to lying in general but to bearing false testimony in court.[25] Israelite justice depended on witnesses to a much larger extent than in modern times.[26] Without surveillance cameras or DNA tests, establishing guilt or innocence depended on honest witnesses and their integrity. Some of these matters are elaborated in Deuteronomy. For example, a death sentence is so important it requires two or three unanimous witnesses (Deut. 17:6; 19:15). In addition, anyone who accuses another of murder must cast the first stone (17:7). If the accusation is "false," the accuser bears the punishment the accused would have borne had the accusation been accurate. No frivolous lawsuits in ancient Israel!

As with the other commandments, the focus of this one is not solely on "personal morality" for the sake of being good. It is rather on how one's behavior affects the health and well-being of the fledgling Israelite community as a whole. When people in a public setting are in a dispute over land or property and, in the course of seeking a fair and just resolution, the parties involved or witnesses intentionally distort the truth, perhaps for personal gain, social cohesion is threatened. God is preparing his people not just

---

25. Stamm and Andrew, *The Ten Commandments*, 107–11; Harrelson, *The Ten Commandments*, 143. The word šeqer is also used in 5:9, where it is translated "lies."

26. See Douma, *The Ten Commandments*, 313–16.

to be nice to each other. He is training them to be his people in *Canaan*, to be order amid chaos, to be a holy people and a kingdom of priests so that by looking at them, the nations will come to know the true God.

(10) *Tenth commandment (v. 17)*. The last commandment is the only one that seems to be restricted to the heart rather than to actions. Coveting (*ḥamad*) refers to an inward desire that, if fanned, will lead to action.[27] Still, the command is concrete, not abstract. In driving home the importance of this command, the Israelite is taken on a tour of his surroundings. Look around you: your neighbor's wife, his servants, his animals—in fact, anything that belongs to him. Coveting his wife will lead to adultery and the breaking of the seventh commandment. Coveting his servants, animals, or other property will lead to breaking the eighth commandment. In this sense, the tenth commandment may be thought of as a "summary commandment."[28]

It is perhaps worth pointing out that the command concerning one's neighbor's wife is specific. The command is not given in the reverse, since this specific sin is committed only when a married woman is involved (see comments on the seventh commandment). It stands to reason, in the original context of this commandment, that desiring an unmarried woman (i.e., one who does not "belong" to a man) is not coveting. Moreover, the command does not address a woman, married or unmarried, desiring the husband of another woman. This is not to say that the Bible condones such behavior, only that such behavior is not treated in the Ten Commandments. They have not been designed to address the full scope of human actions.

It is again worth pointing out that the precise manner in which this desire is manifest is not made clear. How does one monitor whether one is coveting? What has to "happen" in order for the commandment to be broken? Is there a public dimension that might make the matter more open to general scrutiny? Or is this essentially a private matter? If answers to these and other questions were available, much less would be written on the subject.

What seems to me to be of great help in understanding the original purpose of the Ten Commandments is their function in the community. These are commands given by a saving God to a recently saved people for whom he has a national purpose. In this sense, the traditional twofold division of the commands—the first four directed toward God and the last six toward the community—can be justified, at least in part. As God's people, his special possession, the Israelites must know what he requires of them. Being an Israelite is not a matter of private, personal piety. It has vertical and horizontal

---

27. On the various possible shades of meaning see Durham, *Exodus*, 297.
28. Ibid., 298. I do not think, however, that breaking the tenth commandment necessarily leads to the breaking of *any* of the other nine, as Durham suggests.

dimensions, and obedience to God is required on both fronts. After all, if Israelites cannot behave properly toward their God and cannot treat each other as "special people," as God treats them, how can they ever be a light to the Gentiles? How can they ever be a kingdom of priests in a world that does not know the true God?

The Epilogue (20:18–21)

VERSES 18–21 FORM the conclusion to this section. The chronology of these verses is not clear. Verse 19 seems to indicate that the people are within earshot of the words that God has just spoken, which requires that the words have been spoken not privately to Moses on the top of the mountain (where the people were not permitted to go), but publicly with Moses and the people, who hear the words at the base of the mountain.

The Hebrew word for "lightning" (plural of *lappid*, v. 18) is unusual. Its only other use in the Pentateuch is in Genesis 15:17, where it refers to the "torch" that passed between the animal carcasses that Abraham had cut in half. In both passages *lappid* represents God's physical, though mediated, presence. The use of the word in only these two instances suggests a connection between the two (although this is far from certain). Perhaps the allusion is nothing more than another reminder to the reader that the God of the Exodus is the God of the patriarchs.

The people beg Moses not to have God to speak to them again. It is apparently such a frightful experience that they fear for their lives. As we have seen in 19:16, this is not the reaction one might have expected. Certainly God's enemies should flee from his face, but his own special people!?

Moses' answer to the people confirms that such fear and trembling in God's presence is an improper response: "Do not be afraid" (v. 20). Moses does not say, "Yes, O Israel, quake and tremble. You have met your God and he is to be feared." Yet note the reason Moses gives to allay their fear: "God has come to test you, so that the fear of God will be with you to keep you from sinning."

Two points cry for attention here. (1) It seems that, on the one hand, the Israelites are not to be afraid, but on the other, it is the *fear of God* that will keep them from sinning. So, "Don't be afraid of God so you can fear him."[29] There is clearly some sort of paradox here. (2) What kind of "test" is Moses talking about? The Hebrew verb *nsh*, often translated "to test," should not be understood in the sense of "finding out" how the Israelites will perform or react to something. God is not revealing himself in thunder and lightning to

---

29. The same Hebrew root for fear (*yr'*) is used in vv. 18 and 20.

see how the people will react. It is much more convincing to translate the word here as "experience."[30]

In other words, verse 20 can be paraphrased: "Do not be afraid. God is giving you a taste of himself so that this memory will stick with you to keep you from sinning." The people's fear is to be tempered by the fact that God is giving them this experience for a reason. A debilitating fear will give way to a healthy fear, one that will result in faithfulness on their part. Again, this is not morality for its own sake, but for the sake of God's accomplishing his higher purpose. The Israelites are to fear God and obey him so that the nations will one day do likewise (though this passage does not address these issues directly).

In verse 21, Moses makes another journey up the mountain, this time for a more extended visit, to receive another body of legal material, conventionally referred to as the "Book of the Covenant" (see 24:7). How long he stays on the mountain this time is not clear. The problem is compounded by the fact that 24:1–2 speaks of a subsequent ascent[31] without any reference that Moses has come back down. Despite this confusion, with the giving of the Ten Commandments, the stage is set for the extended series of commands and instructions to be given to Moses for the remainder of the book. With the exception of the actions described in chapters 32–34 and the closing comments about the tabernacle (40:34–38), the rest of Exodus describes Moses' role as mediator of God's instructions to the people.

Bridging Contexts

THE BIBLICAL AFTERLIFE of the Ten Commandments. There are two ways of approaching the relevance of Exodus 20. We can treat the topic of law in general (since the topic is introduced here) as it unfolds in the rest of Scripture, or we can focus specifically on the Ten Commandments. The former would be appropriate, since a proper understanding of the function of law in the Old Testament provides a proper framework from which to make suggestions about application of the Ten Commandments. Nevertheless, I prefer to focus more directly on the Ten Commandments themselves and leave general comments on the nature of law for the discussion of the Book of the Covenant (20:22–23:19). For better or worse, the Ten Commandments have taken on a life of their own, detached

---

30. Durham, *Exodus*, 303; M. Greenberg, "נסה in Exodus 20:20 and the Purpose of the Sinaitic Theophany," *JBL* 79 (1960): 273–76. See Deut. 28:56 and 1 Sam. 17:39 as examples where *nsh* means trying something out or getting used to it.

31. Actually, the ascent does not occur until 24:9–18, but it is announced in 24:1–2.

from the surrounding material and even from the book of Exodus as a whole. My reason for isolating the Ten Commandments here is certainly not to add to this misapprehension, but in part to help correct it.

As implied above, the Ten Commandments should not be understood as isolated moral maxims, instructions for personal piety, commands in order for people to win God's favor. They are given in a historical and redemptive context and should be understood in that context. They are given to people *already* redeemed, not *so that* they might be redeemed. They are also given to the people as a whole, and the actions of individuals have broader repercussions. The focus of many of these commands is to foster social cohesion, which serves not merely to make the Israelites "nice people," but agents of world change, image-bearers of God to be a light to the nations.

The Ten Commandments are repeated, almost verbatim, in Deuteronomy 5:6–21, at another stage in Israel's history. There the laws are given to Israel not on Mount Sinai/Horeb, but toward the close of the forty-year desert period (cf. Deut. 1:3). As we read in 29:1, the law of Deuteronomy is a conscious reaffirmation of what had been given forty years earlier: "These are the terms of the covenant the LORD commanded Moses to make with the Israelites in *Moab, in addition to* the covenant he had made with them at *Horeb*" (italics added). Although these words describe more directly the laws, blessings, and curses of Deuteronomy 11–28, they also apply to the laws as a whole, including the Ten Commandments.

This truth is strongly suggested by the prologue to the Ten Commandments in Deuteronomy 5:1–3:

> Moses summoned all Israel and said: Hear, O Israel, the decrees and laws I declare in your hearing today. Learn them and be sure to follow them. The LORD our God made a covenant *with us* at Horeb. It was not with our fathers that the LORD made this covenant, but *with us, with all of us* who are alive here today. (italics added)

The commands that follow are given "today ... in your hearing ... with all of us who are alive here today." They are consciously connected to what happened on Mount Sinai.

But if Deuteronomy 5:6–21 is a repetition of Exodus 20:1–17, why are the two versions not identical? This is a good question, though it will not occupy us here (I trust it will be treated in the Deuteronomy volume in this series!).[32] Rather, we should note that the Ten Commandments are repeated in Deuteronomy at a crucial time in Israel's history. These words were first

---

32. The sources cited in the Original Meaning section typically spend some time discussing this issue.

given at the beginning of Israel's journey to Canaan, a journey that was to take a few weeks at most. Their entrance, however, was delayed by forty years. At the end of this period Moses repeats the Ten Commandments to those living at that time (all those under twenty years old at the time of the desert rebellion, see Num. 14:29).

In light of this setting, the prologue (Deut. 5:1–3, cited above) is most interesting. It shows that the version of the Ten Commandments given in Deuteronomy is no mere repetition of those given in Exodus. Moses is not saying, "Let me review with you what I told *them* forty years ago, so *you too* can hear what they heard." Moses wants to make the Ten Commandments their own, an immediate possession of those who were *not* adults at Mount Sinai forty years earlier. This is the meaning of 5:3. If we step back, this is an amazing statement. It was with the "fathers" that God made the covenant, that is, the Sinai covenant. The whole point of the forty-year wandering in the desert was to assure that all those of adult age would *not* be alive upon entering the land. Hence, most of those standing before Moses in Deuteronomy 5 are *by definition* not those with whom the Sinai covenant was made.

A similar sentiment is expressed in Deuteronomy 11:2–7. Here Moses recounts the defeat of the Egyptians by God's hand (vv. 2–4) and the punishment of Dathan and Abiram in the desert (vv. 5–6; cf. Num. 16). He concludes in verse 7: "But it was your own eyes that saw all these great things the LORD has done." Again, what can this mean? It is most certainly *not* the people to whom Moses is speaking in Deuteronomy 11, who themselves witnessed the Exodus referred to in verses 2–4. What is going on here?

This is no slip of the pen, nor is the writer a fool. In fact, it seems to be a recurring theme in Deuteronomy that the present Israelite community, those living at the end of the forty-year wandering, are treated as if they were the original community. There is a theologically potent reason for this. Had the desert rebellions not occurred, the Ten Commandments of Exodus 20 would have been given within a relatively short time of the Israelite's triumphant entry into the land. But because of the intervening wandering period, it was necessary not only to recap the commandments for the benefit of the later generation, but to treat that later generation as if they had been present at the foot of Mount Sinai, to "re-create" the original Exodus community when Israel was standing at the brink of the land. Hence, it is with *them* that God made the covenant at Sinai. It is *they* who saw the great things God has done.

The Ten Commandments in Deuteronomy, in other words, are more than a restatement or reiteration; they are a *recontextualizing* of the commands. This new context is a continuation of the redemptive context initiated at the Exodus. The desert period, a parenthesis in God's redemptive plan, is now behind the Israelites. They now revert back to "Plan A," which is a continuation of the sequence Exodus-Law-Conquest of Canaan. This recontextualization of the law shows, as does the original context in Exodus, that the law is no abstract guide to living a good life, but an integral element of God's redemptive plan. The Ten Commandments, in both cases, are set in a narrative and redemptive context.

The Ten Commandments can be found either implicitly or explicitly in other parts of the Old Testament. Still, what is striking is how infrequently the rest of the Old Testament seems to make an overt appeal to the ten words. For example, references to the "law of Moses" or a related term are infrequent. Of the prophets, only Daniel 9:11, 13 and Malachi 4:4 use this phrase. Moreover, there are no references at all to Sinai (although Mal. 4:4 does mention Horeb). There are a few references in the historical books, but this number is also not overwhelming (e.g., 1 Kings 2:3; 8:9; 2 Kings 14:6; 18:6, 12; 21:8; 23:25; Ezra 7:6; Neh. 1:7; 8:1). The Psalms and wisdom literature make at best allusions to the Sinai law (e.g., Ps. 50:16–20), but even these are few and far between. If Sinai is so central to Israel's identity as the people of God, why is so little made of it in subsequent books?

Having said this, however, we do find in the Old Testament a degree of reflection on at least some of the Decalogue. Of particular importance seems to have been the first two commandments and the fourth. The ancient Israelites constantly struggled to remain faithful to God. The fact that the first two reiterate a similar point suggests that this most basic element of Israel's existence—that Yahweh alone is their God—had to be emphasized. Idolatry, whether the worship of other gods or the worship of the true God by means of an idol, was a recurring sin in Israel, denying the very basis of their existence.

The impulse toward idolatry surfaces already in the golden calf episode (Ex. 32). In Numbers 25:1–3, Israel worships Baal of Peor. At the end of Joshua, after the Conquest, Joshua reminds Israel of the need to remain faithful to Yahweh and not to worship other gods (Josh. 24:14–15). But within a generation of their entrance into the land they fall into old habits. The entire cycle of sin, punishment, and redemption in Judges is instigated by forsaking God and serving Baal and Asherah (Judg. 2:10–15). Throughout the monarchy, the kings of Israel and Judah are judged in large part by the degree to which they are faithful in leading Israel in proper worship. The exile of both the northern and southern kingdoms is precipitated by their worshiping false gods (2 Kings 17:7–23; 21:1–15; 23:26). The prophets routinely denounce the kings for their failure to keep the first two commandments.

Although not as widely mentioned, the Sabbath law is also a recurring theme in the Old Testament. We have already seen its importance to Exodus as a whole. We see its importance emphasized again in Leviticus, both as a day of rest for the Israelites (Lev. 23:3, 32) and as applied to "rest" for the land (25:2–7; 26:34). Keeping the Sabbath is also a concern for the Israelites returning from the Exile, as Nehemiah makes clear (e.g., Neh. 10:31; 13:15–22). The prophets make similar pronouncements (see Isa. 56:2, 6; 58:13; Jer. 17:21–27).

References to the other seven commandments are not forgotten in the Old Testament, though they do take a back page. In a sense the effects of disobedience of all ten can be seen throughout the Old Testament (see, e.g., Ps. 15; 50:16–20; 81:9–10).

More important than which commands are specifically mentioned, where, and how often, is the fact that these commands are given to Israel in order to distinguish them from the other nations. Because Israel is God's people, they are to reflect God's nature in their conduct. In this way they will bear witness to the nations that Yahweh is God and no other, which will lead to the nations acknowledging that God exists. It is the redemptive-theological dimension of these commands that must be emphasized. They are given to a redeemed people in order that they may more fully bear the image of God as they live among the nations of the world. They are never intended to make Israel a "nice" nation, nor are they to be imposed on the nations apart from their own prior heartfelt acknowledgment that Yahweh alone is to be worshiped. Israel's task as a holy nation is to be a light to the Gentiles. The Ten Commandments are a means toward that end.

The Ten Commandments are referred to a number of times in the New Testament. This should cause no surprise. Leaving aside the complex relationship between Israel's law and the gospel, a reiteration of the Ten Commandments in the New Testament makes sense. The church is the new Israel, and as such, the gift of the law given to the Israelites is transposed into a new context. Moreover, seeing the law reiterated rather than obviated in the context of God's grace in Christ underscores the proper relationship between law and grace.

If law can be so prominent within the New Testament, it seems difficult to maintain any sort of strict law/grace dichotomy between the Old and New Testaments. Law in the New Testament must be seen in the context of grace, just as it was in the Old Testament. This is why both Jesus (Matt. 5:21–30; 15:1–9; 19:18–19) and Paul (Rom. 13:8–14; Eph. 6:1–4) can call on the new people of God, the church—made up of Jews and Gentiles in fulfillment of God's plan—to keep these commandments. In fact, Jesus even makes some of them more stringent (Matt. 5:21–30). These commands are not given so we can be good citizens, but so that we can reflect even more fully the image of God in which we participate through our union with the risen Christ.

THE TEN COMMANDMENTS TODAY. As we apply the Ten Commandments to our lives as Christians in today's world, it is important that we keep in mind what they are. They are a charter of conduct for a people already redeemed, who already participate in God's redemptive plan by being walking and talking examples of what it means to be created in God's image. They are, in other words, commands of God to be understood in a redemptive context, a context that defines their promulgation in the Old Testament and reiteration in the New.

There is no dearth of popular books and pamphlets on the Ten Commandments and how they can provide guidelines for conduct today.[33] These commandments, after all, seem to be a ready and waiting treasure chest of moral principles. My interest here is not to add to (nor to critique) these specific suggestions of how these laws are to be transposed from their ancient setting to today. I would rather make some observations concerning the principle of *who* should be expected to keep them and *why*.

Fully in keeping with the way in which commands are articulated in both the Old and New Testaments, we must confess that the Ten Commandments are not bare "guidelines" for how we should act, but are means by which we as God's people come to understand God better. They are a reflection of him, and since we in Christ are re-created in his image, we ought to honor and keep these laws. As Vern Poythress argues, "all the commandments reflect the perfect righteousness of Jesus Christ."[34] Rather than "spiritualizing" the Ten Commandments or making them too abstract, such a Christological perspective is the proper starting point from which the *church* is to view them. Yet, in my view, fundamental misunderstandings surrounding the purpose of the Ten Commandments abound in our society, perpetuated by well-intentioned Christians. I would like to mention two related misunderstandings.

---

33. Some examples are: W. Barclay, *The Ten Commandments for Today* (Grand Rapids: Eerdmans, 1973); F. Catherwood, *First Things First: The Ten Commandments in the 20th Century* (Downers Grove, Ill.: InterVarsity Press, 1979); J. Davidman, *Smoke on the Mountain: An Interpretation of the Ten Commandments* (Philadelphia: Westminster, 1953); S. Goldman, *The Ten Commandments* (Chicago: Univ. of Chicago Press, 1956); E. F. Palmer, *Old Law—New Life: The Ten Commandments and New Testament Faith* (Nashville: Abingdon, 1984); E. Schaeffer, *Lifelines: God's Framework for Christian Living* (Westchester, Ill.: Crossway, 1982). J. Douma, *The Ten Commandments: Manual for the Christian Life* (Phillipsburg, N.J.: Presbyterian & Reformed, 1996); Michael G. Moriarty, *The Perfect 10: The Blessings of Following the Ten Commandments* (Grand Rapids: Zondervan, 1999). I do not mean to imply that all these works are of equal value.

34. V. S. Poythress, *The Shadow of Christ in the Law of Moses* (Phillipsburg, N.J.: Presbyterian & Reformed, 1991), 92.

(1) As difficult as it may be to accept, we must remember that the Ten Commandments are not primarily concerned with personal, private morality. To be sure, it is individuals who keep them, but God's purpose of giving them and implementing them should never be reduced to a simple matter of individual righteousness. As we have seen, there is a corporate dimension involved when God's people speak of the Ten Commandments. His law is to be followed not so that individuals can show their worth before God, and certainly not so that they can either earn or secure their salvation, but so that God's people can show the world the kind of God they worship. This God is not always friendly but can be demanding and uncompromising.

Too often, however, we use the Ten Commandments today as a basis by which to judge the "personal morality" of others. This is bad enough when we do this with respect to the church, but it is even worse when we judge those outside of the family of God. The sexual sins of politicians have been a regular theme in the news as I write this, and a number of Christian commentators remark that such activity is against God's law and should therefore be punished. In fact, there is even a degree of surprise in their voices, as if it is "normal" for Americans to be ready, willing, and able to keep the law. This is misguided. I am neither shocked nor offended when any public official— or anyone else, for that matter—who does not claim the name of Christ (or perhaps does so only nominally) breaks one of the Ten Commandments. Frankly, breaking those laws is the least of their worries.

We should never wonder when God's law is broken by people who were never intended to keep it in the first place. Moreover, by chiding these individuals for doing so, are we not sending the wrong gospel message, that being right with God is primarily a matter of proper conduct? Are we not, contrary to the place of the law in both the Old and New Testaments, putting the cart before the horse? We are saying to them that God demands a high moral standard *apart from the work of Christ*, that proper behavior is what makes us right with God. But the opposite is true. Apart from being in Christ *first* we are incapable of good works that please God. Such legalistic, pull-yourself-up-by-your-moral-bootstraps theology is only too natural for human beings; it is our nature to want to do it ourselves. Should we perpetuate such a thing?

Expecting unbelievers to keep God's law, or even to respect it, blurs the sharp divide between those who are God's people and those who are not. Even if they can keep the law in an external, superficial way, this is not to say that they do what really matters, which is to keep the law in a manner *pleasing to God*. To single out the Ten Commandments and set them up as a standard of conduct for unbelievers or American society in general indicates not only a misunderstanding of the purpose of the Ten Commandments, but of the good news itself. Christ died and rose to provide another way. We should do nothing to make that way obscure.

(2) This brings us to another example: the Ten Commandments in public schools. This is another hot-button issue that will quickly make you life-long enemies if you say the wrong things in the wrong company. At the risk of losing a friend or two, let me say that I do not think the Ten Commandments should be displayed in public schools. By this point it should go without saying that I feel strongly that they should be kept (although precisely *how* they should be kept is a matter of constant reflection). The point, however, is that they should be kept by the right *people* and for the right *reasons*. It is not really for me a matter of the "separation of church and state"—a wonderful idea in its original intention, but one that has been distorted in our day—as much as a matter of the separation of those who are in Christ from those who are not.

What do we hope to accomplish by imposing God's law on those who do not know him? To make better citizens? To make better-behaved children? Neither of these goals is wrong. In fact, they are important. They are not, however, the goal of the gospel, which is to change those who are not God's people into those who are. Better people and citizens, these things are by-products (again, important ones) of the spread of the gospel.

If I may put the matter somewhat differently, placing the Ten Commandments in public schools represents a misuse and misunderstanding of the purpose of these laws; it is, therefore, tantamount to promoting a false religion. It is not Judaism, and it certainly is not Christianity. It may be a "Judeo-Christian ethic"—a thoroughly nonbiblical concept—but such an ethic has no life if it is presented as anything other than the gift of God for those already redeemed by grace. God's laws are for his people. Those who do not know him are walking tombs. They do not need whitewashing but complete renovation, from the inside out. They do not need their moral gyroscopes pushed in the right direction, but the Spirit of the risen Christ breathed into them.

Exodus 20:22–23:19

THEN THE LORD said to Moses, "Tell the Israelites this: 'You have seen for yourselves that I have spoken to you from heaven: ²³Do not make any gods to be alongside me; do not make for yourselves gods of silver or gods of gold.

²⁴'''Make an altar of earth for me and sacrifice on it your burnt offerings and fellowship offerings, your sheep and goats and your cattle. Wherever I cause my name to be honored, I will come to you and bless you. ²⁵If you make an altar of stones for me, do not build it with dressed stones, for you will defile it if you use a tool on it. ²⁶And do not go up to my altar on steps, lest your nakedness be exposed on it.'

²¹:¹"These are the laws you are to set before them:

²"If you buy a Hebrew servant, he is to serve you for six years. But in the seventh year, he shall go free, without paying anything. ³If he comes alone, he is to go free alone; but if he has a wife when he comes, she is to go with him. ⁴If his master gives him a wife and she bears him sons or daughters, the woman and her children shall belong to her master, and only the man shall go free.

⁵"But if the servant declares, 'I love my master and my wife and children and do not want to go free,' ⁶then his master must take him before the judges. He shall take him to the door or the doorpost and pierce his ear with an awl. Then he will be his servant for life.

⁷"If a man sells his daughter as a servant, she is not to go free as menservants do. ⁸If she does not please the master who has selected her for himself, he must let her be redeemed. He has no right to sell her to foreigners, because he has broken faith with her. ⁹If he selects her for his son, he must grant her the rights of a daughter. ¹⁰If he marries another woman, he must not deprive the first one of her food, clothing and marital rights. ¹¹If he does not provide her with these three things, she is to go free, without any payment of money.

¹²"Anyone who strikes a man and kills him shall surely be put to death. ¹³However, if he does not do it intentionally, but God lets it happen, he is to flee to a place I will designate.

¹⁴But if a man schemes and kills another man deliberately, take him away from my altar and put him to death.

¹⁵"Anyone who attacks his father or his mother must be put to death.

¹⁶"Anyone who kidnaps another and either sells him or still has him when he is caught must be put to death.

¹⁷"Anyone who curses his father or mother must be put to death.

¹⁸"If men quarrel and one hits the other with a stone or with his fist and he does not die but is confined to bed, ¹⁹the one who struck the blow will not be held responsible if the other gets up and walks around outside with his staff; however, he must pay the injured man for the loss of his time and see that he is completely healed.

²⁰"If a man beats his male or female slave with a rod and the slave dies as a direct result, he must be punished, ²¹but he is not to be punished if the slave gets up after a day or two, since the slave is his property.

²²"If men who are fighting hit a pregnant woman and she gives birth prematurely but there is no serious injury, the offender must be fined whatever the woman's husband demands and the court allows. ²³But if there is serious injury, you are to take life for life, ²⁴eye for eye, tooth for tooth, hand for hand, foot for foot, ²⁵burn for burn, wound for wound, bruise for bruise.

²⁶"If a man hits a manservant or maidservant in the eye and destroys it, he must let the servant go free to compensate for the eye. ²⁷And if he knocks out the tooth of a manservant or maidservant, he must let the servant go free to compensate for the tooth.

²⁸"If a bull gores a man or a woman to death, the bull must be stoned to death, and its meat must not be eaten. But the owner of the bull will not be held responsible. ²⁹If, however, the bull has had the habit of goring and the owner has been warned but has not kept it penned up and it kills a man or woman, the bull must be stoned and the owner also must be put to death. ³⁰However, if payment is demanded of him, he may redeem his life by paying whatever is demanded. ³¹This law also applies if the bull gores a son or daughter. ³²If the bull gores a male or female slave, the owner must pay thirty shekels of silver to the master of the slave, and the bull must be stoned.

³³"If a man uncovers a pit or digs one and fails to cover it
and an ox or a donkey falls into it, ³⁴the owner of the pit must
pay for the loss; he must pay its owner, and the dead animal
will be his.

³⁵"If a man's bull injures the bull of another and it dies, they
are to sell the live one and divide both the money and the
dead animal equally. ³⁶However, if it was known that the bull
had the habit of goring, yet the owner did not keep it penned
up, the owner must pay, animal for animal, and the dead animal will be his.

²²:¹"If a man steals an ox or a sheep and slaughters it or sells
it, he must pay back five head of cattle for the ox and four
sheep for the sheep.

²"If a thief is caught breaking in and is struck so that he
dies, the defender is not guilty of bloodshed; ³but if it happens after sunrise, he is guilty of bloodshed.

"A thief must certainly make restitution, but if he has nothing, he must be sold to pay for his theft.

⁴"If the stolen animal is found alive in his possession—
whether ox or donkey or sheep—he must pay back double.

⁵"If a man grazes his livestock in a field or vineyard and lets
them stray and they graze in another man's field, he must
make restitution from the best of his own field or vineyard.

⁶"If a fire breaks out and spreads into thornbushes so that it
burns shocks of grain or standing grain or the whole field, the
one who started the fire must make restitution.

⁷"If a man gives his neighbor silver or goods for safekeeping
and they are stolen from the neighbor's house, the thief, if he
is caught, must pay back double. ⁸But if the thief is not found,
the owner of the house must appear before the judges to
determine whether he has laid his hands on the other man's
property. ⁹In all cases of illegal possession of an ox, a donkey,
a sheep, a garment, or any other lost property about which
somebody says, 'This is mine,' both parties are to bring their
cases before the judges. The one whom the judges declare
guilty must pay back double to his neighbor.

¹⁰"If a man gives a donkey, an ox, a sheep or any other animal to his neighbor for safekeeping and it dies or is injured or
is taken away while no one is looking, ¹¹the issue between
them will be settled by the taking of an oath before the LORD
that the neighbor did not lay hands on the other person's

property. The owner is to accept this, and no restitution is required. [12]But if the animal was stolen from the neighbor, he must make restitution to the owner. [13]If it was torn to pieces by a wild animal, he shall bring in the remains as evidence and he will not be required to pay for the torn animal.

[14]"If a man borrows an animal from his neighbor and it is injured or dies while the owner is not present, he must make restitution. [15]But if the owner is with the animal, the borrower will not have to pay. If the animal was hired, the money paid for the hire covers the loss.

[16]"If a man seduces a virgin who is not pledged to be married and sleeps with her, he must pay the bride-price, and she shall be his wife. [17]If her father absolutely refuses to give her to him, he must still pay the bride-price for virgins.

[18]"Do not allow a sorceress to live.

[19]"Anyone who has sexual relations with an animal must be put to death.

[20]"Whoever sacrifices to any god other than the LORD must be destroyed.

[21]"Do not mistreat an alien or oppress him, for you were aliens in Egypt.

[22]"Do not take advantage of a widow or an orphan. [23]If you do and they cry out to me, I will certainly hear their cry. [24]My anger will be aroused, and I will kill you with the sword; your wives will become widows and your children fatherless.

[25]"If you lend money to one of my people among you who is needy, do not be like a moneylender; charge him no interest. [26]If you take your neighbor's cloak as a pledge, return it to him by sunset, [27]because his cloak is the only covering he has for his body. What else will he sleep in? When he cries out to me, I will hear, for I am compassionate.

[28]"Do not blaspheme God or curse the ruler of your people.

[29]"Do not hold back offerings from your granaries or your vats.

"You must give me the firstborn of your sons. [30]Do the same with your cattle and your sheep. Let them stay with their mothers for seven days, but give them to me on the eighth day.

[31]"You are to be my holy people. So do not eat the meat of an animal torn by wild beasts; throw it to the dogs.

[23:1]"Do not spread false reports. Do not help a wicked man by being a malicious witness.

²"Do not follow the crowd in doing wrong. When you give testimony in a lawsuit, do not pervert justice by siding with the crowd, ³and do not show favoritism to a poor man in his lawsuit.

⁴"If you come across your enemy's ox or donkey wandering off, be sure to take it back to him. ⁵If you see the donkey of someone who hates you fallen down under its load, do not leave it there; be sure you help him with it.

⁶"Do not deny justice to your poor people in their lawsuits. ⁷Have nothing to do with a false charge and do not put an innocent or honest person to death, for I will not acquit the guilty.

⁸"Do not accept a bribe, for a bribe blinds those who see and twists the words of the righteous.

⁹"Do not oppress an alien; you yourselves know how it feels to be aliens, because you were aliens in Egypt.

¹⁰"For six years you are to sow your fields and harvest the crops, ¹¹but during the seventh year let the land lie unplowed and unused. Then the poor among your people may get food from it, and the wild animals may eat what they leave. Do the same with your vineyard and your olive grove.

¹²"Six days do your work, but on the seventh day do not work, so that your ox and your donkey may rest and the slave born in your household, and the alien as well, may be refreshed.

¹³"Be careful to do everything I have said to you. Do not invoke the names of other gods; do not let them be heard on your lips.

¹⁴"Three times a year you are to celebrate a festival to me.

¹⁵"Celebrate the Feast of Unleavened Bread; for seven days eat bread made without yeast, as I commanded you. Do this at the appointed time in the month of Abib, for in that month you came out of Egypt.

"No one is to appear before me empty-handed.

¹⁶"Celebrate the Feast of Harvest with the firstfruits of the crops you sow in your field.

"Celebrate the Feast of Ingathering at the end of the year, when you gather in your crops from the field.

¹⁷"Three times a year all the men are to appear before the Sovereign LORD.

¹⁸"Do not offer the blood of a sacrifice to me along with anything containing yeast.

"The fat of my festival offerings must not be kept until morning.

¹⁹"Bring the best of the firstfruits of your soil to the house
of the LORD your God.

"Do not cook a young goat in its mother's milk.

WE COME NOW to a complex body of laws known
as the Book of the Covenant. It covers a wide
variety of legal issues, including worship, protection of property, and personal injury. Although
many of these laws seem to pertain to mundane social matters, we would mis-
represent these laws if we saw them as anything less than closely connected
to Israel's redemption from Egypt. Like the Ten Commandments, the Book
of the Covenant has to be seen in its redemptive context, as a gift of God to
a people already redeemed. Whatever "secular" content these laws may have
is our own modern penchant for driving a wedge between the sacred and the
secular, something foreign to Israel's worldview.

Having said this, however, it is also clear that many of these laws are of
a specifically social character; that is, they govern Israel's daily dealings with
other Israelites. This yields at least two observations. (1) Many of the laws
are specific, envisioning concrete situations (e.g., 21:22–25). In fact, their very
specificity may give us a clue as to the nature of the whole. Since not all
variables can be recorded in this (or any other) body of law, presumably the
Book of the Covenant is not designed to cover every possible situation the
Israelites are likely to encounter. The Book of the Covenant, in other words,
seems to be a compendium of laws that are representative of the entire corpus.[1] There are, it is fair to say, principles that underlie these laws, and the
specific instances cited are intended to highlight these principles.[2]

---

1. On this, see M. Fishbane, *Biblical Interpretation in Ancient Israel* (Oxford: Clarendon,
1985), 95; Sarna, *Exodus*, 117.

2. On the significance of "omissions" in the Book of the Covenant, see the discussion
by Sarna (*Exploring Exodus*, 168–71). Sarna also discusses the many affinities between Israelite
law and ancient Near Eastern law (both in terms of actual content and the nature of law
codes in general; ibid., 158–89; see also S. Paul, *Studies in the Book of the Covenant in Light of
Cuneiform and Biblical Law* [VTSup 18; Leiden: Brill, 1970])—an interesting subject but one
that will not occupy our attention here. A succinct list of the major ancient Near Eastern
legal corpora may be found in Cassuto, *Commentary on Exodus*, 258–59. A helpful sampling
of the various critical issues surrounding the Book of the Covenant may be found in B. M.
Levinson, ed., *Theory and Method in Biblical and Cuneiform Law: Revision, Interpolation and Development* (JSOTSup 181; Sheffield: Sheffield Academic, 1994). The fact that Israelite law shares
a number of traits with ancient Near Eastern law in general should be no surprise in view
of the similarities we have seen elsewhere in Exodus (e.g., Moses' birth narrative) and will
see later on in the tabernacle.

(2) These laws seem to fit a setting in which Israel is settled in the land. For example, 22:5 presumes some type of property ownership and the planting of vineyards, something that would not have occurred in the desert. This is not to say, however, that the post-Conquest relevance of these laws necessarily implies a post-Conquest composition. Note that even though forty years of desert wandering intervened between the giving of these laws and the entrance into Canaan, God's intention was to bring the Israelites into the land soon after the instructions were given in Exodus. Although these laws would apply to the Israelites only after they have entered the land, the giving of the Book of the Covenant at this point in their journey anticipates that the entrance to the land will occur within a brief time period.[3]

One may well question limiting the Book of the Covenant to 20:22–23:19. The term as it appears in 24:7 seems to cover not just 20:22–23:19 but the entire discourse from 20:2 to 23:33. Moreover, in 24:1 Moses' next ascent of Sinai begins, thus starting a new section. Nevertheless, I have chosen to designate 20:22–23:19 as the Book of the Covenant, as is conventionally done. This will keep the legal material together for ease in organization, even though it may run the risk of encouraging the reader to divorce the laws from their narrative context, a connection Exodus seems eager to maintain.

One further organizational obstacle that must be addressed here concerns the structure of the Book of the Covenant as a whole. It is tempting to subsume the laws under a number of headings, as is done in the NIV. These headings are indeed helpful in places but hardly adequate in dealing with the complexity of the material, which to a certain extent resists any simple scheme.[4] I have chosen a different set of headings, adapted from those of J. Sprinkle.[5]

A. Worship: Idols and Altars (20:22–26)
B. Social Responsibility (21:1–22:17)
1. Freedom and Servitude for Hebrew Slaves (21:1–11)
2. Humans Injuring Other Humans (21:12–27)
3. Various Injuries Involving Animals (21:28–36)
4. Concerning Matters of Property (22:1–17)

---

3. The Israelites spent eleven months at Sinai (cf. Ex. 19:1 with Num. 10:11). It is uncertain how long the journey from Sinai to Canaan would have taken them had they not been made to wander in the desert, but a journey of a few weeks is well within the realm of possibility.

4. For example, many of the laws in 22:16–31 do not concern "social responsibility."

5. J. Sprinkle, *"The Book of the Covenant": A Literary Approach* (JSOTSup 174; Sheffield: JSOT, 1994). His organization is followed by J. G. Janzen, *Exodus* (Westminster Bible Companion: Louisville: Westminster/John Knox, 1997), 159. Sprinkle's work is particularly interesting in that it draws a number of helpful (but not always convincing) conclusions regarding the structure of the Book of the Covenant as a whole.

C. **Worship and Social Responsibility** (22:18–23:19)
  1. Worship: Sorceresses, Bestiality, and False Sacrifices (22:18–20)
  2. Social Responsibility: Oppression and Loans (22:21–28)
  3. Worship: Offerings, Firstborn, Holiness (22:29–31)
  4. Social Responsibility: Testimony in Court, an Enemy's Animal, Oppression (23:1–9)
  5. Worship: Sabbaths and Festivals (23:10–19)

It is no accident that the Book of the Covenant begins and ends with matters of worship. Nor is it accidental that social and cultic matters are interwoven throughout the text, particularly in part C. The structure of the Book of the Covenant reminds us that secular and sacred intertwine. More precisely, there is no "secular" realm in ancient Israel. God's law to Israel pertains to *all* matters of conduct.

A. Worship: Idols and Altars (20:22–26)

VERSE 22 BEGINS a new speech between God and Moses. The injunction against idols and altars follows upon the theophany of 20:18–19. The people are afraid of God, and it is this sight that serves as motivation in verse 22 not to make false gods or improper altars.

Verse 23 is a reiteration of the first two commandments (20:3–6). It goes without saying that this reiteration indicates their importance for understanding what follows, not only through 20:26 but to the end of the Book of the Covenant. Both the Ten Commandments and the Book of the Covenant begin the same way, with a declaration that Yahweh and Yahweh alone is worthy of Israel's worship and is therefore to be obeyed.

In one sense, the connection between the two injunctions of 20:23–26 is obvious: Both idols and altars concern proper worship. But whereas the worship of God alone has clear justification in the context, the rules concerning altars is not only somewhat unexpected but not at all clear as to its significance. In view of the fact that the bulk of the Book of the Covenant concerns social regulations, perhaps a word or two concerning such matters could have been voiced here or even a condensation of commandments 5–10 (e.g., love your neighbor). Instead, we see a cryptic (for us) command about the proper and improper construction of altars: An altar is to be made of earth or of stone; if the latter, it must be uncut stone rather than dressed stone, and no steps are to be built.

Why are instructions on altars needed here at all? After all, the specifics of sacrifice play a minor role at best throughout Exodus in general and the Book of the Covenant specifically. Still, talk of sacrifice is not wholly unexpected.

For one thing, these laws and the book of Exodus as a whole are meant to prepare Israel for entering the land and living there in accordance with God's purpose. The sacrificial system will play a major role from here on out in Israel's life. Note also that the Book of the Covenant ends with a brief description of the three festivals (23:14–17) and some miscellaneous cultic matters (23:18–19), so such things are not wholly foreign to the subject matter of the Book of the Covenant. Finally, the fact that the sacrifices mentioned are burnt and fellowship offerings is significant, for these are the offerings associated with the worship of God (see Lev. 1 and 3), which is the topic of 20:23.

As for the specific regulations, a fair degree of speculation must accompany any comments. Why only altars of earth or uncut stone? And why no steps? The most reasonable explanation is that these stipulations are anti-Canaanite.[6] By building their altars this way, the Israelites are making a definitive statement that the worship of their God is different from the practices of their neighbors. Moreover, the problem with stepped altars is that those walking up the steps would have their "nakedness ... exposed" (v. 26). This is not simply a matter of prudishness or social embarrassment; it may also be a polemic against Canaanite cultic practices, which sometimes included sexual rituals.[7] Later in Israel's history, stepped altars were used, but God had instructed the priests to wear linen undergarments to avoid indecent exposure (cf. Lev. 6:10; 9:22).

The central point of this section is that the attention the writer pays to worship at the outset of the Book of the Covenant indicates the proper context within which to view the laws that follow. There is, in other words, a triad of (1) *redemption* from Egypt that prepared Israel for meeting God, (2) proper *worship* of God, and (3) *law*. These three elements are not to be dissociated from each other if any one of these elements is to be understood properly.

B. Social Responsibility (21:1–22:17)

1. FREEDOM AND servitude for Hebrew slaves (21:1–11). The remainder of the Book of the Covenant pertains to the various "laws" that Moses is to give the people. The Hebrew word used in 21:1 to describe these laws is the common *mišpaṭim* rather than *dᵉbarim* ("words") used to introduce the Ten Commandments.

Why does this main body of regulations begin with a lengthy discussion of Hebrew slavery? Why not begin with matters of murder (v. 12)?[8] In the

---

6. See Durham, *Exodus*, 320. The matter is discussed in more depth in Sprinkle, *The Book of the Covenant*, 35–49.

7. Sarna, *Exodus*, 117 and note.

8. By contrast, the Mesopotamian Code of Hammurabi, a legal corpus often compared to the Book of the Covenant and dated to the mid-second millennium B.C., treats slaves last.

context of the book, the reason seems obvious: The Israelites were slaves themselves in Egypt. Their first thought should be to take great care not to do what Egypt had done to them (see also 22:21; 23:9). Note especially 23:9: "Do not oppress an alien; you yourselves know how it feels to be aliens, because you were aliens in Egypt." If the Israelites are to take care not to mistreat aliens, they must understand that such proper conduct toward others must begin at home, in their treatment of each other.

Having said this, however, one curious element strikes us immediately. If Israel ought to be so concerned not to abuse others as they had been in Egypt, why not abolish slavery altogether? The regulations given in 21:1–11 assume the existence of slaves and hence condones the practice. This cannot be explained away. We are once again reminded of the foundational shortcoming of liberation theology. The Exodus is not about releasing oppressed slaves so they can be "free." If that were the case, slavery would have been done away with completely. Moreover, it is also a reminder to traditional Christianity that there is more to reading the Old Testament than simply appropriating its surface teaching on any matter. Many American Christians, particularly in the latter half of the nineteenth century, used passages such as this to demonstrate "biblically" their right to hold slaves.

It seems that people, even "free" Israelites, could be owned by other Israelites. But this fact does not occupy the writer's attentions. His focus is on the proper treatment of these slaves, and it is here that Israel's humanitarian[9] thrust may be placed in contrast to the nations around them, particularly Egypt. For one thing, there is no Israelite perpetual slavery. In the seventh year (a clear application of the fourth commandment), a male slave is to go free without any legal obligation. The only stipulation is that he go as he came. If he came with a wife, she leaves with him. If a wife was given to him, she and any children must remain.

The slave, however, does have the right to remain a slave by publicly declaring his allegiance in a ceremony that involves the piercing of his ear with an awl (21:5–6). The precise nature of this ceremony is not known, although it clearly signified submission on the part of the slave and perhaps some type of brand mark (see Deut. 15:17; Ps. 40:6). The "judges" before whom they are to appear may be translated "God" rather than "judges," since the Hebrew word is *ʾelohim* (cf. NIV note). "God" is the preferred translation for some scholars, who envision a ceremony at the door of the sanctuary.[10]

---

9. "Humanitarian" is an inadequate way of putting it. At least in our culture, the term implies expressions of human compassion that may very well be devoid of any overt religious content. This is the opposite of how I am using the term in this context.

10. Durham, *Exodus*, 321.

This is possible in the abstract, but the matter is inconclusive. In my view, the scale tips in favor of the NIV's translation, since *ʾelohim* most likely means "judges" in 22:8–9. On the other hand, I prefer the translation "God" in 22:28 since there blasphemy is the crime. In the final analysis, the details elude us.

Whatever ethical misgivings modern readers may have regarding verses 1–6 are augmented in verses 7–11. Male slaves may go free in the seventh year, but female slaves may not. (This gender distinction does not seem to be carried through in Deut. 15:12.) Why? Moreover, it seems that Hebrew fathers could sell their own daughters into slavery!

Despite this, however, the point of the law is not to question the existence of this social condition, but to give clear guidelines for how people in such a condition must be treated. Although a daughter is sold to a man, this does not give the owner the right to do as he pleases. She is not to be mistreated. If he no longer wants her, she must be "redeemed" and not just discarded or sold to foreigners (a clear indication that the female slave in question is an Israelite woman), which probably means that she may be bought back by her family.

Moreover, if the female slave becomes a wife of the owner's son, she ceases being a slave and becomes the owner's daughter. There is a grammatical ambiguity in verse 10, which begins "if he marries another woman." Who is the "he"? If it refers to the owner, this would imply that the owner has the right to marry the slave. If so, there would be some justification for understanding "servant" in verse 7 (*ʾamah*) as a "slave-wife."[11] The immediate context makes this unlikely, however, for the marriage in view in verse 9 is that of a son. Hence, "if he marries another woman" probably refers to the son's taking another wife. In other words, the Israelite daughter sold into slavery either becomes the owner's servant or the son's wife. In either case, however, she is to be treated in such a way that her basic rights as a human being are protected. If she is not treated well, she may go free without any payment.

What is missing here is a detailed account of how foreign slaves are to be treated. Indeed, it is a question whether aliens were even to be used as slaves, since merely their oppression is mentioned in 22:21 and 23:9, not their enslavement. But these matters do not occupy the writer. His focus is on the proper, godly treatment of those Israelites on the lowest rung of the social ladder. They are fellow countrymen, the people of God, a part of the kingdom of priests and the holy nation (see 19:6).

2. Humans injuring other humans (21:12–27). Like the previous section, this one also deals with proper treatment of fellow Israelites—this time personal injury in general. Since verses 20–21 and 26–27 focus on situations specifically related to slaves, we must assume that the other laws in

---

11. This is the view of Sprinkle (*The Book of the Covenant*, 51) and Durham (*Exodus*, 321–22).

this section hold for all Israelites. Hence, the law against killing does not apply only to free Israelites but to any Israelite who kills any other.

It is helpful to think of these laws as an application of the fifth (esp. vv. 15, 17) and sixth commandments, though we should not apply this formula too rigidly. The kidnapping law in verse 16 probably falls under the eighth commandment (see comments on 20:15). Also, adultery and coveting are not represented at all in the Book of the Covenant. It is, therefore, best not to think of this book as simply an elaboration on the Ten Commandments.

The first point made here is a distinction between an intentional, premeditated killing and unintentional, accidental killing. The former is met with nonnegotiable punishment. If the latter happens, however, such a person will have the opportunity to take refuge in some not yet specified location ("cities of refuge," described in more detail in Num. 35:6–32; Deut. 19:1–13). The end of Exodus 21:13 ("he is to flee to a place I will designate") seems to anticipate these passages. We see then a qualification of the absolute principle, "You shall not murder." If that homicide is accidental, it is apparently forgiven, although this passage does not fill out the details.

One's conduct towards one's parents is also prominent here. Verses 15 and 17 mandate death to anyone who attacks or curses his or her parents. The NIV text note suggests "kills" as an alternate translation to "attacks," and this is likely correct. The root *nkh* regularly (but by no means always) refers to killing, especially in Exodus (e.g., 2:12; 12:12), though this same root does not refer to killing in 21:18–19 (NIV, "hits"). In any event, this law should probably be read in light of the previous law of verses 12–14.

What it means to curse one's parents is ambiguous. Following a number of commentators, it seems best to think of this as some egregious act of disrespect or repudiation, a "serious breach of filial duty," enough to warrant death—for example, neglecting their duty to care for their parents in old age.[12] But as is typical not only in the legal sections but throughout Exodus, the details are left unexpressed. Also, precisely why the kidnapping law of verse 16 was inserted between the two laws concerning parents is not clear.

The laws mentioned in verses 12–17 are grievous enough to result in certain death to the perpetrator. The remaining laws in this section (vv. 18–27) deal with more ambiguous matters. Again, they do not cover any and every circumstance, but merely a sampling. For example, if an altercation occurs, clearly intended to harm but does not result in death, there is no death penalty but some restitution must be made for loss of time and for proper healing to take place. One nagging gap in this law, especially if it is intended

---

12. See Sprinkle, *The Book of the Covenant*, 77–78, who follows H. C. Brichto, *The Problem of "Curse" in the Hebrew Bible* (JBLMS 13; Philadelphia: SBL, 1963), 118–99.

to be strictly followed, is the lack of any specificity regarding the amount and type of restitution. How is this law to be carried out?

The case of killing one's servants is ambiguous as well (vv. 20–21). This law requires that the owner be "punished" if he beats his slave *and* he or she dies. This raises two issues. (1) If the slave survives, there is no punishment. Hence, in this respect the slave is not given restitution as is the free man. Why? Because the slave's "loss" is not his own, since he belongs to the master (v. 21). (2) What precisely is this punishment? If the slave dies, the master is punished. If the slave does not die, he is not punished, which seems to imply that punishment cannot mean the death penalty. If "punishment" meant "death," there would be no need to mention it in the event of the slave's survival, since death would not be meted out in the case of mere injury, even with a free man. But then what *is* that punishment? Again, the details are frustratingly unclear.

Verses 22–25 are among the best known in the Book of the Covenant for two reasons: Many find a biblical argument against abortion in verse 22, and verses 23–25 contain the famous phrase "eye for eye, tooth for tooth."

Verse 22 suffers from some of the same ambiguities as does the rest of the Book of the Covenant and should therefore be used with great caution in any modern debate. (1) What the NIV translates "and she gives birth prematurely" (see text note, "she has a miscarriage") is difficult to find in the Hebrew. The phrase literally is, "and her children come out." It does seem that the "coming out" is the result of striking, but this is in the context of a fight between two men where the woman is an innocent bystander, so its relevance for abortion is questionable.

(2) The phrase "but there is no serious injury" (v. 22) is ambiguous. The Hebrew does not tell us *who* the injured party is, whether the child or the mother. If the mother is in view, which is grammatically possible, then the state of the child, whether miscarried or merely born prematurely, is not important. If, however, the child's injury is in view, the subsequent verses concern proper restitution for the child. If it is not seriously injured, some fine is imposed by the husband and court. If it is seriously injured, the "law of retaliation" goes into effect, which is straightforward, though how "an eye for an eye" could be implemented in such a case is not at all clear.

The whole matter is actually more complicated than I have laid out here. Similar instances in ancient Near Eastern law call for the restitution of some monetary payment in the event the fetus does not survive, but it is not clear to what extent these laws should have bearing on 21:22 (is biblical law mirrored in the ancient Near Eastern law or an advance upon it?). In the final analysis, however, I take the following argument by J. Sprinkle to be the most cogent approach to the proper interpretation of this passage:

I take אסון [ʾswn, what the NIV translates as "injury"] to apply solely to the woman, the plural ילדיה [yldyh, "her children" in my translation above] implying an abstract "child-product, fruit of the womb," or the like, an apt term for a stillborn baby. Most premature births before modern medical science would result in the death of the fetus, and the many parallel cuneiform laws which have influenced biblical formulations all assume the death of the fetus. Hence the death of the child at the premature birth is assumed [i.e., the law of retribution pertains only to the mother].[13]

Although this law is clearly meant to maintain the dignity and worth of human life, it is ambiguous in its details. But as for abortion, however strongly I and many others deplore it, it can only be applied to the modern debate if it can be shown what relevance an unintentional killing of a fetus has for a woman's "choice." Also, even if it were relevant for the debate, a convincing argument would have to be mounted for why the principles behind this law should be adhered to but not many of the others in the Book of the Covenant (e.g., 22:16–17).

The remaining law in this section (vv. 26–27) concerns personal injury to a servant. Only injury to an eye and tooth are mentioned, but these terms clearly are meant to refer back to the fuller expression of the law of retribution in verses 23–25.[14] The point is that if a servant is injured, rather than requiring equal injury of the master, the servant is simply to be let go. Rather than being a picture of the slave's worth, the opposite seems to be the case.[15] The slave's injury is not on the same level as a free man's, otherwise the restitution would be the same. The freedom granted the servant simply means that the master who did the injuring suffers merely financial loss; he can always get another servant. The servant, however, is without an eye or tooth. Moreover, he or she must now find some other manner of support.

3. Various injuries involving animals (21:28–36). We move from injuries inflicted between human beings (slave and free) to injuries involving animals, either inflicted by them or to them. These laws clear up a matter left ambiguous in the preceding laws concerning the value of a slave's life. In

---

13. Sprinkle, *The Book of the Covenant*, 93.

14. Sprinkle takes "eye" and "tooth" as "defining upper and lower limits: for as much as an eye, or for as little as a tooth, if you permanently damage him, you must set him free" (ibid., 96).

15. I do not agree with Durham that this law constitutes "a remarkably humanitarian provision" (*Exodus*, 324). Still, the fact that the law of retribution is enacted at all in the case of servants certainly speaks to a humanitarianism of a sort, especially since similar concerns are not evinced in Babylonian law.

verses 28–32, two types of bulls are referred to, the one that gores a human in an isolated incident and the one who has had a habit of goring. In the first case, the bull is put to death but the owner is not held responsible. In the second case, both the bull and the owner must be put to death. A payment option may be exercised, however (presumably at the wishes of the victim's family), thus "redeeming" the negligent owner's life. If, however, the bull gores a servant, the bull is killed but the owner has only to pay a fine of thirty shekels of silver to the owner of the deceased slave. The clear implication is that the life of a free person is worth more than that of the servant.

Whereas injury by animals as a result of human negligence deserves some recompense, so too injury done to animals by negligent humans (vv. 33–34). We are not told why someone would dig or uncover a pit, nor are we told why such a situation deserves specific attention in the Book of the Covenant. The point simply is that, like the loss of a slave, the loss of an animal means a financial loss for the owner. Hence, some financial compensation is in order.

The final scenario is loss of one animal by another (vv. 35–36). Having begun with human against human, the laws then treat in turn animal against human, human against animal, and now animal against animal. In the case of a one-time goring resulting in death (mere injury does not come into view here), the live animal is to be sold and both parties are to divide up the money and the carcass. But if the bull had a habit of goring (by which I take it to mean, both here and above, one or more previous instances of goring), the owner of the live animal may keep the carcass, but he must pay the entire fine to the other owner.

4. Concerning matters of property (22:1–17). This section extends not simply to verse 15, as is indicated by the NIV headings, but through verse 17. The NIV is somewhat generous in its estimation of the status of certain classes of women in Israelite society. The only reason for separating the case of a virgin from the cases of property in verses 1–15 is the assumption that virgin daughters are more than simply property. This may be the case, but the specific law in verses 16–17 has more in common structurally with what precedes than with what follows. These two verses close the preceding unit with the same Hebrew syntax as verses 1–15 (the formula "if ... then ..."). This ceases abruptly in verse 18 when commands are used.

Although these laws are united by syntactical concerns, their topics are free-floating. In general they all concern matters of protection to property, but a variety of scenarios is described. The basic categories are as follows: theft (vv. 1–4), carelessness leading to property damage (vv. 5–6), the safe-keeping of one person's property by another (vv. 7–15), and seduction of a virgin (vv. 16–17).

Verses 1–4 deal with stealing. Verse 2 concerns the killing of the intruder, which is only permissible at night. The logic behind this law seems to be that if the intruder is identifiable, retributive justice should be left for the proper channels. Perhaps this law is intended to discourage vigilante justice. Moreover, death is not the proper penalty for thievery, at least not according to the law of retribution announced in the previous section. That killing the thief at night is permissible appears to give the victim great liberty to defend his own property, as well as obviating any threat to his own life. This law maintains a victim's rights to self-defense.

The other laws in verses 1–4 deal with matters of restitution. Stealing and then selling livestock results in a fivefold or fourfold restitution. If the stolen animal is found alive, the thief must pay back double (so that he understands the element of risk in his theft if he gets caught). If the thief cannot make restitution, he must be sold into slavery to pay for his debt.

Negligence is also a crime (vv. 5–6). We have seen this in the previous section regarding animals who have a habit of goring. Since damage to property is in view here rather than personal injury, the penalty is material restitution rather than death. Two scenarios are in view. The first is allowing one's livestock to graze in another's field or vineyard. The second is a fire that breaks out, presumably other than arson, in which case the one responsible must make restitution. The type of restitution is something like the law of retribution: Whatever is damaged, whether by grazing or fire,[16] must be paid back in kind.

Trust between fellow Israelites was an important matter, and one can see why certain laws were enacted to help prevent bad blood from developing (vv. 7–9). The basic thrust is that when someone entrusts you with something for safekeeping, you are ultimately responsible. If theft is involved, the thief himself, if caught, must pay back double. But if he is not caught, the one to whom the goods were entrusted becomes a suspect (v. 8). It is then up to the judge to determine his guilt or innocence. Whoever is guilty must pay back double. Verse 9 seems to extend the principle to all cases of wrongful possession, that is, to any case where the property of one is claimed to be in the possession of another. In either case, the point is the same. Regardless of how it got there, if it can be proved that someone is in illegal possession of someone else's property, that person will pay double.[17]

---

16. The Hebrew root for both "graze" and "burn" in vv. 5–6 is *bʿr*, an obvious play on words.

17. It should be noted that here, as well as elsewhere in the Book of the Covenant, it is not clear whether double payment includes the property in question (a net gain of 100% for the victim) or double in addition to the property (a net gain of 200%).

If the safekeeping of livestock is involved, the matter is more complicated (vv. 10–15). With animals there is always the potential of death or injury. In this case, it must first be settled whether the one entrusted was immediately responsible. This is determined by the taking of an oath before the Lord (the details of such a ceremony are nowhere given). If the person is innocent, no restitution is required. If, however, the animal is stolen from him while under his care, he must make restitution. It should be pointed out that if an animal is stolen from the one to whom it is entrusted, it results in a fine, whereas the stealing of silver or goods is cause for an investigation (vv. 7–9). It is not stated why this is the case. Death of the animal at the hands of a wild beast, however, is not a punishable offense, provided evidence can be put forth.

A related matter concerns not the safekeeping of an animal but the borrowing of an animal (vv. 14–15). If the animal dies or is injured while its owner is present as a witness, there is no restitution, since the owner himself has witnessed that the borrower is not culpable. If, however, the owner is not present, restitution must be made.

These scenarios differ from the laws of verses 10–13. If someone is entrusted with someone else's livestock, the initiator of the transaction is the owner of the livestock. That is why the one entrusted with the livestock is given every benefit of the doubt in the case of injury or death (an oath is taken). If, however, the borrower initiates the transaction, it is the lender who is given the benefit of the doubt. This makes sense, since the borrower may have ulterior motives for borrowing (like neighbors we have probably all had, who borrow but never seem to get around to returning the item, only to find months later that it is "lost"). If the animal was not borrowed but hired, money has already changed hands, and this is sufficient compensation to the owner who suffers the loss. It is assumed that the one who hired the animal did not do so to kill or injure it, which would be a complete waste of his money.

Finally, we come to the matter of the virgin (vv. 16–17). A virgin who is not pledged to be married and who is seduced by a man shall become that man's wife (this is not rape, hence some consent on the part of the woman is implied). It is important to understand this law from the point of view of the wronged party: It is not the virgin who suffers a loss in such a situation but her father. As I suggested above, this law falls under the category of "property damage," not "social responsibility." If a virgin has sexual relations with a man outside of marriage, she is "damaged goods," which means the father will not be able to exact the bride-price for her. That is why the man who seduced her will have to make restitution *to him*, not to her (v. 17). Marriage, which would help the daughter save face, is something the father can refuse, but the bride-price must be paid to him nonetheless.

C. Worship and Social Responsibility (22:18–23:19)

1. WORSHIP: SORCERESSES, bestiality, and false sacrifices (22:18–20). With 22:18 we begin the final section of the Book of the Covenant, which interweaves social and cultic matters. As mentioned above, this section demonstrates the close association of what we might call "secular" matters and matters of proper worship. For ancient Israelites, all of life is rooted in worship. The quality of one's worship is shown at least in part in one's conduct toward others.

These three laws are brief. The first command is against sorceresses. The Hebrew root is *kšp*, which occurs only thirteen times in the Old Testament.[18] That similar figures are mentioned in Exodus 7:11 suggests some rationale for why they would be mentioned here, but it is not clear why these individuals are female. Nor is it explained just what sorcery entails. If we allow 7:11 to offer a suggestion, sorcery probably involves calling on forces other than Yahweh, which thus constitutes an act of false worship.

According to Leviticus 18:23–25, bestiality (Ex. 22:19) is a cultic offense. It is also a religious practice of Israel's neighbors, and thus must be avoided along with many other things that blur the line between the true worship of the true God and the false worship of false gods.[19] But no explicit reason for this law is given, likely because none is needed. There is more to the prohibition than simply the fact that bestiality is a sick, demented, gross act. Since this act is grievous enough to warrant the death penalty, something more significant than mere social convention is at work. This law should be understood within a cultic context.

The third law is the most explicitly cultic of the three:[20] Sacrificing to other gods is punishable by death. Note that the Hebrew root *ḥrm* is used here to describe the death penalty rather than *mwt*, which has been used elsewhere in the Book of the Covenant. This root indicates the surrendering of something to God for the purpose of utter and complete destruction (cf. NIV note).[21] Throughout Joshua, for example, this word is used with respect to the destruction of Canaanite cities. Anything that is potentially hostile to God is dealt with in this way. The irony here is that it is Israelites themselves who are treated in this way, not people from the outside.

---

18. The other passages (in the Heb. Masoretic Text) are Ex. 7:11; Deut. 18:10; 2 Kings 9:22; 2 Chron. 33:6; Isa. 47:9, 12; Jer. 27:9; Dan. 2:2; Micah 5:11 [Eng. 12]; Nahum 3:4 [2x]; Mal. 3:5.

19. Durham, *Exodus*, 328. Sprinkle also discusses the matter briefly and gives the example from Ugaritic literature of Baal with a heifer (*The Book of the Covenant*, 164–65).

20. Janzen suggests that the third law makes explicit the cultic nature of the previous two (*Exodus*, 172).

21. See R. L. Harris et al., eds., *Theological Dictionary of the Old Testament* (Chicago: Moody, 1980), 1:324.

2. Social responsibility: oppression and loans (22:21–28). Immediately after these cultic laws is a series of laws aimed at the proper treatment of others, whether Israelites or foreigners living within their borders. The first one (v. 21) concerns mistreatment and oppression of aliens. We are not told what form this mistreatment might take. "Alien" (Heb. *ger;* see again 2:22) is a common word in the Old Testament and pertains to someone without rights to land or property. This, of course, is exactly what Israel was in Egypt, and the law makes that connection explicit. Hence, we may conclude that mistreatment and oppression probably refer to harsh enslavement.

Aliens represent a disadvantaged portion of the population. Another such group is widows and orphans (vv. 22–24). Having no husband or parent makes a person particularly susceptible to those who prey on the weak, an unfortunate human trait no less true then than it is today. This is why this command is accompanied by a warning: Oppression of these people will not go unnoticed. God will hear their cry, as he did Israel's in 2:23–25. The same fate awaits these oppressors as that which fell on the Egyptians. They will be killed, thus making their own wives widows and their children orphans.

Verses 25–27 concern proper treatment of the "needy," those severely disadvantaged economically. If a poor man is loaned money, he is to be charged no interest. Presumably, the proper motive for lending money to the poor is to help one's neighbor and not to make a profit.[22] It was customary to take a pledge in a loan transaction, a form of collateral. The fact that someone would give a cloak as a pledge rather than something more valuable indicates his destitute state. But that cloak is to be returned by sunset so that he may sleep warmly. (One rightly wonders how functional a pledge would be that could only be kept for several hours.)

These three laws highlight what we have seen throughout the book of Exodus: God loves his people dearly. He is protective of them against any abuse, including abuse at the hands of fellow Israelites. God's people must not show any sign that they are becoming like the Egyptians, who oppressed them. This includes both in how they worship and in how they treat others, whether fellow Israelites or aliens living among them.

Verse 28 forms the conclusion to this section. I follow both Sprinkle and Brichto in saying that this verse is not an independent law but the conclusion to the laws concerning the disadvantaged.[23] The warning to the Israelites not to blaspheme God or curse the rulers pertains to the previ-

---

22. This is not to say, however, that interest could not be charged to those who could afford it. The Book of the Covenant is silent on that matter.

23. Sprinkle, *The Book of the Covenant*, 167–68; see also Durham, *Exodus*, 329.

ously stated laws. Blasphemy should not be understood as simply some abstract verbal assault on God, but a failure to follow God's law. So, too, cursing the rulers shows contempt for civil authorities whose job it is to uphold God's law.

3. Worship: offerings, firstborn, holiness (22:29–31). The Israelites are reminded here that their best belongs to God. Verse 29 refers to more than simply grain and wine offerings. The Hebrew is difficult, but it literally says "your fullness and your dripping," likely meaning the *firstfruits* of the field and the vine. Don't hold the best for yourself, but give it to God.

The same holds for the firstborn of Israel's sons. We have already seen in 13:1–16 that the firstborn belong to God, which means they must be sacrificed. Of course, a human firstborn was to be redeemed with (i.e., substituted by) a lamb, as could a firstborn donkey (13:12–13). This law, therefore, is a reiteration of the one found earlier in Exodus, and we should assume that the passing reference here should be read in light of its fuller explication in chapter 13.[24] Firstborn cattle and sheep also belong to God, but they must stay with their mothers for seven days and given over on the eighth day. There is a clear parallel here with circumcision on the eighth day (Gen. 17:12), another type of dedication to God. This period of time likely represents a period of completeness after which the subject is adequately "prepared" to be given to God.[25]

Verse 31 contains another reminder—that Israel is to be God's "holy people" (an echo of 19:6). Actually, the Hebrew here has "holy men" rather than "holy people" (*goy*) as in 19:6 (see comments there), but the ideas are congruent.

But what are we to make of the specific law mentioned in verse 31b? Why should the meat of torn animals be such an issue? This law must be read in light of what we see in Leviticus 17:15 and 22:8. Eating meat torn by wild animals (carrion) makes one unclean. Moreover, priests specifically are prohibited from such practice (22:8). This priestly practice is a fitting injunction for all Israel, which is a "kingdom of priests." Why eating torn meat results in uncleanness is not explained here or elsewhere in the Old Testament, unless we understand such eating to be in violation of the law against eating meat with blood in it (see 17:11–14). It may also be another comment on pagan practices from which Israel should distance itself.

4. Social responsibility: testimony in court, an enemy's animal, oppression (23:1–9). The final cycle of laws pertaining to social responsibility focuses mainly on matters of legal justice. As with other laws we have seen

---

24. Sprinkle, *The Book of the Covenant*, 174–75.
25. Ibid., 175.

in the Book of the Covenant, but more explicitly here, there must have been some sort of developed system of filing grievances, although the Old Testament gives us little to go on to fill out the picture.

Verses 1–3 are apodictic laws, that is, simple commands ("do not . . ."), as opposed to the case laws ("if . . . then . . ."). Together with the apodictic laws of verses 6–8, these pertain to giving testimony in court. When called upon to give testimony one must not side with either the "wicked man," the crowd, or, perhaps somewhat surprisingly, even a poor man, simply for the sake of doing so or by giving into some pressure.

The "wicked man" referred to in verse 1 is a misleading translation. The Hebrew *rašaᶜ* in legal contexts refers simply to the perpetrator of the crime, that is, the guilty party. Hence, the man's "wickedness" is not a general moral indictment, but must be understood in the context of legal matters. The godly Israelite is to make no attempt at perverting justice by making the guilty look innocent. This law, and the others that follow, are explications of the ninth commandment: "You shall not give false testimony against your neighbor."

It is, I suppose, always tempting to follow the crowd. As is typical of the Book of the Covenant, we are not given details as to possible motives one might have for following the crowd, but the scene is depicted nonetheless. If one is called upon to testify in a trial, justice can never be served if the witness gives in to social pressure and simply sides with the majority. God's people are called upon to do what *is* right, not what *feels* right.

Verse 3 is a bit surprising in the context of other laws we have seen in the Book of the Covenant. The rights of the poor are emphasized, but here the Israelites are warned not to take this to the extreme. Some commentators, including the editors of *Biblia Hebraica Stuttgartensia*, suggest replacing the word "poor" with "great," that is, those of good social standing. This will bring the law in verse 3 in line with the tenor of the Book of the Covenant as a whole. It is tempting to make this change, since the difference between "poor" and "great" in Hebrew is simply one letter (*dl* vs. *gdl*, respectively). There is, however, no manuscript evidence of any textual corruption. Moreover, no one should assume that the rights of the poor are emphasized to the point that favoritism can be shown them! This is no more justice than is abuse of the poor. Note also Leviticus 19:15 (although the Hebrew is different): "Do not pervert justice; do not show partiality to the poor or favoritism to the great, but judge your neighbor fairly."

Verse 3 should not strike us as odd. God is not "on the side of the poor no matter what." Rather, God is just. As we have noted elsewhere, the implicit critique of modern liberation theology is clear. Verse 3 must, however, be read in conjunction with verse 6. Although the poor are not to be shown favoritism, they are not to be denied justice either. Their case cannot be kept from court simply because they are poor and of little account in society. All of Israel is God's, and all are to be treated equally.

Verse 7 is the inverse of verse 1. The just Israelite who follows God's law will not give testimony that will make a guilty man look innocent (v. 1), nor will he make an innocent man look guilty (v. 7). To do the latter will lead to God's punishment. One common reason for perverting justice, in the ancient world as well as today, is bribery (v. 8). But God's justice does not have a price tag. One must not be tempted by personal material gain to subvert Israel's social-religious structure.

Verses 4—5 are case laws. They envision situations in which one Israelite should go out of his way to help another. In fact, you are even to help your enemy. The identity of the enemy is not given, but we should presume that these laws concern members of the Israelite community, not foreigners. These verses are aimed not at the welfare of animals but that of the enemy. "Love your enemies" is not a sentiment found only in the New Testament. Why are these laws placed here in the context of legal practice? It is not clear. Perhaps verses 4—5 are striking examples of the impartiality commanded in the surrounding laws.[26] The unity that God's covenant people are to express toward each other extends even to those who do not like each other. Again, what is right, not how one feels, determines behavior.

Finally, it is worth pointing out that verses 4—5 do not express enforceable law. This is what makes these two case laws different from most of the others in the Book of the Covenant. No penalty is mentioned, since the behavior described can hardly be monitored. These laws aim further than mere legal dealings. They get closer to the heart of the matter: treating all Israelites with love, whether one loves them or not.

The final verse of this section repeats the essence of 22:21. In this context, however, it serves as a fitting conclusion to 23:1—8: Israelites are to deal fairly (lovingly) with everyone in their midst: fellow countrymen, whether poor or rich (vv. 1—3, 6—8); enemies (vv. 4—5); and even non-Israelites, the "aliens." As a kingdom of priests, they are not to oppress those to whom they are to reflect the glory of God. Having experienced firsthand "man's inhumanity to man," they are to turn around and exemplify the opposite behavior: God's love for all.

5. Worship: Sabbaths and festivals (23:10—19). The Book of the Covenant ends with a number of regulations concerning worship, namely, laws regarding the Sabbath, the three annual festivals, and stipulations regarding sacrifice, presumably relating to these festivals.

---

26. Ibid., 178, 182.

The Book of the Covenant has in view the Israelites as settled in Canaan. The purpose of these laws is to prepare them for proper conduct after entering the land, which, were it not for subsequent rebellion, would have occurred soon after the giving of these laws. It is from such a perspective that verses 10–12 should be understood. Already at this stage in their journey, the Israelites are being prepared to respect the land God is giving them and the people living there.

The stated purpose for leaving the land unplowed during the seventh year is so that the poor can eat their fill. This "Sabbath year" is an extension of the fourth commandment (see Lev. 25:1–7). Note, therefore, that the means by which the Israelites are to "keep it holy" (see Ex. 20:8) is not by offering the produce of the seventh year to God, in the form of a cultic offering, but by leaving it for the poor. The emphasis we have seen on protection of the disadvantaged throughout the Book of the Covenant is strikingly evident here. Allowing even wild animals to eat of the produce may indicate a broader humanitarianism implicit in this law.

Verse 12 refers to the Sabbath day and essentially repeats what we have seen in 20:8–11. As reticent as the author of Exodus is generally, such repetition underscores the importance the Sabbath plays in this book. There is, however, an interesting difference between this passage and the fourth commandment. In 20:11, the motivation for ceasing work is the pattern of creation: God himself rested on the seventh day, so Israel should as well. In 23:12, however, the motive is to "refresh" beasts of burden, slaves, and aliens.[27] We should be careful not to pit the humanitarian concerns of 23:12 against the more "theological" motive of 20:11. They most certainly complement each other.

Verse 13 serves as a sort of transition to the cultic matters of verses 14–19. But it is not clear whether "everything" refers to the entire content of the Book of the Covenant, the laws covered thus far, the immediately preceding Sabbath laws, or something else. From a syntactical point of view, it is difficult to separate the first sentence of verse 13 (in the NIV) from the following two. The Hebrew word translated "everything" is *kol*, a word that means many things (e.g., all, each, every, both) and certainly need not imply "every last thing." In other words, the meaning of this word is determined by its context. I suggest, therefore, that it serves to introduce the following topic: faithfulness to God. Specifically, Israel is not to invoke the names of other gods— a reiteration of the first two commandments.

It is fitting to end the Book of the Covenant with a reminder to the Israelites that they are a worshiping community, a reality that extends to

---

27. This humanitarian motive is reflected in the version of the fourth commandment in Deut. 5:12–15.

every area of life, but that is most clearly seen in the ceremonies by which they worship God. The word "invoke" (v. 13) is a translation of the Hebrew Hiphil verb *hazkir*. It is used elsewhere in Exodus only in 20:24, where the NIV translates it "cause . . . to be honored." God's name is to be honored by the Israelites. Such honor must not be given to other gods. They are not even to speak the names of these gods.

This leads us to a number of cultic regulations that the Israelites are commanded to keep (vv. 14–17; these same ceremonies will again be mentioned in 34:18–26, after the golden calf episode). The three annual feasts correspond to three different stages in Israel's agricultural year. The command to keep these festivals is given in verses 14 and 17, thus framing the description of the festivals themselves.

The first feast is the Feast of Unleavened Bread. This ceremony is to be understood in conjunction with the Passover night described in Exodus 12. We have already seen in 12:17–20 how no bread with yeast is to be eaten from the fourteenth to the twenty-first day of the first month (called Abib, 23:15; cf. 12:2). Lack of yeast symbolizes the haste with which the Israelites were commanded to leave Egypt. This ceremony is a yearly commemoration of that deliverance. The allusion to offerings at the end of verse 15 indicates that the Feast of Unleavened Bread is more than a private celebration of Passover, but a community festival complete with offerings of some sort. The offerings of verse 15 are most likely agricultural in nature.

The Feast of Harvest is also referred to as the Feast of Weeks (34:22). It was held seven weeks after the first festival. Jewish tradition connects this feast to the giving of the law on Sinai, which is a tempting connection in view of the fact that the Israelites arrived at Sinai two months to the day after they left Egypt. Still, the Sinai/Feast of Harvest connection finds no direct support in the Old Testament.[28] This feast entails offering to God the firstfruits of one's produce, the full harvest coming in the fall during the Feast of Ingathering (v. 16). Thus, it symbolizes the harvest that is to come. It is a tangible, concrete evidence of what is ahead. (This is why—to digress for a moment—Paul refers to Christ's resurrection as "the firstfruits of those who have fallen asleep" [1 Cor. 15:20]. Christ's resurrection is the tangible, concrete evidence of the full harvest to come, the resurrection of all believers, Paul's general topic in 1 Cor. 15.)

The Feasts of Harvest and of Ingathering (the latter also referred to as the Feast of Booths, to symbolize Israel's living in temporary shelters; see Lev. 23:43) are intimately tied to the possession of the land, as we have seen

---

28. The New Testament refers to this feast by yet another name, Pentecost (Acts 2:1; 20:16; 1 Cor. 16:8).

throughout the Book of the Covenant. The land's ability to produce is a gift from God. Therefore, it is not to be abused (Ex. 23:10–11). Moreover, it is at these agriculturally significant times that Israel is to be reminded that all these gifts come from God. Israel is truly to thank God for its "daily bread." Every element of life, whether social or agricultural, is to be lived out in God's presence. He is the source and the goal of everything they do. The law comes *from* God, and through obedience Israel will move closer *to* him.

The four final laws given in verses 18–19 are somewhat odd, but they should not be thought of as detached from the previous laws.[29] The injunction against yeast (v. 18) certainly reflects the Feast of Unleavened Bread. Nor may the fat remain until morning (see 12:9–10). The reference to firstfruits (23:19) likewise suggests a connection to the Feast of Harvest. The Israelites must make sure they bring the best of the firstfruits as an offering to "the house of the LORD" (an apparent reference to the tabernacle, the major topic of conversation in chs. 25–40).

The final law in the Book of the Covenant is one that for some captures the obscurity (and contemporary irrelevance) of the Israelite legal system: "Do not cook a young goat in its mother's milk." What does this mean? The best we can do is guess. It seems to be tied somehow to the Feast of Ingathering, since the previous laws in verses 18–19 are linked to the other feasts. But this does not really help us in understanding the law itself. A number of explanations have been suggested, but they are all speculative.[30] In the final analysis, the original meaning of this law remains obscure, and we will make no attempt to nail it down. It seems to have been a practice of Israel's neighbors as is suggested in a Ugaritic text, so it may be that this injunction is a polemic against pagan practices.[31]

Bridging Contexts

THE LAW AND the Christian. When we as Christians turn to the Book of the Covenant, our attention is focused sooner or later on the relevance of these laws for the Christian life. This, of course, is a matter well worth addressing, but we must be careful not to be premature. What will properly bridge the ancient and modern contexts is, first, an understanding of the Book of the Covenant in its own context, which is the book of Exodus specifically as well as the Old Testament as a whole, and then the meaning of the law in light of the coming of Christ.

---

29. Durham considers vv. 18–19 to be miscellaneous laws and resists connecting them to the preceding feasts (*Exodus*, 333–34).

30. Durham lists magic, reaction against Dionysius, or reaction against Canaanite custom (ibid., 334). The latter has some support in the context (see 23:33; 34:15).

31. Cassuto, *Commentary on Exodus*, 305.

(1) Within the context of Exodus, as we have seen above, the Book of the Covenant is part of a triad of concepts that dominate the book as a whole: redemption, worship, law. Neither in Exodus nor anywhere else in the Old Testament should the law be viewed in the abstract.

Obedience to law is something God requires of his people, not just so that they have something to do, but that they may have a proper relationship with him. It is because God has redeemed Israel that he is worthy of their obedience, and that obedience has both vertical and horizontal dimensions. And proper worship of God is not left to Israel's whim, nor is it to be something that is simply styled after the manner in which Israel's neighbors worship their gods. Rather, it is important that a major component of the Book of the Covenant be regulations concerning worship. We must remember the refrain of the Exodus narrative itself: "Let my people go, *so that they may worship me.*" Israel is a worshiping community, and the Book of the Covenant contains the stipulations that direct the Israelites as they perform that function.

Interwoven with these vertically oriented stipulations are laws that govern Israel's conduct among themselves. It is wrong to divorce these "social" laws from the same context in which we view the laws on worship that make up the rest of the Book of the Covenant. The Book of the Covenant is *one* body of law. It is *in its entirety* Israel's response to the God of redemption. Its structure is, in this respect, a fuller expression of Jesus' words in Matthew 22:37–40. In a test by an "expert in the law," Jesus was once asked, "Teacher, which is the greatest commandment in the Law?" Jesus responded with these familiar words:

> "Love the Lord your God with all your heart and with all your soul and with all your mind. This is the first and greatest commandment." And the second is like it: "Love your neighbor as yourself." All the Law and the Prophets hang on these two commandments.

We see this already in the Book of the Covenant: a vertical and horizontal dimension to the law.

The law given to Israel on Mount Sinai is an event for which God's people have been prepared. It is not an afterthought; it is the purpose for their redemption. There are two things to be kept in mind about the place of the Book of the Covenant in Exodus. (a) Law is a response to redemption, not a precondition for redemption, a point made repeatedly in previous chapters. (b) Law is a positive undertaking for Israel. It is not a burden, but liberation, freedom. It is God's pattern of vertical and horizontal conduct for his people. Since the Israelites have been redeemed, it is now a path toward a fuller realization of God's universal plan of redemption, a plan that will only truly come into its own with the coming of Christ.

(2) But what of the broader context in which to understand the law, the Old Testament as a whole? To be sure, a number of the laws contained in the Book of the Covenant are found elsewhere in the Old Testament, at least in substance (Deuteronomy, Leviticus, Psalms, the Prophets). But merely noting the repetition of some laws here and there will not help us understand what purpose they have in God's overarching scheme of redemption.

When we frame the discussion this way, we are invoking an issue that has separated Christians from Jews—and from each other—for two thousand years: the meaning and significance of the law. How (or even if!) the laws of the Book of the Covenant are to be applied here and now is a question that can be addressed only after this preliminary question is addressed. Applying this or that law is a risky endeavor without first considering the Christian framework within which Old Testament law as a whole should be understood.

The application of the Book of the Covenant will be left for the Contemporary Significance section, whereas here we will attempt to provide the proper *framework* for understanding this unit. The problem with such a discussion, however, is that it is difficult to get one's arms around the entire issue. Any topic that has been so debated over the centuries and that so many have found difficult to resolve must therefore be a tricky and nuanced topic. What follows is a general outline of thinking generated by our observations on the role of the Book of the Covenant in Exodus.

What we have seen above with respect to the Book of the Covenant in the context of the Exodus from Egypt is also true of law in general in the Old Testament as a whole. (1) It is a "post-redemptive" phenomenon. (2) It is not legalistic, in the sense in which many Christians use the term, but a gift from God.

(1) It is universally true throughout the Old Testament that the law is Israel's possession. It is meant to be obeyed by God's people. The nations surrounding Israel—the Egyptians, Assyrians, Canaanites, or Babylonians—are never condemned for their failure to capitulate to the Sinaitic law. They are rather condemned essentially because of their treatment of the Israelites, specifically for their attempts at annihilating Israel. This much is clear, for example, by looking at the so-called "oracles against the nations" in Isaiah 13–23 (excluding the prophecy about Jerusalem in ch. 22) and Jeremiah 46–51.

These nations are judged because of specific behavior that affects Israel's existence as the people of God. They are judged because they want to destroy Israel through war. This, obviously, God cannot allow. They are also judged because of idolatry. What ignites God's anger, however, is not the fact that such idolatry breaks such laws as Exodus 20:3—6 or 22:20. These are *Israel's* laws. The problem with the nations' idolatry is that it infests the true worship of the true God that Israel is supposed to exemplify. If such false worship were adopted in any way by Israel—a constant temptation throughout her history—this would lead to Israel's destruction.

These, then, are the reasons the nations meet with God's displeasure. It must be remembered that it is the nations that God ultimately wants to redeem (cf. Gen. 12:3). Hence, God's judgment against them must be understood as a function of their direct opposition to his intention to create for himself a people belonging to him, whose influence will then spread to the ends of the earth. When we read the Old Testament, therefore, with its "heavy emphasis" on law, we should not think of this emphasis as being in any way opposed to grace. Grace (redemption) precedes law. This is why the law applies to God's people only. This is no less true of law in the Old Testament in general as it is of the Book of the Covenant in Exodus.

(2) The second point, touched on elsewhere in this commentary, bears repeating. The law was never a burden. It became burdensome when Israel ceased obeying, but this is simply a consequence of disobedience. To be sure, Israel's initial meeting with God on Mount Sinai produced great fear in their hearts, but that is because they came face-to-face with God on his holy mountain, not because they were given laws to obey. True, it took time for the Israelites to get used to the fact that their covenant, redeeming God made demands on them. The initial reception of these commands was not met with tremendous enthusiasm, although the people did unanimously pledge themselves to obedience (24:3, 7). Moreover, within a brief period we see the Israelites blatantly disregarding God's law in chapter 32 (golden calf episode).

Such an attitude toward the law is a recurring theme throughout the Old Testament, but we must remember that this is a function of Israel's sin. That the law may have seemed to the Israelites from time to time as an annoying or even oppressive burden is not a property of law as such. In time, Israel came to learn more deeply that the law was a gift, not a poison. Or, in the words of Deuteronomy 32:47: "They are not just idle words for you—they are your life." The Old Testament is replete with passages that extol the law as a thing not only to be obeyed, but to be studied and loved (e.g., Ps. 119).

As we read the many stipulations that make up the Book of the Covenant, this is not a lull in the action. We as Christians may look on these laws as an intrusion in the narrative that may be profitably skipped over. For ancient Israelites, however, the law on Mount Sinai represents the beginning of the climax of the book, a climax that carries through to the end of the book with the regulations regarding the construction of the tabernacle. Rather than a collective sigh or show of indifference, the ears of the original audience would have perked up at this stage. Now they can know what God, their Savior, wants them to do, in their conduct both with him and with each other. These are not just idle words, but life itself.

(3) Yet we cannot leave the matter there. That the law in the Old Testament is so highly esteemed is difficult for many Christians to square with what certainly appears to be a negative evaluation of the law in the New Testament. One does not need to search far in the New Testament to find critical remarks about the law. The following is a small sampling of passages:

> He has made us competent as ministers of a new covenant—not of the letter but of the Spirit; for the letter kills, but the Spirit gives life. (2 Cor. 3:6)

> Now we know that whatever the law says, it says to those who are under the law, so that every mouth may be silenced and the whole world held accountable to God. Therefore no one will be declared righteous in his sight by observing the law; rather, through the law we become conscious of sin. But now a righteousness from God, apart from law, has been made known.... (Rom. 3:19–21)

> For we maintain that a man is justified by faith apart from observing the law. (Rom. 3:28)

> It was not through law that Abraham and his offspring received the promise that he would be heir of the world, but through the righteousness that comes by faith. For if those who live by law are heirs, faith has no value and the promise is worthless, because law brings wrath. And where there is no law there is no transgression. (Rom. 4:13–15)

When we phrase the discussion this way, we have entered a debate that has been raging since the beginning of Christianity: What is the relationship between the law and the gospel? The fact that Paul devoted so much attention to it in his letters indicates that it was a frequent and necessary topic of discussion in the first century. That the law is a positive, liberating element in the Old Testament is beyond debate. But likewise, the ineffectiveness of the law in view of the coming of Christ is nonnegotiable as well. How can the two be held together?

When we keep in mind the magnitude of this issue, it becomes clear that the best that can be done here is to give some suggestive, "big picture" types of comments to bring the issue into better focus and to lead us into the subject of application in the following section. As I see it, a proper understanding of the Old Testament in light of the coming of Christ should keep in mind the following.[32]

(a) The law is not a wholly negative entity in the New Testament. One cannot speak of a sweeping law/gospel dichotomy that puts the Old Testament and New Testament economies at odds. Paul's own view of the law, in fact, is complex and resists simplistic evaluation. He has both positive and negative statements to make about its role for those who are "in Christ." We must remember that mixed in with his "negative" statements on the law are positive comments (e.g., a reference to the fifth commandment in Eph. 6:1–3 and to Ex. 22:28 in Acts 23:4–5).

(b) Jesus saw himself and his mission, in some sense, as the fulfillment of Old Testament law. He tells us in Matthew 5:17–20 how he relates to the law:

> Do not think that I have come to abolish the Law or the Prophets; I have not come to abolish them but to fulfill them. I tell you the truth, until heaven and earth disappear, not the smallest letter, not the least stroke of a pen, will by any means disappear from the Law until everything is accomplished. Anyone who breaks one of the least of these commandments and teaches others to do the same will be called least in the kingdom of heaven, but whoever practices and teaches these commands will be called great in the kingdom of heaven. For I tell you that unless your righteousness surpasses that of the Pharisees and the teachers of the law, you will certainly not enter the kingdom of heaven.

This is not the easiest of passages to understand, but several general conclusions can be drawn. (i) Jesus was not "anti-law." He saw himself as fulfilling the law of Moses and the teaching of the prophets (v. 17). (ii) In some sense, even the very details of the law are of vital importance. In fact, they will remain "until heaven and earth disappear" (v. 18). The law is not to be taken lightly. (iii) There are consequences for those who do not obey or who teach others not to obey. These will be "least in the kingdom of heaven"

---

32. If readers would like to dig a bit deeper into this important issue, the following essays are good places to start. They summarize well the elements of the debate and provide helpful bibliographies for further reading: F. Thielman, "Law," in *Dictionary of Paul and His Letters*, ed. G. F. Hawthorne, R. P. Martin, and D. G. Reid (Downers Grove, Ill.: InterVarsity, 1993), 529–42; N. T. Wright, *The Climax of the Covenant* (Minneapolis: Fortress, 1992); D. J. Moo, "Law," in *Dictionary of Jesus and the Gospels*, ed. J. B. Green, S. McKnight, and I. H. Marshall (Downers Grove, Ill.: InterVarsity, 1992), 450–61; the various essays in W. G. Strickland, *The Law, the Gospel, and the Modern Christian* (Grand Rapids: Zondervan, 1993). The following points are an elaboration of my comments in "Law of God," *New International Dictionary of Old Testament Theology and Exegesis*, ed. W. VanGemeren (Grand Rapids: Zondervan, 1997), 4:899. The preceding pages of that essay (893–99) provide the argumentation for these conclusions.

(v. 19). The "kingdom of heaven" refers to those who are a part of God's kingdom here and now. It is also clear that Jesus is not speaking here of what to do in order to enter this kingdom, but of proper conduct for those *already a part of the kingdom*. As in the Old Testament, law is not a condition for entering God's family, but the rules for those who are in God's family. (iv) True obedience to the law, which is what Jesus sets out to explain throughout the Sermon on the Mount (chs. 5–7), exceeds that of the so-called experts (Pharisees), who understood law merely in the outward, legalistic sense.

(c) Paul's statements about the law should not be understood apart from the context in which he addressed those statements. The apostle was not engaged in abstract theological speculation, nor was he concerned to discuss "the concept of the law." He was rather a pastor-theologian addressing particular people with particular problems. Extreme condemnation of the law, such as we find in his letter to Galatians, must be understood in connection with the Judaizing influence in Galatia. Hence, at least part of Paul's polemics against law is really an argument against an improper estimation of the law's effectiveness in first-century Judaism. Such a contextual understanding of Paul's statements on the law also holds for as "systematic" a letter as Romans. Paul here is writing to a church with which he is likely not familiar, and his concern is to make sure they are well rooted in the basics of the gospel, which in his day (as in ours) was always running the risk of losing its grace-centered core.

(d) Having said all this, however, we must take care not to lose sight of the radical nature of the gospel. However positively or ambiguously the New Testament portrays the relationship between law and gospel, the coming of Christ inaugurated an era that rendered obsolete any soteriological scheme, including the Old Testament, that proceeded apart from that event. There is, in other words, both continuity and discontinuity between the era before the coming of Christ and after his coming in terms of the relationship between law and gospel. This is certainly not to say that the gospel "corrected" the legalism of the Old Testament. But it is to say that the death and resurrection of Christ were something new and amazing, even if they were at the same time the ultimate goal for which God had been preparing his people throughout the Old Testament. It is, to use Paul's words, "a righteousness from God, *apart from law ... to which the Law* and the Prophets testify" (Rom. 3:21, italics added).

What then is the Christian's response to the law? We are saved not by any of our own efforts, but by Christ's supreme effort on the cross. But as Christians, we take God's law to heart, not legalistically, but as a pattern of conduct in God's world. That pattern is perhaps best expressed in the "law of love" (Matt. 5:43–48; 7:12; 22:40), for as we love others, we will be perfect as our Father in heaven is perfect (5:48).

THE LAW AND THE CHRISTIAN. To this point I have resisted speaking specifically about the actual laws in the Book of the Covenant. This has been intentional. It is important to communicate that the Book of the Covenant is not meant to be mined today for those laws that seem applicable. It is hard to see how we as Christians can do theological justification to Exodus 20:22–23:19 when we take a sampling of a few laws that seem to be generally compatible in today's world while ignoring or even downplaying those that do not. We are all comfortable with "Do not blaspheme God or curse the ruler of your people" (22:28). Some of us might like to see the death penalty for bestiality enforced (22:19). But few of us would feel comfortable with treating virgin daughters as property (22:16–17). And how many Christian bankers would relieve their struggling Christian brothers and sisters from paying interest on a loan (22:25)? Indeed, would they even get past the application process?!

The law reflects the nature of God, but it does so in a historical context. The Book of the Covenant is *God's* law, but it reveals God to a people living at a particular point in time and for whom he has a particular purpose. One should not simply assume, therefore, that these laws necessarily "apply" to our world today. To say this is not to denigrate the law, but to understand it properly. Those who insist that these laws must be kept today will likely be inconsistent when they themselves attempt to obey them, particularly if they do not own slaves, bulls, oxen, sheep, or donkeys (frequent topics throughout 21:2–22:15).

Of course, one way around this matter is to argue that it is not the laws themselves that need to be applied, but the *principles* underlying them. This is a common way of handling Old Testament law in general, so it is likely not without merit, but I will not take this approach here. Little would be added by repeating the efforts of others. But more important, looking for principles does not really settle the matter of how the law ought to be applied. In fact it introduces a number of problems of its own.

(1) Just what is a "principle" that underlies a law? It is not always easy to discern with any confidence the principle on which to base a present-day application. This is so for three reasons. (a) Many of the laws are too vague or difficult to understand. We have already seen this problem with respect to a number of laws in the Book of the Covenant (e.g., 21:22, the law often understood as support for biblical condemnation of abortion). Since it is difficult to understand the precise nature of this and other laws, to what extent can principles be derived from them?

(b) Some of the laws have a clear underlying principle, but the principles are so general as to be of little use as a guide for conduct. An example is

22:20: "Whoever sacrifices to any god other than the LORD must be destroyed." The underlying principle might be something like, "Yahweh is the only God to be worshiped," but discerning this underlying principle does not give any guidance as to how this principle should be applied today. Moreover, one does not need *this law* to make the point. In other words, in what sense can we say that we are applying the Book of the Covenant when this law refers to sacrifice and the death penalty? What good is a vague principle detached from the specifics from which the principle itself is derived?

(c) Some laws are so irrelevant that they resist any application, even the law's principle. Finding a timeless principle in 22:29–31, for example, stretches common sense, unless one appeals to a general, vague notion of holiness (see v. 31). But applying such a principle would be done essentially at the expense of the specifics of the law itself.

(2) Another reason for not looking for principles in the Book of the Covenant is that I doubt if this is the reason these laws were given in the first place. These laws were specific to Israel's impending entrance into the Promised Land. They were given to serve a purpose for the Israelites at this particular stage in redemptive history. Moses did not say, "Here are some specific laws God wants you to obey, but remember to look for the underlying principles and struggle to apply the *principles* to your lives." In fact, the reason why principles are sought at all is because of the obvious time-boundedness of the laws, combined with the assumption that since Israel applied these laws, we must do so in some sense as well. The appeal to principles seems the only way, but in doing so we should acknowledge that our application is based on something the original audience would likely not have recognized. Such an approach to obedience to the law may "feel" biblical, but it actually requires a "rewriting" of the text to be able to live by it.

(3) A final reason why I do not feel fully comfortable with looking for principles in the Book of the Covenant is because such an approach does not struggle enough with what the death and resurrection of Christ has to say about law. Again, we are treading on eggshells when we discuss the relationship between the law and the gospel, but tread every Christian must. Does extracting principles from the Old Testament law do justice to the significance of what Jesus did? Is this the best we can do, living as we do in the brilliant light of the resurrection?

These are questions worth asking, but to this point I have been hedging about how precisely to apply the law. The reason for my hesitancy is simple: The New Testament opinion on the matter seems ambiguous. The very fact that Paul in his letters cites specific laws certainly implies that the law is something that can, or even should, be brought into the Christian life, and nothing I have said to this point is directed at undermining this. The question I have is not so much *whether* the law is relevant, but *how*. That is the difficult question. I assume it says something to us on some level, but what is that level? How do we get the law from there to here?

To put the problem another way, it is the data of the New Testament itself that complicate the matter. The New Testament is not at all clear on how the law is to be applied by Christians. It presents at least three models. This is the first point to be acknowledged in the debate. (a) In the New Testament occasional letters, sometimes the law seems to have no place (e.g., Rom. 10:4). (b) Yet at other times Paul authoritatively cites a specific law as binding on Christians (e.g., Eph. 6:2). (c) And in at least one instance he even seems to apply a principle. In 1 Corinthians 9:9 (see also 1 Tim. 5:18), Paul cites Deuteronomy 25:4: "Do not muzzle an ox while it is treading out the grain." What does this law mean as far as Paul is concerned?

> Is it about oxen that God is concerned? Surely he says this for us, doesn't he? Yes, this was written for us, because when the plowman plows and the thresher threshes, they ought to do so in the hope of sharing in the harvest. If we have sown spiritual seed among you, is it too much if we reap a material harvest from you? If others have this right of support from you, shouldn't we have it all the more?
>
> But we did not use this right. On the contrary, we put up with anything rather than hinder the gospel of Christ. (1 Cor. 9:9–12)

Paul insists that the point of the law is some underlying principle and *not* the specifics of the law itself. Of course, one could simply argue that Paul is appealing to this law for rhetorical effect, a fruitful avenue of inquiry in my view, but this may be more skirting the issue than an honest attempt to deal with this passage.

We should not attempt to apply the Book of the Covenant until we have some idea of how we are warranted to do so in light of the resurrection. Yet, when we turn to the pages of the New Testament for guidance, we find the three different models just listed. The last thing I want to do is add to the confusion by suggesting an approach to the law that will cover the diverse data we find in the New Testament. After all, there is a reason why this has been a topic of ongoing debate for the entire existence of the church: It is a tricky topic!

When all is said and done, when I read the Book of the Covenant, the first thought that pops into my mind is not, "How do I bring these laws into my life; how do I follow them today?" Rather, the first thing I think of is, "Now I see better how God dealt with his people soon after the Exodus." This is not to say that none of these laws has any relevance to our conduct, but I am not about to draw up a list of laws that apply or those that don't. Nor am I going to abstract principles from these laws to apply to current situations. I remain convinced that what we as Christians are supposed to glean from the Book of the Covenant is an understanding of the nature of God and what he requires of his people, what Jesus summarized as loving God and treating your neighbor as yourself.

The Book of the Covenant teaches us that God requires his people to behave properly toward God and with each other. This is true religion. This is true worship. And, as most Christians understand, what constitutes proper behavior is more often than not a matter of spiritual wisdom and Christian maturity rather than having an exhaustive manual to cover each scenario (even the Book of the Covenant does not do that!). And, most important, as with the Israelites, the Christian's view of the law must first be rooted in the knowledge of what God has already done, apart from the law. He has called us from darkness into light.

Exodus 23:20–33

"SEE, I AM sending an angel ahead of you to guard you along the way and to bring you to the place I have prepared. ²¹Pay attention to him and listen to what he says. Do not rebel against him; he will not forgive your rebellion, since my Name is in him. ²²If you listen carefully to what he says and do all that I say, I will be an enemy to your enemies and will oppose those who oppose you. ²³My angel will go ahead of you and bring you into the land of the Amorites, Hittites, Perizzites, Canaanites, Hivites and Jebusites, and I will wipe them out. ²⁴Do not bow down before their gods or worship them or follow their practices. You must demolish them and break their sacred stones to pieces. ²⁵Worship the LORD your God, and his blessing will be on your food and water. I will take away sickness from among you, ²⁶and none will miscarry or be barren in your land. I will give you a full life span.

²⁷"I will send my terror ahead of you and throw into confusion every nation you encounter. I will make all your enemies turn their backs and run. ²⁸I will send the hornet ahead of you to drive the Hivites, Canaanites and Hittites out of your way. ²⁹But I will not drive them out in a single year, because the land would become desolate and the wild animals too numerous for you. ³⁰Little by little I will drive them out before you, until you have increased enough to take possession of the land.

³¹"I will establish your borders from the Red Sea to the Sea of the Philistines, and from the desert to the River. I will hand over to you the people who live in the land and you will drive them out before you. ³²Do not make a covenant with them or with their gods. ³³Do not let them live in your land, or they will cause you to sin against me, because the worship of their gods will certainly be a snare to you."

THIS SECTION, WHICH serves as a fitting conclusion to the Book of the Covenant, mentions God's
promise of sending his angel and two prominent
themes that we have seen previously in Exodus:
worship of Yahweh only and the gift of land.

Worship and land have formed the backdrop for much of the Book of the
Covenant and even Exodus as a whole. (1) Regarding worship, the Israelites
were redeemed from Egypt so that they might "serve" Yahweh rather than
Pharaoh. The jealous God was fighting for his people in order to turn their
attention toward him. Redemption leads to worship. The Book of the
Covenant is also concerned with Israel's proper conduct toward their God.
Even the horizontal responsibilities the Israelites have toward each other
have implications for how they relate vertically to God. Both are expressions of worship.

(2) The reference to the land in this section, although brief, brings into
sharper focus what has already been seen. In 15:14–16, as Israel stepped out
onto the shores of the Red Sea, their attention was drawn to the next stage
of its journey. Also, as noted in the previous section, the impending realization of the promise of the land is implicit throughout the Book of the
Covenant, since its laws form a manifesto for how the Israelites are to conduct themselves in the land they are about to receive.

By focusing on these two central themes of worship and land, the writer
not only reiterates what he has said before but prepares his readers for what
is to come. Proper worship of God will form his main concern throughout
chapters 25–40, where the central topic is the instructions regarding the
tabernacle. The question of entrance into the land, although not a focus of
the remainder of Exodus, will dominate Numbers and Deuteronomy as well
as Joshua and Judges. To put it another way, whereas the first eighteen chapters of Exodus prepared Israel for its climactic appearance before God on the
mountain, this section begins our journey down the mountain, symbolically
speaking, by giving more detailed attention to the possession of the land.

Verses 20–26 fall into two parts, each with a command followed by consequences of either obeying or disobeying the command. (1) Listening to
the angel will result in the nations being driven out of Canaan (vv. 20–23).
(2) By worshiping Yahweh alone, Israel is promised well-being, long life,
and offspring (vv. 24–26). The object of obedience in the first part is the
angel, in the second it is God. Both are to be obeyed if Israel hopes to realize God's plan for them, which is possession and enjoyment of the land.

Although not a dominant character, the angel has been intimately
involved in Israel's redemption throughout Exodus. He was there at Moses'

call (3:2) and was involved in Israel's redemption (14:19–20). Hence, it is fitting that he guide Israel on the next stage in their journey, the way toward Canaan (see also 32:34; 33:2).

The people are told to listen carefully to what the angel says and obey him (v. 21). Obviously the angel will be speaking to them in some sense. It is not clear how we are to take this, however, since we do not read in the Pentateuch about the angel of Yahweh communicating with the people, giving them commands, and so forth, but of God doing so. Perhaps this is an indication of the close identification of the angel and Yahweh, for their roles are somewhat interchangeable. Moreover, the simple fact that the two are so closely juxtaposed in this section (Israel must obey *both* in order to enter the land) is a serious step toward equating them. Note too the close identification at the end of verse 21, that Yahweh's "Name is in him." Reminiscent of chapter 3, where the angel and the divine name are first brought together, this statement serves to make the equation of the two figures unavoidable. Finally, the curious syntax of verse 22 forces the reader to equate the two: "If you listen carefully to what *he* says and do all that *I* say. . . ." Listening to the angel means obeying God.[1]

What is somewhat striking here is the warning that the angel will not forgive Israel if they rebel. What are we to make of this, especially in light of the fact that forgiveness is precisely what we find throughout Israel's desert experience? Perhaps it simply means that Israel's rebellions will not go unpunished without there being any implication of irrevocable rejection. Yet we should not overlook the severity of this warning. The same Hebrew expression (the verb *naśa²* followed by the preposition *l*) is used in Genesis 18:24 with respect to the destruction of Sodom and Gomorrah. Here we have a dire warning to Israel to obey the angel fully or suffer the horrible consequences.

Hyperbole is not unknown in the Old Testament, and this is what we may be dealing with here. It simply will not do to give a warning in any other way! Imagine God saying, "Listen to the angel, but if you do not, don't worry, I'll forgive you anyway." This could hardly be! A warning *must* be made in no uncertain terms. It is by obeying the angel that Israel will possess the land (vv. 22–23). The angel will wipe out all of Israel's enemies, those who now possess the land of Canaan.

Verse 24 issues another command, not to worship the gods of the Canaanites. This command follows logically upon the preceding topic. Israel's great temptation after entering the land was mixing with its inhabitants and

---

1. Durham refers to the angel as an "extension" of Yahweh (*Exodus*, 335). Sarna points out that the Hebrew word *mrh*, translated "rebel" in 23:21 with reference to the angel, is regularly used in the Old Testament with reference to rebellion against God (*Exodus*, 148).

assuming some or all of their religious practices. To help minimize this influence, the angel will wipe these heathen people out (v. 23). After entering the land, the Israelites are to refrain from Canaanite religions. Their resistance is to take on an active dimension: They are to destroy the Canaanite idols and break their sacred stones (v. 24). As a result, they will receive blessings: well-being, offspring, and long life (v. 26).[2] This is more than merely possessing the land; it is enjoying it and living life to its fullest.

Verses 27–30 continue the theme of Israel's entrance into the land, but it adds a somewhat expected detail: The Conquest will take place little by little (see also Deut. 7:22). As the angel will go ahead of the Israelites in their journey, God says that he will send his "terror" (Hebrew *ʾemah*) ahead of the Israelites to throw the nations into confusion (Ex. 24:27). The same word was used in 15:16, where the topic is also Israel's conquest of Canaan. This "terror" is not some personification of Yahweh or the angel, but the report that Canaan will hear of Yahweh's dealings with the Egyptians.[3] This much is made clear in 15:14–16:

> The nations will hear and tremble;
> > anguish will grip the people of Philistia . . .
> > terror [*ʾemah*] and dread will fall upon them.

As a result the Canaanites will "turn their backs and run" (23:27).

The reference to a "hornet" in verse 28 is not likely literal. The Hebrew word (*ṣirʿah*) only occurs three times in the Old Testament, and its meaning is uncertain.[4] It is probably a graphic symbol of God's defeat of the Canaanites. It, like the "terror" of the preceding verse, buckles the knees of the Canaanites and sends them scurrying for cover.

Verses 29–30 anticipate a problem that this fledgling community will encounter. Their numbers are not yet large enough to take complete and sudden possession of the land. Canaan certainly supports a much larger population than the Israelites who will be displacing them. Simply annihilating or chasing off the inhabitants will leave the land to be overrun by wild animals. Its arable land cannot be cultivated in the absence of a sufficient number of workers and will therefore become desolate. Hence, the Conquest

---

2. Fretheim makes the astute observation that these blessings should be understood in the context of the creation theme begun in chapter 1 (*Exodus*, 252).

3. Fretheim suggests this may refer to some sort of pestilence (ibid., 253).

4. "Hornet" is the meaning suggested in BDB's *Hebrew and English Lexicon*, but this is by no means the clearly preferable translation. Durham translates the word "panic-terror," but without explanation (*Exodus*, 336). Fretheim suggests "pestilence" (*Exodus*, 181). Holladay's lexicon (*A Concise Hebrew and Aramaic Lexicon of the Old Testament* [Grand Rapids: Eerdmans, 1971]) gives the meaning "depression, discouragement."

will take place little by little, in stages—just how many years we are not told—until the population can sustain the land God will give them.

This series of events is played out in the pages of the book of Judges, although there the reason given for a "partial" conquest is Israel's inability (disobedience) to drive out the Canaanites completely, not concern for the health of the land. As the next several books of the Old Testament make clear, the systematic, measured plan of conquest described here meets several roadblocks until its final fulfillment during the reign of David. Even there, one cannot say that the ideal scene depicted here actually takes hold, at least for very long. The implications of this will be discussed in the Bridging Contexts section.

Verses 31—33 reinforce the notion of Israel's complete possession of the land. The general borders God intends for Israel's possession are given. The southern borders will be the "Red Sea," that is, Egypt, and the desert. The western border will be the Mediterranean ("Sea of the Philistines"). The northern border will be the Euphrates ("the River" in Hebrew).[5]

Verses 32—33 remind the Israelites once again about worshiping other gods. This has been a refrain from the Ten Commandments and throughout the Book of the Covenant. It is, therefore, a fitting conclusion to this important scene on Mount Sinai that began in 20:22. What anchors the message of this entire section is Yahweh's insistent teaching to his people that they belong to him and him alone. He is their God who brought them out of Egypt. If they do not remember this foundational fact, if they do not let this truth seep into their hearts, the laws are nothing but hollow precepts and the Promised Land nothing but another plot of earth.

THE ANGEL IS WITH GOD'S PEOPLE. As mentioned above, this is not the first place we have seen the angel active in Exodus.[6] He was there at the call of Moses in chapter 3, at Israel's redemption in chapter 14, and now at Israel's journey to Canaan. The angel's role here continues his redemptive role from the beginning of God's redemptive work in Israel. Regardless of the mystery surrounding his precise identity and despite

---

5. No explicit eastern border is given, but we must presume it is the Jordan. It may be that the Red Sea is a reference to the Gulf of Aqabah, which would represent the southeastern border. If so, the description of the borders moves from the Red Sea in the southeast to the Mediterranean in the northwest, representing the eastern and western borders, and then from the desert in the south to the Euphrates in the north. The desert may also be considered an eastern border, since it in part lies southeast of Canaan.

6. For a discussion of the role that the angel of the Lord plays in the Old Testament, see the comments in Original Meaning section of 3:1—10.

the fact that he is not frequently mentioned in Exodus, he is no doubt a central figure in Israel's redemption. And when we keep in mind the virtual equation of the angel and Yahweh, it follows that the angel's presence is an indication of God's presence with his people from beginning to end. His appearance here reminds Israel of God's faithfulness in bringing to a conclusion what he began in the opening chapters of Exodus.

Like the reference to the angel in 14:19–20, the angel here is also said to go "ahead of" the Israelites. This is another example of what we have seen throughout Exodus. God's honor is at stake here. It is his battle and it is for his sake that Israel was not only to be redeemed from Egypt but will settle within the borders of Canaan, a visible sign to all the nations that Yahweh is the great and only God. The angel goes ahead in order to guard God's people. God will bring them safely to Canaan. Resistance to his plan by outsiders is to be expected (see 17:8–16 and Israel's subsequent history). But none of this is to be a concern for Israel. The angel, God himself, will go before them, guard them, and make sure they get to where they are going. This is more than simply saying that God is *with* his people. He is their buffer and shield going *before* them.

Of the three places where the angel is mentioned in Exodus, 23:20–33 is unique in introducing the notion of obedience. He is stone silent earlier, both in Moses' call and when Israel crossed the sea. But here he begins to take on a more prominent role in Israel's life. He will be a constant, abiding presence with the Israelites, and he will be a figure to whom Israel will now be called to respond. It seems that this "deepening" of Israel's relationship with the angel corresponds to the deepening of their knowledge of the God who brought them out of Egypt and led them to Mount Sinai. Increased knowledge of God and the angel go hand in hand.

These aspects of the angel's role in this passage can be seen elsewhere in Scripture. The angel's abiding presence with the Israelites not only in the initial stages of their redemption but through to the end is a notion that forms the entire backdrop of the redemptive drama of the Old Testament. God never gives up on his people. The Old Testament, as we have seen repeatedly, is a story of God's persistence in forming a people, who are rebellious and thankless at heart, into the people of God. God not only begins the process but sees it through to the end. If he did not, there would be no victory; the goal would never be reached.

The successive stories that unfold on the pages of the Old Testament tell of a God who initiates the relationship with a people and thus calls them his own. Unfortunately, their behavior does not always live up to his expectations, but he never fully rejects them. He disciplines them, to be sure—the parade example being the exile to Babylon—but this constitutes a temporary setback in God's purpose. The reason for even the most *condemning* words of the prophets was to bring Israel *back* to God, not to keep them at arm's distance. The reason for the frequent words of the psalmists concerning divine abandonment is to assure God's people that he has in fact *not* abandoned them. God does not call a people only to leave them to their own devices later on.

This notion of God's abiding presence with his people is expressed even more forcefully by the fact that the angel is said to go "ahead of" the Israelites. The first thing the nations will see as Israel approaches is not Israel's spears or armor or chariots or horses, but Israel's God. He goes before them to intimidate would-be attackers and send them into terror and panic (23:27–28). As we continue reading in Exodus, we find that another figure begins to take on a similar role: the cloud (cf. 14:19–20, where the cloud appears along with the angel). In fact, there is a close identification between the two in this passage:

> Then the *angel* of God, who had been traveling in front of Israel's army, withdrew and went behind them. The *pillar of cloud also moved* from in front and stood behind them, coming between the armies of Egypt and Israel. Throughout the night the cloud brought darkness to the one side and light to the other side; so neither went near the other all night long. (italics added)

As the angel moves, so does the cloud. So, when the cloud begins to take on prominence later in Exodus (and in Numbers), we must keep in mind the close connection these two figures displayed earlier. Note, for example, the closing verses of Exodus (40:36–38):

> In all the travels of the Israelites, whenever the cloud lifted from above the tabernacle, they would set out; but if the cloud did not lift, they did not set out—until the day it lifted. So the cloud of the LORD was over the tabernacle by day, and fire was in the cloud by night, in the sight of all the house of Israel during all their travels.

As the angel is promised to move ahead of the Israelites on their journey to Canaan, the cloud will guide them through their desert journeys. I do not mean to blur the distinctions between these two figures, as if to suggest that they are basically the same. But they do perform a virtually identical function. Both are tangible manifestations of God's presence with his people to bring them to their final goal.

As Israel's story in Exodus continues, we will see a third figure, the ark of the Testimony, occupying a role similar to that of the cloud and the angel. It is first mentioned in 25:10–22, where instructions are given for how it is to be built. Its function is described in 25:22: "There, above the cover between the two cherubim that are over the ark of the Testimony, I will meet with you and give you all my commands for the Israelites." It is the meeting place from which God speak commands to his people. The ark is not simply a piece of furniture to place within the tabernacle, but a physical object to which they can point and say, "This is where we meet God."

Also, we see here some overlap of the ark with the angel's role in 23:22, that of giving commands that the people are expected to obey. Both are vehicles through which God speaks to his people. A further connection between the function of the ark and that of the angel may be seen in Numbers 10:33—36 (italics added):

> So they set out from the mountain of the LORD and traveled for three days. The *ark* of the covenant of the LORD went before them during those three days to find them a place to rest. The *cloud* of the LORD was over them by day when they set out from the camp. Whenever the *ark* set out, Moses said,
>
> "Rise up, O LORD!
> May your enemies be scattered;
> may your foes flee before you."
>
> Whenever it came to rest, he said,
>
> "Return, O LORD,
> to the countless thousands of Israel."

The mixture of figures portrayed in this passage is significant. It describes the Israelites' departure from Sinai, and we read that the ark went *before* them.

This is precisely what the angel is said to do in 23:20 in anticipation of leaving Sinai. Further, not only is the ark said to accompany the Israelites but the cloud, too, is "over them by day." This juxtaposition of the cloud and the ark reinforces the fact that they are indeed two separate entities, but both are involved in Israel's continued progress toward Canaan. Most important is the close identification of the ark with God himself. This is why when the *ark* sets out, Moses says, "Rise up, O LORD!" Again, this is not to equate the ark with God! But the ark is the concrete manifestation of God's presence with his people. These passages, when read in light of the role of the angel in Exodus, form a complex of figures all of which share similar roles in Israel's journey and manifest the presence of God to them.

The main point to be made here is that God goes before his people. He is not just with them; he is the dominant presence. God does not move whenever Israel does; rather, Israel moves when he does. Numbers 14:44—45 records what happens when Israel ignores this order of events. Israel is "presumptuous" in attacking the Amalekites and Canaanites without the ark first moving from the camp. The result of the battle is predictable: The Israelites are beaten back.

Israel's crossing of the Jordan River in Joshua 3 is also worth mentioning here. We have already seen the parallels between the crossing of the Red Sea in Exodus and the crossing of the Jordan by the successive generation. These parallels include the role of ark as going before the people (Josh. 3:6). Israel's crossing of the Jordan is sanctioned by God's guiding presence, as was their crossing of the Red Sea and their departure from Sinai. At every step along the way, God takes the lead, bringing his people to the goal he has planned for them. It is *his* journey, *his* people, *his* plan, *his* honor.

After a series of misadventures and temporary measures (see 1 Sam. 4–6; 2 Sam. 6; 15) the ark finally comes to rest in the Most Holy Place of the temple (1 Kings 8). The fact that the ark now ceases moving ahead of the Israelites means that they have finally arrived at the place to which God has been leading them. God is still with his people, but the people are now settled. The purpose for which the ark was built has been fulfilled. The reason for which Israel was brought out of Egypt has been realized. The people are in the land and God is in their midst.

This brings us to the matter of obedience to the angel. The preceding discussion helps clear up a point mentioned earlier. Exodus 23:20–22 does not really explain what obedience to the angel means. It is not the angel who gives commands but God. But the complex of images seen above brings things into better focus. First, obedience to the angel can refer, at least in part, to Israel's obedience to God in following the angel (cf. Num. 14:44–45 as an example of disobedience). Perhaps this is the command the Israelites are expected to obey.

But I hardly think this is all Exodus 23:22 refers to, since it says, "If you listen carefully to what he says and do *all* that I say." Obedience to the angel is more comprehensive than simply the issue of when the Israelites are to break camp. The connection between the angel, the cloud, and the ark is a more fruitful line of discussion. As with the cloud and the ark, the angel is a tangible manifestation of God's presence with his people, so much so that any of these three objects can simply be equated with God. Recall 3:1–4, where the angel of the Lord appeared to Moses in the burning bush, but it was the Lord who spoke to him from there; or 14:24, where God looks down from the midst of the pillar of cloud. To say that the angel will command the people is nothing other than saying that God himself will speak to them.

There is one final matter concerning obedience that is worth reiterating. It is common in the Old Testament to read of God's people benefiting from their obedience and being punished for their disobedience (e.g., Deut. 7:12–8:20; 28:1–68). God requires obedience, and disobedience leads to death. But these statements must be understood in light of two others. (1) The command to obey and the list of consequences of either obedience or disobedience are given to Israel *after* they have been redeemed. The warnings to obey are only applicable to a people who have already become God's property. Obedience is not a condition for salvation, but expected of those who are saved.

(2) As obviously stern and unyielding as these warnings are, the equally obvious observation cannot escape us: God never fully carries out the threat. God does punish, to be sure, but he always has in his plan the intention to rebuild a people who will eventually be obedient. This is the significance of the theology of the remnant so prevalent in Isaiah. Israel will be punished by exile, but a remnant will return, a purified "stump" will be left (Isa. 6:13), from which will grow an entire nation. To put it another way, God's threat not to forgive rebellion (Ex. 23:21) falls short of the ideal. This is not to say that God is a liar! It is, rather, a snapshot of the good news of the gospel in the Old Testament.

When we turn to the New Testament, we see how these themes are played out in light of the person and work of Christ. The most concrete manifestation of God's presence with his people is Jesus. God actually becomes one of his people. Jesus is fully human (a more concrete image would be hard to come by), and in him God's people see God's glory.

Through the work of the Holy Spirit Christ abides with his people continually. He is with us through every stage in our redemptive journey. He is with us at the beginning: We are called by him into his kingdom. And having called us, he does not leave us to our own strength in holding on to him; he holds on to us and sees the process through to the end. Like the Israelites, the church is a reflection of God's glory. His honor is at stake in maintaining his people.

And just as obedience was expected of the Israelites, it is also expected of the church of Christ. We have looked at this a number of times already. Being in Christ does not mean that obedience is no longer required or that it is optional. The exact opposite is the case (Rom. 6:1–14). Being in Christ means an ever deepening of one's *joyously* obedient relationship with him. In fact, it is *only* God's people to whom the commands are given, for they alone are able to obey.

But what of the blessings for obedience and punishments for disobedience? We have seen a hint of what is to come in Exodus 23 already. The punishment of "no forgiveness" is never fully carried out in the lives of the Israelites. Neither is it carried out in the life of the church. This is because Christ himself shouldered on the cross the *full* burden of God's punishment. It is not that the punishments of the Old Testament are less real to us. Rather, they are more graphic and horrible for Christ who, like the angel, guides us and guards us along the journey. The retribution promised in the Old Testament for disobedience is fully born by Christ alone, the only truly obedient one.

Likewise, the blessings of the Old Testament must also be seen in light of the work of Christ. We partake in the benefits of Christ's obedience and therefore are the beneficiaries of far greater blessing than that envisioned in the Old Testament. We experience more fully the reality to which the Old Testament blessings pointed. Living on this side of the resurrection, we actually see the new day dawning, the arrival of the kingdom of God, the return to the splendor of the Garden of Eden, a reality that was only hinted at in the Old Testament.

The land of God. We noted above that the borders of the land given in Exodus 23:31 are ideal borders. The first such description is in Genesis 15:18, where Abraham is promised the land "from the river of Egypt to the great river, the Euphrates." The "river of Egypt" is not actually in Egypt, but is typically identified as Wadi el-Arish, which forms the southwestern border of Israel. The Euphrates, however, is the northern border. When did Israel's kingdom extend this far north?

According to 1 Kings 4:21 (see also 2 Chron. 9:26), it was during Solomon's reign that the kingdom reached this far north. This seems to have been short-lived, however. More typically, Israel's northern border is said to be Lebo Hamath, a town along the Orontes River, well south of the Euphrates.[7] For example, as early as 1 Kings 8:65, we read that *all* Israel, "from Lebo Hamath to the Wadi of Egypt" (el-Arish), came to the festival to dedicate the temple. These two geographic locations indicate that the entire kingdom in principle came to the festival. But why do we not read "from the Euphrates to the Wadi of Egypt," especially since these are the borders of the land given only four chapters earlier?

Far from being a careless error on the part of the writer, the descriptions of the borders of the land reflect the political realities during Solomon's day. Note 1 Kings 11:23–25, which refers to the opposition of Rezon king of Aram against Solomon. Rezon ruled from Damascus, the capital of Aram, and remained a constant thorn in Solomon's side throughout his reign. So, although in one sense Solomon's kingdom extended far north, his control over that area was not absolute. In fact, it is difficult to determine in what way Solomon "reigned" over the area extending to the Euphrates when from early on in his reign, even back to David's kingship, Damascus actively opposed Israel (see 2 Sam. 8:6; 10:6–7). Also, the fact that Jeroboam II, who reigned over the northern kingdom from 793–753 B.C., "restored the boundaries of Israel from Lebo Hamath to the Sea of the Arabah" (i.e., Dead Sea; 2 Kings 14:25) suggests that Lebo Hamath represented the northernmost "reasonable" boundary of Israel.

---

7. See Num. 13:21; 34:8; Josh. 13:5; 2 Kings 14:25; Ezek. 47:15; 48:1; Amos 6:14.

Another problem is the fact that 1 Kings 4:21, although referring to the land of Aram up to the Euphrates, merely implies Solomon's *rule* over this area. Exodus 23:31 makes clear that the inhabitants of that land would be handed over to the Israelites and driven out. Perhaps this verse should not be taken literally, and the situation of 1 Kings 4:21 can be considered the fulfillment of this divine word. Nevertheless, when we compare these two passages, it does seem as if the ideal of Exodus has not yet been realized, even in 1 Kings 4:21, which itself seems to be an idealized expression of a more tumultuous political situation.

But to come to grips with the meaning of the borders of the land as given in Exodus 23:31, we will have to look beyond the political realities of either Moses' or Solomon's day. In my opinion, it seems that the ideal borders of Israel were never truly realized.[8] At best during the reigns of Solomon and the political renaissance under Jeroboam II do we briefly see these borders realized in principle, but not in detail. Rather than concluding, as some might, that God's plan was thwarted or that an overzealous Judahite writer wanted to present the reign of Solomon in the best possible light, I suggest that this "partial" realization of these borders serves a theological purpose. It forces the readers, both ancient and modern, to look beyond mere geography to something more significant. Dissatisfaction with how the plan *seems* to be unfolding nudges one to reevaluate the entire context in which the fulfillment ought to be expected.

Ultimately, God is not interested in merely one patch of land in the ancient Near East—regardless of whether that land extends to the Euphrates or not! The whole world belongs to him, and it is God's desire that his rule be extended to its four corners. The ideal borders of Israel, which were never attained, are a microcosm of the whole earth. Israel's borders never extend to the Euphrates, because these expansive boundaries represent theologically the ultimate boundaries with which God is concerned.

Conquest of the "land," meaning the earth, must wait for a future time and a future king. In other words, the kingdom of Israel, which in the Old Testament was ruled by a king and was eventually expected to extend in the manner described in 23:31, is fulfilled in the coming of Christ, the true king, to whom the whole world was given as his kingdom (Matt. 28:18; 1 Cor. 15:27; Eph. 1:21–22; Phil. 2:9–10). The fact that the true king has come and now rules the whole world does not mean that the border promises of the Old Testament have somehow been forgotten. What it does mean is that that which was *not* fulfilled in the Old Testament has now been fulfilled to a far greater degree at the death and resurrection of Christ.

---

8. Here I am in agreement with Sarna (*Exodus*, 149). Cassuto says that the ideal was attained during David's reign, but without explanation (*Commentary on Exodus*, 309).

Few Old Testament saints would quibble, I suspect, that Christ's rule over the whole world did not do justice to the less expansive promises given in the Old Testament. It is not the case that the New Testament fulfillment of the land is "merely" spiritual, as if the physical promises of the Old Testament are somehow more real than spiritual realities, but that the New Testament spiritual realities fulfill the Old Testament and then some.

We must take this one step further. Ultimately, God's intention is not just to enthrone King Jesus over the whole world, but over the world to come. The ideal borders of Canaan extend beyond this world into the next. As we have seen elsewhere, this is what the new Jerusalem and the new heaven and earth represent in the book of Revelation. The new world order has come. It is a re-creation of the Garden of Eden itself. It is to this ultimate reality that the land promises, which always seemed to be frustrated in the Old Testament, pointed.

CHRIST, OUR ANGEL. The "angel" is still with God's people. We do not look back at the abiding presence of the angel with the Israelites and heave a sigh of resignation for bygone days. The angel is more deeply felt now than ever before.

The spirit of the risen Christ, the Holy Spirit, is always with us. This is Jesus' final statement to his disciples at the end of Matthew's Gospel: "And surely I am with you always, to the very end of the age" (Matt. 28:20). Christ does now what the angel did for the Israelites. He is truly with us at every step in our journey. He was there at our redemption, not with arms folded waiting to see if we would make the right choice, but calling us into his presence. And having called us, he now walks ahead of us to guard us and guide us home. Such personal application of the angel is already hinted at in the Old Testament.

> The angel of the LORD encamps around those who fear him,
>   and he delivers them. (Ps. 34:7)

> May they [the psalmist's enemies] be like chaff before the wind,
>   with the angel of the LORD driving them away;
> may their path be dark and slippery,
>   with the angel of the LORD pursuing them. (Ps. 35:5–6)

The image offered to us in these passages is not one of "God is my copilot." The angel of the LORD is around his people, driving the enemy away and pursuing them. Christ is not our copilot. Perhaps it is unfair to take this popular image too literally, but taken in its least favorable light, a copilot is someone who helps the main pilot fly the plane. Is this what we mean, that Jesus helps us out while we do the main navigating? If we wish to keep this image, perhaps we could change it. We are *his* copilots. He is the one driving the ship. True, we sit to one side and work the controls, but we do so at his direction. And, as any copilot knows, it is the pilot who is ultimately in charge and responsible for what happens.

Christ is my pilot. Can there be anyone better to whom to entrust our lives? Christ is the guiding and guarding angel to those who know him, and by his presence we are also in God's presence. He is powerful, capable, and compassionate toward them. He is wise, wonderful, and in control—this despite appearances to the contrary.

A number of times I have bumped into a weak and unsatisfying image of God. Many of us remember several years ago the Pan Am flight that blew up in the sky over Scotland. National mourning followed. Many of those who died so tragically in that flight had been college students at Syracuse University taking a holiday trip, which the university offered yearly. (One of my best friends from high school had been on the very flight a couple of years earlier.) After the memorial service for the students, a chaplain was interviewed on the evening news and was asked what he told the grieving families. He said that the most important thing he could tell them was that "God is mourning with you."

Now, this could mean one of two things: either that God is compassionate and caring, or that we are all—God included—caught in this topsy-turvy world of chaos, where bad things happen to good people, and that God is as helpless as the rest of us.[9] Hence, the best he can do is mourn with us, a sort of elderly uncle sharing our pain.

This is not the type of thinking that will change the world. Rather, it is little more than nonsense touted by people who have learned to hold the power of God at bay. Christ is not a weak, helpless bystander. He is the angel, God in the pillar of cloud, the presence of God seated above the ark. He has been raised from the dead and has therefore conquered death. I cannot claim to understand how Christ "reacts" to tragedies (though cf. John 11:35), but we do know that he conquered death. And if this is so, can we really say that he responds to death the way we do? Death, to be sure, is the hated enemy, but Christ conquered death.

To know that Christ is our angel is a source of ever-deepening comfort to the Christian. To understand truly what that means is the goal of our life-

---

9. This is essentially the thesis of Rabbi Harold Kushner's famous book, *When Bad Things Happen to Good People* (New York: Avon, 1983). I do not mean to belittle the personal tragedy that motivated Rabbi Kushner to pen his thoughts (death of his son), but there is little if anything of value that I have found in this book.

long journey of faith. In Exodus, the angel speaks to the Israelites, which, as we have seen, means that the angel is a concrete manifestation of God's presence with his people. Christ speaks to us as well, not as an angel or as seated on the ark in the temple. The Holy Spirit is the ultimate manifestation of God's indwelling presence with his people. Too often, even in evangelical theology, we do not know what to do with the Holy Spirit. He does not always get the press he deserves. But it is his role to maintain that tie we have with God. He manifests God to us, not by speaking to us from the temple, but by taking up residence himself in each and every one of us, the people of God, whom Paul refers to as his "temple" (1 Cor. 3:17; 6:19).

If we carry through this analogy with Exodus—that Christ is our angel and by the Holy Spirit he speaks to us—we come up to the issue of obedience. As the Israelites were expected to obey the angel, so we are to be fully obedient to Christ. But what about the blessings for obedience and the punishments for disobedience. Do such things apply to us today?

On the one hand, I am tempted to say "no." Christ bore God's full punishment for us on the cross, so we should say that the punishments of the Old Testament are no longer our concern. Through Christ's obedience, our (actually Adam's) disobedience is undone and forgotten. The blessings, however, are ours, since we benefit from Christ's obedience.

Yet this perspective does not do justice to the analogy. The command to obey the angel was given to a people already redeemed. It is in their redeemed state that they are still expected to obey the angel or suffer the consequences. Is this something we today should take to heart as well? Scripturally speaking, I think we do.

The New Testament is full of admonitions to Christians to live their lives in the light of the resurrection. It is more than just a matter of "you really ought to." We have no choice; obedience is required. In fact, obedience is the actual demonstration to each other and to the world that we are redeemed people. A difficult passage that has long figured into this discussion is Hebrews 6:4–6, a passage that must be taken with utmost seriousness:

> It is impossible for those who have once been enlightened, who have tasted the heavenly gift, who have shared in the Holy Spirit, who have tasted the goodness of the word of God and the powers of the coming age, if they fall away, to be brought back to repentance, because to their loss they are crucifying the Son of God all over again and subjecting him to public disgrace.

I do not wish to enter into the debate of whether a Christian can lose his or her salvation, but I will say that this passage should be unsettling to any Christian who has been taught to submit to Scripture. It seems to assume that falling away is a real option for those who have "tasted the goodness of the word of God."[10]

This passage should not be dismissed lightly as an aberration of Scripture. We should understand it in a sense similar to the warning we have seen in Exodus. When a responsible Christian sees someone else who has made a credible profession of faith, but who to all appearances acts in a way that is not at all in keeping with that profession, he or she cannot very well say: "Remember that God is with you no matter what. Sure, you're sinning—and you ought to stop—but God will not let go of you, so not to worry." This is not how the "rhetoric of warning" works. Rather, you corner such people, pin them up against the wall (figuratively speaking), and tell them that they are within a hair's width of falling into Satan's hands. You (again, figuratively speaking) slap them silly, dunk their heads in ice water, and scream in their ear.

Is all this to say that there is *no* forgiveness for Christians? In keeping with the Exodus analogy, my answer to this is "no." There is never a point of no return for those who are in Christ. But the word of forgiveness can only be planted in a sinner's heart when repentance has first been sown. The human heart is not at all times equally prepared to hear the same divine message. There is a season in which understanding and forgiveness are appropriate; at other times the message of dire warning is what is needed. I can only suggest that those to whom the book of Hebrews was written were, for some reason, in the latter category. Like all of the New Testament letters, this too is written from a "pastoral" point of view. It is not an abstract theological treatise, but a letter written by someone of spiritual authority to a people he knows well and who knows what it is they need to hear. We are left, as is the case so often in Scripture, with a paradox: The warning of Hebrews 6 is real, but grace will abound all the more.

"Great is the LORD—even beyond the borders of Israel!" (Mal. 1:5). It is perhaps one of the great turnarounds as we go from the Old Testament to the New Testament. The people for whom God is zealous to give a plot of earth in the ancient Near East are commanded to leave it and go to the ends of the earth. The reason for this turnaround is what we have discussed in the previous section. Insofar as the promises are never truly fulfilled, the ultimate fulfillment of these promises must take another form.

To be more accurate, it is not the case that there is a turnaround from the Old Testament to the New. Rather, the Spirit shows us that we should have a different set of expectations. It is not that the promise of land has been aban-

---

10. I am wholly unconvinced by any who argue that the person in view is not actually a Christian but merely acts like one. To taste the heavenly gift, share in the Holy Spirit, taste the goodness of the word and the age to come are things that can only be said of Christians.

doned, but the opposite has happened: The land now includes the whole world, the present one and the one to come. It is hard to think of a more striking way of showing that the gospel of Christ works. The expectation of the Old Testament saints has been exceeded.

This is why it is wrong to think of any land, nation, or political system as being closer to God than another. God is not an American. America is not—nor has it ever been—a "Christian" nation. The good news of the gospel is that no one nation can reserve this title. The Spirit of God is not bound by such things, nor has it been so bound since the coming of Christ. The whole world belongs to God, and he will redeem all of it. It is now the Christian's obligation to go *out* into that world and play his or her role in that redemptive process, by being "Christ's ambassadors" (2 Cor. 5:20), by proclaiming the message of the king. If any analogy is to be drawn between national Israel and today it is not with America but with the church. The church is the new Israel, ruled by the king of God's choosing, Christ.

There is, therefore, no privileged country, nor are there privileged people. Rather, all Christians, regardless of where they are, are "between lands." Every Christian is a citizen in God's world, the one he has redeemed through Christ. Christ has been raised and is enthroned now over all creation (Heb. 2:9). Nevertheless, we await a future time when that spiritual reality will fully invade the world and transform it forever. Every Christian is home and at the same time far from it. Every nation is a "Christian nation," but none has special status or pedigree.

As we journey through our lives as Christians, we must grasp that Christ, our guiding angel, has begun a process whereby we will one day enter the true Promised Land, the one spoken of in the closing chapters of Revelation. In fact, our guiding angel has already entered and prepares a way for us (John 14:2–4). Like the angel of Exodus, he has gone ahead of us. With Christ's victory over death, this process began its unrelenting journey toward the true Canaan. We who are in Christ share in that blessing now even as we will more fully in the world to come.

Exodus 24:1–18

Then he said to Moses, "Come up to the LORD, you and Aaron, Nadab and Abihu, and seventy of the elders of Israel. You are to worship at a distance, ²but Moses alone is to approach the LORD; the others must not come near. And the people may not come up with him."

³When Moses went and told the people all the LORD's words and laws, they responded with one voice, "Everything the LORD has said we will do." ⁴Moses then wrote down everything the LORD had said.

He got up early the next morning and built an altar at the foot of the mountain and set up twelve stone pillars representing the twelve tribes of Israel. ⁵Then he sent young Israelite men, and they offered burnt offerings and sacrificed young bulls as fellowship offerings to the LORD. ⁶Moses took half of the blood and put it in bowls, and the other half he sprinkled on the altar. ⁷Then he took the Book of the Covenant and read it to the people. They responded, "We will do everything the LORD has said; we will obey."

⁸Moses then took the blood, sprinkled it on the people and said, "This is the blood of the covenant that the LORD has made with you in accordance with all these words."

⁹Moses and Aaron, Nadab and Abihu, and the seventy elders of Israel went up ¹⁰and saw the God of Israel. Under his feet was something like a pavement made of sapphire, clear as the sky itself. ¹¹But God did not raise his hand against these leaders of the Israelites; they saw God, and they ate and drank.

¹²The LORD said to Moses, "Come up to me on the mountain and stay here, and I will give you the tablets of stone, with the law and commands I have written for their instruction."

¹³Then Moses set out with Joshua his aide, and Moses went up on the mountain of God. ¹⁴He said to the elders, "Wait here for us until we come back to you. Aaron and Hur are with you, and anyone involved in a dispute can go to them."

¹⁵When Moses went up on the mountain, the cloud covered it, ¹⁶and the glory of the LORD settled on Mount Sinai. For six days the cloud covered the mountain, and on the seventh day the LORD called to Moses from within the cloud.

[17]To the Israelites the glory of the LORD looked like a consuming fire on top of the mountain. [18]Then Moses entered the cloud as he went on up the mountain. And he stayed on the mountain forty days and forty nights.

Original Meaning

AS THE LAST chapter before the section that deals mainly with the building of the tabernacle (chs. 25–40), Exodus 24 is a transitionary chapter of sorts.[1] It revisits a number of things we have seen throughout the book. The covenant, whose stipulations have been recorded in 20:22–23:19, is confirmed through worship, sacrifice, personal dedication, and the writing of the law. But this chapter also looks ahead. As it opens, Moses is called to ascend the mountain yet another time (24:1). He does so in verses 13–18, and during this time on Mount Sinai he receives instructions concerning a number of things that will not only dominate the concluding chapters of Exodus, but the Pentateuch and much of the Old Testament: the building of the tabernacle, the priesthood, and Sabbath regulations. Also during this visit the famous golden calf incident takes place (ch. 32).

Verses 1–2 set the tone for the chapter as a whole. Moses, Aaron, his two oldest sons (Nadab and Abihu), and the seventy elders are to ascend the mountain. At least one of the reasons for doing so is "to worship" (the other being the giving of the tablets, v. 12). It is Israel's presence at the mountain and their worshipful response that drives much of the context of this chapter.

The action depicted here echoes 19:12–24, which contains the rather complicated set of instructions regarding who may and may not approach the mountain and ascend it. The present verses, however, are clear as to who is permitted to do so. Aaron and his two oldest sons are to come up with Moses, as are the seventy elders.

Immediately a few questions come to mind. To whom is God talking here? Verse 1 begins by telling us that he spoke to Moses, and the speech begins this way: *"you and Aaron."* The end of verse 1 and the beginning of verse 2, however, implies that God is not speaking to Moses: *"You* are to worship at a distance, but *Moses* alone is to approach the LORD." The "you" addressed in this sentence is certainly not Moses, but the others, those not permitted further up (the Hebrew "you" is plural). It seems that, although not made explicit, these words are the message that Moses is to bring to the people so they can all hear. God is speaking to the people about who will have access to the mountain.

---

1. Fretheim refers to it as a "swing" chapter (*Exodus*, 255).

Mention of the names Nadab and Abihu should not be totally unexpected. They have already been mentioned in the genealogy of chapter 6 (6:23), though we have not heard anything about them since. Now the reason for earlier specifying Aaron and his sons becomes clearer. These are the priests of God who will be permitted to step closer than their countrymen. What was anticipated in chapter 6 is taking clearer shape in chapter 24.

Less clear is where the seventy elders came from. They may well be the product of Jethro's advice in 18:17—23, although we must remember that the number "seventy" is not mentioned there. Hence, the specificity with which these elders are numbered is unexpected. Nevertheless, it is no more unexpected than, for example, the sudden mention of Joshua and Hur in 17:9—10. I see no reason to attribute this situation to alternate "traditions" (one mentioning seventy elders, the other not specifying the number), as some are tempted to do. This is simply another case of what we have seen throughout the book. The Exodus story was well known to the original audience of the book. This was not the first time they were hearing about it, so not all the gaps needed to be filled in for them.

We should also pause here to remind ourselves of the significance of the partitioning of the mountain. As we have noted earlier, the fact that fewer and fewer people are granted access to Mount Sinai the closer we get to the top is reflected in the construction of the tabernacle (and later the temple). That is, the tabernacle was built with Mount Sinai as a pattern. Without forcing the matter too much, something along the lines of a three-part division seems to be at work in verses 1—2. Moses alone is permitted to go up to "approach the LORD." The priests and elders may come up, but they have to worship at a distance. The people may not come up at all (cf. 19:12). These two verses, therefore, are a fitting opening to the chapter that will lead us to the final main section of the book, the building of the tabernacle.

We might now expect some indication that Moses and the others actually do what God tells them to do in verses 1—2. To read about this, however, we must wait for verse 9. Verses 3—8 "intervene"[2] to fill us in on the action at the foot of the mountain.

Verse 3 clearly implies that Moses, after receiving the instructions of verses 1—2, makes his way down the mountain to tell the people what God has told him, or as the text puts it, "all the LORD's words and laws." Likely "words" and "laws" are a shorthand reference to the Ten Commandments

---

2. Unfortunately, a number of commentators conclude, on the basis that vv. 3—8 are a "break in the action," that they are a clumsy intrusion on what would otherwise be a "coherent" narrative. Such subjective judgments do little to further our understanding of this passage, either in terms of its present form or any hypothetical earlier stage. My use of the word "intervene" is not intended to suggest such a state of affairs.

and the Book of the Covenant: "Words" (*dᵉbarim*) introduces the Ten Commandments in 20:1 and "laws" (*mišpaṭim*) introduces the Book of the Covenant in 21:1. It seems, therefore, that Moses here repeats verbatim the content of these legal corpora. Now for a second time (see 19:8, see comments), the people respond in almost the exact same words of utter enthusiasm as before: "Everything the LORD has said we will do."[3] This enthusiasm is short-lived, as the ensuing chapters will demonstrate.

According to verse 4 Moses wrote down "everything the LORD had said." This can be none other than the contents of the entire previous scene, that is, the Ten Commandments and the Book of the Covenant. This is the second time in Exodus that Moses is said to write (cf. 17:14; 34:28). It also seems that this is what is referred to as the "Book of the Covenant" (20:22–23:19), although the term itself is not introduced until verse 7.

While we are on the subject of writing, we should jump down to verse 12. It is not clear how to square Moses' writing activity in verses 4 and 7 with verse 12, which says that God is the one who will write the "laws and commands" on "tablets of stone." In fact, this seems to be one of the very reasons for which Moses is called up the mountain (the other reason being to receive the instructions for the tabernacle). Although verse 12 is not explicit, the context strongly suggests that the contents of this writing are the Ten Commandments and the Book of the Covenant. Are we to presume that Moses first wrote these things down and later received a divinely written copy for perpetuity? No. Rather, this is another of several ambiguities we have encountered in our reading of Exodus.

In fact, it appears as if the writer intentionally presents the readers with this ambiguity in order to underscore Moses' "divine" activity, something we have seen throughout Exodus. It is both Moses and Yahweh who bring Israel out of Egypt. It is both who divide the sea. Here, it is both who write—the same thing. If anything, rather than ferreting out what precisely Moses or God wrote, it is enough to see in Moses' act of writing his status and authority as Israel's leader.

After recording God's words to him, Moses builds an altar (v. 4). This does not seem to be in response to a specific command of God, unless we look back to 20:24–26. That altar, however, had specific instructions (made of earth and uncut stone), none of which is present in 24:4. Moreover, what we do find in 24:4, twelve pillars representing the twelve tribes, is not mentioned in 20:24–26. Probably no connection should be made between these two passages.

There is, however, some conceptual overlap between the altar built here and the one built in 17:15. For one thing, these are the only two altars Moses

---

3. Ex. 19:8 and 24:3 have only minor differences in the Hebrew text.

is said to build in Exodus. Further, in both passages, building an altar is preceded by Moses' writing, and both look ahead to what Israel will later experience. The battle with the Amalekites in chapter 17, as we have seen, is a preview of the conquest battles. The altar of chapter 24, complete with directions to offer sacrifices on it (vv. 5–8), anticipates the more developed sacrificial system of the following chapters. Instructions for building this more "permanent" altar are given in 27:1–8 (see also 38:1–7).[4]

Upon this altar are to be offered burnt offerings and fellowship offerings. Burnt offerings (cf. 10:25; 18:12) are presumably a well-known practice to the Israelites and therefore need no elaboration in this context. More important, burnt and fellowship offerings are mentioned together in 20:24, where the altar of earth and uncut stone is mentioned. Mention of these two types of offerings in 24:5 not only hearkens back to 20:24, but anticipates what is to come. The following chapters frequently mention burnt offerings in conjunction with the tabernacle (29:18, 25, 42; 30:9; 40:29). Fellowship offerings are also mentioned (29:28). Interestingly, the only other passage in Exodus that mentions *both* in the same verse is 32:6, the golden calf episode, a factor that helps highlight the seriousness of that transgression.

The nature of these burnt and fellowship offerings is significant. Burnt offerings are typically made for atonement for sin and consecration, that is, devotion and commitment to God. Fellowship offerings celebrate fellowship with God. The nature of these two offerings parallels how the blood of the sacrifices was used. One half was sprinkled on the altar, while the other half was put in bowls (v. 6) and was sprinkled on the people (v. 8). The former represents sin atonement (burnt offerings), the latter fellowship.

The sequence is as follow. Moses sprinkles the altar, thus symbolizing Israel's atonement from sin. Next, the Book of the Covenant is read, to which the people respond again with enthusiastic assent (v. 7). Then the blood is sprinkled on the people with these words: "This is the blood of the covenant that the LORD has made with you in accordance with all these words." This blood sprinkled on the people indicates that the fellowship between them and God has just been confirmed. That is why it is called the "blood of the covenant."

We should note also that this covenant is essentially not a matter of a mutual agreement or pact made between God and the Israelites. It is, as we read, "the covenant that the LORD has made with you." It is by his initiative. He is the instigator. What the Israelites are to do is to accept and agree to live by the terms of the covenant that God and God alone has stipulated—these

---

4. Two other altars are mentioned in Exodus. The altar in the golden calf episode (ch. 32) is clearly intended as a contrast to the proper altar God commanded to be built. The altar of incense (30:1–10) is not an altar for sacrifice.

stipulations being the "Book of the Covenant." Israel's choice was never between making a covenant either with other gods or with Yahweh, but between making a covenant with other gods (23:32) or *accepting* the covenant Yahweh graciously, mercifully, lovingly made with them.

Only after this confirmation of the covenant can we proceed to the next scene, a return to what was introduced in verses 1–2: Moses, Aaron and his sons, and the elders worship on the mountain. More to the point, we are told they "went up and saw the God of Israel" (vv. 9–10). At first glance, it is difficult to know what this means precisely, especially since 33:20 seems to say the exact opposite: "No one may see me and live." Moreover, 24:1–2 says that Moses alone is to approach God. Not only does it say nothing about seeing God, it says specifically that the others are to "worship at a distance."

This passage creates some tension, to be sure. We must remember, however, that it is a tension that the passage itself recognizes. This is the significance of verse 11, where the writer goes out of his way to add that those who saw God did *not* die. In other words, for the biblical writer, the fact that they saw God but did not die is worthy of special comment. Thus, it seems that 24:10 and 33:20 are both based on the same premise that seeing God is something that ought to have severe ramifications.

So why are Moses and Israel's leaders permitted to see God at this time? This must be understood in the broader context of the passage. The Israelites are at a crucial point in their redemptive journey. The covenant stipulations have just been given and the covenant confirmed by the sprinkling of blood. By showing himself to the leaders, God is giving them an added dose of his presence to solemnize what has just happened and to prepare them for what is to come. Israel's leaders receive a vivid experience to undergird their own status as figures of authority.

What, then, does it mean to see God? The description given in verses 10–11 does not seem to be complete. In fact, this description is not so much of seeing God but only of seeing his feet and what lies under them! But perhaps this is precisely the point. The leaders do not actually see God in any full sense. In this case, "[seeing] the God of Israel" probably means that they see him in part. Such an understanding removes the notion of contradiction between this passage and 33:20, the latter having to do with seeing God's glory. Thus, 24:10 describes the content of their vision—they see God's feet and the "pavement" below. When meeting the heavenly King, their gaze does not rise higher than his feet.

But even this low view of God is startling: "Under his feet was something like a pavement made of sapphire, clear as the sky itself." Even this vision of God's feet and the ground under his feet is too much for words. The best the writer can do is to say it is *"something like* a pavement." This pavement is described as sapphire, the gem also known as lapis lazuli. This is a striking gem of opaque blue, which was used for a variety of decorative purposes in the ancient Near East. It is no doubt because of its beauty and blue color that it is used to describe not only the clear-as-sky pavement in 24:10 but also the throne of God in Ezekiel 1:26 and 10:1. God resides in the heavens, so that which is under and around him is blue.

In response to this sight, the company on the mountain eat and drink (v. 11). This meal is probably not a common intake of food, nor is it merely a descriptive way of indicating that they survive the ordeal.[5] It is, rather, a "covenant" meal. In the world of the Old Testament, a meal often served to solemnize and ratify an agreement between two parties (cf. 18:12, when Jethro meets Moses and the Israelites in the desert). In fact, a meal is already in view in the fellowship offering mentioned in 24:5. The burnt offerings are "consumed" by God (figuratively speaking, of course!), but the fellowship offering is one in which the people participate. According to 29:32, eating is also something priests do in God's presence. Their eating in God's presence in chapter 24 is, therefore, another hint of what is to come. Whether Moses and the others on the mountain celebrated the fellowship offering in verse 5 is not stated (it refers to the people as a whole), but they certainly eat and drink on the mountain.

After the meal it is time for Moses to leave the others behind and proceed up the mountain (vv. 12–18). The purpose for the ascent is twofold: to receive the stone tablets and to receive the instructions for the building of the tabernacle. These two things represent what is central to the theology of Exodus and the Old Testament as a whole: law and worship. These things are important enough to warrant a private meeting between God and his chosen redeemer.

Apparently, Joshua is allowed to come part of the way, although just how far is not mentioned. His sudden appearance and surprisingly intimate access to God's presence are nevertheless consistent in light of what we know from his role in leading Israel after the death of Moses. The last time Joshua was mentioned—also somewhat abruptly—is 17:9, and in both Hur is also mentioned. This makes the connection between chapters 17 and 24, which we have observed above with respect to the altar, more explicit.

The mention of Joshua and Hur in chapter 24 has a similar function to that of chapter 17. They both preview things to come. Joshua will later be instrumental in the Conquest, of which the battle with the Amalekites in

---

5. In this I am in agreement with Sarna (*Exodus*, 153). I am not sure whether this scene is meant to be contrasted with the fear of the people in 20:18–21, as Janzen suggests (*Exodus*, 184–88).

chapter 17 is itself a preview. Hur is apparently an older man and therefore likely the object of some respect. His old age is clearly implied in light of 31:2, where it is said that he is the grandfather of Bezalel, who, along with Oholiab, is one of the main builders of the tabernacle. Perhaps one of the purposes for mentioning Hur in this context is to provide another connection to the tabernacle section that follows.

While Moses is meeting with God on Sinai, Aaron and Hur are in charge of settling disputes. This is in striking contrast to what we see later in chapter 32. Although Hur is not mentioned there, we see Aaron not only *not* settling disputes but actually adding to controversy by his role in making an idol. As Moses ascends the mountain, he has left things in what he no doubt thinks are trustworthy hands: his older brother Aaron, whom God appointed as his partner, and Hur, a respected member of the community. The anger he shows later is an appropriate response (32:19–20).

As Moses goes further up the mountain (vv. 15–18), he sees the cloud covering it for six days until God calls to him on the seventh day. At this point he enters the cloud and continues his journey upward. He stays on the mountain forty days and nights and does not come down until the instructions for the tabernacle have been given (32:7, 15).

God's presence on the mountain is represented as cloud and fire, both of which we have seen on several occasions already. The cloud and fire were present at Israel's journey out of Egypt. In 16:10, the Israelites caught another glimpse of God in the cloud. It was also in a cloud that the Israelites first met God on Mount Sinai (19:9, 16). Fire represented God's presence not only in Exodus 14 but as far back as Moses' initial encounter with God on Mount Sinai (ch. 3).

The significance of the cloud in chapter 24 is not simply another indication of God's presence with Moses, although it is certainly that as well. It is rather another element in the narrative that sets the stage for what is to come. As we have noted before (ch. 19), there is a clear connection between Mount Sinai and the tabernacle. Both are where God's glory resides in the form of a cloud. According to 24:16, the glory of Yahweh "settles" on the mountain. The Hebrew verb is *šakan*, which is the verbal form of the noun *miškan*, which means "tabernacle" (see 25:9). The cloud's settling on the mountain thus anticipates the settling of the cloud over the tabernacle (see esp. 40:34–38).

Sinai is not a reflection of the tabernacle but the other way around. God meets with his people at Mount Sinai, and the tabernacle is a way of making that presence "portable." God's glory rests on the tabernacle as it does on Mount Sinai. This is why the tabernacle is to be built according to the divine *pattern*, according to what is given Moses *on the mountain* (25:9, 40).

Regarding Moses' forty days and forty nights on the mountain (24:18), it is not clear whether the author intends us to take this number literally. Sarna points out the frequent symbolic use of the number forty,[6] but this does not necessarily imply that all uses of this number are symbolic. The reiteration of the forty-day stay in 34:28 may suggest that the number is to be taken literally. The symbolic use of forty is more likely in the case of years, as can be seen, for example, in the recurring reference to forty years of peace in Judges (Judg. 3:11; 5:31; 8:28). During his stay on Mount Sinai Moses receives the instructions for building the tabernacle, and it is to this important section of the book that we will turn in the next unit of this commentary.

IN THIS SECTION we will focus on two important theological themes: the confirmation of the covenant through eating and the shedding of blood, and the matter of seeing God.

Confirming the covenant. The eating of a meal together in order to solidify an agreement of some sort is a known custom in the ancient Near East. For example, the treaty that Abimelech, king of the Philistines, proposed to Isaac was sealed with a meal, thus signifying there would be peace between them (Gen. 26:26–31). Jacob and Laban observed the same custom and departed in peace although there had been revenge and death on Laban's mind just the day before (Gen. 31, esp. v. 54).

Both Exodus 18:12 and 24:11 differ somewhat from these other examples, however, for the meals mentioned there are held in God's presence. The meal in 24:11, in other words, signifies a contractual agreement between the two parties in question. I do not mean to imply that they are two equal parties who approach the relationship on equal footing. After all, the covenant is entirely by God's initiation. Nevertheless, it is the confirmation of this covenantal relationship between these two parties—Israel and her God—that is the topic of this narrative.

The prophet Isaiah looks forward to a time when the God of Israel will hold another meal, this time inviting the people of the nations to enjoy his presence (see Isa. 25:6–8):

> On this mountain the LORD Almighty will prepare
>   a feast of rich food for all peoples,
> a banquet of aged wine—
>   the best of meats and the finest of wines.
> On this mountain he will destroy

---

6. Sarna, *Exodus*, 155.

> the shroud that enfolds all peoples,
> the sheet that covers all nations;
>   he will swallow up death forever.
> The Sovereign LORD will wipe away the tears
>   from all faces;
> he will remove the disgrace of his people
>   from all the earth.
>   The LORD has spoken.

This, as is typical of much of the Old Testament, is heightened, symbolic language, meant to describe a truly wonderful state of affairs. But whether or not the prophet's description of a meal on a mountain (Mount Zion, i.e., Jerusalem) is literal or figurative, the point is still the same: God intends to extend his relationship with his chosen people, Israel, to include those outside of Israel, that is, all peoples and all nations. The fact that the people of the world will partake in a great feast in God's presence, on his holy mountain, is reminiscent of what we see in Exodus 24:11. We can even say that the pattern we see in Exodus is expanded in Isaiah to bring the full scope of God's redemptive work into clearer focus.

The reflexes of this theme in the New Testament are apparent. In Matthew 8:11, for example, Jesus alludes to an "eschatological" feast such as what we see in Isaiah 25:6–8: "I say to you that many will come from the east and the west, and will take their places at the feast with Abraham, Isaac and Jacob in the kingdom of heaven." This is clearly a feast in which the peoples of the world will partake, even at the expense of the faithless "subjects of the kingdom," who will be excluded. This is also the proper theological perspective from which to view the feeding of the five thousand in John 6:2–4. The fact that Jesus went up a *mountain* to hold a *feast*, and while *looking up* sees a *great crowd* coming toward him is a clear echo of the language used by Isaiah to describe the eschatological meal.[7]

This line of reasoning brings us to the final reference to the eschatological meal in the Bible (Rev. 19:9)—the "wedding supper of the Lamb" (cf. also v. 7), an image that combines the theme of eating with that of marriage. This, in other words, is a truly covenantal meal, and the intensity of the covenant between God (i.e., Christ, the Lamb) and his people is amply communicated by employing the wedding image. Partaking of a meal in God's presence is an intimate and friendly image used in Scripture to describe the bond between God and his people.

---

7. The italicized words indicate the conceptual overlap between John 6:2–4 and Isaiah 25:6–8. Plastaras has convincingly demonstrated this connection, and I follow him in this regard (*The God of Exodus*, 233). Plastaras also appeals to Isa. 60:4.

It is fruitful in this context to revisit the connection between the Passover and the Lord's Supper (see the Bridging Contexts section of 11:1–13:16). Although these are central and pivotal events in their own right, they are also striking examples of a covenant meal such as what we see in 24:11. Both meals occur at the brink of a climactic redemptive event, the Exodus of the Israelites from Egypt and the death and resurrection of Christ. They also occur in intimate settings, with the people of God grouped together apart from the world in preparation for what is about to transpire.

We have already seen the explicit connection Luke makes between the Passover and the Lord's Supper—the latter being the climactic expression of the former (Luke 22:15). In addition, for Luke the Lord's Supper has a decidedly eschatological significance. It is the last meal shared between Christ and his people "until it finds fulfillment in the kingdom of God" (22:16; cf. v. 18). The coming eschatological meal will be the ultimate confirmation of the covenant between God and his people. The Lord's Supper is thus both a continuation of this Old Testament theme (seen most graphically in the Passover) and the first installment of the final meal at Christ's return.

An element essential to both the Passover and the Lord's Supper, and one that is also prominent in Exodus 24, is the shedding of blood. In the Passover, the lamb is to be slaughtered and the blood put on the top and sides of the doorframes (12:22). The Lord's Supper, of course, is followed by the sacrifice of the Lamb of God, whose blood (represented by the wine) also "covered" the sins of the people. The sprinkling of the blood in Exodus 24 should be seen in light of both these ceremonies as an integral element in a covenant celebration.

The sprinkling of blood is repeated numerous times in the Old Testament. Leviticus, for example, speaks often of the sprinkling of the altar with the blood of the sacrifice (see Lev. 1:5). It is not entirely clear just what this practice is supposed to do, but it certainly has something to do with atonement for sin. I would suggest that, since the blood is sprinkled after the sacrifice, the practice represents the atonement that has just occurred.[8] Whatever its precise meaning may be, the imagery is used again and expanded in Isaiah 52:13–15:

---

8. The uncertain meaning of this practice is reflected in the commentaries. J. Milgrom, for example, points out that the blood represents the animal's life (Lev. 17:11). The reason it is sprinkled *against* the altar rather than on the altar is so that the life be "returned to God via the altar lest the slayer-offerer be considered a murderer" (*Leviticus 1–16* [AB 3; New York: Doubleday, 1991], 156). Leviticus, however, does not make such a reason explicit. Moreover, it is not clear what "returning" the animal's life to God means. Likewise, J. E. Hartley comments, "blood rite signifies that the animal's life is poured out to Yahweh," but does not provide explanation of where this notion comes from or what it means (*Leviticus* [WBC 4; Dallas: Word, 1992], 21).

See, my servant will act wisely;
>   he will be raised and lifted up and highly exalted.
Just as there were many who were appalled at him—
>   his appearance was so disfigured beyond that of any man
>   and his form marred beyond human likeness—
so will he *sprinkle many nations,*
>   and kings will shut their mouths because of him.
For what they were not told, they will see,
>   and what they have not heard, they will understand. (italics added)

This passage is studded with a number of interpretive difficulties. The identity of the servant in Isaiah 41–53, for one, is a matter that continues to be debated. At times it seems to refer to the nation of Israel, more specifically the remnant that will return from Babylon, and at other times perhaps an individual.

Without venturing too far into this morass, the original context of Isaiah supports the former option. The remnant Israel is God's servant through whom he will not only restore the fortunes of Israel itself but be a light for the Gentiles. Note Isaiah 49:6:

It is too small a thing for you to be my servant
>   to restore the tribes of Jacob
>   and bring back those of Israel I have kept.
I will also make you a light for the Gentiles,
>   that you may bring my salvation to the ends of the earth.

This reference to the servant's being a "light for the Gentiles" is parallel to 52:15, where the servant will "sprinkle many nations."[9] So what does it mean to sprinkle the nations? Again, this is not clear. It may refer to the process of cleansing with water, such as we see in Numbers 8:7; 19:13, 18, 19. Or it may refer to the people being sprinkled with blood. The latter is relatively infrequent in the Old Testament. Leviticus 8:30 records the sprinkling of blood on Aaron and his sons as a means of consecrating them for their priestly duties. Leviticus 14:7 gives similar instructions for the cleansing of someone who has an infectious disease.

In any event, Isaiah 52:15 tells us that the end result of servant Israel's being "raised and lifted up" (v. 13)—that is, his exaltation after his humiliation in the exile—is that the nations will be sprinkled. Whatever the full significance of these words, it suggests that the nations will in some way be drawn into the orbit of God's redemptive work. The universal dimension of God's redemptive plan, announced as far back as Genesis 12:3, is now coming to

---

9. This is the reading of the Hebrew Masoretic text. The LXX has "and so many nations will be amazed at him."

light. The means through which he will redeem the world is the humiliated and exalted servant, Israel.

It is not difficult to see why the author of Hebrews develops this idea within the context of the death and resurrection of Christ. He appeals directly to the ceremony in Exodus 24 and, as he does throughout the book, guides his readers to see how Christ both fulfilled the Old Testament pattern and went beyond it (Heb. 9:19–22):

> When Moses had proclaimed every commandment of the law to all the people, he took the blood of calves, together with water, scarlet wool and branches of hyssop, and sprinkled the scroll and all the people. He said, "This is the blood of the covenant, which God has commanded you to keep." In the same way, he sprinkled with the blood both the tabernacle and everything used in its ceremonies. In fact, the law requires that nearly everything be cleansed with blood, and without the shedding of blood there is no forgiveness.

The writer then draws out the clear analogy between the cleansing power of the blood of animals and the blood of Christ, who "was sacrificed once to take away the sins of many people" (9:28). For the writer of Hebrews, the covenantal function of the shedding and sprinkling of blood in Exodus 24 foreshadows the work of Christ. The former is temporary and incomplete; the latter is permanent and complete.

The same point seems to be made in Hebrews 10:22, where the author speaks of "having our hearts sprinkled to cleanse us from a guilty conscience." He is likely referring to the sprinkling of Christ's blood, thus continuing the thought he began to develop in 9:19, rather than the sprinkling of water (as in Num. 8:7), especially since he leaves the next clause to pick up on the theme of water cleansing ("having our bodies washed with pure water"). In Hebrews 12:24 as well this book speaks of the "sprinkled blood that speaks a better word than the blood of Abel." First Peter 1:2 also refers to believers being sprinkled by Christ's blood.

The point of all this is that the ceremony in Exodus 24, by which the covenant between Israel and God is confirmed, involves both eating and the sprinkling of blood. The New Testament picks up on both these elements in describing the final covenant confirmation, the death and resurrection of Christ. The church participates in this covenant confirmation both spiritually, by having our hearts sprinkled, and physically, by partaking of the Lord's Supper.

To see God and live. Seeing God is a serious matter in the Old Testament. Typically God's presence is mediated by the angel of the Lord, and even in these cases it is assumed to be of grave consequence. This is because those who saw the angel understood the sight as being tantamount to seeing God himself. We see this in Genesis 16:11–14, where the angel of the Lord appears to Hagar and speaks to her (v. 11), yet she says (v. 13) that it is the Lord who spoke to her. This equation between the Lord and the angel who mediates his presence leads Hagar to say she has "seen" God (v. 13).[10]

Samson's parents likewise see the angel of the Lord and equate that meeting with seeing God (Judg. 13:20–22). They fear for their life, since they understand that no one can see God and live. Jacob's wrestling match with "a man" (perhaps also the angel of the Lord) likewise turns out to be an encounter with God, and Jacob expresses the same surprised reaction as the others at having survived such an encounter. "So Jacob called the place Peniel, saying, 'It is because I saw God face to face, and yet my life was spared'" (Gen. 32:30).

We have already mentioned Exodus 33:20–23 in the context of 24:11, where God himself says what the recipients of the theophanies have always assumed to be the case: "No one may see me and live." A mood of fear, even of death, surrounds a divine encounter with humanity.

This being the case, instances in which God does appear and people do not die are worthy of some reflection. This is particularly the case with passages such as Exodus 24:11, for there is no overt mediation of God's presence. Thus, this meeting between God and his people seems to be of far greater gravity because it is much more immediate.

Moses is the central Old Testament figure who has such "direct" visions of God. Twice he is described as one with whom God speaks "face to face" (Ex. 33:11; Num. 12:8). The former is particularly striking in that it occurs in the same context that proclaims no one may see God and live. It is no accident that both passages are found in contexts in which Moses' authority as God's messenger is being challenged—the golden calf episode and the opposition of Miriam and Aaron. We can conclude, therefore, that the manner in which God's intimacy with Moses is described is in part intended to buttress his authority. This helps us understand the vision of God in 24:11: The appearance of God to Israel's leaders is meant to confirm their status.

Moses is unique in the Old Testament. The manner in which he sees and speaks with God is described as being qualitatively different, at least with respect to his contemporaries. Moreover, the author of Deuteronomy says that Moses was unique not only in his day but at least until the time in which he wrote the following words. "Since then, no prophet has risen in Israel like Moses, whom the LORD knew face to face" (Deut. 34:10).

Isaiah's vision of God on his throne is also striking (Isa. 6:1–5). He sees God seated on his throne in a memorable scene because of its uniqueness in

---

10. With the case of Gen. 16:13, the issue should not be pressed too adamantly, since the Hebrew of this verse is difficult.

the Old Testament. Still, this vision does not achieve the level of immediacy as we see with Moses. For one thing, Isaiah 6 does not describe a face-to-face encounter, but a *vision* that drives the prophet to his knees (v. 5). Moreover, the vision is at least partially mediated by the seraphs, not only as they hovered over God's throne but also as they touched Isaiah's mouth with a coal from the altar to atone for his sin (v. 7).

Leaving aside the matter of the intimacy of the visions, it is important to keep in mind that these visions occur at certain junctures that have particular significance in God's redemptive plan for Israel. The appearances of God to Moses, of course, are in the context of the Exodus, the central salvific event in the Old Testament. Isaiah's vision inaugurates his prophetic ministry, which will include God's bringing the Israelites out of another foreign nation, Babylon. The theophanies of Gideon and Samson, although occurring at less crucial points in Israel's history, are also in a context of the deliverance of God's people from their enemies.

In light of this, I suggest that each appearance of God in the Old Testament signals that an important salvific event is about to transpire, a subsequent stage in God's developing plan of salvation. The fact that the most personal and immediate theophanies involve Moses attests to the central importance both of the Exodus as the paradigmatic salvific event in creating Israel as a nation and of Moses as the quintessential paradigm for all subsequent mediators of this salvation (see again Deut. 34:10).

Many parallels between Moses and Christ have been noted in various places throughout this commentary. Another parallel concerns the matter of seeing God. The degree of immediacy with which Moses beheld God and conversed with him points us to the greater immediacy enjoyed by Christ, the Son of God. John even seems to have a passage such as Exodus 33:20 in mind when he writes the following words: "No one has ever seen God, but God the One and Only, who is at the Father's side, has made him known" (John 1:18). This by all counts is an explicit ascription of divinity to Christ, referring to him as "God the One and Only, who is at the Father's side." It is he alone who has seen God and then made him known to his people.

Jesus himself reiterates the point a few chapters later: "No one has seen the Father except the one who is from God; only he has seen the Father" (John 6:46). This is more than speaking with God face to face as Moses did. It is God himself (Christ) abiding at the Father's side. As the Old Testament stresses, even Moses was limited in what he was permitted to see. In Exodus 24:10–11 it was God's feet; in 33:23 it was his back. As privileged as Moses was, his view of God was a mere shadow of what the true mediator of the covenant, God in Christ, was able to see. It is to be expected that at this climactic stage of God's plan of salvation the final mediator would have such a clear gaze at God's glory.

By being the one who could see God so clearly, Christ's authority as God's chosen mediator is also supported. This is why Christ appeals to his intimacy with the Father when his authority is challenged, which is precisely what we have seen in the Old Testament. John 6:46, cited above, is not simply a bit of good theology. It is found in the midst of a debate Jesus is having with Jews who were challenging his authority (see 6:41, 43, 52). It is he who has truly seen God, so all opposition should cease.

Because Christ is the one who truly sees the Father, he and he alone is properly equipped to mediate that image to the people (see again John 1:18). Christ's role is not simply to see God better than anyone else, but to see God and mediate that vision to those "born of God" (1:13). Because he has gazed fully into the face of the Father, Christ was able to come to earth and to allow us to gaze on "the glory of the One and Only, who came from the Father, full of grace and truth" (v. 14). In other words, Christ's uniquely intimate view of God has equipped him to turn to God's creation and pass that gaze along. The intimacy Adam and Eve enjoyed before the Fall is beginning to be restored in Christ, the second Adam.

OUR HEARTS HAVE been sprinkled. The contemporary significance of the covenant meal has already been suggested in the context of the Passover (see comments on Ex. 12). The most meaningful and significant present-day application of the covenant meal is the fact that the covenant has already been confirmed in the death and resurrection of Christ. The application of this aspect of Exodus 24, therefore, should not be sought so much on the private level but on the communal and theological level. We do not continually confirm our covenant with God; this was done once for all in Christ. What the church does do, however, is celebrate the Lord's Supper as a continual reminder both of what God has done in Christ and of the final eschatological meal to be shared by the universal church in the presence of God at the end of the present world order.

But the confirmation of the covenant in Exodus 24 has a second element, as we noted above: the shedding and sprinkling of blood. This too points us to the great reality of what God has done in Christ, and little more needs to be added. But there are two New Testament passages that apply this theme to the life of the believer: Hebrews 10:22 and 1 Peter 1:2. Our hearts have been "sprinkled" by Christ's blood.

We should not lose sight of the fact that the New Testament, by speaking this way, clearly intends the readers to see their own status as Christians in light of what is outlined in Exodus 24 and the other passages mentioned above. The writers do not merely wish to make a certain point more poignant or graphic by using a particular Old Testament theme as an *illustration*. Rather, they are saying that the Old Testament theme itself should be understood as achieving its full significance by what God has done in Christ. That final, climactic revelation of God is then passed on to his people, who are in union with Christ. What the practice of sprinkling achieved in the Old Testament is taken to a new level in the lives of believers.

What, then, does this sprinkling achieve in the lives of believers today? Hebrews 10:22 puts it this way: "Let us draw near to God with a sincere heart in full assurance of faith, *having our hearts sprinkled* to cleanse us from a guilty conscience" (italics added). The use of the perfect participle *rherantismenoi* (from *rhantizo*, to cleanse or sprinkle) is important. The perfect tense is typically used in the New Testament to convey "the notion of a state of affairs resultant upon the action."[11] In other words, the past action has a continued result in the present. A way to convey this meaning perhaps better is to translate the phrase "having *had* our hearts sprinkled," thus implying that the sprinkling was a one-time, past event that has recurring present implication.

The context of this passage clearly supports this interpretation. The writer of Hebrews is encouraging his readers to have confidence to draw near to God *now*. On what basis do they have this confidence? Their hearts *have been sprinkled*, thus cleansing them from a guilty conscience. This sprinkling is a once-for-all act. It is Christ's death and the shedding of his blood that is continually at work in us.

The significance of this for Christians today is to realize that they are finally, truly, "OK" with God. The writer does not mean by the phrase "guilty conscience" that feeling we all get, indeed *should* get, when we as Christians do something wrong. His view is more foundational. He is looking at the big picture rather than our own private struggling with daily temptations: Our hearts *have been* cleansed from a guilty conscience. In fact, it is precisely *despite* what we might feel to be the case that the author of Hebrews admonishes his readers to draw near to God. To be able to say with the author of Hebrews and with Peter (1 Peter 1:2) that we have been sprinkled by Christ's blood is a bold and liberating affirmation of the blessings bestowed on God's people.

Try as we might, we just don't catch on. The gospel is the message of grace from beginning to end, but that thought does not always penetrate our hearts and minds to the point that it begins affecting our actions. When God commanded Moses to sprinkle the people with blood in Exodus 24, he was making a definitive and unequivocal statement: Israel is his. Likewise, to be sprinkled by Christ's blood is no less a definitive and unequivocal state-

---

11. M. Zerwick, *Biblical Greek* (Rome: Scripta Pontificii Instituti Biblici, 1963), 97.

ment—if anything, it is more so. Being a Christian means being fully liberated from any sense of guilt before God, not because we are somehow good enough, but because of Christ's blood. And this is a once-for-all act, a favorite theme in the book of Hebrews (Heb. 7:27; 9:26; 10:10). It is the real, present, and recurring benefit of what was acted out on the cross.

Our guiltlessness is a fact that should dictate our perceptions and self-image. Something, however, sometimes gets lost in the translation from doctrine to practice. We all fall short of fully appropriating God's great gift in our day-to-day lives. It is true, of course, that our society makes far too little of guilt, as if it is a remnant of an unsophisticated, religious age. On the other hand, it is possible to make too much of it, to dwell on it. Guilt can cause neurotic behaviors and tendencies, which is understandable if there is no true sense of where this feeling comes from, why we have it, and how to get rid of it.

Christians are not perfect. One's problems do not magically go away after an altar call. We struggle with many of the same things everyone else struggles with. A persistent, nagging, guilty conscience, however, should *not* be one of them. Freedom from guilt before God is foundational to the Christian experience—foundational in the sense that it is the beginning point. It is the gift God gives us that starts us down the path of an ever-deepening relationship with him. It is therefore unthinkable to go back and question that foundation at every bad turn.

We are God's people, called to be in union with Christ; God is working in us greater and greater depths of Christian experience. Along this journey, we do indeed sin. But when this happens, our hearts do not become "unsprinkled." We do not need another dose of the blood of Christ in order to be OK with God. That has already been irrevocably taken care of. In fact, it is because our guilt has truly been taken care of that the guilt we feel when we sin can be properly handled. Again, this is the point of Hebrews 10:19–22. The author's main concern is to alert his readers how they can have *confidence* to approach God. We, too, when we sin, can approach God with repentance imbued with confidence, not with fear of backlash.

Seeing God. If only we could see God, actually see him, then we would know he is really there and all our speculation would be over—so our thinking goes. But why does he remain hidden? Why doesn't he just show himself to us?

To see God—to gaze on him with our physical eyes—has been a fascination and longing for people since the dawn of history. Every ancient culture—Mesopotamian, Egyptian, Greek, Roman, and so forth—has ventured to satisfy this longing by making some physical representation of the gods they worship. The God of Israel, however, was not as accommodating. First, he commanded Israel not to make any image of him (Ex. 20:4–6), not to attempt to "capture" God by modeling him after something God had created. Moreover, he kept himself hidden from his people, appearing to them in fire and smoke, not face to face. The few exceptions—that is, Moses' glimpses of God—prove the rule. One does not "see God." For whatever reason, he has not designed things this way.

In the New Testament, things change, yet they stay the same. Looking at John 1:18 again, we see that, although no one has seen God, Christ has—and he makes God known to us. There is a clear tension in John 1. We cannot see God, yet Christ makes him known. Moreover, Christ is the Word who was both with God and was God from the beginning (v. 1). He is also the one in whom we see "glory" (v. 14), a clear reference to the many passages in the Old Testament that speak of God's revealing his glory. So, the tension remains. In Christ we see the glory of God himself, yet we cannot say that we see God.

This paradox has practical implications. Seeing God is a matter of knowing Christ. If anything, this is a forceful argument for his deity. God cannot be known or seen apart from Jesus of Nazareth, which is either an egocentric and ridiculous claim or one that must be seriously reckoned with. We cannot "jump" to seeing God if we bypass the only means by which he has made this possible. There is no unmediated gaze of God apart from the Word, who is the glory of God and who makes God known to us. To put it another way, Christ is the standard by which we come to see and understand God. When we look at Christ, we can say, "This is what God is like." As Jesus said to Philip, "Anyone who has seen me has seen the Father" (John 14:9).

As straightforward as this sounds, we often labor under the opposite impression. Do we not often hold an idea in our minds of what God is like, one formed perhaps from childhood images (as a child I used to equate God with beams of sunlight), hearsay, or some other vague notions we have conjured up? The question is not what we *think* God is like, but how God has chosen to reveal what he is like. This, according to John's Gospel, is through Christ.

The gaze of God that he gives us in Christ is a more powerful image than the glimpses Moses had. Christ is the culmination of God's self-revelation. In light of this, John's words elsewhere are all the more striking: "No one has ever seen God; but if we love one another, God lives in us and his love is made complete in us" (1 John 4:12). We should allow the wonder of this passage to sink in. As in his Gospel, John affirms that no one has seen God. You cannot simply peel back the curtain, so to speak, and catch a peek. But in his first letter John follows up this thought not as he did in the Gospel, by pronouncing Jesus as the One who makes God known. Rather, he brings the "unseeableness" of God down to our everyday lives. While no one has seen God, *if we love one another, we see God in each other.*

In other words, it is by loving each other, meaning the church's love for its members and not a general "all you need is love" idea, that somehow that chasm between seeing God and not seeing God is crossed. How is God seen? First and foremost in Christ, but also, in a practical, day-to-day sense, by the conduct of God's people toward one another.

We can all perhaps think back how love and thoughtfulness from God's people was like a cool drink on a hot day, a spiritual shot in the arm when we were really down. It is, for example, common among God's people to struggle with spiritual issues. It is hard to imagine anyone who has been a Christian for even a brief time not to admit that they don't always "feel" God's presence with them. Well, how do we get this feeling back? First John 4:12 tells us: love. A timely phone call by a trusted and respected friend from church does wonders to remind us that God is real. Musing privately about the metaphysical reality of God and asking abstract theological questions usually does not get us very far. God has set things up so that we see him through the love of others, his church, those whom he has re-created to bear his image.

Moreover, it is not only in receiving love from others that we see God. It is also by loving others. Do you feel distant from God? Don't just wait for someone else to reach out to you. *You* reach out to someone else. This seems to be the clear thrust of John's words. By taking the step of loving our brothers and sisters "God lives in us." We, too, can see God—regularly. We do not need to climb a mountain or look up, expecting the heavens to part with bright flashes of light in order to see God. The coming of Christ has already put the exclamation point on that. But now that he has come, his Spirit lives in his people, and it is through the love that God's people show each other that God is seen. This thought should be a great motivator for us to live lives overflowing with love. It should spur us on not to brood but to act, whether we feel like it or not.

Exodus 25:1–31:18; 35:1–40:33

ⓦ

The Tabernacle

THE MATTER OF the tabernacle spans thirteen of the remaining sixteen chapters of Exodus. The ultimate goal toward which God is leading his redeemed people is possession of the land. On the way toward that end we have the more immediate goal of the giving of the law and the building of the tabernacle and religious system it represents, both of which will be of central importance once the land is conquered. As I hope to make clear, the building of the tabernacle is more than simply a matter of building a worship site in the desert. It is a piece of heaven on earth. Even though the list of building materials, lampstands, and incense altars may seem repetitive and tedious to modern readers, it is precisely the mass of this material that alerts us that we have arrived at the heart of the matter from the ancient point of view.

This being said, however, the length and repetitive nature of this material pose a problem for organizing this section of the commentary. For one thing, chapters 35–40 essentially repeat the content of chapters 25–31 with only insignificant and minor additions and/or deletions.[1] I have thus decided to group together the parallel sections under one heading. For example, immediately below we begin with the writer's treatment of the "offerings for the tabernacle," which is his topic not only in 25:1–9 but also 35:4–9. To treat each passage in a separate Original Meaning section is both tedious and pointless.

To say this, however, is not to minimize the organization that the biblical writer himself deemed necessary. In fact, I must confess it goes against my grain to treat this material in the way I have planned. It is far too common for commentaries and other monographs to deal with the entire tabernacle section first and then treat as almost an appendix the "intervening" chapters 32–34, without trying to account for why the biblical writer set things up the way he did. My point in organizing the material in this way is not to lend credence to such a misapprehension of the biblical text but to facilitate the goals of this commentary as a whole.

Chapters 25–40 manifest a basic structure. Chapters 25–31 record the instructions for building the tabernacle; chapters 35–40, its actual build-

---

1. One exception is 35:10–29, which treats the collection of materials for the tabernacle. This is not a significant addition to chs. 25–31, however, since the collection of materials is only relevant in the context of the actual *building* of the tabernacle in chs. 35–40.

ing. Sandwiched between them is, among other things, the story of the golden calf, a story of rebellion and eventual forgiveness. This is not just a story of any sort of rebellion, but of the Israelites attempting to set up an *alternate* cultic system to the one given in chapters 25–40, a point to which we will return.

Note also another clear organizational element in these chapters. The rebellion section of chapters 32–34 is framed by passages on the importance of keeping the Sabbath (31:12–18 and 35:1–3; see outline earlier in this commentary). This is hardly an accident. Precisely what this structure means to communicate to the reader, however, is not spelled out in the narrative itself. I will attempt to develop this notion elsewhere, but let me anticipate that discussion by suggesting here that the references to the Sabbath are intended to connect the building of the tabernacle to creation. Building the tabernacle, in other words, is an act of re-creation, culminating in the Sabbath command—a new seventh day, as it were. The close affinity between creation and Exodus (creation and redemption) is something we have seen throughout this book, so it is no great surprise to see it developed here at its climactic stages.[2]

Sabbath / tabernacle / creation / redemption, all related.

Another reason for organizing this section in the way described is that it will help us focus more directly on application. As we have seen elsewhere in Exodus, not every section of the book lends itself easily to concrete application (see introductory comments on the plagues in 7:8–10:29). Likewise, the laws in the Book of the Covenant cannot be directly applied to the life of the Christian today (see comments on 22:16–17). The proper starting point for applying both the plagues and the laws in Exodus is to grasp the *overall* theological message of these sections, not to single out a law here, a plague there.

 **Original Meaning** I PLAN ON taking here the same approach with the tabernacle as I did with the plagues and the Book of the Covenant. I will treat the entire tabernacle section first, section by section, as to its original meaning. In the Bridging Contexts and Contemporary Significance sections we will look at the theology of the tabernacle as a whole and ask what that theology has to say to Christians in a contemporary setting.

---

2. This is by no means a new idea with me, as I will note at various places of our discussion below. Rabbinic literature, for example, delights in making connections between the building of the tabernacle and creation.

In applying the tabernacle, I have little interest in "finding Jesus" in every detail.[3] I also have little interest in finding contemporary significance for the altar of incense as distinct from the significance of the lampstand. Such an approach is not only tedious but wholly out of sync with the original significance of the tabernacle. Both the tabernacle and the articles it contained were not meant to be applied personally to the life of the Israelite, as if to say, "What does the ark mean to you?" They were, rather, means by which Israel's relationship with God could move to a higher and deeper level. The question for us to ask, then, is not, "What do I do with it?" but, "What does this tell me about God and how he deals with his people?" In other words, "What is the theology of the tabernacle?"

Offerings for the Tabernacle (25:1–9; 35:4–9)

25:1The LORD said to Moses, 2"Tell the Israelites to bring me an offering. You are to receive the offering for me from each man whose heart prompts him to give. 3These are the offerings you are to receive from them: gold, silver and bronze; 4blue, purple and scarlet yarn and fine linen; goat hair; 5ram skins dyed red and hides of sea cows; acacia wood; 6olive oil for the light; spices for the anointing oil and for the fragrant incense; 7and onyx stones and other gems to be mounted on the ephod and breastpiece.

8"Then have them make a sanctuary for me, and I will dwell among them. 9Make this tabernacle and all its furnishings exactly like the pattern I will show you.

35:4Moses said to the whole Israelite community, "This is what the LORD has commanded: 5From what you have, take an offering for the LORD. Everyone who is willing is to bring to the LORD an offering of gold, silver and bronze; 6blue, purple and scarlet yarn and fine linen; goat hair; 7ram skins dyed red and hides of sea cows; acacia wood; 8olive oil for the light; spices for the anointing oil and for the fragrant incense; 9and onyx stones and other gems to be mounted on the ephod and breastpiece.

---

3. Seeing Christ in the details of the tabernacle is taken to an unconvincing extreme by W. Scott, *The Tabernacle: Its Structure, Vessels, Coverings, Sacrifices and Services* (London: Alfred Holness, n.d.), esp. 22–25. A more sober approach is offered by C. E. Fuller, *The Tabernacle in the Wilderness* (Westwood, N.J.: Revell, 1955). A wonderful example of how Christ ought to be perceived in the tabernacle may be seen in V. Poythress, *The Shadow of Christ in the Law of Moses* (Phillipsburg, N.J.: Presbyterian and Reformed, 1991).

This is the beginning of what God speaks to Moses upon entering the cloud (24:18). The reader is provided with a list of the materials that are to be brought before God for the purpose of building the tabernacle and related items. It is a fitting introduction to the tabernacle section in that the list of materials amounts to an overview of what is to come. And this is no list of simple, everyday items one might expect of desert dwellers. We have precious metals, expensive yarns and linen,[4] acacia wood,[5] olive oil, spices, precious stones, and gems. The only possible source of these items that can be inferred from the text is the Egyptians themselves, whom the Israelites plundered (12:36), although it bears mentioning that nowhere is this connection made explicit.

God commands Moses to build the tabernacle[6] precisely according to the pattern he will give (25:9). The reason for such precision seems to be implied in verse 8: "And I will dwell among them." God intends to be present with his people in a way he has not been before. The suitable abode for God is one that reflects the "pattern" given to Moses. This is an early indication that the tabernacle is an earthly symbol of a greater, heavenly reality; we will return to this idea at various points. It is somewhat striking, however, that the pattern is to be adhered to "exactly," while the instructions are extremely vague on many points.

One important point should be mentioned here, mainly because this will be developed more clearly later on and seems to form a central concern of the biblical writer. Commentators for centuries have noticed that the phrase "the LORD said to Moses" occurs seven times in chapters 25–31. The first six concern the building of the tabernacle and its furnishings (25:1; 30:11, 17, 22, 34; 31:1), while the final introduces the Sabbath command (31:12). It seems clear that the purpose of this arrangement is to aid the reader in making the connection between the building of the tabernacle and the seven days of creation, both of which involve six creative acts culminating in a seventh-day rest.[7]

---

4. Colored yarn was extremely expensive in antiquity. The dye came from a labor-intensive process of extracting the color from marine shells, where thousands were needed to dye just one robe (Sarna, *Exodus*, 157).

5. Acacia is an especially hard and durable, and, perhaps most important, lightweight wood, thus making it ideal for the purpose of building a portable sanctuary (ibid., 158).

6. In vv. 8–9 the words "sanctuary" (*miqdaš*) and "tabernacle" (*miškan*) are clearly used interchangeably.

7. P. J. Kearney has gone so far as to argue that chapters 25–40 as a whole correspond in great detail to the opening chapters of Genesis: chs. 25–31 are creation, chs. 32–33 are the Fall, and 34–40 are restoration ("Creation and Liturgy: The P Redaction of Ex 25–40," *ZAW* 89 [1977]: 375–87). Some of these connections may be too forced, however (see J. D. Levenson, *Creation and the Persistence of Evil: The Jewish Drama of Divine Omnipotence* [New York: HarperCollins, 1988], 82–83).

It should also be mentioned that the theme of sanctuary building by divine pattern and over a seven-day span is not unique to Israel. As early as approximately 2200 B.C. the Sumerian King Gudea of Lagash undertook a similar project, as did the Ugaritic gods in honor of Baal.[8] As we have seen elsewhere in Exodus, the manner in which God reveals himself to his people, at least in terms of its basic structures and patterns, would not seem odd to the ancient Israelites.

incarnational analogy.

The Ark (25:10–22; 37:1–9)

25:10"Have them make a chest of acacia wood—two and a half cubits long, a cubit and a half wide, and a cubit and a half high. 11Overlay it with pure gold, both inside and out, and make a gold molding around it. 12Cast four gold rings for it and fasten them to its four feet, with two rings on one side and two rings on the other. 13Then make poles of acacia wood and overlay them with gold. 14Insert the poles into the rings on the sides of the chest to carry it. 15The poles are to remain in the rings of this ark; they are not to be removed. 16Then put in the ark the Testimony, which I will give you.

17"Make an atonement cover of pure gold—two and a half cubits long and a cubit and a half wide. 18And make two cherubim out of hammered gold at the ends of the cover. 19Make one cherub on one end and the second cherub on the other; make the cherubim of one piece with the cover, at the two ends. 20The cherubim are to have their wings spread upward, overshadowing the cover with them. The cherubim are to face each other, looking toward the cover. 21Place the cover on top of the ark and put in the ark the Testimony, which I will give you. 22There, above the cover between the two cherubim that are over the ark of the Testimony, I will meet with you and give you all my commands for the Israelites.

37:1Bezalel[9] made the ark of acacia wood—two and a half cubits long, a cubit and a half wide, and a cubit and a half high. 2He overlaid it with pure gold, both inside and out, and

---

8. The relevant texts may be found in Pritchard, *Ancient Near Eastern Texts*, 264 and 133–34, respectively. See Cassuto, *Commentary on Exodus*, 322–24, for this and other parallels. Cassuto also points out parallels throughout his commentary on the tabernacle.

9. Bezalel and Oholiab were appointed to build the tabernacle and its furnishings. They are introduced in 31:1–11 and 35:30–36:7.

made a gold molding around it. ³He cast four gold rings for it and fastened them to its four feet, with two rings on one side and two rings on the other. ⁴Then he made poles of acacia wood and overlaid them with gold. ⁵And he inserted the poles into the rings on the sides of the ark to carry it.

⁶He made the atonement cover of pure gold—two and a half cubits long and a cubit and a half wide. ⁷Then he made two cherubim out of hammered gold at the ends of the cover. ⁸He made one cherub on one end and the second cherub on the other; at the two ends he made them of one piece with the cover. ⁹The cherubim had their wings spread upward, overshadowing the cover with them. The cherubim faced each other, looking toward the cover.

We now begin with specifics. The first thing to be mentioned is the ark. This may strike us as a bit unexpected. We would expect first to have the instructions for the tabernacle, since this structure will house the articles like the ark. The "displacement" of the ark here is further suggested by the fact that the actual building of the ark in 37:1–9 *follows* the building of the tabernacle in 36:8–38. So the sequence here is reversed. Why?

Apparently the writer wants to stress the importance of the ark. As Durham puts it, the ark is the "supreme post-Sinai symbol of the Presence of Yahweh."[10] It is, after all, the only furnishing located in the Most Holy Place. By placing the ark first, the reader's attention is drawn to the central concern of the tabernacle narrative. The ark is the focus of God's presence with his people, the central point of contact between heaven and the tabernacle, the earthly symbol of heaven.

The holiness of the ark is no doubt why it is not to be touched. You cannot simply walk up to it, pick it up, and move it as you might a basket of laundry. Rather, a system of rings and poles is necessary to transport it. As we read in the well-known story of Uzzah, to touch the ark means death (2 Sam. 6:3–7; 1 Chron. 13:9–10).

As with the tabernacle in general, the ark also has ancient Near Eastern parallels. In King Tut's tomb, for example, was found a cedar chest complete with rings and poles.[11] Depositing the law inside a sacred place (cf. 25:16, 21) is also known from other ancient sources.[12] The same is true of the cherubim that sit atop the cover of the ark. These were common symbols in the

---

10. Durham, *Exodus*, 350.

11. Sarna, *Exodus*, 160.

12. Ibid. The "Testimony" (25:16, 21) to be placed in the ark is the tablets of the law.

ancient world, and the Israelites were no doubt familiar with them. Moreover, the sudden reference to these creatures (in the Pentateuch cherubim also occur in Gen. 3:24 and Num. 7:89[13]) implies that they need no explanation for the Israelite readers. Cherubim appear not only over the cover but throughout the design of the tabernacle, a sign that the tabernacle is a symbolic representation of God's heavenly dwelling.

The presence of the cherubim also emphasizes the holiness of the ark. Over the ark, which measures approximately 3'9" long by 2'4" wide and high, is the "atonement cover," so called because the Hebrew word *kapporet* derives from the root *kpr*, which often refers to atonement in the Old Testament. From above this cover, between the cherubim, God will meet with his people and speak with them (25:22). It is God's location above the cover and between the cherubim that has led some scholars to regard the cover as God's throne and the ark itself his footstool.[14] This is not just a scholarly conjecture. A number of passages speak of God being *enthroned* between the cherubim (1 Sam. 4:4; 2 Sam. 6:2; Ps. 80:1; 99:1).

We know little else about these cherubim and why God chooses this image in particular for such an important and holy purpose. Perhaps the most we can say is that they are angelic, heavenly beings who live in God's presence (much like the seraphs of Isa. 6:1–7). Since any image of God was strictly forbidden, the best Israel can do is make an image of those beings closest to him. Thus, his holiness is emphasized. Moreover, the fact that the law, God's supreme self-revelation to his people, is kept inside the ark also indicates that the ark is the "center of gravity" of God's presence with his people.

The Table (25:23–30; 37:10–16)

25:23"Make a table of acacia wood—two cubits long, a cubit wide and a cubit and a half high. 24Overlay it with pure gold and make a gold molding around it. 25Also make around it a rim a handbreadth wide and put a gold molding on the rim. 26Make four gold rings for the table and fasten them to the four corners, where the four legs are. 27The rings are to be close to the rim to hold the poles used in carrying the table. 28Make the poles of acacia wood, overlay them with gold and

---

13. The appearance of the cherubim in Gen. 3:24 provides another link with the creation narrative; in Num. 7:89 they are once again connected with the ark and the place from where Moses heard the voice of the Lord.

14. Sarna, *Exploring Exodus*, 209–11; M. Haran, *Temples and Temple-Service in Ancient Israel: An Inquiry Into the Character of Cult Phenomena and the Historical Setting of the Priestly School* (Oxford: Clarendon, 1978), 254–59.

carry the table with them. [29]And make its plates and dishes of pure gold, as well as its pitchers and bowls for the pouring out of offerings. [30]Put the bread of the Presence on this table to be before me at all times.

[37:10]They made the table of acacia wood—two cubits long, a cubit wide, and a cubit and a half high. [11]Then they overlaid it with pure gold and made a gold molding around it. [12]They also made around it a rim a handbreadth wide and put a gold molding on the rim. [13]They cast four gold rings for the table and fastened them to the four corners, where the four legs were. [14]The rings were put close to the rim to hold the poles used in carrying the table. [15]The poles for carrying the table were made of acacia wood and were overlaid with gold. [16]And they made from pure gold the articles for the table—its plates and dishes and bowls and its pitchers for the pouring out of drink offerings.

The table is constructed apparently for the singular purpose of holding the bread of the Presence (25:30). Its dimensions are 3' long by 1'6" wide and 2'3" high; it is made of acacia wood overlaid with pure gold. Like the ark, it has a system of rings and poles for carrying. It will be placed in the Holy Place along with the lampstand and the incense altar.

This passage is cryptic in a number of places. For example, what are the plates and dishes mentioned in 25:29 used for? According to Leviticus 24:9, priests are to eat of the bread, but this information is not given here.[15] Also, the pitchers and bowls mentioned in the same verse are for "the pouring out of offerings," but just what type of offerings is not mentioned (37:16 gives a little more information by speaking of "drink offerings"[16]).

Likewise no explanation is given here for "the bread of the Presence." According to Leviticus 24:6, twelve loaves of bread (two rows of six) are to be placed on the table, the number no doubt representing the tribes of Israel. According to 24:8–9, this bread is to be set out afresh weekly, on the Sabbath, and the priests are to dispose of it properly, that is, by eating it within the

---

15. According to 1 Sam. 21:2–7, Ahimelech agreed to allow David and his men eat of it "provided the men have kept themselves from women" (v. 4).

16. On this, M. Haran comments: "It is somewhat puzzling how a drink-offering could be included in the rite performed inside the temple, since the offering of libations on the incense-altar is forbidden by [Exod. 30:9], while the outer altar must have had its own libatory vessels. The most probable explanation is that these inner libatory vessels were placed on the table merely to serve as a *reminder* of drink-offering.... [The] wine was not actually poured out on any altar. It was apparently consumed by male priests in a holy place, just as were the loaves of shewbread [another name for the bread of the Presence]" (*Temples and Temple-Service*, 216–17).

confines of the tabernacle. The term *bread of the Presence* is an ambiguous term, which may simply mean "bread that is in the presence [of God]." We should not look at this in mystical terms, as if God is present "in" the bread. It is the bread that is placed before God, who is in the Most Holy Place, over the ark.

As to any further significance of the bread we are given little information. Clearly, the placement of the bread on the table at the entrance of the Most Holy Place indicates its status relative to the other furnishings of the tabernacle. Janzen may be correct by suggesting that the table and bread indicate hospitality toward God, though this is conjectural.[17] Another approach may be more helpful. This is the second time within the span of two chapters (cf. 24:11) that we have seen Israel's leaders partaking in a meal in God's presence. Perhaps the bread of the Presence along with the drink offering implied in 25:29 are elements in another covenant meal between God and Israel's leaders. The bread and the wine, situated as they are just outside the Most Holy Place, are a continual reminder of the covenant that the holy God, who is located behind a curtain just several feet away, has made with his people.

The Lampstand (25:31–40; 37:17–24)

25:31"Make a lampstand of pure gold and hammer it out, base and shaft; its flowerlike cups, buds and blossoms shall be of one piece with it. 32Six branches are to extend from the sides of the lampstand—three on one side and three on the other. 33Three cups shaped like almond flowers with buds and blossoms are to be on one branch, three on the next branch, and the same for all six branches extending from the lampstand. 34And on the lampstand there are to be four cups shaped like almond flowers with buds and blossoms. 35One bud shall be under the first pair of branches extending from the lampstand, a second bud under the second pair, and a third bud under the third pair—six branches in all. 36The buds and branches shall all be of one piece with the lampstand, hammered out of pure gold.

37"Then make its seven lamps and set them up on it so that they light the space in front of it. 38Its wick trimmers and trays are to be of pure gold. 39A talent of pure gold is to be used for the lampstand and all these accessories. 40See that you make them according to the pattern shown you on the mountain.

37:17They made the lampstand of pure gold and hammered it out, base and shaft; its flowerlike cups, buds and blossoms

17. Janzen, *Exodus*, 197.

were of one piece with it. [18]Six branches extended from the sides of the lampstand—three on one side and three on the other. [19]Three cups shaped like almond flowers with buds and blossoms were on one branch, three on the next branch and the same for all six branches extending from the lampstand. [20]And on the lampstand were four cups shaped like almond flowers with buds and blossoms. [21]One bud was under the first pair of branches extending from the lampstand, a second bud under the second pair, and a third bud under the third pair— six branches in all. [22]The buds and the branches were all of one piece with the lampstand, hammered out of pure gold.

[23]They made its seven lamps, as well as its wick trimmers and trays, of pure gold. [24]They made the lampstand and all its accessories from one talent of pure gold.

The lampstand and its lamps are made of pure gold with no wood. This is because these items are small enough, although a talent of gold (about 75 pounds) is needed. There is no clear indication of their symbolic meaning. All that 25:37 says is that the lamps are to "light the space in front if it [the lampstand itself]." Is this all there is to it? Why is lighting this space so important? Is it merely to give a friendly glow to the Holy Place?[18]

The matter of tending the lamps is serious business. As we read in Leviticus 24:1–4, it is the high priest's responsibility to do so "from evening till morning, continually" (v. 3). It is unfortunate that the Bible does not satisfy our curiosity by telling us what all this means. Perhaps it is no more significant than to light the Holy Place so the priests can see what they are doing after the sun has set! But if so, why the solemnity? Their function is likely ritualistic and symbolic, though precisely what we do not know.

If we can say nothing further about the function of the lampstand, something more may be said about its design. Carol Meyers has argued on the basis of the botanical imagery of the lampstand that it represents a "stylized tree of life design and symbolizes such themes as the fertility of nature and the sustenance of life."[19] Meyer's thesis is convincing to many, but it, too, is not explicit in the text. In the final analysis, Levenson's acute observation on the "muteness" of the biblical text, both here and elsewhere, is worthy of serious consideration:

---

18. Janzen suggests that the light is "a welcome sign that someone is home" (ibid., 198). This suggestion continues the hospitality theme Janzen adduces to explain the bread (see previous footnote). There is no way of evaluating this comment. Durham says it symbolizes "Yahweh's Presence in perpetual wakefulness" (*Exodus*, 365).

19. C. Meyers, "Lampstand," *ABD*, 4:142. She treats the matter more fully in *The Tabernacle Menorah* (ASORDS 2; Missoula: Scholars, 1976). See also Levenson, *Creation*, 94.

This muteness, this refusal to relate meanings, may be another example of the demythologizing current in biblical thought. By keeping a tight control upon the cosmogonic significance of the Temple[20] appurtenances, the text stresses in austere fashion their subordination to the free and sovereign will of YHWH, the creator who majestically refuses to accord *intrinsic* meaning to his creation.[21]

In other words, the fact that there is mystery may be precisely the point. What the lampstand represents is something God may or may not be pleased to reveal. And even if such significance is hidden from Israel, it has no bearing on how they are to behave. The lampstand is to be made as he said and the light is to be kept burning. Perhaps the mystery will be further revealed as Israel continues to obey God's command. But for now, "See that you make them according to the pattern shown you on the mountain" (Ex. 25:40).

The Tabernacle (26:1–37; 36:8–38)

26:1"Make the tabernacle with ten curtains of finely twisted linen and blue, purple and scarlet yarn, with cherubim worked into them by a skilled craftsman. ²All the curtains are to be the same size—twenty-eight cubits long and four cubits wide. ³Join five of the curtains together, and do the same with the other five. ⁴Make loops of blue material along the edge of the end curtain in one set, and do the same with the end curtain in the other set. ⁵Make fifty loops on one curtain and fifty loops on the end curtain of the other set, with the loops opposite each other. ⁶Then make fifty gold clasps and use them to fasten the curtains together so that the tabernacle is a unit.

⁷"Make curtains of goat hair for the tent over the tabernacle—eleven altogether. ⁸All eleven curtains are to be the same size—thirty cubits long and four cubits wide. ⁹Join five of the curtains together into one set and the other six into another set. Fold the sixth curtain double at the front of the tent. ¹⁰Make fifty loops along the edge of the end curtain in one set and also along the edge of the end curtain in the other set. ¹¹Then make fifty bronze clasps and put them in the loops to fasten the tent together as a unit. ¹²As for the additional length of the tent curtains, the half curtain that is left over is to hang down at the rear of the tabernacle. ¹³The tent curtains will be a cubit longer on

---

20. Levenson freely moves between his observations on the significance of the tabernacle and the temple.

21. Levenson, *Creation*, 95.

both sides; what is left will hang over the sides of the tabernacle so as to cover it. [14]Make for the tent a covering of ram skins dyed red, and over that a covering of hides of sea cows.

[15]"Make upright frames of acacia wood for the tabernacle. [16]Each frame is to be ten cubits long and a cubit and a half wide, [17]with two projections set parallel to each other. Make all the frames of the tabernacle in this way. [18]Make twenty frames for the south side of the tabernacle [19]and make forty silver bases to go under them—two bases for each frame, one under each projection. [20]For the other side, the north side of the tabernacle, make twenty frames [21]and forty silver bases— two under each frame. [22]Make six frames for the far end, that is, the west end of the tabernacle, [23]and make two frames for the corners at the far end. [24]At these two corners they must be double from the bottom all the way to the top, and fitted into a single ring; both shall be like that. [25]So there will be eight frames and sixteen silver bases—two under each frame.

[26]"Also make crossbars of acacia wood: five for the frames on one side of the tabernacle, [27]five for those on the other side, and five for the frames on the west, at the far end of the tabernacle. [28]The center crossbar is to extend from end to end at the middle of the frames. [29]Overlay the frames with gold and make gold rings to hold the crossbars. Also overlay the crossbars with gold.

[30]"Set up the tabernacle according to the plan shown you on the mountain.

[31]"Make a curtain of blue, purple and scarlet yarn and finely twisted linen, with cherubim worked into it by a skilled crafts-man. [32]Hang it with gold hooks on four posts of acacia wood overlaid with gold and standing on four silver bases. [33]Hang the curtain from the clasps and place the ark of the Testimony behind the curtain. The curtain will separate the Holy Place from the Most Holy Place. [34]Put the atonement cover on the ark of the Testimony in the Most Holy Place. [35]Place the table outside the curtain on the north side of the tabernacle and put the lampstand opposite it on the south side.

[36]"For the entrance to the tent make a curtain of blue, purple and scarlet yarn and finely twisted linen—the work of an embroiderer. [37]Make gold hooks for this curtain and five posts of acacia wood overlaid with gold. And cast five bronze bases for them.

36:8All the skilled men among the workmen made the tabernacle with ten curtains of finely twisted linen and blue, purple and scarlet yarn, with cherubim worked into them by a skilled craftsman. 9All the curtains were the same size—twenty-eight cubits long and four cubits wide. 10They joined five of the curtains together and did the same with the other five. 11Then they made loops of blue material along the edge of the end curtain in one set, and the same was done with the end curtain in the other set. 12They also made fifty loops on one curtain and fifty loops on the end curtain of the other set, with the loops opposite each other. 13Then they made fifty gold clasps and used them to fasten the two sets of curtains together so that the tabernacle was a unit.

14They made curtains of goat hair for the tent over the tabernacle—eleven altogether. 15All eleven curtains were the same size—thirty cubits long and four cubits wide. 16They joined five of the curtains into one set and the other six into another set. 17Then they made fifty loops along the edge of the end curtain in one set and also along the edge of the end curtain in the other set. 18They made fifty bronze clasps to fasten the tent together as a unit. 19Then they made for the tent a covering of ram skins dyed red, and over that a covering of hides of sea cows.

20They made upright frames of acacia wood for the tabernacle. 21Each frame was ten cubits long and a cubit and a half wide, 22with two projections set parallel to each other. They made all the frames of the tabernacle in this way. 23They made twenty frames for the south side of the tabernacle 24and made forty silver bases to go under them—two bases for each frame, one under each projection. 25For the other side, the north side of the tabernacle, they made twenty frames 26and forty silver bases—two under each frame. 27They made six frames for the far end, that is, the west end of the tabernacle, 28and two frames were made for the corners of the tabernacle at the far end. 29At these two corners the frames were double from the bottom all the way to the top and fitted into a single ring; both were made alike. 30So there were eight frames and sixteen silver bases—two under each frame.

31They also made crossbars of acacia wood: five for the frames on one side of the tabernacle, 32five for those on the other side, and five for the frames on the west, at the far end of the tabernacle. 33They made the center crossbar so that it extended from end to end at the middle of the frames. [34]They overlaid the frames with gold and made gold rings to hold the crossbars. They also overlaid the crossbars with gold.

[35]They made the curtain of blue, purple and scarlet yarn and finely twisted linen, with cherubim worked into it by a skilled craftsman. [36]They made four posts of acacia wood for it and overlaid them with gold. They made gold hooks for them and cast their four silver bases. [37]For the entrance to the tent they made a curtain of blue, purple and scarlet yarn and finely twisted linen—the work of an embroiderer; [38]and they made five posts with hooks for them. They overlaid the tops of the posts and their bands with gold and made their five bases of bronze.

It is only after the instructions for the ark, table, and lampstand are given that we finally come to the tabernacle itself. The amount of space devoted to its description only begins to tell the story of its vital significance for Israel's religious practices.

The tabernacle is basically a series of curtains and frames. The curtains covering the entire structure are to be made of fine linen and colored yarn. Cherubim are to be worked into them, an ever-present reminder that the tabernacle is an earthly representation of the heavenly tabernacle. This first layer of curtains must be covered on the outside by a second layer made of goat hair, most likely to protect the inner curtains from the elements. There are apparently two further layers of ram skins and hides of sea cows covering the layer of goat hair (26:14). These curtains are to be kept together by a system of bronze clasps and loops.

The frames and crossbars that support the curtains are to be made of acacia wood, doubled in the corners for strength. The crossbars are overlaid with gold and kept together with gold rings. Despite the information given, just how the structure holds together is not clear.

After giving the instructions for the frame and the large curtains that form the roof and walls, the Lord reminds Moses once again to adhere strictly to this plan (26:30). This is a fitting reminder here, since 26:31 commences with instructions concerning the curtain to separate the Holy Place from the Most Holy Place. This curtain seems to be made in the same manner as the first layer of curtains described in 26:1. Another similarly constructed curtain is to be placed at the entrance of the tent (i.e., between the Holy Place and the outer court). Note that this curtain has no cherubim worked into it since this is one step removed from the Most Holy Place.

In current Old Testament scholarship, only the most extreme pessimists cast serious doubt on the historicity of the tabernacle. This happy state of affairs has not always been the case. Julius Wellhausen, for example, considered the tabernacle as a figment of the Priestly writer's (P source) cultic imagination, an attempt to read the splendor of the temple back into the Mosaic era, perhaps to lend ancient support to the practices for which the Priestly class was known. But this view has given way to greater care in assessing the evidence. Recent research has demonstrated that worship in tent shrines in the ancient Semitic world was normal.[22]

Much has been made of the dimensions of the tabernacle, and rightly so (see the diagram below).[23] The entire structure measured 150' on the north and south sides and 75' on the east and west, thus forming a rectangle made up of two squares 75' by 75'. The one square constituted the outer court, in which was placed the altar of burnt offering, roughly a 7'6" square structure, and the wash basin at the entrance of the Holy Place. Inside the other square was the Holy Place, a rectangle measuring 30' by 15', the same proportions as the tabernacle as a whole. The adjoining Most Holy Place measured a perfect 15' square.

Tabernacle Diagram

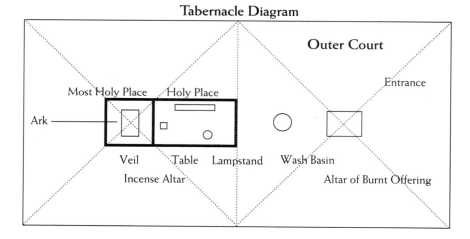

---

22. R. E. Friedman, "Tabernacle," *ABD*, 6:294–98; Sarna, *Exploring Exodus*, 196–200. The latter writes, "In light of all the foregoing variegated data, it is beyond cavil that the Israelite wilderness tabernacle, both as an institution and in its mode of construction, was well rooted in the cultural and religious traditions of the ancient Near East" (199–200). In a related matter, see also Friedman's interesting argument that the tabernacle was not discarded after the building of the temple but placed inside it ("Tabernacle," 6:298–99; *Who Wrote the Bible* [Englewood Cliffs, N.J.: Prentice Hall, 1987], 174–87). A helpful survey of the history of critical scholarship of the tabernacle may be found in M. H. Woudstra, "The Tabernacle in Biblical-Theological Perspective," *New Perspectives on the Old Testament*, ed. J. B. Payne (Waco, Tex.: Word, 1970), 88–103, esp. 88–91.

23. This diagram is adapted from Sarna, *Exploring Exodus*, 192.

As we have noted elsewhere (see Original Meaning section of 24:1–18), the three-part structure of the tabernacle, moving from lesser to greater degrees of holiness, reflects the gradations of holiness on Mount Sinai. The tabernacle is modeled after a higher, cosmic reality: the dwelling place ✓ of God.

This brings us to a matter of great importance for understanding the meaning of the tabernacle in its original setting. The precise measurements of the structure combined with the symbolism of the curtains and the furnishings are not without deep significance. The tabernacle seems to represent a microcosm of creation itself. The splendor and beauty of the materials used—fine fabrics, precious metals, and stones—affirm the goodness of the created world. The precise and perfect dimensions of the tabernacle indicate a sense of order amid chaos.

In pointing this out I am not offering suggestions as to how we might approach the theological significance of the tabernacle today. Rather, I am suggesting, as others have done, that to think of the tabernacle as an act of cosmic re-creation is precisely what the building of the tabernacle originally intended to convey. We have already seen a couple of examples of the creation theme in the tabernacle ("created" in seven segments; the cherubim). The ornate and orderly structure of the tabernacle itself is another. More examples will follow.

The connection between tabernacle and creation is aptly assessed by Levenson.[24] According to him, the tabernacle (actually, his focus is on the temple, but the point holds nonetheless) and creation are two "building projects." They are not simply parallel, however, as if the former is a scaled down model of the latter.

> Rather, they implicate each other, and neither is complete alone. The microcosm is the idealized cosmos . . . the world as it was meant to be, a powerful piece of testimony to God the creator, a palace for the victorious king. To view creation within the precincts of the Temple is to summon up an *ideal world* that is far from the mundane reality of profane life and its persistent evil. It is that ideal world which is the result of God's creative labors.[25]

In the midst of a fallen world, in exile from the Garden of Eden—the original "heaven on earth"—God undertakes another act of creation, a building project that is nothing less than a return to pre-Fall splendor. The tabernacle,

---

24. This entire topic is treated by Levenson in ch. 7, "Cosmos and Microcosm" (*Creation*, 78–99).
25. Ibid., 99.

therefore, is laden with redemptive significance, not just because of the sacrifices and offerings within its walls, but simply because of what it is: a piece of holy ground amid a world that has lost its way. If this is a correct understanding of the tabernacle, we begin to see why the writer of Exodus devotes so much space to its description.

Altar of Burnt Offering (27:1–8; 38:1–7)

27:1"Build an altar of acacia wood, three cubits high; it is to be square, five cubits long and five cubits wide. 2Make a horn at each of the four corners, so that the horns and the altar are of one piece, and overlay the altar with bronze. 3Make all its utensils of bronze—its pots to remove the ashes, and its shovels, sprinkling bowls, meat forks and firepans. 4Make a grating for it, a bronze network, and make a bronze ring at each of the four corners of the network. 5Put it under the ledge of the altar so that it is halfway up the altar. 6Make poles of acacia wood for the altar and overlay them with bronze. 7The poles are to be inserted into the rings so they will be on two sides of the altar when it is carried. 8Make the altar hollow, out of boards. It is to be made just as you were shown on the mountain.

38:1They built the altar of burnt offering of acacia wood, three cubits high; it was square, five cubits long and five cubits wide. 2They made a horn at each of the four corners, so that the horns and the altar were of one piece, and they overlaid the altar with bronze. 3They made all its utensils of bronze—its pots, shovels, sprinkling bowls, meat forks and firepans. 4They made a grating for the altar, a bronze network, to be under its ledge, halfway up the altar. 5They cast bronze rings to hold the poles for the four corners of the bronze grating. 6They made the poles of acacia wood and overlaid them with bronze. 7They inserted the poles into the rings so they would be on the sides of the altar for carrying it. They made it hollow, out of boards.

The altar measures 7'6" square and is 4'6" tall; it is to be located in the outer court. This altar is for offering burnt offerings, an appropriate act of sin atonement considering the fact that God "resides" only several yards away in the Most Holy Place. Details of this sacrifice are presented in Leviticus 1:1–17.

One of its curious characteristics is a horn at each of its four corners. Why are they there? Do they perform a function? Are they merely ornamental, or are they in some way symbolic? We read in 29:12 and Leviticus 4:7, for example, that blood is to be put on the horns, thus suggesting some type of redemptive symbolism, but just what is not clear. We do know that clinging to the horns of the altar was a way of seeking refuge in God's presence from some harm (1 Kings 1:50–51; 2:28). We are not told, however, what about the symbolism of the horns inspires such action. Sarna suggests that they are a "symbol of strength, power, and fertility" (1 Sam. 2:10) as well as providing a means by which the sacrifice can be bound to the altar.[26]

One area where the worlds of biblical studies and archaeology come together is with respect to altars. Although the Israelite altar of burnt offering from the tabernacle has not been found, others like it have been discovered. A horned altar was found in Tel Dan in 1974.[27] An altar found in Arad not only has horns but is five cubits square (as is the altar of Ex. 27:1).[28] Another horned altar was found at Beersheba.[29] The presence of horned altars in antiquity is well established, which lends credence to the historicity of the altar described here.

One final point to consider is the relationship of this altar with that given in 20:24–25. There it is commanded that the altar be made of earth. If stones are used, dressed stones may not be used, lest the altar be defiled by the use of tools. Nothing there is said about acacia wood or bronze overlay. One way of handling this apparent discrepancy is to suggest that the altar of 20:24–25 is not the one of 27:1–8. This may be correct, but one is left wondering if the former will ever be built. Cassuto has offered an ingenious suggestion. According to 27:8, the altar is to be hollow. At whatever site the tabernacle comes to rest, the hollow wood and bronze structure will be filled with earth and stone, thus satisfying both descriptions.[30] Cassuto's suggestion, however, suffers from the fact that his reconstructed altar looks like neither biblical description. His harmonization is strained, but rejecting it does not bring us any closer to a solution.

---

26. Sarna, *Exodus*, 172. Regarding the practical function, Sarna cites Ps. 118:27. The NIV reads, "The LORD is God, and he has made his light shine upon us. *With boughs in hand, join in the festal procession up* to the horns of the altar" (italics added). The alternate reading in the NIV is *"Bind the festal sacrifice with ropes and take it* to the horns of the altar," which is also Sarna's translation: "Bind the festal offering to the horns of the altar with cords." Sarna's translation is the most straightforward handling of the Hebrew.

27. A. Biran, "An Israelite Horned Altar at Dan," *BA* 37 (1974): 106–7.

28. Y. Aharoni, "Arad: Its Inscriptions and Temple," *BA* 31 (1968): 2–32.

29. Y. Aharoni, "The Horned Altar at Beersheba," *BA* 37 (1974): 2–6; Y. Yadin, "Beer-Sheba: The High Place Destroyed by King Josiah," *BASOR* 222 (1976): 5–17.

30. Cassuto, *Commentary on Exodus*, 362.

The Courtyard (27:9–19; 38:9–20)

27:9"Make a courtyard for the tabernacle. The south side shall be a hundred cubits long and is to have curtains of finely twisted linen, 10with twenty posts and twenty bronze bases and with silver hooks and bands on the posts. 11The north side shall also be a hundred cubits long and is to have curtains, with twenty posts and twenty bronze bases and with silver hooks and bands on the posts.

12"The west end of the courtyard shall be fifty cubits wide and have curtains, with ten posts and ten bases. 13On the east end, toward the sunrise, the courtyard shall also be fifty cubits wide. 14Curtains fifteen cubits long are to be on one side of the entrance, with three posts and three bases, 15and curtains fifteen cubits long are to be on the other side, with three posts and three bases.

16"For the entrance to the courtyard, provide a curtain twenty cubits long, of blue, purple and scarlet yarn and finely twisted linen—the work of an embroiderer—with four posts and four bases. 17All the posts around the courtyard are to have silver bands and hooks, and bronze bases. 18The courtyard shall be a hundred cubits long and fifty cubits wide, with curtains of finely twisted linen five cubits high, and with bronze bases. 19All the other articles used in the service of the tabernacle, whatever their function, including all the tent pegs for it and those for the courtyard, are to be of bronze.

38:9Next they made the courtyard. The south side was a hundred cubits long and had curtains of finely twisted linen, 10with twenty posts and twenty bronze bases, and with silver hooks and bands on the posts. 11The north side was also a hundred cubits long and had twenty posts and twenty bronze bases, with silver hooks and bands on the posts.

12The west end was fifty cubits wide and had curtains, with ten posts and ten bases, with silver hooks and bands on the posts. 13The east end, toward the sunrise, was also fifty cubits wide. 14Curtains fifteen cubits long were on one side of the entrance, with three posts and three bases, 15and curtains fifteen cubits long were on the other side of the entrance to the courtyard, with three posts and three bases. 16All the curtains around the courtyard were of finely twisted linen. 17The bases for the posts were bronze. The hooks and bands on the posts

were silver, and their tops were overlaid with silver; so all the
posts of the courtyard had silver bands.

[18]The curtain for the entrance to the courtyard was of blue,
purple and scarlet yarn and finely twisted linen—the work of
an embroiderer. It was twenty cubits long and, like the curtains of the courtyard, five cubits high, [19]with four posts and
four bronze bases. Their hooks and bands were silver, and
their tops were overlaid with silver. [20]All the tent pegs of the
tabernacle and of the surrounding courtyard were bronze.

As mentioned above, the courtyard is a rectangle of 150' on the north and
south ends, and 75' on the east and west. The courtyard, therefore, is the
entire enclosure, not to be confused with the outer court (see diagram above).
The entrance to the courtyard is to be centered on the east side, 30' long.
Most of this description concerns the making of curtains and the system of
posts, bases, and hooks for keeping the structure together.

Oil for the Lampstand (27:20–21)

[27:20]"Command the Israelites to bring you clear oil of
pressed olives for the light so that the lamps may be kept
burning. [21]In the Tent of Meeting, outside the curtain that is
in front of the Testimony, Aaron and his sons are to keep the
lamps burning before the LORD from evening till morning.
This is to be a lasting ordinance among the Israelites for the
generations to come.

It is not clear why the instructions for the oil are not given immediately
following the instructions for the lampstand. Clear olive oil is to be used, as
it produces little smoke and gives off better light. Such a stipulation is not
given for the anointing oil or the oil added to the grain offerings, likely
because the lampstand is located in the Holy Place whereas the other oils are
used mainly in the court.[31] It is not known where the Israelites got the olives
from, but Sarna suggests they brought the oil from Egypt.[32] As mentioned
above, the lamps are to be kept burning by Aaron, although here Aaron's sons
are included (cf. Lev. 24:1–4, which mentions only Aaron; no doubt this
designation includes his sons as well).

Here for the first time the tabernacle is referred to as "the Tent of Meeting," although the term will be used another thirty-two times before the end

---

31. Haran, *Temples and Temple-Service*, 208.
32. Sarna, *Exodus*, 175.

of the book. Once again a new piece of information is placed before the reader somewhat suddenly. The choice of this term does not seem particularly significant here. To call the tabernacle the Tent of Meeting is not an indication of what the Israelites did, but what God did. As Sarna puts it, the term "stresses the oracular function of the Tabernacle."[33]

Priestly Garments (28:1–43; 39:1–31)

28:1"Have Aaron your brother brought to you from among the Israelites, along with his sons Nadab and Abihu, Eleazar and Ithamar, so they may serve me as priests. [2]Make sacred garments for your brother Aaron, to give him dignity and honor. [3]Tell all the skilled men to whom I have given wisdom in such matters that they are to make garments for Aaron, for his consecration, so he may serve me as priest. [4]These are the garments they are to make: a breastpiece, an ephod, a robe, a woven tunic, a turban and a sash. They are to make these sacred garments for your brother Aaron and his sons, so they may serve me as priests. [5]Have them use gold, and blue, purple and scarlet yarn, and fine linen.

[6]"Make the ephod of gold, and of blue, purple and scarlet yarn, and of finely twisted linen—the work of a skilled craftsman. [7]It is to have two shoulder pieces attached to two of its corners, so it can be fastened. [8]Its skillfully woven waistband is to be like it—of one piece with the ephod and made with gold, and with blue, purple and scarlet yarn, and with finely twisted linen.

[9]"Take two onyx stones and engrave on them the names of the sons of Israel [10]in the order of their birth—six names on one stone and the remaining six on the other. [11]Engrave the names of the sons of Israel on the two stones the way a gem cutter engraves a seal. Then mount the stones in gold filigree settings [12]and fasten them on the shoulder pieces of the ephod as memorial stones for the sons of Israel. Aaron is to bear the names on his shoulders as a memorial before the LORD. [13]Make gold filigree settings [14]and two braided chains of pure gold, like a rope, and attach the chains to the settings.

[15]"Fashion a breastpiece for making decisions—the work of a skilled craftsman. Make it like the ephod: of gold, and of

---

33. Ibid., 176.

blue, purple and scarlet yarn, and of finely twisted linen. ¹⁶It is to be square—a span long and a span wide—and folded double. ¹⁷Then mount four rows of precious stones on it. In the first row there shall be a ruby, a topaz and a beryl; ¹⁸in the second row a turquoise, a sapphire and an emerald; ¹⁹in the third row a jacinth, an agate and an amethyst; ²⁰in the fourth row a chrysolite, an onyx and a jasper. Mount them in gold filigree settings. ²¹There are to be twelve stones, one for each of the names of the sons of Israel, each engraved like a seal with the name of one of the twelve tribes.

²²"For the breastpiece make braided chains of pure gold, like a rope. ²³Make two gold rings for it and fasten them to two corners of the breastpiece. ²⁴Fasten the two gold chains to the rings at the corners of the breastpiece, ²⁵and the other ends of the chains to the two settings, attaching them to the shoulder pieces of the ephod at the front. ²⁶Make two gold rings and attach them to the other two corners of the breastpiece on the inside edge next to the ephod. ²⁷Make two more gold rings and attach them to the bottom of the shoulder pieces on the front of the ephod, close to the seam just above the waistband of the ephod. ²⁸The rings of the breastpiece are to be tied to the rings of the ephod with blue cord, connecting it to the waistband, so that the breastpiece will not swing out from the ephod.

²⁹"Whenever Aaron enters the Holy Place, he will bear the names of the sons of Israel over his heart on the breastpiece of decision as a continuing memorial before the LORD. ³⁰Also put the Urim and the Thummim in the breastpiece, so they may be over Aaron's heart whenever he enters the presence of the LORD. Thus Aaron will always bear the means of making decisions for the Israelites over his heart before the LORD.

³¹"Make the robe of the ephod entirely of blue cloth, ³²with an opening for the head in its center. There shall be a woven edge like a collar around this opening, so that it will not tear. ³³Make pomegranates of blue, purple and scarlet yarn around the hem of the robe, with gold bells between them. ³⁴The gold bells and the pomegranates are to alternate around the hem of the robe. ³⁵Aaron must wear it when he ministers. The sound of the bells will be heard when he enters the Holy Place before the LORD and when he comes out, so that he will not die.

³⁶"Make a plate of pure gold and engrave on it as on a seal: HOLY TO THE LORD. ³⁷Fasten a blue cord to it to attach it to the turban; it is to be on the front of the turban. ³⁸It will be on Aaron's forehead, and he will bear the guilt involved in the sacred gifts the Israelites consecrate, whatever their gifts may be. It will be on Aaron's forehead continually so that they will be acceptable to the LORD.

³⁹"Weave the tunic of fine linen and make the turban of fine linen. The sash is to be the work of an embroiderer. ⁴⁰Make tunics, sashes and headbands for Aaron's sons, to give them dignity and honor. ⁴¹After you put these clothes on your brother Aaron and his sons, anoint and ordain them. Consecrate them so they may serve me as priests.

⁴²"Make linen undergarments as a covering for the body, reaching from the waist to the thigh. ⁴³Aaron and his sons must wear them whenever they enter the Tent of Meeting or approach the altar to minister in the Holy Place, so that they will not incur guilt and die.

"This is to be a lasting ordinance for Aaron and his descendants.

³⁹:¹From the blue, purple and scarlet yarn they made woven garments for ministering in the sanctuary. They also made sacred garments for Aaron, as the LORD commanded Moses.

²They made the ephod of gold, and of blue, purple and scarlet yarn, and of finely twisted linen. ³They hammered out thin sheets of gold and cut strands to be worked into the blue, purple and scarlet yarn and fine linen—the work of a skilled craftsman. ⁴They made shoulder pieces for the ephod, which were attached to two of its corners, so it could be fastened. ⁵Its skillfully woven waistband was like it—of one piece with the ephod and made with gold, and with blue, purple and scarlet yarn, and with finely twisted linen, as the LORD commanded Moses.

⁶They mounted the onyx stones in gold filigree settings and engraved them like a seal with the names of the sons of Israel. ⁷Then they fastened them on the shoulder pieces of the ephod as memorial stones for the sons of Israel, as the LORD commanded Moses.

⁸They fashioned the breastpiece—the work of a skilled craftsman. They made it like the ephod: of gold, and of blue, purple and scarlet yarn, and of finely twisted linen. ⁹It was

square—a span long and a span wide—and folded double. [10]Then they mounted four rows of precious stones on it. In the first row there was a ruby, a topaz and a beryl; [11]in the second row a turquoise, a sapphire and an emerald; [12]in the third row a jacinth, an agate and an amethyst; [13]in the fourth row a chrysolite, an onyx and a jasper. They were mounted in gold filigree settings. [14]There were twelve stones, one for each of the names of the sons of Israel, each engraved like a seal with the name of one of the twelve tribes.

[15]For the breastpiece they made braided chains of pure gold, like a rope. [16]They made two gold filigree settings and two gold rings, and fastened the rings to two of the corners of the breastpiece. [17]They fastened the two gold chains to the rings at the corners of the breastpiece, [18]and the other ends of the chains to the two settings, attaching them to the shoulder pieces of the ephod at the front. [19]They made two gold rings and attached them to the other two corners of the breastpiece on the inside edge next to the ephod. [20]Then they made two more gold rings and attached them to the bottom of the shoulder pieces on the front of the ephod, close to the seam just above the waistband of the ephod. [21]They tied the rings of the breastpiece to the rings of the ephod with blue cord, connecting it to the waistband so that the breastpiece would not swing out from the ephod—as the LORD commanded Moses.

[22]They made the robe of the ephod entirely of blue cloth—the work of a weaver—[23]with an opening in the center of the robe like the opening of a collar, and a band around this opening, so that it would not tear. [24]They made pomegranates of blue, purple and scarlet yarn and finely twisted linen around the hem of the robe. [25]And they made bells of pure gold and attached them around the hem between the pomegranates. [26]The bells and pomegranates alternated around the hem of the robe to be worn for ministering, as the LORD commanded Moses.

[27]For Aaron and his sons, they made tunics of fine linen—the work of a weaver—[28]and the turban of fine linen, the linen headbands and the undergarments of finely twisted linen. [29]The sash was of finely twisted linen and blue, purple and scarlet yarn—the work of an embroiderer—as the LORD commanded Moses.

> [30]They made the plate, the sacred diadem, out of pure gold
> and engraved on it, like an inscription on a seal: HOLY TO THE
> LORD. [31]Then they fastened a blue cord to it to attach it to
> the turban, as the LORD commanded Moses.

This lengthy section treats the garments that Aaron (28:1–39) and his sons (28:40–43) are to wear when ministering in the tabernacle. The description of the priestly garments is a wonderful example of what we have been seeing throughout Exodus. The combination of terseness and specificity "suggests that these instructions were set down for people who knew what was being described."[34] As we have seen with the tabernacle itself, precisely what these garments look like cannot be said with any precision.

Although the description of the garments may not be entirely clear, their purpose is spelled out nicely in 28:2: The garments are to give Aaron "dignity and honor," and they are to be prepared in advance of his consecration (v. 3). No doubt the manner in which this dignity and honor are conferred is by the use of expensive materials. Moreover, these materials are not just costly, but they also parallel the materials used to make the tabernacle: gold, blue, purple, and scarlet yarn, fine linen, onyx, and other precious stones.

This similarity between the priestly garments and the tabernacle is hardly accidental, and thus we catch a glimpse of the meaning of these garments. By being decked out as the tabernacle itself, the high priest in his service becomes the focus of God's presence for the people of God—a mini-tabernacle, as it were. I am not suggesting that we extend the analogy to say that the Spirit of God resides "in" the priest as he does in the Most Holy Place. Their garments, rather, reflect the holiness of the place in which they are called to minister. One might well ask, "How *else* should we expect them to dress? Everyday clothes?" Out of the question!

Several particulars are worth noting. The ephod is likely an apron-like garment.[35] As with a number of other elements throughout chapters 25–40, similar garments are known from Ugaritic and Assyrian texts. We are not told here what its purpose is, but other biblical texts indicate that it is a means of finding out God's will (1 Sam. 23:9–11; 30:7–8). The high priest functions not only in a sacrificial role but also as a conduit for God's revelation to the people.

---

34. Durham, *Exodus*, 384–85. Or as M. Haran puts it, perhaps less generously, "We are faced with a unique combination of long-winded description on the one hand and total omission of various particulars on the other" (*Temples and Temple-Service*, 150, quoted in Fretheim, *Exodus*, 263). One can understand Haran's exasperation, as the purpose of his work is to describe in detail the nature of Israel's temple worship. Haran's treatment of the garments may be found on pp. 165–74.

35. Haran, *Temples and Temple-Service*, 166.

Over the ephod is a "breastpiece for making decisions" (v. 15). This garment sports four rows of three stones, each of which is engraved with the name of one of the tribes of Israel. Also placed in the breastpiece are the Urim and Thummim (v. 30). This verse gives a tantalizing piece of information: "Thus Aaron will always bear the means of making decisions for the Israelites over his heart before the LORD." The Urim and Thummim have been a point of scholarly debate for some time. Recently C. Van Dam has argued that the act of decision making did not involve the casting of lots, a commonly accepted notion. The process involved, rather, a gem that verified, through giving off light, "that the message given by the high Priest was indeed from God."[36]

Of course, this matter must be left open in view of the paucity of information we have. What can be said, however, apart from their role in decision making, is that the Urim and Thummim must certainly have predated Moses. The people must have known what they were and how they were to be used, since they simply appear here in Exodus 28 without any explanation (see also Lev. 8:8; Num. 27:21; Deut. 33:8).[37]

Another cryptic piece of information occurs in 28:35: Aaron is to wear a robe beneath the ephod, whose decorations include gold bells. Their purpose, apparently, is to ring when he enters or leaves the Most Holy Place "so that he will not die." Does this mean that if the bells are not heard, the priest will die? Why? Perhaps the best solution is one proposed by Haran and Sarna,[38] that the warning about death pertains not only to the bells but to all the strict demands of the priestly ritual. As Haran puts it, "the omission of *any one* of the details of the inner ritual complex would have fatal consequences."[39]

Next we read of the plate of pure gold, on the front of the turban, on which is engraved: "HOLY TO THE LORD" (v. 36). What precisely is so designated? This should be probably connected to the notion of bearing guilt mentioned in verse 38. But this does not make things clear either. What guilt needs to be born? Perhaps it is to make these sacred gifts acceptable to God. This seems to be the intention of the final part of verse 38. The words on Aaron's forehead are a reminder to God that the offerings Aaron is bringing are "acceptable to the LORD."

The final garments mentioned are tunics, sashes, headbands, and the undergarments. What is conspicuously absent from the list is shoes, perhaps because of what has already been suggested in 3:5: "Take off your sandals, for

---

36. C. Van Dam, *The Urim and Thummim: A Means of Revelation in Ancient Israel* (Winona Lake, Ind.: Eisenbrauns, 1997), 230. See also Cassuto for a concise and helpful summary of the biblical evidence (*Commentary on Exodus*, 378–82).

37. Van Dam, *The Urim and Thummim*, 236.

38. Haran, *Temples and Temple-Service*, 218; Sarna, *Exodus*, 183.

39. Haran, *Temples and Temple-Service*, 218.

the place where you are standing is holy ground." These words were spoken to Moses as he approached God on Mount Horeb. As we have seen, the tabernacle is an earthly representation of a heavenly reality—a portable Mount Horeb/Sinai. Although 3:5 is not explicitly reiterated in chapter 28, this connection seems a fruitful avenue of approach. The priests stand in God's presence and must conduct themselves appropriately.

Consecration of the Priests (29:1–46)

29:1"This is what you are to do to consecrate them, so they may serve me as priests: Take a young bull and two rams without defect. 2And from fine wheat flour, without yeast, make bread, and cakes mixed with oil, and wafers spread with oil. 3Put them in a basket and present them in it—along with the bull and the two rams. 4Then bring Aaron and his sons to the entrance to the Tent of Meeting and wash them with water. 5Take the garments and dress Aaron with the tunic, the robe of the ephod, the ephod itself and the breastpiece. Fasten the ephod on him by its skillfully woven waistband. 6Put the turban on his head and attach the sacred diadem to the turban. 7Take the anointing oil and anoint him by pouring it on his head. 8Bring his sons and dress them in tunics 9and put headbands on them. Then tie sashes on Aaron and his sons. The priesthood is theirs by a lasting ordinance. In this way you shall ordain Aaron and his sons.

10"Bring the bull to the front of the Tent of Meeting, and Aaron and his sons shall lay their hands on its head. 11Slaughter it in the LORD's presence at the entrance to the Tent of Meeting. 12Take some of the bull's blood and put it on the horns of the altar with your finger, and pour out the rest of it at the base of the altar. 13Then take all the fat around the inner parts, the covering of the liver, and both kidneys with the fat on them, and burn them on the altar. 14But burn the bull's flesh and its hide and its offal outside the camp. It is a sin offering.

15"Take one of the rams, and Aaron and his sons shall lay their hands on its head. 16Slaughter it and take the blood and sprinkle it against the altar on all sides. 17Cut the ram into pieces and wash the inner parts and the legs, putting them with the head and the other pieces. 18Then burn the entire ram on the altar. It is a burnt offering to the LORD, a pleasing aroma, an offering made to the LORD by fire.

¹⁹"Take the other ram, and Aaron and his sons shall lay their hands on its head. ²⁰Slaughter it, take some of its blood and put it on the lobes of the right ears of Aaron and his sons, on the thumbs of their right hands, and on the big toes of their right feet. Then sprinkle blood against the altar on all sides. ²¹And take some of the blood on the altar and some of the anointing oil and sprinkle it on Aaron and his garments and on his sons and their garments. Then he and his sons and their garments will be consecrated.

²²"Take from this ram the fat, the fat tail, the fat around the inner parts, the covering of the liver, both kidneys with the fat on them, and the right thigh. (This is the ram for the ordination.) ²³From the basket of bread made without yeast, which is before the LORD, take a loaf, and a cake made with oil, and a wafer. ²⁴Put all these in the hands of Aaron and his sons and wave them before the LORD as a wave offering. ²⁵Then take them from their hands and burn them on the altar along with the burnt offering for a pleasing aroma to the LORD an offering made to the LORD by fire. ²⁶After you take the breast of the ram for Aaron's ordination, wave it before the LORD as a wave offering, and it will be your share.

²⁷"Consecrate those parts of the ordination ram that belong to Aaron and his sons: the breast that was waved and the thigh that was presented. ²⁸This is always to be the regular share from the Israelites for Aaron and his sons. It is the contribution the Israelites are to make to the LORD from their fellowship offerings.

²⁹"Aaron's sacred garments will belong to his descendants so that they can be anointed and ordained in them. ³⁰The son who succeeds him as priest and comes to the Tent of Meeting to minister in the Holy Place is to wear them seven days.

³¹"Take the ram for the ordination and cook the meat in a sacred place. ³²At the entrance to the Tent of Meeting, Aaron and his sons are to eat the meat of the ram and the bread that is in the basket. ³³They are to eat these offerings by which atonement was made for their ordination and consecration. But no one else may eat them, because they are sacred. ³⁴And if any of the meat of the ordination ram or any bread is left over till morning, burn it up. It must not be eaten, because it is sacred.

³⁵"Do for Aaron and his sons everything I have commanded you, taking seven days to ordain them. ³⁶Sacrifice a bull each day

as a sin offering to make atonement. Purify the altar by making atonement for it, and anoint it to consecrate it. [37]For seven days make atonement for the altar and consecrate it. Then the altar will be most holy, and whatever touches it will be holy.

[38]"This is what you are to offer on the altar regularly each day: two lambs a year old. [39]Offer one in the morning and the other at twilight. [40]With the first lamb offer a tenth of an ephah of fine flour mixed with a quarter of a hin of oil from pressed olives, and a quarter of a hin of wine as a drink offering. [41]Sacrifice the other lamb at twilight with the same grain offering and its drink offering as in the morning—a pleasing aroma, an offering made to the LORD by fire.

[42]"For the generations to come this burnt offering is to be made regularly at the entrance to the Tent of Meeting before the LORD. There I will meet you and speak to you; [43]there also I will meet with the Israelites, and the place will be consecrated by my glory.

[44]"So I will consecrate the Tent of Meeting and the altar and will consecrate Aaron and his sons to serve me as priests. [45]Then I will dwell among the Israelites and be their God. [46]They will know that I am the LORD their God, who brought them out of Egypt so that I might dwell among them. I am the LORD their God.

Chapter 29 is devoted to the sacrifices involved in the consecration of the priests; their actual consecration is mentioned only in passing in 40:12–16. This is a deviation from the pattern we have seen: instructions in chapters 25–31, execution in chapters 35–40.[40] This can be easily explained, however. The focus of chapters 35–40 is on the building of the tabernacle and its furnishings. The matter of the consecration of the priests occurs several chapters later in Leviticus. Note, too, that much of Leviticus is an extended conversation between God and Moses at the Tent of Meeting, the tabernacle. Leviticus picks up where Exodus leaves off.

Aaron and his sons are to be consecrated by a series of sacrifices and offerings, an anointing with oil, and the donning of the tunics, headbands, and sashes. The entire ceremony is neatly summarized in 29:1–9. The end of verse 9 already begins to focus the reader's attention on Aaron's descendants, not just his own sons but in perpetuity: "The priesthood is theirs by a lasting ordinance" (cf. also vv. 29–30, 42).

---

40. The detailed description of the following of these commands are not given until Lev. 8.

The sacrifices are of three types: a bull for a sin offering, a ram for a burnt offering, and another ram for a wave offering. This sequence is significant. The sin offering cleanses the priests from sin; it is understandable why the ordination process begins this way. Next, the burnt offering is an expression of devotion and commitment on the part of the worshiper. The second ram, along with a loaf of bread, a cake made with oil, and a wafer, are to be a wave offering.

It is not clear what a wave offering is. The phrase occurs about twenty times in the Pentateuch, but no description is given. Obviously an act of waving is involved, but what purpose does the offering itself have? According to Leviticus 7:28–36, a wave offering is a type of fellowship offering, the purpose of which concerns the establishing of communion between God and his people. This is the expected finale to the consecration ceremony. The element of communion is further indicated in Exodus 29:31–34, where Aaron and his sons eat a meal made up of the fellowship offering. As we have seen in 24:11, Israel's leaders eat in God's presence.

The fact that the ordination process takes seven days (29:35–37) is worth noting. It is not the case that every mention of the number seven in the Old Testament or even in Exodus is automatically an allusion to creation (cf. Jethro's seven daughters in 2:16). Perhaps in this context the number seven simply expresses "completeness." But why does the number seven embody such meaning? The reason is that the world was created in a seven-day pattern. Seven is the number of completeness because it is the number of creation. *Seven* Furthermore, when we keep in mind that Exodus as a whole and the tabernacle in particular abound in creation imagery, it is appropriate to suggest such a connection here. The ordination ceremony of the priest lasts seven days, since he is to be a priest in the tabernacle, the microcosm of the universe.

Verses 38–43 describe the institution of the regular morning and evening sacrifices "for the generations to come" (v. 42). Here we have apparently left the topic of the consecration of the priests. What justifies the shift in topic is the reference to sacrifices on the altar throughout this section. It also helps draw together the twin topics of the consecration of the priests and of the tabernacle, a point made explicit in verse 44. The daily sacrifices are the focus of the priests' duties; it therefore stands to reason to bring these two strands together.

Verses 42–46 reiterate a number of themes treated elsewhere. The tabernacle (once again called the Tent of Meeting) is the place where God's glory dwells and where he has chosen to meet with his people. It is God's presence, his glory, that actually consecrates the tabernacle (v. 43; cf. v. 44: "I will consecrate"). It is not the ceremonies that consecrate the tabernacle or the priests but God himself, no doubt through the ceremonies. In other words, there is nothing magical or manipulative on the part of the people to make it happen. It is God's tabernacle, his priesthood, his people. He will prepare his people to be a suitable dwelling for himself.

The final three verses of chapter 29 are a fitting end to the topic at hand. The writer ties together the tabernacle and priesthood with the Exodus itself. The tabernacle and the priests have been consecrated and God now dwells with his people. Now the people are to think back at what God has done in bringing them out of Egypt. In this way the people will *know* that Yahweh is their God (v. 46). As we have noted many times, the purpose of the Exodus was not simply to free slaves. It was to bring God's people into a covenant relationship with him through the law, tabernacle, and priesthood.

Altar of Incense (30:1–10; 37:25–28)

30:1"Make an altar of acacia wood for burning incense. 2It is to be square, a cubit long and a cubit wide, and two cubits high—its horns of one piece with it. 3Overlay the top and all the sides and the horns with pure gold, and make a gold molding around it. 4Make two gold rings for the altar below the molding—two on opposite sides—to hold the poles used to carry it. 5Make the poles of acacia wood and overlay them with gold. 6Put the altar in front of the curtain that is before the ark of the Testimony—before the atonement cover that is over the Testimony—where I will meet with you.

7"Aaron must burn fragrant incense on the altar every morning when he tends the lamps. 8He must burn incense again when he lights the lamps at twilight so incense will burn regularly before the LORD for the generations to come. 9Do not offer on this altar any other incense or any burnt offering or grain offering, and do not pour a drink offering on it. 10Once a year Aaron shall make atonement on its horns. This annual atonement must be made with the blood of the atoning sin offering for the generations to come. It is most holy to the LORD."

37:25They made the altar of incense out of acacia wood. It was square, a cubit long and a cubit wide, and two cubits high—its horns of one piece with it. 26They overlaid the top and all the sides and the horns with pure gold, and made a gold molding around it. 27They made two gold rings below the molding—two on opposite sides—to hold the poles used to carry it. 28They made the poles of acacia wood and overlaid them with gold.

This altar measures about 1'6" square and 3' tall. It is to be placed in the Holy Place (30:6) and therefore must be constructed of gold. Like the altar of burnt offering, it has horns.

Sarna considers the items mentioned in chapter 30 to be an appendix.[41] One might have expected *all* the items in the tabernacle to be described before the instruction on consecrating the priests in chapter 29. The fact that these items are mentioned later, however, at least raises the possibility of Sarna's suggestion. Perhaps these items are mentioned after chapter 29 because none of them are needed in consecrating the priests. If so,[42] its effect is to place emphasis on the importance of the consecration of the priests. The reason for organizing the various descriptions of the tabernacle and its furnishings is to bring the instructions regarding priestly consecration into the picture as quickly as possible. This, if anything, reminds us that the tabernacle and the priesthood are twin concepts in the book of Exodus. Chapters 25–40 are not just about the building of the tabernacle, but the institution of an entire cultic system.

The incense itself (30:8) is not treated fully until 30:34–38. A question left unanswered is the symbolism of the incense: What is its purpose? Is it to counter the smell of dead animals that permeates the tabernacle? Its use was certainly common in the ancient Near East. It has been suggested that the placement of the altar immediately between the priest and the Most Holy Place indicates that the incense performs a protective function: Its smoke conceals the atonement cover from the priest so he will not die (cf. Lev. 16:12–13).[43] It is a barrier that the high priest crosses only once a year on the Day of Atonement. Little else can be said about the subject.

Atonement Money (30:11–16)

> [30:11]Then the LORD said to Moses, [12]"When you take a census of the Israelites to count them, each one must pay the LORD a ransom for his life at the time he is counted. Then no plague will come on them when you number them. [13]Each one who crosses over to those already counted is to give a half shekel, according to the sanctuary shekel, which weighs twenty gerahs. This half shekel is an offering to the LORD. [14]All who cross over, those twenty years old or more, are to give an offering to the LORD. [15]The rich are not to give more than a half

---

41. Sarna, *Exodus*, 193.

42. But 29:4 refers to the washing of priests at the entrance of the Tent of Meeting, which may imply the existence of the basin for washing described in 30:17–21.

43. K. Nielsen, "Incense," *ABD*, 3:406–7; Haran, *Temples and Temple-Service*, 244.

> shekel and the poor are not to give less when you make the
> offering to the LORD to atone for your lives. [16]Receive the
> atonement money from the Israelites and use it for the service
> of the Tent of Meeting. It will be a memorial for the Israelites
> before the LORD, making atonement for your lives."

This brief reference to atonement money (which does not occur in chs. 35–40) seems somewhat out of place. The passage begins with the second "creative word" given to Moses from God (see 25:1 for the first). As we noted earlier, there are seven occurrences of the phrase, "Then the LORD said to Moses," which correspond to the seven days of creation.

The passage begins, "When you take a census." Why would they do this? A census might be taken as preparation for war (Num. 1:2–3, 44–47), but is that relevant here? Whatever the reason, the context clearly implies that it is a dangerous undertaking, since a census is to be accompanied by a ransom payment. Each person counted is to give a half shekel as a "ransom for his life."[44] In this way a plague on the people will be avoided.

The description of this procedure calls to mind 2 Samuel 24:1–17, where David is punished with three days of plague for taking a census of his fighting men. But if this episode is relevant for understanding Exodus 30:11–16, it would seem more reasonable to read simply, "Do not take a census, for it is wrong to do so." Rather, we find here the assumption that a census will be taken from time to time, and some provision needs to be taken in order to avoid calamity. It may be that the ransom is a reminder to Israel not to rely on its own strength.[45]

The more pertinent question is what all of this has to do with the tabernacle. Verse 16 justifies the logic of including a description of atonement money: The money is to be used for "the service of the Tent of Meeting." We are not told precisely what the money will be used for (purchase of oil? gold? yarns and linens?), but that it involves the tabernacle is clear. But the money is to be used for more than purchasing power. It is also a "memorial for the Israelites before the LORD" (v. 16). At the risk of sounding redundant, just what this means is not certain.

If I may put the pieces together, the money is a reminder to the Israelites that atonement has been made for their lives. This is circular, however, since the very reason atonement is needed is because a census has been taken. Of course, this scenario assumes that the content of verse 16 is directly related to what comes before. If I may put a slightly different spin on it, it seems that the human pen-

---

44. A shekel is 2/5 of an ounce. A gerah is 1/50 of an ounce; thus 20 gerahs equal one shekel. Hence, half a shekel is equal to 10 gerahs.

45. See also Janzen, *Exodus*, 219–20.

chant for assessing self-worth is something God will "tax" for the good of the tabernacle and as a prodding reminder to the people of who really has worth.

The Basin for Washing (30:17–21; 38:8)

30:17Then the LORD said to Moses, 18"Make a bronze basin, with its bronze stand, for washing. Place it between the Tent of Meeting and the altar, and put water in it. 19Aaron and his sons are to wash their hands and feet with water from it. 20Whenever they enter the Tent of Meeting, they shall wash with water so that they will not die. Also, when they approach the altar to minister by presenting an offering made to the LORD by fire, 21they shall wash their hands and feet so that they will not die. This is to be a lasting ordinance for Aaron and his descendants for the generations to come."

38:8They made the bronze basin and its bronze stand from the mirrors of the women who served at the entrance to the Tent of Meeting.

The basin for washing is to be placed in the courtyard between the curtain to the Holy Place and the altar of burnt offering. The priests are to use it to wash themselves before entering the Holy Place. As with other elements of the tabernacle ceremony, there is no room for negotiation: If they do not wash, they will die.

This washing likely has a practical as well as a ceremonial function. The slaughter that takes place at the altar will certainly leave the priests bloody. Washing the blood off will make them more presentable. But again, this explanation is a conjecture and finds no explicit basis in the text. The washing may also symbolize the cleansing from sin (cf. 29:4).

No dimensions for the basin are given. Since it is not in the inner courts of the tabernacle, it is not made of gold but of bronze. Throughout these chapters, the material used to make the tabernacle and the furnishings reflect the gradations of holiness of the structure itself.

The parallel description of the wash basin in 38:8 offers a surprising piece of information not found in its counterpart in 30:17–21: The bronze basin and stand are to be made from "the mirrors of the women who served at the entrance to the Tent of Meeting." Once again, we are given a tantalizing tidbit only to have any hope of further explanation dashed. Mirrors in the ancient world were not made of glass but of polished bronze. Hence, this verse explains the source of the bronze. But who were these women and what does it mean that they "served"?

First Samuel 2:22 is routinely brought into the discussion, since it also mentions women serving at the entrance to the Tent of Meeting (this verse and Ex. 38:8 are similar in Hebrew). The problem with this connection, however, is that 1 Samuel 2:22 speaks of the sin of Eli's sons in engaging in sexual activity with these women. The reference, in other words, is to the ubiquitous ancient Near Eastern practice of cult prostitution. We can safely rule out this option, since otherwise the biblical record of what constitutes proper worship of God would be completely overturned. But this verse may simply refer to a *perversion* of an otherwise commonly accepted (although to us unknown) practice involving some sort of service of women at the tabernacle. The wisest course to take is to agree with Durham:

> [The] best we can do with Exod 38:8 is to note its obvious purpose [i.e., to explain the source of the bronze] and then to confess ignorance, until some further information is available, as to who the women at the opening of the Tent of Appointed Meeting were, why they were there, what they were doing, and whether their mirrors were for personal or ritual use.[46]

Although disappointed not to be able to say more, I am willing to follow Durham's advice.

The Anointing Oil and Incense (30:22–38; 37:29)

30:22Then the LORD said to Moses, 23"Take the following fine spices: 500 shekels of liquid myrrh, half as much (that is, 250 shekels) of fragrant cinnamon, 250 shekels of fragrant cane, 24500 shekels of cassia—all according to the sanctuary shekel—and a hin of olive oil. 25Make these into a sacred anointing oil, a fragrant blend, the work of a perfumer. It will be the sacred anointing oil. 26Then use it to anoint the Tent of Meeting, the ark of the Testimony, 27the table and all its articles, the lampstand and its accessories, the altar of incense, 28the altar of burnt offering and all its utensils, and the basin with its stand. 29You shall consecrate them so they will be most holy, and whatever touches them will be holy.

30"Anoint Aaron and his sons and consecrate them so they may serve me as priests. 31Say to the Israelites, 'This is to be my sacred anointing oil for the generations to come. 32Do not pour it on men's bodies and do not make any oil with the same

---

46. Durham, *Exodus*, 488.

formula. It is sacred, and you are to consider it sacred. [33]Whoever makes perfume like it and whoever puts it on anyone other than a priest must be cut off from his people.'"

[34]Then the LORD said to Moses, "Take fragrant spices—gum resin, onycha and galbanum—and pure frankincense, all in equal amounts, [35]and make a fragrant blend of incense, the work of a perfumer. It is to be salted and pure and sacred. [36]Grind some of it to powder and place it in front of the Testimony in the Tent of Meeting, where I will meet with you. It shall be most holy to you. [37]Do not make any incense with this formula for yourselves; consider it holy to the LORD. [38]Whoever makes any like it to enjoy its fragrance must be cut off from his people."

[37:29]They also made the sacred anointing oil and the pure, fragrant incense—the work of a perfumer.

The basin for washing began with the third repetition of the creation-phrase, "Then the LORD said to Moses" (30:17). Instructions concerning the anointing oil (30:22) and the incense (30:34) are the fourth and fifth instances. I have grouped these two together for the sake of convenience, since the two are mentioned together in one sentence in 37:29.

The recipe for the oil is about sixteen pounds of cinnamon and spices and one gallon of olive oil—an expensive and even extravagant recipe. The purpose of the oil is to anoint the tabernacle and the furnishings, thereby consecrating them (as was the high priest, 29:7). Both are to be set apart for a holy purpose.

The anointing oil and the incense are to be kept only for cultic functions. It is not to be used for self-adornment of any sort, the penalty being to be "cut off from his people" (cf. this same phrase in 12:15, 19, regarding the keeping of the Passover). If we may bring 31:14 into the discussion here, being cut off apparently means more than banishment; it denotes being put to death: "Observe the Sabbath, because it is holy to you. Anyone who desecrates it must be put to death; whoever does any work on that day must be cut off from his people."

This is not totally surprising, since we have seen similar harsh penalties throughout this section. Death is the expected penalty for not following God's directions fully. One may be tempted to ask, "What is the big deal about anointing oil and incense?" This is not a biblical question to ask. The fact of the matter is that the oil and incense *are* worthy of such respect on Israel's part. I would add that the fact that both the oil and incense begin with the creation-phrase is itself an indication of their relative importance.

I must confess, however, that I do not see the logic of why the seven creative words are dispersed as they are. The following elements in chapters

25–31 are introduced by the creation formula: offerings for the tabernacle (25:1), atonement money (30:11), wash basin (30:17), anointing oil (30:22), incense (30:34), appointment of Bezalel and Oholiab (31:1), and Sabbath (31:12). Although the overall theological significance of this pattern of seven seems clear, why certain elements and not others are introduced in this manner is difficult to determine.

Bezalel and Oholiab (31:1–11; 35:30–36:7)

31:1Then the LORD said to Moses, 2"See, I have chosen Bezalel son of Uri, the son of Hur, of the tribe of Judah, 3and I have filled him with the Spirit of God, with skill, ability and knowledge in all kinds of crafts—4to make artistic designs for work in gold, silver and bronze, 5to cut and set stones, to work in wood, and to engage in all kinds of craftsmanship. 6Moreover, I have appointed Oholiab son of Ahisamach, of the tribe of Dan, to help him. Also I have given skill to all the craftsmen to make everything I have commanded you: 7the Tent of Meeting, the ark of the Testimony with the atonement cover on it, and all the other furnishings of the tent—8the table and its articles, the pure gold lampstand and all its accessories, the altar of incense, 9the altar of burnt offering and all its utensils, the basin with its stand—10and also the woven garments, both the sacred garments for Aaron the priest and the garments for his sons when they serve as priests, 11and the anointing oil and fragrant incense for the Holy Place. They are to make them just as I commanded you."

35:30Then Moses said to the Israelites, "See, the LORD has chosen Bezalel son of Uri, the son of Hur, of the tribe of Judah, 31and he has filled him with the Spirit of God, with skill, ability and knowledge in all kinds of crafts—32to make artistic designs for work in gold, silver and bronze, 33to cut and set stones, to work in wood and to engage in all kinds of artistic craftsmanship. 34And he has given both him and Oholiab son of Ahisamach, of the tribe of Dan, the ability to teach others. 35He has filled them with skill to do all kinds of work as craftsmen, designers, embroiderers in blue, purple and scarlet yarn and fine linen, and weavers—all of them master craftsmen and designers. 36:1So Bezalel, Oholiab and every skilled person to whom the LORD has given skill and ability to know how to carry out all the work of constructing the sanctuary are to do the work just as the Lord has commanded."

²Then Moses summoned Bezalel and Oholiab and every
skilled person to whom the LORD had given ability and who
was willing to come and do the work. ³They received from
Moses all the offerings the Israelites had brought to carry out
the work of constructing the sanctuary. And the people continued to bring freewill offerings morning after morning. ⁴So
all the skilled craftsmen who were doing all the work on the
sanctuary left their work ⁵and said to Moses, "The people are
bringing more than enough for doing the work the LORD commanded to be done."

⁶Then Moses gave an order and they sent this word
throughout the camp: "No man or woman is to make anything
else as an offering for the sanctuary." And so the people were
restrained from bringing more, ⁷because what they already
had was more than enough to do all the work.

Two men, Bezalel and Oholiab, are singled out for the task of putting all
the information together and building the tabernacle and all its furnishings
and other elements (the list in 31:7–11 is quite complete). To do so they are
filled with the Spirit of God (31:3, perhaps the same Spirit of God that was
present at creation in Gen. 1:2).[47] Perhaps such divine skill is needed in view
of the paucity of information given.[48] More likely is the fact that what needs
to be built is of great importance and seriousness. Not just anyone can rush
into this occupation foolishly. On the other hand, the seriousness of the
matter may have discouraged most from even attempting such a task were
it not for special divine empowerment.

We know precious little of Bezalel and less of Oholiab. The latter is
mentioned only in Exodus and the former is mentioned outside of Exodus
only incidentally (1 Chron. 2:20; 2 Chron. 1:5). If it is even valid to seek
significance in the etymology of names (a last resort when other information is lacking), Bezalel probably means "in the shadow/protection of
El [ʾel, a name for God]." Oholiab can mean either "father is my tent" or
perhaps "father is a tent." Thus, the names themselves may be an allusion
to the tabernacle.[49]

---

47. Elsewhere in the Pentateuch, the phrase "the Spirit of God" occurs only in Gen. 1:2;
41:38; Num. 24:2. Its use twice here (Ex. 31:3; 35:31) possibly implies that the creative force
present at creation is likewise present in the building of the tabernacle.

48. Cassuto points out that the descriptions that lack details are where Moses is shown
the likeness of the object, thus implying that special skill is needed to execute those plans
(*Commentary on Exodus*, 321).

49. Sarna, *Exodus*, 200.

The Sabbath (31:12–18; 35:1–3)

31:12Then the LORD said to Moses, 13"Say to the Israelites, 'You must observe my Sabbaths. This will be a sign between me and you for the generations to come, so you may know that I am the LORD, who makes you holy.

14"'Observe the Sabbath, because it is holy to you. Anyone who desecrates it must be put to death; whoever does any work on that day must be cut off from his people. 15For six days, work is to be done, but the seventh day is a Sabbath of rest, holy to the LORD. Whoever does any work on the Sabbath day must be put to death. 16The Israelites are to observe the Sabbath, celebrating it for the generations to come as a lasting covenant. 17It will be a sign between me and the Israelites forever, for in six days the LORD made the heavens and the earth, and on the seventh day he abstained from work and rested.'"

18When the LORD finished speaking to Moses on Mount Sinai, he gave him the two tablets of the Testimony, the tablets of stone inscribed by the finger of God.

35:1Moses assembled the whole Israelite community and said to them, "These are the things the LORD has commanded you to do: 2For six days, work is to be done, but the seventh day shall be your holy day, a Sabbath of rest to the LORD. Whoever does any work on it must be put to death. 3Do not light a fire in any of your dwellings on the Sabbath day."

As mentioned previously, the instructions concerning the building of the tabernacle end with the command to keep the Sabbath. The is the seventh passage of the tabernacle section to begin with the creation-formula, "Then the LORD said to Moses."

The plural "Sabbaths" refers to the regular keeping of the Sabbath day week in and week out, not to a multiplicity of differing Sabbath days. The observance of the Sabbath will be a lasting "sign" between God and Israel. Verses 16–17 spell this out: The Sabbath is a sign of the covenant God has made with Israel. God's conduct toward Israel in bringing them out of Egypt and establishing them as his people, an event that culminates here in the construction of the tabernacle and the institution of Israel's religious system, is tied to creation in verse 17.

It is most fitting that the Sabbath be the sign of this covenant. Israel, as we have noted, is a new creation. This is a new people of God, whom he intends to use to undo the work of the first man. Also, the tabernacle is a microcosm of the created order, a parcel of edenic splendor established amid the chaos of the world. The Sabbath is not just a reminder of the original creation in Genesis 1 and 2, but a reminder of God's re-creation of the cosmos in the tabernacle.

The purpose of the Sabbath is "so you may know that I am the LORD, who makes you holy" (31:13). It is, in other words, a reminder of who God is and what his intentions are for his people. We also see here what Jesus meant when he said, "The Sabbath was made for man, not man for the Sabbath" (Mark 2:27). The regular keeping of the Sabbath serves a purpose for our benefit, to help us along in a deeper understanding of who God is.

Failure to keep the Sabbath ("desecration," 31:14), therefore, is to be met with severe punishment, death—or, as we have seen also with the oil and incense, being "cut off from his people." This penalty seems harsh, but not when we realize what the Sabbath was intended to do. By not keeping the Sabbath, the Israelite was showing that he or she was not interested in "know[ing] that I am the LORD." Desecration means to do work, though as we saw under the fourth commandment, the Bible does not provide us a list of what constitutes work. In this respect, attempts in the history of Judaism to define what precisely is work are understandable.

The instructions concerning the building of the tabernacle and its furnishings end in 31:18. The two tablets of the Testimony are to be placed in the ark. It is worth mentioning again that 35:1 picks up right where 31:18 leaves off without missing a beat—as if to say that the intervening episode of rebellion (chs. 32—34) and the near dissolving of the covenant relationship on God's part (see 32:9—14) are forgotten. The framing of the rebellion narrative with the Sabbath law indicates that God's plan is now going forth unabated.

An unusual detail is added in 35:3. Work, of course, is the way in which the Sabbath day is desecrated. But why the cryptic reference to lighting a fire? Does lighting a fire constitute work, as if to say, perhaps, that one cannot cook on the Sabbath?[50] In my opinion, "lighting a fire" is too specific and unexpected a detail to refer simply to one particular type of work that might be done on the Sabbath. Much more plausible is the connection made by Levenson.[51] The Ugaritic story of the building of Baal's palace speaks of fire consuming the structure for six days and subsiding the seventh.[52] As Levenson comments,

> The extinction of the flames on the seventh day of casting Baal's temple is strangely reminiscent of the biblical prohibitions against kindling a fire, baking, or boiling on the Sabbath.[53]

---

50. This is Durham's opinion (*Exodus*, 475).
51. See Levenson, *Creation*, 78—80.
52. Pritchard, *Ancient Near Eastern Texts*, 134.
53. Levenson, *Creation*, 79.

Apparently, what Levenson suggests is that the prohibition in 35:3 against lighting fires on the Sabbath reflects a story such as we see in the Ugaritic text. This is not to say, of course, that the Israelites read the Baal story and appropriated it for their own purpose. Rather, as we have seen elsewhere in Exodus, Israel's religious experience reflected the religious and cultural setting in which they lived.

Finally, the reference to the Sabbath at the end of the first part of the tabernacle section has further significance beyond that of continuing the connection of Exodus to creation. The building of the tabernacle, as we have seen, is a microcosm of the created world—heavenly order amid earthly chaos. It is a true sanctuary where Israel continually experiences its connection to their God, who brought them out of Israel. The tabernacle is like no other place on earth. It is built according to a divine plan to reflect a heavenly reality. It is a piece of holy ground.

To put it another way, the tabernacle is holy space. The Sabbath, by contrast, is holy time. By building the tabernacle and setting apart one day in seven, God is truly recreating heaven in *space* and *time*. Weekly Sabbath worship is on holy ground in holy time. There is no more holy spot on the face of the earth than the tabernacle on the Sabbath. We can see how important the tabernacle, and later the temple, was to Israel's identity as God's people. We can also see how utterly devastating the destruction of the temple by the Babylonians was. By entering the tabernacle, Israel entered God's house; by keeping the Sabbath, Israel entered God's rest.

Collecting of Materials (35:10–29)

35:10"All who are skilled among you are to come and make everything the LORD has commanded: ¹¹the tabernacle with its tent and its covering, clasps, frames, crossbars, posts and bases; ¹²the ark with its poles and the atonement cover and the curtain that shields it; ¹³the table with its poles and all its articles and the bread of the Presence; ¹⁴the lampstand that is for light with its accessories, lamps and oil for the light; ¹⁵the altar of incense with its poles, the anointing oil and the fragrant incense; the curtain for the doorway at the entrance to the tabernacle; ¹⁶the altar of burnt offering with its bronze grating, its poles and all its utensils; the bronze basin with its stand; ¹⁷the curtains of the courtyard with its posts and bases, and the curtain for the entrance to the courtyard; ¹⁸the tent pegs for the tabernacle and for the courtyard, and their ropes; ¹⁹the woven garments worn for ministering in the sanctuary—

both the sacred garments for Aaron the priest and the garments for his sons when they serve as priests."

²⁰Then the whole Israelite community withdrew from
Moses' presence, ²¹and everyone who was willing and whose
heart moved him came and brought an offering to the LORD
for the work on the Tent of Meeting, for all its service, and
for the sacred garments. ²²All who were willing, men and
women alike, came and brought gold jewelry of all kinds:
brooches, earrings, rings and ornaments. They all presented
their gold as a wave offering to the LORD. ²³Everyone who
had blue, purple or scarlet yarn or fine linen, or goat hair,
ram skins dyed red or hides of sea cows brought them.
²⁴Those presenting an offering of silver or bronze brought it
as an offering to the LORD, and everyone who had acacia
wood for any part of the work brought it. ²⁵Every skilled
woman spun with her hands and brought what she had
spun—blue, purple or scarlet yarn or fine linen. ²⁶And all
the women who were willing and had the skill spun the goat
hair. ²⁷The leaders brought onyx stones and other gems to
be mounted on the ephod and breastpiece. ²⁸They also
brought spices and olive oil for the light and for the anointing oil and for the fragrant incense. ²⁹All the Israelite men
and women who were willing brought to the LORD freewill
offerings for all the work the LORD through Moses had commanded them to do.

This is the first passage in the second part of the tabernacle section that
is not treated in the first part, although 35:11–19 is similar to 31:6–10. The
narrative of the collection of the building materials logically precedes the presentation of Bezalel and Oholiab in 35:30–36:7, but the latter was treated
above in conjunction with its parallel in 31:1–11.

Verses 10–19 review what the Israelites are to build: the tabernacle, its furnishings, and the priestly garments. Verses 20–29 recount the actual col-
lecting of the materials necessary to do the work. The emphasis here seems
to be on the willingness of the Israelites to give and the participation of both
men and women. Women are particularly singled out by the writer as spin-
ners of yarn and goat hair (vv. 25–26).

The reference to acacia wood is interesting (v. 24). How is this to be
understood? Are we to think of Israelites carrying planks of wood out of
Egypt? The tree was common in the Sinai peninsula, so it is conceivable
that the Israelites felled the trees and shaped the planks, even though this

is not described in the Exodus narrative. Verse 24 refers merely to "every-one who had acacia wood," a statement that does not imply the cutting of planks.

Also, verse 28 seems to suggest that the oil for the light and anointing are not pounded by the Israelites but are simply in their possession. This implies that these materials were part of the plunder brought from Egypt.

List of Materials Used (38:21–31)

38:21These are the amounts of the materials used for the tabernacle, the tabernacle of the Testimony, which were recorded at Moses' command by the Levites under the direction of Ithamar son of Aaron, the priest. 22(Bezalel son of Uri, the son of Hur, of the tribe of Judah, made everything the LORD commanded Moses; 23with him was Oholiab son of Ahisamach, of the tribe of Dan—a craftsman and designer, and an embroiderer in blue, purple and scarlet yarn and fine linen.) 24The total amount of the gold from the wave offering used for all the work on the sanctuary was 29 talents and 730 shekels, according to the sanctuary shekel.

25The silver obtained from those of the community who were counted in the census was 100 talents and 1,775 shekels, according to the sanctuary shekel—26one beka per person, that is, half a shekel, according to the sanctuary shekel, from everyone who had crossed over to those counted, twenty years old or more, a total of 603,550 men. 27The 100 talents of silver were used to cast the bases for the sanctuary and for the curtain—100 bases from the 100 tal-ents, one talent for each base. 28They used the 1,775 shekels to make the hooks for the posts, to overlay the tops of the posts, and to make their bands.

29The bronze from the wave offering was 70 talents and 2,400 shekels. 30They used it to make the bases for the entrance to the Tent of Meeting, the bronze altar with its bronze grating and all its utensils, 31the bases for the sur-rounding courtyard and those for its entrance and all the tent pegs for the tabernacle and those for the surrounding courtyard.

We have here a list not only of the materials used but of their weights. This list is recorded by the priests under the direction of Ithamar, one of Aaron's four sons. It takes 300 shekels to make one talent. The approximate weights of the material listed, in today's measures, are as follows:[54] 2,193.25 pounds of gold; 7,544.38 pounds of silver;[55] 5,310 pounds of bronze. To put it in perspective, the total weight in precious metals the Israelites carried out of Egypt was about 15,000 pounds. This may seem like an excessively heavy amount in the abstract, but it comes to only approximately .025 pounds for every adult male Israelite—pocket change. There is no need to suggest, as some have done, that these weights are exaggerated numbers.

plunder

The Work Is Completed (39:32–43)

39:32So all the work on the tabernacle, the Tent of Meeting, was completed. The Israelites did everything just as the LORD commanded Moses. 33Then they brought the tabernacle to Moses: the tent and all its furnishings, its clasps, frames, crossbars, posts and bases; 34the covering of ram skins dyed red, the covering of hides of sea cows and the shielding curtain; 35the ark of the Testimony with its poles and the atonement cover; 36the table with all its articles and the bread of the Presence; 37the pure gold lampstand with its row of lamps and all its accessories, and the oil for the light; 38the gold altar, the anointing oil, the fragrant incense, and the curtain for the entrance to the tent; 39the bronze altar with its bronze grating, its poles and all its utensils; the basin with its stand; 40the curtains of the courtyard with its posts and bases, and the curtain for the entrance to the courtyard; the ropes and tent pegs for the courtyard; all the furnishings for the tabernacle, the Tent of Meeting; 41and the woven garments worn for ministering in the sanctuary, both the sacred garments for Aaron the priest and the garments for his sons when serving as priests.

42The Israelites had done all the work just as the LORD had commanded Moses. 43Moses inspected the work and saw that they had done it just as the LORD had commanded. So Moses blessed them.

---

54. One talent is approximately 75 pounds. One shekel is 2/5 of an ounce (i.e., it takes 40 shekels to make one pound).

55. Each Israelite who crossed the Red Sea gave one beka (= 1/2 shekel). One hundred talents and 1,775 shekels comes to 301,775 shekels (one talent = 3000 shekels, hence 100 talents = 300,000 shekels). Since a beka is 1/2 a shekel, the total number of Israelite men who crossed the sea (assuming "men" in v. 26 is to be taken literally) is twice the number of shekels, hence the number 603,550.

This reference to the completed work (esp. vv. 33–41) includes a list more complete than the ones found in 31:7–11 and 35:11–19. This passage recounts Israel's obedience, provides a summary of what is made, and relays Moses' inspection. Verse 32 explicitly equates the tabernacle and the Tent of Meeting.

We have seen a number of creation connections. Several more are found here. (1) In verse 32, the work is "completed." The Hebrew root (klh) is also used in Genesis 2:2 for the completion of God's creative work.[56] (2) Moses inspects the work and sees (rʾh) that the Israelites have completed the work well, according to plan. This is an allusion to God's inspecting his creative work and "seeing" (rʾh) that it was good (e.g., Gen. 1:31). (3) Moses "blesses" (brk) the people after completing the work as God "blessed" (brk) his creation (Gen. 1:22, 28; 2:3). These allusions to creation are not accidental. They confirm that the biblical writer wishes the reader to view the construction of the tabernacle as an act of creation.

The Tabernacle Is Set Up (40:1–33)

40:1Then the LORD said to Moses: 2"Set up the tabernacle, the Tent of Meeting, on the first day of the first month. 3Place the ark of the Testimony in it and shield the ark with the curtain. 4Bring in the table and set out what belongs on it. Then bring in the lampstand and set up its lamps. 5Place the gold altar of incense in front of the ark of the Testimony and put the curtain at the entrance to the tabernacle.

6"Place the altar of burnt offering in front of the entrance to the tabernacle, the Tent of Meeting; 7place the basin between the Tent of Meeting and the altar and put water in it. 8Set up the courtyard around it and put the curtain at the entrance to the courtyard.

9"Take the anointing oil and anoint the tabernacle and everything in it; consecrate it and all its furnishings, and it will be holy. 10Then anoint the altar of burnt offering and all its utensils; consecrate the altar, and it will be most holy. 11Anoint the basin and its stand and consecrate them.

12"Bring Aaron and his sons to the entrance to the Tent of Meeting and wash them with water. 13Then dress Aaron in the sacred garments, anoint him and consecrate him so he may serve me as priest. 14Bring his sons and dress them in tunics.

---

56. See Cassuto, Commentary on Exodus, 476–77; Levenson, Creation, 85–86.

¹⁵Anoint them just as you anointed their father, so they may serve me as priests. Their anointing will be to a priesthood that will continue for all generations to come." ¹⁶Moses did everything just as the LORD commanded him.

¹⁷So the tabernacle was set up on the first day of the first month in the second year. ¹⁸When Moses set up the tabernacle, he put the bases in place, erected the frames, inserted the crossbars and set up the posts. ¹⁹Then he spread the tent over the tabernacle and put the covering over the tent, as the LORD commanded him.

²⁰He took the Testimony and placed it in the ark, attached the poles to the ark and put the atonement cover over it. ²¹Then he brought the ark into the tabernacle and hung the shielding curtain and shielded the ark of the Testimony, as the LORD commanded him.

²²Moses placed the table in the Tent of Meeting on the north side of the tabernacle outside the curtain ²³and set out the bread on it before the LORD, as the LORD commanded him.

²⁴He placed the lampstand in the Tent of Meeting opposite the table on the south side of the tabernacle ²⁵and set up the lamps before the LORD, as the LORD commanded him.

²⁶Moses placed the gold altar in the Tent of Meeting in front of the curtain ²⁷and burned fragrant incense on it, as the LORD commanded him. ²⁸Then he put up the curtain at the entrance to the tabernacle.

²⁹He set the altar of burnt offering near the entrance to the tabernacle, the Tent of Meeting, and offered on it burnt offerings and grain offerings, as the LORD commanded him.

³⁰He placed the basin between the Tent of Meeting and the altar and put water in it for washing, ³¹and Moses and Aaron and his sons used it to wash their hands and feet. ³²They washed whenever they entered the Tent of Meeting or approached the altar, as the LORD commanded Moses.

³³Then Moses set up the courtyard around the tabernacle and altar and put up the curtain at the entrance to the courtyard. And so Moses finished the work.

The narrative of the tabernacle concludes, appropriately, by recounting how it is set up. Verses 1–11 are the detailed commands given by God to Moses concerning what needs to be done: The tabernacle is to be set up, the furnishings put in their places, and both the tabernacle and the furnishings are to be anointed. Verses 12–15 follow with the commands concerning the anointing of the priests. After the summary acknowledgment that Moses obeys God fully (v. 16), the details of the set-up are recounted (vv. 17–33).

There is also creation language here. In fact, this section ends (v. 33) by repeating almost verbatim the language of Genesis 2:2. Compare the Hebrew transliteration of both verses:

Exodus 40:33:	*waykal mošeh ʾet ham-mᵉlaʾka*	So Moses finished the work.
Genesis 2:2:	*waykal ʾᵉlohim bayyom haššᵉbiᶜi mᵉlaʾkᵉto*	So God *on the seventh day* finished *his* work.

Only Genesis 2:2 has the clause "on the seventh day," but both say that God/Moses *finished* (Heb. root *klh*) *work* (Heb. *mlʾkh*). Moses' overseeing the construction of the tabernacle is like God building the universe.

We also see that the tabernacle is set up "on the first day of the first month in the second year" (v. 17). As we saw in 12:2, the Exodus inaugurated a new calendar in Israelite life: The month in which the Exodus took place would be the first month of the year. The deliverance of Israel from Egypt marked a new beginning for God's people, a "new creation." It is no surprise, therefore, that the tabernacle, itself a microcosm of creation, is also set up one year later on the first day of the first month. It, too, is a new creation.

A final creation connection here is perhaps more subtle, but worth pointing out. We see not only in this passage but throughout the tabernacle section that marked attention is given to the precision by which the tabernacle and its furnishings are to be made and where precisely the furnishings are to be placed in the tabernacle. This uncompromising attention to details is another indication that the tabernacle is an act of creation: It reflects the order that God originally created in the universe. There is no room for human disorder or for chaos to invade this holy space. Everything must be exactly as God has commanded. The order of the tabernacle reflects God's very nature, a nature that creation itself reflects.

Bridging Contexts

THE THEOLOGY OF **the tabernacle and temple.** The tabernacle (and later, the temple) and the priestly service are at the heart of ancient Israelite religious practice. The notion, so common among Christians, that these institutions were mainly about endless sacrifices and tedious rituals and can therefore be safely dismissed misunderstands not only their significance in the Old Testament but the purpose of Christ's coming. These institutions were, rather, symbols of a higher—and ultimately mysterious—reality. They were truly the means by which God and his people "connected."

To draw the tabernacle into the orbit of the Christian life, however, does not mean simply transferring its surface meaning to today's world. We must understand what the tabernacle *represents*. What does it teach us about God, and how do those lessons develop as biblical revelation progresses? In other words, we need to answer the question, "What did the tabernacle 'do' for Israel?" It is, therefore, the theology of the tabernacle that holds our interest.

Of course, from Exodus 25 on, the tabernacle and priestly regulations remain recurring topics of discussion. The duties of the priests are more fully described in Leviticus and the early chapters of Numbers. The institution founded at the foot of Mount Sinai, one year after the Exodus, marches full steam for several generations, from the Exodus to the desert period, then on to the Conquest, the judges, and the early years of the monarchy.

Eventually, the portable tabernacle is replaced by the temple, a structure intended to be permanent.[57] The construction of the temple is given a much briefer account than that of the tabernacle (see 1 Kings 5−8). Also, specific instructions as to how it should be built are missing, the emphasis being mainly on the fact that Solomon built it rather than David (see 2 Sam. 7:12−13). Most likely it was constructed according to the pattern of the tabernacle, the obvious differences being the materials used (e.g., stone and cedar for the temple) and its size (the temple being roughly twice as large).

Despite these understandable changes, however, what the tabernacle represented remains essentially unchanged with the construction of the temple. Hence, it is perfectly legitimate, indeed necessary, to speak of the theology of the tabernacle and of the temple in the same breath, for the latter is a conscious continuation of the former.

We have seen that the tabernacle was an earthly representation of heavenly reality. It was a microcosm of the created order—hence, a microcosm of the only spotless point in creation, Eden. This is not to say, however, that the intended ideal was always met. It is fair to say that God's great revelation in Exodus 25−40, the establishment of the tabernacle and the priesthood, became *institutionalized* over time. This state of affairs prompted prophetic critique. Relatively little is mentioned by the prophets about the tabernacle,

---

57. I should point out here again the interesting theory of R. E. Friedman that the tabernacle was not discarded when the temple was built but was placed inside. It seems unreasonable that the tabernacle, made by God's command and according to his divine design, would simply have been tossed aside. See "Tabernacle," *ABD*, 6:298−99; *Who Wrote the Bible*, 174−87.

the temple, and the priestly system. But what little there is, is critical of what these institutions *had become* (see Isa. 1:10–17; Hos. 6:6; Amos 5:21–24; Mic. 6:6–8; see also Ps. 40:6; 50:7–15; 51:16–17).

In making this observation we should be careful to avoid the common Christian criticism that these institutions *in and of themselves* are tedious and ineffective. The prophetic critique is against *abuse* of the system, the notion that God can be controlled or manipulated apart from a true heart devotion to him. In fact, such prophetic critique presumes the legitimacy of the system itself. The tabernacle, despite being built as a perfect rectangle, was never intended to be a "box" in which God, like the pagan gods around them, could be safely stored away and called upon to serve the people's purpose. If anything, the many allusions to creation in the tabernacle's construction reminded Israel of the exact opposite: The God worshiped within is Creator of heaven and earth.

The temple was the center of Israel's religious activity. Without it, they would cease to be an active, worshiping people of God. Without it, the purpose for which they were brought out of Egypt no longer existed. This is why the Exile and destruction of the temple was such a devastating event. For hundreds of years God had been seated above the ark, between the cherubim. Where would he be now? Where would the priests go to offer the daily sacrifices and the all-important rituals of the Day of Atonement? We will have little sympathy with this state of affairs if we assume that these things were merely dead ritual, but we must never forget that these rituals were instituted at God's command and that the tabernacle was an earthly representation of God's heavenly dwelling built by his design. Now it is gone. Devastating!

During the Exile Israel's self-identity took a heavy beating. Afterward one of Israel's first orders of business was to rebuild the temple, a task recorded in Ezra and Haggai. Clearly, the reestablishment of the temple ritual was important. The problem, however, was that the second temple was a mere shadow of the first one, as is implied in Haggai 2:3: "Who of you is left who saw this house in its former glory? How does it look to you now? Does it not seem to you like nothing?" Temple worship continued to be vital to Israelite life throughout the late biblical and intertestamental period, but it never again achieved the grandeur and attention it once had.

On at least two occasions, Jesus is referred to as either the new temple or the tabernacle. Well known are Jesus' words in John 2:19: "Destroy this temple, and I will raise it again in three days." This was misunderstood by the Jews as a claim to be able to rebuild the literal temple, but John quickly adds that the temple of which Jesus spoke was his body (v. 21). John 1:14 is also important here, although its impact is lost in English: "The Word became flesh and *made his dwelling* among us" (italics added). The Greek verb translated "made his dwelling" is *skenoo*, which is related to the noun *skene*, the word used throughout the Septuagint (Greek translation of the Hebrew Old Testament) for the tabernacle. In other words, Jesus came and "tabernacled" among his people.[58]

To talk like this does more than simply add a bit of drama to shock the readers. The intention is that Jesus be seen as the new—and improved—tabernacle/temple. This is not to reject the Old Testament versions of the temple as merely ritualistic and now, thankfully, done away with. It is, rather, to understand the reality to which the Old Testament structures pointed, a reality that reaches its climax in Christ. Hence, John continues in John 1:14: "We have seen his glory." The glory that resided above the ark in the Most Holy Place, to which the high priest alone had access once a year, is now walking the streets of Jerusalem for all to see, a truly "portable" tabernacle!

The coming of Christ is not a dulling of the majesty of the Old Testament tabernacle but a heightening of what it stood for. True, the ornate decorations and furnishings are not here, but something far better is. Inasmuch as the tabernacle was an earthly representation of a heavenly reality, how much more so is Christ, who—to continue John's words in 1:14—"came from the Father, full of grace and truth." Christ fulfills the purpose for which the tabernacle was built.

We should also keep in mind here the role of the priests in the tabernacle. We saw earlier that their garments, particularly those of the high priest, were made of the same material as the tabernacle. In a manner of speaking, the priests embodied the tabernacle. What the tabernacle was made for—to connect the people with God—is also what the priests did by properly performing their duties in that tent. Like a priest,[59] Christ also embodies the tabernacle, not by how he is dressed but by who he is. His clothes are not reminders of the heavenly reality; rather, he himself as God and man *is* the manifestation of that reality. That which the tabernacle and the priesthood together symbolized only partially is embodied fully by Christ alone.

At Christ's return, another chapter will be written on this theme. At the descent of the new Jerusalem, there will be no temple in this new city, for "the Lord God Almighty and the Lamb are its temple" (Rev. 21:22). At the end of our age and the dawn of the new, what the tabernacle and temple represented in the Old Testament, the very presence of God, will be present with God's people without mediation. God himself will live with his people. These

---

58. See also L. Morris, *The Gospel According to John* (rev. ed.; Grand Rapids: Eerdmans, 1995), 91–93.

59. Jesus is called "high priest" in Heb. 2:17; 3:1; 4:14–15; 5:5, 10; 7:26, 28; 8:1; 9:11.

words are no doubt intended to provoke the imagination rather than satisfy our intellectual curiosity. Just how this will look is hard to say. What John does make clear, however, is that at the consummation, the very thing that shaped Israelite self-identity will no longer be needed, because something better will be here, which was first seen when Christ came to earth.

Between the first and second comings of Christ there is another state of affairs. Christ, the new temple, has ascended to the Father. His presence, however, has not left his people, for he has sent his Spirit to abide with us. In fact, he abides *in* us. This is what Paul means in his description of the church in 1 Corinthians 3:16–17: "Don't you know that you[60] yourselves are God's temple and that God's Spirit lives in you? If anyone destroys God's temple, God will destroy him; for God's temple is sacred, and you are that temple." This is not just a way of saying that the church is "special" to God. Paul is saying that the church now becomes God's holy dwelling, God's temple.

Paul continues the thought in 1 Corinthians 6:19: "Do you not know that your body is a temple of the Holy Spirit, who is in you, whom you have received from God? You are not your own." The apostle here applies the temple theme to the individual Christian, for the topic here is sexual conduct for individual believers. His point is that between the first and second comings of Christ, the church both collectively and individually realizes the intimacy between God and his people that was first experienced at the building of the tabernacle.

In knowing that Christ fulfills the tabernacle/temple, we can point out a few ways in which some of the specifics of the tabernacle and its symbolism come into sharper focus in Christ. As I mentioned earlier, I do not advocate finding specific Christological significance in, for example, the lampstand or the anointing oil. Even though such an approach has been taken, I see little value in it. We are after the big picture—how the symbolism of the tabernacle as a whole comes to fulfillment in Christ.

As I have argued, the idea of creation is important for understanding the tabernacle. The tabernacle represents God's presence on earth, just as the coming of Christ does. Also, the tabernacle represents a new creation, which comes into clearer focus in Christ. He who was "in the beginning" (John 1:1) comes now to "tabernacle" with his people (1:14). He is a piece of heaven on earth and, like one drop of dye in a glass of water, he has come so that his creative force may spread through all of creation, making all things new (2 Cor. 5:17; Rev. 21:5).

To use another element discussed above, Christ is himself holy and sacred ground, in whom the glory of God resides. With the spread of the gospel,

---

60. The Greek "you" is plural, indicating that the church at Corinth as a body is meant.

God's glory can now be seen in new temples everywhere, that is, wherever men and women repent and come to know God, wherever people gather together to worship. God's sacred space is no longer restricted to a building in one part of the world. Nor is it embodied only in his Son, as it was for a brief time two thousand years ago. By the work of the Holy Spirit, God's sacred space has spread over all the earth. Indeed, the redemption of the earth was his plan all along. As it was once before, the earth is now again God's holy dwelling.

WE ARE THE TABERNACLE OF GOD. How does one "apply" the tabernacle? As we have just seen, the New Testament points us in the direction we should go. Christ fulfills the symbolism of the tabernacle/temple, and Christians, because they are in Christ, have also become the dwelling place of God, the "temple" (to use Paul's word). What does it mean for God to take up residence in us? How does this work out concretely in our lives?

A proper understanding of the theology of the tabernacle does not provide us with specific guidelines for what we ought to do. A contemporary application of the tabernacle would be strained indeed if we looked to the curtains or furniture for clues as to how we should live. For example, the weekly replenishing of the bread of the Presence is not a sign that we should tithe, nor is the lampstand a sign that "the light of God" should always shine in us. And as beautiful and ornate as the tabernacle/temple was, it is not a justification for the opulence of some modern churches. Any such "application" misses not only the original significance of the tabernacle but how the Bible as a whole, especially the New Testament, has understood that significance.

Applying the tabernacle must be approached from a different angle. Rather than tell us *what* we ought to do, it tells us *why* we ought to do it. It is the tabernacle as a whole that we should seek to apply. It is the big picture that gives us a proper theological framework within which to view our daily activities. A proper understanding of tabernacle theology motivates us to live so as to please God. It does this simply by *reminding us* of who God is and who we are in relation to him. An understanding of the tabernacle helps shape our minds to reflect more the way God wants us to think.

No one should think that such an approach to application is merely "cerebral." I often hear people say, "That's just head knowledge. I want something I can sink my teeth into, something I can do! I need something I can tell the people Sunday morning!" That point is well taken, but sometimes the best way to make it happen is to take a step back from the hustle and bustle and remember—meditate on who God is and what he has done for us. The Bible itself gives numerous examples, particularly in the Psalms, of the importance of catching the vision and remembering who God is (Ps. 8; 19; 24; 105; 106; 144–150). We should think of "application" as including such reflection. Sometimes what the Bible does is change how we *think* about God, ourselves, and the world we live in. Only after our thinking is properly adjusted can we behave in ways that reflect that thinking.

Thus, the tabernacle—what it looked like, how it functioned, what it represented—is one reminder of who God is. There is perhaps no thought more important than to be clear on the question of what God is like. What is the picture of God that we see in the tabernacle?

For one thing, we have noted repeatedly that the tabernacle is a microcosm of creation. In it we see the God of all creation dwelling on earth in a structure intended to reflect the perfect created order—a piece of heaven on earth. Then, at the climactic stage in redemptive history, God took up residence in Christ, the temple who "tabernacled" among his people. He is not a building constructed to reflect heavenly glory. He himself is from heaven and is therefore the concrete manifestation of what the tabernacle symbolized. And finally, inexplicably, the God of creation has built us up to be his house so he can take up residence in us. He has fashioned us with material far more precious than gold or silver, dyed yarn or fine linen, in the image of the risen Christ so that even we reflect a piece of heaven. We are worthy of the Spirit's indwelling because we have been re-created by the power of God into heavenly beings.

What does this mean? The paths to understanding and applying this profound mystery are endless. But I want to point out two implications for how we, as tabernacles, should reflect the order of God amid the chaos around us: how we worship and how we live.

(1) The tabernacle was a place of worship, a place of giving God praise and acknowledging that he alone is worthy. It was a place of "connecting" with God. Worship may be described as the place where heaven and earth meet. This is why we "go to church" on Sunday. When the saints of God meet on Sunday mornings, they, like the Israelites before them, are worshiping in holy time and space. It is holy time because, like the Sabbath, it is the one day in seven set apart for worship. It is holy space in the sense that church buildings set apart from common use are dedicated to the worship of God. I do not mean that the modern church building is analogous to the tabernacle; Christ is the analogy, as are those who are in Christ. I only mean that there is something different, something "set apart," something holy about Christians meeting together at an appointed time and place each week.

I don't always feel like going to church. Sometimes I think it is boring. Sometimes I just want a break. (I thank God my salvation does not depend on whether or not I have these feelings!) At times like these I preach to myself, encouraging myself about what going to church means. I remind myself of the profound mystery of God's dwelling among his people. Church is not a place where programs happen. It is not a place to go and be noticed by others. It is not a place to meet people. It is not even a place where we "listen to sermons." It is *where heaven and earth meet.* To be sure, one implication of our being tabernacles of the Spirit is that each of us is a concrete reminder that God has come to earth. But God has chosen to do this not only individually but corporately. Christians come together to experience communally the reality that God dwells with us.

This is why we go to church—not because we "have to" or because we will feel guilty if we don't. We do it because it is the ordained manner by which we enter into God's time and God's space. Sunday is a foretaste of eternity, where all of time and space will be completely, tangibly under God's rule. We go to church regularly not to put notches on our belts, but because the weekly rhythm becomes a part of us; it seeps into our routines, not so that it can simply become "routine," but so it can shape us into the people of God.

Going to church is also a testimony to the chaotic world around us. As redeemed people we participate in heavenly reality. Worshiping God collectively one day in seven is a sign to the world that there is something other, something higher, than the private universes people create for themselves. Whether in the end the world is attracted to this alternative is the Lord's doing, not ours. But we bear visible, tangible witness that God's order is not the order of the world. We demonstrate that we follow different rules, God's rules, and in doing so God is glorified.

(2) We also reflect divine order by how we live day to day in a fallen world. When we think of our bodies as the temple of God, it puts sinning in a different perspective. This is really Paul's point in 1 Corinthians 6:18–20, where he equates individual Christians at Corinth with the temple. Some in Corinth were engaging in sexual immorality. Paul's rebuke essentially amounts to this: "What, are you crazy?! How can you *possibly* think of doing anything like this?! Don't you know God himself resides in you?!"

Paul's attitude here should not be restricted to sexual sin. It should define our attitude concerning *any* kind of sin. God is not out there, up in the sky somewhere looking down occasionally at what we are doing, so "make sure you're good." God has chosen to take up residence in us. This is a way of getting at the intimacy that God shares with his people.

Some things are unthinkable in God's house. No one, for example, would put a condom machine alongside the pulpit of a church (although in our day and age, I am not so sure). Well, we are God's house, and some things should be unthinkable for us. In fact, if we wish to expand the analogy with the Old Testament tabernacle, *any* sin is repulsive. Just like the construction of the tabernacle and its furnishings, not even the slightest deviation from the divine norm can be tolerated. To introduce sin to the holy dwellings God has made us is unthinkable.

Most Christians, at least on paper, readily acknowledge that all sins are equal. As a matter of practice, however, we devise our own hierarchy. We would rather have our children cheat on their taxes than on their spouses. Lying is OK if it is against an impersonal company, but not if against your parents. To be honest, such hierarchies exist because we all sense that some sins get more at the heart of things than others. I also think it is "less wrong" to steal a pencil from work than to break into someone's house and steal their personal belongings. The point to keep in mind, however, is that we are God's temple and that everything in it has its place and order. Throughout the tabernacle narrative we read recurring reminders that Moses is to follow the divine pattern exactly, without the slightest deviation. As God's temple, we should also strive to follow God's pattern even to the smallest detail.

Such knowledge should not make us paranoid about whether we are living perfect lives. That will not happen. We sin unconsciously all the time, and the blood of Christ atones continually for us. But what of those situations that come up constantly, where a conscious decision has to be made, a fork in the road between the right thing and the wrong thing? These are the times when we hear that all too familiar argument going on inside our heads: "Should I or shouldn't I?" "I know I should trust God, but I just don't have the motivation." These are the times in our lives to put on the brakes and say: "No. I won't do it. I am going to do the right thing, no matter what. The Spirit of God resides in me."

The fact that the Spirit of God resides in our bodies also reminds us that our physical bodies are worthy of such honor. Again, no one is clear as to what it means for God to dwell in us. I do not mean to present a childish picture of God pulling up a chair somewhere behind our solar plexus. But neither do I not want to play down what Paul assumes in 1 Corinthians 6:19 about the importance of our bodies: "Do you not know that your body is a temple of the Holy Spirit, who is in you, whom you have received from God? You are not your own."

Our society exhibits two extremes with respect to the physical body. On the one hand, our bodies and its desires are the center of the universe, our only goal being to satisfy its urgings. Much advertising is based on this assumption. On the other hand, the opposite notion also prevails, that what is important is getting in touch with our inner selves, to find spiritual solace that our bodies cannot give us. The latter has affinities with certain quarters of ancient Greek philosophy that tended to downplay the importance of the flesh and amplify the mind or soul. There was a dichotomy between body and soul; the soul was the "real you," whereas the body was just a temporary prison from which you yearned to be released. I would suggest that the latter approach, with its ancient roots, is to some extent borne out of the failures of the former.

In any event, Christians, whose bodies are God's temple, should be able to resist either of these extremes. Though our bodies are worthy of divine indwelling, this does not make flesh and blood the center of the universe. If anything, it reminds us that we should hold our personal urgings in check. But it also reminds us that our bodies are good. Our reflection of God's image is both spiritual and physical. We are *entirely* created in God's image. While this does not imply that God has a body, it does mean that the totality of our humanity is by God's design. It was the whole person that God declared "very good" on the sixth day of creation (Gen. 1:31). We do not shun the body, nor do we worship it. The fact that God somehow, mysteriously dwells in the human body shows that our physical selves are to be elevated to the appropriate level.

The story of the Bible is nothing less than God's initial intimacy with his creation, the severing of that intimacy, and the steps he takes to restore that intimacy. By living in us, by making us temples of his Spirit, he demonstrates that we are participating in the last chapter of that story.

Exodus 32:1–34:35

WHEN THE PEOPLE saw that Moses was so long in coming down from the mountain, they gathered around Aaron and said, "Come, make us gods who will go before us. As for this fellow Moses who brought us up out of Egypt, we don't know what has happened to him."

²Aaron answered them, "Take off the gold earrings that your wives, your sons and your daughters are wearing, and bring them to me." ³So all the people took off their earrings and brought them to Aaron. ⁴He took what they handed him and made it into an idol cast in the shape of a calf, fashioning it with a tool. Then they said, "These are your gods, O Israel, who brought you up out of Egypt."

⁵When Aaron saw this, he built an altar in front of the calf and announced, "Tomorrow there will be a festival to the LORD." ⁶So the next day the people rose early and sacrificed burnt offerings and presented fellowship offerings. Afterward they sat down to eat and drink and got up to indulge in revelry.

⁷Then the LORD said to Moses, "Go down, because your people, whom you brought up out of Egypt, have become corrupt. ⁸They have been quick to turn away from what I commanded them and have made themselves an idol cast in the shape of a calf. They have bowed down to it and sacrificed to it and have said, 'These are your gods, O Israel, who brought you up out of Egypt.'

⁹"I have seen these people," the LORD said to Moses, "and they are a stiff-necked people. ¹⁰Now leave me alone so that my anger may burn against them and that I may destroy them. Then I will make you into a great nation."

¹¹But Moses sought the favor of the LORD his God. "O LORD," he said, "why should your anger burn against your people, whom you brought out of Egypt with great power and a mighty hand? ¹²Why should the Egyptians say, 'It was with evil intent that he brought them out, to kill them in the mountains and to wipe them off the face of the earth'? Turn from your fierce anger; relent and do not bring disaster on your people. ¹³Remember your servants Abraham, Isaac and Israel, to whom you swore by your own self: 'I will make your

descendants as numerous as the stars in the sky and I will give your descendants all this land I promised them, and it will be their inheritance forever.'" ¹⁴Then the LORD relented and did not bring on his people the disaster he had threatened.

¹⁵Moses turned and went down the mountain with the two tablets of the Testimony in his hands. They were inscribed on both sides, front and back. ¹⁶The tablets were the work of God; the writing was the writing of God, engraved on the tablets.

¹⁷When Joshua heard the noise of the people shouting, he said to Moses, "There is the sound of war in the camp."

¹⁸Moses replied:

> "It is not the sound of victory,
>> it is not the sound of defeat;
>> it is the sound of singing that I hear."

¹⁹When Moses approached the camp and saw the calf and the dancing, his anger burned and he threw the tablets out of his hands, breaking them to pieces at the foot of the mountain. ²⁰And he took the calf they had made and burned it in the fire; then he ground it to powder, scattered it on the water and made the Israelites drink it.

²¹He said to Aaron, "What did these people do to you, that you led them into such great sin?"

²²"Do not be angry, my lord," Aaron answered. "You know how prone these people are to evil. ²³They said to me, 'Make us gods who will go before us. As for this fellow Moses who brought us up out of Egypt, we don't know what has happened to him.' ²⁴So I told them, 'Whoever has any gold jewelry, take it off.' Then they gave me the gold, and I threw it into the fire, and out came this calf!"

²⁵Moses saw that the people were running wild and that Aaron had let them get out of control and so become a laughingstock to their enemies. ²⁶So he stood at the entrance to the camp and said, "Whoever is for the LORD, come to me." And all the Levites rallied to him.

²⁷Then he said to them, "This is what the LORD, the God of Israel, says 'Each man strap a sword to his side. Go back and forth through the camp from one end to the other, each killing his brother and friend and neighbor.'" ²⁸The Levites did as Moses commanded, and that day about three thousand of the people died. ²⁹Then Moses said, "You have been set apart

to the LORD today, for you were against your own sons and brothers, and he has blessed you this day."

³⁰The next day Moses said to the people, "You have committed a great sin. But now I will go up to the LORD; perhaps I can make atonement for your sin."

³¹So Moses went back to the LORD and said, "Oh, what a great sin these people have committed! They have made themselves gods of gold. ³²But now, please forgive their sin—but if not, then blot me out of the book you have written."

³³The LORD replied to Moses, "Whoever has sinned against me I will blot out of my book. ³⁴Now go, lead the people to the place I spoke of, and my angel will go before you. However, when the time comes for me to punish, I will punish them for their sin."

³⁵And the LORD struck the people with a plague because of what they did with the calf Aaron had made.

³³:¹Then the LORD said to Moses, "Leave this place, you and the people you brought up out of Egypt, and go up to the land I promised on oath to Abraham, Isaac and Jacob, saying, 'I will give it to your descendants.' ²I will send an angel before you and drive out the Canaanites, Amorites, Hittites, Perizzites, Hivites and Jebusites. ³Go up to the land flowing with milk and honey. But I will not go with you, because you are a stiff-necked people and I might destroy you on the way."

⁴When the people heard these distressing words, they began to mourn and no one put on any ornaments. ⁵For the LORD had said to Moses, "Tell the Israelites, 'You are a stiff-necked people. If I were to go with you even for a moment, I might destroy you. Now take off your ornaments and I will decide what to do with you.'" ⁶So the Israelites stripped off their ornaments at Mount Horeb.

⁷Now Moses used to take a tent and pitch it outside the camp some distance away, calling it the "tent of meeting." Anyone inquiring of the LORD would go to the tent of meeting outside the camp. ⁸And whenever Moses went out to the tent, all the people rose and stood at the entrances to their tents, watching Moses until he entered the tent. ⁹As Moses went into the tent, the pillar of cloud would come down and stay at the entrance, while the LORD spoke with Moses. ¹⁰Whenever the people saw the pillar of cloud standing at the entrance to the tent, they all stood and worshiped, each at the

entrance to his tent. [11]The LORD would speak to Moses face to face, as a man speaks with his friend. Then Moses would return to the camp, but his young aide Joshua son of Nun did not leave the tent.

[12]Moses said to the LORD, "You have been telling me, 'Lead these people,' but you have not let me know whom you will send with me. You have said, 'I know you by name and you have found favor with me.' [13]If you are pleased with me, teach me your ways so I may know you and continue to find favor with you. Remember that this nation is your people."

[14]The LORD replied, "My Presence will go with you, and I will give you rest."

[15]Then Moses said to him, "If your Presence does not go with us, do not send us up from here. [16]How will anyone know that you are pleased with me and with your people unless you go with us? What else will distinguish me and your people from all the other people on the face of the earth?"

[17]And the LORD said to Moses, "I will do the very thing you have asked, because I am pleased with you and I know you by name."

[18]Then Moses said, "Now show me your glory."

[19]And the LORD said, "I will cause all my goodness to pass in front of you, and I will proclaim my name, the LORD, in your presence. I will have mercy on whom I will have mercy, and I will have compassion on whom I will have compassion. [20]But," he said, "you cannot see my face, for no one may see me and live."

[21]Then the LORD said, "There is a place near me where you may stand on a rock. [22]When my glory passes by, I will put you in a cleft in the rock and cover you with my hand until I have passed by. [23]Then I will remove my hand and you will see my back; but my face must not be seen."

[34:1]The LORD said to Moses, "Chisel out two stone tablets like the first ones, and I will write on them the words that were on the first tablets, which you broke. [2]Be ready in the morning, and then come up on Mount Sinai. Present yourself to me there on top of the mountain. [3]No one is to come with you or be seen anywhere on the mountain; not even the flocks and herds may graze in front of the mountain."

[4]So Moses chiseled out two stone tablets like the first ones and went up Mount Sinai early in the morning, as the LORD

had commanded him; and he carried the two stone tablets in his hands. ⁵Then the LORD came down in the cloud and stood there with him and proclaimed his name, the LORD. ⁶And he passed in front of Moses, proclaiming, "The LORD, the LORD, the compassionate and gracious God, slow to anger, abounding in love and faithfulness, ⁷maintaining love to thousands, and forgiving wickedness, rebellion and sin. Yet he does not leave the guilty unpunished; he punishes the children and their children for the sin of the fathers to the third and fourth generation."

⁸Moses bowed to the ground at once and worshiped. ⁹"O Lord, if I have found favor in your eyes," he said, "then let the Lord go with us. Although this is a stiff-necked people, forgive our wickedness and our sin, and take us as your inheritance."

¹⁰Then the LORD said: "I am making a covenant with you. Before all your people I will do wonders never before done in any nation in all the world. The people you live among will see how awesome is the work that I, the LORD, will do for you. ¹¹Obey what I command you today. I will drive out before you the Amorites, Canaanites, Hittites, Perizzites, Hivites and Jebusites. ¹²Be careful not to make a treaty with those who live in the land where you are going, or they will be a snare among you. ¹³Break down their altars, smash their sacred stones and cut down their Asherah poles. ¹⁴Do not worship any other god, for the LORD, whose name is Jealous, is a jealous God.

¹⁵"Be careful not to make a treaty with those who live in the land; for when they prostitute themselves to their gods and sacrifice to them, they will invite you and you will eat their sacrifices. ¹⁶And when you choose some of their daughters as wives for your sons and those daughters prostitute themselves to their gods, they will lead your sons to do the same.

¹⁷"Do not make cast idols.

¹⁸"Celebrate the Feast of Unleavened Bread. For seven days eat bread made without yeast, as I commanded you. Do this at the appointed time in the month of Abib, for in that month you came out of Egypt.

¹⁹"The first offspring of every womb belongs to me, including all the firstborn males of your livestock, whether from herd or flock. ²⁰Redeem the firstborn donkey with a lamb, but

if you do not redeem it, break its neck. Redeem all your first-born sons.

"No one is to appear before me empty-handed.

²¹"Six days you shall labor, but on the seventh day you shall rest; even during the plowing season and harvest you must rest.

²²"Celebrate the Feast of Weeks with the firstfruits of the wheat harvest, and the Feast of Ingathering at the turn of the year. ²³Three times a year all your men are to appear before the Sovereign LORD, the God of Israel. ²⁴I will drive out nations before you and enlarge your territory, and no one will covet your land when you go up three times each year to appear before the LORD your God.

²⁵"Do not offer the blood of a sacrifice to me along with anything containing yeast, and do not let any of the sacrifice from the Passover Feast remain until morning.

²⁶"Bring the best of the firstfruits of your soil to the house of the LORD your God.

"Do not cook a young goat in its mother's milk."

²⁷Then the LORD said to Moses, "Write down these words, for in accordance with these words I have made a covenant with you and with Israel." ²⁸Moses was there with the LORD forty days and forty nights without eating bread or drinking water. And he wrote on the tablets the words of the covenant—the Ten Commandments.

²⁹When Moses came down from Mount Sinai with the two tablets of the Testimony in his hands, he was not aware that his face was radiant because he had spoken with the LORD. ³⁰When Aaron and all the Israelites saw Moses, his face was radiant, and they were afraid to come near him. ³¹But Moses called to them; so Aaron and all the leaders of the community came back to him, and he spoke to them. ³²Afterward all the Israelites came near him, and he gave them all the commands the LORD had given him on Mount Sinai.

³³When Moses finished speaking to them, he put a veil over his face. ³⁴But whenever he entered the LORD's presence to speak with him, he removed the veil until he came out. And when he came out and told the Israelites what he had been commanded, ³⁵they saw that his face was radiant. Then Moses would put the veil back over his face until he went in to speak with the LORD.

THIS SECTION OF Exodus is punctuated by two famous stories: the golden calf (ch. 32) and Moses' radiant face (34:29–35). The former is the quintessential example of rebellion in the Old Testament; the latter is somewhat firmly pressed on our Christian consciousness because of Paul's reference to it in 2 Corinthians 3:7–18.

Chapters 32–34 cannot be separated without affecting the integrity of the whole. To chop up this narrative into smaller units—however convenient—will only disrupt the message they are intended to convey: rebellion, mediation, and restoration. Hence, we must proceed as we have with the plagues, law, and the tabernacle by dealing with a large amount of material in one block.

The rapid pace with which we move from the final instructions for the tabernacle (31:18) to the rebellion at the foot of the mountain (ch. 32) is almost numbing. The reader is not at all prepared for what is about to transpire. There is a brief notation of Moses' delay in coming down the mountain (32:1a), and suddenly we find ourselves caught up in an event that could threaten to unravel God's entire plan. There is no deliberation, no plotting, no indication as to what actually motivates the Israelites to do what they did. All we read is that they see that Moses has been delayed and so they gather around Aaron to make their request.[1]

Aaron fashions a calf out of gold, and the Israelites proclaim it to be the god that brought them out of Egypt. This amounts to an attempt to undo what has just taken place in the preceding thirty-one chapters: the Exodus, the covenant, and the initiation of God's presence in the tabernacle. In fact, with respect to the last point, that this rebellion is placed in the middle of the tabernacle section suggests it is a rebellion against what the tabernacle represents, or perhaps the message of Exodus as a whole that culminates in the tabernacle. In any event, for one brief but horrifying moment, God almost gives them what they seem to want, were it not for Moses' mediation.

Our own familiarity with the story may lead us to the hasty conclusion that this is nothing less than a gross act of rebellion, a move to reject the God of Israel and join up with the pagan gods of the surrounding peoples. There is, of course, truth to this, but more seems to be going on here. We must remember that Moses is the only means of contact that the Israelites have with God. In fact, if we look back at 20:19, it was at Israel's own request that Moses act as a buffer: "Speak to us yourself and we will listen. But do not have

---

1. Actually, the Hebrew may suggest a more ominous meeting. The Israelites gather *against* (the preposition ʿal) Aaron. This was not a friendly group coming to make a request but a hostile group, perhaps threatening Aaron into compliance. Keeping this in mind may help exonerate Aaron in his interrogation by Moses later, though not completely!

God speak to us or we will die." But now Moses is taking a long time to return from his meeting with God. In light of this, it is possible to read the story not as an act of godless rebellion, but as an act of panic on the part of a people who fear they have lost their contact with God.[2]

There is more to Israel's act, however, than simply missing Moses and panicking at the thought of being disconnected to God. They approach Aaron and refer to Moses as "this fellow Moses," a phrase that in both Hebrew and English certainly communicates a sense of derision and contempt. It may well be that their reaction is a mixture of some panic and a contempt for Moses. We have already seen such contempt in Exodus and will see it again later in the Pentateuch. Perhaps the contempt here is a result of the delay. It is like a child waiting to be picked up from school. The parent is over an hour late. The child panics, becomes worried, and then just gets angry, taking it out on the parent when he or she arrives.

However we explain their motives, the Israelites will later be punished by God for what they are about to do. This root problem is what we have seen earlier in 14:10–14: a lack of trust in God. By making the golden calf, the Israelites adopt a pagan *representation* of their God, who had already demonstrated in no uncertain terms his mastery over the pagan gods of Egypt.

Aaron responds to this threatening situation in a way that, perhaps, we can hardly blame him for. He tells the people to take off their gold earrings, which he will then use to form an idol in the shape of a calf. In light of the repeated references to gold in the tabernacle section, it is hard not to see the connection. By building the calf out of gold the people want what the tabernacle was intended to do—provide a concrete point of contact between the people and God.

The choice of a calf is not arbitrary. It was a common idol image in the ancient Near East.[3] It is commonly accepted by Old Testament scholars today that the ancients did not *equate* an idol with the god, but it was some sort of earthly *representation* of that god. Specifically, it was thought that calves or bulls functioned as pedestals for the gods seated or standing over them. In this sense, the calf is analogous to the ark (the fact that both are made of gold strengthens this connection).

This is important to remember because it is unlikely that the calf *itself* is being declared "god" by the Israelites, as if they actually think that *it* has brought them out of Egypt. Rather, like the ark, it is the place above which

---

2. Sarna comments that Israel was experiencing a "spiritual void" (*Exploring Exodus*, 215). Durham suggests it was a "frightened impatience" (*Exodus*, 419).

3. The same can be said for the fact that earrings were used to make the idol. According to Gen. 35:4, earrings had pagan cultic significance (Sarna, *Exodus*, 203).

God is enthroned, thus ensuring his presence with them. The calf is thus a pagan *representation* of the true God. Put otherwise, the Israelites are not saying that this calf and *not* Yahweh brought them out of Egypt, but that Yahweh's *presence* is now associated with this piece of gold. By making the golden calf, Israel has broken not the first commandment but the second.

Aaron asks for gold and the people respond willingly, an act that parallels nicely the freewill offering the people will make for the tabernacle. It is becoming more clear that the calf represents an alternate point of contact between God and his people. But what does it mean for the Israelites to say, "*These* are your *gods*, O Israel"? What does it mean to call one calf "gods"? We can look at this issue grammatically. The Hebrew word for "God" and "gods" is the same, *ʾelohim*. The form is grammatically plural, and whether the sense of the word is singular or plural depends on the surrounding context. What adds to the confusion is that the pronoun "these" and the verb "brought you up" are also plural. In this case, therefore, because of the plural pronoun and verb, *ʾelohim* seems to suggest a plurality of gods.[4]

Such a statement may have been as odd for ancient readers as for us. Perhaps it is intended to make us stop and think what a terrible thing is happening. As Sarna suggests, "The plural usage may be a scribal device to emphasize the unacceptable nature of the object."[5] In other words, the biblical writer is accentuating the Israelites' sin. What they are doing is horrible. It is not just idolatry, one of the standard practices of pagan religion, but polytheism as well!

Moreover, the Israelites claim that "these gods" are the ones who have "brought [them] up out of Egypt." Again, I do not think this means that they are claiming that this calf and not Yahweh has been responsible for their deliverance, only that this calf is the earthly representation of Yahweh. But this does not make the offense any less severe! We must remember how the Ten Commandments begins: "I am the LORD your God, who brought you out of Egypt" (20:2). Israel's act here is more than simply idolatry. By constructing a calf of gold and claiming that this pagan symbol can in any way be remotely associated with their deliverance from Egypt, the Israelites are in effect turning the Exodus experience on its head. They are going back to the first words God spoke on the mountain, the heart of the law in Exodus, and saying, "No, we see things differently." It is hard to imagine a worse thing they could have done.

---

4. Sarna, however, leaves open the possibility that "the plural forms with *ʾelohim* are found in a monotheistic context several times in the Bible" (*Exodus*, 204; cf. Gen. 20:13 as an example).

5. Ibid. See also Sarna, *Exploring Exodus*, 244, n. 138.

To put it another way, by building the calf and reciting what was earlier said in Exodus 20:2, Israel is fashioning a new, false religion according to the pattern of what God revealed to them earlier. This continues in the following verses. In verse 5 Aaron builds an altar, a parallel to the altar that will be built for the tabernacle. He proclaims that there will be a "festival to the LORD" (*ḥag layhwh*) the next day (cf. the same or similar expression in 10:9; 12:14; 13:6). Throughout Exodus we read the refrain that Israel is to leave Egypt to hold a festival to the Lord. That festival is the Passover and the Feast of Unleavened Bread. But the Israelites at the foot of Mount Sinai turn it into something else.

At least two of the phrases in verse 6 are reminiscent of what we have seen in chapter 24, which is a celebration of the confirmation of the covenant God made with the Israelites. In 24:4–5 Moses rises *early* and sacrifices *burnt and fellowship offerings*. The similar wording in 32:6 suggests that the festival here is a reversal—indeed, a perversion—of the true celebration of chapter 24. Israel's actions are systematically, step by step, undoing what has been done.

The same goes for the eating and drinking mentioned at the end of 32:6. Remember that this is what the leaders of Israel did in 24:11 after they were given a brief glimpse of God himself. Now the Israelites, who were not given that earlier glimpse, fashion themselves as being "in God's presence" and partake of a covenant meal of their own. An added twist is that they also engage in what the NIV translates as "revelry." The Hebrew word is *ṣaḥeq*, which in a number of places has connotations of sexual activity (see Gen. 26:8; 39:14, 17). To say the least, this is not the festival Israel was intended to celebrate at the foot of God's holy mountain.

God reports the activities of the Israelites in verses 1–6 to Moses (vv. 7–10). By referring to the Israelites as "your people" (i.e., Moses' people), we see already an ominous hint of what is to come. Israel is no longer "*my* [God's] people." Up to this point in Exodus God has been zealous to refer to Israel as "my people" or even "my firstborn son" (4:22), but here he has had enough. They have "become corrupt" (v. 7). They have been "quick to turn away" (v. 8). The drama of Israel's sudden turnabout after all that has happened to them, after all they have seen, should leave our heads shaking. In verse 9 God continues to use derisive language to speak of Israel, referring to them as "*these* people," a phrase that brings to mind the Israelites' reference to Moses as "*this* fellow" (v. 1).

God's solution is to have his "anger ... burn against them" (v. 10) and start over with Moses: "Then I will make *you* [Moses] into a great nation." The devastation of Israel's actions cannot be stated more clearly. God's words here reiterate the promise to the patriarchs that we have seen again and again in the course of the book. The Exodus is about God's keeping a promise to the patriarchs—a theological impetus that has driven the march out of Egypt and the trek to the Promised Land. By saying what he does to Moses, God is in effect going back to Genesis 12 and posing Moses as a new Abraham. God is threatening to wipe out the Israelites and to start over again.

But this is not where the story ends. Moses comes through. Rebellion is followed by mediation. Earlier in Exodus Moses argued with God out of his own selfish, almost petty motives (3:11–4:17). Now, however, he argues with God on behalf of the people—he has learned to put their interests first. He does this by reminding God that rejecting Israel at this point will have widespread implications. He reminds the Lord, perhaps gently, that Israel is *"your* people, whom *you* brought out of Egypt"* (v. 11, italics added). He reminds God of the very things that God himself regularly enjoins the Israelites to remember, that God delivered Israel with "great power and a mighty hand." He also reminds the Lord that his own honor is at stake. Had he not just finished dismantling the Egyptian army and their gods? Will he now turn around and give these very same enemies a reason to rejoice in Yahweh's defeat? Never!

Moses bases his argument ultimately on the very element that God seems to have discounted in the previous verses: the promise to the patriarchs (v. 13). In fact, Moses quotes God's own words to Abraham, that he promised to make Abraham's descendants as numerous as the stars and give them the Promised Land (see Gen. 12:7; 15:5).

Moses' argument has the desired outcome. God turns from his anger and does not bring about the threatened disaster (v. 14). What can we say about this change of heart? It certainly seems that Moses, through argument and pleading, has been able to get God to alter his plans. To put it in plain English, Moses gets God to change his mind. There is really no other way to read this, and we should not try to avoid it.

This may, it is true, introduce a problem or two in our own thinking about the nature of God. As the standard line of thinking goes, if God can be convinced to act in a way he has originally intended not to act, then we cannot think of him as sovereign in any true sense. He is just merely "powerful" but not all-knowing. The portrait of God presented here in 32:11–14 seems to have more in common with the capriciousness of Greek and Roman gods, prone to fits of anger and who must be appeased, than to the steady, sovereign Creator of the universe.

How can God's sovereignty be reconciled to the fact that he here changes his mind? In thinking this through one should keep in mind that this is a *true* dilemma. God is not merely acting in verse 10 when he says that he will destroy Israel. He is not goading Moses into pleading with him. He means it. As far as we know, God's intention is to destroy Israel.

I suggest that we should look at this in the broadest context possible. The Bible gives us a varied portrait of the nature of God. At times we seem to be peering into heaven itself. At other times, the Bible presents God in human pictures. The dialogue of verses 11–14 is more in keeping with the latter category than the former. The reason for this here seems to be that the writer is focusing his attention on Moses' role as intercessor, not on the inner workings of God's psyche (as if that is *ever* the topic in the Bible!). Moses has finally begun to grow into the role he so adamantly rejected when he first met God on Mount Horeb.

However we seek to understand this interchange, Moses' pleading works. He then turns to go down the mountain with the two tablets in his hands, which have God's writing on both the front and back. The author mentions this in order to prepare the reader for the devastation of the breaking of these tablets (v. 19). Moses will smash something very sacred.

On his way down the mountain, Moses meets up with Joshua (v. 17), which is where we expect to find him (cf. 24:13). Joshua is unaware of what is happening in the camp below. Moses knows, of course, but Joshua has been given no advanced warning. He surmises, on the basis of the sounds that he hears, that there must be war in the camp—a conclusion perhaps expected of a military leader. Moses informs Joshua of what is actually happening (32:18):

> It is not the sound of victory,
> > it is not the sound of defeat;
> > it is the sound of singing that I hear.

No, Joshua, this is not war. It is neither victory nor peace. It is "singing." What kind of singing could it be that it would have been mistaken by a warrior for battle sounds?!

Moses' description of the type of sound he hears is significant. We should not, on the basis of this description, envision a group of people singing raucous songs down below, wine goblets swaying back and forth. "Singing" is probably an allusion to the singing Israel did after the victory at the sea (the same root [ʿanah] is used in this verse and in 15:21). As we have seen, the Israelites have already taken certain steps to fashion their new cultic trappings to imitate what they have experienced by God's hand. Here is another example. The Israelites look to the calf and say, as it were, "These are your gods, O Israel, who brought you up out of Egypt—you are the ones who defeated Pharaoh and his army in the sea." As in their celebration of God's victory over the Egyptians in chapter 15, their celebration of *this* "god of the Exodus" is complete with singing. The parody is becoming more obvious.

Moses reacts to what he sees in the camp by throwing the tablets to the ground, breaking them to pieces. Moreover, his "anger burns" against the people (v. 19; cf. the similar reference to God's anger in v. 10). But whereas Moses successfully appeased God's wrath, Moses, upon actually seeing the depth to which his people have sunk, does not follow his own advice.

The breaking of the tablets is more than just a graphic, even impulsive, depiction of intense anger. Like so much of this narrative, it is symbolic. By smashing the tablets on which is written the law—by God's finger, no less—the law is symbolically undone. Moses' act says to the Israelites that if they are not prepared to obey the law, they do not deserve to have it.

This would not bring a sense of relief to them, as if now they are finally rid of the burden of God's law. Rather, this shocks them into a clearer understanding of just what it is they have done. True, they may have been able to imitate the portions of their Exodus experience, albeit wholly inadequately, by making the calf and proclaiming it to be the god of the Exodus. They may have used gold to imitate the splendor of the ark and the tabernacle, and they may have appointed Aaron priest of their new religion. But one thing they have not been able to duplicate, which is essential to the Exodus experience, is the law. Their actions are wholly contrary to that law. The smashing of the tablets, with one resounding crash, tells the Israelites below that the party is over. Their attempt to create a religion of their own design has failed.

One curious element concerns the grinding of the golden calf into powder, mixing it with water, and making the Israelites drink it. This is obviously some sort of ritual that the text itself does not explain, but that to the original audience was clear enough. A number of commentators point out the similarity between verse 20 and the following Ugaritic text that describes the goddess Anat's treatment of the god Mot:[6]

> She seizes Motu,[7] son of 'Ilu:
> with a knife she splits him,
> with a winnowing-fork she winnows him.
> with fire she burns him,
> with grindstones she pulverizes him,
> in the field she sows him.

This text provides a helpful background for what we read in 32:20. Pulverizing something into powder and scattering it implies "total annihilation."[8] True, the two texts are in no way to be understood as exact parallels. Anat

---

6. The following translation is from W. W. Hallo and K. L. Younger, eds., *The Context of Scripture: Volume 1: Canonical Compositions From the Biblical World* (Leiden: Brill, 1997), 270. The text may also be found in Pritchard, *Ancient Near Eastern Texts*, 140.

7. Typically, the names in this text are transliterated Mot and Il, names more recognizable to most. This translation reproduced here, however, preserves case endings.

8. Sarna, *Exodus*, 207. See also 2 Kings 23:15.

kills an enemy and grinds him into power; Moses smashes the golden calf and grinds it into powder. Anat scatters the powder in a field; Moses mixes it with water.

Why are the Israelites made to drink the concoction, and what does that mean? The Ugaritic parallel gives us no help here. It may be helpful, however, to bring Numbers 5:12–31 into the discussion. This section describes an elaborate ceremony whereby a woman suspected of adultery is made to drink a mixture of water and dust from the tabernacle in order to determine her guilt or innocence. Even though Exodus 32 does not draw on this ceremony, it may well be the significance of the act described here.

In verses 27–28 the Levites kill three thousand men. Why just this number, and who is unfortunate enough to be counted among that number? Taking our cue again from Numbers 5:12–31, it may be that the guilty parties are exposed by the drinking ceremony, thus enabling the Levites to know whom to kill.[9] How ironic that the law they have rejected is now the means by which their guilt is ascertained. They may have rejected the law, but they cannot escape its power.

Verses 21–24 record a confrontation between Moses and Aaron that appears somewhat pathetic and almost comical on the surface: "What did these people do to you, that you led them into such great sin?" Moses suggests that Aaron's actions are a way of getting back at the Israelites, whom he calls "these people" (again a derisive term). Perhaps the question is sarcastic: "Aaron, you know better! You are the high priest! The only way I can see you doing something so stupid, to commit such a 'great sin,'[10] is that 'these people' did something to you first!"

Aaron responds by trying to appease Moses' anger, as Moses did earlier with God. Aaron more or less reports things as they happened. He even tells Moses that, yes, he told the Israelites to take off their gold jewelry. What he does not tell Moses, however, is that he had a hand in the actual making of the calf. He claims there that all he did was throw the gold into the fire and "out came this calf" (v. 24).

There are two ways of looking at Aaron's response. Either this answer is so lame that it serves no other purpose than to portray Aaron as a weasel and

---

9. Ibid., 209. On the basis of Judg. 16:27, Fretheim suggest that three thousand is a "stereotyped number" (*Exodus*, 289). This number occurs nineteen times in the Bible, and at times seems to mean simply a large number rather than a literal three thousand (see 1 Kings 4:32; perhaps also Job 1:3; Acts 2:41). Other times, however, the number should be taken more or less literally (e.g., Num. 35:5; Josh. 7:3–4; 1 Sam. 13:2). This matter cannot be definitively clarified either way.

10. This phrase can have sexual connotations as it does in Gen. 20:9 (NIV "great guilt"). If there are sexual overtones here, they are not literal but metaphorical: Israel has committed spiritual adultery.

to expose the utter madness of the act, or it has a more serious meaning. I am strongly inclined toward the former, not only because Aaron's answer does indeed appear ridiculous (a circular argument, I know), but also because Moses himself gives no response, as if to say that he will not even dignify it with an answer.

H. Brichto, however, feels the latter option has greater merit.[11] To him, Aaron's answer is not a lame excuse but a claim that the event is a miracle. Moses' silence, therefore, is an indication that he *accepts* the story, not that he rejects it. The fact that it is a miracle, however, does not legitimate the idol, but serves "to demonstrate that faithlessness to His will is unreasonable even when reason itself is called into question by the occurrence of a miracle."[12]

Brichto's argument is worthy of serious consideration, though I am still more inclined to think of Aaron's words as an attempt to divest himself of any blame. Aaron is in effect saying, "Hey, don't look at me. I don't know how it got there." What convinces me of this interpretation is that Aaron has changed the story, deliberately *concealing* the fact that he fashioned the calf with a tool (v. 4). Note also the writer's comment that Aaron let the people "get out of control" (v. 25), which suggests that he (the writer) does not buy the story.

In the wake of this disaster, it is the Levites who rally to Moses' side. They are the ones who will exact punishment. The narrative seems to imply that Moses issues a general call for volunteers, but only the Levites—all of them—respond. Are we to conclude that no one else from any of the other tribes is "for the LORD"? It seems so, at least if we press the matter literally. Yet we have seen throughout Exodus the writer's use of hyperbole. Such a device is never used randomly but purposefully. The purpose here is to accent the faithfulness, amid the chaos of rebellion, of the Levites, to whom God has charged the maintenance of the tabernacle. The fact that all the Levites come forward indicates that God's house is still in order. The rebellion is grievous and serious, but it is not the final word. The guilty parties will be put to death—and by those responsible for maintaining order in the community, the Levites.

The death penalty here is not extreme, at least in the context of Exodus. We should recall that the instructions for the tabernacle must be carried out in detail on pain of death. No less can be expected for those whose actions attempt to overturn the covenant itself. Thus, after the grisly sentence is carried out, the Levites are in effect rewarded for their faithful service. They are "set apart to the LORD" (v. 29). This is an unmistakable echo of the setting

---

11. H. Brichto, "The Worship of the Golden Calf: A Literary Analysis of a Fable on Idolatry," *HUCA* 54 (1983): 1–44, esp. 13–15.

12. Ibid., 15.

apart of the priests in 28:41, where the same Hebrew idiom is used for consecration: "fill your hand."

The next day Moses announces his intention to go up the mountain to make atonement for the people (32:30). The text implies two levels of guilt in the making of the golden calf. The "more guilty" party, perhaps those directly or extensively involved, have been put to death by the Levites. The rest of the Israelites are apparently also guilty in some sense, otherwise atonement would not have to be made; but they are not so guilty as to deserve death along with the three thousand. Perhaps the remaining Israelites are guilty by virtue of the notion of "collective guilt" so prevalent in the Old Testament, or perhaps because they engage in the revelry but to a lesser extent. Still, it is hard to avoid the clear implication of verse 31 that those remaining after the Levite purge are guilty of having made "gods of gold."

Most commentators see a connection between Moses' atonement for the people and the ark.[13] The Hebrew root for both atonement and the cover of the ark is *kpr*. As the high priest would enter the tabernacle and make atonement for the people, Moses once again ascends Mount Sinai, the proto-tabernacle, to do the same.

In his attempt to make atonement by pleading for the life of his people, Moses' argument essentially amounts to "take me instead." He has certainly changed from his first encounter with God on Mount Horeb. He is neither timid nor reluctant to be the mediator between God and his people, and he is showing his commitment to the task by his willingness to pay the ultimate price. To be blotted out of the book of life is not asking to be eternally condemned (as we might be tempted to think), but to die (see Isa. 4:3; Jer. 22:30; Ezek. 13:9; cf. Ps. 69:28). This stands to reason from the context, for death was precisely the penalty inflicted on the three thousand. The Lord responds by rejecting Moses' offer (Ex. 32:33). Sinners, not the guiltless, will be blotted out—for now at least.

That is the only explanation God gives. The Lord then tells Moses to continue on the journey with the angel leading them (v. 34). The guilt of the people, however, will not be swept under the rug; in time they will be punished. It seems that a compromise of sorts has been reached between God and Moses. The mediator has negotiated a solution that will guarantee Israel's existence and keep God close by them, but God still reserves his right to punish later on.

The timing and form of this punishment is indicated in verse 35: "The LORD struck the people with a plague." We do not know what type of plague,

---

13. See Janzen, *Exodus*, 241–42.

but it is obviously not a destruction on the grand scale that might be inferred from the previous verses. We do not know how many or even if anyone died. What is most interesting about verse 35 is the syntax. The NIV presents one valid option: "And the LORD struck the people with a plague because of what they *did with* the calf Aaron made." The Hebrew allows for another option: "And the LORD struck the people with a plague because they *made* (ʿśh) the calf that Aaron *made* (ʿśh)." Both the people and Aaron are said to "make" the calf. But how can the people make the calf that Aaron made? I suggest that the ambiguity is intentional. It lays blame equally on both Aaron and the people.

The story continues with tension and suspense (33:1–6). It seems as though things have been patched up between God and his people. He tells them to "leave this place" (i.e., "Mount Horeb," v. 6) and continue on their journey to the Promised Land. The angel will go before them and drive out the inhabitants of the land. The opening verses of this passage reiterate the earlier promise to Moses in 3:8, which is itself a reiteration of God's recurring promise to the patriarchs. All seems well and good.

Nevertheless there is a problem. God announces that he himself will not be going with them (33:3). Perhaps we see hints of this already in verse 1, where God refers to Israel as "*the* people *you* [Moses] brought up out of Egypt" rather than "*my* people *I* brought up out of Egypt." Note also verse 2, where God promises to send "*an* angel" rather than "*the* angel."[14]

This hinting gives way to the blunt announcement in verse 3: "I will not go with you." The significance of this turn of events cannot be stressed too highly. The whole purpose of the Exodus was for God and his people to be together. God's presence with them will be firmly established in the proposed tabernacle. By saying "go ahead, but you're going without me," the events of the previous thirty-one chapters are being undone. This is not merely a setback; it means the end of the road.

The reason God gives for not going with them is twofold: They are a stiff-necked, stubborn people, and God is afraid he "might destroy [them] on the way." Again, we see a very "human" portrait of God. The Lord does not know how he might react at some point in the journey; he does not seem to trust himself to control his anger. Thus, it is better that he not go at all. We should resist the temptation to gloss over this description of God. This is God's Word and this is how he is described. We should not dismiss it on the basis of what we "know" God to be like. As we have seen above, the writer is not

---

14. Sarna suggests this is significant (*Exodus*, 211). I am open to this, although I would exercise caution in making such an argument on the basis of the presence or absence of the definite article in Hebrew.

concerned to reveal to us the absolute, abstract essence of God, but God in the context of his dealings with his people.

The people's response is appropriate. They mourn, and as a posture of mourning, they do not adorn themselves in any ornaments (perhaps jewelry), and what ornaments they do wear they strip off. We are left not really knowing what will happen to Moses or the Israelites. It is a tension that will be maintained and developed further in 34:6–7. But for now, the worst is over. Moses intercedes for the people and God is appeased. There is a collective sigh of relief, but the relationship has not yet been fully restored.

The relevance of verses 7–11, which refer to the tent that Moses pitches outside the camp, is a source of bafflement. Commentators regularly point out how strange this section is in the context of what has just transpired.[15] Certainly, the significance of this passage is not easy to discern. What, if anything, does it contribute to the flow of the story?

There are two ways of approaching this question. (1) It may be, as Fretheim suggests, that these verses are a lull in the action, intended to augment the tension with which the previous section ended.[16] Hence, it is unnecessary to ponder the possible *logical* connection of this section to its surrounding context.

(2) Others argue, however, that this passage does indeed follow logically from the golden calf narrative. I side with this latter approach. Although this brief episode serves to create a dramatic tension of sorts, it does more. God has just threatened to break off communication with his people. The tabernacle that is to be built, instructions for which were given over seven chapters, no longer seems certain of being completed. The fact that Moses pitches a tent and calls it a "tent of meeting" is no accident. It should be understood as an alternate "tabernacle" in which at least Moses can have access to God.[17] The people do not have such access; this tent is pitched "some distance away" (v. 7). The cloud accompanies Moses alone, not the people (v. 9). The people simply watch from home and worship as Moses enters.

It is the events of chapter 32 that prompt the action of 33:7–11. The people have nearly driven God to the point of no return. God must now "connect" to the people at a distance, in a simple tent, with Moses alone in the vicinity. Still, the fact that *any* step is taken to restore the relationship is a source of encouragement. The fact that a temporary tent of

---

15. Durham calls this an insertion that disrupts "an otherwise carefully directed narrative mosaic" (*Exodus*, 443).

16. Fretheim, *Exodus*, 295.

17. Sarna, *Exodus*, 211; Cassuto, *Commentary on Exodus*, 429. The Hebrew has that Moses pitches the tent *lo* (lit., "for him"). This is not reflected in the NIV.

meeting is set up and that God does meet with Moses as a representative of the people signals to the reader that God has not entirely abandoned Israel. This so-called "tent of meeting" will soon give way to the splendor of the tabernacle, the true Tent of Meeting. The cloud will soon descend to guide the entire camp.

In the tent the Lord speaks to Moses "face to face" (v. 11), no doubt an expression of intimacy and not to be understood literally.[18] This statement is not merely intended to make some disconnected comment about Moses' status before God. It is meant to give the proper setting for the deeply personal conversation that follows. For this reason, I am not convinced that verses 7–11 describe a recurring event, which is how the NIV interprets it: "Moses *used to take a tent* . . . *whenever* Moses went out . . . *whenever* the people saw . . . the LORD *would speak* to Moses" (italics added). I do admit, though, that the NIV's translation is possible.[19]

But verses 10–11 can also indicate a single action and can be translated:

> *So* the people saw the pillar of cloud standing at the entrance to the tent; they all stood and worshiped, each at the entrance to his tent. *Then* the LORD *spoke* to Moses face to face, as a man speaks with his friend. Then Moses *returned* to the camp, but his young aide Joshua son of Nun did not leave the tent.

If this translation is accepted, verses 12–23 recount the conversation between Moses and God implied in verse 11. If the translation in the NIV is accepted, a stronger case is made for verses 7–11 being essentially a lull in the action and no more.

The conversation between God and Moses begins with the latter issuing a challenge. "You have been telling me, 'Lead these people,' but you have not let me know whom you will send with me." What is Moses asking for here? Does he want to know who will go before them and lead, such as the angel? Perhaps. But Moses may also be asking, "I know you want me to lead, but which people are going out with me?" The Hebrew verb *šlḥ* (send) has elsewhere in Exodus referred to the *people* God is sending out of Egypt (e.g., 5:1). In other words, Moses wants to know who will be left after the purge of 33:5? Whom will Moses be leading out? Are there any Israelites left who are still deserving of that honor?

---

18. This is a point about which there is universal agreement. See Durham, *Exodus*, 443; Sarna, *Exodus*, 212.

19. The verbal sequence (imperfects followed by a series of waw-consecutives plus the perfect, and infinitive constructs preceded by the temporal preposition *k*) could certainly indicate a recurring event.

Such an understanding of 33:12 provides a different perspective from which to read the conversation to follow. When Moses continues, "You have said, 'I know you by name and you have found favor with me,'"[20] he seems to be saying, "I know how special *I* am to you, but what about everybody else?" Moses does not want to make the journey alone. He sees no honor in being the only one to reach Canaan. So, he reminds God in verse 13, "Remember that this nation is your people."

In this respect, God's response in verse 14 can be seen as somewhat of a veiled denial to Moses' pleading: "My Presence will go with *you*, and I will give *you* rest." In other words, we have here the answer to what God was pondering in verse 5. He has made his decision: The people will be left behind. This is what God means when he says he will go with *you*: It is Moses alone (the Hebrew word "you" is singular). It is *he* who will be given rest. Rest should not be understood psychologically, as if God is promising that Moses' mind will be put to ease.[21] It is an expression used in the Pentateuch (Deut. 3:20; 12:10; 25:10) for entering the land and receiving rest from engaging enemies in war.[22] Hence, what God seems to be saying to Moses, albeit subtly, is, "Don't worry Moses. I'll be with *you*."

This perspective also helps makes sense of verses 15–17. Moses responds by asking that God's Presence go up "with *us*," meaning all the people, not just Moses. He is not giving in. If in verse 14 God was promising that his presence would be with *all* the people (taking the singular "you" as a plural, which is certainly possible in Hebrew), why does Moses keep pressing the point in verse 15? Why would he ask for the very thing that God has just conceded? It makes more sense to read verse 14 as referring to Moses alone and verse 15 to be Moses' gentle retort.

In other words, the argument of verses 12–16 serves the singular purpose of ensuring that the people will not be left behind. The clincher for Moses is verse 16, which, like 32:11–14, is an appeal to God's reputation among the people of the world: If God's Presence is not with *us*, the people, then no one will know that Moses and the people are special.

The argument concludes by God's promising to do as Moses asked (v. 17). Why? Because he is "pleased" with Moses and knows him "by name." God will be present with the people for Moses' sake. Once again, Moses has succeeded in moving God to compassion.

---

20. Nowhere in Exodus do we find these words, so it is not clear what conversation Moses is referring to, unless he is simply summarizing the general attitude God has toward him. The idea of finding favor with God is also seen in Gen. 6:8.

21. This is the view presented by Durham, *Exodus*, 447; Cassuto, *Commentary on Exodus*, 434.

22. Sarna, *Exodus*, 213.

The following verses (vv. 18–23), where Moses asks to see God's glory, must be understood within this context.[23] This is not simply to satisfy his curiosity or some deep spiritual longing. He is in effect asking God for some demonstration of the promise he has just made. He is asking God to "put it in writing."

God's response to Moses' request is a bit unexpected. Moses asks to see God's glory, by which is meant no doubt some visible sign of God's presence with his people. Earlier (e.g., 16:10; 24:16), God's glory took the form of the cloud. In 24:17 it was the fire. But here God says that he will cause all his "goodness" to pass in front of Moses. What does this mean? Sarna suggests that it carries covenantal overtones.[24] That is, having God's goodness pass in front[25] implies that the covenant between God and the people is being reestablished.

Moreover, God again proclaims his name, "the LORD," to Moses. This is an allusion to the initial encounter in 3:14–15, where God first proclaimed his name to Moses. The fact that God here reiterates the key phrase from the beginning of his call to Moses suggests that after the disaster of chapter 32, God is willing to start over, and Moses is once again called upon to lead his people. In chapter 3 God revealed himself in a striking manner, the burning bush. Now Moses receives another revelation of God's presence (33:21–23). In both passages, the divine name Yahweh is proclaimed. This episode amounts, then, to another call narrative. After the worship of the golden calf threatened to undo God's work, God renews his promise to bring the people to the Promised Land under Moses' leadership. The parallels between this covenant renewal and the previous initiation of that covenant will be seen more clearly in 34:1–7.

The meaning of God's words in 33:19b are not clear in the context. What does it mean that his "mercy" and "compassion" are at his will? Does this connect at all to the surrounding words? Is this nothing more than a statement of

---

23. Sarna's comment here is worth reproducing in full: "It may be pointed out that every other instance of a visible *kavod* [Hebrew word for glory] in the Torah is characterized by three features: (1) It is a mass experience; (2) the *kavod* is distant from the observers; and (3) God initiates the manifestation and freely chooses the time and place. Here Moses pleads for an exclusively individual experience, one that is close at hand and that occurs in response to his personal request there and then" (ibid., 214).

24. "In ancient Near Eastern treaties and in several biblical texts, the term *tov* [Hebrew word for good] bears a technical, legal meaning of covenantal friendship" (ibid.). Sarna cites among other biblical examples Gen. 32:10 (English v. 9), 13 (English v. 12); Deut. 23:7 (English v. 6).

25. We also read in v. 22 that God's glory "passed by." This may be another example of covenant language. In Gen. 15:17 we see God *passing* between the pieces (Sarna, *Exodus*, 214). The same verb (*ᶜabar*) is used in Ex. 33:19, 22, and Gen. 15:17.

God's arbitrariness, to have compassion on whomever he wills? Although a definitive answer to these questions eludes us, I suggest it is a comment on the Exodus in general. We must resist the temptation to read this statement in terms of personal salvation. The reference here is to the Israelites, those on whom the Lord has had mercy and compassion. It is a summary of what God has done for Israel in bringing them out of Egypt, an act of pure mercy.

Finding the relevance of 33:20 in this context is not easy. It makes sense, however, if we equate what Moses means in verse 18 by "glory" with what God means in verse 20 by "face." Moses asks to see God's glory. God says, however, that he will show Moses his goodness and proclaim his name. His face, however, he cannot see. Moses' request is to a certain extent denied, and for his own good. To see God's face/glory means death.

But this explanation is hard to square with verses 21–23, where God intends to do precisely what he has just said he will not do. He will place Moses in a cleft in a rock and cover him with his hand while his *"glory* passes by." Moses will indeed see God's glory but only the back, not the face. Apparently God has compromised his denial of 33:20. The purpose of this theophany, as suggested above, is to draw more clearly the parallel between Moses' commission in chapter 3 and his "recommission" here in chapter 33.

Verse 23 is a captivating image. God is "there" in some tangible form, passing by in front of Moses. The anthropomorphism is apparent, but we should not conclude, on the basis that God does not have a body, that Moses does not see anything. He most certainly does see something, something that God himself refers to as his back. This is not to imply that God appears to Moses in bodily form, only that he sees something. If we dwell on what precisely Moses sees, we lose sight of the point of the story as a whole. No one knows what it means to speak of God's hand, back, and face, but perhaps this is precisely what is intended. God's appearance is a mystery, a mystery that even Moses himself is able to see only partially.

This is the most elevated glimpse of God Moses has ever had and will have. This is not the burning bush, which prompted Moses' curiosity to take a closer look. This is not a series of disasters, as we saw in the plagues and the parting of the sea. This is not the miraculous giving of manna and quail. Moses has gotten to know the God of Abraham much better since then. He has seen his mighty power and has come to understand better what God intends to do with his people. Their relationship has deepened, and so, too, the degree to which God reveals himself to Moses. So, unlike the relatively "tame" theophany of chapter 3, Moses now catches a glimpse of God that, if God were to remove his hand, would bring death even to him.

As with the theophanies in Exodus 3 and 24, this one serves a similar function. It is a boost of God's presence for the task that lies ahead. In chapter

3 Moses' encounter with God prepares him for return to Egypt and for leading the people out. In chapter 24 the leaders of Israel are permitted a glimpse of God's throne and feet, thus reinforcing their authority for the journey ahead. Now, after the disaster of chapter 32, when all seems lost, Moses is recommissioned with a seriousness not seen in the previous theophanies. His authority as God's chosen leader is thus emphasized amid the near disqualification of the people. It is safe to say that such a heightened vision of God is required, considering the circumstances.

The beginning of chapter 34 reinforces that the covenant between God and Israel is reestablished after the golden calf incident. Once again, Moses will have tablets of stone with the words of God's law written on them. The covenant that was nearly annulled with the breaking of the first set is reinstated. The only difference between these tablets and those mentioned previously is that Moses himself must chisel them out (34:1, 4). The other set simply seemed to be given to him by God (24:12; 31:18; 32:16). The fact that Moses has to chisel them may indicate God's displeasure with him at having smashed them (32:19).

In any event, Moses is once again to travel up the mountain to receive God's law, which calls to mind the first trip, which began in 20:21 and lasted for the next eleven chapters. As in 19:13, all others, even animals, are to keep their distance from the mountain. Moses' second reception of the law is patterned after the first.[26] The parallels with previous episodes continue in verses 5–6: Moses ascends and the cloud once again comes down where he is; the name of God (Yahweh) is proclaimed and Moses witnesses a theophany.

In 34:6–7 we find the resolution of the golden calf episode. We would be remiss not to see these verses as the fulfillment of what God said he would do in 33:19–23. He said he would pass in front of Moses, proclaim his name, and speak about mercy and compassion (33:19). Here in 34:6–7 God proclaims his name—the double repetition of the divine name ("the LORD, the LORD") lending emphasis to what is about to take place.[27] As we noted in chapter 3, "the LORD" (Yahweh) is God's "salvation name." This is precisely what he is once again committing himself to do for Israel, even after the events of chapter 32. Moreover, the Lord is "the compassionate and gracious God, slow to anger, abounding in love and faithfulness, maintaining love to thousands, and forgiving wickedness, rebellion and sin."[28]

---

26. Sarna also notes the parallels between the two trips up the mountain. He adds that Moses is told to be ready in the morning (34:2), as were the people in 19:11, 15–16 (*Exodus*, 215).

27. It is possible that the phrase could be translated "The LORD proclaimed 'the LORD' " but I find this unlikely.

28. It is often pointed out that this list of divine attributes is found in a variety of forms elsewhere in the Old Testament (e.g., Num. 14:18; Neh. 9:17; Ps. 103:8, 17; 145:8; see Fretheim, *Exodus*, 302).

This list of attributes is true not only of God's behavior in chapter 34, but throughout Exodus. The reason he brought Israel out of Egypt in the first place is because he is gracious. That attitude is now rekindled toward his people in the aftermath of the golden calf incident.[29]

Still, in light of the rebellion, this litany includes elements that are motivated by and applicable only to the present context. God emphatically states that he is patient with his people and willing to forgive. But forgiveness does not mean overlooking their sin, nor will he leave the guilty unpunished. In fact, in accordance with the penalty for breaking the second commandment (20:5; see comments there), idolatry requires the penalty to extend to the "third and fourth generation" (34:7).

Moses' response in verses 8–9 seems strange. He appears to be petitioning God for what he has just granted.[30] After all, the word of forgiveness certainly implies that God is going to continue with his original plan to bring Israel not only out of Egypt but into Canaan. Are Moses' words superfluous here? I do not want to overread this passage, but Moses' plea is not simply a waste of words. It seems best to read this verse in the same way as Moses' request in 33:18. Despite God's words of forgiveness, Moses wants some added evidence or proof that God will go with his people. He wants God to "document" in some way his intentions.

Perhaps Moses has some doubts. It is not too much to suggest that he may not be exemplifying a strong faith here. We know from how Moses' life ends that his lack of faith and his disobedience will disqualify him from entering Canaan. This may also help explain an interesting detail, that Moses avoids using the divine name Yahweh and uses rather the Hebrew word *ʾadonay*, translated "Lord" in the NIV (rather than "LORD," which stands for Yahweh). Moses uses this word three other times in Exodus, in each case when expressing some doubt as to his mission (4:10, 13; 5:22).[31]

God responds to Moses' doubt not by reprimanding him but by giving him what he wants, some sign of his continued presence with his people. He will make "a covenant" with the people (34:10). To put it more accurately, he will *renew* the covenant. What follows in verses 11–28 is essentially a repetition of a number of things we have seen in previous sections of Exodus—in the Passover section (vv. 18–20, 25), Ten Commandments (vv. 14, 17,

---

29. Hence, Fretheim may be overstating the case when he says that God's mercy in 34:6–7 is a "fundamentally new emphasis" (ibid.).

30. Durham, *Exodus*, 455.

31. I do not agree with Cassuto that *ʾadonay* is "the customary expression for addressing God" (*Commentary on Exodus*, 440).

21), and the Book of the Covenant (vv. 22–24, 26).[32] Even the reference to "wonders" in 34:10, although referring to what God "will do" for Israel, calls to mind the wonders of the plagues and the crossing of the Red Sea (see 3:20; 15:11, the only other occurrences of the root *pl'* in Exodus).

Such tedious repetition is not clumsy writing, nor is it designed to bore the reader. Rather, it virtually forces the reader to understand what is happening as a *renewal* of the covenant. The repetition of the laws in 34:10–28, including references to the Exodus and Conquest[33] and the command to Moses to "write" (vv. 27–28), is a *synopsis* of the main events of the Exodus as a whole. In renewing the covenant, the substance of the original covenant is reiterated. The message is clear: Despite Israel's sin, God is moving forward with the plan.

As before (24:18), Moses stays on the mountain for forty days and nights, although this time we read that he neither eats bread nor drinks water (34:27–28). This indicates that "he was lifted above the everyday plane of life and tangibly approached the Divine sphere," an experience that certainly helps us understand the change in Moses' appearance described in verses 29–35.[34] After receiving the synopsis of the law, Moses writes it on the tablets he chiseled and makes his way back down the mountain.

This time, however, he is not greeted with the sound of "singing." Instead, the people are afraid. Why? Because Moses' face has become radiant (34:30). Moses is God's chosen mediator. The lack of respect the people had toward him in chapter 32 will not be repeated. Although the reason why Moses' face shines is not made explicit in the text, it is probably to impress on the people that God's authority and presence rest unequivocally with Moses. Thus, the people's response is appropriate: fear. It is only after Moses assures the leaders that there is nothing to fear that the people come near and hear him speak (vv. 31–32). A little fear is good for them. They must relearn what they first experienced in chapter 19: Being at the foot of the mountain is serious business. They are receiving God's law.

How is Moses' face radiant. Is it a brilliant light? A soft glow? Does he have a halo in the popular sense? What contributes to this uncertainty is the Hebrew verb *qaran* in 34:29, translated "radiant" in the NIV. This verb only

---

32. I will not discuss these repeated elements, as they have already been treated when they first occurred.

33. The most notable difference between the laws of 34:10–26 and those given previously is the added emphasis here on the attitude the Israelites are to take with respect to the nations. In light of the golden calf incident, where Israel quickly adopted pagan religious practices, this emphasis is understandable. Also, the repetition of the Feasts of Unleavened Bread and of Weeks is presumably a corrective to the "feast" of ch. 32 (Sarna, *Exodus,* 218).

34. Cassuto, *Commentary on Exodus,* 447.

occurs four times in the Hebrew Old Testament, three times in this passage and in Psalm 69:31. In the latter, it is a verbal noun and means "horn," which is the meaning of the cognate noun *qeren*. Because of the close affinity between *qeren*, whose meaning is certain, and the verb *qaran*, some medieval artists depicted Moses as having horns![35]

In actuality, the reference is likely to some sort of glow. Note Habakkuk 3:4, where the same noun clearly refers to "rays" of light. Moreover, illumination is known from Mesopotamian sources to indicate "a characteristic attribute of divinity," typically evinced in kings as a sign of their legitimate authority.[36] This seems to be what is happening in 34:29—35. Moses' glow is actually an afterglow from being in God's presence. As Cassuto remarks, "something of the Divine glory remained with him."[37]

What, then, are we to make of the veil? Its purpose is to cover Moses' face in the presence of the people after he enters "the LORD's presence" (v. 34). The veil is not needed when he speaks with God; but when he speaks to the people, Moses' radiant face causes the same frightful reaction. Within the broader context of Exodus, we may think of Moses' veil functioning in a similar way to the veil or curtain in the tabernacle. Just as the people could not enter the Most Holy Place to behold God's glory, now they cannot behold the glory of God reflected in Moses. He has, therefore, become the embodiment of the tabernacle; his role as mediator has reached a level and depth not yet attained.[38] We should also presume, even though the veil is not mentioned again, that this state of affairs lasts until Moses' death.[39]

It is only after the covenant has been renewed and the relationship between God and his people has been repaired that the plans for building the tabernacle can be carried through to completion. For the remainder of the book, there is not a hint of this near disaster. As noted in the previous section, the story of rebellion and restoration is immediately preceded and succeeded by the regulations concerning the Sabbath (31:12—17; 35:1—3). This is not a haphazard arrangement. The fact that the action picks up *after* the rebellion

---

35. See R. Mellinkoff, *The Horned Moses in Medieval Art and Thought* (Berkeley: Univ. of California Press, 1970). See also Sarna, *Exodus*, 221.

36. Sarna, *Exodus*, 221.

37. Cassuto, *Commentary on Exodus*, 449.

38. The connection between Moses' veil and that of the tabernacle is made by Janzen (*Exodus*, 263). This is intriguing and well worth considering. Nevertheless, I am uncomfortable pressing the matter too far. The word for "veil" in chapter 34 is *masveh* and appears only in this passage (3 times). The word used to refer to the veil separating the Most Holy Place from the Holy Place, which the NIV translates "curtain," is *paroket*. If the writer intends the reader to make this appealing connection, we would expect him to use the same word in both places.

39. Sarna, *Exodus*, 221; Janzen, *Exodus*, 262.

in the same place as *before* the rebellion means that Moses' intercession has been completely successful. The people are *totally* restored. The subsequent silence concerning this event adds to this notion. Forgiveness is complete.

The main thrust of chapters 32–34 now becomes clear. It is not so much a story of rebellion as it is a story of God's forgiveness and Moses' role in making this happen. It is in these chapters that Moses' role as intercessor, as mediator of the covenant, reaches its zenith. If we wish to point to the episode that makes Moses truly special, that makes him deserving of all the honor, attention, and respect he has received through the ages, it is his shielding an ungrateful people from the end they most certainly deserve, even if it means taking their place and bearing the full weight, horror, and ignominy of God's anger. The world will not see the likes of this again for many generations.

GOD'S MEDIATOR. Things were going along so well for the Israelites, and then this had to happen. Why? What does this episode tell us about God's people? More important, what does it tell us about God himself and how he deals with his people?

One Christian interpretive tradition has held that this story of the golden calf shows that the law and the sacrificial system (the tabernacle) simply do not work. No sooner are they given than the Israelites turn around and rebel. This is little more than a caricature, however. The story is in no way intended to communicate that the *law* doesn't work. If anything, it shows that the *Israelites* don't work! Rebellion so soon after the giving of the law is not an indication of the law's ineffectiveness. The law and the sacrificial system are good and holy. They reflect a heavenly pattern. They are from God. The problem is with the people.

Nor do we have here a portrait of a vengeful, stern-faced God, who continually needs to be persuaded not to wipe out his people. The God described here is not one who is prone to turn on his people at any moment, so they had better walk on eggshells. Reflect for a moment on chapters 1–31. Israel's deliverance from Egypt is a response to a promise God made to the patriarchs. The defeat of the Egyptian army in the sea and the triumphal march out of Egypt and up to Mount Sinai are the climactic moment in the realization of that promise. Something big is happening here.

Remember too that the Exodus is an act of re-creation. The allusions to creation throughout this story (plagues, parting of the sea, the law, and the tabernacle) all signal that the generation coming out of Egypt is privy to something unique, something that should have disarmed them of any thought of rebellion. In seeing the Exodus as an act of re-creation, we must see chapter 32 in the same light. If the preceding chapters connect Israel's deliverance to creation, their sin represents the "Fall" of God's people once again. As T. Fretheim puts it, "The garden scene [of chs. 25–31] become a tangled mess.... It is Genesis 3 all over again."[40]

To understand the intensity of God's reaction, we must keep this broad perspective in mind. We must look at the degree to which God has revealed himself in the preceding chapters, not just to Moses but to the people. In a manner of speaking, God has been pouring his heart out. He hand-picked a man to act as deliverer and mediator. He opened up the powers of heaven against the Egyptians. He brought heaven to earth for them in the form of the law and the tabernacle. Yet, no sooner does he do these things than the *people*, not God, become fickle. This is not only a story of the people's *rebellion* against God, but of their *rejection* of something God has been planning and working out since the time of Abraham. It is a rejection of God himself.

That is why God is extremely angry with his people, and understandably so. It is not an arbitrary anger; God is not lashing out. God's intense anger even against his own people indicates not how angry this powerful God can become with these puny humans, but how severe a sin Israel's act is. God's anger, in other words, has purpose and focus. His people shall be no more. His promise to the patriarchs will be kept, but he threatens to start the process all over again with Moses. What needs explaining in this story is not God's anger but the fact that he turns from his anger at Moses' pleading. This is what moves the story forward and brings it to a resolution in chapter 34. It is also what brings us to chapters 35–40 and the *completion* of the tabernacle. Without Moses, the tabernacle would get no further than the architect's plans, cast aside on a drawing room floor. But Moses comes to the rescue—and changes God's mind.

How are we to understand the nature of Moses' intercession? We read in 32:30 that he approaches God to "make atonement" for the sin of the people. Atonement is the purpose of the tabernacle and priestly role in offering sacrifices. By making atonement for the people, Moses, *even before the tabernacle is built*, acts out the purpose for which it is intended—to keep the people connected to God. He acts, in other words, as the high priest atoning for the people's sins.

How specifically does he intend to make atonement? Is it through sacrifice, the manner prescribed by God himself? Yes and no. In the span of a few verses we see a hint of that toward which the Old Testament sacrificial system eventually leads. Moses offers a sacrifice—himself. If God will not forgive the people on the basis of Moses' pleading, then perhaps he will make

---

40. Fretheim, *Exodus*, 226–27.

Moses the focal point of his anger, thus sparing the people. By being blotted out of the book of life, perhaps he can bring life to his people. The death of one will bring life to the many.

The Christological dimension of this interchange between God and Moses is obvious, but by no means superficial. Exodus 32:30–32 offers an early indication of what is necessary to make proper atonement for sin—not the sacrifice of an animal, but of a person. In fact, the sacrificial system of the Old Testament as a whole is a precursor to what true atonement is supposed to look like. Moses' offer is not simply a flash forward to the time of Christ. Rather, at the very inception of the sacrificial system, it is a glimpse into the heart of the heavenly reality to which the earthly sacrificial system points.

Christ fulfills the sacrificial system, to be sure, but there is so much more to it than that. We think too quickly of the Old Testament sacrifices as being imperfect, partial representations, temporary measures, if you will, of what eventually comes to completion in Christ. There is, of course, truth to this. This section, however, gives us another angle: The manner in which the Old Testament is to be fulfilled—personal sacrifice—is something already embedded in the Old Testament sacrificial system itself. In other words, the atoning death of Christ did not undo the law but brought it to its final and ultimate expression.

So far there is little here that catches us off guard. But let us not forget that God *rejects* Moses' offer to be a substitute (32:33–34)! "Only the guilty can be punished, Moses. What do you mean by simply stepping in and taking the people's place?" Moses' death will not make things right because his actions did not make things wrong in the first place. God says he cannot simply transfer the people's guilt onto one man. Guilt stays with the person who sins and who must pay the price.

Thus, God rejects Moses' offer. But he does so not because he doesn't like the idea. After all, such an offer is the heart of the gospel. Rather, he rejects the offer because Moses is not suited to carry it out. Moses does not have the capital to see it through to the end. He is by no stretch pure and blameless, as the Pentateuch will elsewhere bear out (Num. 20:12). The substitute must be one without blemish or fault, like the sacrificial animals of the Old Testament. It must be someone who is *able* to bear the burden of another's guilt.

When we read in 32:33–34 that only the guilty will be punished, the substitutionary death of Christ does not represent a change in God's game plan. This is the great mystery of the death of Christ. He *was* guilty. Our sins were put on him and conversely taken off of us. He was *worthy* of bearing our guilt because he himself was without guilt. Although this is beyond our ability to understand, it is rooted in the Old Testament itself.

Moses' intercessory work is not a one-shot deal. In fact, he is persistent. We see him at work again in 33:12–23, where the subject is who will accompany

Moses into Canaan. It seems that God intends to take only Moses (see also 32:10). But Moses will not take no for an answer. The people *must* come too. This dialogue ends with a promise by God to show his back to Moses. Then a third time Moses intercedes to ensure God's presence with his people (34:8–9). Moses is thorough, to say the least. He acts as a man determined to do the job right. He is faithful to the people under his charge even though they have shown in no uncertain terms that they will turn against him with little provocation.

We read in Hebrews 7:25 that Christ "always lives to intercede" for his people. Moses, too, seems to "live to intercede" in Exodus 32–34. He is there at every turn. Christ's intercession on our behalf is likewise continual and relentless. We do not know what form his heavenly intercession takes, what the dialogue between Christ and the Father looks like, but we know it is perfectly effective. The significant difference between Christ's intercession and that of Moses, as noted above, is that God accepts his Son as a substitute for his people's sin.

One final comparison can be made between Moses' intercession and that of Christ. Moses is in some sense imbued with a "dose of God" (cf. the radiance he displays after coming down from the mountain). He reflects God's glory to the people because he himself has beheld God's glory. It is this experience that will lend crucial support to his authority among the people.

The difference between Moses and Christ is that Moses both *sees* and *reflects* God's glory imperfectly. I am not being too hard on Moses. The intimacy he enjoyed with God was unique in the Old Testament. But the *fullness* of God's glory did dwell in Christ. Note Hebrews 1:3: "The Son is the radiance of God's glory." Christ reflected God's glory to his people fully because he beheld the glory of the Father fully—a fullness best expressed in Christ's own words, "I and the Father are one" (John 10:30). Moses would never have dared say that.

The human portrayal of God. Before we leave this Bridging Contexts section, we ought to reflect on the human portrait of God in Exodus. The give and take between Moses and God in chapters 32–34 is an exchange that must be taken into account as we formulate our notions of what the God of Exodus is like.

If a poll were taken of seminary students, perhaps pastors as well (i.e., those with formal theological education), and if the question asked was, "What is God like?" my strong suspicion is that many of the following attributes of God would be mentioned: omniscient, omnipotent, sovereign, unchanging, eternal, creator, and so forth. Few would add to the list such things as: prone to change his mind, argues with his people, can be frustrated, can regret past actions. Yet all of these latter attributes are just as scripturally defensible.

Too often, it seems to me, despite our biblical literacy, we think of how God *ought to be* rather than how he *has actually revealed himself*. The biblical portrait of God is varied, and I do not deny that God is indeed all of those wonderful attributes we read about in systematic theologies. But what of those other attributes, those less-marketable qualities of God, that never seem to make their way into our systematic theologies but which find constant biblical substantiation? We should not focus on the God *behind* the scenes and thereby lose sight of the God *of* the scenes, the God presented to us in Scripture. Scripture itself is what God has inspired to teach his people what he is like. What he says about himself must be taken into account.

Some implications of this for today will be taken up in the following section. For now, however, it is enough to draw attention to the way in which God is presented in Exodus. He is high, exalted, and mighty. He is also near and approachable. Indeed, he wants to be approached.

IS THE GOD of Exodus 32–34 the Christian God? Is the God of Exodus 32–34 someone we recognize? To put it another way, as terrible as this may sound, is this God one that we feel "comfortable" with? Of course, whether we feel comfortable with this God is beside the point. But with all we as Christians know about the grace of God and his forgiveness, isn't there part of us that reads Exodus 32–34 and finds a God strangely at odds with the gospel? The God we know from the New Testament would certainly have either accepted Moses' offer or provided an alternate way of forgiving his people. But that God actually threatens to wipe them out, needs to be convinced not to act in anger, and then relents at the last minute only to carry through with some punishment, gives one pause to consider whether the God portrayed here is actually relevant to contemporary Christian living.

I maintain that this section of Exodus certainly is relevant, but not in the sense that it tells us how God acts *now*. Applying the Bible does not mean that we simply transport the action of this story into our contemporary setting. Rather, Exodus 32 is relevant today because in it we see how God does *not* act now. This is not to drive a wedge between the Testaments and to proclaim the story passé. It is rather to understand this one story in the context of the whole. In other words, Exodus 32–34 is not to be *applied* in any conventional sense of the word. We do not read the story, make a mental image of God being angry, and then imagine him acting similarly in contemporary settings of our choosing. Rather, it is to help us to see what God is like, what he expects, and how Christ completes the picture. In doing so the significance of the story is not rejected but properly understood.

There are two pitfalls to be avoided in understanding the golden calf story. (1) It does not apply to the world as a whole. A sex shop opens up down the street; the school board votes 5 to 2 to distribute condoms in junior high school; movies rated PG 13 are beginning to look more like R and R-rated movies are beginning to look like soft porn; people all around us are advocating new and strange gods, personal gods, *any* god but the Christian God. The proper Christian reaction to these phenomena in our society is not to call down God's wrath on the revelry below. We are not to look to Exodus 32 and think, "This is how God handles debauchery in any and every time."

As we have seen in a number of other places in Exodus, this is a book written for Israelites and about Israelites. Its application is not for anyone except God's people. We saw this with the Ten Commandments. It is a misapplication to think that the law given to God's people should be used as a standard by which to judge unbelievers. Likewise, the golden calf story does not show us how God deals with pagans caught up in their own raucous behavior. It does not show the world that he is a God of wrath, ready to strike at a moment's notice against sin. Rather, it is a story of God's reaction to how *his people* behave in the face of all that he has shown them.

The story, therefore, cannot be applied today to whatever contemporary cause we happen to be displeased with. Levites slaying their brothers with swords does not give justification for Christians today going on a crusade against some public sin. The message of the story is not, "No compromise! God does not tolerate sin, so neither will we!" The fact that God still punishes the people despite Moses' pleadings to forgive does not mean that we can have an aggressive zero-tolerance for our sinful neighbors, coworkers, or relatives.

(2) Inasmuch as Exodus 32–34 does not apply to the world at large, neither does it apply to the church, at least not in the sense of inserting ourselves into the role of Israel and saying, "God will punish us too if we rebel." God is not ready to pounce on us the moment we slip up. Although the line of application is to be drawn from Israel to the church, this episode does not translate over to the church's life.

We must keep in mind at least one key theological difference between Exodus 32–34 and the church. Israel's sin at the foot of Mount Sinai occurs before there is any official means of sin atonement. The tabernacle has not yet been built, and the priestly system has not yet been inaugurated. At this point these things have only been planned for. This is why Moses himself needs to step in and say, "I will go up to the LORD; perhaps I can make atonement for your sin." For Israel, the official means of atoning for sin is still in the future. For the church, the final, complete, once-for-all atonement for sin *has* happened. The means of atonement Moses offered, substituting himself for his people, which God did not accept, is what Christ was able to do!

593

This is why we cannot and should not import Exodus 32–34 as a model for how God roots out sin in the church. This story is not inspiration for us to search out the "golden calves of our lives" lest God be angry with us. God is not angry with the church, not because the church is faultless, but because his anger has been completely spent on Christ, the substitute. This is not to say that God is now soft on sin. Exodus 32–34 does show us how intolerant God is of sin in his people.[41] But the gospel shows us that God's ultimate punishment for such sin was carried by his Son precisely so that we will not have to.

To put it another way, the good news of the gospel is that Exodus 32–34 does *not* apply to us today! It is not the nature of God that has changed. Rather, a Mediator has come, by God's design, one "who had no sin to be sin for us" (2 Cor. 5:21). What was hinted at by Moses' rejected offer has happened with a crushing finality that even Moses could not have anticipated. This perspective is not to minimize the story of the golden calf but to see it as Christians ought, in light of the empty tomb.

Apart from the matter of mediation there is another element of Exodus 32–34 that lends itself to contemporary significance, namely, the human portrait of God. I want my own view of God to be shaped by what Scripture says. This is not easy to do. We form ideas in our own heads about what God is like—sometimes these ideas are based on Scripture, sometimes on our own musings—and once formed, these ideas are difficult to re-form.

Western culture tends to be somewhat analytical, to take things apart and see how they work. We are even a suspicious people. We want to unmask things to see what they are really like. Perhaps we approach our knowledge of God in a similar way. God is the Creator, and to be Creator is a sign of ultimate power and authority. No one is higher than God, no one is more powerful. The pages of the Old Testament present a picture of God, however, that does not deal exclusively with such properties. As we have noted above, the God of the Old Testament is one who is engaged in human activity on a human level.

In Exodus 32–34, God is engaged in a debate with Moses over how to handle the Israelites. This is not like the debate they had earlier in Exodus, where God announces to Moses that he will lead the people out of Egypt and patiently listens to Moses' complaints. The purpose of the debate in Exodus 32–34 is not to convince Moses of anything, but God! He is the one who nearly goes too far and has to be brought back to his senses! Why does the Old Testament present God in this way? What are we to derive from it?

---

41. Paul, in 1 Cor. 10:6–10, even uses the golden calf incident as motivation for godly living in the church. And so it is!

If we reflect on our common Christian experience, we will notice that this is how we relate to God. Our picture of him is unavoidably human. Think of prayer. Whenever we ask God to do anything, anything at all, we are engaging him in a conversation that assumes at the outset that our pleadings will have the desired effect of changing his mind. "Oh Lord, please let it not rain tomorrow so our picnic won't have to be canceled." "Father, if it is your will, please let the job interview go well."

Implicit in these two requests is the fact that God has not yet made up his mind, that his will can be shaped somehow. Now, if I were asked, I would have to say that God is bigger than our small requests. He is not swayed every moment to change his mind by the daily inundation of human prayers. But when we *actually* pray, none of this enters our mind. We simply come to God in the only way we know how, as people. We engage God on a human level. Indeed, we assume that he can be engaged in this way.

Even Jesus in Gethsemane prayed a very "human" prayer: "My Father, if it is possible, may this cup be taken from me. Yet not as I will, but as you will" (Matt. 26:39). "*If* it is possible." Didn't Jesus know better? Didn't he know all about God's omnipotence? Jesus, caught as he was in the throes of agony and even despair ("overwhelmed with sorrow," cf. 26:38), *pleads* with God. True, he resigns himself to God's will and plan, as indeed we all must when we pray; yet Jesus still asks God, if at all possible, to take the cup from him. It strikes me as significant that Jesus does *not* pray: "Father, you and I are one. I know your will and I follow it obediently. Give me the strength not to question what you have planned for me. You are sovereign and omnipotent." No. Jesus prays, "If it is possible."

Jesus' human way of praying is an extension of the fact that he is human himself. In a sense, presenting God as human in such passages as Exodus 32–34 is no different from presenting God as human in Christ. When we get down to it, at any and every level, we can do nothing other than think of God and relate to him in strictly human terms. We can take some stabs at what he is "really" like by using words like omnipotent or omniscient, and these things are what makes God nonhuman. These are true attributes of God. But when push comes to shove, when the discussion leaves the abstract level, we look to God as our Father, our Friend, our King—all human images (images he himself sanctions throughout Scripture)—and we relate to him on that basis.

The human portrait of God is one that fits well with our everyday experience. More important, this is how God has chosen to reveal himself. We should not try to get behind that portrait to something more "accurate," more like what we "know" God is "really" like. We must look at what God says about himself and take it to heart. And we are encouraged that when we pray and plead with him, we know that he is in fact listening, that what we say matters. How else can we say that we have a relationship with God?

Paul's application of Exodus 34:29–35. One final matter concerning the application of Exodus 32–34 brings us to 2 Corinthians 3:7–18. This is a passage of obvious relevance, since Paul refers to the incident described in Exodus 34:29–35. The most relevant section begins at 2 Corinthians 3:12. Moses' ministry was fading but was accompanied by glory. The gospel, however, has surpassing glory (vv. 9–11). What Christians have access to (more accurately, what Christians have *been given* access to) is a cause to be bold (v. 12). Why? Because we, unlike Moses, do not put a veil over our faces (v. 13). We should not pass over Paul's remark too quickly. He says, "*We* are not like Moses." The point of comparison is between Moses and the *church*.

How then does this Exodus story apply? It is by way of contrast. Paul points out that the reason Moses wore the veil is so that the Israelites would not see the glory *as it faded away*. The fading glory of Moses is like the fading glory of the law (2 Cor. 3:14–16). The law's glory was true but temporary. Paul argues that the Jews' refusal in his day to see the fading glory of the law was due to the "veil" over their own hearts that prevented them from seeing the law for what it was, temporary.

The heart of the matter is found in verse 18. Christians reflect the Lord's glory with "unveiled faces." We, like Moses, see glory. This is why we, too, reflect glory. The difference is that the glory we reflect does not fade away, so that we do not need to wear a veil. And our glory does not fade away because, unlike Moses, we "are *being transformed* into his likeness with *ever-increasing* glory" (italics added).

To put this another way, Paul looks at the Exodus episode not from the people's point of view but from that of Moses. It is odd, to say the least, that Paul's understanding of the significance of the veil is not explicit, or even implied, in Exodus. In fact, the purpose of the veil in Exodus seems to be to *prevent* the people from seeing the *full* glow of the radiance: They were afraid when Moses spoke to them with his radiant face, and thereafter he wore the veil. Moses then took it off again only when he was in private audience with God in the tabernacle.

Paul, however, is drawing the analogy between Moses and the church and so he looks at this story from Moses' perspective. He sees Moses' recurring meetings with God as an indication that he needed repeated exposure to glory. One shot was not good enough. As the glory faded, the veil would be worn and Moses had to go back for another "dose" of God's glory. But we are not like that. For us a veil need not be worn because our glory does not fade—for we are in Christ.

As is typically the case, Paul sets out the reality of the Christian's status and then draws practical conclusions from this. He does this in 2 Corinthians 4:1–18. Since we are a part of this wonderful turn of events, we do not lose heart (v. 1), meaning we have the courage to persevere in any and every circumstance (see also vv. 8–18). We, therefore, are bold to live out the gospel in word and deed plainly to all those around us. And if they do not understand what we are doing, it is because the gospel is "veiled" to them; their sinful hearts do not allow them to see the glory of Christ that we are being transformed to reflect. The practical issue Paul is grappling with is similar to that which confronted Moses: "Will they listen to what I tell them?" (2 Cor. 4:2–6).

If anything, Paul's application of Exodus 34:29–35 reinforces the notion developed above that this Old Testament episode is applied to the Christian life by way of contrast. It is not the case that this episode and Exodus 32–34 are irrelevant, but that their relevance must be properly perceived—in light of the "surpassing glory" (2 Cor. 3:10) of the cross and the empty tomb.

Exodus 40:34–38

T HEN THE CLOUD covered the Tent of Meeting, and the glory of the LORD filled the tabernacle. ³⁵Moses could not enter the Tent of Meeting because the cloud had settled upon it, and the glory of the LORD filled the tabernacle. ³⁶In all the travels of the Israelites, whenever the cloud lifted from above the tabernacle, they would set out; ³⁷but if the cloud did not lift, they did not set out—until the day it lifted. ³⁸So the cloud of the LORD was over the tabernacle by day, and fire was in the cloud by night, in the sight of all the house of Israel during all their travels.

Original Meaning

THIS PASSAGE IS briefer than any of the others we have looked at. It is a fitting end to this book, however, and so it deserves to be treated separately. It rounds off some preceding elements and poises the reader to enter the remaining stories that will bring the Pentateuch to an end.

As we come to the conclusion of the Exodus story, we find God present with his people in a powerful way. The description of his presence in this passage is reminiscent of what we have seen throughout Exodus. Reference to the cloud, glory, and the Tent of Meeting/tabernacle causes us to glance back at much of what has transpired.

The reappearance of the cloud in particular attracts our attention. God was with his people in the form of a cloud at a number of important places in Exodus: 13:21–22; 14:19, 24; 16:10; 24:16–18; 33:9–10; 34:5. It has been a near constant reminder to Israel that God is with them, his special people. The cloud was with them when they left Egypt and when they came to Mount Sinai. Now, as Israel is poised to continue on to the land of Canaan, it is here again. The recurring appearance of this symbol ties various parts of the book together and communicates loud and clear that the God of the Exodus is still with his people.

The same can be said for the use of the Hebrew root *nsᶜ*, which means to travel or set out on a journey. This root appears, both as a verb ("set out") and as a noun ("travels"), in verses 36–38. As with the cloud, this word has occurred a number of times previously in Exodus (12:37; 13:20; 14:15, 19; 15:22; 16:1; 17:1; 19:2). It, too, indicates that God is moving ahead with the plan he announced earlier. This same root is also a bridge to the rest of the Pentateuch, for it will appear about a hundred more times, particularly in Numbers 9–10 and 33.

Exodus 40:36–38, in other words, prepare us for what will become a dominant element in Numbers and Deuteronomy, the relentless push toward the land of Canaan. The purpose of these closing verses of Exodus is to explain how this will happen. When God moves, the people move. When he stays put, so do they. It is, after all, God's plan and purpose that are being fulfilled. Israel's eventual arrival in the Promised Land will be solely by God's guidance and direction, by his will and in his time.

God's presence is manifest now specifically in the tabernacle, which has been the main topic since chapter 25. God is both over the tabernacle in the cloud and in it (40:34). We have no doubt arrived at a climactic moment. Note especially verse 35: God's presence is so "thick," as it were, that even Moses cannot enter. I do not think this means that Moses is waiting for an invitation to enter.[1] This may have been the case earlier (24:16), but not so here. Moses is unable to enter *because of* the cloud and the glory. If the author's intention is to imply that Moses is waiting for an invitation to enter, his choice of words is a roundabout way of putting it.[2]

Moreover, such an explanation dulls the impact these verses should have. This passage as a whole implies a heightening of God's presence. Something powerful is happening in the midst of the community, and it is fitting that it should be so. In light of what we have seen in chapters 32–34, it is important to remind the people of God's holiness, that there are times when even Moses may not come near. This is a lesson the Israelites, unfortunately, will be slow to learn.

Nevertheless, the fact that God is still present with his people, and in such an intense way, reminds the people of something else: All is forgiven. The Exodus-God, the God who has led his people out of Egypt with fire and cloud (14:19, 24) is still at work (40:38). The mission, at least the first stage, has been completed and the plan is proceeding full steam ahead.

Thus, the first phase of Israel's story comes to an end. Throughout the book we have seen the author's concerted attempts to remind his readers that Israel's deliverance should be seen in light of the events of Genesis, namely, creation and the promise to the patriarchs. Now, one chapter of this

---

1. This is what Durham argues (*Exodus*, 501).

2. Sarna admits to the ambiguity of the verse, although he points out the similar situation with the dedication of the temple in 1 Kings 8:10–11 (*Exodus*, 237). In any event, at what point and for what reason Moses is again granted access to the tabernacle is not the focus of this passage; thus, I will refrain from offering a conjecture.

grand story is closing and another is beginning, so our gaze is directed forward to the next phase in Israel's journey.

Along that journey, Israel's prophets and psalmists will from time to time call Israel back to remember what God did in bringing them out of Egypt. They will be challenged to remember that neither Egypt's might nor Israel's stubbornness—nor even God's own anger—have been able to thwart his plan. After all, he made a promise to Abraham. Nothing will get in the way. This is the story of the Exodus.

SINCE THIS PASSAGE is the conclusion of the book, its purpose is not to introduce new themes but to bring old ones to an end. This stands to reason, and so the discussion here will not be drawn out. The bridging of contexts for 40:34–38 is connected both logically and thematically to the flow of the action not only of the preceding section but of the entire book.

Saying this, however, does not end the matter. One may still wonder why, of all the ways to end the book, the writer has chosen *this* conclusion. What is he saying? Is there some point he wants to leave with the readers before moving to the next phase of the story? This central thrust to his conclusion, I think is this: The God who brought the Israelites out of Egypt is at the same time both holy and near.

(1) Verses 34–35 are a final reminder of God's holiness. Access to God, even by Moses, is not something that can be taken for granted. In a manner of speaking, God is *too* present in the tabernacle and so Moses cannot enter. There is a point that Moses himself cannot cross, a boundary set by God that keeps even his chosen redeemer at a distance. The fact that Moses is kept away is not the result of residue wrath after the golden calf incident. That is long past. In the interim the tabernacle has been built, and what we read in 40:35 should be seen in this light.

The reason Moses cannot enter is because the tabernacle is the portable Mount Sinai, the earthly representation of God's heavenly throne, the microcosm of creation. In other words, the point of verse 35 is to highlight the holiness of God as it is manifest in his earthly dwelling place, not Moses' shortcomings or God's anger. Approaching God in his tabernacle is done on his terms because he is holy.

(2) The guiding function of the cloud and fire tells us that this holy God is nevertheless very near his people. He is with them every step of the way. Moreover, he is in charge of their journey to Canaan. This has been God's story since the beginning. It was he who made the promise to Abraham. It

was he whose power was challenged by Pharaoh. It was he who brought Israel to his mountain and gave them his law. They are now not free to go wherever they please and do whatever they want. This is not what they have been redeemed for. They have been set apart by God to be his people, to "serve" him, as we read so often in Exodus.[3]

The description of God in this passage is one that is well at home in the pages of the Old Testament, and one that any reader will recognize. A holy God who directs and guides his people in his own time and in his own way is a thread that runs through so much of the Old Testament that to amplify this theme would require us to study nearly every major section. Furthermore, we have seen these same characteristics in so many places in Exodus that to repeat these efforts here is pointless. What is important is the finality of this passage for the book as a whole. It does not introduce a new picture of God but puts an exclamation point on what the book has been trying to communicate since the beginning.

In the same way, the Christological perspective has been explored throughout this commentary. Christ fulfills so completely what Moses' ministry was set up to do that the comparison between the two figures in the New Testament is often made by way of contrast. Christ is not simply a "new Moses," in the sense that he does the same things only better. He is more. Yet Christ also does what Moses could not do and is thus a better mediator.

This is evident in view of Moses' inability to enter the tabernacle (40:35). Christ, by contrast, is himself the fullness of God's glory. Even Moses, who earlier reflected God's glory so intensely that he had to wear a veil because the people were afraid, cannot bear the weight of God's glory in the tabernacle at this point. True, the point of 40:34–35 is not to highlight Moses' inadequacies. Rather, their focus is to show us, at the close of the book, the holiness of God presented throughout. But looking at this passage from the vantage point of the gospel we see how Christ "goes one better." He is the final mediator of the covenant and the glory of God fills him. There is never a question whether he is able to enter fully into the Father's presence.

---

3. As we have noted in several places in this commentary, it is a common misunderstanding to think of Israel's departure from Egypt as a declaration of independence from any "oppressive" power. Such is how liberation theology understands the book's message. But Israel's deliverance results in an "enslavement" of another type, to the God who delivered them. They are now to serve him.

WHAT DO THE closing verses of Exodus have to say to us? In a number of places in this commentary I have appealed to the book of Hebrews to help us understand what the Christian's understanding of the Exodus should be. This is because Hebrews 3:1–4:13 is an explicit and relatively extensive "commentary" on the Exodus, at least more so than any other portion of the New Testament. The basic analogy that the writer of Hebrews draws is that Israel's desert wanderings correspond to the daily life of the church on its way to "Canaan."

In a manner of speaking, the end of Exodus is among the more applicable parts of the book. Verses 34–38 have something to say to us, since we, too, have been delivered and are waiting to arrive at the final destination. We, like the Israelites, are poised to reach our rest.

On this journey, we follow our holy Redeemer as he guides us to the Promised Land. Admittedly, there is no cloud overhead, but we have the Spirit of Christ dwelling in us. He brings us to the goal of our salvation just as surely as the cloud guided the Israelites to their ultimate destination. The people of God should take great comfort in this. The God of Exodus is still guiding. God is present with his people wherever they go, for he still leads and guides them, not to Canaan but to a "better country—a heavenly one" (Heb. 11:16).

As I turn the final page of the book of Exodus, after struggling to come to grips with its meaning (and I will continue to struggle), I begin to see something I had not noticed before. The end of Exodus is not just the end of the story but the beginning of many others. This is true not only for the Israelites, whose ups and downs are catalogued for us in Scripture, but for us as well. We who have been redeemed by Christ are also poised daily for the journeys we take toward our final goal. Israel's Exodus, as ours, is for a purpose, to bring us "onward and upward." This is a recurring theme in C. S. Lewis's *Chronicles of Narnia* series. And as we reach the end of Exodus, I am reminded of how Lewis ends his series, on the final page of *The Last Battle*:

> Now at last they were beginning Chapter One of the Great Story, which no one on earth has read; which goes on forever; and which every chapter is better than the one before.[4]

This is the message of Exodus. This is the message of the gospel.

---

4. C.S. Lewis, *The Last Battle* (New York: Macmillan, 1956), 184.

Scripture Index

Subject Index

Note: This index does not include such entries as Aaron, Egypt, Mount Sinai, Moses, law, Pharaoh, pillar of cloud and fire, plagues, tabernacle, Ten Commandments, etc.; since these are so pervasive throughout the book, the user can better look up specific passages where words such as these occur.

Author Index